Get the eBook FREE!

(PDF, ePub, Kindle, and liveBook all included)

We believe that once you buy a book from us, you should be able to read it in any format we have available. To get electronic versions of this book at no additional cost to you, purchase and then register this book at the Manning website.

Go to https://www.manning.com/freebook and follow the instructions to complete your pBook registration.

That's it!
Thanks from Manning!

Pipeline as Code

Pipeline as Code

CONTINUOUS DELIVERY WITH JENKINS, KUBERNETES, AND TERRAFORM

MOHAMED LABOUARDY

MANNING
SHELTER ISLAND

For online information and ordering of this and other Manning books, please visit
www.manning.com. The publisher offers discounts on this book when ordered in quantity.
For more information, please contact

    Special Sales Department
    Manning Publications Co.
    20 Baldwin Road
    PO Box 761
    Shelter Island, NY 11964
    Email: orders@manning.com

 Manning Publications Co.
    20 Baldwin Road
    PO Box 761
    Shelter Island, NY 11964

Development editor:	Karen Miller
Technical development editor:	Christopher Haupt
Review editor:	Mihaela Batinić
Production editor:	Deirdre S. Hiam
Copy editor:	Sharon WIlkey
Proofreader:	Keri Hales
Technical proofreader:	Werner Dijkerman
Typesetter and cover designer:	Marija Tudor

ISBN 9781617297540
Printed in the United States of America

brief contents

PART 1 GETTING STARTED WITH JENKINS 1

  1 ■ What's CI/CD? 3
  2 ■ Pipeline as code with Jenkins 21

PART 2 OPERATING A SELF-HEALING JENKINS CLUSTER 47

  3 ■ Defining Jenkins architecture 49
  4 ■ Baking machine images with Packer 70
  5 ■ Discovering Jenkins as code with Terraform 100
  6 ■ Deploying HA Jenkins on multiple cloud providers 140

PART 3 HANDS-ON CI/CD PIPELINES 195

  7 ■ Defining a pipeline as code for microservices 197
  8 ■ Running automated tests with Jenkins 231
  9 ■ Building Docker images within a CI pipeline 271
 10 ■ Cloud-native applications on Docker Swarm 309
 11 ■ Dockerized microservices on K8s 355
 12 ■ Lambda-based serverless functions 401

PART 4 MANAGING, SCALING, AND MONITORING JENKINS 439

 13 ■ Collecting continuous delivery metrics 441
 14 ■ Jenkins administration and best practices 467

contents

preface   xiii
acknowledgments   xv
about this book   xvi
about the author   xix
about the cover illustration   xx

PART 1   GETTING STARTED WITH JENKINS 1

1   **What's CI/CD?   3**

   1.1   Going cloud native   4

         Monolithic   4 ▪ Microservices   5 ▪ Cloud native   8
         Serverless   10

   1.2   Defining continuous integration   12

   1.3   Defining continuous deployment   13

   1.4   Defining continuous delivery   14

   1.5   Embracing CI/CD practices   15

   1.6   Using essential CI/CD tools   16

         Choosing a CI/CD tool   17 ▪ Introducing Jenkins   18

2   **Pipeline as code with Jenkins   21**

   2.1   Introducing the Jenkinsfile   22

         Blue Ocean plugin   26 ▪ Scripted pipeline   29 ▪ Declarative
         pipeline   31

2.2 Understanding multibranch pipelines   36

2.3 Exploring the GitFlow branch model   38

2.4 Test-driven development with Jenkins   39

The Jenkins Replay button   40 ▪ *Command-line pipeline linter   41* ▪ *IDE integrations   43*

PART 2   **OPERATING A SELF-HEALING JENKINS CLUSTER** 47

3   *Defining Jenkins architecture   49*

3.1 Understanding master-worker architecture   50

3.2 Managing Jenkins workers   52

SSH   52 ▪ *Command line   53* ▪ *JNLP   53* ▪ *Windows service   54*

3.3 Architecting Jenkins for scale in AWS   55

Preparing the AWS environment   64 ▪ *Configuring the AWS CLI   65* ▪ *Creating and managing the IAM user   66*

4   *Baking machine images with Packer   70*

4.1 Immutable infrastructure   71

4.2 Introducing Packer   72

How does it work?   73 ▪ *Installation and configuration   74 Baking a machine image   75*

4.3 Baking the Jenkins master AMI   85

Configuring Jenkins upon startup   85 ▪ *Discovering Jenkins plugins   88*

4.4 Baking the Jenkins worker AMI   96

5   *Discovering Jenkins as code with Terraform   100*

5.1 Introducing infrastructure as code   101

Terraform usage   102

5.2 Provisioning an AWS VPC   103

AWS VPC   104 ▪ *VPC subnets   108* ▪ *VPC route tables   111 VPC bastion host   114*

5.3 Setting up a self-healing Jenkins master   117

5.4 Running Jenkins with native SSL/HTTPS   124

5.5   Dynamically autoscaling the Jenkins worker pool   128

*Launch configuration   128 ▪ Auto Scaling group   131
Autoscaling scaling policies   133 ▪ Workers CPU
utilization load   136*

6   *Deploying HA Jenkins on multiple cloud providers   140*

6.1   Google Cloud Platform   141

*Building Jenkins VM images   141 ▪ Configuring a GCP network
with Terraform   147 ▪ Deploying Jenkins on Google Compute
Engine   153 ▪ Launching automanaged workers on GCP   157*

6.2   Microsoft Azure   162

*Building golden Jenkins VM images in Azure   162 ▪ Deploying
a private virtual network   166 ▪ Deploying a Jenkins master
virtual machine   171 ▪ Applying autoscaling to Jenkins
workers   178*

6.3   DigitalOcean   183

*Creating Jenkins DigitalOcean Snapshots   183 ▪ Deploying a
Jenkins master Droplet   186 ▪ Building Jenkins worker
Droplets   190*

PART 3   HANDS-ON CI/CD PIPELINES 195

7   *Defining a pipeline as code for microservices   197*

7.1   Introducing microservices-based applications   199

7.2   Defining multibranch pipeline jobs   203

7.3   Git and GitHub integration   205

7.4   Discovering Jenkins jobs' XML configuration   215

7.5   Configuring SSH authentication with Jenkins   219

7.6   Triggering Jenkins builds with GitHub webhooks   222

8   *Running automated tests with Jenkins   231*

8.1   Running unit tests inside Docker containers   233

8.2   Automating code linter integration with Jenkins   238

8.3   Generating code coverage reports   240

8.4   Injecting security in the CI pipeline   242

8.5   Running parallel tests with Jenkins   244

8.6   Improving quality with code analysis   246

8.7   Running mocked database tests   248

8.8   Generating HTML coverage reports   250

8.9   Automating UI testing with Headless Chrome   254

8.10   Integrating SonarQube Scanner with Jenkins   260

9 Building Docker images within a CI pipeline   271

9.1   Building Docker images   273

Using the Docker DSL   273 ▪ *Docker build arguments   277*

9.2   Deploying a Docker private registry   279

Nexus Repository OSS   279 ▪ *Amazon Elastic Container
Registry   286* ▪ *Azure Container Registry   288* ▪ *Google
Container Registry   290*

9.3   Tagging Docker images the right way   291

9.4   Scanning Docker images for vulnerabilities   296

9.5   Writing a Jenkins declarative pipeline   301

9.6   Managing pull requests with Jenkins   305

10 Cloud-native applications on Docker Swarm   309

10.1   Running a distributed Docker Swarm cluster   310

10.2   Defining a continuous deployment process   321

10.3   Integrating Jenkins with Slack notifications   335

10.4   Handling code promotion with Jenkins   341

10.5   Implementing the Jenkins delivery pipeline   346

11 Dockerized microservices on K8s   355

11.1   Setting up a Kubernetes cluster   356

11.2   Automating continuous deployment flow with Jenkins   360

Migrating Docker Compose to K8s manifests with Kompose   371

11.3   Walking through continuous delivery steps   372

11.4   Packaging Kubernetes applications with Helm   381

11.5   Running post-deployment smoke tests   387

11.6   Discovering Jenkins X   390

12 Lambda-based serverless functions   401

12.1   Deploying a Lambda-based application   402

12.2   Creating deployment packages   407

Mono-repo strategy   407 ▪ *Multi-repo strategy   413*

12.3 Updating Lambda function code 417

12.4 Hosting a static website on S3 420

12.5 Maintaining multiple Lambda environments 423

12.6 Configuring email notification in Jenkins 434

PART 4 MANAGING, SCALING,
AND MONITORING JENKINS 439

13 *Collecting continuous delivery metrics 441*

13.1 Monitoring Jenkins cluster health 442

13.2 Centralized logging for Jenkins logs with ELK 452

*Streaming logs with Filebeat 454 ▪ Streaming logs with the
Logstash plugin 461*

13.3 Creating alerts based on metrics 462

14 *Jenkins administration and best practices 467*

14.1 Exploring Jenkins security and RBAC authorization 468

*Matrix authorization strategy 469 ▪ Role-based authorization
strategy 471*

14.2 Configuring GitHub OAuth for Jenkins 472

14.3 Keeping track of Jenkins users' actions 475

14.4 Extending Jenkins with shared libraries 476

14.5 Backing up and restoring Jenkins 480

14.6 Setting up cron jobs with Jenkins 484

14.7 Running Jenkins locally as a Docker container 487

index 493

preface

Ten years ago, I wrote my first makefile to automate the testing, building, and deployment of a C++ application. Three years later, while working as a consultant, I came across Jenkins and Docker and discovered how to take my automation skills to the next level with CI/CD principles.

The beauty of CI/CD is that it's simply a rigorous way of recording what you're already doing. It doesn't fundamentally change how you do something, but it encourages you to record each step in the development process, enabling you and your team to reproduce the entire workflow later at scale. Over the next few months, I started writing blog posts, doing talks, and contributing to CI/CD-related tools.

However, setting up a CI/CD workflow has always been a very manual process for me. It was done via defining a series of individual jobs for the various pipeline tasks through a graphical interface. Each job was configured via web forms—filling in text boxes, selecting entries from drop-down lists, and so forth. And then the series of jobs were strung together, each triggering the next, into a pipeline. This made the troubleshooting experience a nightmare and reverting to the last known configuration in case of failure a tedious operation.

A few years later, the *pipeline-as-code* practice emerged as part of a larger "as code" movement that includes *infrastructure as code*. I could finally configure builds, tests, and deployment in code that is trackable and stored in a centralized Git repository. All the previous pains were alleviated.

I became a fan and believer of pipeline as code, as I transitioned from being a software engineer, tech leader, and senior DevOps manager to now co-leading my first startup as CTO. Pipeline as code became an important part of each project I was part of.

I had the chance to work on different types of architecture—from monolithic, to microservices, to serverless applications—having built and maintained CI/CD pipelines for large-scale applications. Along the way, I accumulated tips and best practices to follow while going through the journey of continuous everything.

The idea of sharing that experience is what triggered this book. Implementing pipeline as code is challenging for many teams, as they require the use of many tools and processes that all work together. The learning curve takes a lot of time and effort, leading people to wonder whether it's worth it. This book is a handbook experience on how to build a CI/CD pipeline from scratch, using the most widely adopted CI solution: Jenkins. I hope the result will help you embrace the new paradigm of building CI/CD pipelines.

acknowledgments

First and foremost, I want to thank my wife, Mounia. You've always supported me, always patiently listened while I struggled to get this done, and always made me believe I could finish this. I love you.

Next, I'd like to acknowledge my editor at Manning, Karen Miller. Thank you for working with me, and thank you more for being patient when things got rough during the pandemic. Your commitment to the quality of this book has made it better for everyone who reads it. Thanks as well to all the other folks at Manning who worked with me on the production and promotion of the book: Deirdre Hiam, my project editor, Sharon Wilkey, my copyeditor, Keri Hales, my proofreader, and Mihaela Batinić, my reviewing editor. It was truly a team effort.

Finally, I'd like to thank my family, including my parents and brothers, for finding the inner strength to listen to me talk about the book at every gathering.

To all the reviewers: Alain Lompo, Alex Koutmos, Andrea Carlo Granata, Andres Damian Sacco, Björn Neuhaus, Clifford Thurber, Conor Redmond, Giridharan Kesavan, Gustavo Filipe Ramos Gomes, Iain Campbell, Jerome Meyer, John Guthrie, Kosmas Chatzimichalis, Maciej Drożdżowski, Matthias Busch, Michal Rutka, Michele Adduci, Miguel Montalvo, Naga Pavan Kumar Tikkisetty, Ryan Huber, Satej Kumar Sahu, Simeon Leyzerzon, Simon Seyag, Steve Atchue, Tahir Awan, Theo Despoudis, Ubaldo Pescatore, Vishal Singh, and Werner Dijkerman, your suggestions helped make this a better book.

about this book

Pipeline as Code was designed to be a hands-on experience through practical examples. It will teach you the ins and outs of Jenkins and be your best companion to build a solid CI/CD pipeline for cloud-native applications.

Who should read this book

Pipeline as Code is designed for all levels of DevOps and cloud practitioners who want to improve their CI/CD skills.

How this book is organized

The book has four parts that cover 14 chapters.

Part 1 takes you through basic CI/CD principles and discusses how Jenkins can help implement them:

- Chapter 1 gives an overview of continuous integration, deployment, and delivery practices. It also discusses how Jenkins can help you in embracing those DevOps practices.
- Chapter 2 introduces the pipeline-as-code approach and how it can be achieved with Jenkins. It also covers the differences between declarative and scripted Jenkins pipelines.

Part 2 covers how to deploy a self-healing Jenkins cluster on the cloud by using an infrastructure-as-code approach:

- Chapter 3 goes deep into Jenkins distributed builds architecture, with a full example on AWS.
- Chapter 4 introduces the immutable infrastructure approach with HashiCorp Packer, including how to bake a Jenkins machine image with all the needed dependencies to run a Jenkins cluster out of the box.

- Chapter 5 demonstrates how to deploy a secure and scalable Jenkins cluster on AWS with HashiCorp Terraform.
- Chapter 6 describes in deep detail the process of deploying a Jenkins cluster on different cloud providers, including GCP, Azure, and DigitalOcean.

Part 3 focuses on building CI/CD pipelines from scratch for cloud-native applications, including Dockerized microservices running in Swarm or Kubernetes and Serverless applications:

- Chapter 7 defines the foundation for building a CI workflow for a containerized microservices. It covers how to define a multibranch pipeline on Jenkins and how to trigger the pipeline upon a push event.
- Chapter 8 demonstrates how to run automated tests inside Docker containers. Various tests are described, including UI testing with headless Chrome, code coverage, static code analysis with SonarQube, and security analysis.
- Chapter 9 covers building Docker images within CI pipelines, managing their versions, and scanning for security vulnerabilities. It also discusses how to automate reviews of GitHub pull requests with Jenkins.
- Chapter 10 walks through the deployment process of Dockerized applications to Docker Swarm with Jenkins. It demonstrates how to maintain multiple runtime environments and how to achieve continuous deployment and delivery.
- Chapter 11 goes deep into automating the deployment of applications on Kubernetes with Jenkins pipelines, including how to package and version Helm charts and run post-deployment tests. It also demonstrates the usage of Jenkins X and how it compares to Jenkins.
- Chapter 12 covers how to build CI/CD pipelines for a serverless-based application and how to manage multiple Lambda deployment environments.

Part 4 covers maintaining, scaling, and monitoring a Jenkins cluster running in production with ease:

- Chapter 13 explores how to build interactive dashboards to continuously monitor Jenkins for anomalies and performance issues using Prometheus, Grafana, and Slack. It also covers how to stream Jenkins logs to a centralized logged platform based on the ELK stack.
- Chapter 14 covers how to secure Jenkins jobs with a granular RBAC mechanism. It also explores how to back up, restore, and migrate Jenkins jobs and plugins.

About the code

This book is a hands-on experience that provides many examples of code. These appear throughout the text and as separate code listings. Code appears in a `fixed-width font just like this`, so you'll know when you see it.

All of the source code used in the book is available on the Manning website (https://www.manning.com/books/pipeline-as-code), or in my GitHub repository (https://github.com/mlabouardy/pipeline-as-code-with-jenkins). This repository is a labor of love, and I appreciate the work done by all who catch bugs, make performance improvements, and help with documentation. Everything is ideal for contributions!

liveBook discussion forum

Purchase of *Pipeline as Code* includes free access to a private web forum run by Manning Publications where you can make comments about the book, ask technical questions, and receive help from the author and from other users. To access the forum, go to https://livebook.manning.com/#!/book/pipeline-as-code/discussion. You can also learn more about Manning's forums and the rules of conduct at https://livebook.manning.com/#!/discussion.

Manning's commitment to our readers is to provide a venue where a meaningful dialogue between individual readers and between readers and the author can take place. It is not a commitment to any specific amount of participation on the part of the author, whose contribution to the forum remains voluntary (and unpaid). We suggest you try asking the author some challenging questions lest his interest stray! The forum and the archives of previous discussions will be accessible from the publisher's website as long as the book is in print.

Other online resources

Need additional help?

- Check out my blog (https://labouardy.com/), where I regularly share the latest news about Jenkins and the best practices to follow while building CI/CD workflows.
- A weekly DevOps newsletter (https://devopsbulletin.com) can help you stay up-to-date with the latest wonders in the pipeline-as-code space.
- The Jenkins tag at StackOverflow (https://stackoverflow.com/questions/tagged/jenkins) is a great place to both ask questions and help others.

about the author

MOHAMED LABOUARDY is CTO and cofounder of Crew.work, and a DevSecOps evangelist. He is the founder of Komiser.io, and an author of multiple books about serverless and distributed applications. He enjoys contributing to open source projects and is a regular conference speaker. You can also find him on Twitter (@mlabouardy).

about the cover illustration

The figure on the cover of *Pipeline as Code* is captioned "Bohémien de prague," or a Bohemian from Prague. The illustration is taken from a collection of dress costumes from various countries by Jacques Grasset de Saint-Sauveur (1757–1810), titled *Costumes de Différents Pays,* published in France in 1797. Each illustration is finely drawn and colored by hand. The rich variety of Grasset de Saint-Sauveur's collection reminds us vividly of how culturally apart the world's towns and regions were just 200 years ago. Isolated from each other, people spoke different dialects and languages. In the streets or in the countryside, it was easy to identify where they lived and what their trade or station in life was just by their dress.

The way we dress has changed since then and the diversity by region, so rich at the time, has faded away. It is now hard to tell apart the inhabitants of different continents, let alone different towns, regions, or countries. Perhaps we have traded cultural diversity for a more varied personal life—certainly for a more varied and fast-paced technological life.

At a time when it is hard to tell one computer book from another, Manning celebrates the inventiveness and initiative of the computer business with book covers based on the rich diversity of regional life of two centuries ago, brought back to life by Grasset de Saint-Sauveur's pictures.

Part 1

Getting started with Jenkins

This first part of this book takes you through the DevOps essential concepts. You'll learn about CI/CD practices and how they allow you to integrate small pieces of code at one time and ease technical debt. After that, I'll introduce the new approach of building CI/CD pipelines, pipeline as code, and how it can be implemented with Jenkins. Finally, I'll lay the groundwork for a well-designed CI/CD workflow by introducing the GitFlow branching model.

What's CI/CD?

1

This chapter covers

- The path organizations have taken to evolve from monolith to cloud-native applications
- The challenges of implementing CI/CD practices for cloud-native architectures
- An overview of continuous integration, deployment, and delivery
- How CI/CD tools like Jenkins can bring business value to organizations that undertake the journey of continuous everything

Software development and operations have experienced several paradigm shifts recently. These shifts have presented the industry with innovative approaches for building and deploying applications. More importantly, two significant paradigm shifts have consolidated capabilities for developing, deploying, and managing scalable applications: cloud-native architecture and DevOps.

Cloud-native architecture emerged with cloud adoption, with cloud providers like Amazon Web Services (AWS), Google Cloud Platform (GCP), and Microsoft Azure taking ownership of the infrastructure. Open source tools like Kubernetes, Docker, and Istio offer horizontal scaling ability, letting developers build and run modern scalable applications without worrying about the underlying infrastructure. As a result, operational overhead is reduced, and the development velocity of applications is increased.

DevOps bridged the divide between developers and ops teams, and brought back harmony through collaboration, automated tools, and iterative and Agile development and deployment.

With these two significant, powerful approaches combined, organizations now have the capability to create scalable, robust, and reliable applications with a high level of collaboration and information sharing among small teams. However, to build, test, and safely deploy cloud-native applications, two essential DevOps practices must be implemented in a cloud-native manner: continuous integration (CI) and continuous deployment/delivery (CD).

The first part of this book takes you through the evolution of cloud-native applications. You'll learn about the main principles of CI/CD and how automation invented the way those principles are implemented through the *pipeline-as-code* approach. This first chapter lays the foundation. It introduces basic principles of DevOps and cloud-native approaches, in addition to selecting the tools for implementing CI/CD pipelines.

1.1 Going cloud native

Before exploring the essential characteristics of cloud-native applications and how CI/CD practices contribute to standardizing feedback loops for developers and enabling fast product iterations, we will cover the changes the software development model went through and the challenges associated with each model, starting with the monolithic approach.

1.1.1 Monolithic

In the past, organizations used to build their software in a *monolithic* way: all functionalities were packaged in a single artifact and deployed in a single server running one process. This architecture comes with many drawbacks and limitations:

- *Development velocity*—Adding new features on top of an existing application is next to impossible. Application modules are tightly coupled and, most of the time, not documented. As a result, adding new features is often slow, expensive, and requires extra synchronization when working with multiple developers within distributed teams on a large codebase. Moreover, the release cycle can take months, if not several years, because of the application's large codebase. This delay puts companies at risk of being surpassed by new competitors and ultimately undercuts the company's profits.

- *Maintainability*—Modules in a monolithic architecture are frequently tightly coupled, which makes them hard to maintain and test. Plus, upgrading to new technology is limited to the framework used to develop the application (no polyglot programming).
- *Scaling and resiliency*—Applications are designed with no scalability in mind, and the application may face downtime if traffic increases. The monolithic application works as a single unit and is developed in a single programming language using a single tech stack. As a result, to achieve partial horizontal scaling, the whole application needs to be scaled (inefficient usage of server resources).
- *Cost-effectiveness*—The application is expensive to maintain in the long run (for example, finding an experienced COBOL developer is time-consuming and expensive).

In the late 2000s, many web giants (including Facebook, Netflix, Twitter, and Amazon) came onto the tech scene with innovative ideas, aggressive strategies, and a "move fast" approach that led to the exponential growth of their platforms. These companies introduced a new architecture pattern that is known today as *microservices*. So, what exactly is microservices architecture?

1.1.2 Microservices

James Lewis and Martin Fowler defined microservices architecture as follows in 2014:

> *In short, the microservice architectural style is an approach to developing a single application as a suite of small services, each running in its own process and communicating with lightweight mechanisms, often an HTTP resource API. These services are built around business capabilities and independently deployable by fully automated deployment machinery. There is a bare minimum of centralized management of these services, which may be written in different programming languages and use different data storage technologies.*

This architecture uses the same technique of "divide and conquer" to tackle the complexity of an application. An application is split into smaller, independent, and composable services/fragments, each responsible for a specific functionality or task of the application (organized around business capabilities).

Those microservices communicate using an application programming interface (API), typically over HTTP or HTTP/2 (for example, gRPC, RESTful APIs, Google Protocol Buffers, or Apache Thrift), or through message brokers (such as Apache ActiveMQ or Kafka). Each microservice can be implemented in a different programming language running on a different OS platform.

In contrast to microservices, the monolithic architecture means the code's components are designed to work together as one cohesive unit, sharing the same server resources (memory, CPU, disk, and so forth). Figure 1.1 illustrates the differences between monolith and microservices architectures.

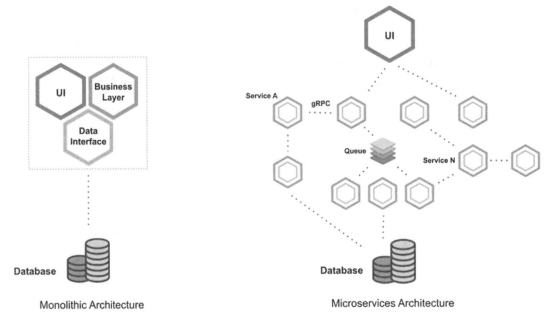

Figure 1.1   Comparing monolith and microservices architectures

Microservices architecture is an extension of *service-oriented architecture* (SOA). Both architectures rely on services as the main component, but they vary greatly in terms of service characteristics:

- *Granularity*—Service components within a microservices architecture are generally single-purpose services that do one thing. In SOA, service components can range in size, anywhere from small application services to very large enterprise services.
- *Sharing*—SOA enhances component sharing, whereas microservices architecture tries to minimize sharing through bounded context (loosely coupled services or modules) with minimal dependencies.
- *Communication*—Microservices rely on lightweight protocols such as HTTP/REST and simple messaging, while SOA architectures rely on enterprise service bus (ESB) for communication; early versions of SOA used object-oriented protocols to communicate with each other, such as Distributed Component Object Model (DCOM) and object request brokers (ORBs). Later versions used messaging services such as Java Message Service (JMS) or Advanced Message Queuing Protocol (AMQP).
- *Deployment*—SOA services are deployed to application servers (IBM WebSphere Application Server, WildFly, Apache Tomcat) and virtual machines. On the other hand, microservices are deployed in containers. This makes microservices more flexible and lighter than SOA.

NOTE For more details about microservices architecture, I recommend reading *Microservices in Action* by Morgan Bruce and Paulo A. Perreira (Manning, 2018). It covers what makes a microservice, how it can be composed by an individual or a dedicated team, the constant back-and-forth comparison between a monolithic application, and things to consider when deploying your microservices.

The advantages of microservices convinced some big enterprise players such as Amazon, Netflix, and Uber to adopt the methodology. Following their footsteps, other companies are working in the same direction: evolving from monolithic to flexible microservice-based architecture.

But what makes it so special? Compared to more monolithic design structures, microservices architecture comes with the following benefits:

- *Scalability*—Applications built as microservices can be broken into multiple components so that each component can be deployed and scaled independently without service interruption. Also, for stateless microservices, usage of Docker or Kubernetes can offer horizontal scaling within seconds.
- *Fault tolerance*—If one microservice fails, the others will continue to work because of loosely coupled components. A single microservice can be easily replaced by a new one without affecting the whole system. As a result, modernization in microservices architecture can be incremental, while modernization in monolithic architecture can cause service outages.
- *Development velocity*—Microservices can be written in different languages (polyglot programming) and use different databases or OS environments. If one microservice is, for example, CPU intensive, it could be implemented in highly productive languages such as Golang or C++, while other components could be implemented in lightweight programming languages such as JavaScript or Python. So companies can easily hire more developers and scale development. Also, because microservices are autonomous, developers have the freedom to independently develop and deploy services without bumping into each other's code (avoiding synchronization hell within the organization) and having to wait for one team to finish a chunk of work before starting theirs. As a result, team productivity increases, and vendor or technology stack lock-in reduces.
- *Continuous everything*—Microservices architecture combined with Agile software development enable continuous delivery. The software release cycle in microservice applications becomes much smaller, and many features can be released per day through CI/CD pipelines with open source CI tools like Jenkins.

To summarize, microservices make solving big problems easier, increase productivity, offer flexibility in choosing technologies, and are great for cross-functional teams. At the same time, running microservices in a distributed cloud environment can be a tough challenge for organizations. Here are some of the potential pain areas associated with microservices designs:

- *Complexity*—Increased complexity over a monolithic application due to the number of services involved. As a result, enormous effort, synchronization, and automation are required to handle interservice communication, monitoring, testing, and deployment.
- *Operational overhead*—Deploying a microservice-based application can be complex. It needs a lot of coordination among multiple services. Each service must be isolated with its own runtime environment and resources. Hence, traditional deployment solutions like virtualization can't be used and must be replaced with containerization solutions like Docker.
- *Synchronization*—Microservices require cultural changes in organizations seeking to adopt them. Having multiple development teams working on different services requires a huge effort to ensure that communication, coordination, and automated processes are in place. Cultures like Agile and DevOps practices are mandatory to take on microservice-based applications.

NOTE While Docker comes with no learning curve, it can quickly become a nightmare when handling deploying microservices among a cluster of machines or nodes.

Most of these drawbacks were addressed with the consumption of cloud computing services offered by AWS and with the rise of open source tools—particularly Kubernetes. It brought a completely new approach to managing infrastructure and enabled applications to be architected in a distributed manner. As a result, a new software architecture style arose in 2014: cloud-native applications.

1.1.3   *Cloud native*

The Cloud Native Computing Foundation (CNCF), a Linux Foundation project founded in 2015 to help advance container technology, defines *cloud native* as follows:

> *Cloud-native technologies empower organizations to build and run scalable applications in modern, dynamic environments such as public, private, and hybrid clouds. Containers, service meshes, microservices, immutable infrastructure, and declarative APIs exemplify this approach. These techniques enable loosely coupled systems that are resilient, manageable, and observable. Combined with robust automation, they allow engineers to make high-impact changes frequently and predictably with minimal toil.*

Cloud native is a paradigm for building applications as microservices and running them on containerized and dynamically orchestrated platforms that fully exploit the advantage of the cloud computing model. These applications are developed using the language and framework best suited for the functionality. They're designed as loosely coupled systems, optimized for cloud scale and performance, use managed services, and take advantage of continuous delivery to achieve reliability and faster time to market.

The overall objective is to improve the speed, scalability, and finally, profit margin. Figure 1.2 illustrates an example of a cloud-native application.

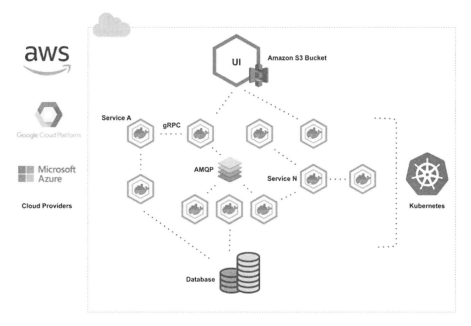

Figure 1.2   Overview of a cloud-native application

Cloud-native applications are packaged in lightweight containers and efficiently deployed as microservices. They use a lightweight API to expose their functionality, and binary and nonbinary protocols to communicate with each other internally. A step further, the applications are managed on elastic cloud infrastructure through Agile DevOps processes having continuous delivery workflows.

> **NOTE**   Docker has become the standard for container technology. It has revolutionized the way we think about developing microservices, and enables us to easily deploy microservices locally, on premises, or in the cloud.

Kubernetes (https://kubernetes.io/) is one of the preferred platforms for running workloads that function as cloud-native applications. It's an open source container orchestration platform originally developed at Google. It ensures high-end automated deployment, scaling, and management of containerized applications. This new paradigm of building and deploying applications comes with many benefits:

- *No operational overhead*—Developers can focus on developing features and adding business value instead of dealing with infrastructure provisioning and management.
- *Security compliance*—Simplified security monitoring is required because the various parts of an application are isolated. A security problem could happen in one container without affecting other areas of the application.
- *Autoscaling*—Containers can be deployed into a fleet of servers in different availability zones or even multiple isolated data centers (regions). As a result,

cloud-native apps can take advantage of the elasticity of the cloud by scaling resources in or out during a use spike without the need to procure and provision physical servers. Also, by adopting cloud services, the business can go global in minutes with lower adaptation costs and increased revenue and without worrying about scalability.

- *Development speed*—The application architecture is easy to understand since each container represents a small piece of functionality, and is easy for developers to modify, so they can help a new team member become productive quickly. Also, adopting cloud-native technologies and practices enables companies to create software in-house, allowing business people to closely partner with IT people, keep up with competitors, and deliver better services to their customers.
- *Resiliency*—Cloud-native microservices allow for failure at a granular level. They do this by providing adequate isolation between each service and offer multiple design patterns that might improve the components' availability and resilience such as Circuit Breaker (https://martinfowler.com/bliki/CircuitBreaker.html), Throttling (www.redhat.com/architect/pros-and-cons-throttling), and Retry patterns. Companies like Netflix used it to develop a new approach called *chaos engineering* to build a resilient streaming platform.

Figure 1.3 shows the differences between monolithic, microservices, and cloud-native architectures.

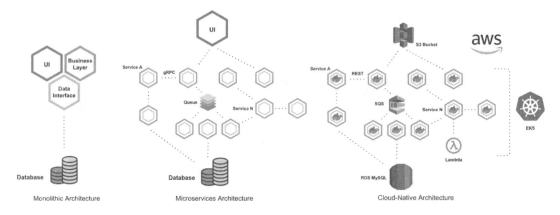

Figure 1.3   Monolith, microservices, and cloud-native architectures

To summarize, cloud-native architecture allows you to dynamically scale and support large numbers of users, events, and requests on distributed applications. A real-world example of the adoption of cloud-native architecture is the serverless model.

1.1.4   Serverless

The *serverless* computing model was kicked off with AWS Lambda in 2014. In this architecture, developers can write cost-efficient applications without provisioning or maintaining a complex infrastructure.

Cloud providers deploy customers' code to fully managed, ephemeral, time-boxed containers that live only during the invocation of the functions. Therefore, businesses can grow without customers having to worry about horizontal scaling or maintaining complex infrastructure.

> **NOTE** Serverless doesn't mean "no ops." You're just outsourcing sysadmin with serverless services. You will still deal with monitoring, deployment, and security.

An application built based on serverless architecture may end up looking like figure 1.4.

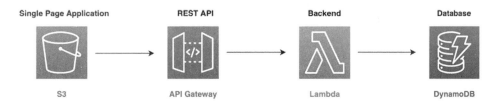

Single Page Application	REST API	Backend	Database
S3	API Gateway	Lambda	DynamoDB

Figure 1.4 An example of a serverless application

Instead of maintaining a dedicated container or instance to host your static web application, you can combine an Amazon Simple Storage Service (S3) bucket to benefit from scalability at a cheaper cost. The HTTP requests coming from the website go through Amazon API Gateway HTTP endpoints that trigger the right AWS Lambda function to handle the application logic and persist data to a fully managed database service such as DynamoDB. For particular use cases, going serverless can make sense for several reasons:

- *Less operational overhead*—The infrastructure is managed by the cloud provider, and this reduces the overhead and increases developer velocity. OS updates are taken care of, and patching is done by the function-as-a-service (FaaS) provider. This results in decreased time to market and faster software releases and eliminates the need for a system administrator.
- *Horizontal autoscaling*—Function becomes the unit of scale that leads to small, loosely coupled, stateless components that, in the long run, lead to scalable applications. Plus, the scaling mechanism is shifted to the cloud provider, which decides how to use its infrastructure effectively to serve the client's requests.
- *Cost optimization*—You pay for only the compute time and resources that you consume. As a result, you don't pay for idle resources, which significantly reduces infrastructure costs.
- *Polyglot*—Another benefit is the ability to choose a different language runtime depending on the use case. One part of the application can be written in Java, while another in Python; it doesn't really matter as long as the job gets done.

NOTE   A big concern while going serverless is vendor lock-in. Although you should favor development speed and efficiency above all, it's important to choose a vendor based on your use case.

Cloud-native architectures, in general, are gaining massive adoption, but the learning curve for many teams is steep. Plus, the shift to cloud-native architecture can be a double-edged sword for many organizations, and one of the challenges when moving to a fully cloud-native approach can be CI/CD.

But what do these practices mean? And how can they be applied when you're building cloud-native applications?

1.2   *Defining continuous integration*

Continuous integration (CI) is the practice of having a shared and centralized code repository, and directing all changes and features through a complex pipeline before integrating them into the central repository (such as GitHub, Bitbucket, or GitLab). A classic CI pipeline is as follows:

1 Triggers a build whenever a code commit occurs
2 Runs the unit tests and all pre-integration tests (quality and security tests)
3 Builds the artifact (for example, Docker image, zip file, machine learning training model)
4 Runs acceptance tests and pushes the result to an artifact-management repository (such as a Docker Registry, Amazon S3 bucket, Sonatype's Nexus, or JFrog Artifactory)

Figure 1.5 shows an example of a CI pipeline for a containerized application.

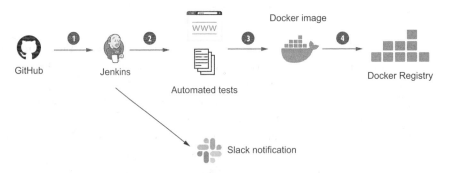

Figure 1.5   Basic CI workflow for cloud-native applications

Basically, CI automatically monitors the commits that each developer makes and launches automated tests. Automated testing is an integral part of CI/CD pipelines. Without automated tests, CI/CD pipelines will lack quality checks, which are important in order for the application to be released.

You can implement various types of testing to ensure that your software meets all the initial requirements. Here are the most famous ones:

- *Unit tests*—These test each piece of the source code. They consist of testing individual functions and methods. You could also output your test coverage and validate that you're meeting your code coverage requirements.
- *Quality tests*—Check that the code is well formatted, follows best practices, and has no serious coding errors. This is also called *static code analysis*, as it helps to produce high-quality code by looking for patterns in code that might generate bugs.
- *Security tests*—Inspect source code to uncover common security vulnerabilities and common security flaws (for example, leaked usernames and passwords).
- *UI tests*—Simulate user behavior through the system to ensure that the application works correctly in all supported browsers (including Google Chrome, Mozilla Firefox, and Microsoft Internet Explorer) and platforms (such as Windows, Linux, and macOS) and that it delivers the functionality promised in user stories.
- *Integration tests*—Check that services or components used by the application work well together and no defects exist. For example, an integration test might test an application's interaction with the database.

Manually executing all these tests can be time-consuming and counterproductive. Therefore, you should always use a testing framework that suits your application requirements to perform those tests on a scale in a repeatable and reliable way.

> **NOTE** Chapter 8 covers how to run automated tests with Jenkins and Headless Chrome, as well as how to integrate SonarQube for code analysis.

Once tests are successful, the application will be compiled and packaged, and a releasable artifact will be generated and versioned in a remote repository.

1.3 Defining continuous deployment

Continuous deployment (CD) is an extension of continuous integration. Every change that passes all stages of your continuous integration pipeline is released automatically to your staging/preproduction environment.

In such a process, there's no need to decide what will be deployed and when. The pipeline will automatically deploy whatever build components/packages successfully exit the pipeline. Figure 1.6 illustrates a typical CI/CD pipeline for microservices running in Kubernetes.

This CI workflow has four steps, and the CD pipeline is the deployment to Kubernetes (step 5). However, a pure continuous deployment approach is not always appropriate for everyone.

For example, many clients would not appreciate new versions falling into their laps several times a week, and prefer a more predictable and transparent release cycle.

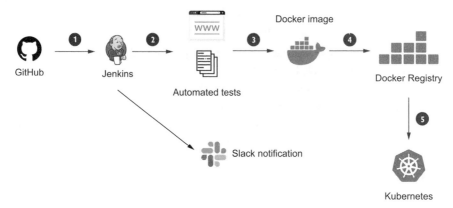

Figure 1.6   Basic CI/CD workflow for cloud-native applications

Commercial and marketing considerations might also play a role in when a new release should actually be deployed.

While continuous deployment may not be right for every company, continuous delivery is an absolute requirement of DevOps practices. Only when you continuously deliver your code can you have true confidence that your changes will be serving value to your customers within minutes of pushing the "go" button, and that you can actually push that button any time the business is ready for it.

1.4   *Defining continuous delivery*

Continuous delivery (CD) is similar to continuous deployment but requires human intervention or a business decision before deploying the release to production. Figure 1.7 shows how the CI/CD practices relate to each other.

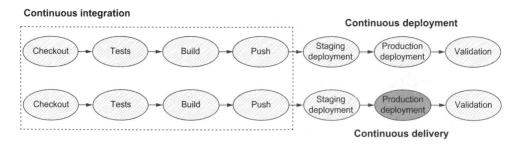

Figure 1.7   The continuous deployment maturity model

> **NOTE**   A Monitor and Optimize stage can occur in a sophisticated CI/CD workflow. This step consists of collecting and analyzing metrics and feedback to eliminate risks and waste and to optimize the release time.

1.5 Embracing CI/CD practices

CI/CD and continuous delivery can bring more agility to cloud-native applications through daily builds, which leads to the following:

- Detecting anomalies at an earlier stage (reducing the risk) and minimizing technical debt through unit and functional tests. According to Atlassian (www.atlassian.com/software-development/practices), 75% of development teams face issues with bugs, defects, or delays when it's time to release.
- Building features your users actually want. This often results in better user interaction and quicker feedback regarding released features, which can help the product team focus on the most demanded features and build a high-quality product.
- Having a production-ready package available. This is an excellent way to accelerate the time to market.
- Increasing product quality and reliability through quality and stress tests, and tracking with better visibility into project status and health.
- Driving innovation from feedback while building high-quality products through each iteration.

However, the journey from a manual to a highly automated deployment process can take several months. Therefore, companies need to be iterative in adopting CI/CD, as illustrated in figure 1.8.

You should always prioritize the steps in CI/CD. First and foremost, automate the process for compiling the source code. Ideally, you will develop new features and fix multiple bugs per day. Manually, this process takes a few minutes to a couple of hours. Also, you should prioritize functional testing before UI testing, as it often changes and

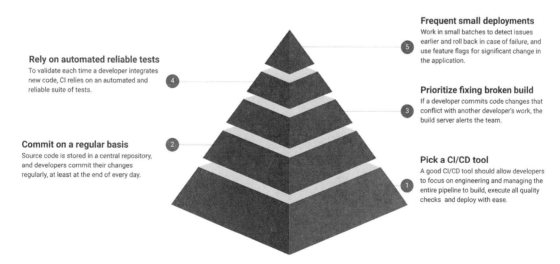

Frequent small deployments
Work in small batches to detect issues earlier and roll back in case of failure, and use feature flags for significant change in the application.

Rely on automated reliable tests
To validate each time a developer integrates new code, CI relies on an automated and reliable suite of tests.

Prioritize fixing broken build
If a developer commits code changes that conflict with another developer's work, the build server alerts the team.

Commit on a regular basis
Source code is stored in a central repository, and developers commit their changes regularly, at least at the end of every day.

Pick a CI/CD tool
A good CI/CD tool should allow developers to focus on engineering and managing the entire pipeline to build, execute all quality checks and deploy with ease.

Figure 1.8   Introducing CI/CD to an organization

thus requires frequent pipeline changes. So make sure to break your CI/CD steps into smaller segments and automate in patches to make the best use of your resources.

Another concern is that the complexity of CI/CD will be increasing, from handling singular applications to dozens of microservices (multiple pipelines). Therefore, adapting your CI/CD tools and processes is mandatory to keep pace.

Moreover, you need to have a clear road map of your product with a proven track record of development success. Your end customers should be able to consume constant product changes. Therefore, using CI/CD requires a high degree of discipline, dedication to quality, and a learning curve (new skill sets). If you can't handle that, stop thinking about CI/CD immediately.

As a result, moving to CI/CD should not be an isolated decision, made alone by the DevOps team. A successful rollout of CI/CD must be a decision for your whole organization and should be made only when your entire organization agrees to it.

Although you need to keep some concerns in mind, the benefits of CI/CD almost always outweigh the challenges. To realize the full promise of cloud-native applications, you must implement CI/CD practices that are best suited to your unique business goals.

In this book, we will go through some real-world use cases for building CI/CD pipelines for most adopted cloud-native architectures, such as Dockerized microservices with both Docker Swarm and Kubernetes, as well as Lambda-based serverless applications. We will also cover how to manage and scale a CI tool with less maintenance hassle to help you increase deployment speed. But first, what makes a modern CI tool, and which one are we going to use?

> **NOTE**   While monoliths may not be trendy, many companies still have monolith flagship products and can still benefit tremendously from a well-architected CI/CD solution. So most of the examples in the book can also be applied to modernizing monolithic applications.

1.6   *Using essential CI/CD tools*

A lot of excellent CI tools are out there. Some have been here for a long time, and others are relatively new. It's a bit redundant to say that a modern CI tool must be fast, user-friendly, and flexible, since those are the features we already expect out of the box. CI tools can be divided into the following three main categories:

- Cloud-managed solutions like AWS CodePipeline (https://aws.amazon.com/codepipeline/), Google Cloud Build (https://cloud.google.com/build), and Microsoft Azure Pipelines (https://azure.microsoft.com/services/devops/pipelines/).
- Open source solutions such as Jenkins (www.jenkins.io), Spinnaker (https://spinnaker.io/), or GoCD (www.gocd.org).
- Software-as-a-service (SaaS) solutions like Travis CI (https://travis-ci.org/), CircleCI (https://circleci.com/), and TeamCity (www.jetbrains.com/teamcity/).

1.6.1 Choosing a CI/CD tool

Figure 1.9 shows the most popular CI/CD tools on the market today. These tools are the mature ones, with the essential capabilities for your project.

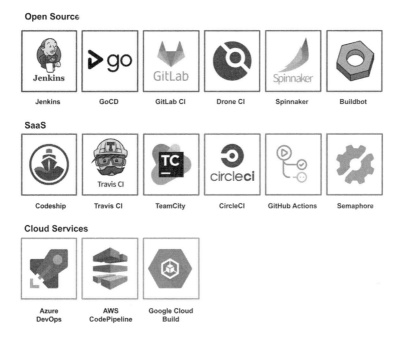

Figure 1.9   Top CI/CD tools in 2021

Plenty of excellent CI tools are available, so you need to pick the best one based on the following factors:

- *Team experience and skills*—While many tools use configuration YAML files to declare the CI/CD pipeline, they might require some sysadmin skills to set up and provision the needed infrastructure to run the CI/CD platform. Also, maintaining the underlying infrastructure might cause a lot of headaches and become a bottleneck for your company's growth once your project codebase becomes bigger (scaling capabilities), as you need to maintain distributed CI/CD complex pipelines across multiple nodes or servers.
- *Target platform*—Consider the operating system your application or project is running on (some CI tools don't support macOS and ARM architecture), and the use of a self-hosted infrastructure or a cloud provider.
- *Programming language and architecture*—Most CI tools support the top cutting-edge languages including Java, Ruby, Python, PHP, and JavaScript. However, some tools like TeamCity offer better integration and support for Java and .NET

projects. Similarly, Bamboo, as a creation of Atlassian, has native support for Jira and Bitbucket. Additionally, the deployment solution can be a factor in choosing the right CI tool for your project. Tools like Drone (www.drone.io) and GitLab CI (https://docs.gitlab.com/ee/ci/) offer native Docker support with an integrated Docker registry.

1.6.2 *Introducing Jenkins*

Although no single tool can satisfy the needs of every project, in this book, we will rely heavily on *Jenkins*. It's considered one of the most popular CI tools on the market today, with over one million users. It was written in Java, making it a cross-platform (Windows, Linux, and macOS) continuous integration tool.

Originally a part of the Hudson project, the community and codebase split following trademark conflicts with Oracle after it acquired Sun Microsystems. Hudson was originally released in 2005, while the first release as Jenkins was made in 2011.

> **NOTE** Hosted SaaS platforms can be beneficial if you're willing to pay a bit of extra money for someone else to maintain and update the solution. Businesses tend to choose this option when they need a UI superior to what Jenkins offers and when they lack infrastructure skills. But a major benefit of self-hosting solutions like Jenkins is that you have more control and flexibility over your own data security and job pipelines.

A rich set of plugins enables Jenkins to support any type of language or technology such as Docker, Maven, Git, Mercurial, and AWS. Being an open source project makes it customizable and easy for developers to extend by creating custom plugins. Here are some of Jenkins key features:

- Extensible with a huge community-contributed plugin resource (more than 1,400 plugins).
- A free and open source tool as well as a paid enterprise edition offered by CloudBees (www.cloudbees.com/jenkins) with speedy customer support.
- Has an active community that helps developers reduce the time to build a working CI/CD workflow.
- Can be deployed on premises or in the cloud with an easy configuration through the user interface or the command line.
- Supports distributed builds with master-worker architecture with a built-in parallelism mechanism.
- A powerful and flexible tool with complete control over workflow that can serve every CI/CD need.
- Works on many platforms and has the support for a wide variety of tools and frameworks.
- Supports containers as build agents for teams planning to use Docker.
- Seamless integration with GitHub, GitLab, Bitbucket, and most of the source code management (SCM) systems and Apache Subversion (SVN).

- Flexible user management, user roles assignment, sorting users into groups, different ways of user authentication (including LDAP, GitHub OAuth, and Active Directory).
- The CI process can be defined using the Groovy language in files within the repository itself or through text fields in the Jenkins web UI, thanks to the Jenkins pipeline workflow.

NOTE If you like to test a small application for one particular platform, you won't need the complexity of running a Jenkins server.

Another key feature of Jenkins is *pipeline as code*. We're going to use this approach to create Jenkins jobs. The cool part of using this approach is that our entire Jenkins jobs configuration can be created, updated, and version-controlled along with the rest of the application source code.

It is helpful to note that Jenkins must be hosted on a server, so it often needs the attention of someone with infrastructure skills. You can't just set it up and then expect it to run itself; the system requires frequent updates and maintenance. The main barrier to entry for most teams is the initial setup, procrastination, or failed previous attempts to set it up. People tend to know it's good, but many teams neglect it for more urgent coding work. Perhaps someone on your team tried to deploy Jenkins at some point but did not successfully maintain it. Maybe the wasted effort gave your boss a bad impression about it.

The reasons people do not implement Jenkins are usually very practical. That's why, throughout this book, we will be using the magical power of infrastructure as code with open source tools like Terraform and Packer to set up our entire CI infrastructure out of thin air on most popular public cloud providers such as AWS, GCP, and Microsoft Azure.

Another problem we will tackle in this book is how to write tests. Writing tests is something most developers want to do, but often don't find the time to do. Understandably, coding the actual application is usually a higher priority for the business. Also, tests break, meaning when the functionality under test changes, it needs to be updated. If functionality is not updated, it stops delivering value. We will cover how to run various types of tests within CI/CD pipelines and how to integrate external code analysis tools.

To sum up, implementing CI/CD for cloud-native architecture requires a cultural and mindset shift, especially from management. Managers have to allow time for this "unproductive stuff" to be done.

Still, the brief sacrifice of time translates into long-term benefits for the whole company. With Jenkins, your code becomes easier to maintain, and fewer bugs sneak into production. Your team becomes more integrated, and builds take less time. Your business can ship faster and keep up with the changing needs of your customers (by shipping code faster, organizations can quickly respond to changes and keep products on the market).

CI/CD is not an expense but an investment. And the return on investment (ROI) for implementation can be counted in time saved, errors avoided, and higher-quality products delivered more easily to your clients.

Summary

- Cloud-native architectures are changing the landscape, forcing organizations to think about new models and new delivery methods.
- Continuous integration, delivery, and deployment are practices designed to help increase the velocity of development and the release of well-tested, usable products.
- Choosing the right CI/CD tool is critical to the long-term success of cloud-native applications and should be based on platform complexity, integration, learning curve, pricing, and work-time efficiency.
- Jenkins can leverage the team's current workflow to best exploit the automation features and create a solid CI/CD pipeline.

Pipeline as code with Jenkins

2

This chapter covers

- How pipeline as code works with Jenkins
- An overview of Jenkinsfile structure and syntax
- Introduction to Blue Ocean, the new Jenkins user experience
- Declarative versus scripted Jenkins pipelines
- Integration of a GitFlow model within Jenkins projects
- Tips for productivity and efficiency while writing Jenkinsfiles for complex CI/CD pipelines

There's no doubt that cloud computing has had a major impact on the way companies build, scale, and maintain technology products. The ability to click a few buttons to provision machines, databases, and other infrastructure has led to an increase in developer productivity we've never seen before.

While it was easy to spin up simple cloud architectures, mistakes can easily be made while provisioning complex ones. Human error will always be present, especially when you can launch cloud infrastructure by clicking buttons on the cloud provider's web console.

The only way to avoid these kinds of errors is through automation, and infrastructure as code (IaC) is helping engineers automatically launch cloud environments quickly and without mistakes. The growth of DevOps and the adoption of its practices have led to more tooling that can implement the IaC paradigm to a larger degree.

In the past, setting up CI/CD workflow has been a manual process. It was commonly done via defining a series of individual jobs for the various pipeline tasks. Each job was configured via web forms—filling in text boxes, selecting entries from dropdown lists, and so forth. And then the series of jobs were strung together, each triggering the next, into a pipeline.

Jenkins somewhat lagged in this area until the release of Jenkins 2. Although widely used and a primary workflow tool for creating CI/CD pipelines, this way of creating and connecting Jenkins jobs to form a pipeline was challenging. It did not meet the definition of IaC. Job configurations were stored only as Extensible Markup Language (XML) files within the Jenkins configuration area. This meant that the files were not easily readable or directly modifiable. And the Jenkins application itself provided the user's primary view and access to them.

> **NOTE** Jenkins 2 is the name we are generally applying to newer versions that support the pipeline-as-code functionality, as well as other features.

Because it's an important part of each project, the pipeline configuration should be managed as code and rolled out automatically. This also allows us to manage the pipeline itself, applying the same standards that apply to application code. That's where pipeline as code comes into play.

2.1 *Introducing the Jenkinsfile*

Pipeline as code (PaC) describes a set of features that allow Jenkins users to define pipelined job processes with code, stored and versioned in a source repository. These features allow Jenkins to discover, manage, and run jobs for multiple source repositories and branches—eliminating the need for manual job creation and management.

PaC helps you automate the CI/CD workflows in a repeatable, consistent manner, which has many benefits:

- *Speed*—You can quickly and easily write a CI/CD workflow for sandbox, staging, and production environments, which can help you deliver your product on time.
- *Consistency*—PaC completely standardizes the setup of CI/CD, so there's a reduced possibility of any human errors or deviations.
- *Risk management*—Because the pipeline can be version-controlled, PaC allows every change to your CI/CD workflow to be documented, logged, tracked, and tested just like application code. Hence, you can revert to a working version in case of failure.
- *Efficiency*—It minimizes the introduction of human errors and helps your application's deployment run more smoothly.

The bottom line is simple: adopting the PaC paradigm will create a culture that generates better software, and will save you a lot of money, time, and headaches trying to implement complex CI/CD workflows through UIs and web forms. So how does PaC work with Jenkins?

To use PaC with Jenkins, projects must contain a file named Jenkinsfile in the code repository top-level folder. This template file contains a set of instructions, or steps, called *stages* that will be executed on Jenkins every time the development team pushes a new feature to the code repository. Because Jenkinsfile is living along with the source code, we can always pull, edit, and push the Jenkinsfile within source control, just as we would for any other file. We can also do things like code reviews on the pipeline script.

Jenkinsfile uses a domain-specific language (DSL) based on the Groovy programming language to define the entire CI/CD workflow. Figure 2.1 is an example of a classic CI/CD workflow.

Figure 2.1   CI/CD workflow

Those phases can be described in a Jenkinsfile by using the `stage` keyword. A *stage* is a block that contains a series of steps. It can be used to visualize the pipeline process. The following listing is an example of a simple Jenkinsfile for figure 2.1.

Listing 2.1   Jenkinsfile stages

```
node('workers'){
    try {
        stage('Checkout'){
            checkout scm
        }

        stage('Quality Test'){
            echo "Running quality tests"
        }

        stage('Unit Test'){
            echo "Running unit tests"
        }

        stage('Security Test'){
            echo "Running security checks"
        }

        stage('Build'){
            echo "Building artifact"
        }

        stage('Push'){
            echo "Storing artifact"
        }
```

```
        stage('Deploy'){
            echo "Deploying artifact"
        }

        stage('Acceptance Tests'){
            echo "Running post-integrations tests"
        }
    } catch(err){
        echo "Handling errors"
    } finally{
        echo "Cleaning up"
    }
}
```

We'll dive deep into the syntax in the next chapter, but for now, let's focus on what the stages are doing:

- *Checkout*—Pulls the latest changes from the source code repository, which can be GitHub, Bitbucket, Mercurial, or any SCM.
- *Quality tests*—Contains instructions on how to execute static code analysis to measure code quality, and identify bugs, vulnerabilities, and code smell. It can be automated by integrating external tools like SonarQube to fix code-quality violations and reduce technical debt.
- *Unit tests*—In this stage, unit tests are executed. If tests are successful, a code coverage report will be generated that can be consumed by Jenkins plugins to show a visual overview of the project's health and keep track of the code coverage metrics as your project grows. Code coverage can be an indication of how much your application code is executed during your tests, and can give some indication as to how well your team is applying good testing practices such test-driven development (TDD) or behavior-driven development (BDD).
- *Security tests*—Responsible for identifying project dependencies and checks if any known, publicly disclosed vulnerabilities exist. A security report will be published with the total number of findings grouped by severity (critical, high, medium, or low). A well-known open source Jenkins plugin is OWASP Dependency-Check (http://mng.bz/MvR7).
- *Build*—In this phase, the needed dependencies will be installed, the source code will be compiled, and an artifact will be built (Docker image, zip file, Maven JAR, and so forth).
- *Push*—The artifact built in the previous stage will be versioned and stored in a remote repository.
- *Deploy*—In this stage, the artifact will be deployed to a sandbox/testing environment for quality assurance or to production after the user has approved the deployment.
- *Acceptance tests*—After the changes are deployed, a series of smoke and validation tests will be executed against the deployed application to verify that the application is running as expected. The tests can be simple health checks with cURL commands or sophisticated API calls.

If any of these stages throws an exception or error, the pipeline build's status will be set to fail. This default behavior can be overridden by using `try-catch` blocks. The `finally` block can be used to clean up the Jenkins workspace (temporary files or build packages) or to execute post-script commands such as sending Slack notifications to alert the development team about the build status.

> **NOTE** Don't worry if you don't completely understand the steps of the Jenkinsfile in listing 2.1. You will get an in-depth explanation of how to implement each stage in chapters 7, 8, and 9.

One of the things that makes Jenkins a leader when it comes to CI tools is the ecosystem behind it. You can customize your Jenkins instance with free open source plugins. A must-have plugin is Pipeline Stage View (https://plugins.jenkins.io/pipeline-rest-api), shown in figure 2.2. It allows you to have a visualization of your pipeline stages. This plugin is handy when you have complex build pipelines and want to track the progress of each stage.

The pipeline output is organized as a matrix, with each row representing a run of the job, and each column mapped to a defined stage in the pipeline. When you run some builds, the stage view will appear with Checkout, Quality Test, Unit Test, Security Test, Build, Push, and Deploy columns, and one row per build showing the status of those stages. When hovering over a stage cell, you can click the Logs button to see log messages printed in that stage.

> **NOTE** Part 3 of this book covers how to create a Jenkins job and define a pipeline like the one in figure 2.2.

Figure 2.2 Jenkins Pipeline Stage View

You can take this UI further and install the Blue Ocean plugin (https://plugins .jenkins.io/blueocean/) to have a fast and intuitive comprehension of the CI/CD stages, as shown in figure 2.3. This plugin requires Jenkins version 2.7 or later.

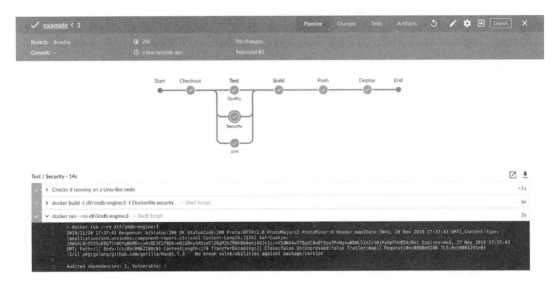

Figure 2.3   Blue Ocean plugin's detailed view of the pipeline

> **NOTE**   Chapter 5 covers how to install and configure the Jenkins Blue Ocean plugin.

2.1.1 *Blue Ocean plugin*

You can also troubleshoot pipeline failure by clicking the stage in red to easily identify the problem without going through thousands of output logs.

One of the big concerns while choosing Jenkins is the user interface, which many users consider outdated, unintuitive, and hard to navigate when you have many projects. That's why the Jenkins core team launched Blue Ocean in April 2017 for a new, modern Jenkins user experience.

Blue Ocean is a new user experience for Jenkins, based on a modern design that allows users to graphically create, personalize, visualize, and diagnose CD pipelines. It comes bundled with the Jenkins Pipeline plugin or as a separate plugin (www.jenkins .io/doc/book/blueocean/getting-started/).

> **NOTE**   The Jenkins Classic UI exists side-by-side at its usual place at JENKINS_ URL/jenkins. The Blue Ocean plugin is available by appending `/blue` to the end of the Jenkins server URL.

Anyone in your team can create a CI/CD pipeline with just several clicks. Blue Ocean has seamless integration with Git and GitHub. It prompts you for credentials to access

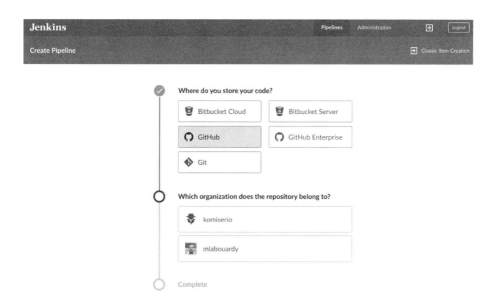

Figure 2.4 New pipeline in Blue Ocean mode

your repositories on the Git server in order to create pipelines based on those repositories (figure 2.4).

You can also create a complete CI/CD pipeline from start to finish by using the
intuitive and visual pipeline editor (figure 2.5). It's a great way to write pipeline proto-
types and debug pipeline stages before generating a working Jenkinsfile.

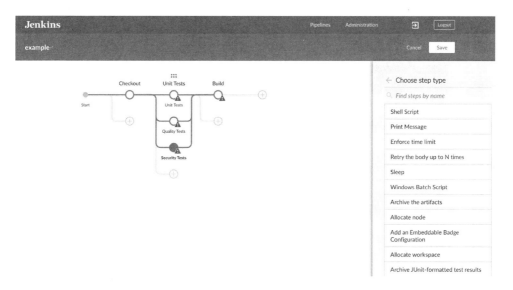

Figure 2.5 Defining stages with pipeline editor

Any pipeline created with the visual editor can also be edited in your favorite text editor, bringing all the benefits of PaC. Figure 2.6 shows an example of the pipeline script generated by pressing Ctrl-S for Windows users and Command-S for macOS users.

You can now copy the content and paste it in a new file called Jenkinsfile in your code repository, alongside the source code. Alternatively, you can upload the file directly from the Blue Ocean editor by supplying an appropriate description and the target Git branch (figure 2.7).

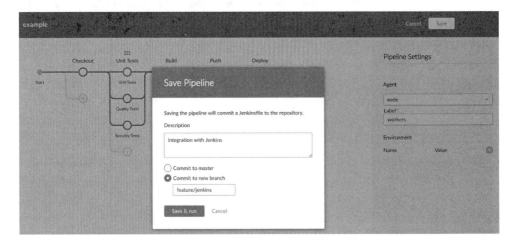

```
pipeline {
    agent {
        node {
            label 'workers'
        }
    }
    stages {
        stage('Checkout') {
            steps {
                echo 'clone project'
            }
        }

        stage('Unit Tests') {
            parallel {
                stage('Unit Tests') {
                    steps {
                        echo 'run unit tests'
                    }
                }

                stage('Quality Tests') {
                    steps {
                        echo 'run quality tests'
                    }
```

Figure 2.6   Jenkinsfile generated from the pipeline editor

Figure 2.7   Committing the Jenkinsfile to the Git repository

Once the file is committed, the pipeline will be triggered, and the stages defined in the pipeline will be executed.

Keep in mind that Blue Ocean doesn't support all features of Jenkins such as administration, nodes management, or credential settings. However, you can always switch back to the classic Jenkins UI by clicking the exit icon at the top right of the Blue Ocean navigation bar.

> **NOTE** This is just a sneak peek of Blue Ocean's main features. In chapter 7, we will dig deeper into each feature.

Now that you're familiar with how a Jenkinsfile works, let's see how to write your own pipeline as code with Jenkins. Jenkins 2 allows two styles of structure and syntax for building out workflows. These are referred to as scripted and declarative pipelines.

2.1.2 Scripted pipeline

A *scripted pipeline* is a traditional way of writing pipeline code. In this pipeline, the Jenkinsfile is written on the Jenkins UI instance. The pipeline steps are wrapped in a node block (denoted by the opening and closing braces). Here, a node refers to a *Jenkins agent* (formerly referred to as a *slave instance*).

The node gets mapped to the Jenkins cluster by using a label. A *label* is simply an identifier that has been added when configuring the node in Jenkins via the Manage Nodes section, as shown in figure 2.8.

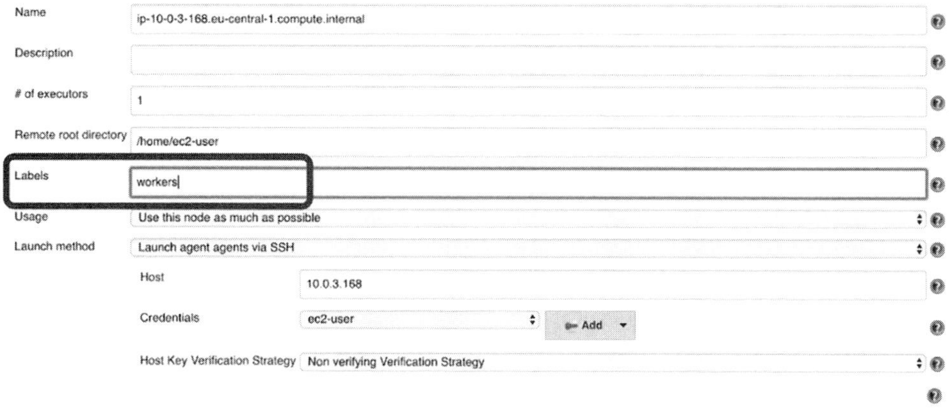

Figure 2.8   Assigning labels to Jenkins workers

> **NOTE** The next chapter covers how the Jenkins distributed mode works and how node agents can be used to offload work from Jenkins.

The steps inside the node block can include and make use of any valid Groovy code. The pipeline can be defined by creating a new pipeline project and typing the code in the Pipeline Editor section, as shown in figure 2.9.

Pipeline

Definition   Pipeline script

```
1 ▾ node('workers'){
2       git "https://github.com/mlabouardy/komiser.git"
3       docker.build('komiser')
4   }
```

☑ Use Groovy Sandbox

Pipeline Syntax

Save   Apply

Figure 2.9   Using an inline Jenkinsfile with Pipeline scripts

Although this simple node block is technically valid syntax, Jenkins pipelines generally
have a further level of granularity—stages. A *stage* is a way to divide the pipeline into
logical functional units. It also serves to group steps and Groovy code together to create targeted functionality. Figure 2.10 shows an example of the preceding pipeline
using stages.

Pipeline

Definition   Pipeline script

```
1 ▾ node('workers'){
2 ▾     stage('Checkout'){
3           git "https://github.com/mlabouardy/komiser.git"
4       }
5
6 ▾     stage('Build'){
7           docker.build('komiser')
8       }
9   }
```

☑ Use Groovy Sandbox

Pipeline Syntax

Figure 2.10   Using the `stage` keyword to define logical units

The pipeline has two stages:

- *Checkout*—For cloning the project GitHub repository
- *Build*—For building the project Docker image

How much of the pipeline's logic goes into a particular stage is up to the developer. However, the general practice is to create stages that mimic the separate pieces of a traditional pipeline.

The scripted pipeline uses stricter Groovy-based syntaxes because it was the first pipeline to be built on the Groovy foundation. Since this Groovy script was not typically desirable to all users, the declarative pipeline was introduced to offer a simpler and more optioned Groovy syntax.

> **NOTE** Chapter 14 covers how to write a shared Jenkins library with custom Groovy scripts for code modularity.

2.1.3 *Declarative pipeline*

A *declarative pipeline* is a relatively new feature (introduced in Pipeline 2.5, https://plugins.jenkins.io/workflow-aggregator) that supports the PaC approach. It makes the pipeline code easier to read and write for new Jenkins users.

This code is written in a Jenkinsfile that can be checked into a version-control system (VCS) such as SVN or an SCM system such as GitHub, GitLab, Bitbucket, or others. Figure 2.11 is an example of a Jenkinsfile located at the root folder of a GitHub repository.

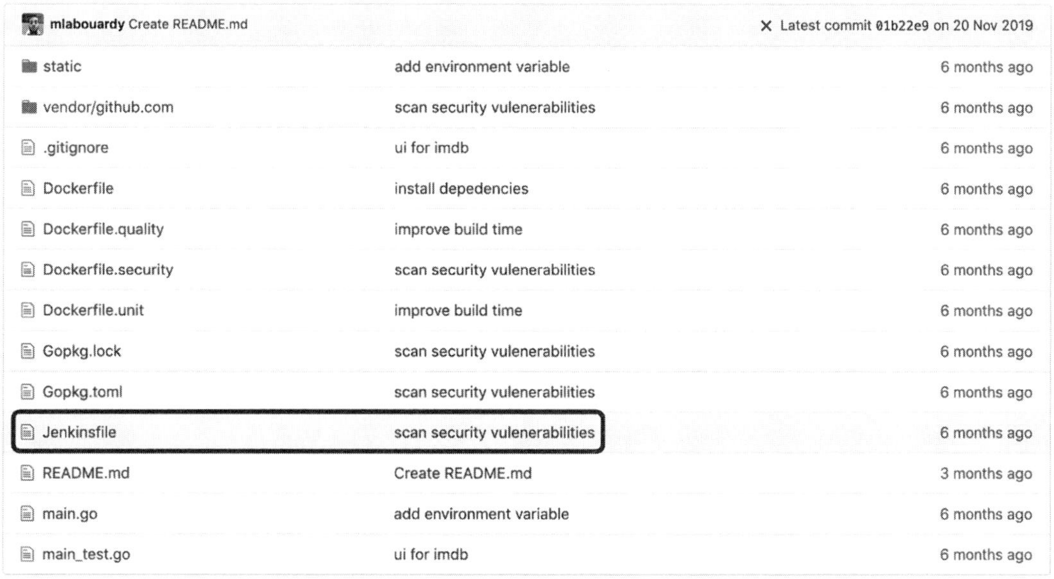

mlabouardy Create README.md		X Latest commit 01b22e9 on 20 Nov 2019
📁 static	add environment variable	6 months ago
📁 vendor/github.com	scan security vulnerabilities	6 months ago
📄 .gitignore	ui for imdb	6 months ago
📄 Dockerfile	install depedencies	6 months ago
📄 Dockerfile.quality	improve build time	6 months ago
📄 Dockerfile.security	scan security vulnerabilities	6 months ago
📄 Dockerfile.unit	improve build time	6 months ago
📄 Gopkg.lock	scan security vulnerabilities	6 months ago
📄 Gopkg.toml	scan security vulnerabilities	6 months ago
📄 Jenkinsfile	scan security vulnerabilities	6 months ago
📄 README.md	Create README.md	3 months ago
📄 main.go	add environment variable	6 months ago
📄 main_test.go	ui for imdb	6 months ago

Figure 2.11 A Jenkinsfile stored in a source-control repository

In declarative syntax, you cannot use Groovy code such as variables, loops, or conditions. You are restricted to the structured sections/blocks and the DSL (Jenkins domain-specific language) steps.

Figure 2.12 shows the differences between scripted and declarative pipelines. Declarative pipelines are restricted and have well-defined structures (for example, all DSL statements must be enclosed in a `steps` directive).

Scripted	Declarative

```
node('node label'){
stage('id #1'){
//DSL statements
}
stage('id #2'){
//DSL statements
}


// OR


//DSL statements without stage block


// OR


//Loops, conditions, variables, etc
def variable = value


if(variable){
//DSL statements
}else{
//DSL statements
}


def list = []
for(int i=0;i<list.size();i++){
//DSL statements
}
}
```

```
pipeline{
agent{
label 'node label'
}


environment{
ENV_VARIABLE_A = 'v.
}


stages{
stage('id #1'){
agent{
label 'node label 1
}
environment{}
steps{
//DSL statements
}
}
stage('id #2'){
agent{
label 'node label 2
}
environment{}
steps{
//DSL statements
}
}
}


post {
always {
//DSL statements
}
success {
//DSL statements
}
failure {
//DSL statements
}
}
}
```

Figure 2.12   Differences between scripted and declarative pipelines

Declarative pipelines provide a more restrictive syntax, as each pipeline must use these predefined block attributes or sections:

- `agent`
- `environment`
- `post`
- `stages`
- `steps`

The `agent` section defines the worker or machine where the pipeline will be executed. This section must be defined at the top level inside the pipeline block or overridden at the stage level. The agent can be any of the following:

- Jenkins worker or node (refer to chapter 3 for distributed builds on Jenkins)
- Docker container based on a Docker image or a custom Dockerfile (covered in chapter 9)
- Pod deployed on a Kubernetes cluster (covered in chapter 14)

For example, you can define the pipeline to run on a custom Docker container, as shown in the following listing.

Listing 2.2 Declarative pipeline agents definition

```
pipeline{
    agent {
        node {
            label 'workers'
        }

        dockerfile {
            filename 'Dockerfile'
            label 'workers'
        }

        kubernetes {
            label 'workers'
            yaml """
            kind: Pod
            metadata:
            name: jenkins-worker
            spec:
            containers:
            - name: nodejs
              image: node:lts
              tty: true
            """
        }
    }
}
```

> **NOTE** Refer to the official documentation for more information about the agent syntax: www.jenkins.io/doc/book/pipeline/syntax/.

The `environment` section contains a set of environment variables needed to run the pipeline steps. The variables can be defined as sequences of key-value pairs. These will be available for all steps if the environment block is defined at the pipeline top level; otherwise, the variables can be stage-specific. You can also reference credential variables by using a helper method `credentials()`, which takes as a parameter the ID of the target credential, as shown in the following listing.

Listing 2.3   Environment variables definition

```
pipeline{
    environment {
        REGISTRY_CREDENTIALS= credentials('DOCKER_REGISTRY')
        REGISTRY_URL = 'https://registry.domain.com'
    }

    stages {
        stage('Push'){
            steps{
                sh 'docker login $REGISTRY_URL --username
    $REGISTRY_CREDENTIALS_USR --password $REGISTRY_CREDENTIALS_PSW'
            }
        }
    }
}
```

The Docker registry username and password are accessible automatically by referencing the `REGISTRY_CREDENTIALS_USR` and `REGISTRY_CREDENTIALS_PSW` environment variables. Those credentials are then passed to the `docker login` command to authenticate with the Docker Registry before pushing a Docker image.

The `post` section contains commands or scripts that will be run upon the completion of a pipeline or stage run, depending on the location of this section within the pipeline. However, conventionally the `post` section should be placed at the end of the pipeline. Examples of commands that can be used within the `post` section are those that provide Slack notifications, clean up the job workspace, and execute post-scripts based on the build status. The pipeline build status can be fetched by using either the `currentBuild.result` variable or the post-condition blocks `always`, `success`, `unstable`, `failure`, and so forth.

The following listing is an example Slack notification. The instructions wrapped by the `always` directive will run no matter the status of the build and will not interfere with the final status.

Listing 2.4   Post build actions in a declarative pipeline

```
pipeline{
    post {
        always {
            echo 'Cleaning up workspace'
        }
```

```
        success {
            slackSend (color: 'GREEN', message: \
                "${env.JOB_NAME} Successful build")
        }
        failure {
            slackSend (color: 'RED', message: "${env.JOB_NAME} Failed build")
        }
    }
}
```

This code references the env.JOB_NAME variable, which contains the Jenkins job name.

NOTE Chapter 10 has a dedicated section on how to implement Slack notifications with Jenkins.

The stages section is the core of the pipeline. This section defines what is to be done at a high level. It contains a sequence of more stage directives for each discrete part of the CI/CD workflow.

Finally, the steps section contains a series of more steps to be executed in a given stage directive. The following listing defines a Test stage with instructions to run unit tests and generate code coverage reports.

Listing 2.5 Running automated tests within a pipeline

```
pipeline{
    agent any
    stages {
        stage('Test'){
            steps {
                sh 'npm run test'
                sh 'npm run coverage'
            }
        }
    }
}
```

These are the most used directives and sections while writing a declarative pipeline. Additional directives will be covered throughout this book. For an overview of all available blocks, refer to Pipeline Syntax documentation (www.jenkins.io/doc/book/pipe line/syntax/#stages).

Both declarative and scripted styles can be used to build CI/CD pipelines in either the web UI or with a Jenkinsfile. However, it's generally considered a best practice to create a Jenkinsfile and check it into the source-control repository to have a single source of truth and be able to track all changes (auditing) that your pipeline went through.

NOTE In chapters 7 through 11, you will learn how to write a scripted pipeline from scratch for various application architectures and how to convert a Jenkinsfile from a scripted to a declarative format.

2.2   *Understanding multibranch pipelines*

When you're building your application, you must separate your deployment environments to test new changes without impacting your production. Therefore, having multiple environments for your application makes sense. To be able to achieve that, you need to structure your code repository to use multiple branches, with each branch representing an environment. For instance, the master branch corresponds to the current production code.

While it's easier nowadays to replicate multiple infrastructure environments with the adoption of cloud computing and IaC tools, you still need to configure your CI tools for each target branch.

Fortunately, when using a Jenkinsfile, your pipeline definition lives with the code source of the application going through the pipeline. Jenkins will automatically scan through each branch in the application code repository and check whether the branch has a Jenkinsfile. If it does, Jenkins will automatically create and configure a subproject within the multibranch pipeline project to run the pipeline for that branch. This eliminates the need for manual pipeline creation and management.

Figure 2.13 shows the jobs in a multibranch pipeline project after executing against the Jenkinsfiles and source repositories. Jenkins automatically scans the designated repository and creates appropriate projects for each branch in the repository that contains a Jenkinsfile.

Figure 2.13   Jenkins automatically creates a job for each branch with a Jenkinsfile.

In figure 2.13, Jenkins will trigger a build whenever a new code change occurs on any of the develop, preprod, or master branches. In addition, each branch might have different pipeline stages. For example, you might perform a complete CI/CD pipeline for the master branch and only a CI pipeline for the develop branch (see figure 2.14). You can do this with the help of a multibranch pipeline project.

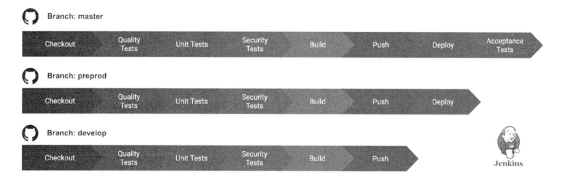

Figure 2.14   Each Git branch can have its own Jenkinsfile stages.

A multibranch pipeline can also be used to validate pull requests before merging them to target branches. You can configure Jenkins to launch pre-integration tests against the application's code and block the pull request merge if the tests failed, as in figure 2.15.

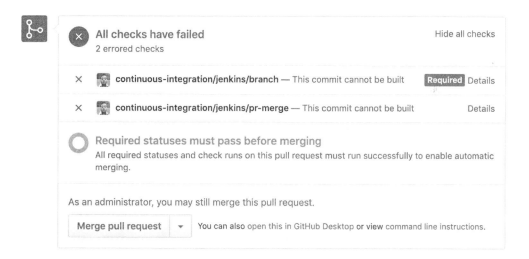

Figure 2.15   Jenkins build status in GitHub pull request

NOTE   Chapter 9 covers using multibranch pipelines to validate pull/change requests.

Now that you're familiar with the basics of the Jenkins multibranch pipeline, you must follow Git branching guidelines to have a common vision and methodology within the development team. So which Git branching strategies should you use for your development cycle?

2.3   *Exploring the GitFlow branch model*

A couple of Git branching strategies exist. The most interesting and used one is Git-Flow. It consists of the following essential branches:

- *Master*—A branch that corresponds to the current production code. You can't commit directly except for hotfixes. Git tags can be used to tag all commits in the master branch with a version number (for instance, you can use the semantic versioning convention detailed at https://semver.org/).
- *Preprod*—A release branch, a mirror of production. It can be used to test all new features developed on the develop branch before merging them to the master branch.
- *Develop*—A development integration branch containing the latest integrated development code.
- *Feature/X*—An individual feature branch being developed. Each new feature resides in its own branch, and it's generally created from the latest develop branch.
- *Hotfix/X*—When you need to solve something in production code, you can use the hotfix branch and open a pull request for the master branch. This branch is based on the master branch.

> **NOTE**   A complete example demonstrating the use of GitFlow with the Jenkins multibranch pipeline project is given in chapters 7 through 11.

The overall flow of GitFlow within Jenkins can be summarized as follows:

- A develop branch is created from the master branch.
- A preprod branch is created from the develop branch.
- A developer creates a new feature branch based on the development branch. When a feature is completed, a pull request is created.
- Jenkins automatically runs pre-integration tests in this individual feature. If the tests are successful, Jenkins marks the commits as successful. The development team will then review the changes and merge the pull request of the new feature branch to the develop branch and delete the feature branch.
- A build will be triggered on the develop branch, and the changes will be deployed to the sandbox/development environment.
- A pull request is created to merge the develop branch into the preprod branch.
- When the develop branch is merged to the preprod branch, the pipeline will be triggered to deploy the new features to the staging environment upon the completion of the pipeline.
- Once the release is being validated, the preprod branch will be merged to master, and changes will be deployed to the production environment after user approval.
- If an issue in production is detected, a hot branch is created from the master branch. Once the hotfix is complete, it will be merged to both the develop and master branches.

NOTE   You can use the GitFlow wrapper around the Git command line (available on multiple operating systems) to create a project blueprint with all needed branches.

Figure 2.16 summarizes how GitFlow works.

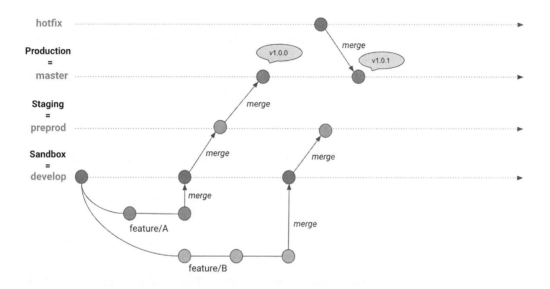

Figure 2.16   Overview of GitFlow branches

GitFlow does not solve all problems with branching. But it offers you a more logical branch structure and a great workflow organization model when working within a big team. In addition, many feature branches are developed concurrently, which makes parallel development easy. For smaller projects (and smaller teams), GitFlow can be overkill. Hence, in upcoming chapters, we will usually use three main branches:

- *Master* branch, to store the official release history and the source code of an application running in a production environment
- *Preprod* branch, to store new integrated features running in the staging environment and ready to be merged to the master branch
- *Develop* branch, for the latest delivered development changes and mirror of the application running in a sandbox environment

2.4   *Test-driven development with Jenkins*

Using Jenkinsfiles has one potential downside: it can be more challenging to discover problems up-front when you are working in the external file and not in the environment of the Jenkins server. One approach to dealing with this is developing the code within the Jenkins server as a pipeline project first. Then, you can convert it to a Jenkinsfile afterward.

You can also use Blue Ocean mode as a playground, as seen earlier in this chapter, to set up a Jenkinsfile from scratch with a modern and intuitive pipeline editor. Another approach to test a new pipeline is a declarative pipeline linter application that you can run against Jenkinsfiles, outside Jenkins, to detect problems early.

2.4.1   *The Jenkins Replay button*

Sometimes, when working on Jenkins jobs, you might find yourself stuck in this cycle of committing the Jenkinsfile, pushing it, and running the job over and over again. It can be a time-consuming and tedious workflow, especially if your build time is inherently long. Plus, your Git history will get filled with junk commits (unnecessary debugging commits).

What if you could work on your Jenkinsfile in a "sandbox" and test the Jenkinsfile live on the system? A neat little feature allows you to modify the Jenkins file and rerun the job. You can do it over and over until you are happy with the results and then commit the working Jenkinsfile without breaking anything.

Now, this is a little easier. If you have a Pipeline build that did not proceed exactly as you expected, you can use the Replay button in the build's sidebar, shown in figure 2.17.

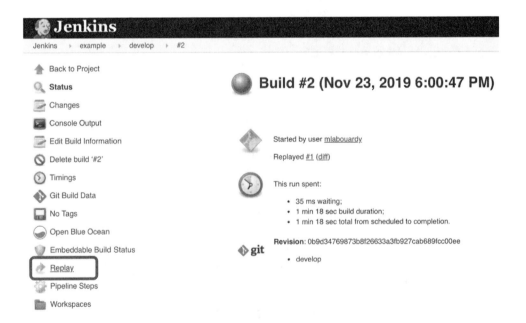

Figure 2.17   Rerunning the build with a Replay button

It is somewhat similar to the Rebuild button but allows you to edit the Jenkinsfile content just before running the job. Therefore, you can use the built-in Jenkinsfile block in the UI (figure 2.18), to test your pipelines out there before committing them to source control like GitHub.

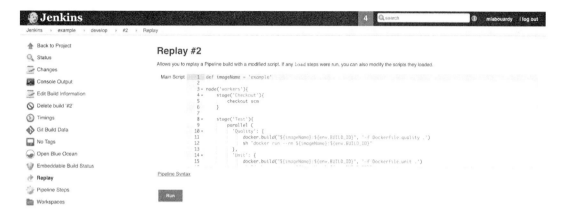

Figure 2.18   **Updating the Jenkinsfile before replaying the pipeline**

You can change your pipeline's code and click the Run button and rerun the job. Once you are satisfied with the changes, you update the Jenkinsfile with the applied changes and commit them to your SCM.

   The Replay button feature allows for quick modifications and execution of an existing pipeline without changing the pipeline configuration or creating a new commit. It's ideal for rapid iteration and prototyping of a pipeline.

2.4.2   *Command-line pipeline linter*

For advanced users, you can use the Jenkins RESTful API to validate the Jenkinsfile syntax by issuing an HTTP/HTTPS POST request with the parameters shown in figure 2.19.

> **NOTE**   To get the API endpoint working on a Jenkins server with cross-site request forgery (CSRF) protection enabled, you need to request a crumb issuer and include it in the Authorization header in the issued HTTP request. To generate this crumb, you need to request the following URL: JENKINS_URL/jenkins/crumbIssuer/api/json.

Figure 2.19 is an example of how to use the Jenkins Linter API to validate Jenkinsfile syntax. We're using Postman in this example, and the Jenkinsfile form data has been loaded from the developer machine.

Figure 2.19   Example of using Jenkins Linter API

The API response will return both errors and warnings, which can save time during the development and allows you to follow best practices while writing a Jenkinsfile.

Specifying the real password is still supported, but it is not recommended because of the risk of revealing the password, and the human tendency to reuse the same password in different places. Another way of validating the Jenkinsfile is to run the following command from the terminal session (cURL is available for most operating systems):

```
curl -X POST -L --user USERNAME:TOKEN JENKINS_URL/pipeline-model-converter/
    validate
-F "jenkinsfile=<Jenkinsfile"
```

NOTE   Chapter 7 covers another way of creating a Jenkins API token from the Jenkins web dashboard.

The Jenkins command-line interface (CLI), www.jenkins.io/doc/book/managing/cli/, can also be used with the `declarative-lint` option to lint a declarative pipeline from the command line before actually running it. You can issue this command to lint a Jenkinsfile via the CLI with SSH:

```
ssh -p $JENKINS_SSHD_PORT $JENKINS_HOSTNAME declarative-linter < Jenkinsfile
```

Replace the `JENKINS_HOSTNAME` and `JENKINS_SSHD_PORT` variables based on the URL and port where you are running Jenkins. You can also use localhost as a URL if you are running Jenkins on your machine.

2.4.3 IDE integrations

The Jenkins CLI or API does a great job of reducing the turnaround times when writing a Jenkinsfile, but its usage has its own inconveniences. You need tools like SSH to make a connection to your Jenkins server, and you need to remember the correct command to validate your Jenkinsfile.

Fortunately, you can install extensions on your favorite integrated development environment (IDE) to automate the validation process. For instance, on Visual Studio Code (VSCode), you can install Jenkins Validation Linter from the marketplace. This extension, shown in figure 2.20, validates Jenkinsfiles by sending them to the Pipeline Linter endpoint of a Jenkins server.

> **NOTE** Similar extensions and packages are available to validate a Jenkinsfile for Eclipse, Atom, and Sublime Text.

Figure 2.20 Jenkins Pipeline Linter extension for VSCode

Once the extension is installed, you must provide Jenkins server settings, including the server URL (with the following format: JENKINS_URL/pipeline_model_converter/validate) and credentials (Jenkins username and password, or token if CSRF protection is enabled) by clicking Preferences from the top navigation bar, and selecting Settings, as shown in figure 2.21.

Text Editor
  Cursor
  Find
  Font
  Formatting
  Diff Editor
  Minimap
  Suggestions
  Files
Workbench
Window
Features
Application
Extensions
  CSS
  Emmet
  Git
  Go
  Grunt
  Gulp
  HTML
  Jake
  Jenkins Pipeline...
  JSON
  LESS
  Markdown
  Merge Conflict
  Node debug
  Npm
  PHP
  Reference Search...

Jenkins Pipeline Linter Connector

Jenkins › Pipeline › Linter › Connector: Crumb Url
The url of the crumb service (i.e. http://<your_jenkins_server:port>/crumbIssuer/api/xml?
xpath=concat(//crumbRequestField,%22:%22,//crumb))

Jenkins › Pipeline › Linter › Connector: Pass
Password (can be left blank if you don't want to put your password in your settings)

Jenkins › Pipeline › Linter › Connector: Strictssl
[✓] Set to false to allow invalid ssl connections

Jenkins › Pipeline › Linter › Connector: Token
Token (can be left blank if you don't want to put your token in your settings)

Jenkins › Pipeline › Linter › Connector: Url
Linter url (i.e. http://<your_jenkins_server:port>/pipeline-model-converter/validate)

https://jenkins.slowcoder.com/pipeline-model-converter/validate

Jenkins › Pipeline › Linter › Connector: User
Username

mlabouardy

JSON

Figure 2.21   Jenkins Pipeline Linter configuration

Once settings are configured, you can type the `Validate Jenkinsfile` command on the command palette search bar (keyword shortcut ⇧⌘P), as shown in figure 2.22.

Figure 2.22   VSCode command palette

The linter will report the pipeline validation results in the terminal, as shown in figure 2.23.

```
Jenkinsfile ×
manning > chapter2 > Jenkinsfile
1    def imageName = 'example'
2
3    pipeline{
4        agent{
5            label 'workers'
6        }
7
8        stages{
9            stage('Checkout'){
10               steps{
11                   checkout scm
12               }
13           }
14
15           stage('Build'){
16               docker.build(imageName)
17           }
18
19           stage('Deploy'){
20               echo "Deploying ..."
21           }
22       }
23   }
```

```
PROBLEMS   OUTPUT   DEBUG CONSOLE   TERMINAL                                            Jenkins Pipeline Linter  ▲▼

Errors encountered validating Jenkinsfile:
WorkflowScript: 16: Method calls on objects not allowed outside "script" blocks. @ line 16, column 13.
            docker.build(imageName)
            ^

WorkflowScript: 15: Unknown stage section "error". Starting with version 0.5, steps in a stage must be in a 'steps' block. @ line 15, column 9.
        stage('Build'){
        ^

WorkflowScript: 19: Unknown stage section "echo". Starting with version 0.5, steps in a stage must be in a 'steps' block. @ line 19, column 9.
        stage('Deploy'){
        ^

WorkflowScript: 15: Expected one of "steps", "stages", or "parallel" for stage "Build" @ line 15, column 9.
        stage('Build'){
        ^

WorkflowScript: 19: Expected one of "steps", "stages", or "parallel" for stage "Deploy" @ line 19, column 9.
        stage('Deploy'){
        ^
```

Figure 2.23   Example of Jenkins Linter's output

NOTE   In chapter 8, you will learn how to write unit tests for CI pipelines and use the Jenkins Pipeline Unit (https://github.com/jenkinsci/JenkinsPipeline Unit) testing framework to mock the pipeline executor locally.

Summary

- Infrastructure as code influenced CI/CD tools to embrace the pipeline-as-code concepts.
- A Jenkinsfile uses Groovy syntax and utilizes shared Jenkins libraries to customize a CI/CD workflow.
- Declarative pipelines encourage a declarative programming model. Scripted pipelines follow a more imperative programming model.

- The Blue Ocean editor can facilitate a quick and easy setup of a new Jenkins pipeline with minimal hassle.
- A feature branch workflow facilitates pull requests and more efficient collaboration.
- GitFlow offers a dedicated channel for hotfixes to production without interrupting the rest of the workflow or waiting for the next release cycle.
- The Jenkins UI, Replay button, and code linters can be used to test new pipelines before committing them to source control, enabling you to avoid a bunch of unnecessary debugging commits.

Part 2

Operating a self-healing Jenkins cluster

You've read through part 1 and now feel comfortable with some of the core concepts and principles of pipeline as code. It's time to get your hands dirty and deploy a Jenkins cluster from scratch with infrastructure-as-code tools on the cloud, including Amazon Web Services, Google Cloud Platform, Microsoft Azure, and DigitalOcean.

Along the way, you'll discover how to scale Jenkins workers dynamically and how to architect Jenkins for scale with distributed build mode. We'll then look at Jenkins essential plugins and how to provision a preconfigured Jenkins cluster with all needed dependencies and configurations using Packer and Groovy scripts.

Defining Jenkins architecture

This chapter covers

- Understanding how Jenkins distributed builds work
- Understanding the roles of Jenkins master and worker nodes
- Architecting Jenkins in the cloud for scale
- Configuring multiple Jenkins masters
- Preparing an AWS environment and CLI configuration

In a distributed microservices architecture, you may have multiple services to build, test, and deploy regularly. Hence, having multiple build machines makes sense. While you can always run Jenkins in a standalone mode, running all builds on a central machine may not be the best option and will result in having a single point of failure (a single Jenkins server cannot handle the entire load for larger and heavier projects). Fortunately, Jenkins can also be configured to run distributed builds across a fleet of machines/nodes by setting up a master/worker cluster, as shown in figure 3.1.

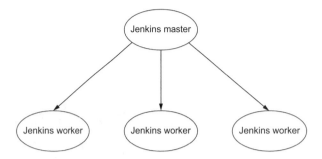

Figure 3.1   Distributed master-worker architecture

Jenkins uses a master-worker architecture to manage distributed builds. Each component has a specific role:

- *Jenkins master*—Responsible for scheduling build jobs and distributing builds to the workers for the actual execution. It also monitors the workers' states, and collects and aggregates the build results in the web dashboard.
- *Jenkins worker*—Also known as a *slave* or *build agent*, this is a Java executable that runs on a remote machine, listens for requests coming from the Jenkins master, and executes build jobs. You can have as many workers as you want (up to 100+ nodes). Workers can be added and removed on the fly. Therefore, the workload will be distributed to them automatically, and the workers will take the load off the master Jenkins server.

> **NOTE**   In 2016, the Jenkins community decided to start removing offensive terminology within the project. The *slave* term was deprecated in Jenkins 2.0 and replaced by *agent*.

To sum up, Jenkins can be deployed in a standalone mode. However, when you want to run multiple build jobs regularly in different environments to meet the requirements of the build environment for different projects, then a single Jenkins server cannot simply handle the workload. That's why in this book, we will be focusing on *master-worker architecture*.

3.1   *Understanding master-worker architecture*

In a master-worker architecture, the web dashboard is running on the Jenkins master instance. The master's role is to handle scheduling build jobs, dispatching and delegating builds to the workers for the actual execution, monitoring the workers' state (online or offline), and recording and presenting the build results. Even in a distributed architecture, a master instance of Jenkins can also execute build jobs directly.

Jenkins workers can be added and configured on the Jenkins dashboard or through a Jenkins RESTful API. The worker's role is to execute build jobs assigned by the master. You can configure a project to always run on a particular node by assigning labels to nodes. Labels are a powerful feature; they are virtual group names. You can assign multiple labels to a worker node while configuring it. Labels can also be used to restrict the build job to run on a worker node associated with a specific label name—for instance, to restrict a job to be built on a CPU-optimized instance.

To add a worker, you can click Manage Jenkins in the admin page menu, and then click Manage Nodes and Add New Node. Fill in the configuration information, including a name for the node, the workspace name, and the IP address of the node. Then, enter a label like `workers` (you can assign multiple labels in the Labels entry box by separating them with spaces). Figure 3.2 shows how to add a new worker to Jenkins.

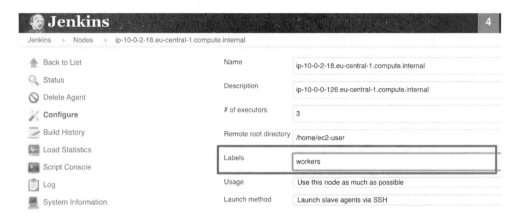

Figure 3.2 Using labels for Jenkins jobs assignments

By assigning the `workers` label to the node, you can reference it easily in your Jenkinsfile. In a declarative pipeline, you can restrict the pipeline to run on nodes with the `workers` label by setting up the `agent` directive as follows:

```
pipeline{
    agent{
        label 'workers'
    }
    stages{
        stage('Checkout'){}
    }
}
```

The scripted pipeline, however, uses the `node` block wrapper with the label name as a parameter to define the execution environment for the pipeline:

```
node('workers'){
    stage('Checkout'){}
}
```

If more build jobs are requested for the same node, Jenkins will automatically create a job queue. By default, each node can execute one job; however, you can increase the node's capacity for running jobs by setting the field labeled # of Executors. In the previous example, the node is configured with three executors, which means up to three jobs can be executed at once. If four jobs are started, the first three will execute, and the fourth will be added to the build queue. Once nodes become available, Jenkins will execute the remaining jobs in the order they were requested.

To be able to add a worker to the Jenkins cluster, the workers and master need to establish bidirectional communication through TCP/IP. Another requirement is that Java should be installed on the worker machine. Because Java is a platform-agnostic programming language, a Jenkins cluster might consist of workers that run on a variety of OS platforms such as Windows, Linux, or macOS. This architecture comes with multiple benefits, such as having a heterogeneous build farm that supports all of the environments that you might need to run builds/tests with a different OS or CPU architecture.

In the example in figure 3.3, using a worker to represent each of your required environments results in having several environments and configurations to test, build, and deploy your projects. The delegation behavior of build jobs depends on the configuration of each project; some projects may choose to "stick" to a particular machine for a build using labels, while others may choose to roam freely among available workers.

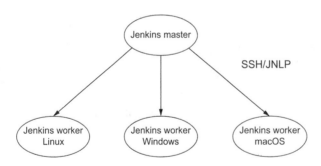

Figure 3.3 You can set up multiple workers running different operating systems by using SSH or Java Network Launch Protocol (JNLP)

3.2 *Managing Jenkins workers*

Several strategies are available when it comes to managing Jenkins workers, depending on your target operating systems and other architectural considerations. These strategies affect the way you configure your workers, so we need to consider each separately.

3.2.1 *SSH*

If you are working in a UNIX environment, the most convenient way to start a Jenkins worker is undoubtedly to use Secure Shell (SSH). Jenkins has its own built-in SSH client, and almost all UNIX environments support SSH (usually sshd) out of the box.

The worker needs to be reachable from the master server, and you will have to supply the hostname, login, and password. You can also provide a path to the SSH private key file on the master instance to use public/private key authentication, as shown in figure 3.4.

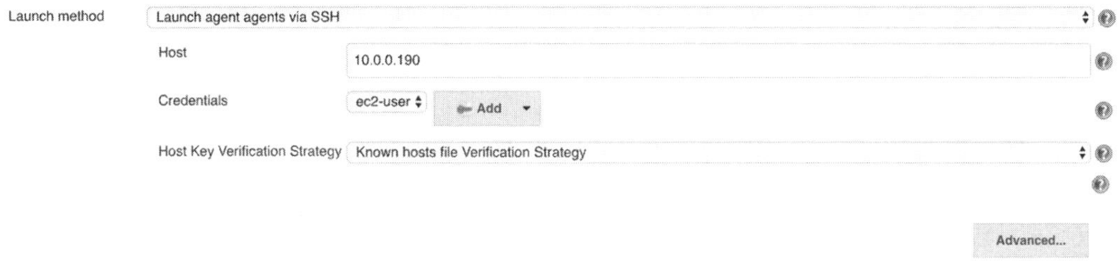

Figure 3.4   Launching a Jenkins worker via SSH

> **NOTE**   In chapter 5, we will use the SSH launch method to set up a Jenkins cluster.

3.2.2   *Command line*

You can add a worker by having Jenkins execute a command from the master, as shown in figure 3.5. Use this approach when the master is capable of remotely executing a process on another machine. However, the remoting mode has been deprecated since Jenkins 2.54 (so it might not a valid option in the newest version of Jenkins).

Launch method   Launch agent via execution of command on the master

Launch command   ssh ec2-user@10.0.0.190 java -jar ~/bin/agent.jar

Figure 3.5   Launching a Jenkins worker via the command line

3.2.3   *JNLP*

Another option is to start an agent from the worker machine itself by using Java Web Start (JWS). This approach is useful if the master cannot reach the worker—for example, if the worker machine is running on the other side of a firewall. It works no matter what operating system your worker is running on. However, it is more suitable for managing Windows workers.

This approach does suffer from a few major drawbacks: the worker machine cannot be started or restarted automatically by Jenkins. If the worker goes down, the master instance cannot restart it. When you do this on a Windows machine, you need to start the Jenkins worker manually at least once. This requires opening a browser on the machine, opening the worker node page on the Jenkins master, and launching the worker using a very visible JNLP icon. However, once you have launched the worker, you can install it as a Windows service.

3.2.4   *Windows service*

Jenkins can also manage a remote Windows worker as a Windows service, using the Windows DCOM Server Process Launcher service, which is installed out of the box on Windows. When you choose this option, you need to provide a Windows hostname, username, and password, as you can see in figure 3.6.

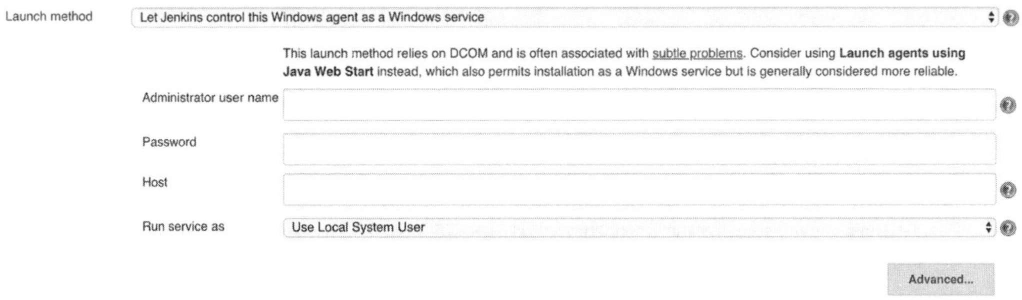

Figure 3.6   Starting a Windows worker

This launching mode is convenient, as it does not require you to physically connect to the Windows machine to set it up. However, it does have limitations—in particular, you cannot run any applications requiring a graphical interface.

Once the workers are added to the Jenkins cluster, the master will proactively monitor their statuses and take a worker offline if it considers the worker incapable of safely executing a build job. You can fine-tune exactly what Jenkins monitors on the Manage Nodes page, shown in figure 3.7.

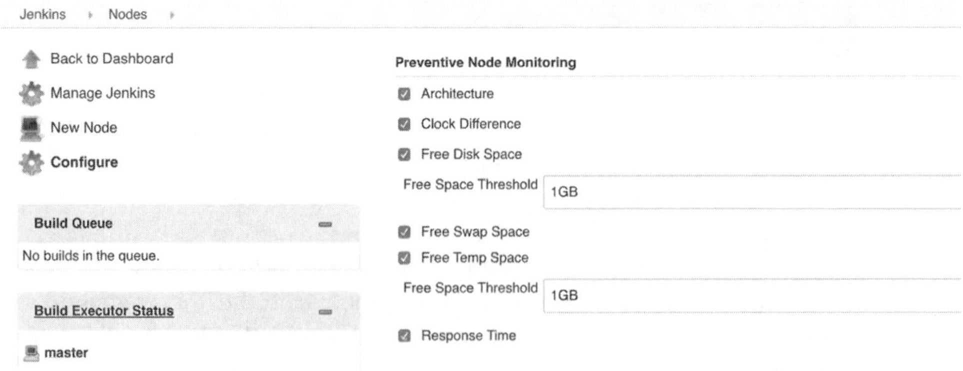

Figure 3.7   Defining node-monitoring thresholds

Jenkins monitors the available disk space of $JENKINS_HOME on each worker, as well as the disk space of the temporary directory and swap space. It also keeps tabs on the system clock difference between the master and workers. Finally, it monitors the round-trip network response time from the master to the worker. If any of these criteria is below a certain threshold, the worker will be marked offline.

Finally, it's worth mentioning that by default Jenkins uses the workers as much as possible. Whenever a build can be executed by a specific worker, Jenkins will use it.

To control how Jenkins is scheduling builds on available workers, you can configure the Usage field, shown in figure 3.8, to use the Only Build Jobs with Label Expressions Matching This Node option to restrict jobs to a worker that matches its name and/or label. This can become handy if you want to reserve a worker for a certain kind of Jenkins job. Furthermore, if you set the # of Executors field's value to 1, you can ensure that only one job will be executed at any given time. As a result, no other builds will interfere.

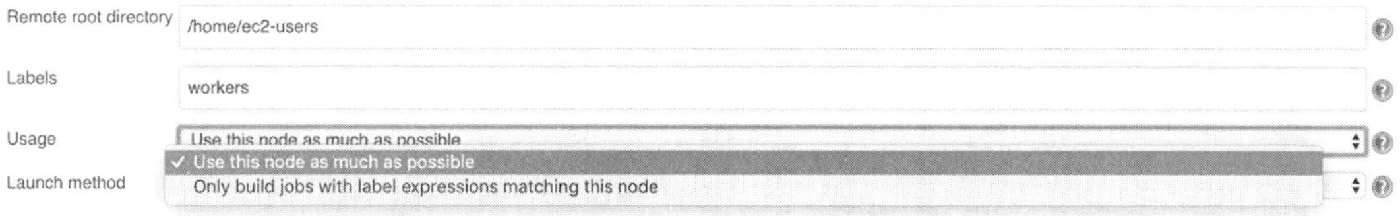

Remote root directory	/home/ec2-users	?
Labels	workers	?
Usage	Use this node as much as possible	?
	✓ Use this node as much as possible	
Launch method	Only build jobs with label expressions matching this node	?

Figure 3.8 Configuring Jenkins worker usage

3.3 *Architecting Jenkins for scale in AWS*

So far, we have covered how Jenkins distributed builds work. This section covers how to architect Jenkins for scale on AWS. Therefore, you will need an AWS account to follow the examples. With a new AWS account, the Free Tiers should cover all the examples at no cost to you. For more information on the AWS Free Tier, and a step-by-step guide on how to create a new AWS account, visit https://aws.amazon.com/free/.

> **NOTE** Although this section focuses on AWS, this content can also be used to help set up a Jenkins cluster in other cloud providers. Chapter 6 provides a step-by-step guide.

The simple architecture you can deploy is a standalone or single-node setup. You simply need to deploy a Jenkins server on an Amazon Elastic Compute Cloud (EC2) instance from the AWS Marketplace (https://aws.amazon.com/marketplace), shown in figure 3.9.

The AWS Marketplace contains preconfigured Amazon Machine Images (AMIs) from popular categories such as security, networking, storage, machine learning, business intelligence, database, and DevOps. You can quickly launch a Jenkins server with

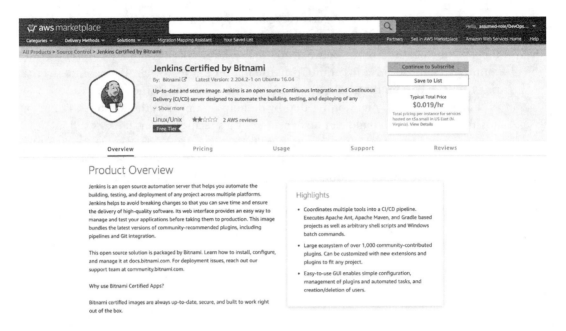

Figure 3.9   Jenkins Amazon Machine Image available on AWS Marketplace

just a few clicks, by selecting the Jenkins Long-Term Support (LTS) release and the machine instance type (based on resource requirements).

You can also install Jenkins on a base machine image by using a package manager (for example, APT or Yum). Jenkins installers are available for several Linux distributions as well as Windows and macOS. Otherwise, you can set up a Jenkins playground with a Jenkins official Docker image.

> **NOTE**   Chapter 4 covers how to create your own Jenkins machine image from scratch with HashiCorp Packer.

Once you have installed Jenkins on an EC2 instance, you will need to configure the security group attached to the instance to allow traffic on port 8080. This is the port where the Jenkins dashboard is exposed to.

A *security group* acts as a firewall that controls the traffic allowed to reach the EC2 instances (figure 3.10). To control traffic, we create rules in the security group. For this case, the following security rules need to be added:

- Allow inbound (ingress) traffic on port 8080 (Jenkins dashboard port number).

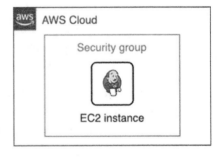

Figure 3.10   The Jenkins standalone architecture on AWS consists of an EC2 instance behind a security group.

- (Optional) Allow inbound SSH traffic from your computer's public address so that you can connect to your Jenkins instance for debugging or maintenance.
- By default, a security group includes an outbound rule that allows all outbound (egress) traffic.

You might set up a network access-control list (ACL) with rules similar to your security group to add an additional layer of security to your instance. The security group acts as a firewall for your Amazon EC2 instance, controlling both inbound and outbound traffic at the instance level. ACL acts as a firewall for associated subnets, controlling both inbound and outbound traffic at the subnet level.

> **NOTE** While you can scale the Jenkins master vertically to absorb the loading pike of build jobs, there is a limit to how much an instance can be scaled.

While this architecture works for smaller projects, it can't scale for larger and complex projects. Therefore, we will deploy a Jenkins cluster to share the load across multiple workers. Instead of scheduling builds jobs on a Jenkins master instance, they will be assigned to Jenkins workers. As a result, additional EC2 instances (figure 3.11) will be deployed as build servers or Jenkins agents.

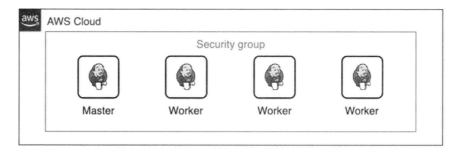

Figure 3.11 Jenkins distributed architecture on AWS

This architecture is much better. However, distributed builds are generally used to absorb extra load (for example, in build activity) by dynamically adding extra machines as required. Hence, the number of workers shouldn't be fixed in advance. We want to add or remove workers based on the number of jobs waiting in the queue or the CPU utilization of the worker's cluster. That's why, instead of deploying workers independently, we will deploy them inside an AWS Auto Scaling group (ASG); see https://aws.amazon.com/autoscaling/.

The ASG feature comes with EC2 and allows you to deploy a group of EC2 instances that are treated as a logical grouping for the purpose of automatic scaling. In addition, Amazon EC2 Auto Scaling helps to ensure that you have the correct number of instances by specifying the minimum and maximum number of instances at any given time.

To create and terminate Jenkins workers on demand based on build jobs, we can create scaling policies. A *scaling policy* is a set of instructions for adjusting the size of instances in the ASG in response to an Amazon CloudWatch alarm (http://mng.bz/g1rl).

An Amazon CloudWatch alarm will monitor the CPU usage of the EC2 instances, for example. Then it will trigger a scale-out or scale-in event to add or remove a worker to the Jenkins cluster automatically. For instance, if the average CPU utilization of the Jenkins workers is over 80%, a scale-out event will be triggered, and a new worker will be deployed and added to the Jenkins cluster. Similarly, if the average CPU utilization of the Jenkins workers is less than 20%, a scale-in event will be triggered, and unused workers will be removed (providing infrastructure cost optimization).

> **NOTE**   When creating an alarm on the Auto Scaling group, the alarm uses aggregated metrics across all Jenkins worker instances (average CPU utilization). This way, it won't add instances just because one worker is too busy.

When the CPU utilization is less than 20%, the scale-in policy takes effect, and the ASG terminates on the available instances. If you did not assign a specific termination policy to the ASG, it uses the default termination policy. This means the ASG selects the instance to terminate based on the following factors:

- The instance that is closed to the next billing hour.
- Longest/oldest running EC2 instance.
- Oldest launch configuration. The *launch configuration* is the blueprint or template that describes what a Jenkins worker instance should look like.

However, you can use Amazon EC2 termination protection to protect a Jenkins worker from being accidentally terminated. Refer to the official guide for instructions: http://mng.bz/ePwz.

We can also configure the scaling policies based on memory utilization. However, memory utilization is one of the metrics not available by default in CloudWatch. Since AWS does not have access to the instance at the OS level, only metrics that can be monitored through the hypervisor layer (such as CPU and network utilization) are recorded.

We have various ways to solve this problem. The most used one is to install a metrics collector agent on the EC2 instances. For more details on how to fetch the memory utilization, check out chapter 13.

> **NOTE**   To be able to add workers automatically, the worker machine will run a shell script at boot time and use the Jenkins RESTful API to autoregister to the cluster with the machine's private IP address (known as *cluster discovery*). Chapters 4 and 5 explain this part in depth.

Figure 3.12 illustrates how to dynamically scale Jenkins workers by using CloudWatch scaling policies.

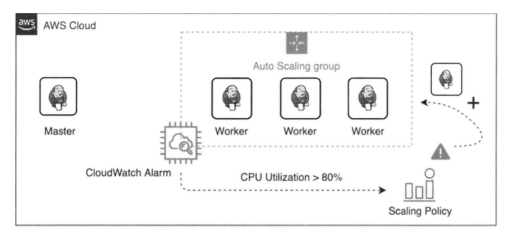

Figure 3.12   Jenkins workers belong to an AWS autoscaling group and will be scaled dynamically based on the average CPU utilization of the group.

We can also use custom metrics such as the number of jobs waiting in the build queue to trigger scaling policies. To get this information, you can use an open source solution such as Prometheus (https://prometheus.io/docs/introduction/overview/) to export Jenkins cluster metrics and make a Lambda function to consume/scrape those metrics. From the Lambda function, you can trigger scale-out or scale-in events on the Jenkins worker autoscaling group by using the AWS API/SDK.

> **NOTE**   Chapter 13 covers how to monitor a Jenkins cluster's health and how to use the Prometheus exporter plugin on Jenkins to expose server-side metrics.

Figure 3.13 demonstrates how to scale Jenkins workers dynamically based on a custom metric.

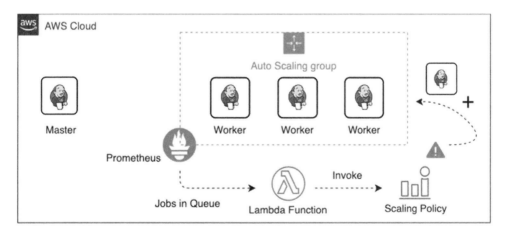

Figure 3.13   You can scale Jenkins workers dynamically based on the number of jobs waiting in the build queue by integrating Prometheus and AWS Lambda.

So far, the architecture is promising. However, it's not secure and resilient. To secure our Jenkins cluster, we will deploy the architecture inside a virtual private cloud (VPC) and within a private subnet precisely. In reality, by default, any EC2 instance is deployed in the AWS default VPC. But we will create a nondefault VPC that suits our specific requirements, using specific Classless Inter-Domain Routing (CIDR) block range and subnet sizes.

Amazon VPC (https://aws.amazon.com/vpc) lets you provision a logically isolated section of the AWS cloud where you can launch AWS resources in a virtual network that you can define. You have complete control over your virtual networking environment, including a selection of your own IP address range, creation of subnets, and configuration of route tables and network gateways.

An important point to note here is that a VPC is still a part of the AWS cloud. It is not physically separate hosting provided by AWS; it is a logically isolated part of the EC2 infrastructure. This isolation is done at the network layer and is similar to a traditional datacenter's network isolation; it's just that we, as end users, are shielded from the complexities of it. Figure 3.14 shows the network topology of AWS VPC.

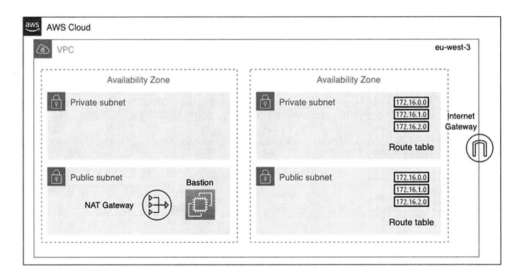

Figure 3.14   The virtual private cloud consists of private and public subnets.

We will create an AWS VPC with multiple subnets. A *subnet* is nothing more than a range of valid IP addresses. For resiliency, these subnets will be deployed in different availability zones in the selected AWS region.

Next, we deploy an internet gateway (IGW) and attach it to the VPC. The IGW will be used primarily to provide internet connectivity to Jenkins instances (this might be needed if your build jobs running in Jenkins workers require downloading external packages from the internet). Plus, the IGW maps the instance's private IP address with an associated public or Elastic IP address (http://mng.bz/p9QG) and then routes traffic outside the subnet to the internet. Finally, we create a public route table with rules to direct network traffic from public subnets to the IGW, as shown in table 3.1.

Table 3.1   Public route table

Destination	Target	Remark
10.0.0.0/16	local	Allow traffic to flow with this particular subnet (10.0.0.0/16)
0.0.0.0/0	IGW ID	Allow subnet traffic to flow through the internet.

But what about instances in the private subnets? That's where a Network Address Translation (NAT) instance or gateway comes into play. The NAT gateway/instance will be created inside a public subnet and will forward the outbound traffic and not allow any traffic from the internet to reach the private subnets. This means instances will have access to the internet without being exposed to the public (no public IP address is given). Once the NAT gateway is deployed, we need to add an entry to the private subnets route table to point to the NAT gateway; see table 3.2.

Table 3.2   Private route table

Destination	Target	Remark
10.0.0.0/16	local	Allow traffic to flow with this particular subnet (10.0.0.0/16)
0.0.0.0/0	NAT ID	Allow subnet traffic to flow through the NAT gateway/instance

Because Jenkins instances will be deployed into private subnets that are isolated from the internet, we cannot SSH directly to them from local desktops. A basic solution is to deploy a special instance that acts as a proxy you can use to SSH into your Jenkins instances. This special instance is called a *bastion host*, or *jump box*. This instance will be deployed in your public subnet and will basically route only SSH traffic from your local network over the Jenkins instances by setting up a secure SSH tunnel/bridge.

> **NOTE** An advanced solution is to deploy OpenVPN to establish a secure TLS VPN session to securely access your private Jenkins instances. Refer to "Setting Up OpenVPN Access Server in Amazon VPC" at http://mng.bz/OQVn for instructions.

Once the VPC is configured, we can go ahead and deploy a dedicated EC2 instance running the Jenkins server on a private subnet. Alongside, an ASG of Jenkins workers will be deployed across multiple private subnets. We configure scaling policies with CloudWatch alarms to dynamically scale Jenkins workers based on the build activity. Figure 3.15 summarizes the current deployment architecture.

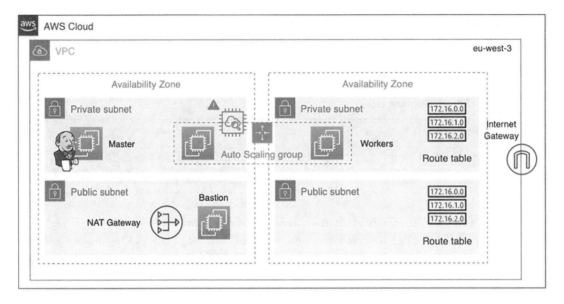

Figure 3.15   This Jenkins cluster deployed in private subnets consists of an ASG of workers and an EC2 instance holding the Jenkins dashboard.

We can take this architecture further, and configure a public-facing Elastic load balancer in front of the Jenkins instance to access the Jenkins web dashboard. This way, your Jenkins instance does not have to be directly exposed to the internet.

> **NOTE** It's possible to have multiple Jenkins instances even though Jenkins core doesn't support multiple masters by default. Then, use the load balancer to fetch requests and distribute them among multiple Jenkins masters.

The load balancer will listen on both the HTTP (80) and HTTPS (443) ports and send incoming requests to the instance on port 8080. That way, it uses an encrypted connection to communicate with the Jenkins instance. Table 3.3 summarizes the port configurations.

Table 3.3   Load balancer listener configuration

Load balancer protocol	Load balancer port	Instance protocol	Instance port
HTTP	80	HTTP	8080
HTTPS	443	HTTP	8080

If you specify the HTTPS listener, you will need to select a private Secure Sockets Layer (SSL) certificate. The load balancer uses the certificate to terminate the connection and then decrypt requests from clients before sending them to the Jenkins instance. You can get a free SSL certificate with AWS Certificate Manager (ACM); you can also import your own certificate.

The load balancer has a publicly resolvable DNS name, so it can route requests from clients over the internet to a Jenkins instance that is registered with the load balancer. Also, it will be useful while setting up a GitHub webhook for continuously triggering Jenkins builds upon push events.

> **NOTE** If you plan to stick with a private Jenkins instance, chapter 7 explains how to set up a GitHub webhook for a Jenkins instance running behind a firewall.

Finally, if you would like to use a friendly DNS name to access your load balancer, instead of the default DNS name automatically assigned to your load balancer, you can create a custom domain name and associate it with the DNS name for your load balancer. The DNS configuration can be done on Amazon Route 53 (https://aws.amazon .com/route53/). Figure 3.16 shows the final architecture diagram.

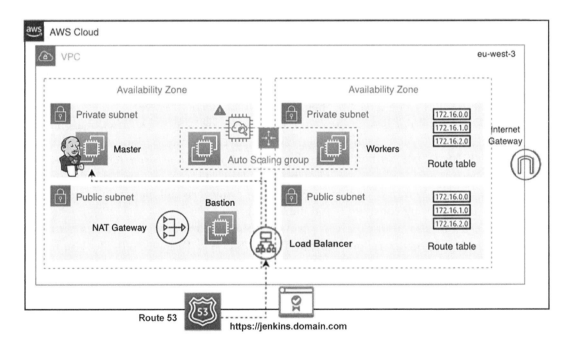

Figure 3.16   Jenkins cluster deployment on a custom VPC

Adding workers to a Jenkins cluster is the typical way to scale Jenkins. However, you can set up multiple Jenkins masters with a proxy (typically, HAProxy or NGINX) to actively monitor the primary master and reroute requests to backup masters if the

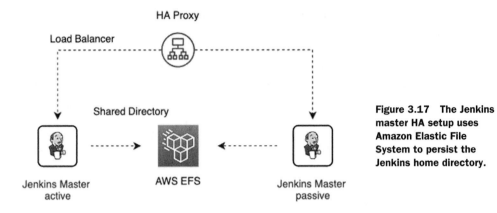

Figure 3.17 The Jenkins master HA setup uses Amazon Elastic File System to persist the Jenkins home directory.

active master goes down. The Jenkins architecture for master instances will look like figure 3.17.

As you can see, the first tier is the reverse proxy. Whenever an incoming request for the build occurs, it will first reach the proxy. Then, the proxy will decide the instance to which the request can be routed. Here, one of the masters will be in the active state to serve requests, and the other one will be passive. Whenever a problem exists with the active master and it goes down, the other master will become active, and requests will resume. (We also can deploy Jenkins masters inside an ASG to ensure that a minimum number of masters is always available for backup). These requests will then be served by the master that has become active.

The second tier is Amazon Elastic File System, or EFS (https://aws.amazon.com/efs/), which is used as a storage solution to persist the Jenkins home directory $JENKINS_HOME so both Jenkins masters can access and store Jenkins jobs. This storage solution can be mounted on multiple Jenkins instances concurrently. Amazon EFS, like any Network File System (NFS) server, supports full filesystem access semantics such as strong consistency and file locking.

EFS can also be used if you plan to deploy Jenkins on a Kubernetes cluster or Docker-based orchestration platforms like AWS ECS or Fargate. As the Jenkins master container can be launched on any node in the cluster, EFS can be used to persist the Jenkins data directory to preserve its state.

> **NOTE** Chapter 14 covers how to mount EFS in the $JENKINS_HOME directory to ensure that 100% of data is shared and can't be lost in case of failure.

Now that the Jenkins architecture is clear, next we will prepare our AWS environment, and then install and configure the tools needed for upcoming chapters.

3.3.1 *Preparing the AWS environment*

This section will walk you through installing and configuring the AWS command line. The command-line interface (CLI) is a solid and mandatory tool that we'll use in upcoming chapters. It will save us substantial time by automating the deployment and configuration of a Jenkins cluster on AWS with HashiCorp Terraform and Packer as well as defining CI/CD steps for cloud-native applications.

3.3.2 *Configuring the AWS CLI*

The AWS CLI (https://aws.amazon.com/cli/) is a powerful tool for managing your AWS services and resources from a terminal session. It was built on top of the AWS API, and hence everything that can be done through the AWS Management Console (https://console.aws.amazon.com/console/home) can be done with the CLI; this makes it a handy tool that can be used to automate and control your AWS infrastructure through scripts. Later chapters provide information on the use of the CLI with Jenkins to manage cloud-native applications in AWS.

Let's go through the installation process for the AWS CLI; you can find information on its configuration and testing in the AWS Management Console section. To get started, refer to the official documentation and follow the instructions to install the AWS CLI based on your operating system (http://mng.bz/Yw8N).

Once the AWS CLI is installed, you need to add the AWS CLI binary path to the PATH environment variable as follows:

- For Windows, press the Windows key and type `Environment Variables`. In the Environment Variables window, highlight the PATH variable in the System Variables section. Edit it and add a path by placing a semicolon right after the last path, and then enter the complete path to the folder where the CLI binary is installed.
- For Linux, Mac, or any UNIX system, open your shell's profile script (.bash_profile, .profile, or .bash_login) and add the following line to the end of the file:

```
export PATH=~/.local/bin:$PATH
```

Finally, load the profile into your current session:

```
source ~/.bash_profile
```

Verify that the CLI is correctly installed by opening a new terminal session and typing the following command:

```
aws --version
```

You should be able to see the AWS CLI version; in my case, 2.0.0 is installed. Let's test it out and list Amazon S3 buckets in the Frankfurt region as an example:

```
aws s3 ls --region eu-central-1
```

The previous command displays the following output:

```
jenkins:~ mlabouardy$ aws s3 ls --region eu-central-1
Unable to locate credentials. You can configure credentials by running "aws configure".
jenkins:~ mlabouardy$
```

When using the CLI, you'll generally need your AWS credentials to authenticate with AWS services. You can configure AWS credentials in multiple ways:

- *Environment credentials*—Use the `AWS_ACCESS_KEY_ID` and `AWS_SECRET_KEY` variables. They can be useful for scripting or temporarily setting a named profile as the default.

> **NOTE** If you set the environment variables at the terminal prompt, the values are saved for only the duration of the current session. To make the environment variable settings persistent across all terminal sessions, store them under /etc/profile or in ~/.bash_profile for the current user.

- *Shared Credentials file*—The AWS CLI stores the credentials in a local file named *credentials* under the .aws folder in your home directory. You can specify a nondefault location for the credentials file by setting the `AWS_SHARED_CREDEN-TIALS_FILE` environment variable to another local path.
- *IAM roles*—If you're using the CLI in an EC2 instance, this removes the need to manage credential files in production. Each Amazon EC2 instance contains metadata that the AWS CLI can directly query for temporary credentials.

In the next section, I will show you how to create a new user for the AWS CLI with the AWS Identity and Access Management (IAM) service.

3.3.3   *Creating and managing the IAM user*

IAM (https://aws.amazon.com/iam/) is a service that allows you to manage users, groups, and their level of access to AWS services. It's strongly recommended that you do not use the AWS root account for any task except billing tasks, as it has the ultimate authority to create and delete IAM users, change billing, close the account, and perform all other actions on your AWS account. Therefore, we will create a new IAM user and grant it the permissions it needs to access the right AWS resources following the principle of least privilege.

> **NOTE** The *principle of least privilege* (PoLP) works by giving a given user only the minimum levels of access—or permissions—needed to perform the required task.

Sign in to AWS Management Console by using your AWS email address and password. Then, open the IAM console from the Security, Identity & Compliance section or type `IAM` in the search bar; figure 3.18 shows the console.

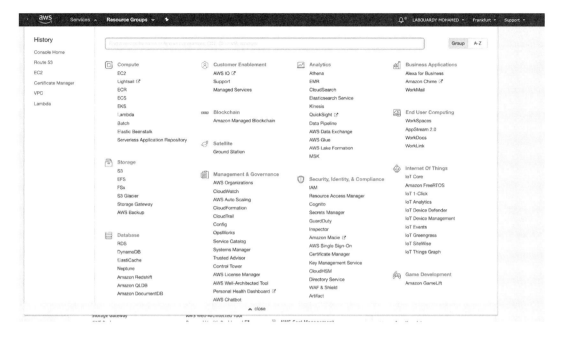

Figure 3.18 AWS Management Console

From the navigation pane, choose Users. Click the Add User button. Then set a name for the user and select Programmatic Access (also select AWS Management Console access if you want the same user to have access to the console), as shown in figure 3.19.

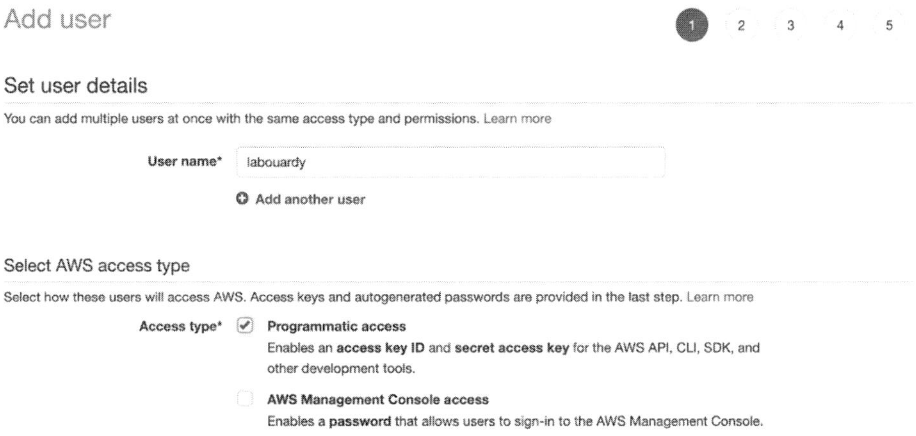

Figure 3.19 Creating a new IAM user

In the Set Permissions section, assign the AmazonS3FullAccess policy to the user, as shown in figure 3.20.

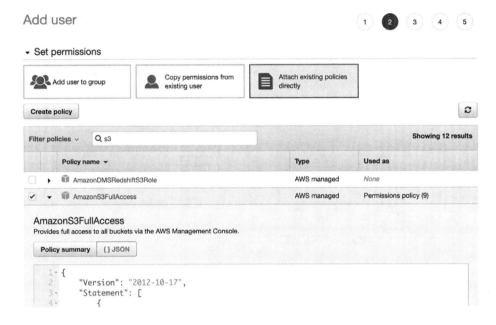

Figure 3.20   Attaching IAM policies to the user

> **NOTE**   It's better to be granular and specify only permissions that are needed to get the job done (leave privilege access). Start with a minimum set of permissions and add more permissions only if necessary.

On the final page, you should see the user's AWS credentials (figure 3.21). Make sure you save the access keys in a safe location, as you won't be able to see them again.

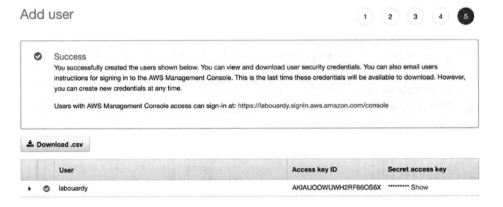

Figure 3.21   AWS credentials generation

> **NOTE** You can create IAM users to represent users, applications, or services. In the next chapter, we will create dedicated IAM users for HashiCorp Terraform and Packer tools.

Next, configure the AWS CLI by using the `aws configure` command. The CLI will store credentials specified in the preceding command in a local file under ~/.aws/ credentials (or in %UserProfile%\.aws\credentials on Windows) with the following content (substitute `eu-central-1` with your AWS region):

```
[default]
region=eu-central-1
aws_access_key_id=ACCESS KEY ID
aws_secret_access_key=SECRET ACCESS KEY
```

> **NOTE** You can override the region in which your AWS resources are located by using the `AWS_DEFAULT_REGION` environment variable of the `--region` command-line option.

That should be it; try out the following command and, if you have an S3 bucket, you should be able to see the credentials listed. Otherwise, the command will return no results:

```
aws s3 ls
```

Now that the AWS environment is set up, let's get down to business and deploy a Jenkins cluster on AWS.

Summary

- Deploying Jenkins in distributed builds mode allows for decoupling orchestration, build executions, and better performance.
- Jenkins is a crucial component of the DevOps chain, and its downtime may have adverse effects on the DevOps environment. To overcome these, you need a high-availability setup for Jenkins.
- AWS CloudWatch provides a rich set of metrics to monitor the health of EC2 instances. The metrics collected can be used to set up alarms and trigger scaling policies upon alarm firing such as scaling Jenkins workers.
- Delegating the workload of building projects to worker nodes is referred to as distributed builds.
- You can configure a build to run on a particular worker machine by using Jenkins labels.
- It's highly recommended to launch your Jenkins deployment within a private subnet in a VPC for security purposes.
- By assigning labels to nodes, you can specify the resources you want to use for specific jobs, and set up graceful queuing for your tests.

Baking machine images with Packer

This chapter covers

- Overview of immutable infrastructure
- Baking Jenkins machine images with Packer
- Discovering Jenkins essentials plugins
- Executing Jenkins Groovy scripts
- Using Packer provisioners to automate Jenkins settings

In the previous chapter, you learned how Jenkins distributed mode architecture works. In this one, we will get our hands dirty and deploy a Jenkins cluster on AWS. As a quick reminder, you learned that the Jenkins cluster is divided into two main components: master and worker. Before diving into the implementation of the distributed builds architecture, we will deploy the standalone mode, shown in figure 4.1, to cover some basics.

To deploy this architecture, we need to provision a server (for example, an EC2 instance in AWS). Then we'll install and configure Jenkins on the machine. While this manual process works, it's not efficient when we want to deploy Jenkins to

Figure 4.1   Jenkins standalone architecture on AWS

scale. Plus, updating or upgrading Jenkins can be lengthy and painful, and things can easily go wrong—breaking your CI/CD pipelines and impacting your product release as a result.

So instead of installing Jenkins after infrastructure creation (EC2 instance deployment) and applying updates on an existing Jenkins instance (in case of upgrades or maintenance), all changes must be packaged in a new machine image. A new Jenkins instance should be deployed based on the new image, and then the old server will be destroyed. This process creates what is known as an *immutable infrastructure.*

4.1   *Immutable infrastructure*

Immutable infrastructure is all about immutable components that are re-created and replaced instead of updated after infrastructure creation. This immutable infrastructure reduces the number of places where things can go wrong. This helps reduce inconsistency and improves reliability in the deployment process.

When an update is necessary for immutable infrastructure, new servers are provisioned with a preconfigured image, and old servers are destroyed. We create a new machine image that is built for deployment and use it for creating new servers. In immutable infrastructure, we are moving the configuration setup after the server creation process to the build process. As all deployments are done by new images, we can keep the history of previous releases in case of reverting to an old build. This allows us to reduce deployment time and the chance of configuration failure, and to scale deployments. Figure 4.2 illustrates the differences between immutable and mutable infrastructures.

Notice that the new Instance B, generated from a "golden" machine image, is provisioned upon the destruction of Instance A in the immutable pattern. Note, too, that there is no Jenkins downtime during instance replacement with well-architected immutable patterns that have multiple instances in service at a given time. By contrast, in the mutable pattern, Instance A isn't replaced. The same instance is modified manually or by using a script or tool, with the Jenkins updated from v1.0 to v2.0.

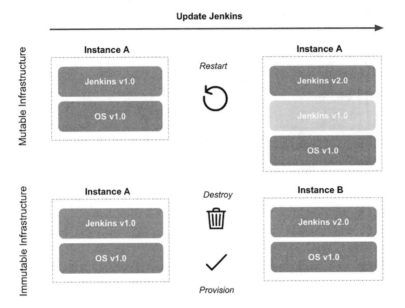

Figure 4.2   Updating via mutable and immutable infrastructures

In this era of cloud computing, many companies are adopting immutable infrastructure to simplify configuration management and improve reliability by using infrastructure as code. With immutable infrastructure, instead of making changes on a running server, we create a new server. Creating immutable infrastructure is hard and needs a sophisticated process for building and testing. The best way to implement immutable infrastructure is to use a well-tested and tried tool.

Multiple tools and frameworks allow you to build immutable infrastructure. The most famous ones are HashiCorp Packer, HashiCorp Vagrant, and Docker. In this book, we will keep our focus on machine images by using Packer. The goal is to illustrate the workflow for building immutable infrastructure and show how it can be fully automated using Packer. However, the same workflow can be applied while using other alternatives.

4.2   *Introducing Packer*

HashiCorp Packer (www.packer.io) is a lightweight and easy-to-use open source tool that automates the creation of any type of machine image for multiple platforms. Packer is not a replacement for configuration management tools like Ansible, Puppet, or Chef. Packer works with these tools to install and configure software and dependencies while creating images.

Packer uses a configuration file to create a machine image. Then it uses builders to spin up an instance on the target platform, and runs provisioners to configure applications or services. Once setup is done, it shuts down the instance and saves the new baked machine instance with any needed post-processing.

Using Packer has many advantages. Here are a few:

- *Fast infrastructure deployment*—Machine images allow us to more quickly launch provisioned and configured machines.
- *Scalable*—Packer installs and configures all needed software and dependencies for a machine during the image-creation process. The same image can be used to spawn any number of instances without doing extra configuration. (The same image can be used to deploy multiple Jenkins workers, for instance.)
- *Multiprovider support*—Packer can be used to create images for multiple cloud providers like AWS, GCP, and Microsoft Azure.

Figure 4.3 illustrates a typical machine image build process with Packer.

Figure 4.3   Building Jenkins machine images with Packer

The drawback of using Packer is managing existing images: you need to manage them yourself by using tags or versions and keep deleting old, unused images (in AWS, you're charged for the storage of the bits that make up your machine image, or AMI).

4.2.1   How does it work?

Figure 4.4 illustrates the process Packer uses to bake machine images.

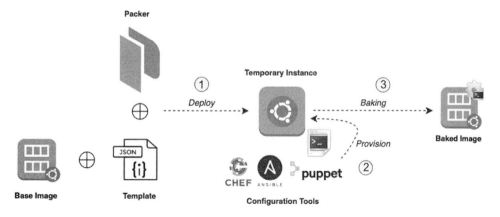

Figure 4.4   Packer baking workflow

Here are the steps in the process:

1   Boot a temporary instance using the base image defined in the template file.
2   Provision the instance by using configuration management tools like Ansible, Chef, or Puppet, or with a simple automated script to configure the instance into the desired state.
3   Create a new machine image from the temporary running instance and shut down the temporary instance after the image is baked.

Once a new machine image is created, booting a new server from this new image will give the same configuration that was already done on the temporary instance. This helps provide a smooth deployment process. This also helps scale our services fast.

The Packer configuration, also known as a template file, can be written in JSON or YAML format. It consists of the following three main components:

- *User variables*—This section is used to parameterize the Packer template file so we can keep secret, environment variables and other parameters out of the template. The section helps with the portability of the template file and helps in separating out the part that can be modified in our template. Variables can be passed through command lines, environment variables, HashiCorp Vault (www.vaultproject.io), or files. The section is a key-value mapping with the variable name assigned to a default value.
- *Builders*—This section contains a list of builders that Packer uses to generate a machine image. Builders are responsible for creating an instance and generating machine images from them. A builder maps to a single machine image. This section contains information including the type (which is the name of the builder), access keys, and credentials required to connect to the platform (AWS, for instance).
- *Provisioners*—This section, which is optional, contains a list of provisioners that Packer uses to install and configure software within a running instance before creating a machine image. The type specifies the name of a provisioner such as Shell, Chef, or Ansible.

NOTE   For a full list of supported builders, refer to the official documentation at www.packer.io/docs/builders/. For a full list of supported provisioners, see www.packer.io/docs/provisioners/.

Packer helps bake configuration into the machine image during image creation time. This helps in creating identical servers in case things go wrong.

4.2.2   Installation and configuration

Packer is written in Go, which is a compiled language. Hence, installing Packer is straightforward; you just need to download the appropriate binary for your system and architecture from www.packer.io/downloads/. Figure 4.5 shows the download page.

Figure 4.5 Packer download page

> **NOTE** Make sure the directory where you installed the Packer binary is on the `PATH` variable.

After installing Packer, verify that the installation is working by opening a new terminal session and checking that Packer is available by issuing the following command:

```
jenkins:~ mlabouardy$ packer
Usage: packer [--version] [--help] <command> [<args>]

Available commands are:
    build      build image(s) from template
    console    creates a console for testing variable interpolation
    fix        fixes templates from old versions of packer
    inspect    see components of a template
    validate   check that a template is valid
    version    Prints the Packer version
```

> **NOTE** At the time of writing this book, the latest stable version of Packer is 1.7.2.

If you get an error that Packer could not be found, your `PATH` environment variable was not set up properly. Otherwise, Packer is installed, and you're ready to go!

4.2.3 Baking a machine image

With Packer installed, let's dive right into it and build our first image. Our first machine image will be an Amazon EC2 AMI with Jenkins pre-installed. To create this AMI, we need to write a Packer configuration file.

NOTE   The following Packer template file has been cropped for brevity. The full template is available in the GitHub repository under the chapter4 folder: http://mng.bz/GO8q.

Create a template.json file and fill it with the following content.

Listing 4.1   Packer template for standalone Jenkins server

```
{
    "variables" : {
        "region" : "AWS REGION",
        "aws_profile": "AWS PROFILE",
        "source_ami" : "AMAZON LINUX AMI ID",
        "instance_type": "EC2 INSTANCE TYPE"
    },
    "builders" : [
        {
            "type" : "amazon-ebs",
            "profile" : "{{user `aws_profile`}}",
            "region" : "{{user `region`}}",
            "instance_type" : "{{user `instance_type`}}",
            "source_ami" : "{{user `source_ami`}}",
            "ssh_username" : "ec2-user",
            "ami_name" : "jenkins-master-2.204.1",
            "ami_description" : "Amazon Linux Image with Jenkins Server",
    ],
    "provisioners" : [                {
            "type" : "shell",
            "script" : "./setup.sh",
            "execute_command" : "sudo -E -S sh '{{ .Path }}'"
        }
    ]
}
```

This template file consists of three main sections:

- variables
- builders
- provisioners

Instead of hardcoding values in the template file, we are using variables that can be overridden at the Packer runtime. In our example, we have defined the variables in table 4.1.

Substitute the value of source_ami with the appropriate Amazon Linux AMI ID. The Amazon Linux AMI ID can be found by heading to AWS Management Console and navigating to the EC2 dashboard. Click Launch EC2 Instance. On the Choose AMI tab, type Amazon Linux AMI in the search bar, shown in figure 4.6.

Table 4.1 Packer variables

Variable	Description
region	The name of the AWS region, such as `eu-central-1`, in which to launch the EC2 instance to create the AMI. While you can always copy an AMI from one region to another, for simplicity the AMI location will be the same as the region where the Jenkins EC2 instance will be deployed to.
aws_profile	The AWS profile used. Check chapter 3 for details about AWS CLI configuration. You can also provide AWS credentials through environment variables or with EC2 metadata if you plan to run Packer inside an EC2 instance. If you plan to use AWS access and secrets keys, keep them out of the template and provide them only during runtime by using the `-var` flag.
instance_type	The EC2 instance type to use while building the AMI, such as a `t2.micro`. A list of supported instance types can be found at https://aws.amazon.com/ec2/instance-types/.
source_ami	The base AMI to use to boot the temporary EC2 instance. In the previous example, we're using the official Amazon Linux image. You may need to change the source AMI ID based on what images exist when this template is run and the AWS region you're using.

Figure 4.6 Amazon Linux image identifier

You can also find the ID programmatically with Packer by using the `source_ami_filter` attribute in the Packer template file. This attribute will automatically populate the `source_ami` attribute based on the defined filters. For instance, the following snippet selects the most recent Amazon Linux AMI (the full template file can be copied from chapter4/standalone/template-with-filter.json):

```
"builders" : [
    {
        "ami_name" : "jenkins-master-2.204.1",
        "ami_description" : "Amazon Linux Image with Jenkins Server",
```

```
        "source_ami_filter": {
            "filters": {
                "virtualization-type": "hvm",
                "name": "Amazon Linux AMI-*",
                "root-device-type": "ebs"
            },
            "owners": ["amazon"],
            "most_recent": true
        }
    }
]
```

If multiple AMIs meet all of the filtering criteria provided in `source_ami_filter`, the `most_recent` attribute will select the newest Amazon Linux image.

Because the target machine image is an Amazon Machine Image, we are using the `amazon-ebs` builder. This is the Amazon EC2 AMI builder that ships with Packer. This builder builds an EBS-backed AMI by launching a source AMI, provisioning on top of that, and repackaging it into a new AMI. Multiple builders are available based on the target platform. Separate builders are available for EC2, VMware, VirtualBox, and others. Packer comes with many builders by default and can also be extended to add new builders.

The `ami_name` attribute in the `builder` section is the name of the resulting AMI that will appear when managing AMIs in the AWS console. The name must be unique. To help make this unique, I have added it as a prefix to the version of the installed Jenkins server, but you can also use the current timestamp with the following format:

```
"ami_name" : "jenkins-master-2.204.1-{{timestamp}}"
```

`{{timestamp}}` will be replaced by the Packer template engine to generate the current UNIX timestamp in Coordinated Universal Time (UTC).

The `provisioners` stage is responsible for installing and configuring all needed dependencies. Packer fully supports multiple modern configuration management tools such as Ansible, Chef, and Puppet. Bash scripts are also supported. To simplify the baking process for the Jenkins AMI, we have defined a bash script called setup.sh with the following content.

> **Listing 4.2 Bash script to install Jenkins LTS**

```
#!/bin/bash
yum remove -y java
yum install -y java-1.8.0-openjdk
wget -O /etc/yum.repos.d/jenkins.repo
http://pkg.jenkins-ci.org/redhat-stable/jenkins.repo
rpm --import https://jenkins-ci.org/redhat/jenkins-ci.org.key
yum install -y jenkins
chkconfig jenkins on
service jenkins start
```

The script is self-explanatory: it installs the Java Development Kit (JDK), which is mandatory to run Jenkins, and then it installs the latest stable version of Jenkins. Here we install the Jenkins LTS release. Although it might lag behind in terms of new features, it provides more stability than weekly releases. The weekly Jenkins releases deliver bug fixes and new features rapidly to users and plugin developers who need them. But for more conservative users, it's preferable to stick to a release line that changes less often and receives only important bug fixes.

Once the Jenkins package is installed with the Yum package manager, the script configures Jenkins to start automatically if the machine has been restarted with the `chkconfig` command.

Now that our template file is defined, we can execute the following command to verify the syntax of the template file:

```
packer validate template.json
```

The command will return a zero exit status to indicate that the template.json syntax is valid.

Before we take this template and build an image from it, we need to assign the AmazonEC2FullAccess policy to the IAM user created in chapter 3 for Packer to be able to deploy an EC2 instance and create a machine image out of it.

Head back to AWS Console, navigate to the IAM dashboard, and jump to the Users section. Then, select the Packer user and attach the policy in listing 4.3, as shown in figure 4.7.

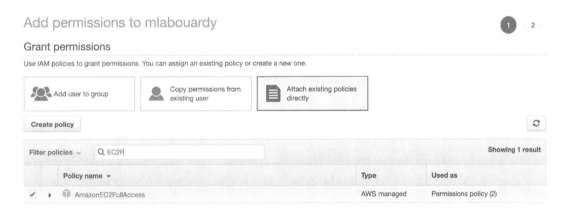

Figure 4.7 Attaching the EC2 policy to an IAM user

> **NOTE** A preferred approach is to provide the minimal set of permissions necessary for Packer to work. The following listing is an IAM policy with the minimal set permissions necessary for the Amazon plugin to work.

Listing 4.3   AWS IAM policy for Packer

```
{
    "Version": "2012-10-17",
    "Statement": [{
        "Effect": "Allow",
        "Action" : [
          "ec2:AttachVolume",
          "ec2:AuthorizeSecurityGroupIngress",
          "ec2:CopyImage",
          "ec2:CreateImage",
          "ec2:CreateKeypair",
          "ec2:CreateSecurityGroup",
          "ec2:CreateSnapshot",
          "ec2:CreateTags",
          "ec2:CreateVolume",
          "ec2:DeleteKeyPair",
          "ec2:DeleteSecurityGroup",
          "ec2:DeleteSnapshot",
          "ec2:DeleteVolume",
          "ec2:DeregisterImage",
          "ec2:DescribeImageAttribute",
          "ec2:DescribeImages",
          "ec2:DescribeInstances",
          "ec2:DescribeInstanceStatus",
          "ec2:DescribeRegions",
          "ec2:DescribeSecurityGroups",
          "ec2:DescribeSnapshots",
          "ec2:DescribeSubnets",
          "ec2:DescribeTags",
          "ec2:DescribeVolumes",
          "ec2:DetachVolume",
          "ec2:GetPasswordData",
          "ec2:ModifyImageAttribute",
          "ec2:ModifyInstanceAttribute",
          "ec2:ModifySnapshotAttribute",
          "ec2:RegisterImage",
          "ec2:RunInstances",
          "ec2:StopInstances",
          "ec2:TerminateInstances"
        ],
        "Resource" : "*"
    }]
}
```

With a properly configured IAM user, it is time to build your first image. This is done by calling the `packer build` command with the template file as an argument:

```
packer build template.json
```

Packer will deploy an EC2 instance based on the configuration specified in the template file, and then execute the bash script on the deployed instance. The output should look similar to the following. Note that this process typically takes a few minutes.

```
    amazon-ebs: Total download size: 60 M
    amazon-ebs: Installed size: 61 M
    amazon-ebs: Downloading packages:
    amazon-ebs: Running transaction check
    amazon-ebs: Running transaction test
    amazon-ebs: Transaction test succeeded
    amazon-ebs: Running transaction
    amazon-ebs:   Installing : jenkins-2.204.1-1.1.noarch                          1/1
    amazon-ebs:   Verifying  : jenkins-2.204.1-1.1.noarch                          1/1
    amazon-ebs:
    amazon-ebs: Installed:
    amazon-ebs:   jenkins.noarch 0:2.204.1-1.1
    amazon-ebs:
    amazon-ebs: Complete!
    amazon-ebs: Starting Jenkins [  OK  ]
==> amazon-ebs: Stopping the source instance...
    amazon-ebs: Stopping instance
==> amazon-ebs: Waiting for the instance to stop...
==> amazon-ebs: Creating AMI jenkins-master-2.204.1 from instance i-04ce242efa89ee5cd
    amazon-ebs: AMI: ami-051933c5e0fc71592
==> amazon-ebs: Waiting for AMI to become ready...
==> amazon-ebs: Modifying attributes on AMI (ami-051933c5e0fc71592)...
    amazon-ebs: Modifying: description
==> amazon-ebs: Modifying attributes on snapshot (snap-0ddcaf514891ce646)...
==> amazon-ebs: Adding tags to AMI (ami-051933c5e0fc71592)...
==> amazon-ebs: Tagging snapshot: snap-0ddcaf514891ce646
==> amazon-ebs: Creating AMI tags
    amazon-ebs: Adding tag: "Tool": "Packer"
    amazon-ebs: Adding tag: "Author": "mlabouardy"
==> amazon-ebs: Creating snapshot tags
==> amazon-ebs: Terminating the source AWS instance...
==> amazon-ebs: Cleaning up any extra volumes...
==> amazon-ebs: No volumes to clean up, skipping
==> amazon-ebs: Deleting temporary security group...
==> amazon-ebs: Deleting temporary keypair...
Build 'amazon-ebs' finished.

==> Builds finished. The artifacts of successful builds are:
--> amazon-ebs: AMIs were created:
eu-central-1: ami-051933c5e0fc71592
```

At the end of running the `packer build` command, Packer outputs the artifacts that were created as part of the build. Artifacts are the results of a build and typically represent the AMI ID. (Your ID will surely be different from the preceding one.) In this example, we have only a single artifact: the AMI was created in the Frankfurt region (`eu-central-1`).

You can use the same template file to create Jenkins machine images for different platforms, all from the same specification. This is a nice feature that allows you to create machine images of different types of providers without repetitive coding. For example, we can modify the template to add Google Compute Cloud and Microsoft Azure builders to it, as shown in the following listing. The full template is available on the GitHub repository (chapter4/standalone/template-multiple-builders.json).

Listing 4.4   Jenkins multiplatform machine image builds

```
{
    "builders": [
        {
            "type": "amazon-ebs",
            "profile": "{{user `aws_profile`}}",
            "region": "{{user `region`}}",
            "instance_type": "{{user `instance_type`}}",
            "source_ami": "{{user `source_ami`}}",
            "ssh_username": "ec2-user",
            "ami_name": "jenkins-master-2.204.1",
            "ami_description": "Amazon Linux Image with Jenkins Server",
        },
        {
            "type": "azure-arm",
            "subscription_id": "{{user `subscription_id`}}",
            "client_id": "{{user `client_id`}}",
            "client_secret": "{{user `client_secret`}}",
            "tenant_id": "{{user `tenant_id`}}",
            "managed_image_resource_group_name": "{{user `resource_group`}}",
            "managed_image_name": "jenkins-master-v22041",
            "os_type": "Linux",
            "image_publisher": "OpenLogic",
            "image_offer": "CentOS",
            "image_sku": "8.0",
            "location": "{{user `location`}}",
            "vm_size": "Standard_B1ms"
        },
        {

            "type": "googlecompute",
            "image_name": "jenkins-master-v22041",
            "account_file": "{{user `service_account`}}",
            "project_id": "{{user `project`}}",
            "source_image_family": "centos-8",
            "ssh_username": "packer",
            "zone": "{{user `zone`}}"
        }
    ]
}
```

Packer will create multiple Jenkins images for multiple platforms in parallel, all configured from a single template. In this example, Packer can make an Amazon Machine Image, Azure image, and Google Compute Engine image in parallel, provisioned with the same script, resulting in a near-identical Jenkins image.

> **NOTE** For a step-by-step guide on how to bake machine images for Azure virtual machines and Google Compute Engine instances, refer to chapter 6.

Once the AMI is created, the temporary EC2 instance will be terminated by Packer, and the baked AMI will be available in the AMIs section under Images on the EC2 dashboard, as shown in figure 4.8.

Figure 4.8   A new baked image is available on the Images section.

Now that our Jenkins AMI has been created, let's test it out and see if Jenkins has been properly installed. Jump to Instances and click the Launch Instance button. Then, select the AMI built by Packer from the My AMIs section, as shown in figure 4.9.

Figure 4.9   The new AMI can be selected from the My AMIs section.

For the instance type, select a general-purpose instance such as `t2.micro`, which is Free Tier eligible. We will cover Jenkins resource requirements in the next chapter.

For now, leave all the other values at their default settings. Navigate to the Add Tags section and type a name for your EC2 instance in the value box. This name, more correctly known as a *tag*, will appear in the console when the instance launches. This makes it easy to keep track of the running Jenkins instance.

Configure the security group (firewall that controls traffic to the instance) to allow traffic on port 8080 from anywhere. Port 8080 is the default port to which the Jenkins web dashboard is exposed.

> **NOTE**   The instance will be deployed inside the default VPC. In chapter 5, we will deploy the Jenkins cluster on a custom VPC from scratch and go through advanced network configurations.

Figure 4.10   Allowing traffic on port 8080

The EC2 instance security group rules should look similar to figure 4.10.

Make sure to allow inbound traffic on port 22 in order to authorize SSH traffic from your computer's public IPv4 address. It's mandatory; otherwise, you won't be able to unlock the Jenkins dashboard later.

Finally, verify the configuration details in the Review section and select an SSH key pair, or create a new one if it's the first time you're launching an EC2 instance. This configuration will allow you to connect to your instance via SSH.

Once the instance is running, point your browser to the instance's public IP address and specify port 8080. The Jenkins setup wizard should pop up on the screen, as shown in figure 4.11. Congrats—you have successfully deployed a Jenkins instance from a custom AMI built with Packer.

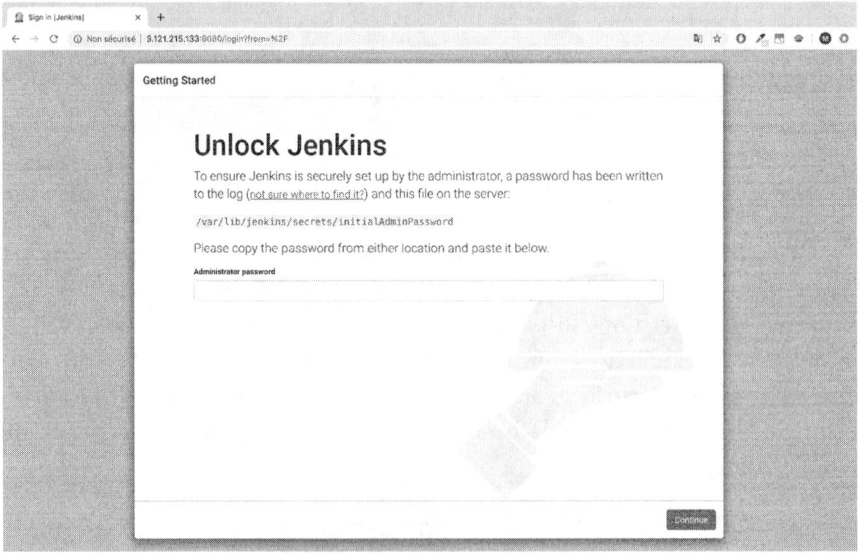

Figure 4.11   Jenkins setup wizard

You will be asked to unlock Jenkins by using an initial password. You can find this password inside the file /var/lib/jenkins/secrets/initialAdminPassword. (The following sections cover how to create a custom admin account for Jenkins.)

So far, we have deployed Jenkins in standalone mode. Figure 4.12 summarizes the currently deployed architecture.

Figure 4.12 Jenkins standalone mode in AWS

> **NOTE** Make sure to terminate the instance when you no longer need it, to stop incurring charges for that instance.

Next, you will learn how to use Groovy scripts to customize and configure Jenkins settings while baking the Jenkins master AMI. Furthermore, we will create another image for Jenkins workers to deploy Jenkins at scale.

4.3 *Baking the Jenkins master AMI*

We can use the AMI built in the previous section, but the ending Jenkins instance will still have many settings requiring manual configuration, including Jenkins admin credentials, needed plugins to set up CI/CD pipelines, and security checks. While you can configure those manually, the purpose of this book is to avoid operational overhead as much as possible. We want to automate the tedious tasks while deploying a highly available and fault-tolerant Jenkins cluster on your favorite cloud provider with few commands by using automation tools like HashiCorp Packer and Terraform.

> **NOTE** When I say *high availability*, I am referring to a Jenkins cluster that can operate continuously without failure.

To fully automate a Jenkins master instance, we will use Jenkins post-initialization scripts. We will leverage the power of Groovy scripts and place them in the $JENKINS_HOME/init.groovy.d directory. This directory will be consumed by Jenkins upon startup. Therefore, it can be used to preconfigure Jenkins to the target desired state.

4.3.1 *Configuring Jenkins upon startup*

These scripts are written in Groovy and are executed inside the same Java Virtual Machine (JVM) as Jenkins, allowing full access to the domain model of Jenkins (we can access classes in Jenkins and all its plugins).

> **NOTE** Another alternative to Groovy scripts is the Jenkins Configuration as Code (JCasC) plugin. For more details, refer to the official guide on GitHub: http://mng.bz/zEJa.

The basic-security.groovy script in listing 4.5 creates a Jenkins user with full admin access. (You need to replace the USERNAME and PASSWORD attributes with your own values.) Furthermore, by default, the anonymous read access is disabled by default, which means Jenkins requires authentication to access the web dashboard. However, you can enable anonymous read access by adding the strategy.setAllowAnony-mousRead(true) instruction before the instance.save() statement.

Listing 4.5   basic-security.groovy script

```groovy
#!groovy

import jenkins.model.*
import hudson.security.*

def instance = Jenkins.getInstance()          ⟵─┘ Gets an instance of
                                                   the Jenkins model
def hudsonRealm = new HudsonPrivateSecurityRealm(false)    Creates a new user
                                                           account by registering
hudsonRealm.createAccount('USERNAME','PASSWORD')    ⟵─┘ a password to the user
instance.setSecurityRealm(hudsonRealm)

def strategy = new FullControlOnceLoggedInAuthorizationStrategy()
instance.setAuthorizationStrategy(strategy)
instance.save()          ⟵─┐ Gives full access
                            to logged-in users
```

In addition to user management, we will also set some basic configurations for hardening Jenkins to protect against CSRF attacks. With CSRF protection enabled, all issued tokens should include a web session to prevent external attackers from obtaining web sessions. However, if your automation script uses a CSRF token for authentication, you can install the Strict Crumb Issuer plugin (available in the list of plugins installed while baking the Jenkins image) to exclude the web session ID from the validation criteria. We will enable CSRF protection with the csrf-protection.groovy script in the following listing.

Listing 4.6   csrf-protection.groovy script

```groovy
#!groovy

import hudson.security.csrf.DefaultCrumbIssuer
import jenkins.model.Jenkins
                                                      Enables CSRF
def instance = Jenkins.getInstance()                  protection by setting
instance.setCrumbIssuer(new DefaultCrumbIssuer(true))  ⟵─┘ up a crumb issuer
instance.save()
```

This option is enabled by default in new installations, starting with Jenkins 2.*x*. You can also enable CSRF by updating JENKINS_JAVA_OPTIONS. Add the following argument:

```
JENKINS_JAVA_OPTIONS="-Dhudson.security.csrf.DefaultCrumbIssuer=true"
```

NOTE If you're using the Jenkins linter feature to validate Jenkinsfiles against a Jenkins server protected from CSRF, you need to use an API token that doesn't require a CSRF token (crumb) since Jenkins 2.96.

Jenkins has a built-in CLI that allows users and administrators to access Jenkins from a script or a shell environment. The use of the CLI is not recommended for security reasons (to prevent remote access). Hence, we will disable it through the disable-cli.groovy script in the following listing.

Listing 4.7   disable-cli.groovy script

```groovy
#!groovy

import jenkins.model.Jenkins

Jenkins jenkins = Jenkins.getInstance()
jenkins.CLI.get().setEnabled(false)
jenkins.save()
```

> **Gets an instance of Jenkins and disabled CLI access**

We will also disable the JNLP and old unencrypted protocols (JNLP-connect, JNLP2-connect, JNLP3-connect, and CLI-connect) to get rid of the warning messages in the web dashboard. The script disable-jnlp.groovy is in the following listing.

Listing 4.8   disable-jnlp.groovy script

```groovy
#!groovy

import jenkins.model.Jenkins
import jenkins.security.s2m.*

Jenkins jenkins = Jenkins.getInstance()
jenkins.setSlaveAgentPort(-1)
HashSet<String> newProtocols = new HashSet<>(jenkins.getAgentProtocols());
newProtocols.removeAll(Arrays.asList(
        "JNLP3-connect", "JNLP2-connect", "JNLP-connect", "CLI-connect"
));
jenkins.setAgentProtocols(newProtocols);
jenkins.save()
```

> **Sets 0 to indicate random available TCP port, -1 to disable this service**

> **Initializes HashSet structure with available agent protocols, removes old unencrypted protocols from the structure, and saves the new list**

Adding credentials to a new, local Jenkins server for development or troubleshooting can be a daunting task. However, with Groovy scripts and the right setup, developers can automate adding the required credentials into the new Jenkins server.

The Groovy script in listing 4.9 creates SSH credentials based on the AWS key pair we will use to deploy Jenkins worker instances. The SSH credentials object is created by using the `BasicSSHUserPrivateKey` constructor, which takes as parameters the credentials scope, username, SSH private key, and passphrase. The use of these SSH credentials will be illustrated in chapter 5.

Listing 4.9   node-agent.groovy script

```groovy
import jenkins.model.*
import com.cloudbees.plugins.credentials.*
import com.cloudbees.plugins.credentials.common.*
import com.cloudbees.plugins.credentials.domains.*
import com.cloudbees.plugins.credentials.impl.*
import com.cloudbees.jenkins.plugins.sshcredentials.impl.*
import hudson.plugins.sshslaves.*;

domain = Domain.global()
store = Jenkins.instance
.getExtensionList('com.cloudbees.plugins.credentials \
                    .SystemCredentialsProvider')[0].getStore()

slavesPrivateKey = new BasicSSHUserPrivateKey(CredentialsScope.GLOBAL,
        "Jenkins-workers",
        "Ec2-user",
        new BasicSSHUserPrivateKey.UsersPrivateKeySource(),
        "", "")
store.addCredentials(domain, slavesPrivateKey)
```

> Creates a Jenkins credential of type
> "SSH Username with private key." The
> constructor takes the username, private key,
> passphrase, and description as arguments.

NOTE   Now every time the Jenkins server is restarted, the scripts will run and apply configuration for you. You don't need to worry about executing these settings manually every time the server restarts.

You can use Groovy init scripts to customize Jenkins and enforce the desired state. Although writing Groovy scripts requires knowing Jenkins internals and API, you've seen how to configure the common tasks and settings with Groovy scripts upon Jenkins initialization. We still need to install plugins to extend Jenkins functionalities in order to be able to build CI/CD pipelines.

4.3.2   *Discovering Jenkins plugins*

Plugins can be easily installed from the Jenkins dashboard. However, the purpose of this section is to build a fully automated Jenkins AMI, because if you want to install many plugins, this manual process can be fairly long and boring. Therefore, we will use a script provided by the Jenkins community to install plugins, including their dependencies. The scripts take, as a parameter, a file containing the list of Jenkins plugins to be installed.

Table 4.2 lists some of the most useful plugins that help developers save time, as well as making their lives easier. The full list is in the GitHub repository at chapter4/distributed/master/config/plugins.txt.

Table 4.2   Essential Jenkins plugins

Plugin	Description
blueocean	Provides the new Jenkins user experience with sophisticated visualizations of CI/CD pipelines and a bundled pipeline editor that makes automating CI/CD workflows approachable by guiding the user through an intuitive and visual process to create a pipeline. Refer to chapter 2 to explore the key features of Blue Ocean mode.
git	Provides access to any Git server with support for fundamental Git operations within Jenkins pipelines. It can pull, fetch, check out, branch, list, merge, tag, and push Git repositories.
ssh-agent	Allows you to provide SSH credentials to builds via ssh-agent in Jenkins. The ssh-agent is a helper program to hold private keys used for public-key authentication.
ssh-credentials	Allows you to store SSH credentials in Jenkins. It is used to launch Jenkins workers via SSH and execute Docker commands on a Kubernetes cluster remotely over SSH.
slack	Provides Jenkins notification integration with Slack. It can be used to send Slack notifications with Jenkins job build status upon the completion of a CI/CD pipeline. This plugin does require some straightforward setup on the Slack side in order to connect and post messages.
credentials-binding	Allows credentials to be bound to environment variables for use from miscellaneous build steps. It gives you an easy way to package up all of a job's secret files and passwords, and access them using environment variables during the build.
github-pullrequest	Fundamental for integrating Jenkins with GitHub repositories, it supports GitHub pull requests, branches, and custom webhooks. GitHub will trigger a new hook each time a pull request is opened, and once Jenkins receives the hook, it will run the associated job.
job-dsl	Allows jobs to be defined in a programmatic form in a human-readable file. It can be used to create complex pipelines for Jenkins freestyle jobs.
jira	Does pretty much what it says on the tin. It allows developers to integrate Jira (www.atlassian.com/software/jira) into Jenkins to update Jira open issues within CI/CD pipelines. It also associates build and deployment information with relevant Jira tickets and exposes key information about the pipeline across Jira boards.
htmlpublisher	Useful for publishing HTML reports that your builds generate at build time. It can be used to generate code coverage HTML reports and track the percentage of tests covering your application source code in a user-friendly way.
email-ext	Can be used to send email notifications. It's highly customizable: you can configure notifications triggers, content, and recipients. Plus, it supports both plaintext and HTML for the email body.
sonar	Allows easy integration of SonarQube (www.sonarqube.org), the open source platform for continuous inspection of code quality and code security.
embeddable-build-status	Generates badges for all your Jenkins jobs that display, in real time, their build status. You can add these badges to your Git repository README.md file.

NOTE   These are just some of the plugins we will use, and upcoming chapters offer dozens more to explore.

More than a thousand plugins are available to support almost every solution, tool, and process for building, deploying, and automating your projects within Jenkins pipelines. The Jenkins Plugins Index, shown in figure 4.13, has over more than 1,800 plugins at https://plugins.jenkins.io/, free for download and use.

Figure 4.13   Jenkins plugins

NOTE   Before installing a Jenkins plugin, make sure to review the changelog in the plugin's description page, as not all plugins may be safe to use. Also, always pick the latest stable version available.

Now you are more familiar with the essential Jenkins plugins. Let's go ahead and install them.

The script in listing 4.10 will go through the file containing a list of Jenkins plugins line by line, and then issue a cURL command to download the plugin from the Jenkins Plugins Index. Finally, the script will copy the downloaded plugin file to the /var/lib/jenkins/plugins folder. The listing illustrates the main function, and the full script can be downloaded from the GitHub repository at chapter4/distributed/master/config/install-plugins.sh.

Listing 4.10   install-plugins.sh script

```bash
#!/bin/bash
installPlugin() {
  if [ -f ${plugin_dir}/${1}.hpi -o -f ${plugin_dir}/${1}.jpi ]; then
    if [ "$2" == "1" ]; then
      return 1
    fi
    echo "Skipped: $1 (already installed)"
    return 0
  else
    echo "Installing: $1"
```

```
    curl -L --silent --output ${plugin_dir}/${1}.hpi  https://
     updates.jenkins-ci.org/latest/${1}.hpi
    return 0
  fi
}
```

The .hpi extension stood for *Hudson plugin* (remember, Jenkins was a fork of the Hudson project). With the move away from Hudson to Jenkins, this became *Jenkins plugin* and hence the .jpi format. Since the Jenkins v1.5 release, all .hpi plugin files are renamed automatically to .jpi at boot time.

By now, we have configured and automated all tasks needed to set up a running Jenkins server out of the box. Therefore, there's no need for the setup wizard at Jenkins startup (see figure 4.11). As a result, we will disable it by writing a Groovy init script. Create a skip-jenkins-setup.groovy script with the following content.

Listing 4.11   skip-jenkins-setup.groovy script

```groovy
#!groovy

import jenkins.model.*
import hudson.util.*;
import jenkins.install.*;

def instance = Jenkins.getInstance()
instance.setInstallState(InstallState.INITIAL_SETUP_COMPLETED)
```

Finally, we will update the Packer template file used in the first section to copy the Groovy scripts described previously to the temporary instance by using the file *provisioner* (www.packer.io/docs/provisioners/file/). Next, we use a shell provisioner to move these files to the init.groovy.d folder. The template.json file should look similar to the following listing.

Listing 4.12   Jenkins master template file

```json
{
    "variables" : {...},                                        ◁─── List of variables should be declared
    "builders" : [                                                   here such as: aws_profile, region,
        {                                                            instance_type, and source_ami
            "type" : "amazon-ebs",
            "profile" : "{{user `aws_profile`}}",
            "region" : "{{user `region`}}",                         Name of the baked machine
            "instance_type" : "{{user `instance_type`}}",           image. The version number
            "source_ami" : "{{user `source_ami`}}",                 (2.204.1) should be replaced
            "ssh_username" : "ec2-user",                            based on the current version
            "ami_name" : "jenkins-master-2.204.1",      ◁───        you have installed.
            "ami_description" : "Amazon Linux Image with Jenkins Server"
        }
    ],
    "provisioners" : [
        {
```

```
            "type" : "file",
            "source" : "./scripts",
            "destination" : "/tmp/"
    },
    {

            "type" : "file",
            "source" : "./config",
            "destination" : "/tmp/"
    },
    {

            "type" : "file",
            "source" : "{{user `ssh_key`}}",
            "destination" : "/tmp/id_rsa"
    },
    {
            "type" : "shell",
            "script" : "./setup.sh",
            "execute_command" : "sudo -E -S sh '{{ .Path }}'"
    }
]
}
```

Copies the Groovy scripts folder from the local machine to /tmp in the host machine

Copies the configuration files from the local machine to /tmp in the host machine

Copies the user private SSH key to the /tmp folder

Executes the setup.sh shell script to copy the files from the /tmp folder to the right folder and installs Jenkins and its dependencies

NOTE The variables section has been omitted for brevity. The full template file can be found on GitHub at chapter4/distributed/master/template.json.

The SSH key can be generated with `ssh-keygen`. The command will provide a series of prompts. Feel free to use the defaults. However, from a security perspective, it's a good idea to enter a passphrase. Table 4.3 provides a complete list of Packer variables.

Table 4.3 Jenkins master Packer variables

Variable	Description
region	AWS region where the Jenkins master machine image will be created, such as `eu-central-1` (aka Frankfurt).
aws_profile	The profile to use in the shared credentials file for AWS. See Amazon's documentation on specifying profiles for more details: https://docs.aws.amazon.com/sdk-for-go/v1/developer-guide/configuring-sdk.html.
instance_type	The EC2 instance type to use while baking the target AMI, such as `t2.micro`, which is Free Tier eligible.
source_ami	The source AMI that the temporary instance will be based on. We're using the official Amazon Linux image. The ID should be updated according to the AWS region you're using. Refer to figure 4.6 for an example.
ssh_key	Private SSH key location (~/.ssh/id_rsa), the same key you will use to SSH to Jenkins worker instances. A Groovy script will be executed at boot time to add the private key as a credential on the Jenkins master to set up the initial connection with Jenkins workers over SSH.

Once files are uploaded to the temporary instance built by Packer, a setup.sh script will be executed to install the Jenkins LTS version. Next, the script installs the Git client (to clone GitHub repositories in advanced chapters). Then, it copies the workers' private SSH key to the /var/lib/jenkins/.ssh folder and set permissions. Finally, it moves Groovy scripts to the initialization folder, installs essentials plugins by executing the install-plugins.sh script, and starts the Jenkins server.

It's worth mentioning that scripts files were uploaded to the /tmp folder; Packer can upload files only to locations that the provisioning user (`ec2-user`) has permission to access. The following listing contains the content of setup.sh.

Listing 4.13 setup.sh script (install Jenkins)

```
#!/bin/bash                                        Installs JDK (minimum v1.8.0), which is
yum remove -y java                                 required for Jenkins to be up and running
yum install -y java-1.8.0-openjdk
wget -O /etc/yum.repos.d/jenkins.repo
http://pkg.jenkins-ci.org/redhat-stable/jenkins.repo
rpm --import https://jenkins-ci.org/redhat-stable/jenkins-ci.org.key
yum install -y jenkins
chkconfig jenkins on
                             Installs Git client, which will be needed to clone
yum install -y git    ◁──┘   project GitHub repositories in upcoming chapters
mkdir /var/lib/jenkins/.ssh
touch /var/lib/jenkins/.ssh/known_hosts
chown -R jenkins:jenkins /var/lib/jenkins/.ssh          Copies the private SSH
chmod 700 /var/lib/jenkins/.ssh                         key used to deploy
mv /tmp/id_rsa /var/lib/jenkins/.ssh/id_rsa             Jenkins workers/agents
chmod 600 /var/lib/jenkins/.ssh/id_rsa                  to JENKINS_HOME
chown -R jenkins:jenkins /var/lib/jenkins/.ssh/id_rsa

mkdir -p /var/lib/jenkins/init.groovy.d              Moves the Groovy
mv /tmp/*.groovy /var/lib/jenkins/init.groovy.d/     scripts to init.groovy.d
mv /tmp/jenkins /etc/sysconfig/jenkins
chmod +x /tmp/install-plugins.sh        Installs needed dependencies
bash /tmp/install-plugins.sh            by running install-plugins.sh      Starts the
service jenkins start                                              ◁──┘   Jenkins service
```

The template directory structure should look like the following. The scripts directory holds initial configuration and seeding scripts. The config folder contains the list of essential plugins to install, as well as the shell script to install plugins from the Jenkins Plugin Index:

```
├── config
│   ├── install-plugins.sh
│   ├── jenkins
│   └── plugins.txt
├── scripts
│   ├── basic-security.groovy
│   ├── csrf-protection.groovy
│   └── disable-cli.groovy
```

```
│    ├── disable-jnlp.groovy
│    ├── node-agent.groovy
│    └── skip-jenkins-setup.groovy
├── setup.sh
└── template.json
```

NOTE   Jenkins captures launch configuration parameters in the /etc/syscon-fig/jenkins file. If you want to add Java arguments, it's the file you're looking for.

Prior to building the AMI, it's a good idea to validate the syntactical correctness of the template file by issuing the `packer validate` command. `Template validated successfully` is the expected output if the template is valid.

Now that the template is validated, we will bake the AMI with the `packer build` command:

`packer `**`build`**` template.`**`json`**

The process can take several minutes. Output similar to this is expected:

```
==> amazon-ebs: Prevalidating any provided VPC information
==> amazon-ebs: Prevalidating AMI Name: jenkins-master-2.204.1
    amazon-ebs: Found Image ID: ami-010fae13a16763bb4
==> amazon-ebs: Creating temporary keypair: packer_5e10856e-9f7d-06d4-88dc-739f5737cad3
==> amazon-ebs: Creating temporary security group for this instance: packer_5e10856f-2ed6-76c3-17d9-eac59e672186
==> amazon-ebs: Authorizing access to port 22 from [0.0.0.0/0] in the temporary security groups...
==> amazon-ebs: Launching a source AWS instance...
==> amazon-ebs: Adding tags to source instance
    amazon-ebs: Adding tag: "Name": "packer-builder"
    amazon-ebs: Instance ID: i-03b1fb7327193394f
==> amazon-ebs: Waiting for instance (i-03b1fb7327193394f) to become ready...
==> amazon-ebs: Using ssh communicator to connect: 18.184.247.211
==> amazon-ebs: Waiting for SSH to become available...
==> amazon-ebs: Connected to SSH!
==> amazon-ebs: Uploading ./scripts/basic-security.groovy => /tmp/basic-security.groovy
basic-security.groovy 419 B / 419 B [========================================================
==> amazon-ebs: Uploading ./scripts/disable-cli.groovy => /tmp/disable-cli.groovy
disable-cli.groovy 174 B / 174 B [===========================================================
==> amazon-ebs: Uploading ./scripts/csrf-protection.groovy => /tmp/csrf-protection.groovy
csrf-protection.groovy 228 B / 228 B [=======================================================
==> amazon-ebs: Uploading ./scripts/disable-jnlp.groovy => /tmp/disable-jnlp.groovy
disable-jnlp.groovy 463 B / 463 B [==========================================================
==> amazon-ebs: Uploading ./scripts/skip-jenkins-setup.groovy => /tmp/skip-jenkins-setup.groovy
skip-jenkins-setup.groovy 182 B / 182 B [====================================================
==> amazon-ebs: Uploading ./config/jenkins => /tmp/jenkins
jenkins 3.09 KiB / 3.09 KiB [=================================================================
==> amazon-ebs: Uploading /Users/mlabouardy/keys/komiser.pem => /tmp/id_rsa
komiser.pem 1.66 KiB / 1.66 KiB [=============================================================
==> amazon-ebs: Uploading ./scripts/node-agent.groovy => /tmp/node-agent.groovy
node-agent.groovy 705 B / 705 B [=============================================================
==> amazon-ebs: Uploading ./plugins.txt => /tmp/plugins.txt
plugins.txt 1.85 KiB / 1.85 KiB [=============================================================
==> amazon-ebs: Uploading ./install-plugins.sh => /tmp/install-plugins.sh
install-plugins.sh 1.18 KiB / 1.18 KiB [=====================================================
==> amazon-ebs: Provisioning with shell script: ./setup.sh
    amazon-ebs: Install Jenkins stable release
    amazon-ebs: Loaded plugins: priorities, update-motd, upgrade-helper
    amazon-ebs: Resolving Dependencies
```

If the script succeeds, Packer should show a message containing the AMI ID, and the Jenkins master AMI will be available in the EC2 dashboard, as shown in figure 4.14.

Figure 4.14   Jenkins master AMI

> **NOTE**   The AMI name should be unique. Therefore, you might need to delete the existing image from your AWS account if it exists already.

Finally, we can spin up an EC2 instance based on the baked AMI. Once the instance is running, point your browser to the instance's public IP address on port 8080. After a while, you'll see the screen in figure 4.15.

Figure 4.15   Jenkins web dashboard

This time, the setup wizard should disappear and many functionalities should be added. Sign in using the admin credentials defined in the basic-security.groovy script from listing 4.5. After login, you can verify that Jenkins credentials are created by going to the Credentials item on the left; see figure 4.16. So far, only the Jenkins

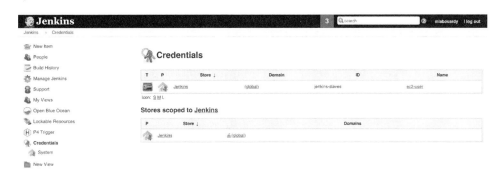

Figure 4.16   Jenkins credentials

worker SSH credential has been created (see listing 4.9), but you can customize the Groovy script to create additional credentials for external services like GitHub, Nexus, or SonarQube.

Moreover, the essential plugins were also installed. Jump to Manage Jenkins from the home page and then navigate to Plugins. You should see a list of plugins installed by default on the Installed tab, as shown in figure 4.17.

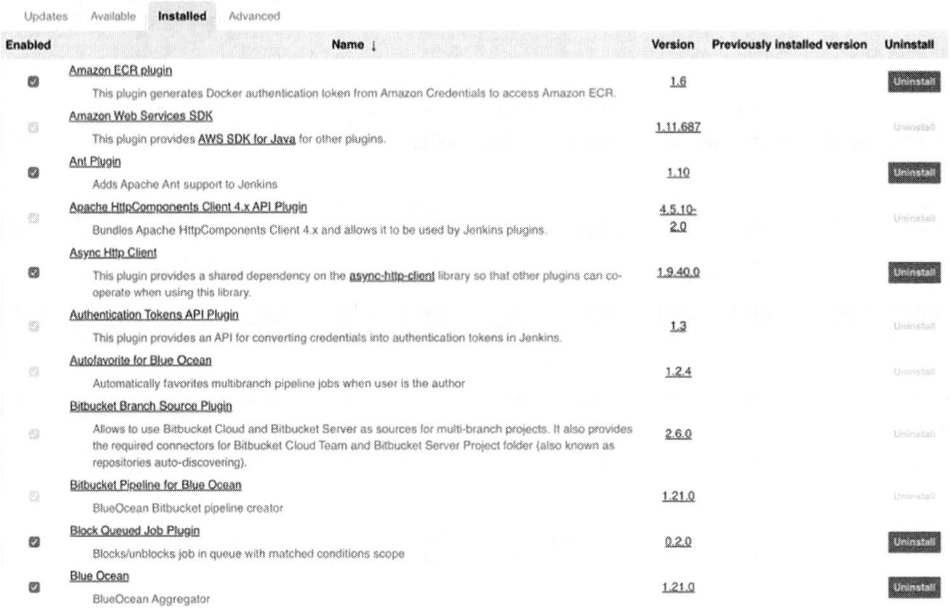

Figure 4.17   Jenkins installed plugins

Now that we have defined a Jenkins configuration as code, we can spawn it as many times as possible, on different machines, with the same result. And we've had no tiresome manual walks through the GUI.

4.4   *Baking the Jenkins worker AMI*

The Jenkins worker AMI baking process should be straightforward; see the following listing. The only requirement for an instance to be a Jenkins worker or build agent is to have a JDK. Modern Jenkins versions require a Java 8 runtime environment.

Listing 4.14   Jenkins worker template file

```
{
    "variables" : {...},
    "builders" : [
        {
```

```
                    "type" : "amazon-ebs",
                    "profile" : "{{user `aws_profile`}}",
                    "region" : "{{user `region`}}",
                    "instance_type" : "{{user `instance_type`}}",
                    "source_ami" : "{{user `source_ami`}}",
                    "ssh_username" : "ec2-user",
                    "ami_name" : "jenkins-worker",
                    "ami_description" : "Jenkins worker's AMI",

        ],
        "provisioners" : [
            {
                "type" : "shell",
                "script" : "./setup.sh",
                "execute_command" : "sudo -E -S sh '{{ .Path }}'"
            }
        ]
}
```

The variables in table 4.4 should be provided during build time within the template file or with the -var flag.

Table 4.4   Jenkins worker Packer variables

Variable	Description
region	AWS region where the Jenkins worker machine image will be created. Similar to the Jenkins master AWS region value.
aws_profile	The profile to use in the shared credentials file for AWS. See Amazon's documentation on specifying profiles for more details: http://mng.bz/O1Yx.
instance_type	The EC2 instance type to use while baking the target AMI, such as t2.micro, which is Free Tier eligible.
source_ami	The source AMI that the temporary instance will be based on. We're using the official Amazon Linux image. The ID should be updated according to the AWS region you're using.

Packer will use the shell provisioner to install the JDK, as well as any tool that you may require to run your builds (Git or Docker, for example). You can take this script further and create a user called jenkins with a home directory to store Jenkins job workspaces, as shown in the following listing.

Listing 4.15   setup.sh script

```
#!/bin/bash
yum remove -y java
yum update -y
yum install -y git docker java-1.8.0-openjdk
usermod -aG docker ec2-user
systemctl enable docker
```

NOTE   Docker is necessary, as we are going to define CI/CD pipelines for Dockerized microservices in upcoming chapters.

Issue the `packer build` command to bake the Jenkins worker AMI. Once the image-baking process is finished, the worker's AMI will be available on the EC2 dashboard, as shown in figure 4.18.

	Name	AMI Name	AMI ID	Source	Owner	Visibility	Status	Creation Date	Platform
		jenkins-master-2.107.2	ami-09483ba4841596a42	305929695733/j...	305929695733	Private	available	September 1, 2019 at 6:02:0...	Other Linux
		jenkins-master-2.204.1	ami-051933c5e0fc71592	305929695733/j...	305929695733	Private	available	December 23, 2019 at 7:22:...	Other Linux
		jenkins-slave	ami-0816e8088a552b822	305929695733/j...	305929695733	Private	available	September 1, 2019 at 6:07:3...	Other Linux
		jenkins-worker	ami-08ab98c3d3d999d42	305929695733/j...	305929695733	Private	available	December 25, 2019 at 4:38:...	Other Linux
		nexus-3.18.1-01	ami-0ba6475c33f76d40d	305929695733/j...	305929695733	Private	available	September 1, 2019 at 6:38:1...	Other Linux
		public-bee-with-hurl.	ami-72765499	305929695733/j...	305929695733	Private	available	May 6, 2018 at 12:18:05 PM ...	Other Linux

Figure 4.18   Jenkins worker AMI

NOTE   After running the preceding examples, your AWS account now has an AMI associated with it. AMIs are stored in S3 by Amazon, so unless you want to be charged about $0.01 per month, you'll probably want to remove these images if they're not needed.

Now that our Jenkins cluster AMIs are ready to use, we will use them in the next chapter to deploy our cluster on AWS with the IaC tool HashiCorp Terraform. Figure 4.19 illustrates how Terraform will be integrated.

If you plan to embrace the immutable infrastructure approach for upgrading Jenkins or installing additional plugins, triggering the provisioning process with Packer can get challenging. That's why you should opt for automation and set up a pipeline with Jenkins to automate the baking workflow for AMI. A basic workflow will use

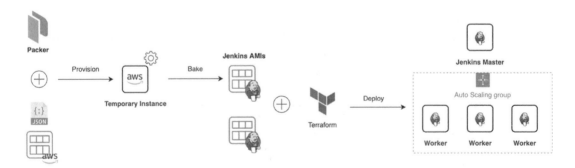

Figure 4.19   Packer will provision a temporary instance from a template file, and provision the instance with all needed configs and dependencies. From there, Terraform will deploy EC2 instances based on the baked image.

GitHub to store Packer template files and trigger a build on Jenkins upon the push event. The job will validate the template changes, start the baking process (1), and create an EC2 instance (2) based on the new baked AMI. Figure 4.20 summarizes the entire workflow.

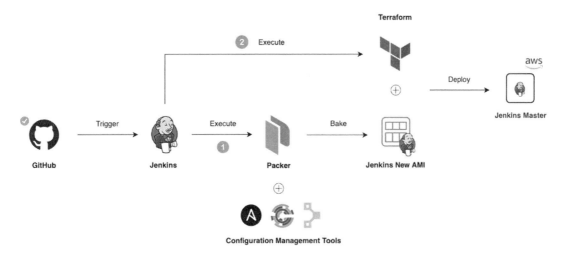

Figure 4.20   Automating the AMIs with Jenkins

NOTE   Chapter 7 covers how to set up GitHub webhooks to continuously trigger Jenkins build jobs when a push or merge event occurs.

Summary

- HashiCorp Packer leverages the power of immutable infrastructure to bake custom machine images with all needed dependencies.
- Setting up Jenkins is a complex process, as both Jenkins and its plugins require tuning and configuration, with dozens of parameters to set within the web UI Manage Jenkins section.
- Configuration scripts in the init.groovy directory are executed in alphabetical order during Jenkins boot time. This is ideal for setting up seeding and configuration job interfaces.
- Jenkins provides thousands of plugins to support building, deploying, and automating any project.
- The weekly Jenkins releases deliver bug fixes and new features rapidly to users and plugin developers who need them. However, the Long-Term Support release is preferred for its stability.

5

Discovering Jenkins as code with Terraform

This chapter covers
- Introducing infrastructure as code (IaC)
- Using HashiCorp Terraform, which enables IaC
- Deploying Jenkins in a secure private network
- Scaling Jenkins workers dynamically with AWS Auto Scaling

In the previous chapter, we used HashiCorp Packer to create custom Jenkins machine images; in this chapter, we will use those images (figure 5.1) to deploy the machines. To do that, we will write declarative definitions of the Jenkins infrastructure we want to exist and use an automation tool to deploy the resources on the given infrastructure-as-a service (IaaS) provider.

In the past, managing IT infrastructure was a hard job. System administrators had to manually manage and configure all of the hardware and software that was needed for the applications to run. However, in recent years, things have changed dramatically. Trends like cloud computing revolutionized—and improved—the way organizations design, develop, and maintain their IT infrastructure. One of the critical components of this trend is called infrastructure as code.

	Name	AMI Name	AMI ID	Source	Owner	Visibility	Status	Creation Date	Platform
☐		jenkins-master-2.107.2	ami-09463ba4641596a42	305929695733/j...	305929695733	Private	available	September 1, 2019 at 6:02:0...	Other Linux
☐		jenkins-master-2.204.1	ami-051933c5e0fc71592	305929695733/j...	305929695733	Private	available	December 23, 2019 at 7:22:...	Other Linux
☐		jenkins-slave	ami-0816e8088a552b822	305929695733/j...	305929695733	Private	available	September 1, 2019 at 6:07:3...	Other Linux
■		jenkins-worker	ami-08ab98c3d3d999d42	305929695733/j...	305929695733	Private	available	December 25, 2019 at 4:38:...	Other Linux
☐		nexus-3.18.1-01	ami-0ba6475c33f76d40d	305929695733/...	305929695733	Private	available	September 1, 2019 at 6:38:1...	Other Linux
☐		public-bee-with-hurl.	ami-72765499	305929695733/...	305929695733	Private	available	May 6, 2018 at 12:18:05 PM ...	Other Linux

Figure 5.1 Jenkins custom machine images

5.1   Introducing infrastructure as code

Infrastructure as code (IaC) allows you to manage your infrastructure by using configuration files. This decreases costs, reduces risks, and deploys faster resources on the cloud. Another benefit is that your infrastructure becomes testable, repeatable, self-healing, idempotent, and, most importantly, easy to understand, because your infrastructure code will essentially be your documentation.

Several IaC tools are available, each with its own implementation (figure 5.2). Some tools are focused on specific clouds, including AWS CloudFormation (https://aws.amazon.com/cloudformation/), Azure Resource Manager (https://azure.microsoft.com/features/resource-manager/), OpenStack Heat (https://wiki.openstack.org/wiki/Heat), and Google Cloud Deployment Manager (https://cloud.google.com/deployment-manager). Others are attempting to bridge all cloud providers and mask their semantic differences to provide a cloud-agnostic implementation. This category includes HashiCorp Terraform, HashiCorp Vagrant, Chef Provisioning, and Pulumi.

Figure 5.2 Infrastructure-as-code tools

In this book, we will focus exclusively on using HashiCorp Terraform to deploy Jenkins components. Terraform provides a flexible abstraction of resources and providers, is platform-agnostic, and supports multiple IaaS providers such as AWS, Microsoft Azure, Google Cloud Platform, and DigitalOcean. Moreover, Terraform is open source and comes with a simple and unified syntax with no steep learning curve for new users and easy-to-access online resources for any infrastructure deployment use case.

NOTE   Configuration management tools like Ansible and Puppet were built to install and manage configuration on existing servers. Terraform focuses on bootstrapping and initialization of servers and other infrastructure resources.

Over the next few sections, you will learn how to use Terraform to deploy a Jenkins cluster on AWS.

5.1.1   Terraform usage

Terraform uses a push approach: the developer or ops engineer describes the desired infrastructure in a template file, and Terraform directly interacts with the cloud provider through its API. For example, if the target cloud provider is AWS, Terraform uses the Terraform AWS provider plugin (https://registry.terraform.io/providers/hashicorp/aws/latest), which, under the hood, uses the AWS official SDK to create/ update or destroy resources.

To maintain the desired state of the infrastructure and detect changes, Terraform generates a JSON file named terraform.tfstate that stores the state of your managed infrastructure and configuration. Terraform uses a diffing technique to detect the changes before any operation. Therefore, individuals and teams can safely and predictably change the infrastructure.

Terraform itself is a CLI tool, which can be downloaded from its official release page (www.terraform.io/downloads.html), as shown in figure 5.3, by installing the

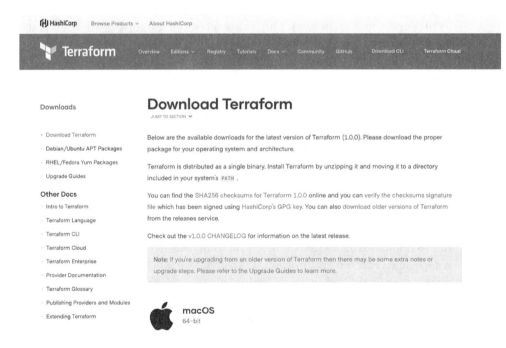

Figure 5.3   Terraform download page

binary for your operating system and architecture. It supports all major operating systems. Windows, macOS, and any Linux distribution are supported in both 32-bit and 64-bit versions.

Once you download the zip archive, unzip it to any convenient folder. Make sure that this folder is available in your `PATH` environment variable. To check whether Terraform is properly installed, issue this command:

```
terraform --version
```

> **NOTE** At the time of writing this book, the latest stable version of HashiCorp Terraform is 1.0.0.

If you get output similar to `Terraform vX.Y.Z`, congrats! You have a working Terraform installation. We're ready to write our Terraform template files.

5.2 *Provisioning an AWS VPC*

As discussed in chapter 3, our Jenkins cluster will be deployed inside a VPC within private subnets; see figure 5.4. We can deploy the cluster in the default VPC created by AWS. However, to have full control of the network topology, we will create a VPC from scratch to isolate the Jenkins cluster from the application workloads we're going to deploy in advanced chapters. The following schema summarizes the target VPC architecture:

> **NOTE** To understand Amazon VPC terminology (subnets, security groups, route tables, and so forth), refer to chapter 3.

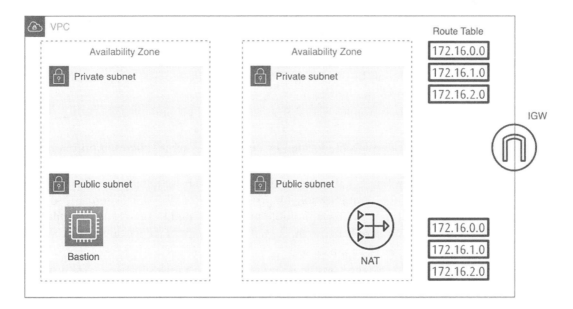

Figure 5.4   AWS virtual private cloud architecture

In essence, this VPC will be divided into subnets. Some subnets will be public, with access to the internet; and some will be private. Then, we define routing rules between subnets to allow traffic to go through either an internet gateway or NAT gateway. We will also deploy a bastion host to be able to SSH to Jenkins private instances without exposing them to the public.

5.2.1   *AWS VPC*

Terraform uses a DSL called *HashiCorp Configuration Language* (HCL), a declarative language to describe infrastructure resources. These resources are described in a simple text file with a .tf extension.

   Instead of writing one big template file, we will use a modular development approach and split our Jenkins cluster deployment into multiple template files. Each file is responsible for deploying a component or an AWS resource of the target infrastructure. First, create a terraform.tf file with the following content:

```
provider "aws" {
  region                   = var.region
  shared_credentials_file = var.shared_credentials_file
  profile                  = var.aws_profile
}
```

> **NOTE**   Through the rest of the chapters, Terraform will store the state locally, which isn't ideal for team collaboration, as the state might contain sensitive information (if you plan to use SCM for versioning). I recommend using a remote backend such as Amazon S3 to store the state.

For Terraform to interact with an IaaS, it needs to have a provider configured. In the preceding code block, we defined AWS as a provider and configured the needed credentials to interact with the AWS API to create AWS resources afterward. The AWS provider supports multiple methods of authentication:

- Static credentials by providing `access_key` and `secret_key` attributes inline in the `aws` provider block.
- Environment variables via `AWS_ACCESS_KEY_ID` and `AWS_SECRET_ACCESS_KEY` variables.
- A shared credentials file located by default at ~/.aws/credentials on Linux and macOS, and %USERPROFILE%\.aws\credentials for Windows users. By default, Terraform will check these locations, but you can optionally specify a different location in the configuration by providing the `shared_credentials_file` attribute. Also, if you have multiple profiles defined in the credentials file, you can specify the profile to use through the `AWS_PROFILE` environment variable by setting the `profile` attribute.
- An EC2 IAM instance profile if you're using Terraform from an EC2 instance. Terraform will fetch the temporary access tokens from the instance's metadata. This is a preferred approach over the preceding strategies when running in an EC2 instance, as you can avoid hardcoding credentials.

Next, we will declare an AWS VPC resource in a vpc.tf file. The following code snippet uses the CIDR block 10.0.0.0/16 for the VPC, but you can choose a different CIDR block:

```
resource "aws_vpc" "default" {
  cidr_block          = var.cidr_block
  enable_dns_hostnames = true

  tags {
    Name   = var.vpc_name
    Author = var.author
  }
}
```

> **NOTE** All available AWS resources can be found in the Terraform AWS documentation at www.terraform.io/docs/providers/aws/index.html.

Note the use of variables instead of hardcoded values to create reusable resources (portability) and give users the flexibility to override them during runtime. We'll define the list of variables in the variables.tf file, shown in the following listing.

Listing 5.1 Terraform variables file

```
variable "region" {
  description = "AWS region"
  type = string
}

variable "cidr_block" {
  description = "VPC CIDR block"
  default     = "10.0.0.0/16"
}
```

Terraform variables are created with a `variable` block. They have a name and an optional type, default value, and description arguments. Table 5.1 provides the full list of variables.

Table 5.1 VPC's Terraform variables

Variable	Type	Value	Description
region	String	None	The name of the region, such as `eu-central-1`, in which to deploy the VPC.
shared_ credentials_file	String	`~/.aws/ credentials`	The path to the shared credentials file. If this is not set and a profile is specified, `~/.aws/ credentials` will be used.
aws_profile	String	`profile`	The AWS profile name as set in the shared credentials file.
cidr_block	String	`10.0.0.0/16`	The CIDR block for the VPC. The allowed block size is between a /16 netmask (65,536 IP addresses) and /28 netmask (16 IP addresses).

Table 5.1   VPC's Terraform variables *(continued)*

Variable	Type	Value	Description
vpc_name	String	management	Ensure that your VPC is using appropriate naming for tagging to manage it more efficiently and adhere to AWS resource tagging best practices.
author	String	None	Name of the owner of the VPC. It's optional, but it's recommended to tag your AWS resources to track the monthly costs by owner or environment.

Before running Terraform, we need to install the AWS plugin for Terraform. You can do this by executing the following command:

```
terraform init
```

This installs the AWS provider plugin and initializes a new configuration:

```
Initializing the backend...

Initializing provider plugins...
- Checking for available provider plugins...
- Downloading plugin for provider "aws" (hashicorp/aws) 2.54.0...

The following providers do not have any version constraints in configuration,
so the latest version was installed.

To prevent automatic upgrades to new major versions that may contain breaking
changes, it is recommended to add version = "..." constraints to the
corresponding provider blocks in configuration, with the constraint strings
suggested below.

* provider.aws: version = "~> 2.54"

Terraform has been successfully initialized!

You may now begin working with Terraform. Try running "terraform plan" to see
any changes that are required for your infrastructure. All Terraform commands
should now work.

If you ever set or change modules or backend configuration for Terraform,
rerun this command to reinitialize your working directory. If you forget, other
commands will detect it and remind you to do so if necessary.
```

> **NOTE** To be able to use Terraform for the examples in this chapter, add the VPCFullAccess policy to the IAM user associated with Terraform.

Use the following command to generate an execution plan of changes that will be applied (for a dry run):

```
terraform plan --var-file="variables.tfvars"
```

You can specify individual variables on the command line with the -var option when running terraform plan. However, because we have a lot of variables to set, it is more convenient and handy to use a variable definitions file called variables.tfvars.

This file contains dynamic variables declared in the variables.tf file such as for the AWS region and credentials file. Any variable for which you define a value needs to exist in variables.tf, as shown in the following listing.

Listing 5.2 Terraform dynamic variables

```
region="YOUR AWS REGION"
shared_credentials_file="PATH TO .aws/credentials FILE"
aws_profile="AWS PROFILE"
author="AUTHOR NAME"
```

NOTE If you named the variable definition files terraform.tfvars or terraform .tfvars.json, they will be loaded automatically by Terraform.

You can also load variables from environment variables. Terraform will parse any environment variables that are prefixed with TF_VAR. For example, if Terraform finds an environment variable named TF_VAR_aws_profile, it will use its value as the string value of the aws_profile variable.

The terraform plan command will display the target plan, which is particularly useful to validate the changes in advance and avoid unwanted changes. The output should look like this:

```
Terraform will perform the following actions:

  # aws_vpc.management will be created
  + resource "aws_vpc" "management" {
      + arn                              = (known after apply)
      + assign_generated_ipv6_cidr_block = false
      + cidr_block                       = "10.0.0.0/16"
      + default_network_acl_id           = (known after apply)
      + default_route_table_id           = (known after apply)
      + default_security_group_id        = (known after apply)
      + dhcp_options_id                  = (known after apply)
      + enable_classiclink               = (known after apply)
      + enable_classiclink_dns_support   = (known after apply)
      + enable_dns_hostnames             = true
      + enable_dns_support               = true
      + id                               = (known after apply)
      + instance_tenancy                 = "default"
      + ipv6_association_id              = (known after apply)
      + ipv6_cidr_block                  = (known after apply)
      + main_route_table_id              = (known after apply)
      + owner_id                         = (known after apply)
      + tags                             = {
          + "Author" = "mlabouardy"
          + "Name"   = "management"
        }
    }

Plan: 1 to add, 0 to change, 0 to destroy.
```

NOTE I highly recommend encrypting the state and plan files because they can potentially store secrets.

We can see that one resource will be created. Now we are comfortable that Terraform is going to do the right thing! We can apply the changes with the following command:

```
terraform apply --var-file="variables.tfvars"
```

Type `yes` to apply the actions, and Terraform will create the AWS VPC resource:

```
Do you want to perform these actions?
  Terraform will perform the actions described above.
  Only 'yes' will be accepted to approve.

  Enter a value: yes

aws_vpc.management: Creating...
aws_vpc.management: Creation complete after 2s [id=vpc-0c11cb69a871f0b24]

Apply complete! Resources: 1 added, 0 changed, 0 destroyed.
```

On the AWS VPC dashboard, you should see an additional VPC called *management* with the 10.0.0.0/16 CIDR block created, as shown in figure 5.5.

Figure 5.5   AWS VPC dashboard

Awesome—we have a custom VPC!

5.2.2   *VPC subnets*

Creating a VPC is not enough; to be able to place Jenkins instances in this isolated network, we also need a subnet. This subnet belongs to a previously created VPC, so we have to pass a VPC ID when we create it. We don't have to hardcode it, though. Terraform, via interpolation syntax, allows us to reference any other resource via its ID.

Create a subnets.tf file with two public subnets and two private subnets in different availability zones for resiliency, as shown in the following listing. Each subnet has its own CIDR block that is a subset of the VPC CIDR block.

Listing 5.3   VPC subnets

```
resource "aws_subnet" "public_subnets" {
  vpc_id                 = aws_vpc.management.id
```

The count.index variable has the distinct index number (starting with 0) and is used to construct a unique CIDR block within the 10.0.0.0/16 range

```
cidr_block              = "10.0.${count.index * 2 + 1}.0/24"
availability_zone       = element(var.availability_zones, count.index)
map_public_ip_on_launch = true           ◁

count = var.public_subnets_count
```
Specify true to indicate that instances launched into the subnet should be assigned a public IP address

```
tags = {
  Name    = "public_10.0.${count.index * 2 +
    1}.0_${element(var.availability_zones, count.index)}"        ◁
  Author = var.author
}
}
```
Gives a unique name to the subnet; for example, public_10.0.0.0_eu-central-1

```
resource "aws_subnet" "private_subnets" {
  vpc_id                  = aws_vpc.management.id
  cidr_block              = "10.0.${count.index * 2}.0/24"
  availability_zone       = element(var.availability_zones, count.index)
  map_public_ip_on_launch = false

  count = var.private_subnets_count

  tags = {
    Name    = "private_10.0.${count.index *
      2}.0_${element(var.availability_zones, count.index)}"
    Author = var.author
  }
}
```

The code uses interpolation with a `count` attribute to give us a parameterized subnet. With this, we can calculate the subnet CIDR block with expressions such as `10.0.${count.index*2+1}.0/24`. You can also use the `cidrsubnet(prefix, newbits, netnum)` method to calculate the subnet address within a VPC CIDR block. (Refer to the documentation at http://mng.bz/WBj0 for more details.)

Set the default number of subnets to 2 and define the availability zones where the subnets will be located as variables in the variables.tf file. (You can use the `aws ec2 describe-availability-zones` command to view the availability zones within your AWS region.) Table 5.2 provides the complete list of Terraform variables.

Table 5.2 Subnet Terraform variables

Variable	Type	Value	Description
availability_zones	List	None	Availability zone for spinning up the VPC subnet
public_subnets_count	Number	2	The number of public subnets to create
private_subnets_count	Number	2	The number of private subnets to create

Run the `terraform plan` command to generate an action plan. This validates the configuration that will apply to the current infrastructure:

```
# aws_subnet.private_subnets[1] will be created
+ resource "aws_subnet" "private_subnets" {
    + arn                             = (known after apply)
    + assign_ipv6_address_on_creation = false
    + availability_zone               = "eu-west-3b"
    + availability_zone_id            = (known after apply)
    + cidr_block                      = "10.0.2.0/24"
    + id                              = (known after apply)
    + ipv6_cidr_block                 = (known after apply)
    + ipv6_cidr_block_association_id  = (known after apply)
    + map_public_ip_on_launch         = false
    + owner_id                        = (known after apply)
    + tags                            = {
        + "Author" = "mlabouardy"
        + "Name"   = "private_10.0.2.0_eu-west-3b"
      }
    + vpc_id                          = "vpc-0c11cb69a871f0b24"
  }

# aws_subnet.public_subnets[0] will be created
+ resource "aws_subnet" "public_subnets" {
    + arn                             = (known after apply)
    + assign_ipv6_address_on_creation = false
    + availability_zone               = "eu-west-3a"
    + availability_zone_id            = (known after apply)
    + cidr_block                      = "10.0.1.0/24"
    + id                              = (known after apply)
    + ipv6_cidr_block                 = (known after apply)
    + ipv6_cidr_block_association_id  = (known after apply)
    + map_public_ip_on_launch         = true
    + owner_id                        = (known after apply)
    + tags                            = {
        + "Author" = "mlabouardy"
        + "Name"   = "public_10.0.1.0_eu-west-3a"
      }
    + vpc_id                          = "vpc-0c11cb69a871f0b24"
  }
```

If you are comfortable with the deployment plan, apply the configuration with the `terraform apply` command. The subnets should be created inside the VPC, as shown in figure 5.6.

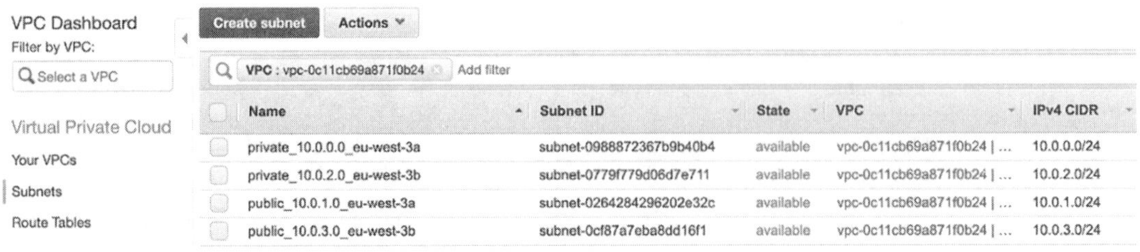

Figure 5.6   **VPC's public and private subnets**

After you've created the VPC and subnets, you need to create private and public route tables to define the traffic-routing mechanism in VPC subnets.

5.2.3 *VPC route tables*

As stated earlier, the typical configuration for a VPC divides it into public and private subnets. To let instances deployed in private subnets have access to the internet without being exposed to the public, we will create private and public route tables for fine-grained traffic control.

Create a public_rt.tf file, define an internet gateway resource, and attach it to the VPC created earlier:

```
resource "aws_internet_gateway" "igw" {
  vpc_id = aws_vpc.management.id

  tags = {
    Name   = "igw_${var.vpc_name}"
    Author = var.author
  }
}
```

Within public_rt.tf, define a public route table and a route that points all traffic (0.0.0.0/0) to the internet gateway:

```
resource "aws_route_table" "public_rt" {
  vpc_id = aws_vpc.management.id

  route {
    cidr_block = "0.0.0.0/0"
    gateway_id = aws_internet_gateway.igw.id
  }

  tags = {
    Name   = "public_rt_${var.vpc_name}"
    Author = var.author
  }
}
```

So far, the public route table is not associated with any subnet. You need to associate it with public subnets in your VPC so that traffic coming from those subnets is routed to the internet gateway:

```
resource "aws_route_table_association" "public" {
  count          = var.public_subnets_count
  subnet_id      = element(aws_subnet.public_subnets.*.id, count.index)
  route_table_id = aws_route_table.public_rt.id
}
```

NOTE I recommend generating an execution plan before deploying resources with Terraform to avoid any surprises when Terraform manipulates infrastructure.

Once you've applied Terraform changes with `terraform apply`, head over to the VPC dashboard and jump to the Route Tables section. You should see the public route table, as shown in figure 5.7.

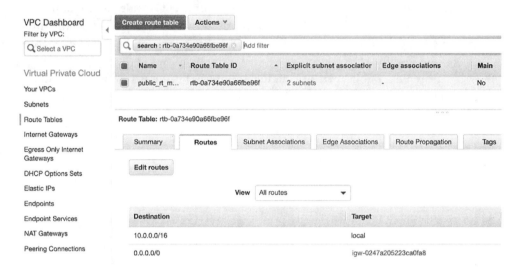

Figure 5.7   VPC's public route table

With the public route table created, go ahead and create the private route table.

Create a private_rt.tf file and define a NAT gateway resource inside a public subnet to enable Jenkins instances that will be deployed in private subnets later to connect to the internet. Then, associate an Elastic IP address with the NAT gateway, shown in the following listing.

Listing 5.4   VPC NAT gateway

```
resource "aws_eip" "nat" {
  vpc = true

  tags = {
    Name   = "eip-nat_${var.vpc_name}"
    Author = var.author
  }
}

resource "aws_nat_gateway" "nat" {
  allocation_id = aws_eip.nat.id
  subnet_id     = element(aws_subnet.public_subnets.*.id, 0)

  tags = {
    Name   = "nat_${var.vpc_name}"
    Author = var.author
  }
}
```

Within the same file, create a private route table with a route that forwards all traffic (0.0.0.0/0) to the ID of the NAT gateway that you created, as shown in the following listing.

Listing 5.5 Private route table

```
resource "aws_route_table" "private_rt" {
  vpc_id = aws_vpc.management.id

  route {
    cidr_block     = "0.0.0.0/0"
    nat_gateway_id = aws_nat_gateway.nat.id
  }
  tags = {
    Name   = "private_rt_${var.vpc_name}"
    Author = var.author
  }
}
```

> **NOTE** If you prefer to manage a NAT instance, you can replace the current route that points to the NAT gateway with a route to the NAT instance.

Finally, assign private subnets to the private route table with the following code block:

```
resource "aws_route_table_association" "private" {
  count         = var.private_subnets_count
  subnet_id     = element(aws_subnet.private_subnets.*.id, count.index)
  route_table_id = aws_route_table.private_rt.id
}
```

The Elastic IP address is a static public IPv4 address, so it may be useful to mask the failure of a NAT gateway by rapidly remapping the address to another NAT gateway.

Use `terraform apply` to apply the infrastructure changes. A private route table should be created, as shown in figure 5.8.

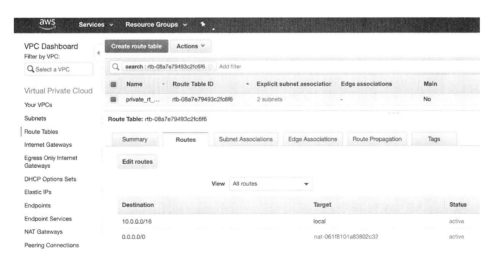

Figure 5.8 VPC's private route table

An additional route table rule should be created to point internet-bound traffic to the NAT gateway. This enables Jenkins instances in the private subnets to have access to the internet.

Our Jenkins cluster will be deployed inside private subnets. Hence, instances won't be publicly accessible from the internet (because the cluster doesn't have a public IP). To securely access Jenkins instances, we will deploy a bastion host.

> **NOTE**   You can skip this solution if you set up a remote access virtual private network (VPN) like OpenVPN Access Server. Refer to the official guide at https://openvpn.net/aws-video-tutorials/byol/ for instructions.

5.2.4   *VPC bastion host*

A *bastion host*, also called a *jump box*, provides secure access to EC2 instances located in private subnets via a single controlled point of entry. A bastion host is a special-purpose machine, deployed in a public subnet, and has access to private instances within private subnets.

These instances are accessed with the help of SSH or RDP protocols. After a connection is established with the bastion host, it allows using SSH or RDP to log in to other instances. In this way, it behaves like a jump box.

In a new bastion.tf file, define an EC2 instance resource within a public subnet to reach it from the outside internet:

```
resource "aws_instance" "bastion" {
  ami             = data.aws_ami.bastion.id
  instance_type = var.bastion_instance_type
  key_name = aws_key_pair.management.id
  vpc_security_group_ids = [aws_security_group.bastion_host.id]
  subnet_id = element(aws_subnet.public_subnets, 0).id
  associate_public_ip_address = true

  tags = {
    Name = "bastion"
    Author = var.author
  }
}
```

The EC2 instance uses an Amazon 2 Linux machine image. We use the `aws_ami` data source to get the AMI ID from the AWS marketplace. The `most_recent` attribute is enabled to use the recent AMI if more than one result is returned:

```
data "aws_ami" "bastion" {
  most_recent = true
  owners = ["amazon"]

  filter {
    name    = "name"
    values = ["amzn2-ami-hvm-*-x86_64-ebs"]
  }
}
```

NOTE If you want to add an extra layer of security for the bastion host, you can bake your own machine image with HashiCorp Packer by using the same procedure described in chapter 4.

While creating the EC2, we attached an SSH key pair to be able to access via SSH to the bastion host with the private key. The key pair uses our public SSH key located under the .ssh folder in the working directory. You can also generate a new one with the `ssh-keygen` command. The following is the Terraform snippet code; the `aws_key_pair` resource takes as a parameter the SSH public-key file location:

```
resource "aws_key_pair" "management" {
  key_name   = "management"
  public_key = file(var.public_key)
}
```

By default, SSH access to newly created EC2 instances is disabled. To allow SSH access to the bastion hosts, we will associate a security group to the running instance. The security group will allow inbound (ingress) traffic on port 22 (SSH) from anywhere (0.0.0.0/0). The CIDR source block can be replaced with your own public IP address/32 or network address to enhance security and prevent security breaches:

```
resource "aws_security_group" "bastion_host" {
  name        = "bastion_sg_${var.vpc_name}"
  description = "Allow SSH from anywhere"
  vpc_id      = aws_vpc.management.id

  egress {
    from_port   = 0
    to_port     = 0
    protocol    = "-1"
    cidr_blocks = ["0.0.0.0/0"]
  }

  ingress {
    from_port   = 22
    to_port     = 22
    protocol    = "tcp"
    cidr_blocks = ["0.0.0.0/0"]
  }

  tags = {
    Name   = "bastion_sg_${var.vpc_name}"
    Author = var.author
  }
}
```

You can use a website such as icanhazip.com to retrieve your machine's public IP address with the following code block:

```
data "http" "ip" {
  url = "http://ipv4.icanhazip.com"
}
```

If you want to use this in a network ingress rule, you can reference the IP address with the `data.http.ip.body` attribute.

Once we have our networking setup ready, declare the new Terraform variables in variables.tf. Refer to chapter5/variables.tf for the complete list of variables.

Then, apply the changes with `terraform apply`. A public EC2 instance should be deployed inside the VPC in a public subnet, as shown in figure 5.9.

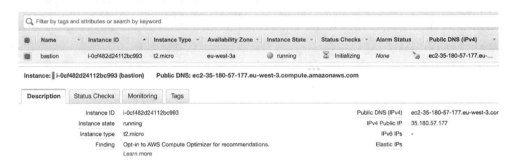

Figure 5.9   Bastion host deployed in a public subnet

We can copy the instance's public IP address directly from the EC2 console. Alternatively, we can use the Terraform outputs feature to display the IP address in the terminal session by defining an outputs.tf file with the following content:

```
output "bastion" {
  value = ${aws_instance.bastion.public_ip}
}
```

To get the instance's IPv4 public IP, you can reissue the `terraform apply` or `terraform output` command:

```
aws_key_pair.bastion: Refreshing state... [id=bastion]
aws_eip.nat: Refreshing state... [id=eipalloc-066cc823616bfb133]
aws_vpc.management: Refreshing state... [id=vpc-0c11cb69a871f0b24]
data.aws_ami.bastion: Refreshing state...
aws_internet_gateway.igw: Refreshing state... [id=igw-0247a205223ca0fa8]
aws_subnet.public_subnets[1]: Refreshing state... [id=subnet-0cf87a7eba8dd16f1]
aws_subnet.public_subnets[0]: Refreshing state... [id=subnet-0264284296202e32c]
aws_subnet.private_subnets[1]: Refreshing state... [id=subnet-0779f779d06d7e711]
aws_security_group.bastion_host: Refreshing state... [id=sg-0e4670a4c5352a2dd]
aws_subnet.private_subnets[0]: Refreshing state... [id=subnet-0988872367b9b40b4]
aws_route_table.public_rt: Refreshing state... [id=rtb-0a734e90a66fbe96f]
aws_nat_gateway.nat: Refreshing state... [id=nat-061f8101a83802c32]
aws_instance.bastion: Refreshing state... [id=i-0cf482d24112bc993]
aws_route_table_association.public[1]: Refreshing state... [id=rtbassoc-052b68eb9265dffb8]
aws_route_table_association.public[0]: Refreshing state... [id=rtbassoc-05350fb22c143b1e7]
aws_route_table.private_rt: Refreshing state... [id=rtb-08a7e79493c2fc6f6]
aws_route_table_association.private[1]: Refreshing state... [id=rtbassoc-0d06b3ee669e8fe99]
aws_route_table_association.private[0]: Refreshing state... [id=rtbassoc-0e9f57cd37637a6bf]

Apply complete! Resources: 0 added, 0 changed, 0 destroyed.

Outputs:

bastion = 35.180.57.177
```

With this Terraform code, we have our bastion host ready and can use it to set up an SSH tunnel to access private instances:

```
ssh -L TARGET_PORT:TARGET_INSTANCE_PRIVATE_IP:22 ec2-user@BASTION_IP
```

> **NOTE** You can take this further and deploy an Auto Scaling group (`min=1` and `max=1`) to ensure that a bastion host instance is always available. Also for cost optimization, you can use Spot instances instead of on-demand instances.

After creating these files, the directory structure should look as follows:

```
terraform.tf
vpc.tf
subnets.tf
private_rt.tf
public_rt.tf
bastion.tf
variables.tf
variables.tfvars
outputs.tf
```

The files can be called anything. We've named them based on the AWS resources declared on each, and for convenience and identification. Remember all files that end in .tf will be loaded by Terraform.

5.3 *Setting up a self-healing Jenkins master*

Now that our VPC has been created, we can deploy a dedicated EC2 instance to host the Jenkins master component within a private subnet, by defining an `aws_instance` resource in the jenkins_master.tf file with the following attributes. The instance is backed by an EBS volume (SSD) of 30 GB, which makes it suitable for a broad range of workloads:

```
resource "aws_instance" "jenkins_master" {
  ami                    = data.aws_ami.jenkins-master.id
  instance_type          = var.jenkins_master_instance_type
  key_name               = aws_key_pair.management.id
  vpc_security_group_ids = [aws_security_group.jenkins_master_sg.id]
  subnet_id              = element(aws_subnet.private_subnets, 0)

  root_block_device {
    volume_type           = "gp3"
    volume_size           = 30
    delete_on_termination = false
  }

  tags = {
    Name   = "jenkins_master"
    Author = var.author
  }
}
```

The 30 GB storage value can change based on the number and size of the projects you will continuously build, because Jenkins settings and build logs are stored on the master by default.

> **NOTE** A proper tagging policy for Jenkins instances is pivotal in cloud cost optimization. It leverages the use of filters within AWS bills and enforces tracking and cost allocation.

The EC2 instance uses the Jenkins master AMI baked by Packer in chapter 4, referenced by the `aws_ami` data resource:

```
data "aws_ami" "jenkins-master" {
  most_recent = true
  owners      = ["self"]

  filter {
    name   = "name"
    values = ["jenkins-master-*"]
  }
}
```

We'll attach a security group to the instance to allow SSH from the bastion host only and inbound traffic on port 8080 (Jenkins web dashboard) from VPC CIDR block; see the following listing.

Listing 5.6   Jenkins security group

```
resource "aws_security_group" "jenkins_master_sg" {
  name        = "jenkins_master_sg"
  description = "Allow traffic on port 8080 and enable SSH"
  vpc_id      = aws_vpc.management.id

  ingress {
    from_port       = "22"
    to_port         = "22"
    protocol        = "tcp"
    security_groups = [aws_security_group.bastion_host.id]
  }

  ingress {
    from_port   = "8080"
    to_port     = "8080"
    protocol    = "tcp"
    cidr_blocks = [var.cidr_block]
  }

  egress {
    from_port = "0"
    to_port   = "0"
```

```
    protocol   = "-1"
    cidr_blocks = ["0.0.0.0/0"]
  }

  tags = {
    Name   = "jenkins_master_sg"
    Author = var.author
  }
}
```

Next, define the instance type used to deploy the EC2 instance as a variable. For the sake of simplicity, t2.large (8 GB of memory and 2vCPU) should be enough, as we won't be allocating executors/workers on the master. Hence, the Jenkins master won't be overloaded by build jobs.

However, the amount of memory Jenkins needs depends on your project build needs and tools required by the same builds. Each build node connection will take two to three threads, which equals about 2 MB or more of memory. You will also need to factor in CPU overhead for Jenkins if a lot of users will be accessing the Jenkins user interface.

That's why we will deploy Jenkins workers later, to delegate builds to workers and keep the bulk of the work off the master itself. Therefore, a general-purpose instance to host a Jenkins master can provide a balance between compute and memory resources.

> **NOTE**   For more information, see the EC2 general-purpose instance documentation: https://aws.amazon.com/ec2/pricing/on-demand/.

The t2.large instance type may be a good option (though this instance type is not part of the AWS Free Tier, so you should terminate it or turn it off when you're done experimenting). Declare it as a variable in the variables.tfvars file:

```
variable "jenkins_master_instance_type" {
  type = string
  description = "Jenkins master EC2 instance type"
  default = "t2.large"
}
```

> **NOTE**   I encourage you to benchmark your project builds on several Amazon EC2 instance types to select the most appropriate configuration.

Generate an execution plan with this command:

```
terraform plan --var-file=variables.tfvars
```

You should see output similar to the following (the full terraform plan has been cropped for brevity):

```
# aws_instance.jenkins_master will be created
+ resource "aws_instance" "jenkins_master" {
    + ami                           = "ami-03717b21bb9b73007"
    + arn                           = (known after apply)
    + associate_public_ip_address   = (known after apply)
    + availability_zone             = (known after apply)
    + cpu_core_count                = (known after apply)
    + cpu_threads_per_core          = (known after apply)
    + get_password_data             = false
    + host_id                       = (known after apply)
    + id                            = (known after apply)
    + instance_state                = (known after apply)
    + instance_type                 = "t2.large"
    + ipv6_address_count            = (known after apply)
    + ipv6_addresses                = (known after apply)
    + key_name                      = (known after apply)
    + network_interface_id          = (known after apply)
    + password_data                 = (known after apply)
    + placement_group               = (known after apply)
    + primary_network_interface_id  = (known after apply)
    + private_dns                   = (known after apply)
    + private_ip                    = (known after apply)
    + public_dns                    = (known after apply)
    + public_ip                     = (known after apply)
    + security_groups               = (known after apply)
    + source_dest_check             = true
    + subnet_id                     = "subnet-0988872367b9b40b4"
    + tags                          = {
        + "Author" = "mlabouardy"
        + "Name"   = "jenkins_master"
      }
    + tenancy                       = (known after apply)
    + volume_tags                   = (known after apply)
    + vpc_security_group_ids        = (known after apply)
```

Since the execution plan looks good, enter `yes`, and you'll see your Jenkins master EC2 instance being deployed. Once the provisioning process is completed, the instance should be available on the EC2 dashboard, as shown in figure 5.10.

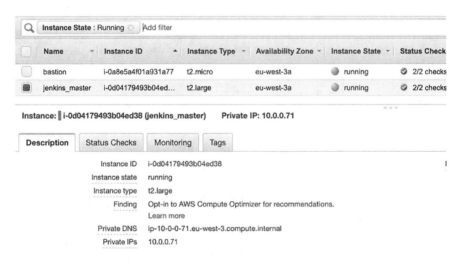

Figure 5.10 Jenkins master EC2 instance

While this instance is private (it has no public IP address), we can set up an SSH tunnel by using the bastion host and executing the following commands (obviously, with different values):

```
ssh -L 4000:10.0.0.71:22  ec2-user@35.180.122.81
ssh ec2-user@localhost -p 4000
```

You can check that Jenkins is running by issuing the `service jenkins status` command. Figure 5.11 shows the output.

```
[jenkins:chapter5 mlabouardy$ ssh ec2-user@localhost -p 4000
The authenticity of host '[localhost]:4000 ([::1]:4000)' can't be established.
ECDSA key fingerprint is SHA256:+7ERU8Oe8K9IoK8ZKr6AskPkI0t+z8w+jZVEyqV0JQY.
Are you sure you want to continue connecting (yes/no)? yes
Warning: Permanently added '[localhost]:4000' (ECDSA) to the list of known hosts.

      __|  __|_  )
      _|  (     /   Amazon Linux AMI
     ___|\___|___|

https://aws.amazon.com/amazon-linux-ami/2018.03-release-notes/
19 package(s) needed for security, out of 36 available
Run "sudo yum update" to apply all updates.
[[ec2-user@ip-10-0-0-71 ~]$
[[ec2-user@ip-10-0-0-71 ~]$
[[ec2-user@ip-10-0-0-71 ~]$ service jenkins status
jenkins (pid  3023) is running...
[ec2-user@ip-10-0-0-71 ~]$ █
```

Figure 5.11   SSH tunnel connection

To access the Jenkins dashboard, we will create a public load balancer in front of the EC2 instance. This Elastic load balancer will accept HTTP traffic on port 80 and forward it to the EC2 instance on port 8080. Also, it automatically checks the health of the registered EC2 instance on port 8080. If the Elastic Load Balancing (ELB) finds the instance unhealthy, it stops sending traffic to the Jenkins instance. Within jenkins_master.tf, declare the load balancer resource:

```
resource "aws_elb" "jenkins_elb" {
    subnets                   = \
      [for subnet in aws_subnet.public_subnets : subnet.id]
    cross_zone_load_balancing = true
    security_groups           = [aws_security_group.elb_jenkins_sg.id]
    instances                 = [aws_instance.jenkins_master.id]

    listener {
      instance_port     = 8080
      instance_protocol = "http"
      lb_port           = 80
      lb_protocol       = "http"
    }
```

```
  health_check {
    healthy_threshold   = 2
    unhealthy_threshold = 2
    timeout             = 3
    target              = "TCP:8080"
    interval            = 5
  }
  tags = {
    Name   = "jenkins_elb"
    Author = var.author
  }
}
```

The load balancer will accept incoming HTTP traffic from anywhere (you should lock the incoming traffic to the specific IP address range from which you expect traffic) by assigning the following security group configuration. Later, we will add an HTTPS listener to use an SSL protocol to establish secure connections over the HTTP layer. Define the load balancer's security group within jenkins_master.tf; here is the resource code block:

```
resource "aws_security_group" "elb_jenkins_sg" {
    name        = "elb_jenkins_sg"
    description = "Allow http traffic"
    vpc_id      = aws_vpc.management.id

    ingress {
      from_port   = "80"
      to_port     = "80"
      protocol    = "tcp"
      cidr_blocks = ["0.0.0.0/0"]
    }

    egress {
      from_port   = "0"
      to_port     = "0"
      protocol    = "-1"
      cidr_blocks = ["0.0.0.0/0"]
    }

    tags = {
      Name   = "elb_jenkins_sg"
      Author = var.author
    }
}
```

Next, update the Jenkins master security group to allow traffic on port 8080 from the load balancer security group ID only:

```
ingress {
    from_port       = "8080"
    to_port         = "8080"
    protocol        = "tcp"
    security_groups = [aws_security_group.elb_jenkins_sg.id]
}
```

Output the load balancer DNS URL by defining a new output section in the outputs.tf file:

```
output "jenkins-master-elb" {
  value = aws_elb.jenkins_elb.dns_name
}
```

After you apply the changes with Terraform, the Jenkins master load balancer URL should be displayed in your terminal session:

```
aws_security_group.elb_jenkins_sg: Creating...
aws_security_group.elb_jenkins_sg: Creation complete after 2s [id=sg-0e5698167b02b43af]
aws_elb.jenkins_elb: Creating...
aws_security_group.jenkins_master_sg: Modifying... [id=sg-0994c23fcd12219db]
aws_security_group.jenkins_master_sg: Modifications complete after 0s [id=sg-0994c23fcd12219db]
aws_elb.jenkins_elb: Creation complete after 2s [id=tf-lb-20200323152023632600000001]

Apply complete! Resources: 2 added, 1 changed, 0 destroyed.

Outputs:

bastion = 35.180.122.81
jenkins-master-elb = tf-lb-20200323152023632600000001-587097020.eu-west-3.elb.amazonaws.com
```

Point your favorite browser to the URL, and you should have access to the Jenkins web dashboard. You can see the Welcome to Jenkins! message on the home page (figure 5.12).

Figure 5.12   Jenkins web dashboard

Awesome! You have a running Jenkins server behind an Elastic Load Balancer.

If your goal is to architect for high availability, you need to maintain a redundant Jenkins master in separate availability zones. However, because the Jenkins master configuration is stored in the $JENKINS_HOME directory instead of a centralized database, you need to use an external plugin such as the High Availability Management plugin from CloudBees (https://docs.cloudbees.com/plugins/ci/cloudbees-ha) or set up the $JENKINS_HOME directory on a shared network drive, so it could be accessible by multiple Jenkins master instances.

> **NOTE**   In chapter 14, we will go through how to use a solution like Amazon Elastic File System (EFS) to mount a volume to share the $JENKINS_HOME folder across multiple instances.

5.4   *Running Jenkins with native SSL/HTTPS*

Having secure access to the Jenkins dashboard is a plus. That's why we will use a free SSL provided by AWS to serve the content with HTTPS at your custom domain name and provide encrypted network connections; see figure 5.13.

> **NOTE**   If you're running Jenkins locally, you can generate a self-signed certificate and deploy a reverse proxy like NGINX. If you opt to go with a different cloud provider, you can generate a certificate issued by a certificate authority (CA) for free with Let's Encrypt.

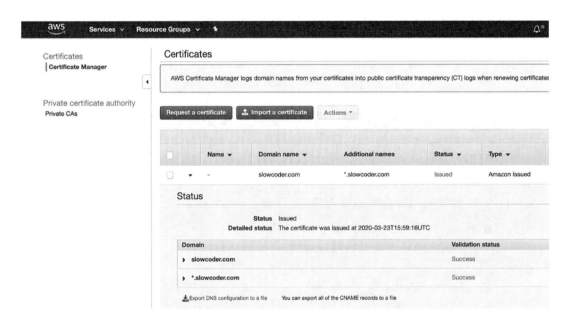

Figure 5.13   Free SSL certificates from AWS Certificate Manager

You can easily get an SSL certificate with AWS Certificate Manager (ACM). This service makes it easy to provision, manage, and deploy SSL/TLS certificates on AWS-managed resources.

Head to the ACM dashboard and click the Request a Certificate button to create a new SSL certificate. Select Request a Public Certificate and add your domain name. You might also want to secure your subdomains by adding an asterisk. Once AWS validates that you own those domain names, the status will change from Pending Validation to Issued. Copy the SSL Amazon Resource Name (ARN).

Update the load balancer resource to enable the HTTPS listener on port 443. Set the ACM SSL ARN on the HTTPS listener. The load balancer uses the certificate to terminate the connection and then decrypt requests from clients before sending them to the Jenkins instance:

```
listener {
    instance_port       = 8080
    instance_protocol   = "http"
    lb_port             = 443
    lb_protocol         = "https"
    ssl_certificate_id = var.ssl_arn
}
```

Exposes an HTTPS listener and forwards incoming requests on port 443 to port 8080 of the EC2 instance.

Add an ingress rule to the load balancer security group to allow incoming HTTPS traffic:

```
ingress {
    from_port   = "443"
    to_port     = "443"
    protocol    = "tcp"
    cidr_blocks = ["0.0.0.0/0"]
}
```

Allows inbound traffic on port 443 from anywhere (0.0.0.0/0)

Then create an A record in the Route 53 service (https://aws.amazon.com/route53/) pointing to the load balancer fully qualified domain name (FQDN). The Terraform code for the DNS record will look like this:

```
resource "aws_route53_record" "jenkins_master" {
  zone_id = var.hosted_zone_id
  name    = "jenkins.${var.domain_name}"
  type    = "A"

  alias {
    name                   = aws_elb.jenkins_elb.dns_name
    zone_id                = aws_elb.jenkins_elb.zone_id
    evaluate_target_health = true
  }
}
```

Sets up an alias record (jenkins.domain.com) that points to the Jenkins load balancer FQDN

> **NOTE** If you don't have a hosted zone in Amazon Route 53, you can skip to the next section and stick with the load balancer FQDN.

This resource block will create an A record, which maps the jenkins.domain.com URL to an AWS alias to the load balancer FQDN.

Finally, define the referenced Terraform variables in the variables.tf file. Table 5.3 lists the variables to define in addition to the variables defined earlier in this chapter.

Table 5.3   DNS Terraform variables

Variable	Type	Value	Description
hosted_zone_id	String	None	The ID of the hosted zone to contain the A record
domain_name	String	None	The domain name to use, such as domain.com
ssl_arn	String	None	ARN of SSL certificate you have created in AWS ACM

Define an `output` section to display the Jenkins public DNS URL by referencing the Route 53 A record resource:

```
output "jenkins-dns" {
  value = "https://${aws_route53_record.jenkins_master.name}"
}
```

Concatenates the alias record name
with the https:// keyword to
construct the Jenkins HTTPS URL

Issue the `terraform apply` command for changes to take effect. It should deploy the needed resources and display the Jenkins dashboard URL:

```
aws_elb.jenkins_elb: Modifying... [id=tf-lb-20200323152023632600000001]
aws_elb.jenkins_elb: Modifications complete after 1s [id=tf-lb-20200323152023632600000001]
aws_route53_record.jenkins_master: Creating...
aws_route53_record.jenkins_master: Still creating... [10s elapsed]
aws_route53_record.jenkins_master: Still creating... [20s elapsed]
aws_route53_record.jenkins_master: Still creating... [30s elapsed]
aws_route53_record.jenkins_master: Creation complete after 37s [id=Z2TR95QTU3UIUT_jenkins.slowcoder.com_A]

Apply complete! Resources: 1 added, 1 changed, 0 destroyed.

Outputs:

bastion = 35.180.122.81
jenkins-dns = https://jenkins.slowcoder.com
jenkins-master-elb = tf-lb-20200323152023632600000001-587097020.eu-west-3.elb.amazonaws.com
```

The Jenkins load balancer now should be listening on both the HTTP (80) and HTTPS (433) ports, as shown in figure 5.14.

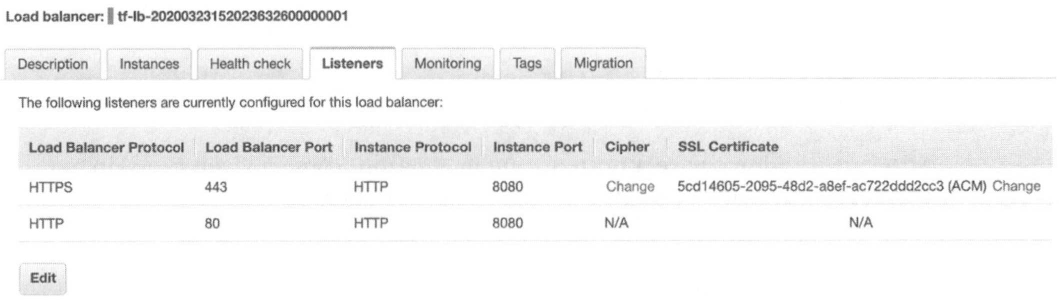

Load balancer: tf-lb-20200323152023632600000001

| Description | Instances | Health check | **Listeners** | Monitoring | Tags | Migration |

The following listeners are currently configured for this load balancer:

Load Balancer Protocol	Load Balancer Port	Instance Protocol	Instance Port	Cipher	SSL Certificate
HTTPS	443	HTTP	8080	Change	5cd14605-2095-48d2-a8ef-ac722ddd2cc3 (ACM) Change
HTTP	80	HTTP	8080	N/A	N/A

Edit

Figure 5.14   Allowing HTTPS and HTTP on ELB

Point your browser to the subdomain name created with Terraform. The Jenkins web dashboard should be served through HTTPS, as shown in figure 5.15.

Figure 5.15   The Jenkins dashboard is now served through HTTPS. If you're using Chrome, you should see a green lock in the URL bar.

So far, we have deployed a private standalone Jenkins master instance behind a public load balancer, as shown in figure 5.16.

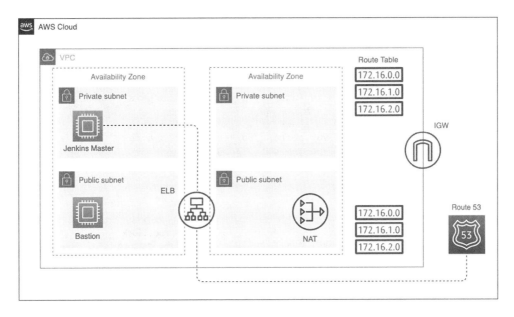

Figure 5.16   Jenkins standalone setup on AWS

In the next section, we will deploy additional Jenkins workers to offload the load from the Jenkins master.

> **NOTE**   Maintaining a regular backup of your Jenkins EBS volume is crucial to ensuring that the Jenkins instance can be restored in the event of data corruption or loss. Refer to the official documentation for instructions: http://mng.bz/807P.

5.5   *Dynamically autoscaling the Jenkins worker pool*

Running a single Jenkins instance is a good start, but in the real world, a single instance is a single point of failure. If that instance crashes or becomes overwhelmed by too many builds, developers can no longer deliver their releases. The solution is to run a cluster of Jenkins workers and adjust the size of the cluster up or down based on resource utilization.

5.5.1   *Launch configuration*

You can certainly deploy Jenkins workers as separate EC2 instances (rerunning the previous steps). However, we want the instances to be deployed and replaced automatically for autorecovery. That's why we will rely on a standard AWS feature called *Auto Scaling groups*.

> **NOTE**   For more details on how the AWS EC2 autoscaling feature works, refer to chapter 3 about architecting Jenkins for scale.

The first step in creating an ASG is to create a launch configuration, which describes how to configure each Jenkins worker instance. Declare an `aws_launch_configuration` resource in the jenkins_workers.tf file:

Configures a blueprint with the baked Jenkins worker AMI and key name that should be used for the instances, and assigns a security group

```
resource "aws_launch_configuration" "jenkins_workers_launch_conf" {
  name            = "jenkins_workers_config"
  image_id        = data.aws_ami.jenkins-worker.id
  instance_type   = var.jenkins_worker_instance_type
  key_name        = aws_key_pair.management.id
  security_groups = [aws_security_group.jenkins_workers_sg.id]
  user_data       = data.template_file.user_data_jenkins_worker.rendered

  root_block_device {
    volume_type          = "gp2"
    volume_size          = 30
    delete_on_termination = false
  }

  lifecycle {
    create_before_destroy = true
  }
}
```

The user data to provide when launching the instance. It will autojoin the running instance to the Jenkins cluster.

Customizes details about the root block device of the instance

> **NOTE**   You should benchmark performance for your projects to determine the appropriate instance type you need, as well as the amount of disk space.

Similarly to the Jenkins master, the workers will be deployed across private subnets and will use the Jenkins worker AMI built with Packer in chapter 4:

```
data "aws_ami" "jenkins-worker" {
  most_recent = true
```

```
owners       = ["self"]

filter {
  name   = "name"
  values = ["jenkins-worker*"]
}
}
```

The data source resource is used to get the ID of the baked Jenkins worker AMI.

To be able to set up the Jenkins cluster, the master needs to set up a bidirectional connection with the workers. Hence, we need to allow SSH from the Jenkins master security group ID (allowing SSH from the bastion host can be helpful for future debugging and troubleshooting):

```
resource "aws_security_group" "jenkins_workers_sg" {
  name        = "jenkins_workers_sg"
  description = "Allow traffic on port 22 from Jenkins master SG"
  vpc_id      = aws_vpc.management.id

  ingress {
    from_port       = "22"
    to_port         = "22"
    protocol        = "tcp"
    security_groups = [aws_security_group.jenkins_master_sg.id,
aws_security_group.bastion_host.id]
  }
```

Allows inbound traffic on port 22 (SSH) from the Jenkins master and bastion host security groups

```
  egress {
    from_port   = "0"
    to_port     = "0"
    protocol    = "-1"
    cidr_blocks = ["0.0.0.0/0"]
  }
```

Allows outbound traffic from anywhere for all protocols (–1)

```
  tags = {
    Name   = "jenkins_workers_sg"
    Author = var.author
  }
}
```

Finally, we define `user-data`, a script that will be executed at boot time on each Jenkins worker instance. The script takes as a parameter the Jenkins admin credentials, Jenkins SSH credential ID, as well as the Jenkins IP address.

The SSH credential ID refers to the credential we created with the Groovy script at initialization time in chapter 4; the credential contains the private SSH key located in the .ssh folder in the working directory. The private SSH key will be used by the Jenkins master to add the Jenkins workers via SSH:

```
data "template_file" "user_data_jenkins_worker" {
  template = "${file("scripts/join-cluster.tpl")}"

  vars = {
    jenkins_url      = "http://${aws_instance.jenkins_master.private_ip}:8080"
    jenkins_username = var.jenkins_username
```

```
        jenkins_password      = var.jenkins_password
        jenkins_credentials_id = var.jenkins_credentials_id
  }
}
```

The scripts/join-cluster.tpl script will fetch the running instance's private IP address from the EC2 metadata (available at 169.254.169.254/latest/meta-data). The script will then issue an HTTP request to Jenkins with the Groovy script in the following listing to add the instance to the cluster.

Listing 5.7   Autojoining Jenkins workers

```
#!/bin/bash
JENKINS_URL="${jenkins_url}"
JENKINS_USERNAME="${jenkins_username}"
JENKINS_PASSWORD="${jenkins_password}"
TOKEN=$(curl -u $JENKINS_USERNAME:$JENKINS_PASSWORD
''$JENKINS_URL'/crumbIssuer/api/xml?xpath= \
concat(//crumbRequestField,":",//crumb)')
INSTANCE_NAME=$(curl -s 169.254.169.254/latest/meta-data/local-hostname)
INSTANCE_IP=$(curl -s 169.254.169.254/latest/meta-data/local-ipv4)
JENKINS_CREDENTIALS_ID="${jenkins_credentials_id}"
```

Replaces the variables with the given values in the user_data_jenkins _worker Terraform resource

Fetches a valid token from the Jenkins master server

Fetches the instance private IP address and hostname from the EC2 metadata

```
curl -v -u $JENKINS_USERNAME:$JENKINS_PASSWORD -H "$TOKEN" -d 'script=
import hudson.model.Node.Mode
import hudson.slaves.*
import jenkins.model.Jenkins
import hudson.plugins.sshslaves.SSHLauncher
DumbSlave dumb = new DumbSlave("'$INSTANCE_NAME'",
"'$INSTANCE_NAME'",
"/home/ec2-user",
"3",
Mode.NORMAL,
"workers",
new SSHLauncher("'$INSTANCE_IP'", 22, "'$JENKINS_CREDENTIALS_ID'"),
RetentionStrategy.INSTANCE)
Jenkins.instance.addNode(dumb)
' $JENKINS_URL/script
```

Issues a GET request on the Jenkins server with a Groovy script in the request payload. The script will add the current instance as a Jenkins agent.

This configuration allows three executors to be run in parallel in each worker. If you plan to use only the master as a job scheduler, you can configure its number of executors setting to 0 to ensure that project builds will happen on only the worker machines. The resource block also defines a workspace directory on the worker instance that the worker agent can use to run build jobs. This configuration uses /home/ec2-user as a workspace. Nothing mission-critical is stored in this directory; everything important is transferred back to the master instance after the build is done, so you usually don't need to be concerned with backing up this directory.

We have also defined a label called `workers`, so each worker instance will join the Jenkins cluster under that label. Hence, you can configure your build jobs to run on only workers' machines.

Next, define the Jenkins master credentials and worker instance type as variables in the variable.tf file. Table 5.4 lists the variables.

Table 5.4 Jenkins workers' Terraform variables

Variable	Type	Value	Description
`jenkins_username`	String	None	Jenkins admin username
`jenkins_password`	String	None	Jenkins admin password
`jenkins_credentials_id`	String	None	Jenkins worker SSH-based credential ID
`jenkins_worker_instance_type`	String	`t2.medium`	Jenkins worker EC2 instance type

NOTE You can significantly reduce your Jenkins workers' costs (up to 90% cost savings) by using Amazon EC2 Spot instances (http://aws.amazon.com/ec2/spot), or by subscribing to Amazon Savings Plans (https://aws.amazon.com/savingsplans/).

Finally, issue `terraform apply` to deploy the Jenkins workers.

5.5.2 Auto Scaling group

Now that the Jenkins workers' blueprint is defined in a launch configuration, we can deploy an Auto Scaling group to deploy similar Jenkins workers based on the launch configuration.

Create the ASG by using the `aws_autoscaling_group` resource within the jenkins_workers.tf file:

```
resource "aws_autoscaling_group" "jenkins_workers" {
  name                = "jenkins_workers_asg"
  launch_configuration =
      aws_launch_configuration.jenkins_workers_launch_conf.name
  vpc_zone_identifier = \
[for subnet in aws_subnet.private_subnets : subnet.id]      Deploys an ASG of two EC2
  min_size            = 2                                    instances (minimum) in
  max_size            = 10                                   different subnets for resiliency
  depends_on = [aws_instance.jenkins_master, aws_elb.jenkins_elb]
  lifecycle {
    create_before_destroy = true
  }
  tag {
    key               = "Name"
    value             = "jenkins_worker"
    propagate_at_launch = true
  }
  tag {
```

```
    key                  = "Author"
    value                = var.author
    propagate_at_launch = true
  }
}
```

This ASG will run 2 to 10 workers (defaulting to 2 for the initial launch), each tagged with the name `jenkins_worker`. The ASG uses a reference to fill in the launch configuration name.

NOTE   The keyword `depends_on` is used to ensure that the Jenkins master instance is running before deploying workers, as the workers need the Jenkins master IP to join the cluster successfully.

The launch configuration is immutable, so you can't modify it after it was created (for example, to upgrade the Jenkins worker instance type or change the base AMI). Therefore, you will need to destroy the launch configuration and create a new one instead; that's why the `create_before_destroy` life cycle setting is used.

To create the autoscaling group, run `terraform apply` on your terminal session:

```
# aws_autoscaling_group.jenkins_workers will be created
+ resource "aws_autoscaling_group" "jenkins_workers" {
    + arn                       = (known after apply)
    + availability_zones        = (known after apply)
    + default_cooldown          = (known after apply)
    + desired_capacity          = (known after apply)
    + force_delete              = false
    + health_check_grace_period = 300
    + health_check_type         = (known after apply)
    + id                        = (known after apply)
    + launch_configuration      = "jenkins_workers_config"
    + load_balancers            = (known after apply)
    + max_size                  = 10
    + metrics_granularity       = "1Minute"
    + min_size                  = 2
    + name                      = "jenkins_workers_asg"
    + protect_from_scale_in     = false
    + service_linked_role_arn   = (known after apply)
    + target_group_arns         = (known after apply)
    + vpc_zone_identifier       = [
        + "subnet-0779f779d06d7e711",
        + "subnet-0988872367b9b40b4",
      ]
    + wait_for_capacity_timeout = "10m"

    + tag {
        + key               = "Author"
        + propagate_at_launch = true
        + value             = "mlabouardy"
      }
    + tag {
        + key               = "Name"
        + propagate_at_launch = true
        + value             = "jenkins_worker"
      }
  }
```

The provisioning process should take a few seconds. When you refresh your EC2 console, you'll see the output in figure 5.17 in the dashboard.

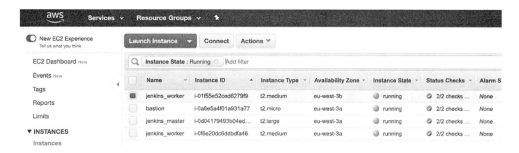

Figure 5.17   Jenkins workers deploying inside an ASG

> **NOTE**   Chapter 14 covers another approach: we'll deploy the worker nodes in Docker containers to use EC2 instances efficiently (with multiple builds to run independently on the same server) as well as to run in a "clean" build environment every time.

Great! We have two Jenkins workers running inside an ASG.

5.5.3   Autoscaling scaling policies

So far, the number of workers is static and fixed. To scale the number of workers dynamically, we will define scaling policies based on CPU utilization. This gives you extra capacity to handle the build of additional jobs without maintaining an excessive number of idle Jenkins workers and paying extra money.

Create a cloudwatch.tf file and define an AWS CloudWatch metric alarm based on CPU utilization. The CloudWatch alarm will trigger a scale-out event to add a new Jenkins worker instance if the average CPU utilization is over 80% for a period of 2 minutes, as shown in the following listing.

Listing 5.8   CloudWatch scale-out alarm

```
resource "aws_cloudwatch_metric_alarm" "high-cpu-jenkins-workers-alarm" {
  alarm_name          = "high-cpu-jenkins-workers-alarm"
  comparison_operator = "GreaterThanOrEqualToThreshold"
  evaluation_periods  = "2"
  metric_name         = "CPUUtilization"
  namespace           = "AWS/EC2"
  period              = "120"
  statistic           = "Average"
  threshold           = "80"

  dimensions = {
    AutoScalingGroupName = aws_autoscaling_group.jenkins_workers.name
  }
```

```
    alarm_description = "This metric monitors workers cpu utilization"
    alarm_actions     = [aws_autoscaling_policy.scale-out.arn]
}

resource "aws_autoscaling_policy" "scale-out" {
  name                      = "scale-out-jenkins-workers"
  scaling_adjustment        = 1
  adjustment_type           = "ChangeInCapacity"
  cooldown                  = 300
  autoscaling_group_name = aws_autoscaling_group.jenkins_workers.name
}
```

NOTE   It's up to you what to monitor, but the metrics most useful for knowing
when you should scale up and add another Jenkins worker or scale down by
terminating a worker are probably CPU utilization, memory utilization, and
network utilization.

Similarly, we define another CloudWatch alarm to trigger a scale-in event to remove a
Jenkins worker if the average CPU utilization is less than 20% for a period of 2 minutes; see the following listing.

Listing 5.9   CloudWatch scale-in alarm

```
resource "aws_cloudwatch_metric_alarm" "low-cpu-jenkins-workers-alarm" {
  alarm_name           = "low-cpu-jenkins-workers-alarm"
  comparison_operator  = "LessThanOrEqualToThreshold"
  evaluation_periods   = "2"
  metric_name          = "CPUUtilization"
  namespace            = "AWS/EC2"
  period               = "120"
  statistic            = "Average"
  threshold            = "20"

  dimensions = {
    AutoScalingGroupName = aws_autoscaling_group.jenkins_workers.name
  }

  alarm_description = "This metric monitors ec2 cpu utilization"
  alarm_actions     = [aws_autoscaling_policy.scale-in.arn]
}

resource "aws_autoscaling_policy" "scale-in" {
  name                      = "scale-in-jenkins-workers"
  scaling_adjustment        = -1
  adjustment_type           = "ChangeInCapacity"
  cooldown                  = 300
  autoscaling_group_name = aws_autoscaling_group.jenkins_workers.name
}
```

The cooldown period is set to 300 seconds to ensure that the ASG doesn't launch or
terminate additional Jenkins workers before the previous scaling activity takes effect.

NOTE   When a scale-in event occurs, the ASG will terminate a Jenkins worker
based on the termination policy. Refer to chapter 3 for more information.

If you run the `terraform apply` command, you'll see that Terraform wants to create two CloudWatch alarms (the output has been cropped for brevity):

```
# aws_cloudwatch_metric_alarm.high-cpu-jenkins-workers-alarm will be created
+ resource "aws_cloudwatch_metric_alarm" "high-cpu-jenkins-workers-alarm" {
    + actions_enabled                    = true
    + alarm_actions                      = (known after apply)
    + alarm_description                  = "This metric monitors workers cpu utilization"
    + alarm_name                         = "high-cpu-jenkins-workers-alarm"
    + arn                                = (known after apply)
    + comparison_operator                = "GreaterThanOrEqualToThreshold"
    + dimensions                         = {
        + "AutoScalingGroupName" = "jenkins_workers_asg"
      }
    + evaluate_low_sample_count_percentiles = (known after apply)
    + evaluation_periods                 = 2
    + id                                 = (known after apply)
    + metric_name                        = "CPUUtilization"
    + namespace                          = "AWS/EC2"
    + period                             = 120
    + statistic                          = "Average"
    + threshold                          = 80
    + treat_missing_data                 = "missing"
  }
```

You can access Amazon EC2 Auto Scaling (figure 5.18) by signing into the AWS Management Console, choosing EC2 from the console home page, and then choosing Auto Scaling Groups from the navigation pane.

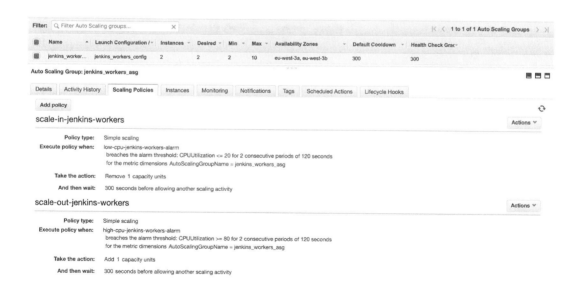

Figure 5.18   Auto Scaling group scaling policies

Next, we will run the Stress tool to test the scaling policies of the workers' ASG.

5.5.4   *Workers CPU utilization load*

SSH to one of the Jenkins workers by setting up an SSH tunnel from a bastion host. Install the Stress tool with the Yum package manager:

```
sudo yum update
sudo yum install -y stress
```

To run the Stress tool, enter the following command. It will generate a thread to max out two CPU cores (which is all we need, as we're using t2.large instances):

```
stress --cpu 2
```

This gives you a chance to see what will happen to the autoscaling policies when real jobs are being built on Jenkins and CloudWatch alarms start triggering.

You can use the top command to monitor the CPU utilization of the process created by the Stress tool or use CloudWatch metrics on the EC2 instance. The CPU utilization will hit 100% for an amount of time, as shown in figure 5.19.

> **NOTE**   CloudWatch basic monitoring refreshes every 5 minutes, and our autoscaling policies require a metric to be met for 2 consecutive minutes, so we had to run stress tests for at least 5 minutes to ensure that our policies had enough time to be triggered.

Figure 5.19   Jenkins worker CPU utilization usage

CloudWatch aggregates metric data points based on the statistic of CPU utilization associated with the CloudWatch alarm. When the alarm is breached, the scale-out policy is triggered, as shown in figure 5.20.

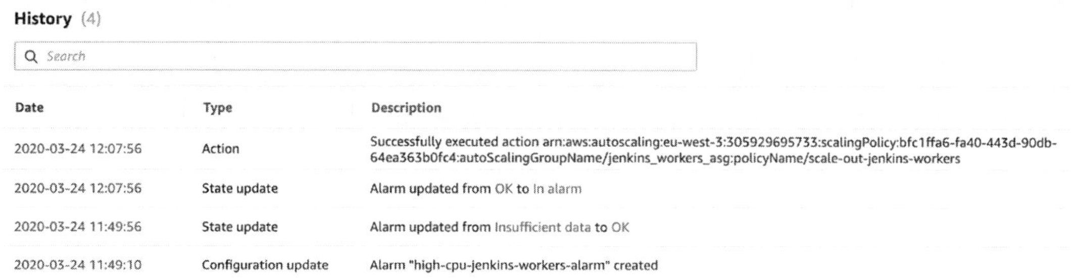

History (4)

Q Search

Date	Type	Description
2020-03-24 12:07:56	Action	Successfully executed action arn:aws:autoscaling:eu-west-3:305929695733:scalingPolicy:bfc1ffa6-fa40-443d-90db-64ea363b0fc4:autoScalingGroupName/jenkins_workers_asg:policyName/scale-out-jenkins-workers
2020-03-24 12:07:56	State update	Alarm updated from OK to In alarm
2020-03-24 11:49:56	State update	Alarm updated from Insufficient data to OK
2020-03-24 11:49:10	Configuration update	Alarm "high-cpu-jenkins-workers-alarm" created

Figure 5.20 CloudWatch scale-out alarm triggered

When the metric value gets to 80%, the desired capacity of the group increases by one instance to two instances; see figure 5.21.

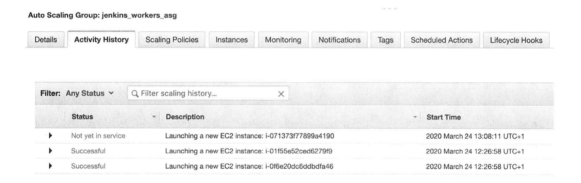

Figure 5.21 Scale-out policy invoked

After the new instance is running, the user-data script will be executed, and the worker will join the cluster, as you can see in figure 5.22.

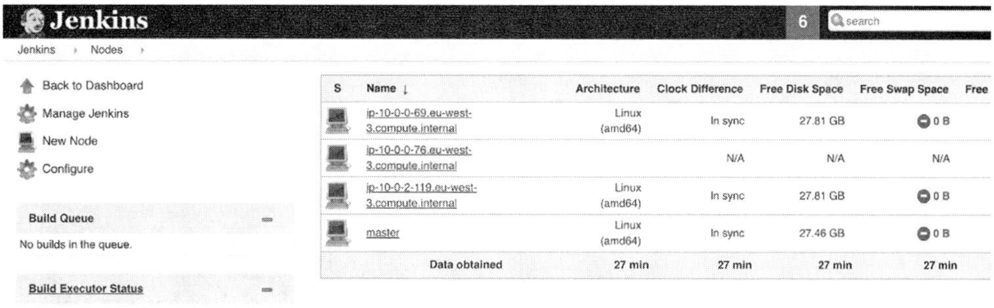

Figure 5.22 The new worker has joined the cluster automatically.

If the metric value gets to 20%, the desired capacity of the group decreases by one instance; see figure 5.23.

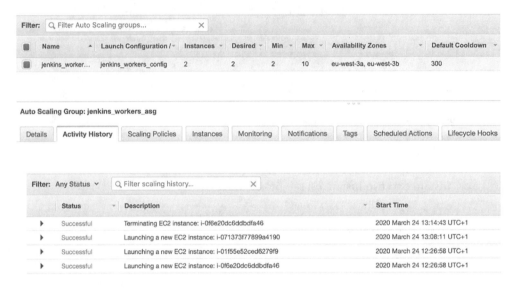

Figure 5.23   Terminating an unused worker because of a scale-in event

As a result, the terminated worker won't be reachable and will be marked offline on the Jenkins web dashboard (figure 5.24).

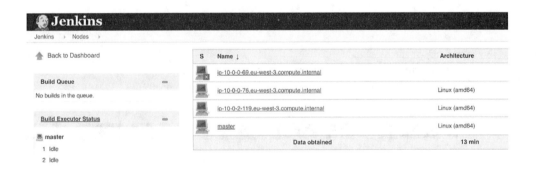

Figure 5.24   The terminated Jenkins worker is unreachable.

NOTE   When you're done experimenting with Terraform, it's a good idea to remove all the resources you created so AWS doesn't charge you for them. Run the `terraform destroy` command to delete the existing AWS infrastructure.

In this chapter, you learned how to deploy a highly available, secure, and resilient Jenkins cluster on AWS by using the IaC tool Terraform and how to use the baked Packer images to deploy workers to scale. Figure 5.25 summarizes the deployed architecture.

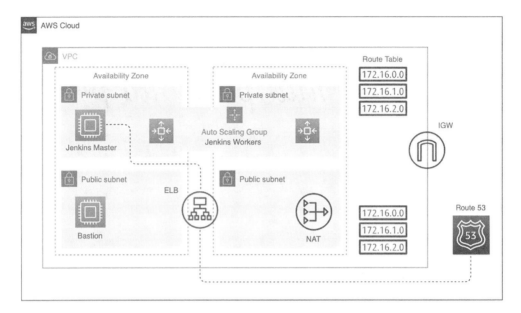

Figure 5.25   Jenkins distributed builds on AWS

Terraform is a vendor-agnostic tool that can manage infrastructure for multiple resource providers. Therefore, in the upcoming chapter, you'll learn to deploy the preceding architecture on other cloud providers such as Microsoft Azure and Google Cloud Platform by using the same configuration files.

Summary

- Infrastructure as code is an approach to defining infrastructure and network components through descriptive or high-level code.
- Terraform is an IaC tool that works with any cloud, be it private, on premises, or a public provider. Terraform allows safe and convenient management of infrastructure resources.
- The Jenkins master should be hosted on an instance that has enough CPU and network bandwidth to handle concurrent users.
- Jenkins workers should be immutable, able to be thrown away quickly and brought up or added into the cluster with as little manual interaction as possible. This can be achieved by leveraging AWS Auto Scaling groups.
- Architect Jenkins for high availability and fault tolerance by spreading Jenkins workers across multiple availability zones.

Deploying HA Jenkins on multiple cloud providers

This chapter covers

- Automating the build process of Jenkins VMs with Packer
- Deploying a Jenkins cluster on Azure, GCP, and DigitalOcean
- Reducing the cost of deploying Jenkins workers by creating them on demand
- Using the same Packer template to create identical Jenkins machine images in different cloud providers

You've already seen how to accomplish fault tolerance by deploying the Jenkins cluster in AWS. The chapter will try to achieve the same required speed and automation on the infrastructure level by using the same tools and processes to automate the creation of a cluster on different cloud providers such as Microsoft Azure, Google Cloud Platform, and DigitalOcean—ranging from infrastructure-as-a-service (IaaS) to platform-as-a-service (PaaS) providers.

You might notice that some parts of this chapter are similar, or even the same as, those you read in the previous chapter. The reason for the partial repetition is to achieve the goal of this book, which is to illustrate the use of Jenkins with cloud-native applications—and because not everyone is adopting AWS as their main cloud provider, I want to make this book useful for others and for those who skipped chapter 5 and jumped right here.

> **NOTE** Using the providers detailed in this chapter carries some benefits and drawbacks. No matter which provider you choose, you'll always encounter issues at some point along the way.

6.1 Google Cloud Platform

We all know that AWS doesn't have the most user-friendly web console. *Google Cloud Platform* (GCP) has managed to outperform AWS by offering a better user experience. GCP consists of a variety of services ranging from computing, to network, to extract-transform-load (ETL) pipelines that are 25% cheaper than its rival (AWS) because of lower-increment billing (10 minutes instead of 1 hour).

Plus, GCP has more expertise when it comes to big data, with services like Big-Query (https://cloud.google.com/bigquery), Cloud Bigtable (https://cloud.google .com/bigtable), and Dataflow (https://cloud.google.com/dataflow). In addition, you can run container workloads on Kubernetes and deploy machine learning (ML) models with TensorFlow; both Kubernetes and TensorFlow originated from Google. However, GCP still lacks features compared to AWS, which is the oldest and most mature cloud vendor on the market.

Why use Jenkins with GCP, then? You can have seamless integration with Kubernetes; with services like Google Kubernetes Engine (GKE), you can run ephemeral Jenkins workers, ensuring that each build runs on a clean environment. Native support for Docker containers is another reason, with services like Container Registry to store and manage Docker images built within CI/CD pipelines. In addition, you can have integrated security and compliance with detailed reports on vulnerability impacts and available fixes of build artifacts. Finally, you pay per usage when you use GCP virtual machines (VMs) to speed up your Jenkins builds.

With that being said, let's head over and deploy a Jenkins cluster with Terraform and Packer on GCP. To get started, sign up for a free account with a Gmail address (https://console.cloud.google.com/). You will automatically get a 12-month free trial with a $300 credit. You need to provide your credit card details, but you won't be charged extra until after your trial period ends or you have exhausted the $300 credit.

> **NOTE** The estimated cost to deploy a Jenkins cluster is $0.00. This cost assumes that you're within the GCP Free Tier limits and that you terminate all resources within 1 hour of deploying the infrastructure.

6.1.1 Building Jenkins VM images

For Packer to build a custom image, it needs to interact with GCP. Therefore, we need to create a dedicated service account for Packer to be authorized to access resources in Google APIs.

Head to the GCP console and navigate to the IAM & Admin dashboard, shown in figure 6.1. In the Service Accounts section, create a new service account with `Packer` as a name, and click the Create button.

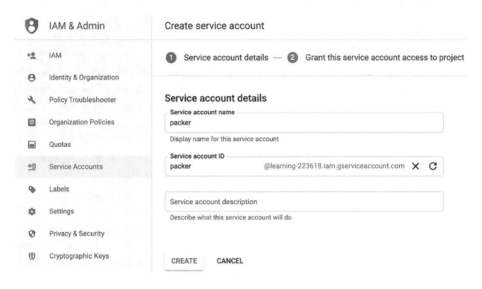

Figure 6.1   **Creating a Packer service account**

Assign the Project Owner role to the service account (or at least select Compute Engine Instance Admin and Service Account User roles) and click the Continue button, as shown in figure 6.2.

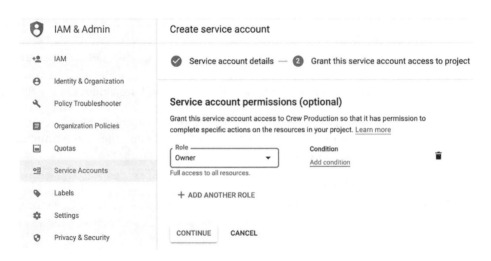

Figure 6.2   **Setting Packer service account permissions**

Each service account is associated with a key (JSON or P12 format), which is managed by GCP. This key is used for service-to-service authentication. Download the JSON key by clicking the Create Key button. The service account file is created and downloaded on the computer. Copy this JSON file and place it in a secure folder. Ensure that the Google Compute Engine API is enabled on your GCP project.

NOTE If you're unfamiliar with Packer, refer to chapter 4 for a step-by-step guide on installation and configuration.

Next update the Packer template file for the Jenkins worker provided in chapter 4's listing 4.16 with the following content, or copy and paste the content from the GitHub repository at chapter6/gcp/packer/worker/setup.sh.

Listing 6.1 Jenkins worker template file

```
{
    "variables" : {
        "service_account" : "SERVICE ACCOUNT JSON FILE PATH",
        "project": "GCP PROJECT ID",
        "zone": "GCP ZONE ID"
    },
    "builders" : [
        {
            "type": "googlecompute",
            "image_name" : "jenkins-worker",
            "account_file": "{{user `service_account`}}",
            "project_id": "{{user `project`}}",
            "source_image_family": "centos-8",
            "ssh_username": "packer",
            "zone": "{{user `zone`}}"
        }
    ],
    "provisioners" : [
        {
            "type" : "shell",
            "script" : "./setup.sh",
            "execute_command" : "sudo -E -S sh '{{ .Path }}'"
        }
    ]
}
```

Defines variables that will be provided at runtime. The values can be fetched from the GCP dashboard.

Runs the shell script in privileged mode to install the Git client, Docker, and needed dependencies

NOTE The JSON account file is not required if you're running the baking process from a Google Compute Engine (GCE) instance with a properly configured GCE service account. Packer will fetch the credentials from the metadata server.

Listing 6.1 uses the `googlecompute` builder to create a machine image on top of the CentOS base image. Then it uses the shell script provided in chapter 4's listing 4.13 to provision the temporary machine to install all needed dependencies—Git, JDK, and Docker.

The power of Packer comes from leveraging template files to create identical virtual machine images independently of the target platform. Therefore, we can use the same template file to build an identical Jenkins image for AWS, GCP, or Azure.

NOTE   The scripted shell is explained in depth in chapter 4. All source code is available on the GitHub repository in the chapter6 folder.

The template file in listing 6.1 uses a set of variables such as the service account key file created earlier, the name of the zone where the builder machine will be provisioned, and the Google Cloud project ID that will own the image. The `service_account` variable can be implicit if you specify the path to the JSON file with the `GOOGLE_APPLICATION_CREDENTIALS` environment variable.

Packer will deploy a temporary instance from CentOS 8. A list of available images can be found on the Images dashboard, as you can see in figure 6.3.

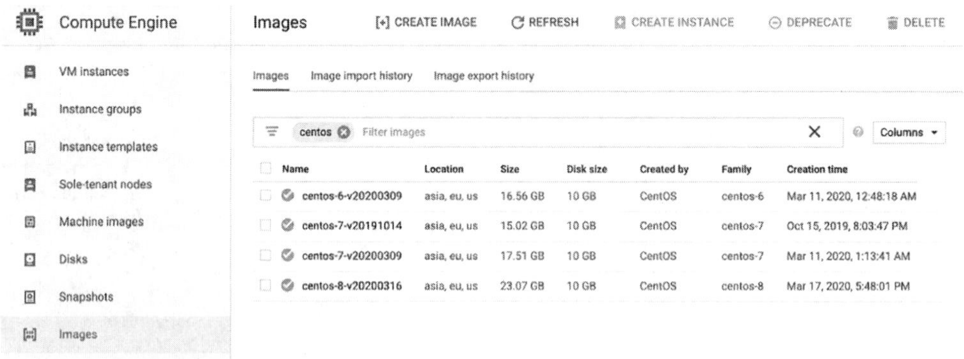

Figure 6.3   CentOS base image from GCE images

NOTE   You can also use the `gcloud compute images list` command to list available images in a specific GCP location.

After supplying all the necessary variables, issue a `packer build` command. The output should be similar to the following output, which has been cropped for the sake of brevity:

```
googlecompute: output will be in this color.

==> googlecompute: Checking image does not exist...
==> googlecompute: Creating temporary SSH key for instance...
==> googlecompute: Using image: centos-8-v20200316
==> googlecompute: Creating instance...
    googlecompute: Loading zone: europe-west3-a
    googlecompute: Loading machine type: n1-standard-1
    googlecompute: Requesting instance creation...
    googlecompute: Waiting for creation operation to complete...
    googlecompute: Instance has been created!
==> googlecompute: Waiting for the instance to become running...
    googlecompute: IP: 34.89.251.218
==> googlecompute: Using ssh communicator to connect: 34.89.251.218
==> googlecompute: Waiting for SSH to become available...
```

Once the baking process is done, the Jenkins worker image should be available on the Google Compute Engine (GCE) console, as you can see in figure 6.4.

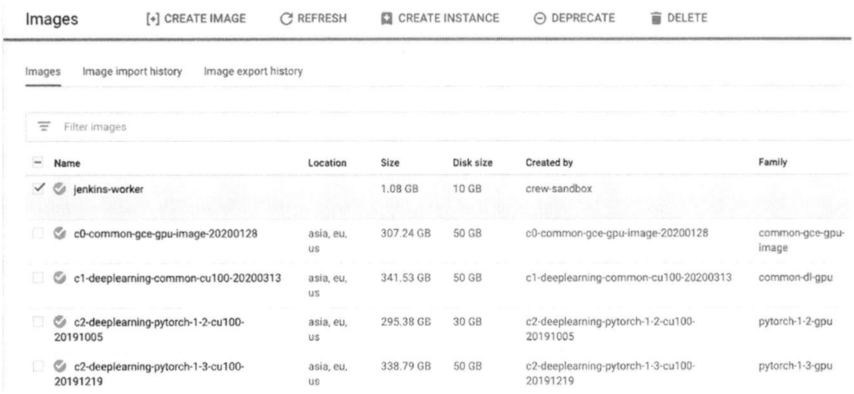

Figure 6.4   Jenkins worker custom image

Next, to build the Jenkins master machine image, we will use the same blueprint provided in chapter 4's listing 4.12. The only difference is the use of `googlecompute` in the `builders` section. The full template file, shown in the following listing, can be downloaded from chapter6/gcp/packer/master/setup.sh.

Listing 6.2   Jenkins master template file

```
{
    "variables" : {
        "service_account" : "SERVICE ACCOUNT JSON PATH",
        "project": "PROJECT ID",
        "zone": "ZONE ID",
        "ssh_key" : "PRIVATE SSH KEY PATH"
    },
    "builders" : [
        {
            "type": "googlecompute",
            "image_name" : "jenkins-master-v22041",
            "account_file": "{{user `service_account`}}",
            "project_id": "{{user `project`}}",
            "source_image_family": "centos-8",
            "ssh_username": "packer",
            "zone": "{{user `zone`}}"
        }
    ],
    "provisioners" : [
        ...
    ]
}
```

NOTE   This code listing already exists in the GitHub repository. You do not need to type it. It is shown for illustration purposes only.

Before we take this template and build an image from it, let's validate the template by running the following command:

```
packer validate template.json
```

With a properly validated template, it is time to build the Jenkins images. This is done by calling the `packer build` command with the template file as an argument. The output should look similar to the following. Note that this process typically takes a few minutes:

```
==> googlecompute: Checking image does not exist...
==> googlecompute: Creating temporary SSH key for instance...
==> googlecompute: Using image: centos-8-v20200316
==> googlecompute: Creating instance...
    googlecompute: Loading zone: europe-west3-a
    googlecompute: Loading machine type: n1-standard-1
    googlecompute: Requesting instance creation...
    googlecompute: Waiting for creation operation to complete...
    googlecompute: Instance has been created!
==> googlecompute: Waiting for the instance to become running...
    googlecompute: IP: 34.89.251.218
==> googlecompute: Using ssh communicator to connect: 34.89.251.218
==> googlecompute: Waiting for SSH to become available...
==> googlecompute: Connected to SSH!
==> googlecompute: Uploading ./scripts => /tmp/
==> googlecompute: Uploading ./config => /tmp/
==> googlecompute: Uploading /Users/mlabouardy/.ssh/id_rsa => /tmp/id_rsa
id_rsa 1.81 KiB / 1.81 KiB [=================================================
==> googlecompute: Provisioning with shell script: ./setup.sh
    googlecompute: Install Jenkins stable release
==> googlecompute: No packages marked for removal.
    googlecompute: No match for argument: java
    googlecompute: Dependencies resolved.
    googlecompute: Nothing to do.
    googlecompute: Complete!
    googlecompute: CentOS-8 - AppStream                3.1 MB/s | 6.6 MB    00:02
    googlecompute: CentOS-8 - Base                     2.5 MB/s | 5.0 MB    00:02
    googlecompute: CentOS-8 - Extras                   5.3 kB/s | 4.8 kB    00:00
    googlecompute: CentOS-8 - PowerTools               1.0 MB/s | 2.0 MB    00:01
    googlecompute: Google Compute Engine               2.9 kB/s | 6.2 kB    00:02
    googlecompute: Google Cloud SDK                     15 MB/s |  33 MB    00:02
```

When Packer is done building the image, head over to the GCP console, The newly created image will be in the Images section, as shown in figure 6.5.

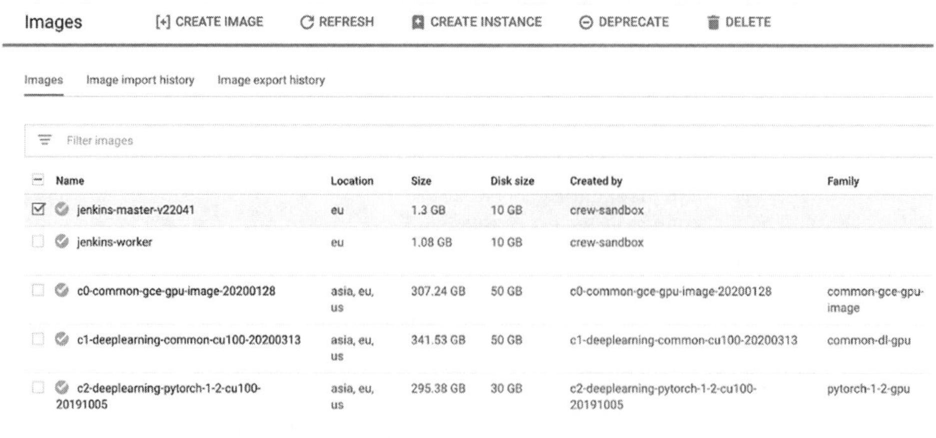

Figure 6.5   Jenkins master custom image

So far, you have learned how to automate the build process for the Jenkins machines images on GCP. In the next section, we will use Terraform to deploy VM instances based on those images. But first, we will deploy a private network on which our Jenkins cluster will be isolated.

6.1.2 Configuring a GCP network with Terraform

At the end of this section, you will have an isolated VPN running in different zones, as shown in figure 6.6.

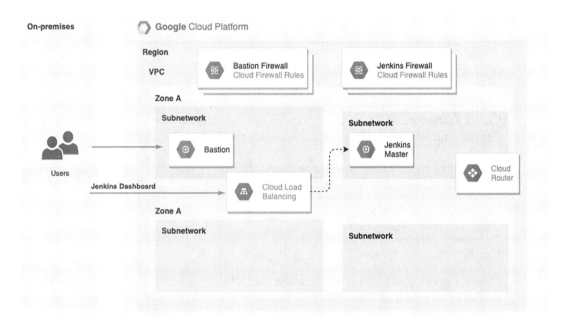

Figure 6.6 The Google VPN architecture consists of multiple subnetworks deployed in different zones. To access private instances, a bastion host can be used.

The VPC will be spun up in a single GCP region. It will be subdivided into subnets, each subnet contained within a single zone. Within a public subnet, a Google compute instance will be deployed with a role of a bastion host to give remote access to instances deployed in private subnets.

On the IAM console, shown in figure 6.7, create a dedicated service account for Terraform with Project Owner permission and download the JSON private key. This file contains credentials that will be needed for Terraform to manage the resources on your GCP project.

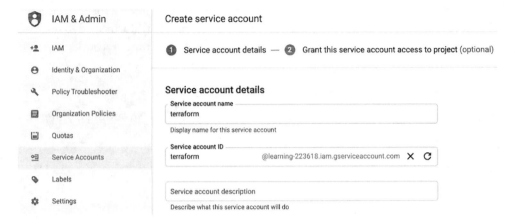

Figure 6.7   Terraform service account

Create a terraform.tf file, declare `google` as a provider, and configure it to use the service account created in the previous step; see the following listing.

Listing 6.3   Declaring Google as a provider

```
provider "google" {
  credentials = file(var.credentials_path)
  project     = var.project
  region      = var.region
}
```

Create a network.tf file and define a regional VPC network, as shown in the following listing. (If you plan to deploy Jenkins instances across multiple GCP regions, you need to change the routing mode to global.)

Listing 6.4   Defining a GCP network named management

```
resource "google_compute_network" "management" {
  name = var.network_name
  auto_create_subnetworks = false
  routing_mode = "REGIONAL"
}
```

Within the same file, declare two public and two private subnets, as shown in the next listing. Each subnet has its own CIDR block that is a subset of the network CIDR block (10.0.0.0/16).

Listing 6.5   Defining public and private subnetworks

```
resource "google_compute_subnetwork" "public_subnets" {
  count = var.public_subnets_count
```

```
  name           = "public-10-0-${count.index * 2 + 1}-0"
  ip_cidr_range  = "10.0.${count.index * 2 + 1}.0/24"
  region         = var.region
  network        = google_compute_network.management.self_link
}

resource "google_compute_subnetwork" "private_subnets" {
  count = var.private_subnets_count
  name           = "private-10-0-${count.index * 2}-0"
  ip_cidr_range  = "10.0.${count.index * 2}.0/24"
  region         = var.region
  network        = google_compute_network.management.self_link
  private_ip_google_access = true
}
```

Defines a unique CIDR range within the 10.0.0.0/16 block using the count.index variable

Before applying the changes with `terraform apply`, declare variables used to parameterize and customize the deployment in variables.tf. Table 6.1 lists the variables.

Table 6.1 GCP Terraform variables

Name	Type	Value	Description
credentials_path	String	None	The path to the service account key file in JSON format. This can be specified using the GOOGLE_CREDENTIALS environment variable.
project	String	None	The default project to manage resources in. If another project is specified on a resource, it will take precedence. This can also be specified using the GOOGLE_PROJECT environment variable.
region	String	None	The default region to manage resources in. If another region is specified on a regional resource, it will take precedence. Alternatively, this can be specified using the GOOGLE_REGION environment variable.
network_name	String	management	Name of the virtual network. The name must be 1–63 characters long and match the regular expression [a-z]([-a-z0-9]*[a-z0-9])?
public_subnets_ count	Number	2	The number of public subnetworks. By default, we will create two public subnets in different zones for resiliency.
private_subnets_ count	Number	2	The number of private subnetworks. By default, we will create two private subnets in different zones for resiliency.

We can now run Terraform to deploy the infrastructure. First, initialize Terraform to download the latest version of the Google Cloud provider plugin:

```
terraform init
```

The command output is given here:

```
Initializing the backend...

Initializing provider plugins...
- Checking for available provider plugins...
- Downloading plugin for provider "google" (hashicorp/google) 3.14.0...

The following providers do not have any version constraints in configuration,
so the latest version was installed.

To prevent automatic upgrades to new major versions that may contain breaking
changes, it is recommended to add version = "..." constraints to the
corresponding provider blocks in configuration, with the constraint strings
suggested below.

* provider.google: version = "~> 3.14"

Terraform has been successfully initialized!
```

Run a `plan` step to validate the configuration syntax and show a preview of what will be created:

```
terraform plan --var-file=variables.tfvars
```

> **NOTE**   To set lots of variables, it is more convenient to specify their values in a variable definitions file (with a filename ending in either .tfvars or .tfvars .json) and then specify that file on the command line with the `-var-file` flag.

Now execute the `terraform apply` command to apply those changes:

```
terraform apply --var-file=variables.tfvars
```

You will see output similar to the following (cropped for brevity):

```
# google_compute_network.management will be created
+ resource "google_compute_network" "management" {
    + auto_create_subnetworks       = false
    + delete_default_routes_on_create = false
    + gateway_ipv4                  = (known after apply)
    + id                            = (known after apply)
    + ipv4_range                    = (known after apply)
    + name                          = "management"
    + project                       = (known after apply)
    + routing_mode                  = (known after apply)
    + self_link                     = (known after apply)
  }
```

It should take only a few moments to provision the private network. When it is finished, you should see something like figure 6.8.

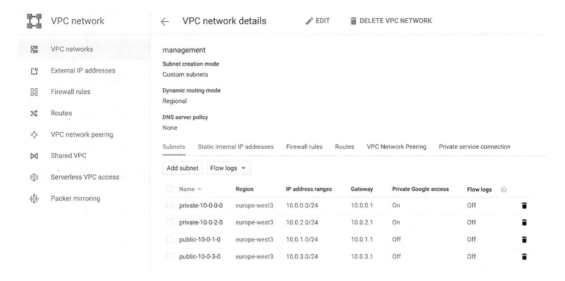

Figure 6.8 VPC network and its public and private subnets

To be able to SSH into private Jenkins instances, we will deploy a bastion host. Create bastion.tf and define a VM instance in a public subnet with a static IPv4 public IP address. To SSH into the bastion instance using Terminal (as opposed to the GCP console), you must generate and upload a public SSH key (located by default under ~/.ssh/id_rsa.pub, or generate a new one with ssh-keygen). The metadata attribute defined in the following listing references the public SSH key.

Listing 6.6   Bastion host resource

```
resource "google_compute_address" "static" {
  name = "ipv4-address"
}
resource "google_compute_instance" "bastion" {
  project      = var.project
  name         = "bastion"
  machine_type = var.bastion_machine_type
  zone         = var.zone
  tags = ["bastion"]
  boot_disk {
    initialize_params {
      image = var.machine_image
    }
  }
  network_interface {
    subnetwork = google_compute_subnetwork.public_subnets[0].self_link

    access_config {
      nat_ip = google_compute_address.static.address
    }
```

```
  }
  metadata = {
    ssh-keys = "${var.ssh_user}:${file(var.ssh_public_key)}"
  }
}
```

Within the same file, create a firewall rule to allow SSH from anywhere on the bastion host, as shown in the following listing. (It's recommended to enable ingress from only the IP address you wish to allow access from.)

Listing 6.7   Bastion host firewall rules

```
resource "google_compute_firewall" "allow_ssl_to_bastion" {
  project = var.project
  name    = "allow-ssl-to-bastion"
  network = google_compute_network.management.self_link

  allow {
    protocol = "tcp"
    ports    = ["22"]
  }                              Allows inbound traffic on
                                 port 22 (SSH) from anywhere
  source_ranges = ["0.0.0.0/0"]

  source_tags = ["bastion"]
}
```

Finally, create an outputs.tf file and use the Terraform `output` variable to act as helper to expose the public IP address of the bastion virtual machine:

```
output "bastion" {
    value = "${google_compute_instance.bastion.network_interface
    .0.access_config.0.nat_ip }"        ◁─┐ Outputs the bastion
}                                            instance's public IP address
```

After the `terraform apply` command has finished, you should see output similar to this:

```
google_compute_address.static: Refreshing state... [id=projects/learning-223618/regions/europe-west3/addresses/ipv4-address]
google_compute_network.management: Refreshing state... [id=projects/learning-223618/global/networks/management]
google_compute_subnetwork.private_subnets[0]: Refreshing state... [id=projects/learning-223618/regions/europe-west3/subnetworks/private-10-0-0-0]
google_compute_subnetwork.private_subnets[1]: Refreshing state... [id=projects/learning-223618/regions/europe-west3/subnetworks/private-10-0-2-0]
google_compute_firewall.allow_ssl_to_bastion: Refreshing state... [id=projects/learning-223618/global/firewalls/allow-ssl-to-bastion]
google_compute_router.private_router: Refreshing state... [id=projects/learning-223618/regions/europe-west3/routers/private-router-management]
google_compute_subnetwork.public_subnets[0]: Refreshing state... [id=projects/learning-223618/regions/europe-west3/subnetworks/public-10-0-1-0]
google_compute_subnetwork.public_subnets[1]: Refreshing state... [id=projects/learning-223618/regions/europe-west3/subnetworks/public-10-0-3-0]
google_compute_router_nat.nat: Refreshing state... [id=learning-223618/europe-west3/private-router-management/nat-management]
google_compute_instance.bastion: Refreshing state... [id=projects/learning-223618/zones/europe-west3-a/instances/bastion]

Apply complete! Resources: 0 added, 0 changed, 0 destroyed.

Outputs:

bastion = 35.246.240.251
```

On the GCE console, a new VM instance should be deployed, as in figure 6.9.

Figure 6.9   Bastion VM instance

With the jump box deployed, we can now access private instances in the VPC network.

6.1.3   *Deploying Jenkins on Google Compute Engine*

Now that the VPC is created, we will deploy a VM instance based on the Jenkins master image within a private subnet and expose a public load balancer to access the Jenkins web dashboard on port 8080, as described in figure 6.10.

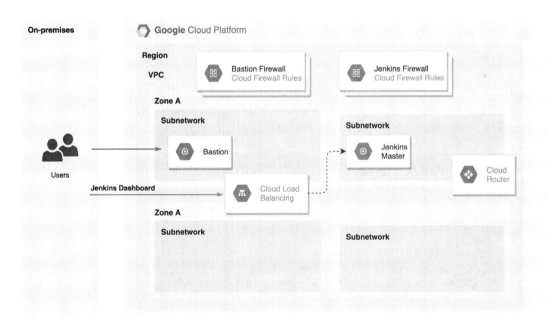

Figure 6.10   Jenkins master VM inside VPC

Create a jenkins_master.tf file and define a private compute instance with the attributes in the following listing.

Listing 6.8 Jenkins master compute instance

```
resource "google_compute_instance" "jenkins_master" {
  project      = var.project
  name         = "jenkins-master"
  machine_type = var.jenkins_master_machine_type
  zone         = var.zone

  tags = ["jenkins-ssh", "jenkins-web"]          ⟵── Attaches jenkins-ssh and jenkins-
                                                     web networks to the VM instance.
  depends_on = [google_compute_instance.bastion]   The groups allow inbound traffic
                                                     on port 22 and 8080 (Jenkins
  boot_disk {                                        dashboard), respectively.
    initialize_params {
      image = var.jenkins_master_machine_image
    }
  }

  network_interface {
    subnetwork = google_compute_subnetwork.private_subnets[0].self_link
  }

  metadata = {
    ssh-keys = "${var.ssh_user}:${file(var.ssh_public_key)}"
  }
}
```

The compute instance uses the following firewall, which allows SSH from the bastion host only and inbound traffic on port 8080 from anywhere. (I recommend restricting the traffic to your network CIDR block.)

Listing 6.9 Jenkins master firewall and traffic control

```
resource "google_compute_firewall" "allow_ssh_to_jenkins" {
  project = var.project
  name    = "allow-ssh-to-jenkins"
  network = google_compute_network.management.self_link

  allow {
    protocol = "tcp"      │ Allows inbound traffic
    ports    = ["22"]     │ on port 22 (SSH)
  }

  source_tags = ["bastion", "jenkins-ssh"]
}

resource "google_compute_firewall" "allow_access_to_ui" {
  project = var.project
  name    = "allow-access-to-jenkins-web"
  network = google_compute_network.management.self_link
```

```
allow {
  protocol = "tcp"
  ports    = ["8080"]        Allows inbound traffic on port 8080,
}                            where the Jenkins dashboard is exposed

source_ranges = ["0.0.0.0/0"]

source_tags = ["jenkins-web"]
}
```

Use `terraform apply` to deploy the Jenkins compute instance. Once the deployment is completed, a new VM will be deployed, as you can see in figure 6.11.

Figure 6.11 Jenkins master VM instance

The instance is deployed inside a private subnetwork. To be able to access the Jenkins web dashboard, we need to deploy a public load balancer in front of the VM instance.

Load balancing on GCP is different than on other cloud providers. The primary difference is that GCP uses forwarding rules instead of routing instances. These forwarding rules are combined with backend services, target pools, and health checks to construct a functional load balancer across an instance group.

First we define a target pool resource that defines the instances that should receive the incoming traffic, as shown in the next listing. In our case, the target pool will consist of the Jenkins master VM instance.

Listing 6.10   Jenkins master target pool

```
resource "google_compute_target_pool" "jenkins-master-target-pool" {
    name             = "jenkins-master-target-pool"
    session_affinity = "NONE"
    region = var.region                        Defines Jenkins master
                                                VM instance as a
    instances = [                              target of the network
        Google_compute_instance.jenkins_master.self_link  ◁─┘ load balancer
    ]

    health_checks = [
        google_compute_http_health_check.jenkins_master_health_check.name
    ]
}
```

The cloud load balancer forwards traffic to the Jenkins master only if it's up and ready to receive the traffic. That's why we define a health-check resource to send health-check requests to the Jenkins master at a specific frequency on port 8080; see the following listing.

Listing 6.11   Jenkins master health check

```
resource "google_compute_http_health_check" "jenkins_master_health_check" {
  name          = "jenkins-master-health-check"
  request_path = "/"
  port = "8080"
  timeout_sec        = 4
  check_interval_sec = 5
}
```

Defines a template for how the Jenkins master should be checked for health, via HTTP

Finally, in the next listing, we define a forwarding rule to direct traffic to the target pool defined earlier.

Listing 6.12   Load balancer forwarding rule

```
resource "google_compute_forwarding_rule" "jenkins_master_forwarding_rule" {
  name   = "jenkins-master-forwarding-rule"
  region = var.region
  load_balancing_scheme = "EXTERNAL"
  target = google_compute_target_pool.jenkins-master-target-pool.self_link
  port_range         = "8080"
  ip_protocol        = "TCP"
}
```

If the incoming packet matches the given IP address, IP protocol, and port range tuple, it will be forwarded to the Jenkins master target pool.

Use `terraform apply` to deploy the public load balancer. On the Network Services dashboard, you should have the configuration shown in figure 6.12.

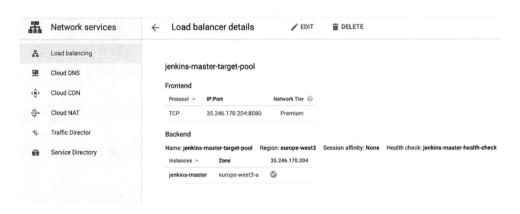

Figure 6.12   Public load balancer with Jenkins VM as a backend

As a backend, the load balancer uses Jenkins master instance and forwards incoming traffic on port 8080 to the backend on the same port. Also, it sets up an HTTP health check on port 8080.

To display the IP address of the load balancer, create an output section in the outputs.tf file:

```
output "jenkins" {
    value = google_compute_forwarding_rule \
.jenkins_master_forwarding_rule.ip_address
}
```

Issue the `terraform output` command on the console, and the Jenkins load balancer IP address should be displayed:

```
Apply complete! Resources: 1 added, 0 changed, 1 destroyed.

Outputs:

bastion = 34.89.153.200
jenkins = 35.246.170.204
```

You can now point your browser to the IP address on port 8080 and see the Jenkins welcome screen. If you see a screen like the one in figure 6.13, you've successfully deployed Jenkins on GCP!

Figure 6.13   Public load balancer IP address to access the Jenkins dashboard

> **NOTE**   The forwarding rule may take several minutes to be provisioned. While it's being created, you might see 404 and 500 errors in the browser.

6.1.4   *Launching automanaged workers on GCP*

Arguably one of the most powerful features of Jenkins is its ability to dispatch build jobs across many workers. It is quite easy to set up a farm of build machines, either to share the load across multiple machines or to run build jobs in different environments. This is an effective strategy that can potentially increase the capacity of your CI infrastructure dramatically.

Demand for Jenkins workers can also fluctuate over time. If you are working with product release cycles, you may need to run a much higher number of workers toward the end of the cycle. Therefore, to avoid paying for extra resources while Jenkins workers are idle, we will deploy Jenkins workers inside an instance group and set up autoscaling policies to trigger scale-out or scale-in events that add or remove Jenkins workers, respectively, based on metrics such as CPU utilization.

> **NOTE**   In chapter 13, we will cover how to use an open source solution like Prometheus to export Jenkins custom metrics, including its integration with the scaling process of Jenkins workers.

Figure 6.14 summarizes the architecture we're going to deploy in this section.

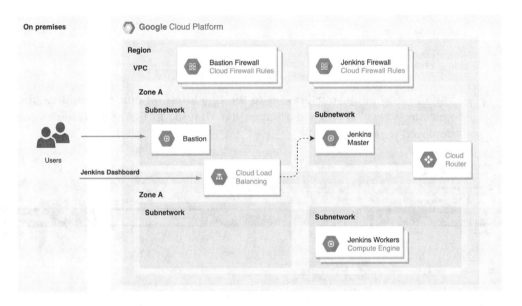

Figure 6.14   Jenkins cluster deployment on Google Cloud

First, create a jenkins_workers.tf file and define the instance template that will be used as a blueprint to define the Jenkins workers configurations; see the following listing.

Listing 6.13   Jenkins worker template configuration

```
resource "google_compute_instance_template" "jenkins-worker-template" {
  name_prefix = "jenkins-worker"
  description = "Jenkins workers instances template"
  region      = var.region

  tags = ["jenkins-worker"]
  machine_type        = var.jenkins_worker_machine_type
```

```
metadata_startup_script =
    data.template_file.jenkins_worker_startup_script.rendered          ◄─┐

disk {
  source_image = var.jenkins_worker_machine_image
  disk_size_gb = 50
}
network_interface {
  network = google_compute_network.management.self_link
  subnetwork = google_compute_subnetwork.private_subnets[0].self_link
}

metadata = {
  ssh-keys = "${var.ssh_user}:${file(var.ssh_public_key)}"
}
}
```

A shell script that will be executed the first time the VM instance is launched. The script will autojoin the instance as a Jenkins agent.

We will deploy the instances inside a private subnetwork and will execute the startup script in the following listing to make the running virtual machine join the cluster. This script is similar to the shell script provided in chapter 5's listing 5.7.

Listing 6.14   Jenkins worker startup script

```
data "template_file" "jenkins_worker_startup_script" {
  template = "${file("scripts/join-cluster.tpl")}"

  vars = {
    jenkins_url             = "http://${google_compute_forwarding_rule.
jenkins_master_forwarding_rule.ip_address}:8080"
    jenkins_username        = var.jenkins_username
    jenkins_password        = var.jenkins_password
    jenkins_credentials_id = var.jenkins_credentials_id
  }
}
```

The join-cluster.tpl template file takes as parameters the Jenkins credentials and URL. The values will be interpolated at runtime.

We will be using the Google Cloud metadata server to fetch the instance name and private IP address. The metadata server request's output is in JSON format, so we'll use the jq utility to parse the JSON and grab the target attributes:

```
INSTANCE_NAME=$(curl -s metadata.google.internal/0.1/meta-data/hostname)
INSTANCE_IP=$(curl -s metadata.google.internal/0.1/meta-data/network
| jq -r '.networkInterface[0].ip')
```

Next, we will define a firewall rule to allow SSH on Jenkins workers from the Jenkins master and bastion host, as shown in the following listing.

Listing 6.15   Jenkins master firewall and traffic control

```
resource "google_compute_firewall" "allow_ssh_to_worker" {
  project = var.project
  name    = "allow-ssh-to-worker"
  network = google_compute_network.management.self_link
```

```
allow {
  protocol = "tcp"              Allows inbound traffic
  ports    = ["22"]             on port 22 (SSH)
}

source_tags = ["bastion", "jenkins-ssh", "jenkins-worker"]
}
```

Then, we define an instance group based on the template file with a target size of two workers by default; see the next listing.

Listing 6.16   Jenkins worker instance group

```
resource "google_compute_instance_group_manager" "jenkins-workers-group" {
  provider = google-beta
  name = "jenkins-workers"
  base_instance_name = "jenkins-worker"
  zone               = var.zone

  version {
    instance_template  = google_compute_instance_template
.jenkins-worker-template.self_link                          ◁──┐
  }                                                              Creates and manages pools of
                                                                 homogeneous VM instances (two
  target_pools = [google_compute_target_pool                     instances) from a common instance
.jenkins-workers-pool.id]                                        template (jenkins-worker-template)
  target_size = 2                                          ◁──┘
}

resource "google_compute_target_pool" "jenkins-workers-pool" {
  provider = google-beta
  name = "jenkins-workers-pool"
}
```

Once the new resources are deployed with `terraform apply`, two worker instances should be running, as shown in figure 6.15.

However, the number of workers is static and fixed, for now. To be able to scale Jenkins workers for heavy build jobs, we will deploy an autoscaler based on CPU

| VM instances | ⬛ CREATE INSTANCE | ⬆ IMPORT VM | ⟳ REFRESH | ▶ START | ⬛ STOP | ⏻ RESET | 🗑 |

☐ Name ∧	Zone	Recommendation	In use by	Internal IP	External IP
☐ ✓ bastion	europe-west3-a			10.0.1.2 (nic0)	34.89.153.200
☐ ✓ jenkins-master	europe-west3-a		jenkins-master-target-pool	10.0.0.2 (nic0)	None
☐ ✓ jenkins-worker-3mf7	europe-west3-a		jenkins-workers, jenkins-workers-pool	10.0.0.3 (nic0)	None
☐ ✓ jenkins-worker-wbpp	europe-west3-a		jenkins-workers, jenkins-workers-pool	10.0.0.4 (nic0)	None

Figure 6.15   Jenkins worker instance groups

utilization. Define the following resource to trigger a scale-out event if the CPU utilization is over 80%. Within jenkins_workers.tf, add the code in the following listing.

Listing 6.17 Jenkins worker autoscaler

```
resource "google_compute_autoscaler" "jenkins-workers-autoscaler" {
  name   = "jenkins-workers-autoscaler"
  zone   = var.zone
  target = google_compute_instance_group_manager.jenkins-workers-group.id

  autoscaling_policy {
    max_replicas    = 6
    min_replicas    = 2
    cooldown_period = 60

    cpu_utilization {
      target = 0.8
    }
  }
}
```

Scales Jenkins worker instances in managed instance groups according to the autoscaling policy. The policy is based on the CPU utilization of the instances.

Once the changes are deployed with Terraform, the autoscaling policy will be configured on the Jenkins worker instance group, as you can see in figure 6.16.

Figure 6.16 Instance group scaling based on CPU utilization

As a result, the workers will automatically join the cluster after the startup script is executed (figure 6.17). Awesome! You are running a Jenkins cluster on GCP.

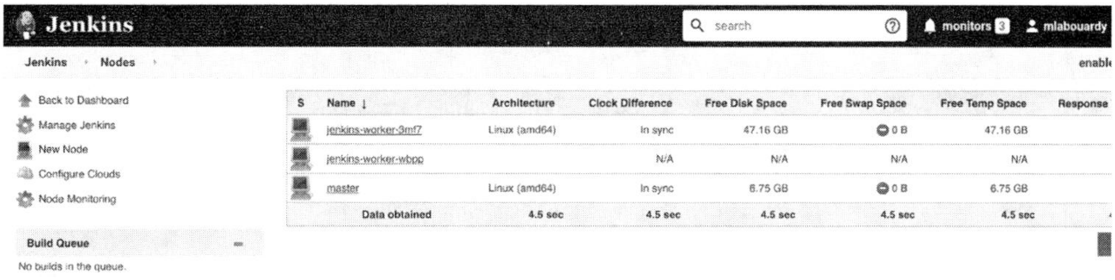

Figure 6.17 Jenkins worker VM instances joined the cluster.

6.2   Microsoft Azure

Both Microsoft Azure and AWS follow a similar approach by offering a variety of cloud-based services under one hood. However, organizations that use Microsoft software typically have an Enterprise Agreement that provides discounts on that software. These organizations can typically obtain significant incentives for using Azure.

If you plan to use Azure, you can deploy the Jenkins solution template from the Azure Marketplace. However, if you're looking to have full control over Jenkins, follow this section to learn how to build a Jenkins cluster from scratch and scale your Jenkins workers on demand based on Azure virtual machines.

> **NOTE** While Azure and Google Cloud have seen a fairly significant amount of growth, AWS is still the leader. This is mainly due to AWS being the first to invest in and shape the cloud computing industry. Google Cloud and Azure have some catching up to do.

Before getting started, if you're new to Azure, you may sign up for an Azure free account (https://portal.azure.com/) to start exploring with a free $200 credit.

6.2.1   Building golden Jenkins VM images in Azure

During the build process, Packer creates temporary Azure resources as it builds the source VM. Therefore, it needs to be authorized to interact with the Azure API.

Create an Azure service principal (SP) with permissions to create and manage resources with the following commands. An SP represents an application accessing your Azure resources. It is identified by a client ID (aka *application ID*) and can use a password or a certificate for authentication.

To create an SP, copy these commands:

```
$sp = New-AzADServicePrincipal -DisplayName "PackerServicePrincipal"
$BSTR = [System.Runtime
.InteropServices.Marshal]::SecureStringToBSTR($sp.Secret)
$plainPassword = [System.Runtime
.InteropServices.Marshal]::PtrToStringAuto($BSTR)
New-AzRoleAssignment -RoleDefinitionName
 Contributor -ServicePrincipalName $sp.ApplicationId
```

You can execute the commands on Azure PowerShell, as shown in figure 6.18.

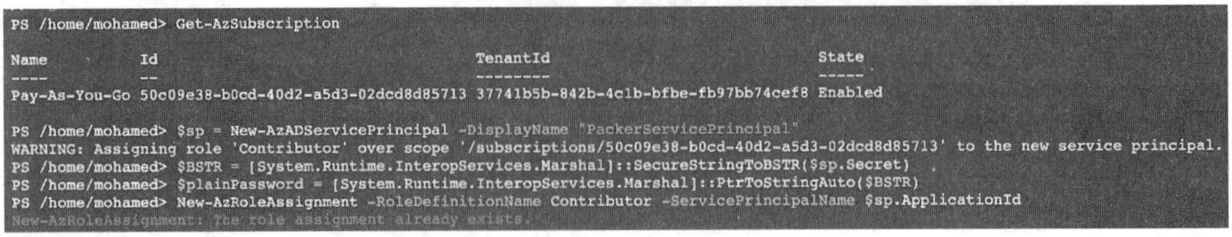

Figure 6.18   Creating Azure credentials

Then output the password and application ID by executing the following commands:

```
$plainPassword
$sp.ApplicationId
```

Save the application ID and password for later.

To authenticate to Azure, you also need to obtain your Azure tenant and subscription IDs, which can be fetched with `Get-AzSubscription` or from Azure Active Directory (AD). AD, shown in figure 6.19, is an identity management service that controls access and security to Azure resources with the right roles and permissions.

Figure 6.19 Packer registration on Azure Active Directory

Note the client ID and key. This will be used as credentials in Packer to provision resources in Azure.

To build the Jenkins worker image, create a template.json file. In the template, you define builders and provisioners that carry out the actual build process. Packer has a builder for Azure called `azure-arm` that allows you to define Azure images. Add the following content to template.json or download the full template from chapter6/azure/packer/worker/template.json.

Listing 6.18 Jenkins worker template with Azure builder

```
{
    "variables" : {
        "subscription_id" : "YOUR SUBSCRIPTION ID",
        "client_id": "YOUR CLIENT ID",
        "client_secret": "YOUR CLIENT SECRET",          List of runtime variables to
        "tenant_id": "YOUR TENANT ID",                  make the Packer template
        "resource_group": "RESOURCE GROUP NAME",        portable and reusable
        "location": "LOCATION NAME"
    },
    "builders" : [
        {
            "type": "azure-arm",
```

```
            "subscription_id": "{{user `subscription_id`}}",
            "client_id": "{{user `client_id`}}",
            "client_secret": "{{user `client_secret`}}",
            "tenant_id": "{{user `tenant_id`}}",
            "managed_image_resource_group_name": "{{user `resource_group`}}",
            "managed_image_name": "jenkins-worker",
            "os_type": "Linux",
            "image_publisher": "OpenLogic",
            "image_offer": "CentOS",
            "image_sku": "8.0",
            "location": "{{user `location`}}",
            "vm_size": "Standard_B1s"
        }
    ],
    "provisioners" : [
        {
            "type" : "shell",
            "script" : "./setup.sh",
            "execute_command" : "sudo -E -S sh '{{ .Path }}'"
        }
    ]
}
```

> **Packer will provision an instance of type Standard_B1s (1 RAM and 1vCPU) based on the CentOS 8.0 machine image.**

If you're running Packer in a virtual machine, you can assign a managed identity to the virtual machine. No configuration properties are required to be set.

The template in listing 6.18 deploys a temporary instance based on CentOS 8.0 and provisions the instance with a shell script to install needed dependencies. The choice of CentOS is not arbitrary. Both Amazon Linux Image and CentOS have similarities, especially the support of the Yum package manager. To use the same scripts provided in previous chapters and keep consistent and identical Jenkins images, we'll use CentOS.

Bake the image with the `packer build` command. Here's an example of the output:

```
azure-arm: output will be in this color.

==> azure-arm: Running builder ...
==> azure-arm: Getting tokens using client secret
==> azure-arm: Getting tokens using client secret
    azure-arm: Creating Azure Resource Manager (ARM) client ...
==> azure-arm: Creating resource group ...
==> azure-arm:  -> ResourceGroupName : 'packer-Resource-Group-gr48cazkyb'
==> azure-arm:  -> Location          : 'centralus'
==> azure-arm:  -> Tags              :
==> azure-arm: Validating deployment template ...
==> azure-arm:  -> ResourceGroupName : 'packer-Resource-Group-gr48cazkyb'
==> azure-arm:  -> DeploymentName    : 'pkrdpgr48cazkyb'
==> azure-arm: Deploying deployment template ...
==> azure-arm:  -> ResourceGroupName : 'packer-Resource-Group-gr48cazkyb'
==> azure-arm:  -> DeploymentName    : 'pkrdpgr48cazkyb'
==> azure-arm: Getting the VM's IP address ...
==> azure-arm:  -> ResourceGroupName  : 'packer-Resource-Group-gr48cazkyb'
==> azure-arm:  -> PublicIPAddressName : 'pkripgr48cazkyb'
==> azure-arm:  -> NicName             : 'pkrnigr48cazkyb'
==> azure-arm:  -> Network Connection  : 'PublicEndpoint'
==> azure-arm:  -> IP Address          : '40.122.174.203'
==> azure-arm: Waiting for SSH to become available...
==> azure-arm: Connected to SSH!
==> azure-arm: Provisioning with shell script: ./setup.sh
    azure-arm: Install Java JDK 8
```

It takes a few minutes for Packer to build the VM, run the provisioners, and bake the Jenkins worker image. Once completed, the image is created in the resource group set in the `resource_group` variable, as shown in figure 6.20.

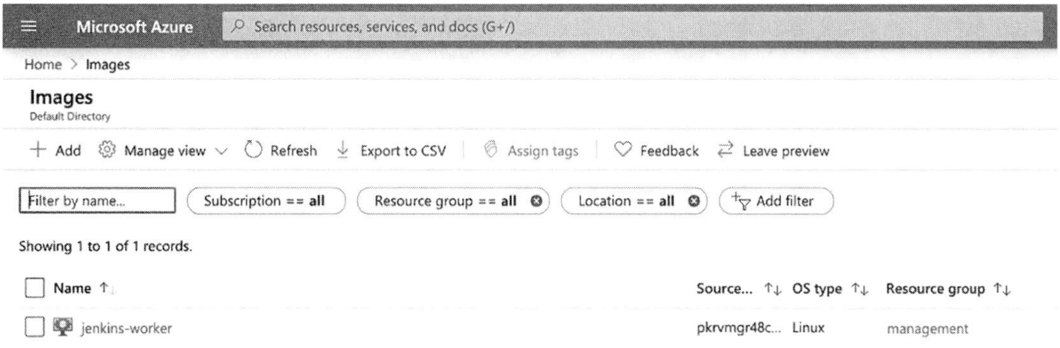

Figure 6.20 Jenkins worker machine image

A similar workflow will be applied to build the Jenkins master image. The following is the template.json file (the complete template is available at chapter6/azure/packer/master/template.json).

Listing 6.19   Jenkins worker template with Azure builder

```
{
    "variables" : {...},
    "builders" : [
        {
            "type": "azure-arm",
            "subscription_id": "{{user `subscription_id`}}",
            "client_id": "{{user `client_id`}}",
            "client_secret": "{{user `client_secret`}}",
            "tenant_id": "{{user `tenant_id`}}",
            "managed_image_resource_group_name": "{{user `resource_group`}}",
            "managed_image_name": "jenkins-master-v22041",
            "os_type": "Linux",
            "image_publisher": "OpenLogic",
            "image_offer": "CentOS",
            "image_sku": "8.0",
            "location": "{{user `location`}}",
            "vm_size": "Standard_B1ms"
        }
    ],
    "provisioners" : [
        ...
    ]
}
```

◁—— List of variables has been omitted for brevity; the complete list is in listing 6.18.

Once the template is defined, bake the image with Packer. The baking process should take a few minutes to create the image. Once the image has been created, it should be available on the Images dashboard from the Azure portal, as shown in figure 6.21.

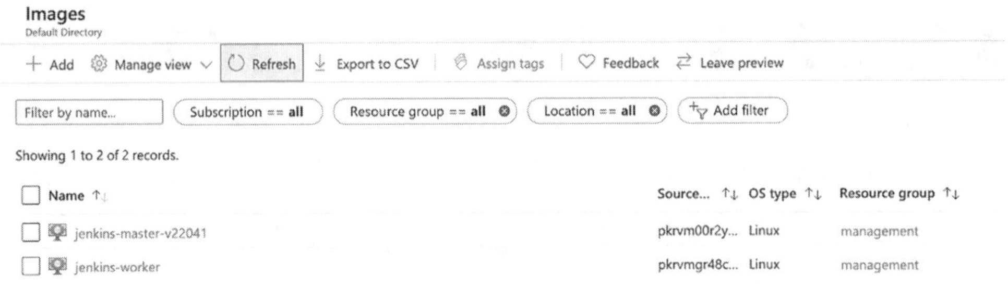

Images
Default Directory
+ Add
Manage view
Refresh
Export to CSV
Assign tags
Feedback
Leave preview
Filter by name...
Subscription == all
Resource group == all
Location == all
Add filter
Showing 1 to 2 of 2 records.
Name
Source...
OS type
Resource group
jenkins-master-v22041
pkrvm00r2y...
Linux
management
jenkins-worker
pkrvmgr48c...
Linux
management

Figure 6.21 Jenkins master machine image

With both Jenkins master and worker images available, you can now create a Jenkins cluster from your custom images with Terraform.

6.2.2 Deploying a private virtual network

Before deploying the Jenkins cluster, we need to set up a private network with the architecture shown in figure 6.22 to secure access to the cluster.

Virtual Network
Public Subnet
Public Subnet
Private Subnet
Private Subnet
AzureBastionSubnet
Azure Bastion

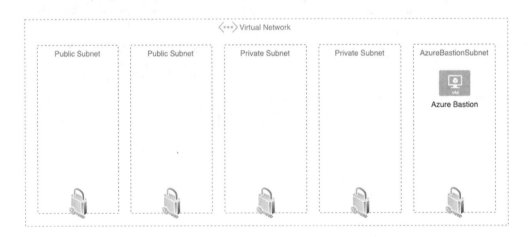

Figure 6.22 VPN on Azure

NOTE To enable Terraform to provision resources into Azure, create an Azure Active Directory service principal by following the same steps described in section 6.2.1.

Create a terraform.tf file and declare azurerm as a provider, as shown in the following listing. The provider section tells Terraform to use an Azure provider. To get values for subscription_id, client_id, client_secret, and tenant_id, see section 6.2.1.

Listing 6.20 Defining an Azure provider

```
provider "azurerm" {
  version = "=1.44.0"

  subscription_id = var.subscription_id
  client_id       = var.client_id
  client_secret   = var.client_secret
  tenant_id       = var.tenant_id
}
```

Run terraform init to download the latest version of the Azure plugin and build the .terraform directory:

```
Initializing the backend...

Initializing provider plugins...
- Checking for available provider plugins...
- Downloading plugin for provider "azurerm" (hashicorp/azurerm) 1.44.0...

Terraform has been successfully initialized!
```

Next, create a virtual_network.tf file on which you define a virtual network called management in the 10.0.0.0/16 address space with public and private subnets and an additional subnet called AzureBastionSubnet reserved for a bastion host, as shown in the following listing.

Listing 6.21 Azure virtual network definition

```
data "azurerm_resource_group" "management" {
  name = var.resource_group
}

resource "azurerm_virtual_network" "management" {
  name                = "management"
  location            = var.location
  resource_group_name = data.azurerm_resource_group.management.name
  address_space       = [var.base_cidr_block]
  dns_servers         = ["10.0.0.4", "10.0.0.5"]      ⟵── List of IP addresses
                                                          of DNS servers
  dynamic "subnet" {
    for_each = [for s in var.subnets: {
      name   = s.name                                 Defines a list of
      prefix = cidrsubnet(var.base_cidr_block, 8, s.number)   subnets within the
    }]                                                        10.0.0.0/16 space
```

```
    content {
      name          = subnet.value.name
      address_prefix = subnet.value.prefix
    }
  }

  subnet {
    name          = "AzureBastionSubnet"
    address_prefix = cidrsubnet(var.base_cidr_block, 11, 224)
  }

  tags = {
    environment = "management"
  }
}
```

Defines a list of subnets within the 10.0.0.0/16 space

Defines a dedicated subnet where the Bastion host will be deployed

NOTE   We can tag our resources in Azure with a key-value pair. It's useful for cost optimization. So we will add the `environment` tag with value management to all the resources we create.

Before applying the changes, declare the variables used to parameterize and customize the Terraform deployment in variables.tf. Table 6.2 lists the variables.

Table 6.2   Azure Terraform variables

Name	Type	Value	Description
subscription_id	String	None	The subscription ID to be used. This can also be sourced from the ARM_SUBSCRIPTION_ID environment variable.
client_id	String	None	The client ID to be used. This can also be sourced from the ARM_CLIENT_ID environment variable.
client_secret	String	None	The client secret to be used. This can also be sourced from the ARM_CLIENT_SECRET environment variable.
tenant_id	String	None	The Tenant/Directory ID to be used. This can also be sourced from the ARM_TENANT_ID environment variable
resource_group	String	None	The name of the resource group in which to create the virtual network.
location	String	None	The location/region where the virtual network is created. Changing this forces a new resource to be created. Refer to Azure Locations documentation for a full list of supported locations.
base_cidr_block	String	10.0.0.0/16	The address space (CIDR block) that is used for the virtual network.
subnets	Map	None	A map holding a list of subnets to create inside the virtual network.

When authenticating as a service principal using a client certificate, the following fields should be set: `client_certificate_password` and `client_certificate_path`.

Now it's time to run the `terraform apply` command. Terraform will call Azure APIs to set up the new virtual network as shown here:

```
# azurerm_virtual_network.management will be created
+ resource "azurerm_virtual_network" "management" {
    + address_space       = [
        + "10.0.0.0/16",
      ]
    + dns_servers         = [
        + "10.0.0.4",
        + "10.0.0.5",
      ]
    + id                  = (known after apply)
    + location            = "centralus"
    + name                = "management"
    + resource_group_name = "management"
    + tags                = {
        + "environment" = "management"
      }

    + subnet {
        + address_prefix = "10.0.0.0/24"
        + id             = (known after apply)
        + name           = "public-10.0.0.0"
      }
    + subnet {
        + address_prefix = "10.0.1.0/24"
        + id             = (known after apply)
        + name           = "public-10.0.1.0"
      }
    + subnet {
        + address_prefix = "10.0.2.0/24"
        + id             = (known after apply)
        + name           = "private-10.0.2.0"
      }
    + subnet {
        + address_prefix = "10.0.28.0/27"
        + id             = (known after apply)
        + name           = "AzureBastionSubnet"
      }
    + subnet {
        + address_prefix = "10.0.3.0/24"
        + id             = (known after apply)
        + name           = "private-10.0.3.0"
      }
  }
```

To verify the results within the Azure portal, browse to the management resource group. The new virtual network is located under this group, as shown in figure 6.23.

To access private Jenkins machines, we need to deploy a gateway or proxy servers, also known as jump boxes or bastion hosts. Fortunately, Azure provides a managed service called Azure Bastion offering Remote Desktop Protocol (RDP) and SSH access to any VM without the need to manage a hardened bastion instance and apply security patches (no operational overhead).

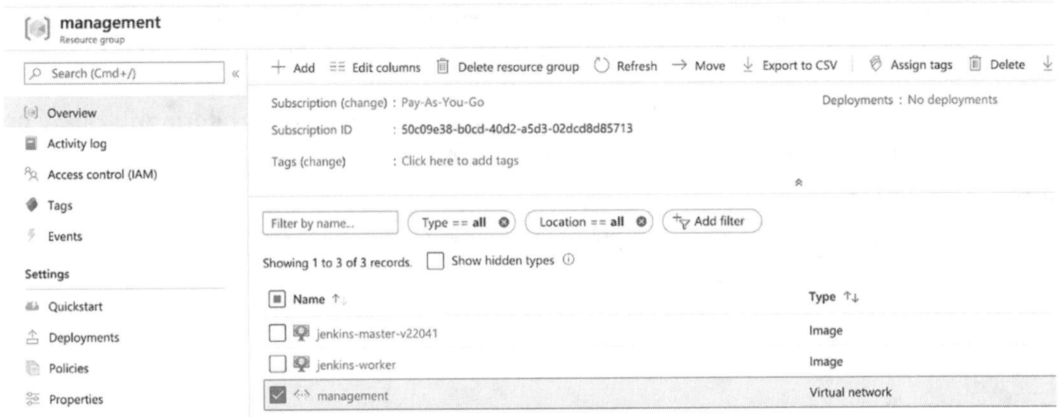

Figure 6.23   Management virtual network

To deploy the Azure Bastion service into the existing Azure virtual network, create a bastion.tf file with the following content. The bastion host service will be deployed into the dedicated `AzureBastionSubnet` subnet:

```
Listing 6.22   Azure Bastion service deployment

resource "azurerm_public_ip" "bastion_public_ip" {
  name                = "bastion-public-ip"
  location            = var.location
  resource_group_name = data.azurerm_resource_group.management.name
  allocation_method   = "Static"          ◁──┐ Requests a static
  sku                 = "Standard"            │ public IP address
}
data "azurerm_subnet" "bastion_subnet" {
  name                 = "AzureBastionSubnet"
  virtual_network_name = azurerm_virtual_network.management.name
  resource_group_name  = data.azurerm_resource_group.management.name
  depends_on = [azurerm_virtual_network.management]
}                                               Reference to a subnet in which
resource "azurerm_bastion_host" "bastion" {      the bastion host will be created. It
  name                = "bastion"              also associates the provisioned public
  location            = var.location              IP address to the bastion host.
  resource_group_name = data.azurerm_resource_group.management.name
  depends_on = [azurerm_virtual_network.management]

  ip_configuration {
    name                 = "bastion-configuration"
    subnet_id            = data.azurerm_subnet.bastion_subnet.id
    public_ip_address_id = azurerm_public_ip.bastion_public_ip.id
  }
}
```

Use a Terraform output variable to act as a helper to expose the bastion IP address by referencing the `azurerm_public_ip` resource.

```
output "bastion" {
    value = azurerm_public_ip.bastion_public_ip.ip_address
}
```

Run `terraform apply` to apply the configuration. A bastion service will be deployed into the `management` resource group, as shown in figure 6.24.

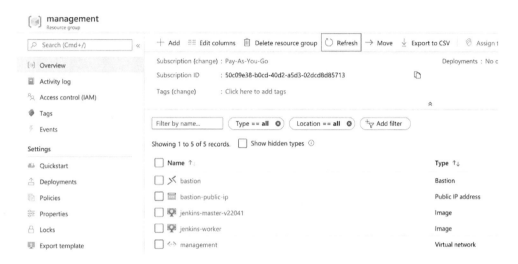

Figure 6.24   Azure bastion host

6.2.3 Deploying a Jenkins master virtual machine

With the VPN being deployed, we can deploy our Jenkins cluster. Figure 6.25 summarizes the target architecture.

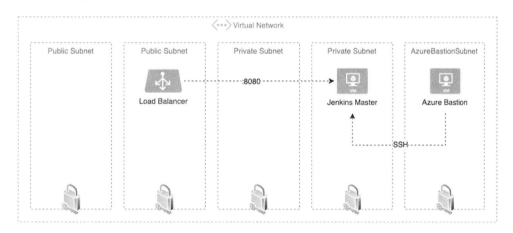

Figure 6.25   Jenkins VM inside a private subnet

Deploy a virtual machine based on the Jenkins master image built with Packer earlier. Define the resource in jenkins_master.tf with the following code.

Listing 6.24 Jenkins master virtual machine

```
data "azurerm_image" "jenkins_master_image" {
  name                = var.jenkins_master_image
  resource_group_name = data.azurerm_resource_group.management.name
}

resource "azurerm_virtual_machine" "jenkins_master" {
  name                = "jenkins-master"
  resource_group_name = data.azurerm_resource_group.management.name
  location            = var.location
  vm_size             = var.jenkins_vm_size

  network_interface_ids = [
    azurerm_network_interface.jenkins_network_interface.id,
  ]

  os_profile {
    computer_name  = var.config["os_name"]
    admin_username = var.config["vm_username"]
  }
  os_profile_linux_config {
    disable_password_authentication = true
    ssh_keys {
      path     = "/home/${var.config["vm_username"]}/.ssh/authorized_keys"
      key_data = file(var.public_ssh_key)
    }
  }

  storage_os_disk {
    name = "main"
    caching           = "ReadWrite"
    managed_disk_type = "Standard_LRS"
    create_option     = "FromImage"
    disk_size_gb      = "30"
  }

  storage_image_reference {
    id = data.azurerm_image.jenkins_master_image.i
  }
  delete_os_disk_on_termination = true
}
```

Disables password authentication and enables SSH as an authentication mechanism

Specifies the type of managed disk that should be created. Possible values are Standard_LRS, StandardSSD_LRS, or Premium_LRS.

Provisions the VM from the baked Jenkins master image

Deletes the OS disk automatically when deleting the VM

NOTE We allowed 30 GB as the disk size for the virtual machine. Jenkins needs some disk space to perform builds and keep archives and build logs.

SSH key data is provided in the ssh_key section, and the username is provided in the os_profile section with password authentication disabled.

The Jenkins virtual machine uses the B-Series Azure VM family with burstable CPU performances. This VM family provides the right balance between computing and network bandwidth. I recommend selecting your VM family type based on your project build needs and requirements.

Listing 6.24 created a VM named `jenkins-master`, and now we'll attach the virtual network interface, as shown in the following listing.

Listing 6.25 Jenkins VM network configuration

```
data "azurerm_subnet" "private_subnet" {
  name                 = var.subnets[2].name
  virtual_network_name = azurerm_virtual_network.management.name
  resource_group_name  = data.azurerm_resource_group.management.name
  depends_on = [azurerm_virtual_network.management]
}

resource "azurerm_network_interface" "jenkins_network_interface" {
  name                = "jenkins_network_interface"
  location            = var.location
  resource_group_name = data.azurerm_resource_group.management.name
  depends_on = [azurerm_virtual_network.management]

  ip_configuration {
    name                          = "internal"
    subnet_id                     = data.azurerm_subnet.private_subnet.id
    private_ip_address_allocation = "Dynamic"
  }
}
```

> **Deploys the Jenkins master instance in a private subnet and assigns a dynamic private IP address**

The virtual network interface connects the Jenkins master to the private network subnet.

Once you provide the needed Terraform variables in variables.tfvars, issue `terraform apply`. Creating the Jenkins VM, shown in figure 6.26, from your Packer image and the expected resources takes a few minutes.

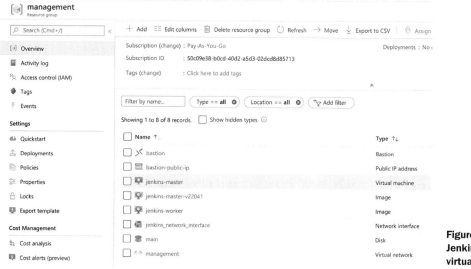

Figure 6.26 Jenkins master virtual machine

The Jenkins virtual machine should be accessible through a Bastion host only. Figure 6.27 confirms that the machine was deployed within a private subnet.

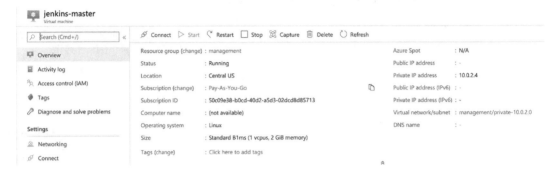

Figure 6.27   Jenkins master deployed in a private subnet

However, to access the Jenkins dashboard, we will deploy a load balancer in front of the VM. Create a loadbalancers.tf file on which you define an Azure load balancer and a security rule to serve the Jenkins dashboard and attach it to a public IP address, as shown in the following listing.

Listing 6.26   Jenkins dashboard load balancer configuration

```
resource "azurerm_public_ip" "jenkins_lb_public_ip" {
  name                = "jenkins-lb-public-ip"
  location            = var.location
  resource_group_name = data.azurerm_resource_group.management.name
  allocation_method   = "Static"
}
resource "azurerm_lb" "jenkins_lb" {                          Associates a public IP
  name                = "jenkins-lb"                          address to the load balancer
  location            = var.location
  resource_group_name = data.azurerm_resource_group.management.name

  frontend_ip_configuration {
    name                 = "publicIPAddress"
    public_ip_address_id = azurerm_public_ip.jenkins_lb_public_ip.id
  }
}
resource "azurerm_lb_rule" "jenkins_lb_rule" {
  name = "jenkins-lb-rule"
  resource_group_name = data.azurerm_resource_group.management.name
  protocol = "tcp"                        The load balancer listens on port
  enable_floating_ip = false              80 for incoming requests and
  probe_id = azurerm_lb_probe.jenkins_lb_probe.id    communicates with the Jenkins
  loadbalancer_id = azurerm_lb.jenkins_lb.id         master instance through port 8080.
  backend_address_pool_id = azurerm_lb_backend_address_pool
```

```
.jenkins_backend.id
  frontend_ip_configuration_name = "publicIPAddress"
  frontend_port = 80
  backend_port = 8080
}
```

> The load balancer listens on port 80 for incoming requests and communicates with the Jenkins master instance through port 8080.

Within the same file, define an Azure backend address pool and assign it to the load balancer. Then set a health check on port 8080, as shown in the following listing.

Listing 6.27 Jenkins dashboard health check

```
resource "azurerm_lb_backend_address_pool" "jenkins_backend" {
 resource_group_name = data.azurerm_resource_group.management.name
 loadbalancer_id      = azurerm_lb.jenkins_lb.id
 name                 = "jenkins-backend"
}
resource "azurerm_lb_probe" "jenkins_lb_probe" {
  resource_group_name = data.azurerm_resource_group.management.name
  loadbalancer_id      = azurerm_lb.jenkins_lb.id
  name                 = "jenkins-lb-probe"
  protocol             = "Http"
  request_path         = "/"
  port                 = 8080
}
```

> The URI used for requesting health status from the backend endpoint

> Port on which the probe queries the backend endpoint

Azure allows for opening ports to traffic via security groups, which can also be managed in the Terraform configuration. Add the following to security_groups.tf and proceed to run `plan/apply` to create the security rule to allow inbound traffic on port 8080 and SSH traffic on TCP port 22.

Listing 6.28 Jenkins master security group

```
resource "azurerm_network_security_group" "jenkins_security_group" {
  name            = "jenkins-sg"
  location        = var.location
  resource_group_name   = data.azurerm_resource_group.management.name

  security_rule {
    name              = "AllowSSH"
    priority          = 100
    direction         = "Inbound"
    access            = "Allow"
    protocol          = "Tcp"
    source_port_range        = "*"
    destination_port_range   = "22"
    source_address_prefix    = "*"
    destination_address_prefix  = "*"
  }
```

> Allows inbound traffic on port 22 (SSH) from anywhere

```
  security_rule {
    name            = "AllowHTTP"
    priority        = 200
    direction       = "Inbound"
    access          = "Allow"
    protocol        = "Tcp"
    source_port_range          = "*"
    destination_port_range     = "8080"
    source_address_prefix      = "Internet"
    destination_address_prefix = "*"
  }
}
```

Allows inbound traffic on port 8080, where the Jenkins web dashboard is served

Finally, assign the security group to the virtual network interface attached to the Jenkins master virtual machine, as shown in the following listing.

Listing 6.29   Jenkins network interface configuration

```
resource "azurerm_network_interface" "jenkins_network_interface" {
  name                = "jenkins_network_interface"
  location            = var.location
  resource_group_name = data.azurerm_resource_group.management.name
  network_security_group_id =
      azurerm_network_security_group.jenkins_security_group.id
  depends_on = [azurerm_virtual_network.management]

  ip_configuration {
    name                        = "internal"
    subnet_id                   = data.azurerm_subnet.private_subnet.id
    private_ip_address_allocation = "Dynamic"
    load_balancer_backend_address_pools_ids =
    [azurerm_lb_backend_address_pool.jenkins_backend.id]
  }
}
```

Assigns the Jenkins security group to the virtual network interface configured in a private subnet

Apply the changes with the `terraform apply` command. Once Terraform completes, your load balancer is ready. Obtain its public IP address from outputs.tf by adding the following code.

Listing 6.30   Jenkins master firewall and traffic control

```
output "jenkins" {
    value = azurerm_public_ip.jenkins_lb_public_ip.ip_address
}
```

Let's verify the resources by using the Azure portal. As you can see in figure 6.28, Terraform created all the expected resources under the `management` resource group.

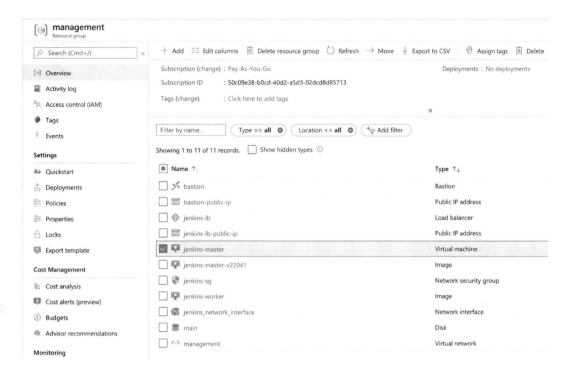

Figure 6.28   Public load balancer pointing to Jenkins master VM

Now point your web browser to the public IP address of the load balancer in the address bar. The default Jenkins home page will be displayed, as shown in figure 6.29.

Figure 6.29   Jenkins dashboard accessible from LB public IP address

You can now sign in with admin credentials defined in the Groovy init scripts while baking the Jenkins master machine image.

6.2.4   *Applying autoscaling to Jenkins workers*

We're ready to deploy Jenkins workers to offload build projects from the master. The workers will be deployed inside an autoscaling set to be provisioned dynamically. Figure 6.30 illustrates the target deployment architecture.

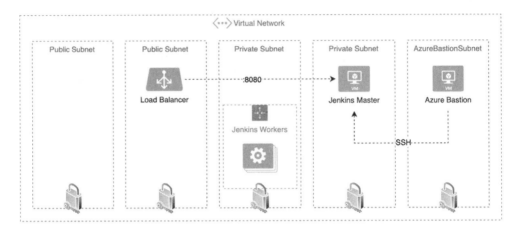

Figure 6.30   Jenkins workers scale set

We need to deploy Jenkins worker machines inside a machine scale set. A Jenkins worker will be based on the Jenkins worker image built earlier with Packer and will be deployed inside a private subnet. Create jenkins_workers.tf with the following content.

Listing 6.31   Jenkins worker machine scale set

```
data "azurerm_image" "jenkins_worker_image" {          References the Jenkins
  name                = var.jenkins_worker_image        worker machine image ID
  resource_group_name = data.azurerm_resource_group.management.name
}
resource "azurerm_virtual_machine_scale_set" "jenkins_workers_set" {
  name                = "jenkins-workers-set"
  location            = var.location
  resource_group_name = data.azurerm_resource_group.management.name
  upgrade_policy_mode = "Manual"
  sku {
    name     = var.jenkins_vm_size
    tier     = "Standard"
    capacity = 2
  }
  storage_profile_image_reference {
    id = data.azurerm_image.jenkins_worker_image.id
  }
  storage_profile_os_disk {
    caching       = "ReadWrite"
    create_option = "FromImage"
```

```
      managed_disk_type = "Standard_LRS"
  }
  os_profile {                                  Disables password authentication
    computer_name_prefix = "jenkins-worker"     and configures the SSH credentials
    admin_username = var.config["vm_username"]
    custom_data = data.template_file.jenkins_worker_startup_script.rendered
  }
  os_profile_linux_config {
    disable_password_authentication = true
    ssh_keys {
      path     = "/home/${var.config["vm_username"]}/.ssh/authorized_keys"
      key_data = file(var.public_ssh_key)
    }
  }
  network_profile {
    name    = "private-network"            Assigns a security group to the VM instances
    primary = true                         and requests private IP addresses
    network_security_group_id =
     azurerm_network_security_group.jenkins_worker_security_group.id
    ip_configuration {
      name = "private-ip-configuration"
      primary = true
      subnet_id = data.azurerm_subnet.private_subnet.id
    }
  }
}
```

NOTE You should test your projects on multiple Azure VM family types to determine the appropriate machine type for Jenkins workers, as well as the amount of disk space.

Each Jenkins worker machine will execute a custom script (chapter6/azure/terraform/scripts/join-cluster.tpl) at runtime to join the Jenkins cluster; see the following listing.

Listing 6.32 Jenkins workers launch script

```
data "template_file" "jenkins_worker_startup_script" {
  template = "${file("scripts/join-cluster.tpl")}"      ◄─┐  Initialization script
                                                           │  to autojoin the VM as
  vars = {                                                 │  a Jenkins agent
    jenkins_url              = "http://
      ${azurerm_public_ip.jenkins_lb_public_ip.ip_address}:8080"
    jenkins_username        = var.jenkins_username
    jenkins_password        = var.jenkins_password
    jenkins_credentials_id  = var.jenkins_credentials_id
  }
}
```

The script will use Azure Instance Metadata Service (IMDS) to fetch information regarding the machine's private IP address and hostname and will issue a POST HTTP request to the Jenkins RESTful API to establish a bidirectional connection with the machine and join the cluster:

```
INSTANCE_NAME=$(curl -s http://169.254.169.254/metadata/instance/compute/name
?api-version=2019-06-01&format=text)
INSTANCE_IP=$(curl -s http://169.254.169.254/metadata/instance/network/
    interface/0/ipv4/ipAddress/0/privateIpAddress
?api-version=2017-08-01&format=text)
```

A security group will be attached to the virtual network interface attached to the scale set. It allows inbound traffic on port 22 (SSH), as shown in the following listing.

Listing 6.33   Jenkins worker security group

```
resource "azurerm_network_security_group" "jenkins_worker_security_group" {
  name        = "jenkins-worker-sg"
  location    = var.location
  resource_group_name    = data.azurerm_resource_group.management.name
  security_rule {
    name       = "AllowSSH"
    priority   = 100
    direction  = "Inbound"
    access     = "Allow"
    protocol   = "Tcp"
    source_port_range           = "*"
    destination_port_range      = "22"
    source_address_prefix       = "*"
    destination_address_prefix  = "*"
  }
}
```

Allows incoming traffic on port 22 (SSH) from anywhere. It's recommended to restrict the access to your network CIDR block.

Once the deployment has completed, the content of the resource group resembles that shown in figure 6.31.

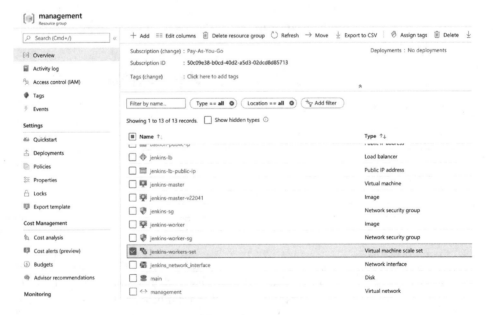

Figure 6.31   Jenkins worker virtual machine scale set

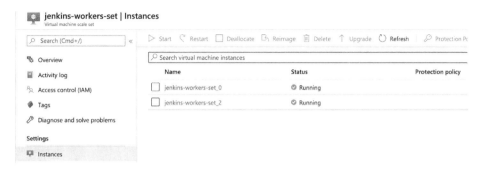

Figure 6.32 Static number of Jenkins workers

By default, two Jenkins workers will be up and running, as shown in figure 6.32.

To be able to scale workers based on build jobs and pipeline running, we will use Azure autoscale policies to trigger a scale-out or scale-in based on CPU utilization of the worker machines. Within jenkins_workers.tf, add the following `resource` block.

Listing 6.34 Jenkins worker autoscaling policies

```
resource "azurerm_monitor_autoscale_setting" "jenkins_workers_autoscale" {
  name                 = "jenkins-workers-autoscale"
  resource_group_name  = data.azurerm_resource_group.management.name
  location             = var.location
  target_resource_id   =
    azurerm_virtual_machine_scale_set.jenkins_workers_set.id

  profile {
    name = "jenkins-autoscale"
    capacity {
      default = 2
      minimum = 2          Defines the minimum and maximum
      maximum = 10         numbers of Jenkins workers
    }
    rule {
      metric_trigger {
        metric_name       = "Percentage CPU"
        metric_resource_id =
      azurerm_virtual_machine_scale_set.jenkins_workers_set.id
        time_grain        = "PT1M"          Monitors the CPU
        statistic         = "Average"       utilization of the
        time_window       = "PT5M"          workers—if it
        time_aggregation  = "Average"       hits 80%, a new
        operator          = "GreaterThan"   Jenkins worker's
        threshold         = 80              VM will be
      }                                     deployed.
      scale_action {
        direction = "Increase"
        type      = "ChangeCount"
        value     = "1"
        cooldown  = "PT1M"
      }
    }
  }
```

```
rule {
  metric_trigger {
    metric_name        = "Percentage CPU"
    metric_resource_id =
  azurerm_virtual_machine_scale_set.jenkins_workers_set.id
    time_grain         = "PT1M"
    statistic          = "Average"
    time_window        = "PT5M"
    time_aggregation   = "Average"
    operator           = "LessThan"
    threshold          = 20
  }

  scale_action {
    direction = "Decrease"
    type      = "ChangeCount"
    value     = "1"
    cooldown  = "PT1M"
  }
}
}
}
```

> **Monitors the CPU utilization of the workers—if it's below 20%, an existing Jenkins worker VM will be terminated.**

Apply the changes with `terraform apply`. Then, head over to the Jenkins worker scale set configuration. In the Scaling section, define a new autoscale policy, as shown in figure 6.33.

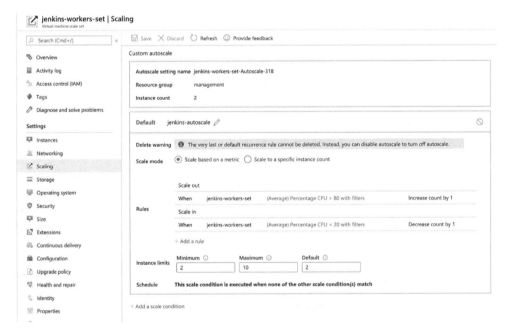

Figure 6.33   Jenkins worker autoscaling policies

NOTE Once you're finished playing with the Jenkins cluster, you will likely want to tear down everything that was created so that you don't incur any further costs.

Great! You are now able to deploy a self-healing Jenkins cluster on Microsoft Azure.

6.3 *DigitalOcean*

When we think of cloud computing providers, we are typically referring to the three giants in the industry: Azure, Google Cloud, and AWS. Unlike those providers that are known to everyone, DigitalOcean (www.digitalocean.com) is relatively new. You might be wondering why you should choose DigitalOcean over other providers. The reason lies in the differences between the three big players and DigitalOcean.

They differ in many aspects. One is small, while the others (AWS, GCP, and Azure) are huge. DigitalOcean provides virtual machines (called *Droplets*). There are no bells and whistles. You do not get lost in a catalog of services, since they are almost nonexistent. Plus, DigitalOcean's interface allows developers to quickly set up machines because of its friendly design. Moreover, it's affordable and has cheaper instances, which is a good starting point for beginner businesses and startups. (If you don't have a DigitalOcean account, you will need to create one; you will get $100 of free credits.)

To use Packer with DigitalOcean, we first need to generate a DigitalOcean API token. This can be done on the DigitalOcean Applications & API page. Click the Generate New Token button to obtain a token with read and write permissions, as shown in figure 6.34.

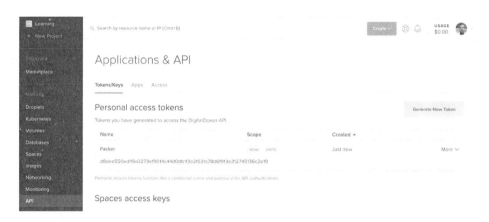

Figure 6.34 Packer API access token

6.3.1 *Creating Jenkins DigitalOcean Snapshots*

We're using the same template covered in listings 6.1 and 6.2; the only difference is the use of the `digitalocean` Packer builder to interact with the DigitalOcean API. The builder takes a CentOS source image and runs the provisioning necessary—installing the tools required for building Jenkins jobs on the image after launching it—and then snapshots it into a reusable image; see the following listing. This reusable image can then be used as the foundation of new Jenkins workers that are launched within Digital-Ocean by using Terraform.

Listing 6.35   Jenkins worker image with DigitalOcean builder

```
{
    "variables" : {
        "api_token" : "DIGITALOCEAN API TOKEN",          │ DigitalOcean API token
        "region": "DIGITALOCEAN REGION"                  │ and target region
    },
    "builders" : [
        {
            "type": "digitalocean",
            "api_token": "{{user `api_token`}}",
            "image": "centos-8-x64",            ◁─── The build Droplet will
            "region": "{{user `region`}}",           be based on CentOS 8.
            "size": "512mb",
            "ssh_username": "root",
            "snapshot_name": "jenkins-worker"
        }
    ],
    "provisioners" : [
        {
            "type" : "shell",
            "script" : "./setup.sh",
            "execute_command" : "sudo -E -S sh '{{ .Path }}'"
        }
    ]
}
```

Include your DigitalOcean API token and target region (refer to the official documentation for a list of supported regions: http://mng.bz/EDRJ). Then run the `packer build template.json` command. You'll get a working Jenkins worker image in your DigitalOcean account in a couple of minutes, as shown in figure 6.35.

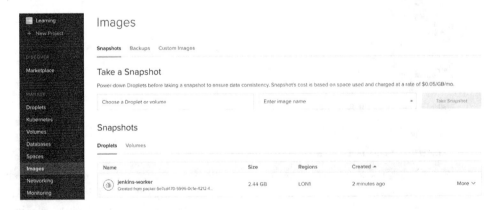

Figure 6.35   Jenkins worker image snapshot

Similarly, update the Jenkins master template referenced in listing 6.2 to use the `digitalocean` builder. The provisioning part creates a Jenkins credential based on a private SSH key used to deploy Jenkins workers. This is needed, as Jenkins needs to set up a bidirectional connection with workers via SSH.

> **Listing 6.36   Jenkins master image with DigitalOcean builder**

```
{
    "variables" : {
        "api_token" : "DIGITALOCEAN API TOKEN",
        "region": "DIGITALOCEAN REGION",
        "ssh_key" : "PRIVATE SSH KEY FILE"
    },
    "builders" : [
        {
            "type": "digitalocean",
            "api_token": "{{user `api_token`}}",
            "image": "centos-8-x64",
            "region": "{{user `region`}}",
            "size": "2gb",
            "ssh_username": "root",
            "snapshot_name": "jenkins-master-2.204.1"
        }
    ],
    "provisioners" : [
        ...
    ]
}
```

This template has been cropped for brevity. The full JSON file can be downloaded from chapter6/digitalocean/packer/master/template.json.

Run the `packer validate` command to make sure that everything is copacetic. Then issue a `packer build` command. Once the build and provisioning part is finished, the Jenkins master snapshot should be ready to be used, as shown in figure 6.36.

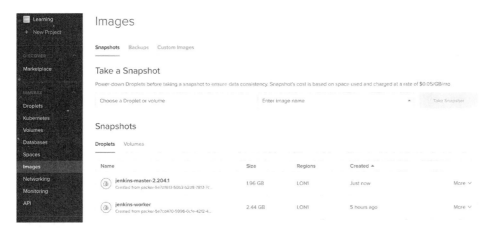

Figure 6.36   Jenkins master image snapshot

6.3.2   *Deploying a Jenkins master Droplet*

In this step, you'll write Terraform template files for automating Jenkins cluster Droplet deployments of the snapshot containing the Jenkins master and worker you just built using Packer.

Define a terraform.tf file and declare DigitalOcean as a provider. The provider needs to be configured with the proper API token before it can be used, as shown in the following listing.

Listing 6.37   Defining the DigitalOcean provider

```
provider "digitalocean" {
  token = var.token
}
```

Run `terraform init` to download the DigitalOcean plugin needed to translate the Terraform instructions into API calls:

```
Initializing the backend...

Initializing provider plugins...
- Checking for available provider plugins...
- Downloading plugin for provider "digitalocean" (terraform-providers/digitalocean) 1.15.1...

The following providers do not have any version constraints in configuration,
so the latest version was installed.

To prevent automatic upgrades to new major versions that may contain breaking
changes, it is recommended to add version = "..." constraints to the
corresponding provider blocks in configuration, with the constraint strings
suggested below.

* provider.digitalocean: version = "~> 1.15"

Terraform has been successfully initialized!
```

Define a single resource of the type `digitalocean_droplet` named `jenkins-master` in the jenkins_master.tf file, as shown in Listing 6.38. Then set its parameters according to the variable values and add an SSH key (using its fingerprint) from your DigitalOcean account to the Droplet resource. The deployed Droplet will be of type `s-1vcpu-2gb`, which comes up with 1 GB of RAM and 1vCPU.

For heavier workloads and larger projects, and to handle concurrent users connecting to the Jenkins web dashboard, a large Droplet type might be required. Refer to the official documentation for the list of available Droplet sizes: http://mng.bz/N4yD.

Listing 6.38   Jenkins master Droplet

```
data "digitalocean_image" "jenkins_master_image" {
  name = var.jenkins_master_image
}
```

```
resource "digitalocean_droplet" "jenkins_master" {
  name    = "jenkins-master"
  image   = data.digitalocean_image.jenkins_master_image.id
  region  = var.region
  size    = "s-1vcpu-2gb"
  ssh_keys = [var.ssh_fingerprint]
}
```

Uses the Jenkins master image backed previously with Packer

Provisions a Droplet with 2 GB of RAM and 1vCPU

On DigitalOcean, you can upload your SSH public key to your account, which lets you add it to your Droplets at creation time (figure 6.37). This lets you log in to your Jenkins master without a password while still remaining secure.

Figure 6.37   Adding a public SSH key

Next, attach a firewall to the Jenkins master Droplet with rules allowing inbound traffic on port 22 and 8080 from anywhere; see the following listing. For security purposes, I recommend limiting SSH incoming traffic to your CIDR network block.

Listing 6.39   Jenkins master Droplet's firewall

```
resource "digitalocean_firewall" "jenkins_master_firewall" {
  name = "jenkins-master-firewall"

  droplet_ids = [digitalocean_droplet.jenkins_master.id]

  inbound_rule {
    protocol        = "tcp"
    port_range      = "22"
    source_addresses = ["0.0.0.0/0", "::/0"]
  }

  inbound_rule {
    protocol        = "tcp"
    port_range      = "8080"
    source_addresses = ["0.0.0.0/0", "::/0"]
  }
```

Allows inbound traffic on port 22 (SSH) from anywhere

Allows inbound traffic on port 8080, where the Jenkins web dashboard is served from

```
outbound_rule {
  protocol              = "tcp"
  port_range            = "1-65535"
  destination_addresses = ["0.0.0.0/0", "::/0"]
}

outbound_rule {
  protocol              = "udp"                          Allows outbound traffic on
  port_range            = "1-65535"                      all ports from anywhere
  destination_addresses = ["0.0.0.0/0", "::/0"]
}

outbound_rule {
  protocol              = "icmp"
  destination_addresses = ["0.0.0.0/0", "::/0"]
}
}
```

Paste the following code to the outputs.tf file to display the IP address of the Jenkins master Droplet when the deployment is complete.

Listing 6.40   Jenkins master public IP address

```
output "master" {
  value = digitalocean_droplet.jenkins_master.ipv4_address
}
```

Define the Terraform variables listed in table 6.3 in a new variable.tf file. Set their values in variables.tfvars to keep secrets and sensitive information out of template files.

Table 6.3   DigitalOcean Terraform variables

Name	Type	Value	Description
token	String	None	This is the DigitalOcean API token. Alternatively, this can also be specified using DIGITALOCEAN_TOKEN environment variables.
region	String	None	The DigitalOcean region in which deploy the Jenkins master.
jenkins_master_image	String	None	The name of the Jenkins master image that was built previously with Packer.
ssh_fingerprint	String	None	SSH ID or fingerprint. To retrieve the info, head to the DigitalOcean Security dashboard.

Run the `terraform plan` command to see the effect of the deployment before execution:

```
# digitalocean_droplet.jenkins_master will be created
+ resource "digitalocean_droplet" "jenkins_master" {
    + backups            = false
    + created_at         = (known after apply)
    + disk               = (known after apply)
    + id                 = (known after apply)
    + image              = "61197862"
    + ipv4_address       = (known after apply)
    + ipv4_address_private = (known after apply)
    + ipv6               = false
    + ipv6_address       = (known after apply)
    + ipv6_address_private = (known after apply)
    + locked             = (known after apply)
    + memory             = (known after apply)
    + monitoring         = false
    + name               = "jenkins-master"
    + price_hourly       = (known after apply)
    + price_monthly      = (known after apply)
    + private_networking = false
    + region             = "lon1"
    + resize_disk        = true
    + size               = "s-1vcpu-2gb"
    + ssh_keys           = [
        + "87:3d:be:dd:2a:1f:31:2f:55:db:2e:34:9e:59:a0:cd",
      ]
    + status             = (known after apply)
    + urn                = (known after apply)
    + vcpus              = (known after apply)
    + volume_ids         = (known after apply)
  }

Plan: 1 to add, 0 to change, 0 to destroy.
```

You can now move on to validating and deploying it on a Droplet with a `terraform apply` command. The deployment process should take a few seconds to finish. Then a new Jenkins master Droplet will be available in the Droplets console, and Terraform should display the IP address of the Jenkins master Droplet, as you can see in figure 6.38.

Figure 6.38 Jenkins master Droplet

Open your favorite browser and connect to the public IPv4 that was returned by the previous command. A preconfigured Jenkins dashboard should be displayed; see figure 6.39.

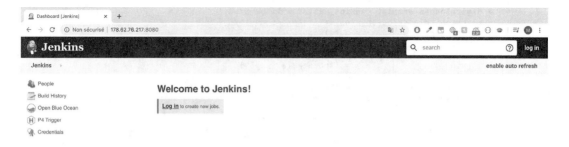

Figure 6.39   Jenkins dashboard access with Droplet public IP

6.3.3   *Building Jenkins worker Droplets*

Now to delegate build jobs to workers and offload the Jenkins master Droplet. Several build workers will be deployed to absorb the build activity.

Create a jenkins_workers.tf file where you define Jenkins worker Droplets. The workers will be launched from the Jenkins worker image.

> **Listing 6.41   Jenkins worker Droplets**

```
data "digitalocean_image" "jenkins_worker_image" {
  name = var.jenkins_worker_image
}

data "template_file" "jenkins_worker_startup_script" {
  template = "${file("scripts/join-cluster.tpl")}"

  vars = {
    jenkins_url           = "http://
      ${digitalocean_droplet.jenkins_master.ipv4_address}:8080"
    jenkins_username      = var.jenkins_username
    jenkins_password      = var.jenkins_password
    jenkins_credentials_id = var.jenkins_credentials_id
  }
}
resource "digitalocean_droplet" "jenkins_workers" {
  count = var.jenkins_workers_count
  name  = "jenkins-worker"
  image = data.digitalocean_image.jenkins_worker_image.id
  region = var.region
  size  = "s-1vcpu-2gb"
  ssh_keys = [var.ssh_fingerprint]
  user_data = data.template_file.jenkins_worker_startup_script.rendered
  depends_on = [digitalocean_droplet.jenkins_master]
}
```

The script is used to make the Droplet autojoin the cluster as a Jenkins agent/worker.

Indicates the number of Jenkins workers to create

In this Droplet configuration, we're using 1 GB of RAM and 1vCPU as configuration for Jenkins workers.

The launch script is passed in the user_data section so it can be executed the first time the Droplet is running.

The count variable is used to define the number of workers to deploy. Each Droplet will execute a shell script at startup. This script is similar to the one provided in previous sections, except for the use of the DigitalOcean metadata server to fetch the Droplet IP address and hostname:

```
INSTANCE_NAME=$(curl -s http://169.254.169.254/metadata/v1/hostname)
INSTANCE_IP=$(curl -s http://169.254.169.254/metadata/v1/
interfaces/public/0/ipv4/address)
```

Finally, to set up a bidirectional connection between Jenkins master and workers, we define a firewall allowing inbound traffic on TCP port 22.

Listing 6.42 Jenkins worker firewall

```
resource "digitalocean_firewall" "jenkins_workers_firewall" {
  name = "jenkins-workers-firewall"

  droplet_ids =
[for worker in digitalocean_droplet.jenkins_workers : worker.id   ]

  inbound_rule {
    protocol          = "tcp"
    port_range        = "22"
    source_droplet_ids = [digitalocean_droplet.jenkins_master.id]
  }
}
```

Allows the Jenkins master to SSH to the Jenkins workers

After a few minutes, the workers' Droplets will finish provisioning, and you'll see output similar to figure 6.40.

Figure 6.40 Jenkins worker Droplets

Go back to the Jenkins dashboard. The new deployed workers should join the cluster after executing the user data script covered in chapter 5's listing 5.7; see figure 6.41.

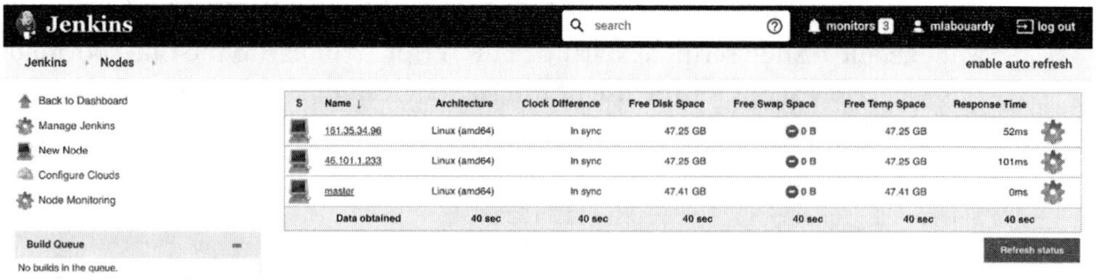

Figure 6.41   Worker Droplets joining the cluster

You can take this architecture further by deploying a load balancer in front of the Jenkins master Droplet to forward traffic to port 8080 and creating a DNS record pointing to the load balancer FQDN; see figure 6.42.

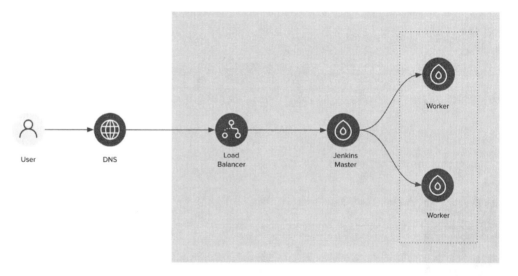

Figure 6.42   Jenkins cluster architecture on DigitalOcean

When you're finished, clean up the infrastructure by running the following:

```
terraform destroy --var-file=variables.tfvars
```

This chapter has covered how to deploy and operate a resilient and self-healing Jenkins cluster from scratch on numerous cloud providers with IaC tools. I've also explained how to architect Jenkins workers for scale with autoscaling policies and metrics alarms. In the next chapter, we will implement pipelines as code on Jenkins for numerous cloud-native applications such as Dockerized microservices and serverless applications.

Summary

- The power of Packer comes from leveraging template files to create identical Jenkins machine images independently of the target platform.
- Deploying Jenkins on Google Cloud Platform comes with seamless native support for Kubernetes.
- Azure offers a variety of cloud-based services and might be a good alternative for running Jenkins on the cloud.
- Running Jenkins on DigitalOcean can be a cost-efficient solution for beginner businesses and startups.

Part 3

Hands-on CI/CD pipelines

You've smashed through parts 1 and 2 but you're still hungry for more. I understand. Thankfully, this part is designed to give you a lot to chew on.

You'll implement CI/CD workflows for real-world, cloud-native applications. In the next few chapters, you'll run automated tests with Docker, analyze your Docker images for security vulnerabilities, and deploy containerized microservices on Docker Swarm and Kubernetes. You'll learn how to automate the deployment process for your serverless applications. This is just a tiny glimpse, so roll up your sleeves and let's dive into this!

7

Defining a pipeline as code for microservices

This chapter covers

- Using a Jenkins multibranch pipeline plugin and GitFlow model
- Defining multibranch pipelines for containerized microservices
- Triggering a Jenkins job on push events using GitHub webhooks
- Exporting Jenkins jobs configuration as XML and cloning Jenkins jobs

The previous chapters covered how to deploy a Jenkins cluster on multiple cloud providers by using automation tools: HashiCorp Packer and Terraform. In this chapter, we will define a continuous integration (CI) pipeline for Dockerized microservices.

In chapter 1, you learned that CI is continuously testing and building all changes of the source code before integrating them into the central repository. Figure 7.1 summarizes the stages in this workflow.

Continuous integration

Figure 7.1   Continuous integration stages

Every change to the source code triggers the CI pipeline, which launches the auto-mated tests. This comes with many benefits:

- Detecting bugs and issues earlier, which results in a dramatic decrease in main-tenance time and costs
- Ensuring that the codebase continues to work and meets the spec requirements as the system grows
- Improving team velocity by establishing a fast-feedback loop

While automated tests come with multiple benefits, they're extremely time-consuming to implement and execute. Therefore, we will use a testing framework based on the target service runtime and requirements.

Once tests are successful, the source code is compiled and an artifact is built. Then it will be packaged and stored in a remote registry for version control and deployment later.

Chapter 8 covers how to write a classic CI pipeline for containerized microservices. The end result will look like the CI pipeline in figure 7.2.

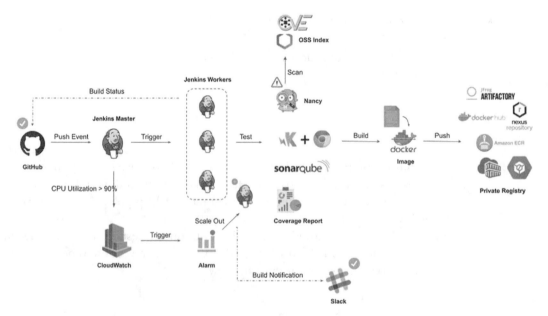

Figure 7.2   Target CI pipeline

These steps cover the most basic flow of a continuous integration process. In the following chapters, once you are comfortable with this workflow, we'll go even further. We'll start by creating our multibranch pipeline from scratch with Jenkins and continuously running pipelines with GitHub webhooks.

7.1 *Introducing microservices-based applications*

It can be challenging to create a reliable CI/CD process for a microservices architecture. The goal of the pipeline is to allow teams to build and deploy their services quickly and independently, without disrupting other teams or destabilizing the application as a whole.

To illustrate how to define a CI/CD pipeline from scratch for containerized microservices, I have implemented a simple web application based on a microservices architecture. We are going to integrate and deploy a web-based application called Watchlist, where users can browse the top 100 greatest movies of all time and add them to their watching list.

The project includes tests, benchmarks, and everything needed to run the application locally and on the cloud. The deployed application will look like figure 7.3.

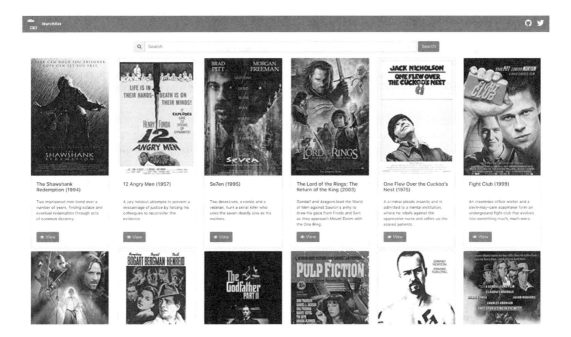

Figure 7.3   Watchlist marketplace UI

Figure 7.4 illustrates the application architecture and flow.

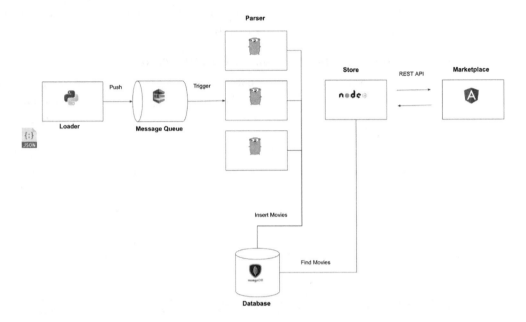

Figure 7.4   The Loader service takes an array of movies in JSON format and forwards them one by one to a message queue (for example, Amazon SQS). From there, a Parser service will consume the items and fetch the movie's details from the IMDb database and save the result into MongoDB. Finally, the data is served through a RESTful API by the Store service and visualized with the Marketplace UI.

NOTE   *Amazon Simple Queue Service* (SQS) is a distributed message queuing service. It is intended to provide a highly scalable managed message queue to resolve issues arising from producer-consumer problems and to decouple distributed application services. See https://aws.amazon.com/sqs/ for more details.

The architecture is composed of multiple services written in different languages to illustrate the advantages of the microservices paradigm and the use of Jenkins to automate the build and deployment process of different runtime environments. Table 7.1 lists the microservices.

Table 7.1   Application microservices

Service	Language	Description
Loader	Python	Responsible for reading a JSON file containing a list of movies and pushing each movie item to Amazon SQS.
Parser	Golang	Responsible for consuming movies by subscribing to SQS and scraping movie information from the IMDb website (www.imdb.com) and storing the metadata (movie's name, cover, description, and so forth) into MongoDB.

Table 7.1 Application microservices *(continued)*

Service	Language	Description
Store	Node.js	Responsible for serving a RESTful API with endpoints to fetch a list of movies and insert new movies into the watch list database in the MongoDB server.
Marketplace	Angular and TypeScript	Responsible for serving a frontend to browse movies by calling the Store RESTful API.

Before we dig deeper into the CI workflow for the application, let's see how the distributed application source code will be organized. When you start moving to microservices, one of the big challenges you will be facing is the organization of the codebase.

Do you create a repository for each service or a single repo for all services? Each pattern has its own advantages and disadvantages:

- *Multiple repositories*—You can have multiple teams independently developing a service (clear ownership). Plus, smaller codebases are easier to maintain, test, and deploy with less team coordination. However, having independent teams might create localized knowledge across the organization and result in teams lacking an understanding of the bigger picture of the project.
- *Mono repository*—Having a single source-control repository comes with a simplified project organization with less overhead from managing project dependencies. It also improves the overall work culture when teams work on a mono repository. However, versioning might become more complicated, and performance and scalability issues may arise.

Both patterns have pros and cons, and neither is a silver bullet. You should understand their benefits and limitations, and use them to make an informed decision on what's best for you and your project.

The way you structure your codebase will impact the design of the CI/CD pipeline. Having a project hosted on a single repository might result in a single pipeline with fairly complex stages. Pipeline size and complexity are often a huge pain point. As the number of services evolves within an organization, the management of pipelines becomes a bigger issue as well. In the end, most pipelines end as a spaghetti mix of npm, pip, and Maven scripts sprinkled with some bash scripts all over the place. On the other side, adopting a multiple-repositories strategy might result in multiple pipelines to manage and code duplication. Fortunately, solutions are available to reduce pipeline management, including using shared pipeline segments and shared Groovy scripts.

> **NOTE** Chapter 14 covers how to write a shared library in Jenkins to share common code and steps across multiple pipelines.

This book illustrates how to build CI/CD pipelines for both patterns. For microservices, we will adopt the multiple repositories strategy. We will cover the mono-repo approach while building CI/CD pipelines for serverless functions.

First, create four Git repositories to store the source code for each service (Loader, Parser, Store, and Marketplace). In this book, I'm using GitHub, but any SCM system can be used, such as GitLab, Bitbucket, or even SVN. Make sure you have Git installed on the machine that you will use to perform the steps mentioned in the following section.

> **NOTE** Throughout this book, we will use the GitFlow model for branch management. For more information, read chapter 2.

Once the repositories are created, clone them to your workspace and create three main branches: develop, preprod, and master branches to help organize the code and isolate the under-development code from the one running in production. This branching strategy is a slimmer version of the GitFlow workflow branching model.

> **NOTE** The complete Jenkinsfile for each service can be found in the chapter7/ microservices folder within the book's GitHub repository.

Use the following commands to create the target branches and push them to the remote repository:

```
git clone https://github.com/mlabouardy/movies-loader.git
cd movies-loader
git checkout -b preprod
git push origin preprod
git checkout -b develop
git push origin develop
```

To view the branches in the Git repository, run this command in your terminal:

```
git branch -a
```

An asterisk (*) will be next to the branch that you're currently on (develop). Output similar to the following should be displayed in your terminal session:

```
[jenkins:movies-loader mlabouardy$ git branch -a
* develop
  preprod
  remotes/origin/develop
  remotes/origin/master
  remotes/origin/preprod
jenkins:movies-loader mlabouardy$
```

Next, copy the code from the book's GitHub repository to each Git repository on the develop branch, and then push the changes to the remote repository:

```
git add .
git commit -m "loading from json file"
git push origin develop
```

The GitHub repository should look like figure 7.5.

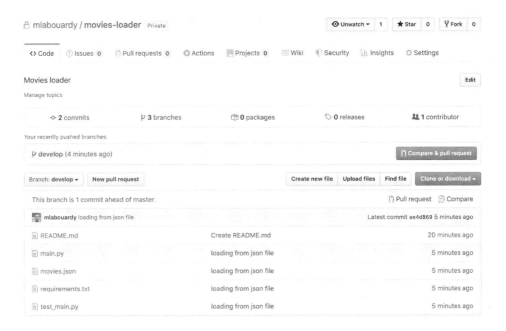

Figure 7.5   The Loader GitHub repository has the service source's code.

NOTE   For now, we push the changes directly to the develop branch. Later, you will see how to create pull requests and set up a review process with Jenkins.

The movies-loader source code is available in the chapter7/microservices/movies-loader folder. Repeat the same process to create the movies-parser, movies-store, and movies-marketplace GitHub repositories.

7.2   Defining multibranch pipeline jobs

To integrate the application source code with Jenkins, we need to create Jenkins jobs to continuously build it. Head over to Jenkins web dashboard and click the New Item button at the top-left corner, or click the Create New Jobs link to create a new job, as shown in figure 7.6.

Figure 7.6   Jenkins new job creation

NOTE   For a step-by-step guide on deploying Jenkins, refer to chapter 5.

On the resultant page, you will be presented with various types of Jenkins jobs to choose from. Enter the name of the project, scroll down, select Multibranch Pipeline, and click the OK button. The Multibranch Pipeline option allows us to automatically create a pipeline for each branch on the source-control repository.

Figure 7.7 shows the multibranch job pipeline for the movies-loader service.

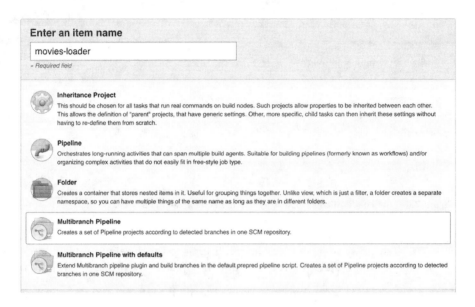

Figure 7.7   Jenkins new job settings

NOTE   The Jenkins Multibranch Pipeline plugin (https://plugins.jenkins.io/workflow-multibranch/) is installed by default on the baked Jenkins master AMI.

I'll briefly summarize the new job types here and then explain each in more detail in upcoming chapters:

- *Freestyle project*—This is a classic way of creating a Jenkins job, wherein each CI stage is represented by using UI components and forms. The job is a web-based configuration, and any modification is done through the Jenkins dashboard.
- *Inheritance project*—The purpose of this project type is to bring true inheritance of properties between multiple job definitions to Jenkins. It allows you to share common properties only once and create Jenkins jobs to inherit them across many projects.
- *Pipeline*—This job type lets you either paste a Jenkinsfile directly into the job UI or reference a single Git repository as the source and then specify a single branch where the Jenkinsfile is located. This job can be useful if you plan to use a trunk-based workflow to manage your project source code.

- *Folder*—This is a way to group multiple projects together rather than a type of project itself. This is different from the view tabs on the Jenkins dashboard, which provide just a filter. Rather, this is like a directory folder on the server, storing nested items.
- *Multibranch pipeline*—This is a type of project we will use through this book. As its name indicates, it allows us to automatically create nested jobs for each Git branch containing a Jenkinsfile.
- *Organization*—Certain source-control platforms provide a mechanism for grouping multiple repositories into organizations. This project type allows you to use a Jenkinsfile in the repositories within an organization and execute a pipeline based on the Jenkinsfile. Currently, the project type supports only GitHub and Bitbucket organizations.

NOTE The trunk-based strategy uses one central repository with a single entry (called a *trunk* or *master*) for all changes to the project.

To be clear, having these new job types available depends on having the requisite plugins installed. If you baked the Jenkins master machine image with the list of plugins provided in chapter 4's section 4.3.2, you will get all the job types discussed in the preceding list.

7.3 Git and GitHub integration

The pipeline script (Jenkinsfile) will be versioned in GitHub. Therefore, we need to configure the Jenkins job to fetch it from the remote repository.

Set a name and description in the General section. Then, select the code source from the Branch Sources section. Configure the pipeline to refer to GitHub for source-control management by selecting GitHub from the drop-down list; see figure 7.8.

Figure 7.8 Branch Sources configuration

For checkout credentials, open a new tab and go to the Jenkins dashboard. Click Credentials and then System. On the Global Credentials page, from the menu on the left, click the Add Credentials link. Next, create a new Jenkins global credential of type Username and Password to access the microservices projects in Git. The GitHub username and password can be set as shown in figure 7.9. However, it's not recommended to use a personal GitHub account.

> **NOTE**   The Jenkins Credentials plugin (https://plugins.jenkins.io/credentials/) is installed by default on the baked Jenkins master machine image. It is part of the essential plugins listed in chapter 4's section 4.3.2.

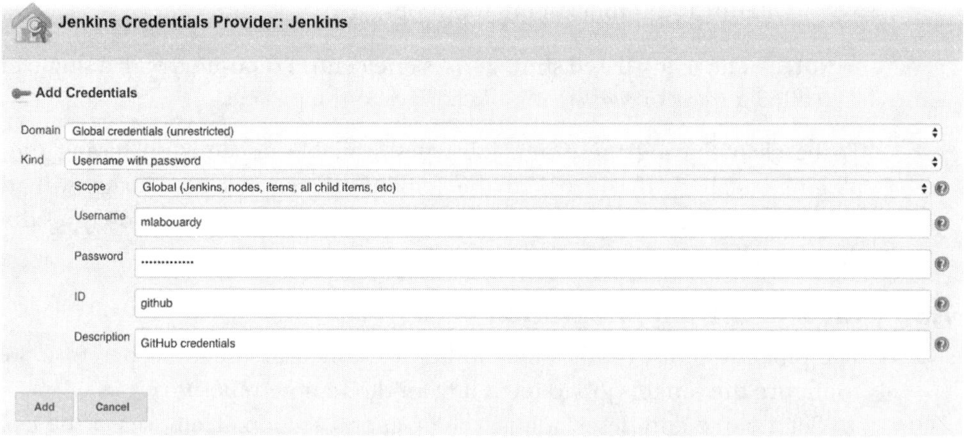

Figure 7.9   Jenkins credentials provider

Therefore, I have created a dedicated Jenkins service account on GitHub and used an access token instead of the account password. You can create the access token by signing in with the GitHub credentials and navigating to Settings. Then, from the left menu, select Developer Settings and select Personal Access Tokens, as shown in figure 7.10.

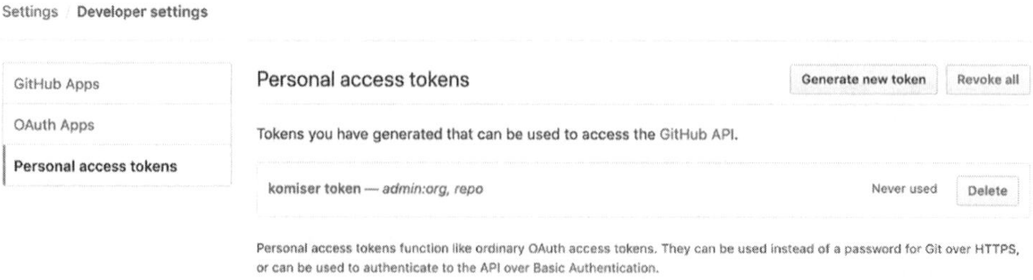

Figure 7.10   GitHub personal access tokens

Click the Generate New Token button, give a name to the access token, and select the `repo` access from the list of authorized scopes, as shown in figure 7.11. For private repositories, you must ensure that the `repo` scope is selected, and not just the `repo:status` and `public_repo` scopes. The token name is helpful, as you'll likely have many of these tokens for many applications.

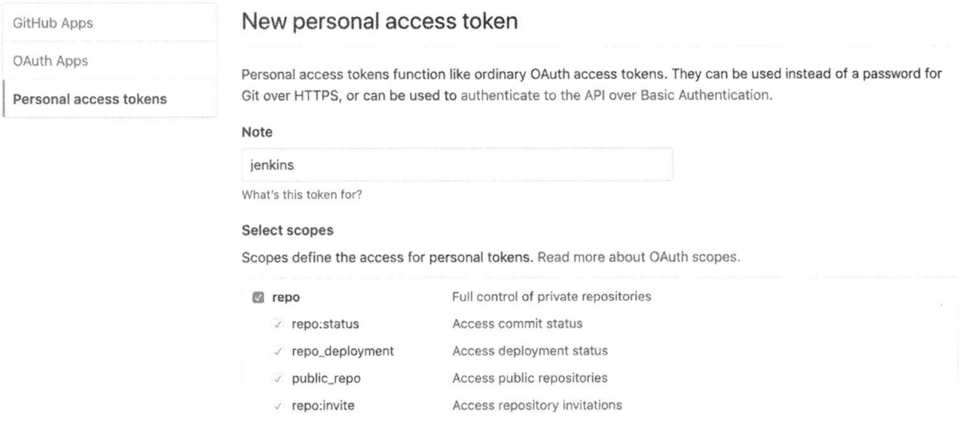

GitHub Apps	**New personal access token**	
OAuth Apps		
Personal access tokens	Personal access tokens function like ordinary OAuth access tokens. They can be used instead of a password for Git over HTTPS, or can be used to authenticate to the API over Basic Authentication.	
	Note	
	jenkins	
	What's this token for?	
	Select scopes	
	Scopes define the access for personal tokens. Read more about OAuth scopes.	
	☑ **repo**	Full control of private repositories
	✓ repo:status	Access commit status
	✓ repo_deployment	Access deployment status
	✓ public_repo	Access public repositories
	✓ repo:invite	Access repository invitations

Figure 7.11 Jenkins dedicated token for GitHub access

As the GitHub warning in figure 7.12 indicates, you must copy the token after you generate it, as you won't be able to see it again. If you fail to do so, your only recourse will be to regenerate the token.

GitHub Apps	**Personal access tokens**	Generate new token	Revoke all
OAuth Apps			
Personal access tokens	Tokens you have generated that can be used to access the GitHub API.		
	Make sure to copy your new personal access token now. You won't be able to see it again!		
	✓ dfffd29cec2845dd080a2e6ea322f2f8ee8e3ab3 📋		Delete
	komiser token — *admin:org, repo*	Never used	Delete

Figure 7.12 Jenkins personal access token

Paste in the GitHub personal access token to the Password field. Give a unique ID to your GitHub credentials by typing a string in the ID field and add a meaningful description to the Description field, as shown in figure 7.13. Then click the Save button.

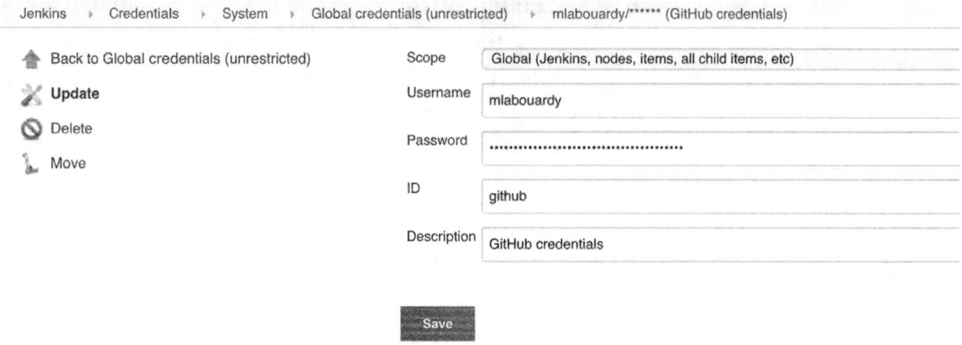

Figure 7.13   GitHub credentials configuration on Jenkins

Go back to the job configuration tab, shown in figure 7.14, and select the credentials you created from the Credentials drop-down list. Set the repository HTTPS clone URL and set the discovering behavior to allow scanning of all repository branches. Then, scroll all the way down and click the Apply and Save buttons.

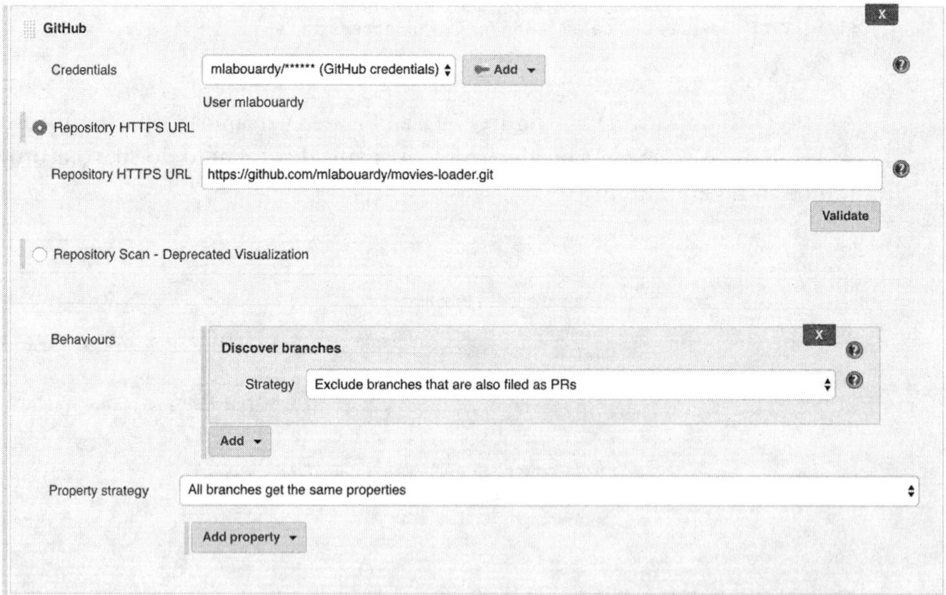

Figure 7.14   GitHub repository configuration on Jenkins

NOTE   We cover Jenkins advanced scanning behaviors and strategies in chapter 9.

Jenkins will scan the GitHub repository, looking for branches with a Jenkinsfile in the root repository. So far, there are none, and we can check that by clicking the Scan Repository Log button from the left sidebar.

> **NOTE** In this book, we will use the concept of pipeline as code instead of representing each CI stage within the UI as in a Jenkins classic freestyle job. The pipeline will be described in a Jenkinsfile.

The log output confirms that no Jenkinsfile has been found yet in the GitHub repository, as shown in figure 7.15.

Figure 7.15 Jenkins repository scanning logs

It's time to create a Jenkinsfile. Using your favorite text editor or IDE, create and save a new text file with the name `Jenkinsfile` at the root of your local movies-loader Git repository. Copy the following scripted pipeline code and paste it into your empty Jenkinsfile.

Listing 7.1 Jenkinsfile using a scripted approach

```
node('workers'){
    stage('Checkout'){
        checkout scm
    }
}
```

> **NOTE** We are using scripted pipeline syntax to write most of the Jenkinsfile. However, the declarative approach will be given when the CI pipeline is completed.

The `Checkout` stage, as its name indicates, will simply check out the code at the reference point that triggered the run. You can customize the checkout process by providing additional parameters. Also, the stages will be executed on Jenkins workers—hence, the use of the `workers` label on the node block. We're assuming we have a Jenkins worker already set up on the Jenkins instance labeled `workers`. If no label is provided, Jenkins will run the pipeline on the first executor that becomes available on any machine (master or worker).

Save your edited Jenkinsfile and push the changes to the develop branch by running the following commands:

```
git add Jenkinsfile
git commit -m "creating Jenkinsfile"
git push origin develop
```

The Jenkinsfile lives with the source code in GitHub. Therefore, like any code, it can be peer-reviewed, commented on, and approved before being merged into main branches; see figure 7.16.

Branch: develop ▾ New pull request		Create new file Upload files Find file Clone or download ▾
This branch is 2 commits ahead of master.		↻ Pull request Compare
👤 mlabouardy creating Jenkinsfile		Latest commit 707f744 3 minutes ago
📄 Jenkinsfile	creating Jenkinsfile	3 minutes ago
📄 README.md	Create README.md	3 hours ago
📄 main.py	loading from json file	3 hours ago
📄 movies.json	loading from json file	3 hours ago
📄 requirements.txt	loading from json file	3 hours ago
📄 test_main.py	loading from json file	3 hours ago

Figure 7.16   Jenkinsfile is stored along with source code

Go back to the Jenkins dashboard, and to trigger the scanning again, click the Scan Repository Now button. By default, this will automatically trigger builds for all newly discovered branches, as shown in figure 7.17.

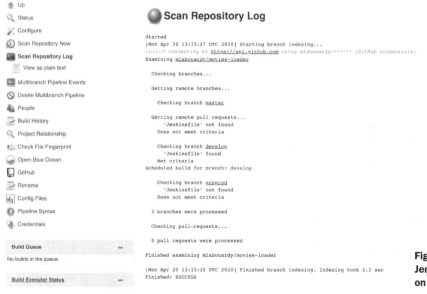

**Figure 7.17
Jenkinsfile detected
on develop branch**

In our current setup, a Jenkinsfile has been found only on the develop branch. If we click the movies-loader job again. Jenkins should have created a nested job for the develop branch, as you can see in figure 7.18. There was no pipeline scheduled for the preprod and master branches since there was no Jenkinsfile on them yet.

Figure 7.18   Build job triggered on the develop branch

NOTE   If you ever have problems with jobs for branches not being created or built automatically, check the Scan Repository Log item from the left job sidebar.

The build should be triggered on the develop branch automatically, and the checkout stage will be executed and turned green. Note that the Git client should be installed on the worker where the build is executed.

The Jenkins Stage view, shown in figure 7.19, lets us visualize the progress of various stages of the pipeline in real-time.

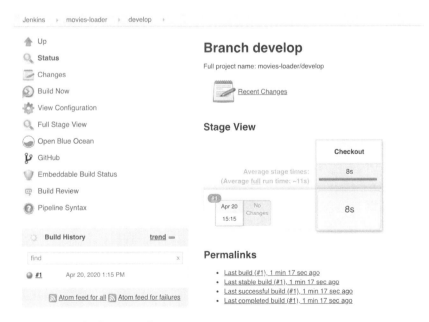

Figure 7.19   Pipeline execution

NOTE   The Jenkins Stage view is a new feature that comes as a part of release 2.*x*. It works only with Jenkins Pipeline and Jenkins Multibranch pipeline jobs.

Click the Checkout stage column to view the stage's logs. You can see that Jenkins has cloned the movies-loader GitHub repository and checked out the develop branch to fetch the latest source code changes from the remote repository, as shown in figure 7.20.

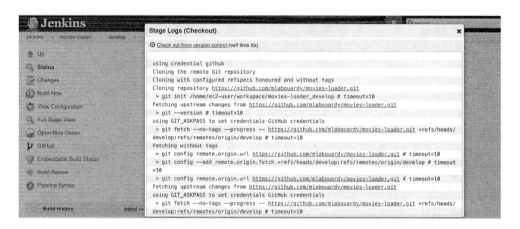

Figure 7.20   Checkout stage logs

To view the complete build log, look for the Build History on the left side. The Build History tab will list all the builds that have been run. Click the last build number; see figure 7.21.

Figure 7.21   Build number settings

Then, click the Console Output item from the left corner. The complete build logs will be displayed, as shown in figure 7.22.

Console Output

```
Branch indexing
13:15:29 Connecting to https://api.github.com using mlabouardy/****** (GitHub credentials)
Obtained Jenkinsfile from 707f744940482e36dc82a6ef5604161c36949828
Running in Durability level: MAX_SURVIVABILITY
[Pipeline] Start of Pipeline
[Pipeline] node
Running on ip-10-0-2-24.eu-west-3.compute.internal in /home/ec2-user/workspace/movies-loader_develop
[Pipeline] {
[Pipeline] stage
[Pipeline] { (Checkout)
[Pipeline] checkout
using credential github
Cloning the remote Git repository
Cloning with configured refspecs honoured and without tags
Cloning repository https://github.com/mlabouardy/movies-loader.git
 > git init /home/ec2-user/workspace/movies-loader_develop # timeout=10
Fetching upstream changes from https://github.com/mlabouardy/movies-loader.git
 > git --version # timeout=10
using GIT_ASKPASS to set credentials GitHub credentials
 > git fetch --no-tags --progress -- https://github.com/mlabouardy/movies-loader.git +refs/heads/develop:refs/remotes/origin/develop #
timeout=10
Fetching without tags
```

Figure 7.22   Build console logs

Now that we have created a Jenkins job for movies-loader, let's create another Jenkins job for the movies-parser service; once again, head over to Jenkins main page and click the New Item button. However, to save time, copy the configuration from the previous job, as shown in figure 7.23.

Figure 7.23   Parser job's creation

Click the OK button. The movies-parser job will reflect all features of the cloned movies-loader job. Update appropriately the GitHub repository HTTPS clone URL, job description, and display name, as shown in figure 7.24.

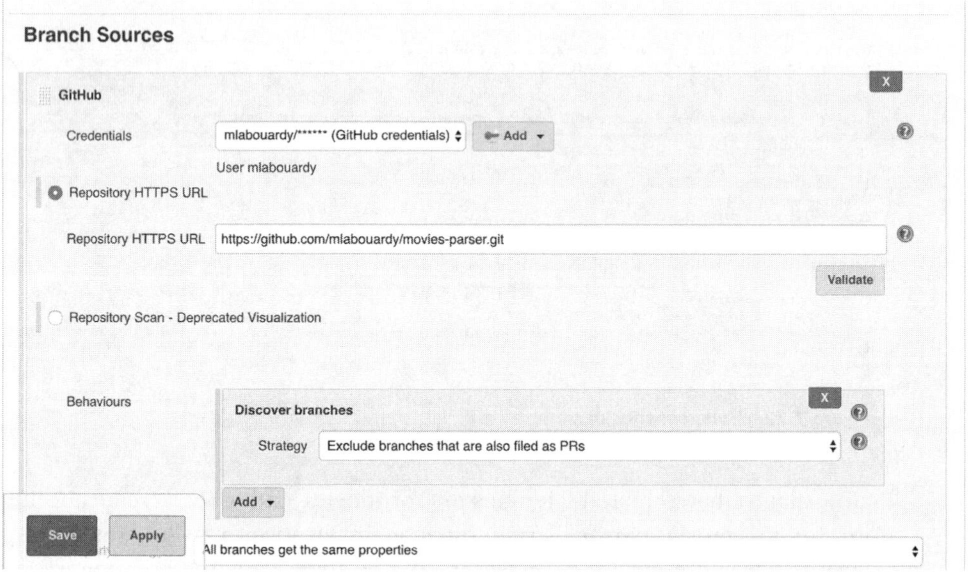

Figure 7.24   Parser job GitHub configuration

Push the same Jenkinsfile used in the previous job to the develop branch of the movies-parser GitHub repository. Then click Apply for changes to take effect.

After saving, the build will always run from the current version of Jenkinsfile into the repository, as shown in figure 7.25.

Figure 7.25   Parser job list of active branches

Follow the same steps to create Jenkins jobs for the movies-store and movies-market-place services.

While Git is the most used distributed version control nowadays, Jenkins comes with built-in support for Subversion. To use source code from a Subversion repository, you simply provide the corresponding Subversion URL—it will work fine with any of the three Subversion protocols of HTTP, SVN, or File. Jenkins will check that the URL is valid as soon as you enter it. If the repository requires authentication, you can create a Jenkins credential of type Username with Password, and select it from the Credentials drop-down list, as shown in figure 7.26.

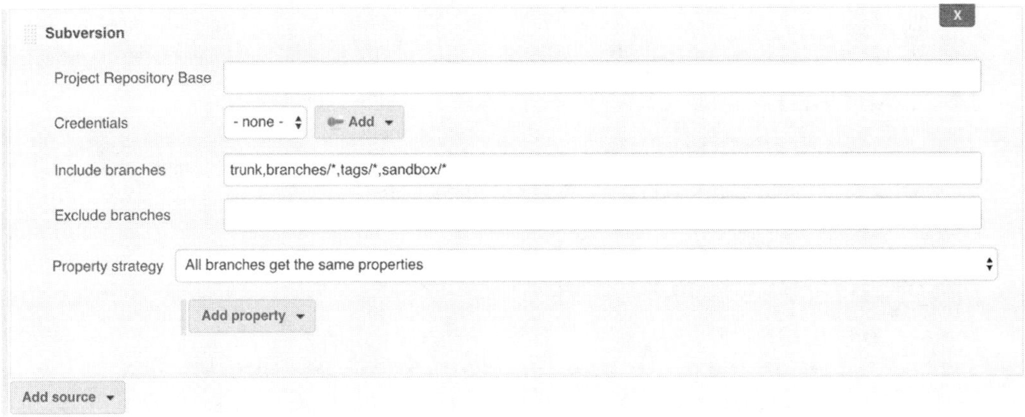

Figure 7.26 SVN repository configuration

You can fine-tune the way Jenkins obtains the latest source code from your Subversion repository by selecting an appropriate value in the Check-out Strategy drop-down list.

7.4   *Discovering Jenkins jobs' XML configuration*

Another way to create or clone a multibranch pipeline job is to export the config.xml file of an existing job. The XML file contains, as you might expect, the configuration details for the build job.

You can view the XML configuration of a job by pointing your browser to JENKINS _DNS/job/JOB_NAME/config.xml. It should dump the job XML definition in the browser page, as shown in figure 7.27.

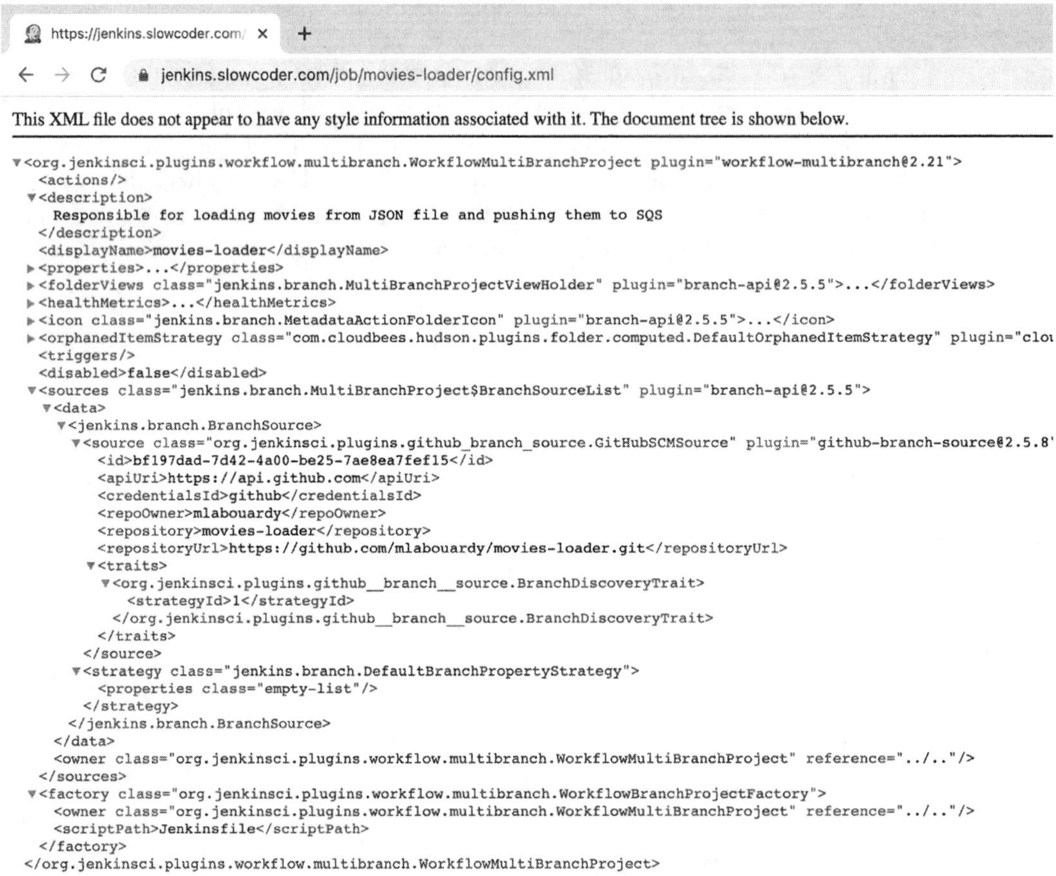

Figure 7.27   Job XML configuration

Save the job definition in an XML file and update the XML tags in table 7.2 with the appropriate values based on the target Jenkins job you're planning to create.

Table 7.2   XML tags

XML tag	Description
`<description>`	Meaningful description explaining in a few words the purpose of the Jenkins job
`<displayName>`	Jenkins job's display name; general practice is to use the name of the repository storing the source code as a value for display name
`<repository>`	Name of the GitHub repository holding the source code, such as movies-store
`<repositoryURL>`	GitHub repository HTTPS clone URL, set in the following format: https://github.com/username/repository.git

NOTE   In chapter 14, we will cover how to use the Jenkins CLI to automate the import and export of multiple jobs and plugins in Jenkins.

The following listing is an example of an XML config file for the movies-store job. It illustrates a typical structure of a Jenkins job XML configuration.

Listing 7.2   Movies store config.xml

```
<?xml version="1.0" encoding="UTF-8"?>
<org.jenkinsci.plugins.workflow
.multibranch.WorkflowMultiBranchProject plugin="workflow-multibranch@2.21">
    <actions />
    <description>Movies store RESTful API</description>       Defines the job's name
    <displayName>movies-store</displayName>                    and description
    <sources class="jenkins.branch
.MultiBranchProject$BranchSourceList" plugin="branch-api@2.5.5">
        <data>
            <jenkins.branch.BranchSource>
                <source class="org.jenkinsci.plugins
.github_branch_source.GitHubSCMSource" plugin="github-branch-source@2.5.8">
                    <id>bf197dad-7d42-4a00-be25-7ae8ea7fef15</id>
                    <apiUri>https://api.github.com</apiUri>      Defines the project
                    <credentialsId>github</credentialsId>        GitHub repository
                    <repoOwner>mlabouardy</repoOwner>            URL (HTTPS format)
                    <repository>movies-store</repository>
                    <repositoryUrl>
https://github.com/mlabouardy/movies-store.git
                    </repositoryUrl>
                    <traits>

    <org.jenkinsci.plugins.github__branch__source.BranchDiscoveryTrait>
                    <strategyId>1</strategyId>
</org.jenkinsci.plugins.github__branch__source.BranchDiscoveryTrait>
                    </traits>                        Tells Jenkins to scan all branches
                </source>                            in the GitHub repository looking
            </jenkins.branch.BranchSource>                 for a Jenkinsfile
        </data>
    </sources>
</org.jenkinsci.plugins.workflow.multibranch.WorkflowMultiBranchProject>
```

NOTE   The XML has been cropped for brevity. The full job XML definition is available in the GitHub repository in chapter7/jobs/movies-store.xml.

Once you have updated the config.xml file with the appropriate values, issue an HTTP POST request with the job XML definition as a payload to the Jenkins URL with a query parameter name equal to the target job's name. Figure 7.28 shows an example for creating a movies-store job with a Postman HTTP API client.

NOTE   If CSRF protection is enabled on Jenkins, you will need to create an API token instead of a crumb issuer token. For more information, refer to chapter 2.

Figure 7.28   Job creation Jenkins RESTful API with Postman

A one-line cURL command can also be used to clone and create a new job:

```
curl -s https:///<USER>:<API_TOKEN>@JENKINS_HOST/job/JOBNAME/config.xml
| curl -X POST 'https:///<USER>:<API_TOKEN>@JENKINS_HOST/
    createItem?name=JOBNAME'
--header "Content-Type: application/xml" -d @-
```

The Jenkins API token (`API_TOKEN` variable) can be created from the Jenkins dashboard by logging with the user that you want to generate the API token for. Then open the user profile page and click Configure to open the user configuration page.

Locate the Add new Token button, give a name to the new token, and click the Generate button, as shown in figure 7.29. Retrieve the token and replace the `API_TOKEN` variable in the preceding cURL commands with the generated token value.

Figure 7.29   Jenkins API token generation

NOTE Jenkins jobs can also be created by copying the XML file directly to the /var/lib/jenkins/jobs/<*Job name*> folder on the Jenkins master instance and restarting Jenkins with the `service jenkins restart` command for changes to take effect.

Once the four Jenkins jobs are created, you should have the jobs shown in figure 7.30 on the Jenkins main page. You can organize these jobs in one view by creating a Jenkins folder. You can create a folder named Watchlist and move these jobs to it.

Figure 7.30 Microservices jobs in Jenkins

To do so, follow these steps: From the sidebar, click New Item, enter `Watchlist` as a name in the text box, and select Folder to create the folder. To move the existing jobs to the folder, click the arrow to the right of the job and select Move. Select Watchlist as the desired folder and click Move.

The microservices jobs will be accessible with the following URL format: JENKINS _DNS/job/Watchlist/job.

The Jenkins CLI can be used to import or export a job even if its usage is deprecated and not recommended for security vulnerabilities (at least for Jenkins 2.53 and older versions). You can run this command to import your Jenkins job XML file:

```
java -jar jenkins-cli.jar -s JENKINS_URL
-auth USERNAME:PASSWORD
create-job movies-marketplace < config.xml
```

An alternative authentication method is to use an access token by replacing the `-auth` option with the `username:token` argument.

7.5 *Configuring SSH authentication with Jenkins*

Previously, you learned to configure GitHub on Jenkins with username and password credentials. We also covered how to create a GitHub API access token with granular permissions. This section covers how to use SSH keys instead to authenticate with project repositories.

> **NOTE** You can generate a one-purpose SSH key for SSH authentication with remote Git repositories by using the `ssh-keygen` command.

First, configure the Jenkins public SSH key on GitHub. You can configure SSH on the GitHub repository by going to the repository settings and adding a deploy key from the Deploy Keys section. Or simply configure the SSH key globally from the user profile settings. Give a name such as `Jenkins` and paste the public key (from the id_rsa.pub file); see figure 7.31.

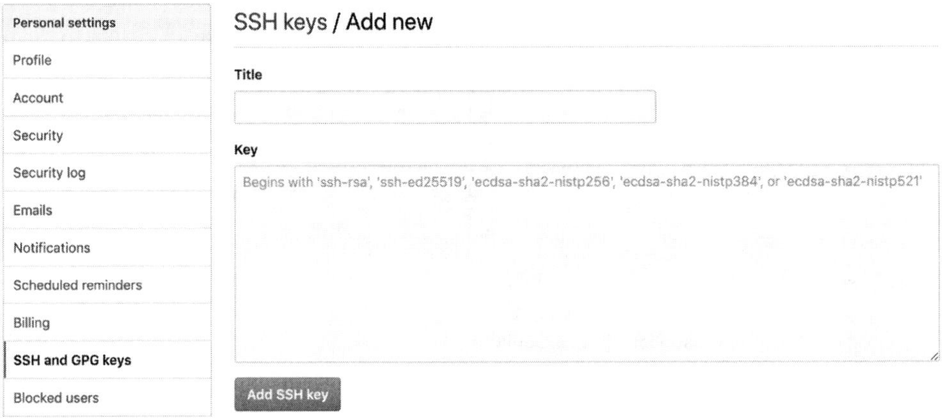

Figure 7.31   GitHub SSH configuration

> **NOTE** Once a key has been attached to one repository as a deploy key, it cannot be used on another repository.

To determine whether the key is successfully configured, type the following command on your Jenkins SSH session. Use the `-i` flag to provide the path to the Jenkins private key:

```
ssh -T -ai PRIVATE_KEY_PATH git@github.com
```

If the response looks something like `Hi username`, the key has been properly configured.

Now go to Credentials from the left pane inside the Jenkins console and click Global. Then select Add Credentials and create a credential of type SSH Username with Private Key. Give it a name and set the value of the SSH private key, as shown in figure 7.32. The Username should be the username for the GitHub account that hosts the project. In the Passphrase text box, write the passphrase given while generating the SSH RSA key. If not set, leave it blank.

Kind	SSH Username with private key

Scope	Global (Jenkins, nodes, items, all child items, etc)

ID	github-ssh

Description	GitHub SSH credentials

Username	mlabouardy

Private Key ● Enter directly

Key

Enter New Secret Below

```
-----BEGIN OPENSSH PRIVATE KEY-----
bJBlbnNzaClrZXktdjEAAAAABG5vbmUAAAAEbm9uZQAAAAAAAABAAABFwAAAAdzc2gtcn
NhAAAAAwEAAOAAAOEAx7vsZEB35DUAT2T+MrUvaFiRtFcwDV2ada4afzih9a3I9Oh6Uc3U
```

Passphrase	

Figure 7.32   Configuring GitHub SSH credentials on Jenkins

Head back to the Jenkins job, and under Branch Sources, choose Git from the drop-down list, set the repository SSH clone URL, and select the saved credentials title name; see figure 7.33.

Figure 7.33 Configuring the Jenkins job to use SSH keys

If you go to the build output, it should clearly list that the SSH key is being used for authentication. The following is sample output highlighting the same:

```
Branch indexing
 > git rev-parse --is-inside-work-tree # timeout=10
Setting origin to git@github.com:mlabouardy/movies-loader.git
 > git config remote.origin.url git@github.com:mlabouardy/movies-loader.git # timeout=10
Fetching origin...
Fetching upstream changes from origin
 > git --version # timeout=10
 > git config --get remote.origin.url # timeout=10
using GIT_SSH to set credentials GitHub SSH credentials
 > git fetch --tags --progress -- origin +refs/heads/*:refs/remotes/origin/* # timeout=10
```

Until now, the `Checkout` stage has been using the credentials and settings configured in the current Jenkins job. If you want to customize the settings and use specific credentials, you can replace it with the following listing.

Listing 7.3   Customized git clone command

```
stage('Checkout') {
    steps {
        git branch: 'develop',
            credentialsId: 'github-ssh',
            url: 'git@github.com:mlabouardy/movies-loader.git'
    }
}
```

This example will clone the develop branch of the movies-loader GitHub repository, using the SSH credentials saved in the github-ssh Jenkins credentials.

7.6   *Triggering Jenkins builds with GitHub webhooks*

So far, we have always built the pipeline manually by clicking the Build Now button. It works but is not very convenient. All team members would have to remember that after committing to the repository, they need to open Jenkins and start the build.

To trigger the jobs by push event, we will create a webhook on the GitHub repository of each service, as illustrated in figure 7.34. Remember, a Jenkinsfile should also be present on the respective branch to tell Jenkins what it needs to do when it finds a change in the repository.

> **NOTE** *Webhooks* are user-defined HTTP callbacks. They are triggered by an event in a web application and can facilitate integrating different applications or third-party APIs.

Figure 7.34   Webhook explained

Navigate to the GitHub repository that you want to connect to Jenkins and click the repository Settings option. In the menu on the left, click Webhooks, as shown in figure 7.35.

GitHub webhooks allow you to notify external services when certain Git events happen (push, merge, commit, fork, and so forth) by sending a POST request to the configured service URL.

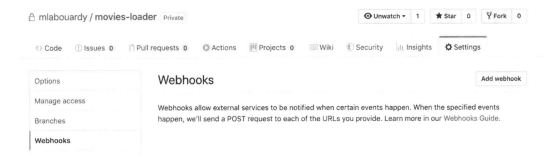

Figure 7.35   GitHub Webhooks section

Click the Add Webhook button to bring up the associated dialog, shown in figure 7.36. Fill in the form with the following values:

- The payload URL should be in the following format: JENKINS_URL/github-webhook/ (make sure it includes the last forward slash).
- The content type can be either application/json or application/x-www-form-urlencoded.
- Select the push event as a trigger and leave the Secret field empty (unless a secret has been created and configured in the Jenkins Configure System > GitHub Plugin section).

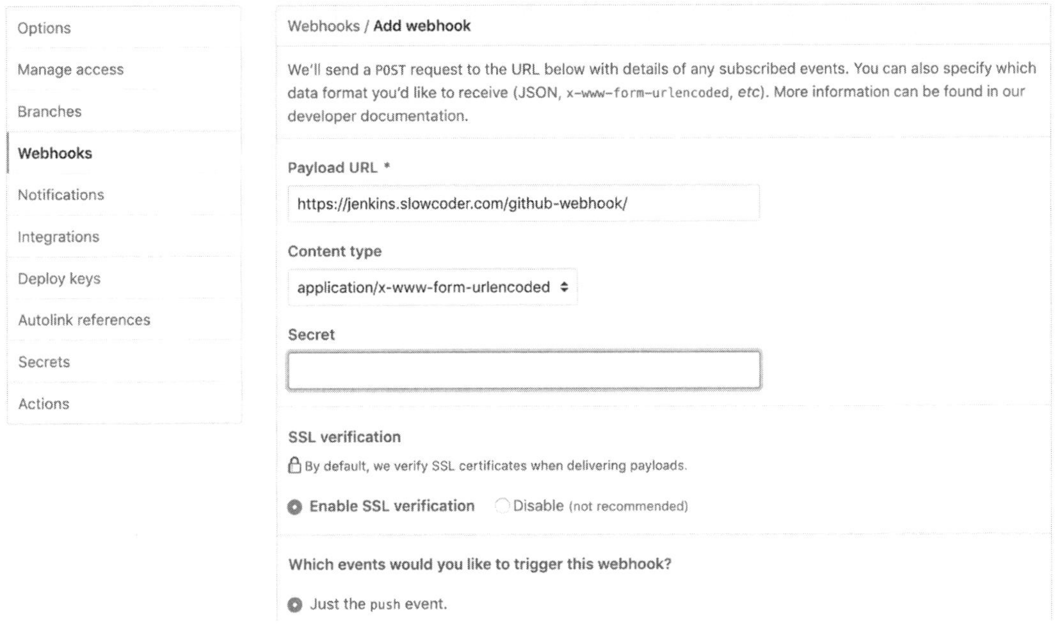

Options

Manage access

Branches

Webhooks

Notifications

Integrations

Deploy keys

Autolink references

Secrets

Actions

Webhooks / **Add webhook**

We'll send a POST request to the URL below with details of any subscribed events. You can also specify which data format you'd like to receive (JSON, x-www-form-urlencoded, *etc*). More information can be found in our developer documentation.

Payload URL *

https://jenkins.slowcoder.com/github-webhook/

Content type

application/x-www-form-urlencoded ⬍

Secret

SSL verification

🔒 By default, we verify SSL certificates when delivering payloads.

● **Enable SSL verification**   ○ Disable (not recommended)

Which events would you like to trigger this webhook?

● Just the push event.

Figure 7.36   Jenkins webhook settings

Leave the rest of the options at their default values and then click the Add Webhook button. A test payload should be sent to Jenkins to set up the hook. If the payload is successfully received by Jenkins, you should see the webhook with a green check mark, as shown in figure 7.37.

Okay, that hook was successfully created. We sent a ping payload to test it out! Read more about it at https://developer.github.com/webhooks/#ping-event.

🔒 mlabouardy / **movies-loader** Private   👁 Unwatch ▾ | 1   ★ Star | 0   ⑂ Fork | 0

<> Code   ⓘ Issues **0**   ⑂ Pull requests **0**   ⊙ Actions   ▥ Projects **0**   ▥ Wiki   🛡 Security   ⅼⅼⅼ Insights   ⚙ Settings

Options	**Webhooks**	Add webhook
Manage access		
Branches	Webhooks allow external services to be notified when certain events happen. When the specified events happen, we'll send a POST request to each of the URLs you provide. Learn more in our Webhooks Guide.	
Webhooks	✓ https://jenkins.slowcoder.com/github-webhook/ *(push)* Edit	Delete
Notifications		

Figure 7.37   Jenkins webhook settings

With these GitHub updates done, if you push some changes to the Git repository, a new event should get kicked off automatically. In this scenario, we update the README.md file:

Recent Deliveries

✓ 📋 2fba89da–8310–11ea–8100–1a550bb73ad1   2020-04-20 16:06:53   ⋯

✓ 📋 de90c880–830f–11ea–8eb4–b5093551f5c1   2020-04-20 16:04:37   ⋯

Go back to your Jenkins project, and you'll see that a new job was triggered automatically from the commit we made at the previous step. Click the little arrow next to the job and choose Console Output. Figure 7.38 shows the output.

The update readme message confirms that the build was triggered automatically upon pushing the new README.md to the GitHub repository. Now, every time you publish your changes to your remote repository, GitHub will trigger your new Jenkins job. Create a similar webhook on the remaining GitHub repositories by following the same procedure.

Figure 7.38   GitHub push event

> **NOTE**   If you want SVN users to continuously trigger Jenkins jobs after every commit, you can either configure Jenkins to periodically poll the SVN server or set up a post-commit hook on the remote repository.

In a different situation, the Jenkins dashboard might not be accessible from a public network. Instead of executing jobs manually, you can set up a public reverse proxy as middleware between the GitHub server and Jenkins, and configure the GitHub webhook to use the middleware URL. Figure 7.39 explains how to use AWS managed services to set up a webhook forwarder for a Jenkins instance within a VPC.

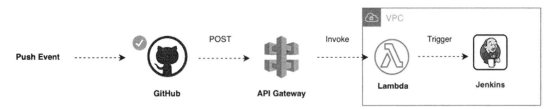

Figure 7.39   GitHub webhook setup with API Gateway

> **NOTE**   You can generalize this approach to other services too, such as Bitbucket or DockerHub—or anything, really, that emits webhooks.

If you're using AWS as a cloud provider, you can use a managed proxy called Amazon API Gateway to invoke a Lambda function when a POST request is invoked on a specific endpoint, as shown in figure 7.40.

Figure 7.40   Triggering a Lambda function with API Gateway

The Lambda function will receive the GitHub payload from API Gateway and relay it to the Jenkins server. The following listing is a function entry point written in JavaScript.

Listing 7.4   Lambda function handler

```
const Request = require('request');
exports.handler = (event, context, callback) => {
    Request.post({
        url: process.env.JENKINS_URL,
        method: "POST",
        headers: {
            "Content-Type": "application/json",
            "X-GitHub-Event": event.headers["X-GitHub-Event"]
        },
        json: JSON.parse(event.body)
    }, (error, response, body) => {
        callback(null, {
            "statusCode": 200,
            "headers": {
                "content-type": "application/json"
            },
            "body": "success",
            "isBase64Encoded": false
        })
    })
};
```

To deploy the GitHub webhook and AWS resources, we will use Terraform. But first, we need to create a deployment package with the Lambda function index.js entry point. The deployment package is a zip file that can be generated with the following command:

```
zip deployment.zip index.js
```

NOTE This section assumes you're familiar with the usual Terraform plan/apply workflow. If you're new to Terraform, refer to chapter 5.

Next, we define a lambda.tf file containing the Terraform resource definition for an AWS Lambda function. We set the runtime to be a Node.js runtime environment (the Lambda handler is written in JavaScript). We define an environment variable named JENKINS_URL with a value pointing to the Jenkins web dashboard URL, as shown in the next listing.

Listing 7.5 Lambda function based on Node.js runtime

```
resource "aws_lambda_function" "lambda" {
  filename = "../deployment.zip"
  function_name = "GitHubWebhookForwarder"
  role = aws_iam_role.role.arn
  handler = "index.handler"
  runtime = "nodejs14.x"
  timeout = 10
  environment {
    variables = {
      JENKINS_URL = var.jenkins_url
    }
  }
}
```

Then, we define an API Gateway RESTful API to trigger the preceding Lambda function when a POST request occurs on the /webhook endpoint. Create a new file, apigateway.tf, in the same directory as our lambda.tf from the previous step and paste the following content.

Listing 7.6 API Gateway RESTful API

```
resource "aws_api_gateway_rest_api" "api" {
  name        = "GitHubWebHookAPI"
  description = "GitHub Webhook forwarder"
}

resource "aws_api_gateway_resource" "path" {
  rest_api_id = aws_api_gateway_rest_api.api.id
  parent_id   = aws_api_gateway_rest_api.api.root_resource_id
  path_part   = "webhook"
}

resource "aws_api_gateway_integration" "request_integration" {
  rest_api_id = aws_api_gateway_rest_api.api.id
  resource_id = aws_api_gateway_method.request_method.resource_id
  http_method = aws_api_gateway_method.request_method.http_method
  type        = "AWS_PROXY"
  uri         = aws_lambda_function.lambda.invoke_arn
  integration_http_method = "POST"
}
```

Finally, in the following listing, we create an API Gateway deployment to activate the configuration and expose the API at a URL that can be used for webhook configuration. We use a Terraform output variable to display the API deployment URL by referencing the API deployment stage.

Listing 7.7   API new deployment stage

```
resource "aws_api_gateway_deployment" "stage" {
    rest_api_id = aws_api_gateway_rest_api.api.id
    stage_name  = "v1"
}

output "webhook" {
    value = "${aws_api_gateway_deployment.stage.invoke_url}/webhook"
}
```

Before issuing the `terraform apply` command, you need to define the variables used in the preceding resources. The variables.tf file will contain the list of variables, which are detailed in table 7.3.

Table 7.3   GitHub webhook proxy's Terraform variables

Variable	Type	Value	Description
`region`	String	none	The AWS region in which to deploy AWS resources. It can also be sourced from the `AWS_REGION` environment variable.
`shared_credentials_file`	String	none	The path to the shared credentials file. If this is not set and a profile specified, ~/.aws/credentials will be used.
`aws_profile`	String	profile	The AWS profile name as set in the shared credentials file.
`jenkins_url`	String	none	The Jenkins URL, which has the format http://IP:8080, or uses HTTPS if an SSL certificate is being used.

When Terraform finishes deploying the AWS resources, a new Lambda function called `GitHubWehookForwarder` should be created with a trigger of type API Gateway, as shown in figure 7.41.

Figure 7.41   `GitHubWebhookForwarder` Lambda function

Furthermore, Terraform will display the RESTful API deployment URL, which you can use to create a webhook on the target GitHub repository, as shown in figure 7.42.

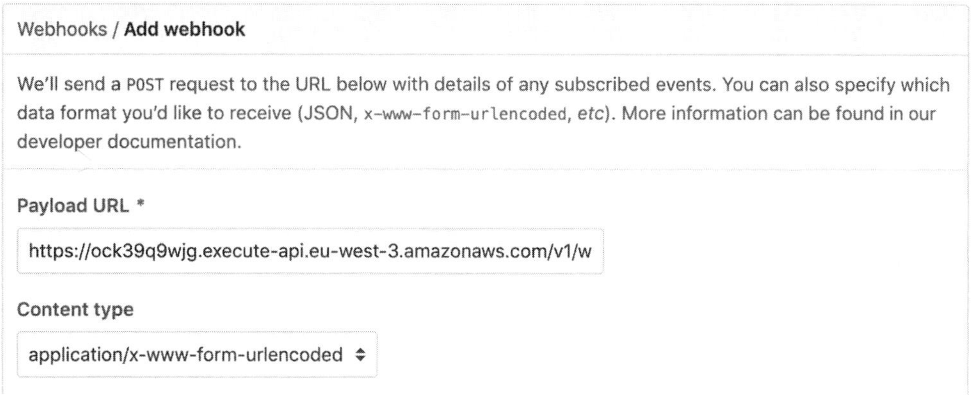

Figure 7.42   GitHub webhook based on API Gateway URL

Webhooks should be flowing now. You can make a change to your repository and check that a build starts soon after. You also can add an extra security layer, by requiring a request secret and validating the incoming request signature on the Lambda function side.

If you're running Jenkins locally, you can use a build trigger to poll SCM and schedule it to run periodically, as shown in figure 7.43. In such a case, Jenkins would regularly check the repository, and if anything changed, it would run the job.

Figure 7.43   Under the job's settings, you can define the interval of checks.

After running the pipeline manually for the first time, the automatic trigger is set. Then it checks GitHub every minute, and for new commits, starts a build. To test that it works as expected, you can commit and push anything to the GitHub repository and see that the build starts.

> **NOTE**   Polling SCM, even if it's less intuitive, might be useful if Git commits are frequent and the build takes a long time, so executing a build upon a push event every time would cause an overload.

So far, you have learned how to integrate Git repositories with Jenkins and define multibranch pipeline jobs. And we have ended up creating our first complete commit pipeline. However, with the current state, it doesn't do much. In the following chapters, we will see what improvements can be made to make the commit pipeline even better, and we will start by running automated tests within the Jenkins pipelines.

Summary

- A webhook is a mechanism to automatically trigger the build of a Jenkins project upon a commit pushed in a remote Git repository.
- The development workflow should be carefully chosen inside the team or organization because it affects the CI process and defines the way the code is developed.
- Using multi-repo or mono-repo strategies to organize the codebase will define the complexity of a CI/CD pipeline as the number of applications evolves within an organization.
- A pipeline can go through the standard code development process (code review, pull requests, automated testing, and so forth) when a Jenkinsfile and application source code live together on the same Git repository.
- Jenkins stores configuration files for the jobs it runs in an XML file. Editing these XML configuration files has the same effect as editing Jenkins jobs through the web dashboard.
- A reverse proxy can be useful to let Git webhooks reach a running Jenkins server behind a firewall.

Running automated tests with Jenkins

This chapter covers

- Implementing CI pipelines for Python, Go, Node.js, and Angular-based services
- Running pre-integration tests and automated UI testing with Headless Chrome
- Executing SonarQube static code analysis within Jenkins pipelines
- Running unit tests inside a Docker container and publishing code coverage reports
- Integrating dependency checks in a Jenkins pipeline and injecting security in DevOps

In the previous chapter, you learned how to set up multibranch pipeline jobs for containerized microservices and for continuously triggering Jenkins upon push events with webhooks. In this chapter, we will run automated tests within the CI pipeline. Figure 8.1 summarizes the current CI workflow stages.

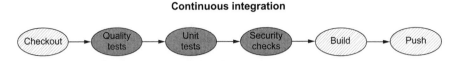

Figure 8.1   The test stages covered in this chapter

Test automation is widely considered a cornerstone of Agile development. If you want to release fast—even daily—with reasonable quality, you have to move to automated testing. On the other hand, giving less importance to testing can result in customer dissatisfaction and a delayed product. However, automating the testing process is a bit more difficult than automating the build, release, and deployment processes. Automating nearly all the test cases used in an application usually takes a lot of effort. It is an activity that matures over time. It is not always possible to automate all the testing. But the idea is to automate whatever testing is possible.

By the end of this chapter, we will implement the test stage in the target CI pipeline shown in figure 8.2.

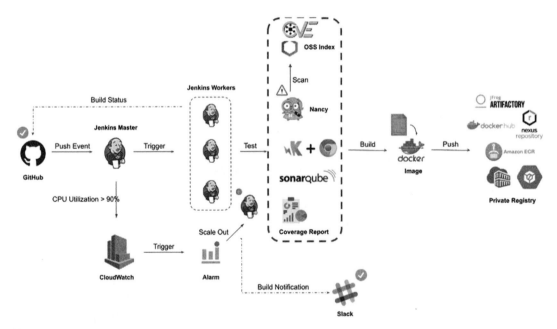

Figure 8.2   Target CI pipeline

Before resuming the CI pipeline implementation, a quick reminder regarding the web distributed application we're integrating with Jenkins: it's based on a microservices architecture and split into components/services written in different programming languages and frameworks. Figure 8.3 illustrates this architecture.

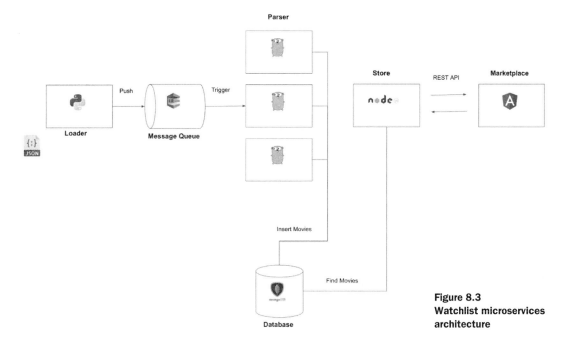

**Figure 8.3
Watchlist microservices
architecture**

In the following sections, you will learn how to integrate various types of tests in our CI workflow. We will start with unit testing.

8.1 Running unit tests inside Docker containers

Unit testing is the frontline effort to identify issues as early as possible. The test needs to be small and quick to execute to be efficient.

The movies-loader service is written in Python. To define unit tests, we're going to use the unittest framework (it comes bundled with the installation of Python). To use it, we import the unittest module, which offers a rich set of methods to construct and run tests. The following listing, test_main.py, demonstrates a short unit test to test the JSON loading and parsing mechanism.

Listing 8.1 Unit testing in Python

```python
import unittest
import json

class TestJSONLoaderMethods(unittest.TestCase):
    movies = []

    @classmethod
    def setUpClass(cls):
        with open('movies.json') as json_file:
            cls.movies = json.load(json_file)

    def test_rank(self):
        self.assertEqual(self.movies[0]['rank'], '1')
```

```
    def test_title(self):
        self.assertEqual(self.movies[0]['title'], 'The Shawshank Redemption')

    def test_id(self):
        self.assertEqual(self.movies[0]['id'], 'tt0111161')

if __name__ == '__main__':
    unittest.main()
```

The `setUpClass()` method allows us to load the movies.json file before the execution of each test method. The three individual tests are defined with methods whose names start with the prefix `test`. This naming convention informs the test runner about which methods represent tests. The crux of each test is a call to `assert-Equal()` to check for an expected result. For instance, we check whether the first movie's title attribute parsed from the JSON file is `The Shawshank Redemption`.

To run the test, we can execute the `python test_main.py` command on Jenkins. However, it requires Python 3 to be installed. To avoid installing the runtime environment for each service we are building, we will run the tests inside a Docker container. That way, we will be using Docker as an execution environment across all Jenkins workers.

On the movies-loader repository, create a Dockerfile.test file by using your favorite text editor or IDE with the following content.

Listing 8.2   Movie loader's Dockerfile.test

```
FROM python:3.7.3
WORKDIR /app
COPY test_main.py .
COPY movies.json .
```

The Dockerfile is built from a Python 3.7.3 official image. It sets a working directory called app, and copies the test files to the working directory.

NOTE   The name convention *Dockerfile.test* is used to avoid name conflict with *Dockerfile*, which is used to build the main application's Docker image.

Now, update the Jenkinsfile given in listing 7.1 and add a new `Unit Test` stage, as shown in the following listing. The stage will create a Docker image based on Dockerfile.test and then spin up a Docker container from the created image to run the `python test_main.py` command to launch unit tests. The `Unit Test` stage uses a DSL-like syntax to define the shell instructions.

Listing 8.3   Movie loader's Jenkinsfile

```
def imageName = 'mlabouardy/movies-loader'

node('workers'){
    stage('Checkout'){
        checkout scm
    }
```

```
    stage('Unit Tests'){
        sh "docker build -t ${imageName}-test -f Dockerfile.test ."
        sh "docker run --rm ${imageName}-test"
    }
}
```

The `docker build` and `docker run` commands are used to create an image and build a container from the image, respectively.

> **NOTE** The `--rm` flag in the `docker run` command is used to automatically clean up the container and remove the filesystem when the container exits.

You can use the `powershell` step in your pipeline on a Windows worker. This step has the same options as the `sh` instruction.

Commit the changes to the develop branch with the following commands:

```
git add Dockerfile.test Jenkinsfile
git commit -m "unit tests execution"
git push origin develop
```

In a few seconds, a new build should be triggered on the movies-loader job for the develop branch. From the movies-loader Multibranch Pipeline job, click the respective develop branch. On the resultant page, you will see the Stage view for the develop branch pipeline, as shown in figure 8.4.

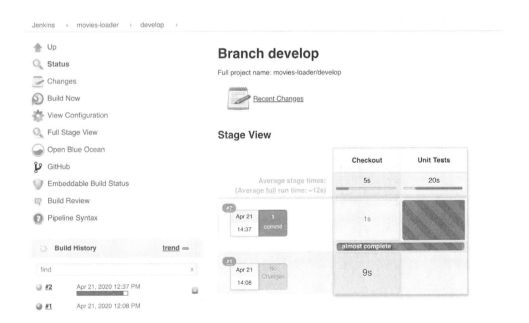

Figure 8.4   Unit test stage execution

Click the Console Output option to view the test results. All three test cases ran, and the status shows as SUCCESS in the logs, as you can see in figure 8.5.

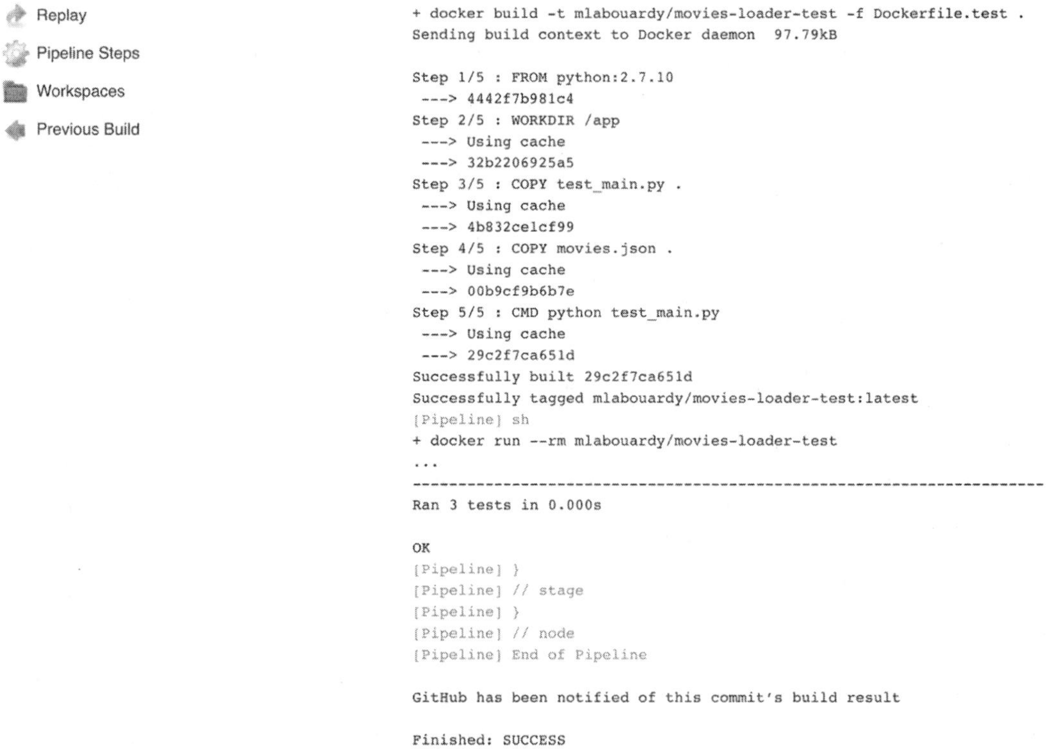

Replay

Pipeline Steps

Workspaces

Previous Build

```
+ docker build -t mlabouardy/movies-loader-test -f Dockerfile.test .
Sending build context to Docker daemon  97.79kB

Step 1/5 : FROM python:2.7.10
 ---> 4442f7b981c4
Step 2/5 : WORKDIR /app
 ---> Using cache
 ---> 32b2206925a5
Step 3/5 : COPY test_main.py .
 ---> Using cache
 ---> 4b832ce1cf99
Step 4/5 : COPY movies.json .
 ---> Using cache
 ---> 00b9cf9b6b7e
Step 5/5 : CMD python test_main.py
 ---> Using cache
 ---> 29c2f7ca651d
Successfully built 29c2f7ca651d
Successfully tagged mlabouardy/movies-loader-test:latest
[Pipeline] sh
+ docker run --rm mlabouardy/movies-loader-test
...
----------------------------------------------------------------------
Ran 3 tests in 0.000s

OK
[Pipeline] }
[Pipeline] // stage
[Pipeline] }
[Pipeline] // node
[Pipeline] End of Pipeline

GitHub has been notified of this commit's build result

Finished: SUCCESS
```

Figure 8.5   Unit test successful execution logs

The shell commands can be replaced with Docker DSL instructions. I advise using them where appropriate instead of running Docker commands via the shell, because they provide high-level encapsulation and ease of use:

```
stage('Unit Tests'){
      def imageTest= docker.build("${imageName}-test",
 "-f Dockerfile.test .")
      imageTest.inside{
          sh 'python test_main.py'
      }
}
```

The `docker.build()` method is similar to running the `docker build` command. The returned value of the method can be used for a subsequent call to create a Docker container and run the unit tests. Figure 8.6 shows a successful run of the pipeline.

```
$ docker run -t -d -u 500:500 -w /home/ec2-user/workspace/movies-loader_develop -v /home/ec2-user/workspace/movies-
loader_develop:/home/ec2-user/workspace/movies-loader_develop:rw,z -v /home/ec2-user/workspace/movies-loader_develop@tmp:/home/ec2-
user/workspace/movies-loader_develop@tmp:rw,z -e ******** -e ******** -e ******** -e ******** -e ******** -e ******** -e ******** -e
******** -e ******** -e ******** -e ******** -e ******** -e ******** -e ******** -e ******** -e ******** -e ******** -e ******** -e
******** -e ******** -e ******** mlabouardy/movies-loader-test cat
$ docker top da810b2d196fb6e261456ad1ca42ed5ca7a07ebeca697aae513b29c382cfac63 -eo pid,comm
[Pipeline] {
[Pipeline] sh
+ python test_main.py
...
--------------------------------------------------------------------
Ran 3 tests in 0.000s

OK
[Pipeline] }
$ docker stop --time=1 da810b2d196fb6e261456ad1ca42ed5ca7a07ebeca697aae513b29c382cfac63
$ docker rm -f da810b2d196fb6e261456ad1ca42ed5ca7a07ebeca697aae513b29c382cfac63
[Pipeline] // withDockerContainer
[Pipeline] }
```

Figure 8.6   Using the Docker DSL to run tests

To show results in a graphical, visual way, we can use the JUnit report integration plugin on Jenkins to consume an XML file generated by Python unit tests.

> **NOTE**   The JUnit report integration plugin (https://plugins.jenkins.io/junit/) is installed by default in the baked Jenkins master machine image.

Update the test_main.py file to use the xmlrunner library, and pass it to the unittest .main method:

```
import xmlrunner
...
if __name__ == '__main__':
    runner = xmlrunner.XMLTestRunner(output='reports')
    unittest.main(testRunner=runner)
```

This will generate test reports in the reports directory. However, we need to address a problem: the test container will store the result of the tests that it executes within itself. We can resolve this by mapping a volume to the reports directory. Update the Jenkinsfile to tell Jenkins where to find the JUnit test report:

```
stage('Unit Tests'){
        def imageTest= docker.build("${imageName}-test",
 "-f Dockerfile.test .")
        sh "docker run --rm -v $PWD/reports:/app/reports ${imageName}-test"
        junit "$PWD/reports/*.xml"
}
```

> **NOTE**   You can also get the report results by using the `docker cp` command to copy the report files into the current workspace. Then, set the workspace as an argument for the JUnit command.

Let's go ahead and execute this. This will add a chart to the project page in Jenkins after the changes are pushed to the develop branch and CI execution is completed; see figure 8.7.

Branch develop

Full project name: movies-loader/develop

 Recent Changes

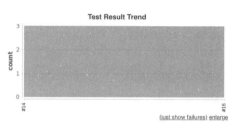

Test Result Trend

Figure 8.7   JUnit test chart analyzer

The historic graph shows several metrics (including failure, total, and duration) related to the test execution over a period of time. You can also click the chart to get more details about individual tests.

8.2   *Automating code linter integration with Jenkins*

Another example of tests to implement within CI pipelines is *code linting*. Linters can be used to check the source code and find typos, syntax errors, undeclared variables, and calls to undefined or deprecated functions. They can help you write better code and anticipate potential bugs. Let's see how to integrate code linters with Jenkins.

The movies-parser service is written in Go, so we can use a Go linter to make sure that the code respects the code style. A linter may sound like an optional tool, but for larger projects, it helps to keep a consistent style over your project.

Dockerfile.test uses golang:1.13.4 as a base image, and installs the `golint` tool and service dependencies, as shown in the following listing.

Listing 8.4   Movie parser's Dockerfile.test

```
FROM golang:1.13.4
WORKDIR /go/src/github.com/mlabouardy/movies-loader
ENV GOCACHE /tmp
WORKDIR /go/src/github/mlabouardy/movies-parser
RUN go get -u golang.org/x/lint/golint
COPY . .
RUN go get -v
```

Add the `Quality Tests` stage to the Jenkinsfile to build a Docker image based on Dockerfile.test with the `docker.build()` command, and then use the `inside()` instruction on the built image to start a Docker container in daemonized mode to execute the `golint` command:

```
def imageName = 'mlabouardy/movies-parser'
node('workers'){
    stage('Checkout'){
        checkout scm
    }
```

```
    stage('Quality Tests'){
        def imageTest= docker.build("${imageName}-test", "-f Dockerfile.test .")
        imageTest.inside{
            sh 'golint'
        }
    }
}
```

NOTE If an `ENTRYPOINT` instruction is defined in Dockerfile.test, the `inside()` instruction will pass the commands defined in its scope as an argument to the `ENTRYPOINT` instruction.

The `golint` execution will result in the logs shown in figure 8.8.

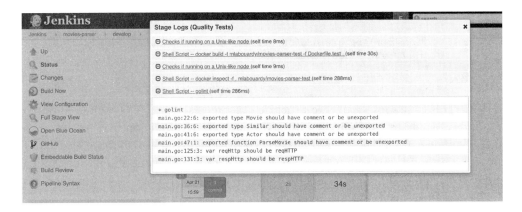

Figure 8.8 The `golint` command output identifies the missing comments

By default, `golint` prints only the style issues, and returns (with a 0 exit code), so the CI never considers that something went wrong. If you specify `-set_exit_status`, the pipeline will fail if an issue is reported by `golint`.

We can also implement a unit test for the movies-parser service. Go has a built-in testing command called `go test` and the package *testing*, which combine to give a minimal but complete unit-testing experience.

Similarly to the movies-loader service, we will write a Dockerfile.test file to execute the `go test` command that will execute tests written in the main_test.go file. The code in the following listing has been cropped for brevity and to highlight the main parts. You can browse the full code in chapter7/microservices/movies-parser/main_test.go.

Listing 8.5 Movie parser's unit test

```
package main

import (
    "testing"
)
```

```
const HTML = `
<div class="plot_summary ">
    <div class="summary_text">
        An ex-hit-man comes out of retirement to track down the gangsters
that killed his dog and took everything from him.
    </div>
    ...
</div>
`
func TestParseMovie(t *testing.T) {
    expectedMovie := Movie{
            Title:       "John Wick (2014)",
            ReleaseDate: "24 October 2014 (USA)",
            Description: "An ex-hit-man comes ...",
    }

    currentMovie, err := ParseMovie(HTML)
    if expectedMovie.Title != currentMovie.Title {
      t.Errorf("returned wrong title: got %v want %v"
, currentMovie.Title, expectedMovie.Title)
    }
}
```

This code shows the basic structure of a unit test in Go. The built-in testing package is provided by Go's standard library. A unit test is a function that accepts the argument of type `*testing.T` and calls the `t.Error()` method to indicate a failure. This function must start with a `Test` keyword, and the latter name should start with an uppercase letter. In our use case, the function tests the `ParseMovie()` method, which takes as a parameter `HTML` and returns a `Movie`'s structure.

8.3   Generating code coverage reports

The `Unit Tests` stage is straightforward: it will execute `go test` inside the Docker container created from the Docker test image. Instead of building the test image on each stage, we move the `docker.build()` instruction outside the stage to speed up the pipeline execution time, as you can see in the following listing.

Listing 8.6   Movie parser's Jenkinsfile

```
def imageName = 'mlabouardy/movies-parser'
node('workers'){
    stage('Checkout'){
        checkout scm
  }

    def imageTest= docker.build("${imageName}-test", "-f Dockerfile.test .")
    stage('Quality Tests'){
        imageTest.inside{
            sh 'golint'
        }
    }
    stage('Unit Tests'){
```

```
        imageTest.inside{
            sh 'go test'
        }
    }
}
```

Push the changes to the develop branch, and the pipeline should be triggered to execute the three stages defined on the Jenkinsfile, as shown in figure 8.9.

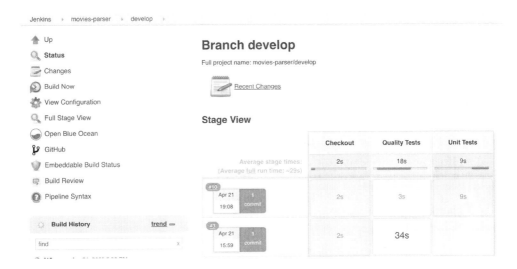

Figure 8.9　Go CI pipeline

The `go test` command output is shown in figure 8.10.

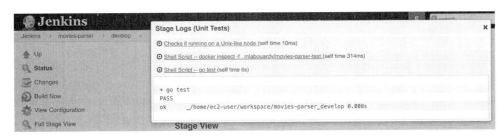

Figure 8.10　`go test` command output

> **NOTE**　Go provides the `-cover` flag to the `go test` command as a built-in functionality to check your code coverage.

If we want to get the coverage report in HTML format, you need to add the following command:

```
go test -coverprofile=cover/cover.cov
go tool cover -html=cover/coverage.cov -o coverage.html
```

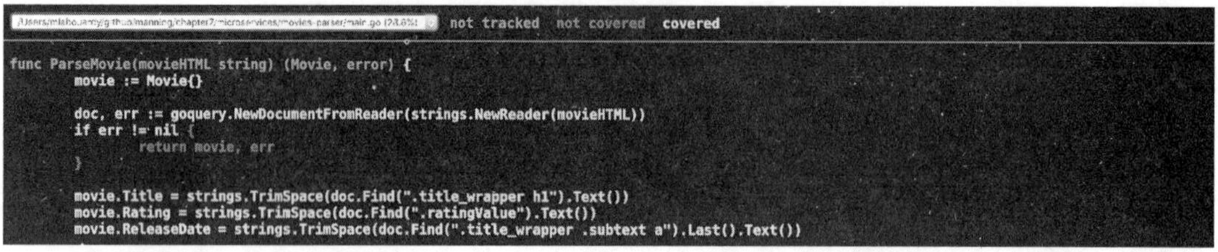

Figure 8.11   The coverage.html content can be served from the Jenkins dashboard at the end of the test stage.

The commands render an HTML page, shown in figure 8.11, that visualizes line-by-line coverage of each affected line in the main.go file.

You can include the previous command in the CI workflow to generate coverage reports in HTML format.

8.4   *Injecting security in the CI pipeline*

It's important to make sure that no vulnerabilities are published to production—at least no critical or major ones. Scanning project dependencies within a CI pipeline can ensure this additional level of security. Several dependency scanning solutions exist, commercial and open source. In this part, we'll go with Nancy.

Nancy (https://github.com/sonatype-nexus-community/nancy) is an open source tool that checks for vulnerabilities in your Go dependencies. It uses Sonatype's OSS Index (https://ossindex.sonatype.org/), a mirror of the Common Vulnerabilities and Exposures (CVE) database, to check your dependencies for publicly filed vulnerabilities.

> **NOTE**   Chapter 9 covers how to use the OWASP Dependency-Check plugin on Jenkins to detect references to dependencies that have been assigned CVE entries.

Step one in the process is to install a Nancy binary from the official release page. Update Dockerfile.test for the movies-parser project to install Nancy version 1.0.22 (at the time of writing this book) and configure the executable on the PATH variable, as shown in the following listing.

Listing 8.7   Movie parser's Dockerfile.test

```
FROM golang:1.13.4
ENV VERSION 1.0.22
ENV GOCACHE /tmp
WORKDIR /go/src/github/mlabouardy/movies-parser
RUN wget https://github.com/sonatype-nexus-community/nancy/releases/download/
     $VERSION/nancy
```

```
linux.amd64-$VERSION -O nancy && \
    chmod +x nancy && mv nancy /usr/local/bin/nancy
RUN go get -u golang.org/x/lint/golint
COPY . .
RUN go get -v
```

To start using the tool, add a `Security Tests` stage on the Jenkinsfile to run Nancy with the Gopkg.lock file as parameter, which contains a list of used Go dependencies in the movies-parser service:

```
stage('Security Tests'){
        imageTest.inside('-u root:root'){
            sh 'nancy /go/src/github/mlabouardy/movies-parser/Gopkg.lock'
        }
}
```

Push the changes to the remote repository. A new pipeline will be started. At the `Security Tests` stage, Nancy will be executed, and no dependency security vulnerability will be reported, as shown in figure 8.12.

```
+ nancy /go/src/github/mlabouardy/movies-parser/Gopkg.lock
  __   __
 /\ \/\ \
 \ \ `\\ \         __        __      ___   __ __
  \ \ , ` \     /'_ `\    /' _ `\   /'___\ /\ \/\ \
   \ \ \`\ \ /\ \L\.\_ /\ \/\ \ /\ \__/ \ \ \_\ \
    \ \_\ \_\\ \__/.\_\ \_\ \_\ \____\ \/`____ \
     \/_/\/_/ \/__/\/_/ \/_/\/_/ \/____/  `/___/> \
                                            /\___/
                                            \/__/
  _       _                      (_   _  _ .  _   _   _/  _
 /_)  /_/ .  / /// //_| /_/ /_/|_  (_x /   / / /_/ //_/ _\
   _/              _/ /
Nancy version: 0.2.0
 [31m!!!!! WARNING !!!!!
Scanning cannot be completed on the following package(s) since they do not use semver.
 [0m[1/9] [1mpkg:golang/github.com/golang/snappy@master [0m
 [2/9] [1mpkg:golang/github.com/jmespath/go-jmespath@c2b33e84 [0m
 [3/9] [1mpkg:golang/github.com/xdg/scram@master [0m
 [4/9] [1mpkg:golang/github.com/xdg/stringprep@master [0m
 [5/9] [1mpkg:golang/golang.org/x/crypto@master [0m
 [6/9] [1mpkg:golang/golang.org/x/lint@master [0m
 [7/9] [1mpkg:golang/golang.org/x/net@master [0m
 [8/9] [1mpkg:golang/golang.org/x/sync@master [0m
 [9/9] [1mpkg:golang/golang.org/x/tools@master [0m

 [1/8] [1mpkg:golang/github.com/PuerkitoBio/goquery@1.5.1 [0m [38;5;251m   No known vulnerabilities against package/version
 [0m[2/8] [1mpkg:golang/github.com/andybalholm/cascadia@1.1.0 [0m [38;5;251m   No known vulnerabilities against package/version
 [0m[3/8] [1mpkg:golang/github.com/aws/aws-sdk-go-v2@0.20.0 [0m [38;5;251m   No known vulnerabilities against package/version
 [0m[4/8] [1mpkg:golang/github.com/go-stack/stack@1.8.0 [0m [38;5;251m   No known vulnerabilities against package/version
 [0m[5/8] [1mpkg:golang/github.com/klauspost/compress@1.10.4 [0m [38;5;251m   No known vulnerabilities against package/version
 [0m[6/8] [1mpkg:golang/github.com/pkg/errors@0.9.1 [0m [38;5;251m   No known vulnerabilities against package/version
 [0m[7/8] [1mpkg:golang/go.mongodb.org/mongo-driver@1.3.2 [0m [38;5;251m   No known vulnerabilities against package/version
 [0m[8/8] [1mpkg:golang/golang.org/x/text@0.3.2 [0m [38;5;251m   No known vulnerabilities against package/version
 [0m
Audited dependencies:8,Vulnerable: [1;31m0 [0m
```

Figure 8.12   Dependencies scanning for known vulnerabilities

If Nancy finds a vulnerability in one of your dependencies, it will exit with a nonzero code, allowing you to use Nancy as a tool in your CI/CD process, and fail builds.

While you should aim to resolve all security vulnerabilities, some security scan results may contain false positives. For example, if you see a theoretical denial-of-service attack under obscure conditions that don't apply to your project, it may be safe to schedule a fix a week or two into the future. On the other hand, a more serious vulnerability that may grant unauthorized access to customer credit card data should be fixed immediately. Whatever the case, arm yourself with knowledge of the vulnerability so you and your team can determine the proper course of action to mitigate the security threat.

Adding the dependency scanning to your pipeline (figure 8.13) is a simple first step to reduce your attack surface. This is easy to implement, as it requires no server reconfigurations or additional servers to work. In its most basic form, simply install the Nancy binary and roll it out.

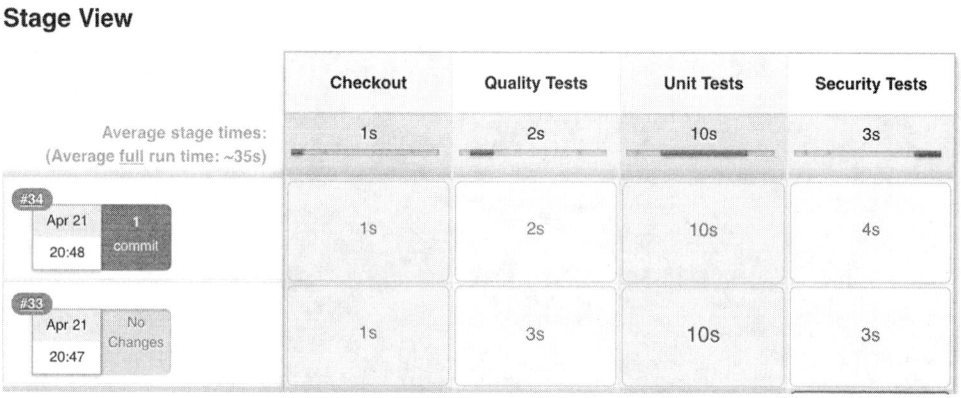

Stage View

	Checkout	Quality Tests	Unit Tests	Security Tests
Average stage times: (Average full run time: ~35s)	1s	2s	10s	3s
#34 Apr 21 20:48 1 commit	1s	2s	10s	4s
#33 Apr 21 20:47 No Changes	1s	3s	10s	3s

Figure 8.13 Security injection in CI pipeline

8.5 *Running parallel tests with Jenkins*

So far, pre-integration tests are running sequentially. One problem we always encounter is how to run all the tests needed to ensure high-quality changes while still keeping pipeline times reasonable and changes flowing smoothly. More tests mean greater confidence, but also longer wait times.

> **NOTE** In chapter 9, we will cover how to use the Parallel Test Execution plugin to run tests in parallel across multiple Jenkins workers.

One of the features of Jenkins pipelines that you see advertised quite frequently is its ability to run parts of your build in parallel by using the `parallel` DSL step.

Update the Jenkinsfile to use the `parallel` keyword, as shown in the following listing. The `parallel` section contains a list of nested test stages to be run in parallel.

Also, you can force your parallel stages to all be aborted when any one of them fails, by adding a `failFast true` instruction.

Listing 8.8 Running tests in parallel

```
node('workers'){
    stage('Checkout'){
        checkout scm
    }

    def imageTest= docker.build("${imageName}-test", "-f Dockerfile.test .")
    stage('Pre-integration Tests'){
            parallel(
                'Quality Tests': {
                    imageTest.inside{
                        sh 'golint'
                    }
                },
                'Unit Tests': {
                    imageTest.inside{
                        sh 'go test'
                    }
                },
                'Security Tests': {
                    imageTest.inside('-u root:root'){
                        sh 'nancy Gopkg.lock'
                    }
                }
            )
    }
}
```

If you push those changes to the remote repository, a new build will be invoked (figure 8.14). However, one disadvantage of the standard pipeline view is that you can't easily see how the parallel steps progress, because the pipeline is linear, like a pipeline. This issue has been addressed by Jenkins by providing an alternate view: Blue Ocean.

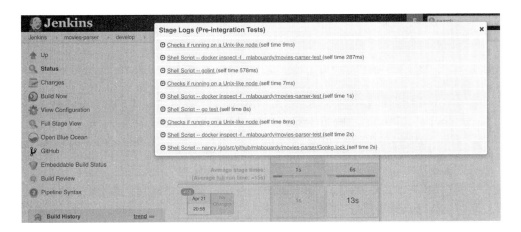

Figure 8.14 Pre-integration tests' parallel execution

Figure 8.15 shows the results for the same pipeline, with parallel test execution in Blue Ocean mode.

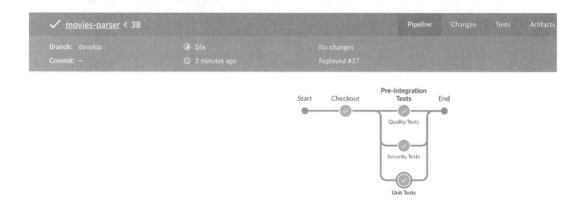

Figure 8.15 Parallel stages in Blue Ocean

This looks nice and provides great visualization for parallel pipeline stages.

8.6 *Improving quality with code analysis*

Apart from continuously integrating code, CI pipelines nowadays also include tasks that perform continuous inspection—inspecting code for its quality in a continuous approach.

The movies-store application is written with TypeScript. We will use Dockerfile.test to build the Docker image to run automated tests, as shown in the following listing.

Listing 8.9   Movie store's Dockerfile.test

```
FROM node:14.0.0
WORKDIR /app
COPY package-lock.json .
COPY package.json .
RUN npm i
COPY . .
```

The first category of tests will be linting the source code. As you saw earlier in this chapter, linting is the process of checking the source code for programmatic, syntactic, stylistic errors. Linting puts the whole service in a uniform format. The code linting can be achieved by writing some rules. Many linters are available, including JSLint, JSHint, and ESLint.

When it comes to linting TypeScript code, ESLint (https://eslint.org/) has a higher-performing architecture than others. For that reason, I'm using ESLint for linting the Node.js project, as shown in the following listing.

Listing 8.10 Movie store's Jenkinsfile

```
def imageName = 'mlabouardy/movies-store'

node('workers'){
    stage('Checkout'){
        checkout scm
    }

    def imageTest= docker.build("${imageName}-test", "-f Dockerfile.test .")

    stage('Quality Tests'){
        imageTest.inside{
            sh 'npm run lint'
        }
    }
}
```

Copy this content to the movies-store Jenkinsfile and push the changes to the develop branch. A new build should be triggered. At the `Quality Tests` stage, we'll see the errors regarding undefined keywords (figure 8.16) such as `describe` and `before`, which are part of the Mocha (https://mochajs.org/) and Chai (www.chaijs.com) JavaScript frameworks. These frameworks are used to describe unit tests (located under the test folder) efficiently and handily.

```
Jenkins  ›  movies-store  ›  develop  ›  #7

[Pipeline] { (Quality Tests)
[Pipeline] sh
+ docker run --rm mlabouardy/movies-store-test npm run lint

> movies-store@1.0.0 lint /app
> eslint .


/app/dao.js
  29:32  error  'process' is not defined  no-undef

/app/index.js
  49:12  error  'process' is not defined  no-undef

/app/test/dao.spec.js
   6:1   error  'describe' is not defined    no-undef
   7:3   error  'before' is not defined      no-undef
   9:5   error  'process' is not defined     no-undef
  10:5   error  'process' is not defined     no-undef
  13:3   error  'beforeEach' is not defined  no-undef
  14:3   error  'afterEach' is not defined   no-undef
  15:3   error  'after' is not defined       no-undef
  20:2   error  'it' is not defined          no-undef
  28:2   error  'it' is not defined          no-undef
  41:2   error  'it' is not defined          no-undef

✖ 12 problems (12 errors, 0 warnings)

npm ERR! code ELIFECYCLE
npm ERR! errno 1
npm ERR! movies-store@1.0.0 lint: `eslint .`
npm ERR! Exit status 1
```

Figure 8.16 ESLint problem detection

ESLint will return an exit 1 code error, which will break the pipeline. To fix the spotted errors, extend ESLint rules by enabling the Mocha environment for ESLint. We use the `key` attribute in eslintrc.json to specify the environments we want to enable by setting `mocha` to `true`:

```
{
    "env": {
        "node": true,
        "commonjs": true,
        "es6": true,
        "mocha": true
    },

}
```

If you push the changes, this time the static code analysis results will be successful, as you can see in figure 8.17.

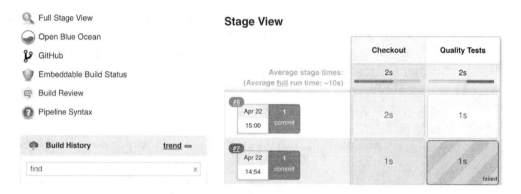

Figure 8.17   CI pipeline execution after fixing ESLint errors

8.7   *Running mocked database tests*

While many developers focus on 100% coverage with unit tests, the code you write must not be tested just in isolation. Integration and end-to-end tests give you that extra confidence by testing parts of your application together. These parts may be working just fine on their own, but in a large system, units of code rarely work separately.

Typically, for integration or end-to-end tests, your scripts will need to connect to a real, dedicated database for testing purposes. This involves writing code that runs at the beginning and end of every test case/suite to ensure that the database is in a clean, predictable state.

Using a real database for testing does have some challenges: database operations can be relatively slow, the testing environment can be complex, and operational overhead may increase. Java projects widely use DbUnit with an in-memory database for this purpose (for example, H2, www.h2database.com/html/main.html). Reusing a good solution from another platform and applying it to the Node.js world can be the way to go here.

Mongo-unit (www.npmjs.com/package/mongo-unit) is a Node.js package that can be installed by using Node Package Manager (npm) or Yarn. It runs MongoDB in memory. It makes integration tests easy by integrating well with the Mocha framework and providing a simple API to manage the database state.

> **NOTE** In chapter 9 and 10, we will run sidecar containers in Jenkins pipelines, such as a MongoDB database, to run end-to-end tests.

The following listing is a simple test (/chapter7/microservices/movies-store/test/dao.spec.js), written with Mocha and Chai, that uses the mongo-unit package to simulate MongoDB by running an in-memory database.

Listing 8.11 Mocha and Chai unit tests

```
const Expect = require('chai').expect
const MongoUnit = require('mongo-unit')
const DAO = require('../dao')
const TestData = require('./movies.json')

describe('StoreDAO', () => {
  before(() =>  MongoUnit.start().then(() => {
    process.env.MONGO_URI = MongoUnit.getUrl()
    DAO.init()
  }))
  beforeEach(() => MongoUnit.load(TestData))
  afterEach(() => MongoUnit.drop())
  after(() => {
    DAO.close()
    return MongoUnit.stop()
  })
 it('should find all movies', () => {
   return DAO.Movie.find()
    .then(movies => {
      Expect(movies.length).to.equal(8)
      Expect(movies[0].title).to.equal('Pulp Fiction (1994)')
    })
 })
})
```

Next, we update the Jenkinsfile to add a new stage that executes the `npm run test` command:

```
stage('Integration Tests'){
        sh "docker run --rm ${imageName}-test npm run test"
}
```

The npm run test command is an alias; it runs the Mocha command line against test cases in the test folder (figure 8.18). The command is defined in package.json, provided in the following listing.

Listing 8.12 Movie store's package.json

```
"scripts": {
    "start": "node index.js",
    "test": "mocha ./test/*.spec.js",
    "lint": "eslint .",
    "coverage-text": "nyc --reporter=text mocha",
    "coverage-html": "nyc --reporter=html mocha"
}
```

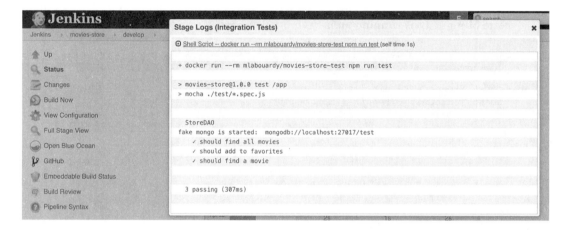

Figure 8.18 Unit testing using the Mocha framework

> **NOTE** If your tests depend on other services, Docker Compose can be used to simplify the startup and connection of all the services that the application depends on.

8.8 Generating HTML coverage reports

We create a new stage to run the coverage tool with a text output format:

```
stage('Coverage Reports'){
        sh "docker run --rm ${imageName}-test npm run coverage-text"
}
```

This will output the text report to the console output, as shown in figure 8.19.

> **NOTE** Istanbul is a JavaScript code coverage tool. For more information, refer to the official guide at https://istanbul.js.org.

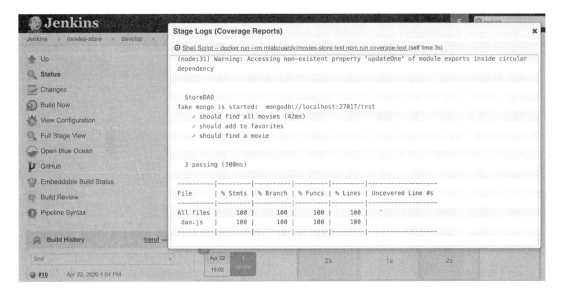

Figure 8.19 Istanbul coverage reports in text format

The metrics that you might see in your coverage reports could be defined as in table 8.1.

Table 8.1 Coverage report metrics

Metric	Description
Statements	The number of statements in the program that are truly called, out of the total number
Branches	The number of branches of the control structures executed
Functions	The number of functions called, out of the total number of functions defined
Lines	The number of lines of source code that are being tested, out of the total number of lines present inside the code

By default, Istanbul uses a text reporter, but various other reporters are available. You can view the full list at http://mng.bz/DKoE.

To generate the HTML format, we will map a volume to /app/coverage, which is the folder in which Istanbul will generate the reports. Then, we'll use the Jenkins HTML Publisher plugin to display the generated code coverage reports, as shown in the following listing.

Listing 8.13 Publishing code coverage HTML reports

```
stage('Coverage Reports'){
      sh "docker run --rm
-v $PWD/coverage:/app/coverage ${imageName}-test
```

```
npm run coverage-html"
        publishHTML (target: [
          allowMissing: false,
          alwaysLinkToLastBuild: false,
          keepAll: true,
          reportDir: "$PWD/coverage",
          reportFiles: "index.html",
          reportName: "Coverage Report"
        ])
}
```

The publishHTML command takes the target block as the main parameter. Within that, we have several subparameters. The allowMissing parameter is set to false, so if something goes wrong while generating the coverage report and the report is missing, the publishHTML instruction will throw an error.

At the end of the CI pipeline, an HTML file will be generated and consumed by the HTML Publisher plugin, as shown in figure 8.20.

```
[Pipeline] publishHTML
[htmlpublisher] Archiving HTML reports...
[htmlpublisher] Archiving at BUILD level /home/ec2-user/coverage to /var/lib/jenkins/jobs/movies-
store/branches/develop/builds/16/htmlreports/Coverage_20Report
```

Figure 8.20   HTML report generation with Istanbul

The HTML report will then be accessible from Jenkins, by clicking the Coverage Report item from the left panel; see figure 8.21.

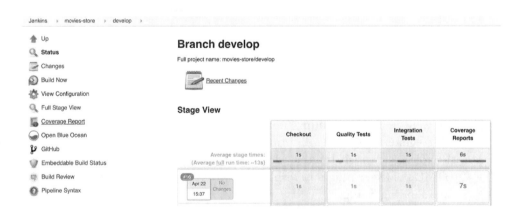

Figure 8.21   The coverage report can be accessible from the Jenkins panel.

NOTE The Cobertura plugin (https://plugins.jenkins.io/cobertura/) can also be used to publish HTML reports. Both plugins show the same results.

We can drill down to identify the uncovered lines and functions, as shown in figure 8.22.

Back to develop | index

All files dao.js

100% Statements 5/5   **100%** Branches 0/0   **100%** Functions 2/2   **100%** Lines 5/5

Press *n* or *j* to go to the next uncovered block, *b*, *p* or *k* for the previous block.

```
1  1x   const Mongoose = require('mongoose')
2
3  1x   const movieSchema = new Mongoose.Schema({
4           title: String,
5           id: String,
6           poster: String,
7           releaseDate: String,
8           rating: String,
9           genre: String,
10          description: String,
11          videos: [String],
12          similar: [
13            {
14                title: String,
15                poster: String,
16            }
17          ],
```

Figure 8.22 Deep dive inside the coverage report

> **NOTE**   Several tools exist to create coverage reports, depending on the language you use (for example, SimpleCov for Ruby, Coverage.py for Python, and JaCoCo for Java).

You can take this further and run stages in parallel to reduce the waiting time of running tests, as shown in the following listing.

Listing 8.14 Running pre-integration tests in parallel

```
stage('Tests'){
      parallel(
          'Quality Tests': {
              sh "docker run --rm ${imageName}-test npm run lint"
          },
          'Integration Tests': {
              sh "docker run --rm ${imageName}-test npm run test"
          },
          'Coverage Reports': {
              sh "docker run --rm
-v $PWD/coverage:/app/coverage ${imageName}-test
npm run coverage-html"
              publishHTML (target: [
                  allowMissing: false,
                  alwaysLinkToLastBuild: false,
                  keepAll: true,
                  reportDir: "$PWD/coverage",
                  reportFiles: "index.html",
                  reportName: "Coverage Report"
              ])
          }
      )
}
```

Figure 8.23 shows the end result of running this job in the Blue Ocean view.

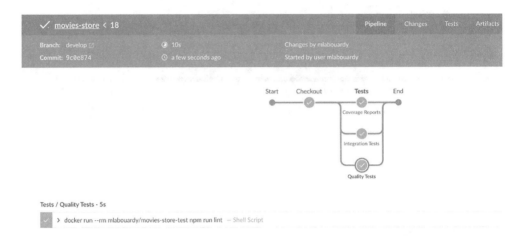

Figure 8.23   Running tests in parallel

8.9   *Automating UI testing with Headless Chrome*

For the Angular application, we will create a Dockerfile.test file that installs the Angular CLI (https://angular.io/cli) and the needed dependencies to run automated tests; see the following listing.

Listing 8.15   Movie marketplace's Dockerfile.test

```
FROM node:14.0.0
ENV CHROME_BIN=chromium
WORKDIR /app
COPY package-lock.json .
COPY package.json .
RUN npm i && npm i -g @angular/cli
COPY . .
```

The linting state is similar to the previous part; we will use the TSLint linter, which comes installed by default for Angular projects. Hence, we will run the `npm run lint` alias command defined in package.json, as shown in the following listing.

Listing 8.16   Movie marketplace's package.json

```
"scripts": {
    "start": "ng serve",
    "build": "ng build",
    "test": "ng test --browsers=ChromeHeadlessCI --code-coverage=true",
    "lint": "ng lint",
    "e2e": "ng e2e"
  }
```

We update the Jenkinsfile with the following content.

Listing 8.17   Movie marketplace's Jenkinsfile

```
def imageName = 'mlabouardy/movies-marketplace'
node('workers'){
    stage('Checkout'){
        checkout scm
    }

    def imageTest= docker.build("${imageName}-test", "-f Dockerfile.test .")
    stage('Pre-integration Tests'){
        parallel(
            'Quality Tests': {
                sh "docker run --rm ${imageName}-test npm run lint"
            }
        )
    }
}
```

Let's save this config and run a build. The pipeline should fail and turn red because of the forced rules on TSLint, as shown in figure 8.24.

Figure 8.24   CI pipeline failure

If you click the Quality Tests stage logs, the logs should display errors regarding missing semicolons and trailing whitespace, as shown in figure 8.25.

Figure 8.25   Angular linting output logs

If you wish to let TSLint pass within your code (figure 8.26), you need to update tslint.json to disable forced rules or add the `/* tslint:disable */` instruction at the beginning of each file for TSLint to skip the linting process on those files.

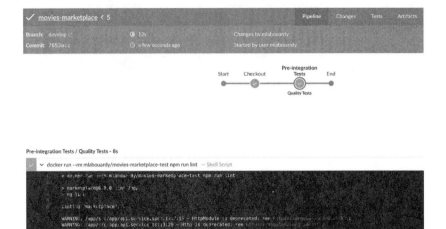

Figure 8.26   Angular linting output logs

For Angular unit testing, we will use the Jasmine (https://jasmine.github.io/) and Karma (https://karma-runner.github.io/latest/index.html) frameworks. Both testing frameworks support the BDD practice, which describes tests in a human-readable format for nontechnical people. The sample unit test (chapter7/microservices/movies-marketplace/src/app/app.component.spec.ts) in the following listing is self-explanatory. It tests whether the app component has a property `text` with the value `Watchlist` that is rendered in the HTML inside a `span` element tag.

Listing 8.18   Movie marketplace's Karma tests

```
import { TestBed, async } from '@angular/core/testing';
import { RouterTestingModule } from '@angular/router/testing';
import { AppComponent } from './app.component';

describe('AppComponent', () => {
  beforeEach(async(() => {
    TestBed.configureTestingModule({
      imports: [
        RouterTestingModule
      ],
      declarations: [
        AppComponent
      ],
    }).compileComponents();
  }));
```

```
it('should create the app', () => {
  const fixture = TestBed.createComponent(AppComponent);
  const app = fixture.debugElement.componentInstance;
  expect(app).toBeTruthy();
});
it('should render title', () => {
  const fixture = TestBed.createComponent(AppComponent);
  fixture.detectChanges();
  const compiled = fixture.debugElement.nativeElement;
  expect(compiled.querySelector('.toolbar
    span').textContent).toContain('Watchlist');
});
});
```

NOTE   When creating Angular projects with the Angular CLI, it defaults to creating and running unit tests by using Jasmine and Karma.

Running unit tests for frontend web applications requires them to be tested in a web browser. While it's not an issue on a workstation or host machine, it can become tedious when running in a restricted environment such as a Docker container. In fact, these execution environments are generally lightweight and do not contain any graphical environment.

Fortunately, Karma tests can be run with a UI-less browser, and two main options can be used: Chrome Headless or PhantomJS. The example in the following listing uses Chrome Headless with Puppeteer, which can be configured on a simple flag in the Karma config (chapter7/microservices/movies-marketplace/karma.conf.js).

Listing 8.19   Karma runner configuration

```
module.exports = function (config) {
  config.set({
    basePath: '',
    frameworks: ['jasmine', '@angular-devkit/build-angular'],
    customLaunchers: {
      ChromeHeadlessCI: {
        base: 'Chrome',
        flags: [
          '--headless',
          '--disable-gpu',
          '--no-sandbox',
          '--remote-debugging-port=9222'
        ]
      }
    },
    browsers: ['ChromeHeadless', 'Chrome'],
    singleRun: true,  });
};
```

Headless Chrome needs sudo privileges to be run unless the `--no-sandbox` flag is used. Next, we need to update Dockerfile.test to install Chromium:

```
RUN apt-get update && apt-get install -y chromium
```

NOTE Chromium/Google Chrome has shipped with the headless mode since version 59.

Then, we update the Jenkinsfile to run unit tests with the `npm run test` command. The command will fire up Headless Chrome and execute Karma.js tests. Next, we generate a coverage report in HTML format that will be consumed by the HTML Publisher plugin, as shown in the following listing.

Listing 8.20 Mapping the workspace folder with the Docker container volume

```
stage('Pre-integration Tests'){
      parallel(
            'Quality Tests': {
                sh "docker run --rm ${imageName}-test npm run lint"
            },
            'Unit Tests': {
                sh "docker run --rm
-v $PWD/coverage:/app/coverage ${imageName}-test
npm run test"
                publishHTML (target: [
                    allowMissing: false,
                    alwaysLinkToLastBuild: false,
                    keepAll: true,
                    reportDir: "$PWD/coverage",
                    reportFiles: "index.html",
                    reportName: "Coverage Report"
                ])}
      )
}
```

Once changes are pushed to the GitHub repository, a new build will be triggered and unit tests will be executed, as shown in figure 8.27.

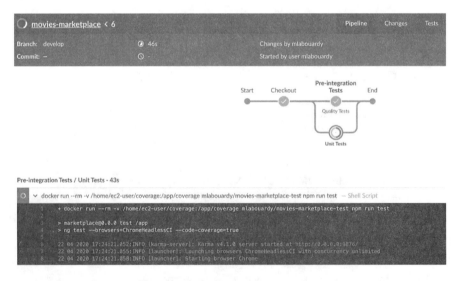

Figure 8.27 Running headless Chrome inside a Docker container

The Karma launcher will run the tests on the Headless Chrome browser and display the code coverage statistics, as shown in figure 8.28.

Figure 8.28 Successful execution of the Karma unit tests

Also, a generated HTML report will be available in the Artifacts section in the Blue Ocean view, shown in figure 8.29.

Figure 8.29   Coverage report alongside other artifacts

If you click the coverage report link, it should display the statements and functions coverage by Angular components and services, as shown in figure 8.30.

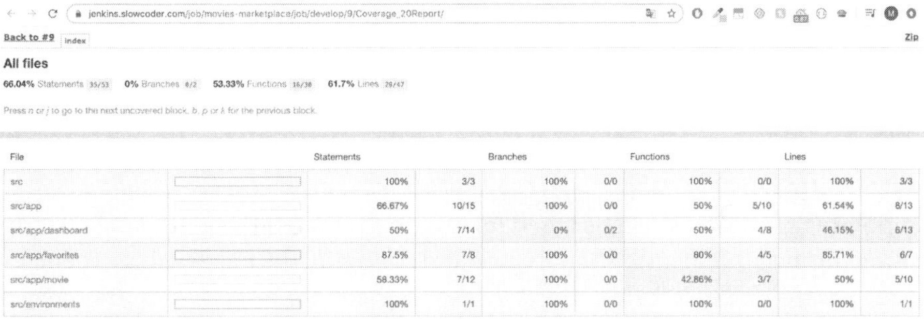

File		Statements		Branches		Functions		Lines	
src		100%	3/3	100%	0/0	100%	0/0	100%	3/3
src/app		66.67%	10/15	100%	0/0	50%	5/10	61.54%	8/13
src/app/dashboard		50%	7/14	0%	0/2	50%	4/8	46.15%	6/13
src/app/favorites		87.5%	7/8	100%	0/0	80%	4/5	85.71%	6/7
src/app/movie		58.33%	7/12	100%	0/0	42.86%	3/7	50%	5/10
src/environments		100%	1/1	100%	0/0	100%	0/0	100%	1/1

Figure 8.30 Coverage statistics by filename

With this done, it is now possible to run the unit tests with Chromium inside a Docker container.

8.10   *Integrating SonarQube Scanner with Jenkins*

While code linters can give you a high-level overview of the quality of your code, they're still limited if you want to perform deep static code analysis and inspection to detect potential bugs and vulnerabilities. That's where SonarQube comes into play. it will give you a 360-degree vision of the quality of the codebase by integrating external libraries like PMD, Checkstyle, and FindBugs. Every time code gets committed, code analysis is performed.

> **NOTE**   SonarQube can be used to inspect code in more than 20 programming languages, including Java, PHP, Go, and Python.

To deploy SonarQube, we will bake a new AMI with Packer. Similarly to previous chapters, we create a template.json file with the content in the following listing (chapter8/sonarqube/packer/template.json).

Listing 8.21   Jenkins worker's Packer template

```
{
    "variables" : {...},
    "builders" : [
        {
            "type" : "amazon-ebs",
            "profile" : "{{user `aws_profile`}}",
            "region" : "{{user `region`}}",
            "instance_type" : "{{user `instance_type`}}",
            "source_ami" : "{{user `source_ami`}}",
            "ssh_username" : "ubuntu",
            "ami_name" : "sonarqube-8.2.0.32929",
            "ami_description" : "SonarQube community edition"
        }
    ],
    "provisioners" : [
        {
            "type" : "file",
            "source" : "sonar.init.d",
            "destination" : "/tmp/"
        },
        {
            "type" : "shell",
            "script" : "./setup.sh",
            "execute_command" : "sudo -E -S sh '{{ .Path }}'"
        }
    ]
}
```

The temporary EC2 instance will be based on Amazon Linux AMI and uses a shell script to provision the instance to install SonarQube and configure the needed dependencies.

The setup.sh script will install SonarQube from the official release page. For this example, SonarQube 8.2.0 will be installed. SonarQube supports PostgreSQL, MySQL, Microsoft SQL Server (MSSQL), and Oracle as a backend. I opted to go with PostgreSQL to store configurations and report results. Then, the script creates a directory named sonar, sets permissions, and configures SonarQube to start automatically; see the following listing.

Listing 8.22 Installing SonarQube LTS

```
wget https://binaries.sonarsource.com/
Distribution/sonarqube/$SONAR_VERSION.zip -P /tmp
unzip /tmp/$SONAR_VERSION.zip
mv $SONAR_VERSION sonarqube
mv sonarqube /opt/

apt-get install -y unzip curl
sh -c 'echo "deb http://apt.postgresql.org/pub/repos/apt/
 `lsb_release -cs`-pgdg main" >> /etc/apt/sources.list.d/pgdg.list'
wget -q https://www.postgresql.org/media/keys/ACCC4CF8.asc
-O - | sudo apt-key add -
apt-get install -y postgresql postgresql-contrib
systemctl start postgresql
systemctl enable postgresql
cat > /tmp/db.sql <<EOF
CREATE USER $SONAR_DB_USER WITH ENCRYPTED PASSWORD '$SONAR_DB_PASS';
CREATE DATABASE $SONAR_DB_NAME OWNER $SONAR_DB_USER;
EOF
sudo -u postgres psql postgres < /tmp/db.sql

mv /tmp/sonar.properties /opt/sonarqube/conf/sonar.properties
sed -i 's/#RUN_AS_USER=/RUN_AS_USER=sonar/' sonar.sh
sysctl -w vm.max_map_count=262144
groupadd sonar
useradd -c "Sonar System User" -d /opt/sonarqube -g sonar -s /bin/bash sonar
chown -R sonar:sonar /opt/sonarqube
ln -sf /opt/sonarqube/bin/linux-x86-64/sonar.sh /usr/bin/sonar
cp /tmp/sonar.init.d /etc/init.d/sonar
chmod 755 /etc/init.d/sonar
update-rc.d sonar defaults
service sonar start
```

NOTE The full shell script is available on the GitHub repository along with a step-by-step guide. Also, make sure you have at least 4 GB of memory to run the 64-bit version of SonarQube.

Once you define the needed Packer variables, issue a packer build command to start the provisioning process. Once the AMI is baked, it should be available on the EC2 dashboard in the Images section, as shown in figure 8.31.

Figure 8.31   SonarQube machine image

From there, use Terraform to deploy a private EC2 instance based on the SonarQube AMI, as shown in the following listing.

Listing 8.23   SonarQube EC2 instance resource with Terraform

```
resource "aws_instance" "sonarqube" {
  ami                    = data.aws_ami.sonarqube.id
  instance_type          = var.sonarqube_instance_type
  key_name               = var.key_name
  vpc_security_group_ids = [aws_security_group.sonarqube_sg.id]
  subnet_id              = element(var.private_subnets, 0)

  root_block_device {
    volume_type         = "gp2"
    volume_size         = 30
    delete_on_termination = false
  }

  tags = {
    Name   = "sonarqube"
    Author = var.author
  }
}
```

Then, define a public load balancer to forward incoming HTTP and HTTPS (optional) traffic to the instance on port 9000 (the port to which the SonarQube dashboard is exposed). Also, create an A record in Route 53 pointing to the load balancer FQDN.

Issue the `terraform apply` command to provision the instance and other resources. The instance should be deployed in a few seconds, as shown in figure 8.32.

Name	Instance ID	Instance Type	Availability Zone	Instance State	Status Checks	Alarm Status	Public DNS (IPv4)
bastion	i-04cb68cc8ac1d79bb	t2.micro	eu-west-3a	running	2/2 checks ...	None	ec2-35-180-33-152.eu-...
jenkins_master	i-0aa7ecdfbb8e74bb9	t2.large	eu-west-3a	running	2/2 checks ...	None	
jenkins_worker	i-04241bea527fd058a	t2.medium	eu-west-3a	running	2/2 checks ...	None	
jenkins_worker	i-0f18182f68cf2a9a8	t2.medium	eu-west-3b	running	2/2 checks ...	None	
sonarqube	i-0ee0c0253678e09b4	t2.large	eu-west-3a	running	Initializing	None	

Figure 8.32   SonarQube private EC2 instance

On the terminal, you should have the URL of the public load balancer in the Outputs section, as shown in figure 8.33.

```
aws_security_group.elb_sonarqube_sg: Creating...
aws_security_group.elb_sonarqube_sg: Creation complete after 1s [id=sg-082e62dc156bf43cd]
aws_security_group.sonarqube_sg: Creating...
aws_security_group.sonarqube_sg: Creation complete after 2s [id=sg-0eec135401e424f0f]
aws_instance.sonarqube: Creating...
aws_instance.sonarqube: Still creating... [10s elapsed]
aws_instance.sonarqube: Still creating... [20s elapsed]
aws_instance.sonarqube: Creation complete after 22s [id=i-0ee0c0253678e09b4]
aws_elb.sonarqube_elb: Creating...
aws_elb.sonarqube_elb: Creation complete after 2s [id=tf-lb-20200424121504563600000001]
aws_route53_record.sonarqube: Creating...
aws_route53_record.sonarqube: Still creating... [10s elapsed]
aws_route53_record.sonarqube: Still creating... [20s elapsed]
aws_route53_record.sonarqube: Still creating... [30s elapsed]
aws_route53_record.sonarqube: Creation complete after 39s [id=Z2TR95QTU3UIUT_sonarqube.slowcoder.com_A]

Apply complete! Resources: 5 added, 0 changed, 0 destroyed.

Outputs:

sonarqube = https://sonarqube.slowcoder.com
```

Figure 8.33   SonarQube DNS URL

Head over to the URL and log in with the default credentials (figure 8.34). Right now, no user accounts are configured in SonarQube. However, by default, an admin account exists with the username `admin` and the password `admin`.

Figure 8.34   SonarQube web dashboard

Next, make sure the TypeScript analyzer is enabled from the SonarQube Plugins section, as shown in figure 8.35.

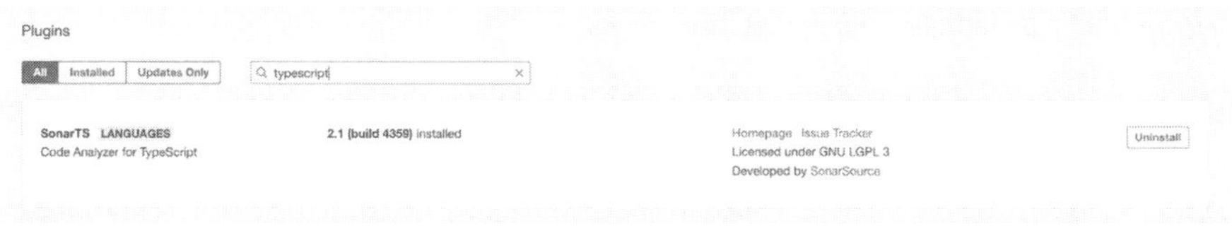

Figure 8.35   SonarQube TypeScript analyzer plugin

Then, generate a new token for Jenkins to avoid using SonarQube admin credentials for security purposes. Go to Administration and navigate to Security. On the same page under the Tokens section is an option to generate a token; click the Generate button, shown in figure 8.36.

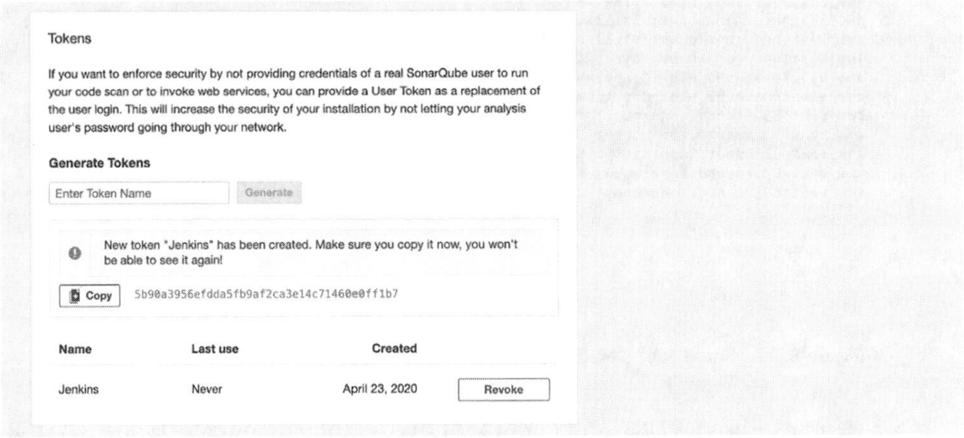

Tokens

If you want to enforce security by not providing credentials of a real SonarQube user to run your code scan or to invoke web services, you can provide a User Token as a replacement of the user login. This will increase the security of your installation by not letting your analysis user's password going through your network.

Generate Tokens

| Enter Token Name | | Generate |

ⓘ New token "Jenkins" has been created. Make sure you copy it now, you won't be able to see it again!

📋 Copy   5b90a3956efdda5fb9af2ca3e14c71460e0ff1b7

Name	Last use	Created	
Jenkins	Never	April 23, 2020	Revoke

Figure 8.36   SonarQube Jenkins dedicated token

The server authentication token should be created as a `Secret text` credential from Jenkins, as shown in figure 8.37.

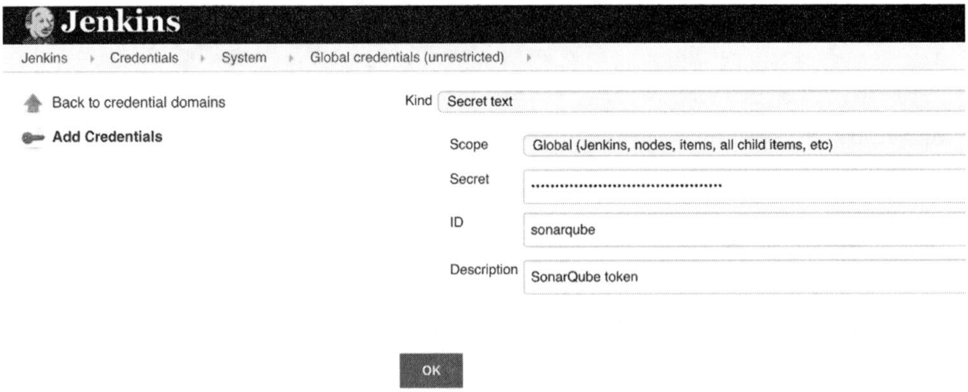

🔗 Jenkins

Jenkins ▸ Credentials ▸ System ▸ Global credentials (unrestricted) ▸

🔼 Back to credential domains

📇 Add Credentials

Kind	Secret text
Scope	Global (Jenkins, nodes, items, all child items, etc)
Secret	....
ID	sonarqube
Description	SonarQube token

OK

Figure 8.37   SonarQube secret text credentials

To trigger the scanning from the CI pipeline, we need to install SonarQube Scanner. You can choose to either install it automatically or provide the installation path for this tool on Jenkins workers. It can be installed by choosing Manage Jenkins > Global

Tool Configuration. Or you can bake a new Jenkins worker image with SonarQube Scanner with the commands shown in the following listing.

Listing 8.24 SonarQube Scanner installation

```
wget https://binaries.sonarsource.com/
Distribution/sonar-scanner-cli/sonar-scanner-cli-2.0.1873-linux.zip -P /tmp
unzip /tmp/sonar-scanner-cli-4.2.0.1873-linux.zip
mv sonar-scanner-4.2.0.1873-linux sonar-scanner
ln -sf /home/ec2-user/sonar-scanner/bin/sonar-scanner /usr/bin/sonar-scanner
```

> **NOTE** The launch configuration of the Jenkins workers is immutable. You will need to clone the launch configuration, update it with newly built AMI, and attach it to the Jenkins workers' Auto Scaling group to create new workers with the Sonar Scanner tool.

Lastly, make Jenkins aware of the SonarQube server installation from the Configure menu in Manage Jenkins, as shown in figure 8.38.

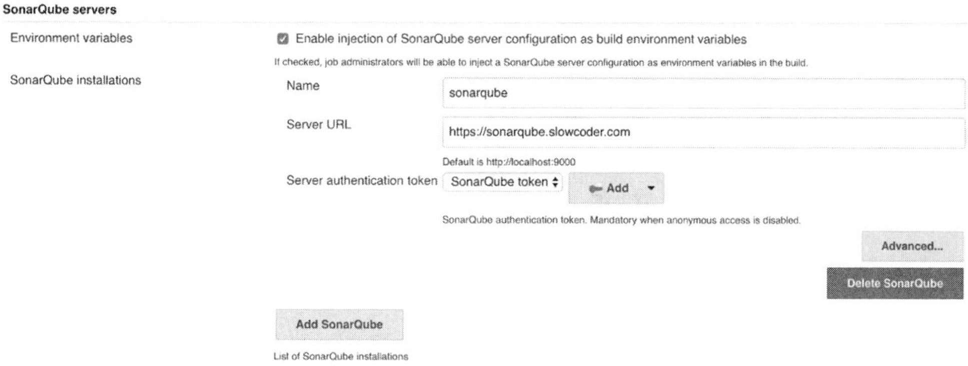

Figure 8.38 SonarQube server settings

Then, create a sonar-project.properties file in the movies-marketplace root folder to publish the coverage report to the SonarQube server. This file contains certain sonar properties, such as which folder to scan and exclude, and the name of the project; see the following listing.

Listing 8.25 SonarQube project configuration

```
sonar.projectKey=angular:movies-marketplace
sonar.projectName=movies-marketplace
sonar.projectVersion=1.0.0
sonar.sourceEncoding=UTF-8
sonar.sources=src
sonar.exclusions=**/node_modules/**,**/*.spec.ts
```

```
sonar.tests=src/app
sonar.test.inclusions=**/*.spec.ts
sonar.ts.tslint.configPath=tslint.json
sonar.javascript.lcov.reportPaths=/home/ec2-user/coverage/marketplace/
    lcov.info
```

Next, update the Jenkinsfile to create a new `Static Code Analysis` stage.

Then inject a SonarQube global configuration (secret token and SonarQube server URL values) with the `withSonarQubeEnv` block and invoke the `sonar-scanner` command to start the analysis process, as shown in the following listing.

Listing 8.26 Triggering SonarQube analysis

```
stage('Static Code Analysis'){
        withSonarQubeEnv('sonarqube') {
            sh 'sonar-scanner'
        }
}
```

You can override property values by using the `-D` flag:

```
sh 'sonar-scanner -Dsonar.projectVersion=$BUILD_NUMBER'
```

This option allows us to attach the Jenkins build number with every analysis that we perform and publish to SonarQube.

After a successful build, the logs will show you the files and folders SonarQube has scanned. After scanning, the analysis report is posted to the SonarQube server we have integrated. This analysis is based on rules defined by SonarQube. If the code passes the error threshold, it's allowed to move to the next step in its life cycle. But if it crosses the error threshold, it's dropped:

```
INFO: Sensor SonarTS [typescript] (done) | time=0ms
INFO: ------------ Run sensors on project
INFO: Sensor Zero Coverage Sensor
INFO: Sensor Zero Coverage Sensor (done) | time=3ms
INFO: CPD Executor Calculating CPD for 5 files
INFO: CPD Executor CPD calculation finished (done) | time=27ms
INFO: Analysis report generated in 103ms, dir size=121 KB
INFO: Analysis report compressed in 42ms, zip size=42 KB
INFO: Analysis report uploaded in 51ms
INFO: ANALYSIS SUCCESSFUL, you can browse https://sonarqube.slowcoder.com/dashboard?id=angular%3Amovies-marketplace
INFO: Note that you will be able to access the updated dashboard once the server has processed the submitted analysis report
INFO: More about the report processing at https://sonarqube.slowcoder.com/api/ce/task?id=AXGrwc7YDDGq9I6LnDBw
INFO: Analysis total time: 6.103 s
INFO: ------------------------------------------------------------------------
INFO: EXECUTION SUCCESS
INFO: ------------------------------------------------------------------------
INFO: Total time: 9.014s
INFO: Final Memory: 13M/44M
INFO: ------------------------------------------------------------------------
```

You can define your custom thresholds by creating Quality Profiles, which are a set of rules that will make the pipeline fail if an issue is raised in your codebase.

NOTE   Refer to this official documentation for a step-by-step guide on how to create SonarQube custom rules with Quality Profiles: http://mng.bz/l9vy.

Finally, on visiting the SonarQube server, the project details should be visible with all the metrics captured from the code coverage report, as you can see in figure 8.39.

Figure 8.39   SonarQube project metrics

Now you can go inside the movies-marketplace project and discover issues, bugs, code smells, coverage, or duplication. The dashboard (figure 8.40) shows where you stand in terms of quality in the glimpse of an eye.

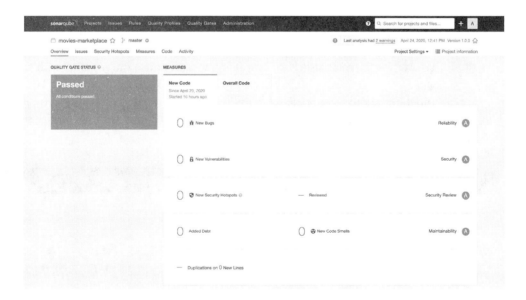

Figure 8.40   SonarQube project deep-dive metrics and issues

Also, when the job is completed, the SonarQube Scanner plugin will detect that a SonarQube analysis was made during the build. The plugin will then display a badge and a widget on the Jenkins job page with a link to the SonarQube dashboard as well as quality gate status, as shown in figure 8.41.

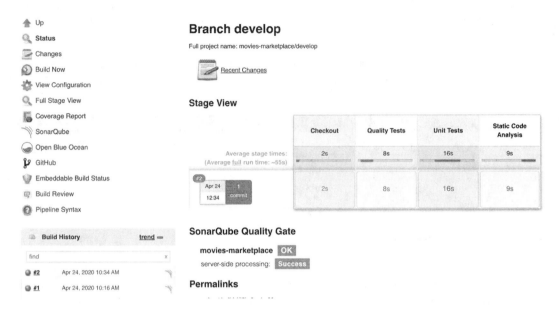

Figure 8.41   SonarQube integration with Jenkins

The SonarQube analysis was quick, but for larger projects, the analysis might take a few minutes to complete.

To wait for the analysis to be completed, we will pause the pipeline with the `with-ForQualityGate` step, which waits for SonarQube analysis to be done. To notify the CI pipeline about the analysis completion, we need to create a webhook on SonarQube to notify Jenkins when project analysis is done, as shown in figure 8.42.

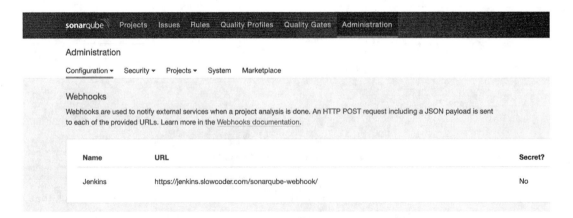

Figure 8.42   SonarQube webhook creation

Next, in the following listing, we update the Jenkinsfile to integrate the `waitFor-QualityGate` step that pauses the pipeline until SonarQube analysis is completed and returns the quality gate status.

Listing 8.27 Adding a quality gate to the Jenkinsfile

```
stage('Static Code Analysis'){
        withSonarQubeEnv('sonarqube') {
            sh 'sonar-scanner'
        }
}
stage("Quality Gate"){
        timeout(time: 5, unit: 'MINUTES') {
            def qg = waitForQualityGate()
            if (qg.status != 'OK') {
                error "Pipeline
aborted due to quality gate failure: ${qg.status}"
            }
        }
}
```

NOTE The quality gate can be moved outside the `node{}` block to avoid occupying a Jenkins worker waiting for SonarQube notification.

Commit the changes and push them to the remote repository. A new build will be triggered, and SonarQube analysis will be kicked off automatically. Once the analysis is completed, a notification will be sent to the CI pipeline to resume the pipeline stages, as shown in figure 8.43.

NOTE We can set up Post-build actions in Jenkins to notify the user about the test results.

Figure 8.43 SonarQube project analysis status

As a result, as soon as a developer commits the code to GitHub, Jenkins will fetch/pull the code from the GitHub repository, perform static code analysis with the help of Sonar Scanner, and send analysis reports to the SonarQube server.

In this chapter, you learned how to run various automated tests and how to integrate external tools like Nancy and SonarQube to inspect code quality, detect bugs, and avoid potential security vulnerabilities while continuously building microservices within Jenkins CI pipelines. In the next chapter, we will build the Docker image after a successful run of tests and push the image to a private remote repository.

Summary

- Docker containers are used to run tests to avoid installing multiple runtime environments for each service we're integrating and keep a consistent execution environment across all Jenkins workers.
- Promoting traditional security practices into CI/CD workflows like external dependencies scanning can enable an additional security layer to avoid security breaches and vulnerabilities.
- Headless Chrome is a way to run UI tests in a headless environment without the full browser UI.
- The parallel DSL step gives the ability to easily run pipeline stages in parallel.
- SonarQube is a code-quality management tool that allows teams to manage, track, and improve the quality of their source code.

Building Docker images within a CI pipeline

This chapter covers

- Building Docker images inside Jenkins pipelines and best practices of writing Dockerfiles
- Using Docker agents as an execution environment in Jenkins declarative pipelines
- Integrating Jenkins build statuses into GitHub pull requests
- Deploying and configuring hosted and managed Docker private registry solutions
- Docker images life cycle within the development cycle and tagging strategies
- Scanning Docker images for security vulnerabilities within Jenkins pipelines

In the previous chapter, you learned how to run automated tests inside Docker containers within CI pipelines. In this chapter, we will finish the CI workflow by building a Docker image and storing it inside a private remote repository for versioning; see figure 9.1.

Continuous integration

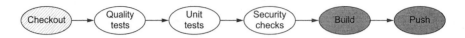

Figure 9.1   The Build and Push stages will be implemented in this chapter.

By the end of this chapter, you should be able to build a similar CI pipeline with these steps:

1 Check out the source code from a remote repository. The CI server fetches the code from the version-control system (VCS) on a push event.
2 Run pre-integration tests such as unit tests, security tests, quality tests, and UI tests inside a Docker container. These might include generating coverage reports and integrating quality-inspection tools like SonarQube for static code analysis.
3 Compile the source code and build a Docker image (automated packaging).
4 Tag the end image and store it in a private registry.

Figure 9.2 summarizes the end result of the CI workflow.

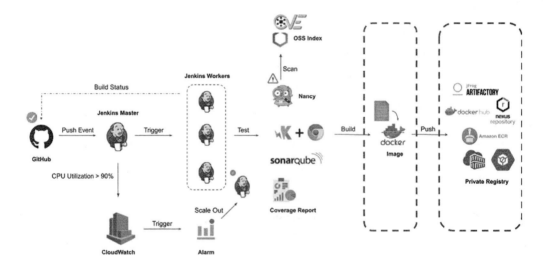

Figure 9.2   The CI pipeline process

The purpose of this CI pipeline is to automate the process of continuously building, testing, and uploading the Docker image to the private registry. Reporting for failures/success happens at every stage.

> **NOTE**   The CI design discussed in this chapter and previous ones can be modified to suit the needs of any type of project; the users just need to identify the right tools and configurations that can be used with Jenkins.

9.1 *Building Docker images*

For now, each push event to the remote repository triggers the pipeline on Jenkins. The pipeline will be executed based on stages defined in the Jenkinsfile. The first stage to be launched will be cloning the code from the remote repository, running automated tests, and publishing coverage reports. Figure 9.3 shows the current CI workflow for the movies-loader service.

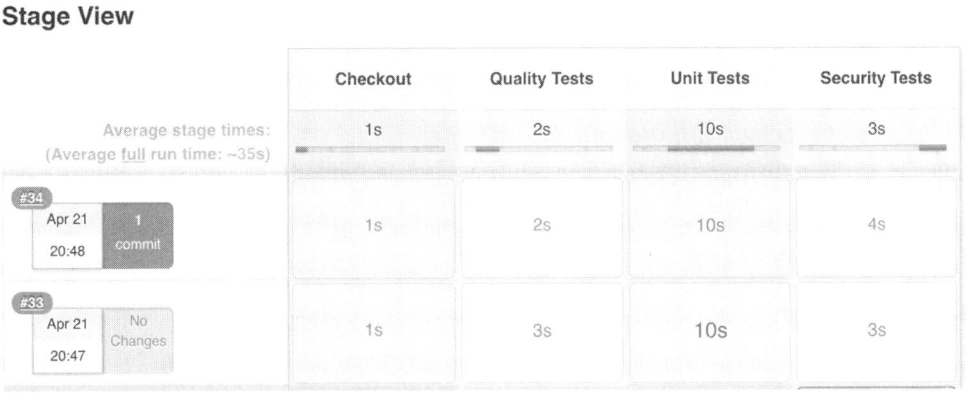

Stage View

	Checkout	Quality Tests	Unit Tests	Security Tests
Average stage times: (Average full run time: ~35s)	1s	2s	10s	3s
#34 Apr 21 20:48 — 1 commit	1s	2s	10s	4s
#33 Apr 21 20:47 — No Changes	1s	3s	10s	3s

Figure 9.3   Current CI workflow

If the tests are successful, the next stage will be building the artifact; in our case, it will be a Docker image.

> **NOTE** When you're building a Docker image for your application, you're building on top of an existing image. A broken base image can lead to production outages (security breaches, for instance). I recommend using an up-to-date and well-maintained image.

9.1.1 *Using the Docker DSL*

To build the main application Docker image, we need to define a Dockerfile with a set of instructions that specify the environment to use and the commands to run. Create a Dockerfile in the top-level directory of the movies-loader project, using the following code.

Listing 9.1   Movie loader's Dockerfile

```
FROM python:3.7.3
LABEL MAINTAINER mlabouardy
WORKDIR /app
COPY requirements.txt .
RUN pip install -r requirements.txt
COPY movies.json main.py ./
CMD python main.py
```

The Python-based application will use Python v3.7.3 as a base image, install the run-time dependencies with the pip manager, and set `python main.py` as the main command for the Docker image.

> **NOTE**   To maintain the consistency of your image builds, create a requirements .txt file with transitively pinned versions of all used dependencies.

The order of instructions in a Dockerfile is important. The Docker image is rebuilt whenever any change occurs in the source code. That's why I placed the `pip install` command in listing 9.1, as the dependencies are not frequently changed. Therefore, Docker will rely on layer caching that will speed up the build time of the image. Refer to the official Docker documentation to learn more about the Docker build cache: http://mng.bz/B10J.

Finally, we add a `Build` stage in the Jenkinsfile, which uses the Docker DSL to build an image based on the Dockerfile in the repository:

```
stage('Build'){
        docker.build(imageName)
}
```

The `build()` method builds the Dockerfile in the current directory by default. You can override this by providing the Dockerfile path as the second argument of the `build()` method.

The changes are pushed to the develop branch with the following commands:

```
git add Jenkinsfile Dockerfile
git commit -m "building docker image"
git push origin develop
```

Then a new build should be triggered, and the image should be built, as shown in figure 9.4.

```
Jenkins  ›  movies-loader  ›  develop  ›  #2

                                     [Pipeline] stage
                                     [Pipeline] { (Build)
                                     [Pipeline] isUnix
                                     [Pipeline] sh
                                     + docker build -t mlabouardy/movies-loader .
                                     Sending build context to Docker daemon  114.2kB

                                     Step 1/7 : FROM python:2.7.10
                                      ---> 4442f7b981c4
                                     Step 2/7 : LABEL MAINTAINER mlabouardy
                                      ---> Running in e2c1a27aa2e2
                                     Removing intermediate container e2c1a27aa2e2
                                      ---> 0899c44ac2cd
                                     Step 3/7 : WORKDIR /app
                                      ---> Running in ab0b93253f21
                                     Removing intermediate container ab0b93253f21
                                      ---> bab38bb0c657
                                     Step 4/7 : COPY requirements.txt .
                                      ---> 54f3f491c8d3
                                     Step 5/7 : RUN pip install -r requirements.txt
```

Figure 9.4 Python Docker image build logs

Branch develop

Full project name: movies-loader/develop

Recent Changes

Stage View

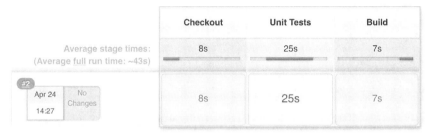

Figure 9.5 Movie loader CI pipeline

So far, we've defined the CI stages in figure 9.5 for the movies-loader CI pipeline. The movies-parser service's Dockerfile will be different, as it's written in Go. Because Go is a compiled language, we won't need it at the runtime of the service. Therefore, we will use Docker's multistage build feature to reduce the Docker image size, as shown in the following listing.

Listing 9.2 Multistage build usage

```
FROM golang:1.16.5
WORKDIR /go/src/github.com/mlabouardy/movies-parser
COPY main.go go.mod .
RUN go get -v
RUN CGO_ENABLED=0 GOOS=linux go build -a -installsuffix cgo -o app main.go

FROM alpine:latest
LABEL Maintainer mlabouardy
RUN apk --no-cache add ca-certificates
WORKDIR /root/
COPY --from=0 /go/src/github.com/mlabouardy/movies-parser/app .
CMD ["./app"]
```

The Dockerfile is split into two stages. The first stage builds the binary with the `go build` command. The second stage uses Alpine as the base image, which is a lightweight image, and then copies the binary from the first stage.

The intermediate layer where the Go build tools and compilation happen is about 300 MB. The final image has a minimal footprint of 8 MB. The end result is the same tiny production image as before, with a significant reduction in complexity. The Go SDK and any intermediate artifacts are left behind and not saved in the final image.

NOTE   The multistage build feature requires Docker engine 17.05 or higher on the daemon and client.

In the previous Dockerfile, stages are not named and are referred to by their integer number (starting with 0 for the first FROM instruction). However, we can name the stages by passing AS *NAME* to the FROM instruction, as shown in the following listing.

Listing 9.3   Naming Docker multistages

```
FROM golang:1.16.5 AS builder
WORKDIR /go/src/github.com/mlabouardy/parser
...
FROM alpine:latest
...
COPY --from=builder /go/src/github.com/mlabouardy/movies-parser/app .
```

Add the Build stage to the project Jenkinsfile, and push the changes to the develop branch. The pipeline will be triggered, and the result of the build should be similar to the one shown in figure 9.6.

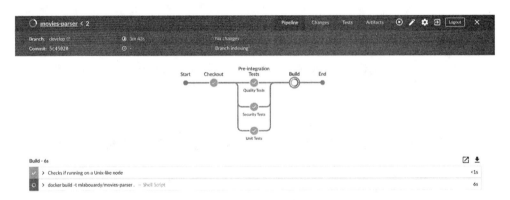

Figure 9.6   Movie parser CI pipeline

NOTE   You could have just as easily based the final image on scratch or distroless images, but I prefer to have the convenience of Alpine. Plus, it's a safe choice for reducing image size.

The movies-store Docker image will use the Node.js base image from DockerHub; we're using the latest LTS node release at the time of writing. I prefer to name a specific version, rather than one of the floating tags like node:lts or node:latest, so that if you or someone else builds this image on a different machine, they will get the same version, rather than risking an accidental upgrade and attendant head-scratching.

NOTE   In most cases, the best choice for a base image is from the official images available in DockerHub (https://hub.docker.com/). They tend to be better controlled than those created by the community.

Then, we install the needed dependencies for runtime by passing `--only=prod`. Finally, we set the `npm start` command to start the express server when the container is created, as shown in the following listing.

Listing 9.4 Movie store's Dockerfile

```
FROM node:14.17.0
WORKDIR /app
COPY package-lock.json package.json .
RUN npm i --only=prod
COPY index.js dao.js ./
EXPOSE 3000
CMD npm start
```

Note that, rather than copying the entire working directory, we are copying only the package.json and package-lock.json files. This allows us to take advantage of cached Docker layers. The package-lock.json file records the versions of all dependencies to ensure that the `npm install` command in Docker builds is consistent.

Once the pipeline changes are versioned and the execution is completed, the CI pipeline so far for movies-store should look similar to the Blue Ocean view in figure 9.7.

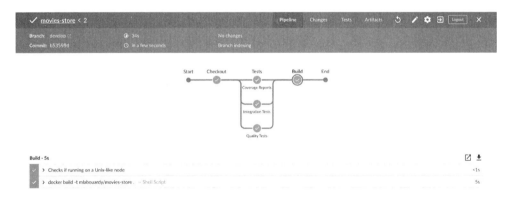

Figure 9.7 Movie store CI pipeline

> **NOTE** During image build, Docker takes all files in the context directory. To increase the Docker build performance, exclude files and directories by adding a .dockerignore file to the context directory.

9.1.2 Docker build arguments

Finally, for the Angular application (aka movies-marketplace), we will once again use the multistage build feature to build the static folder with the `ng build` command. Then we'll copy the folder to an NGINX image to serve the content with a web server; see the following listing.

Listing 9.5   Movie marketplace's Dockerfile

```
FROM node:14.17.0 as builder
ARG ENVIRONMENT
ENV CHROME_BIN=chromium
WORKDIR /app
RUN apt-get update && apt-get install -y chromium
COPY package-lock.json package.json .
RUN npm i && npm i -g @angular/cli
COPY . .
RUN ng build -c $ENVIRONMENT

FROM nginx:alpine
RUN rm -rf /usr/share/nginx/html/*
COPY --from=builder /app/dist /usr/share/nginx/html
EXPOSE 80
CMD ["nginx", "-g", "daemon off;"]
```

> **NOTE** The ENV instruction is available during build and runtime. The ARG
> instruction (listing 9.5) is accessible only during build time.

Because we might have multiple Angular configurations (with different settings) based on the running environment, we will inject a build argument during the build time to specify the target environment as follows:

```
stage('Build'){
        docker.build(imageName, '--build-arg ENVIRONMENT=sandbox .')
}
```

When passing arguments to the build() method, the last value should end with the folder to use as the build context.

Finally, make sure to create a .dockerignore file in the root folder of the project to prevent local modules, debug logs, and temporary files from being copied into the Docker image. To exclude those directories, we create a .dockerignore file with the following content:

```
nodes_modules
coverage
dist
tmp
```

After pushing the changes, the pipeline should look like the Blue Ocean view in figure 9.8.

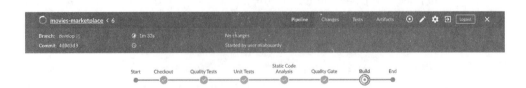

Figure 9.8   Movie marketplace CI pipeline

Now that the project Docker images are built, we need to store them somewhere. Therefore, we will deploy a private registry on which we will store all the images built through the development cycle of the project.

9.2   *Deploying a Docker private registry*

Continuous integration results in frequent builds and packages. Hence, we need a mechanism to store all this binary code (builds, packages, third-party plugins, and so on) in a system akin to a version-control system. Since VCSs such as Git and SVN store code and not binary files, we need a binary repository tool.

   Many solutions exist, such as Nexus or Artifactory. However, they come with challenges including managing and hardening the instance. Fortunately, managed solutions also exist, depending on the cloud provider you're using, such as Amazon Elastic Container Registry (ECR), Google Container Registry, and Azure Container Registry.

> **NOTE**   You can also host your Docker images in DockerHub. If you go with this approach, you can skip this part.

9.2.1   *Nexus Repository OSS*

Nexus Repository OSS (www.sonatype.com/products/repository-oss) is a widely used open source, free artifact repository that can be used to store binaries and build artifacts. It can be used to distribute Maven/Java, npm, Helm, Docker, and more.

> **NOTE**   Since you're already familiar with Docker, you can run Nexus Repository OSS in a Docker container by using the Docker image from Sonatype.

To deploy Nexus Repository OSS, we need to bake a new machine image with Packer. The following listing provides the template.json content (the full template is available in chapter9/nexus/packer/template.json).

Listing 9.6   Nexus Repository OSS Packer template

```
{
    "variables" : {...},
    "builders" : [
        {
            "type" : "amazon-ebs",
            "ami_name" : "nexus-3.22.1-02",
            "ami_description" : "Nexus Repository OSS"
        }
    ],
    "provisioners" : [
        {
            "type" : "file",
            "source" : "./nexus.rc",
            "destination" : "/tmp/nexus.rc"
        },
        {
            "type" : "file",
```

```
        "source" : "./repository.json",
        "destination" : "/tmp/repository.json"
    },
    {

        "type" : "shell",
        "script" : "./setup.sh",
        "execute_command" : "sudo -E -S sh '{{ .Path }}'"
    }
  ]
}
```

This will create a temporary instance based on the Amazon Linux image and provision it with a shell script (listing 9.7) that installs the Nexus OSS version from the official repository and configures it to run a service with init.d, so it restarts after the instance reboots. This example uses version 3.30.1-01. The full script is available in chapter9/nexus/packer/setup.sh.

Listing 9.7   Installing the Nexus Repository OSS version (setup.sh)

```
NEXUS_USERNAME="admin"           Defines Nexus OSS default
NEXUS_PASSWORD="admin123"        credentials (admin/admin 123)
echo "Install Java JDK 8"
yum update -y                              Installs Java JDK 1.8.0, which
yum install -y java-1.8.0-openjdk          is required to run Nexus OSS
echo "Install Nexus OSS"
wget https://download.sonatype.com/nexus/3/latest-unix.tar.gz -P /tmp
tar -xvf /tmp/latest-unix.tar.gz
mv nexus-* /opt/nexus
mv sonatype-work /opt/sonatype-work
useradd nexus                                      Downloads Nexus OSS
chown -R nexus:nexus /opt/nexus/ /opt/sonatype-work/    from the official
ln -s /opt/nexus/bin/nexus /etc/init.d/nexus       repository and extracts
chkconfig --add nexus                              the archive to the target
chkconfig --levels 345 nexus on
mv /tmp/nexus.rc /opt/nexus/bin/nexus.rc
echo "nexus.scripts.allowCreation=true" >> nexus-default.properties
systemctl enable nexus
Systemctl start nexus
```

Then, the script will start Nexus server with the `service nexus restart` command and wait for it to be up and ready, as shown in the following listing.

Listing 9.8   Waiting for the Nexus server to be up (setup.sh)

```
until $(curl --output /dev/null
--silent --head --fail http://localhost:8081); do
    printf '.'
    sleep 2
done
```

Once the server responds, a POST request will be issued to the Nexus Script API to create a Docker hosted repository. The scripting API can be used to automate the creation of complex tasks for the Nexus Repository Manager, as shown next.

Listing 9.9 Nexus OSS script API (setup.sh)

```
curl -v -X POST -u $NEXUS_USERNAME:$NEXUS_PASSWORD
--header "Content-Type: application/json" 'http://localhost:8081/service/
    rest/v1/script'
-d @/tmp/repository.json
```

Performs a POST request on the Nexus server by including the default credentials in the request and the Docker repository config in the request payload

> **NOTE** A comprehensive listing of Nexus REST API endpoints and functionality is documented through the NEXUS_HOST/swagger-ui endpoint.

The request payload is a Groovy script that exposes a Docker hosted registry on port 5000:

```
import org.sonatype.nexus.blobstore.api.BlobStoreManager;
import org.sonatype.nexus.repository.storage.WritePolicy;
repository.createDockerHosted('docker-registry',
5000, 443,
BlobStoreManager.DEFAULT_BLOBSTORE_NAME, true, true, WritePolicy.ALLOW, true)
```

Issue the `packer build` command to bake the AMI. Once the provisioning is finished, the Nexus AMI should be available in the Images section in the AWS Management Console, as shown in figure 9.9.

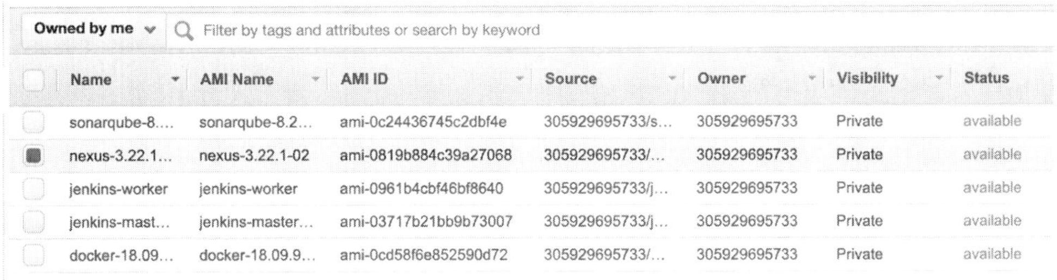

Owned by me | Filter by tags and attributes or search by keyword

Name	AMI Name	AMI ID	Source	Owner	Visibility	Status
sonarqube-8....	sonarqube-8.2...	ami-0c24436745c2dbf4e	305929695733/s...	305929695733	Private	available
nexus-3.22.1...	nexus-3.22.1-02	ami-0819b884c39a27068	305929695733/...	305929695733	Private	available
jenkins-worker	jenkins-worker	ami-0961b4cbf46bf8640	305929695733/j...	305929695733	Private	available
jenkins-mast...	jenkins-master...	ami-03717b21bb9b73007	305929695733/j...	305929695733	Private	available
docker-18.09...	docker-18.09.9...	ami-0cd58f6e852590d72	305929695733/...	305929695733	Private	available

Figure 9.9 Nexus OSS AMI

From there, use Terraform to provision an EC2 instance based on the baked Nexus OSS AMI. Create a nexus.tf file with the content in the following listing.

Listing 9.10 Nexus EC2 instance resource

```
resource "aws_instance" "nexus" {
  ami                    = data.aws_ami.nexus.id
  instance_type          = var.nexus_instance_type
  key_name               = var.key_name
  vpc_security_group_ids = [aws_security_group.nexus_sg.id]
  subnet_id              = element(var.private_subnets, 0)
```

```
root_block_device {
    volume_type          = "gp2"
    volume_size          = 50
    delete_on_termination = false
  }

  tags = {
    Author = var.author
   Name = "nexus"
  }
}
```

NOTE   Running Nexus OSS without a problem requires a minimum of 8 GB of memory. Additionally, I strongly recommend using a dedicated EBS for blob storage (http://mng.bz/dr7Q).

Also, provision a public load balancer to forward incoming HTTP and HTTPS traffic to port 8081 of the EC2 instance, which is the port where the Nexus Repository Manager (dashboard) is exposed. Create a new file, loadbalancers.tf, with the following listing.

Listing 9.11   Nexus Repository Manager public load balancer

```
resource "aws_elb" "nexus_elb" {
  subnets                  = var.public_subnets
  cross_zone_load_balancing = true
  security_groups          = [aws_security_group.elb_nexus_sg.id]
  instances                = [aws_instance.nexus.id]

  listener {
    instance_port     = 8081
    instance_protocol = "http"
    lb_port           = 443
    lb_protocol       = "https"
    ssl_certificate_id = var.ssl_arn
  }

  health_check {
    healthy_threshold   = 2
    unhealthy_threshold = 2
    timeout             = 3
    target              = "TCP:8081"
    interval            = 5
  }

  tags = {
    Name   = "nexus_elb"
    Author = var.author
  }
}
```

Within the same file, add another public load balancer, as shown in the next listing. This will access the Docker private registry pointing to port 5000 of the hosted repository on the Nexus Repository Manager.

Listing 9.12 Docker registry public load balancer

```
resource "aws_elb" "registry_elb" {
  subnets                     = var.public_subnets
  cross_zone_load_balancing = true
  security_groups             = [aws_security_group.elb_registry_sg.id]
  instances                   = [aws_instance.nexus.id]

  listener {
    instance_port     = 5000
    instance_protocol = "http"
    lb_port           = 443
    lb_protocol       = "https"
    ssl_certificate_id = var.ssl_arn
  }
}
```

Use `terraform apply` to provision the AWS resources, the Nexus dashboard, and Docker Registry. URLs should be displayed at the end of the provisioning process in the `Outputs` section, as shown in figure 9.10.

```
aws_route53_record.nexus: Creating...
aws_route53_record.registry: Still creating... [10s elapsed]
aws_route53_record.nexus: Still creating... [10s elapsed]
aws_route53_record.registry: Still creating... [20s elapsed]
aws_route53_record.nexus: Still creating... [20s elapsed]
aws_route53_record.registry: Still creating... [30s elapsed]
aws_route53_record.nexus: Still creating... [30s elapsed]
aws_route53_record.registry: Creation complete after 34s [id=Z2TR95QTU3UIUT_registry.slowcoder.com_A]
aws_route53_record.nexus: Creation complete after 34s [id=Z2TR95QTU3UIUT_nexus.slowcoder.com_A]

Apply complete! Resources: 8 added, 0 changed, 0 destroyed.

Outputs:

nexus = https://nexus.slowcoder.com
registry = https://registry.slowcoder.com
```

Figure 9.10 Nexus Terraform resources

Point your favorite browser to the Nexus URL, and the web dashboard in figure 9.11 should be displayed. The default `admin` password can be found in /opt/sonatype-work/nexus3/admin.password.

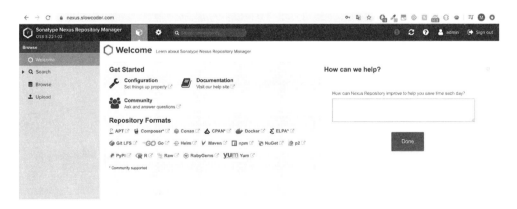

Figure 9.11 Nexus Repository Manager

If you jump to Settings from the cogwheel icon and then Repositories, a new Docker hosted repository should be created. The repository disables tag immutability and allows image tags to be overwritten by a subsequent image push using the same tag. If this option is enabled, an error will be returned if you attempt to push an image with a tag that already exists in the repository. The rest of the configurations should be similar to figure 9.12.

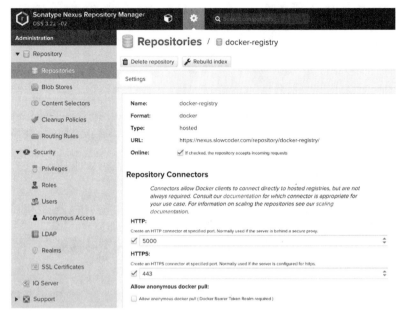

**Figure 9.12
Docker-hosted
registry on Nexus**

To be able to pull and push Docker images to the registry, we will create a custom Nexus role from the Security section. This role, shown in figure 9.13, will give full access to the Docker hosted registry.

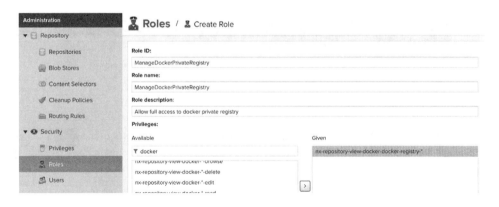

Figure 9.13   Nexus custom role for the Docker registry

> **NOTE** For push and pull operations, only `nx-*-registry-add` and `nx-*-registry-read` permissions are required.

Next, we create a Jenkins user and assign to it the custom Nexus role we just created, as shown in figure 9.14.

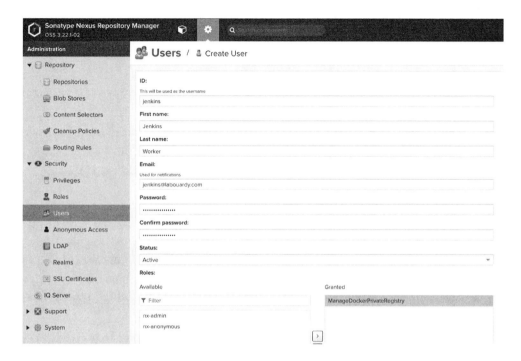

Figure 9.14 Docker registry credentials for Jenkins

We can test out the authentication by jumping back to the terminal session on the local machine and issuing the `docker login` command:

```
[jenkins:terraform mlabouardy$ docker login https://registry.slowcoder.com
 Username: jenkins
[Password:
 Login Succeeded
```

> **NOTE** The hosted Docker repository is exposed on HTTPS by default. However, if you expose the private repository on a plain HTTP endpoint only, you need to configure the Docker daemon to allow insecure connections by passing the `-insecure-registry` flag to the Docker engine.

Finally, on Jenkins, create a registry credential of type Username with Password with the Nexus credentials we created so far for Jenkins (figure 9.15).

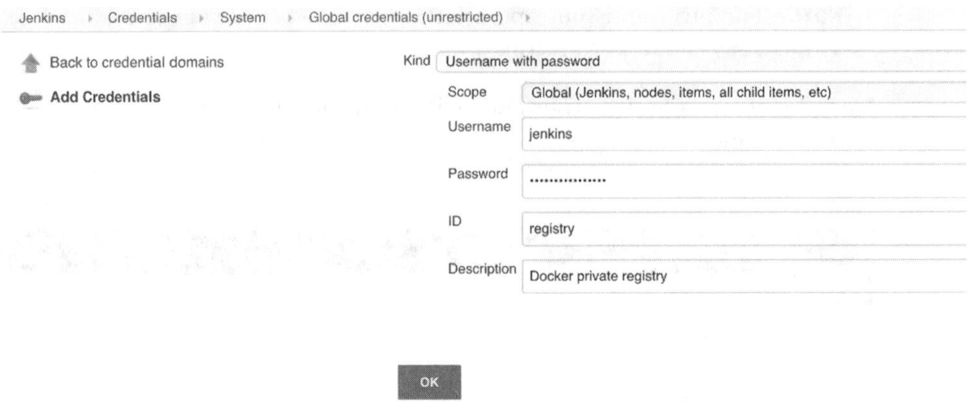

Jenkins ▸ Credentials ▸ System ▸ Global credentials (unrestricted) ▸

🔼 Back to credential domains

👌 **Add Credentials**

Kind	Username with password
Scope	Global (Jenkins, nodes, items, all child items, etc)
Username	jenkins
Password	··············
ID	registry
Description	Docker private registry

OK

Figure 9.15   Docker registry credentials

Another alternative to Nexus Repository OSS is an AWS managed service.

9.2.2   *Amazon Elastic Container Registry*

If you're using AWS, as I am, you can use a managed AWS service called Elastic Container Registry (ECR) to host your private Docker images. From the AWS Management Console, navigate to Amazon ECR (https://console.aws.amazon.com/ecr/repositories). Then, create a repository for each Docker image you want to host or store. In our project, we need to create four repositories, one for each microservice. The service-loader repository, for instance, is shown in figure 9.16.

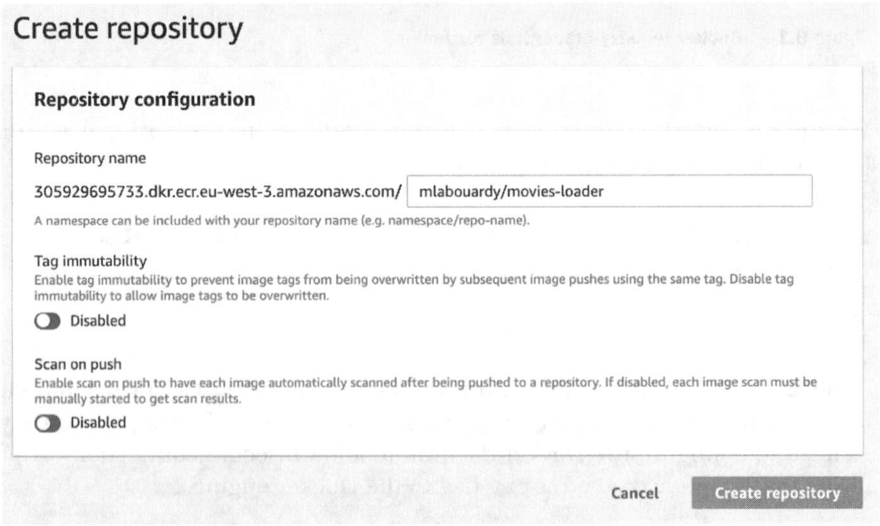

Create repository

Repository configuration

Repository name

305929695733.dkr.ecr.eu-west-3.amazonaws.com/ | mlabouardy/movies-loader

A namespace can be included with your repository name (e.g. namespace/repo-name).

Tag immutability
Enable tag immutability to prevent image tags from being overwritten by subsequent image pushes using the same tag. Disable tag immutability to allow image tags to be overwritten.
⬤ Disabled

Scan on push
Enable scan on push to have each image automatically scanned after being pushed to a repository. If disabled, each image scan must be manually started to get scan results.
⬤ Disabled

Cancel   Create repository

Figure 9.16   ECR new repository

Once the repository is created, you can click the View Push Commands button, and a dialog should pop up with a list of instructions on how to tag, push, and pull images to the remote repository; see figure 9.17.

Figure 9.17 Movie loader ECR repository

Before interacting with the repository, you need to authenticate with ECR. The following command for Mac and Linux users can be used to log in to the remote repository:

```
aws ecr get-login-password --region REGION
| docker login --username AWS --password-stdin
ACCOUNT_ID.dkr.ecr.REGION.amazonaws.com/
mlabouardy/movies-loader
```

NOTE Replace `ACCOUNT_ID` and `REGION` with your Amazon account ID and AWS region, respectively.

For Windows users, here is the command:

```
(Get-ECRLoginCommand).Password |
docker login --username AWS --password-stdin
ACCOUNT_ID.dkr.ecr.REGION.amazonaws.com/mlabouardy/movies-loader
```

Repeat the same procedure to create dedicated ECR repositories per microservice, as shown in figure 9.18.

Repository name	URI	Created at	Tag immutability	Scan on push
mlabouardy/movies-loader	305929695733.dkr.ecr.eu-west-3.amazonaws.com/mlabouardy/movies-loader	04/25/20, 03:39:41 PM	Disabled	Disabled
mlabouardy/movies-marketplace	305929695733.dkr.ecr.eu-west-3.amazonaws.com/mlabouardy/movies-marketplace	04/25/20, 03:41:23 PM	Disabled	Disabled
mlabouardy/movies-parser	305929695733.dkr.ecr.eu-west-3.amazonaws.com/mlabouardy/movies-parser	04/25/20, 03:41:13 PM	Disabled	Disabled
mlabouardy/movies-store	305929695733.dkr.ecr.eu-west-3.amazonaws.com/mlabouardy/movies-store	04/25/20, 03:41:17 PM	Disabled	Disabled

Figure 9.18 ECR repository for each microservice

9.2.3 *Azure Container Registry*

For Azure users, the Azure Container Registry service can be used to store container images without managing a private registry. On the Azure portal (https://portal.azure .com/), navigate to the Container Registries service and click the Add button to create a new registry. Specify the region where you want to deploy the registry and give it a name, as shown in figure 9.19.

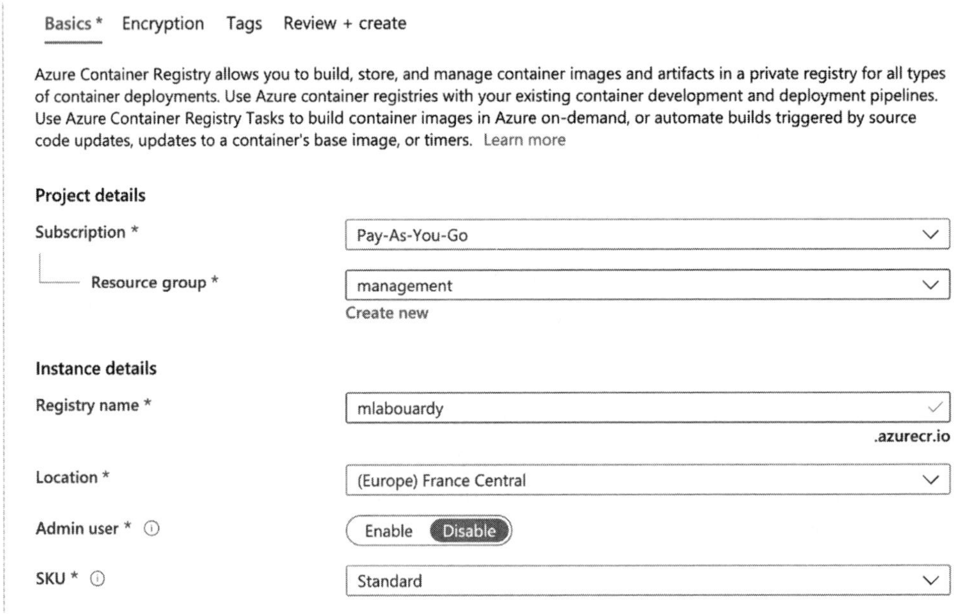

Figure 9.19 Azure new registry configuration

Leave other fields at the defaults and click Create. Once the registry is created, navigate to Access Keys under the Settings section, where you will find the admin username and password that you can use to authenticate to the registry to push or pull Docker images from Jenkins; see figure 9.20.

You can use those credentials in Jenkins to push the image within the CI pipeline. However, I recommend creating a token with granular access control by using role-based access control (RBAC), or the least privilege principle. The admin account is designed for only a single user to access the registry, mainly for testing purposes.

Navigate to the Tokens section and click the Add button to create a new access token. Give it a name and associate the _repositories_push scope to allow the execution of the `docker push` operation only (Jenkins will need to push only images to the registry); see figure 9.21.

Generate a password after you have created a token, as shown in figure 9.22. To authenticate with the registry, the token must be enabled and have a valid password.

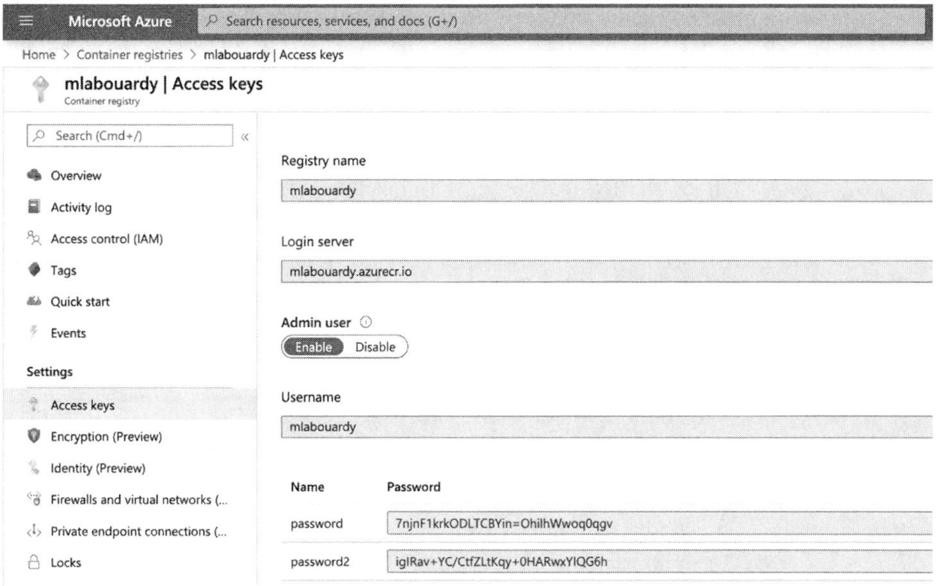

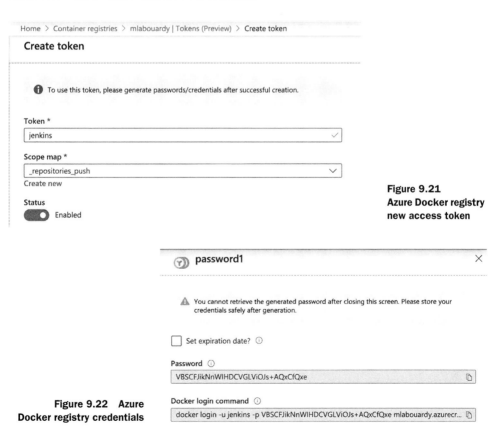

Figure 9.20   Azure Docker registry admin credentials

**Figure 9.21
Azure Docker registry
new access token**

**Figure 9.22   Azure
Docker registry credentials**

After generating a password, copy and save it as Jenkins credentials of type Username with Password. You can't retrieve a generated password after closing the dialog screen, but you can generate a new one.

9.2.4   *Google Container Registry*

For Google Cloud Platform users, a managed service called Google Container Registry (GCR) can be used to host Docker images. To get started, you need to enable API Container Registry (https://cloud.google.com/container-registry/docs/quickstart) for your GCP project and then install the `gcloud` command line. For Linux users, run the following listing.

Listing 9.13   `gcloud` installation

```
curl -O https://dl.google.com/dl/cloudsdk/channels/
rapid/downloads/google-cloud-sdk-344.0.0-linux-x86_64.tar.gz
tar zxvf google-cloud-sdk-344.0.0-linux-x86_64.tar.gz
 google-cloud-sdk
./google-cloud-sdk/install.sh
```

> **NOTE**   For further instructions on how to install the Google Cloud SDK, read the official GCP guide at https://cloud.google.com/sdk/install.

Next, issue the following command to authenticate with the registry. The resulting authentication token is persisted in ~/.docker/config.json and reused for any subsequent interactions against that repository:

```
gcloud auth configure-docker
```

You need to tag the target images with the GCR URI (`gcr.io/[PROJECT-ID]`) and push the images with the `docker push` command. Figure 9.23 shows how to tag and push the movies-loader Docker image to GCR:

```
docker tag mlabouardy/movies-loader
eu.gcr.io/PROJECT_ID/mlabouardy/movies-loader
docker push eu.gcr.io/PROJECT_ID/mlabouardy/movies-loader
```

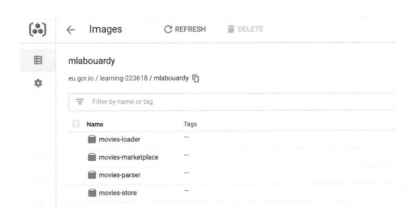

Figure 9.23
Google Container
Registry images

Now that we've covered how to deploy a private Docker registry, we will update the Jenkinsfile for each service to push the image to the remote private registry at the end of a successful CI pipeline execution.

9.3 *Tagging Docker images the right way*

Add a new push stage to the Jenkinsfile with the `withRegistry` block, which authenticates against the registry URL provided in the first parameter by using the credentials provided in the second parameter. Then it persists the changes in ~/.docker/config.json. Finally, it pushes the image with a tag value equal to the build number ID (using the `env.BUILD_ID` keyword). The following listing is the Jenkinsfile for the movies-loader service after implementing the `Push` stage.

Listing 9.14 Publishing Docker image to a registry

```
def imageName = 'mlabouardy/movies-loader'
def registry = 'https://registry.slowcoder.com'
node('workers'){
    stage('Checkout'){
        checkout scm
    }

    stage('Unit Tests'){
        def imageTest= docker.build("${imageName}-test",
"-f Dockerfile.test .")
        imageTest.inside{
            sh 'python test_main.py'
        }
    }

    stage('Build'){
        docker.build(imageName)
    }

    stage('Push'){
        docker.withRegistry(registry, 'registry') {
            docker.image(imageName).push(env.BUILD_ID)
        }
    }
}
```

> **NOTE** The `imageName` and `registry` values must be replaced with your own Docker private registry URL and name of the image to store, respectively.

For this example, the build number is 2; therefore, the movies-loader image is pushed to the registry after tagging it with a tag equal to 2, as shown in figure 9.24.

```
[Pipeline] { (Push)
[Pipeline] withEnv
[Pipeline] {
[Pipeline] withDockerRegistry
$ docker login -u jenkins -p ******** https://registry.slowcoder.com
WARNING! Using --password via the CLI is insecure. Use --password-stdin.
WARNING! Your password will be stored unencrypted in /home/ec2-user/workspace/movies-loader_
86edd538b844/config.json.
Configure a credential helper to remove this warning. See
https://docs.docker.com/engine/reference/commandline/login/#credentials-store

Login Succeeded
[Pipeline] {
[Pipeline] isUnix
[Pipeline] sh
+ docker tag mlabouardy/movies-loader registry.slowcoder.com/mlabouardy/movies-loader:2
[Pipeline] isUnix
[Pipeline] sh
+ docker push registry.slowcoder.com/mlabouardy/movies-loader:2
The push refers to repository [registry.slowcoder.com/mlabouardy/movies-loader]
908027c5b2f4: Preparing
c8924bb9cb10: Preparing
59bc756f6273: Preparing
3a9cf82366b7: Preparing
```

**Figure 9.24
Docker push
command logs**

If we head back to the registry (for example, on Nexus Repository Manager), we can see that a movies-loader image has been successfully pushed (figure 9.25).

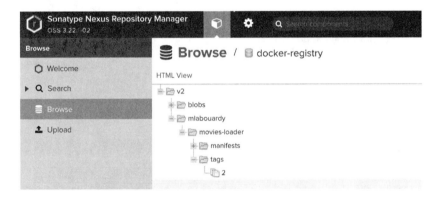

Figure 9.25   Docker image stored in Nexus

While the Jenkins build ID can be used to tag the images, it might not be handy. A better identifier is the Git commit ID. In this example, we will use it to tag the built Docker image. On a declarative and scripted pipeline, this information is not available out of the box. Therefore, we will create a function that uses the Git command line to fetch the commit ID and return it:

```
def commitID() {
    sh 'git rev-parse HEAD > .git/commitID'
    def commitID = readFile('.git/commitID').trim()
    sh 'rm .git/commitID'
    commitID
}
```

From there, we can update the `Push` stage to tag the image with the value returned by the `commitID()` function:

```
stage('Push'){
        docker.withRegistry(registry, 'registry') {
            docker.image(imageName).push(commitID())
        }
}
```

NOTE In chapter 14, we will cover how to create a Jenkins shared library with custom functions to avoid duplication of code in Jenkinsfiles.

Push the changes to the GitHub repository with the following commands:

```
git add Jenkinsfile
git commit -m "tagging docker image with git commit id"
git push origin develop
```

The new CI pipeline stages should look like figure 9.26 for the movies-loader service.

Branch develop

Full project name: movies-loader/develop

Stage View

**Figure 9.26
Movie loader
CI pipeline**

After a successful run on Nexus Repository Manager, a new image with a commit ID should be available (figure 9.27).

Figure 9.27   Commit ID image tag

We will take this further and push the same image with a tag based on the branch name. This tag will be helpful when we tackle continuous deployment and delivery. It will allow us to assign a particular tag per environment:

- *Latest*—Used to deploy the image to the production environment
- *Preprod*—Used to deploy the image to the staging or preproduction environment
- *Develop*—Used to deploy the image to the sandbox or development environment

The `Push` stage code block is as follows:

```
stage('Push'){
        docker.withRegistry(registry, 'registry') {
            docker.image(imageName).push(commitID())

            if (env.BRANCH_NAME == 'develop') {
                docker.image(imageName).push('develop')
            }
        }
}
```

The `env.BRANCH_NAME` variable contains the branch name. Also, you can just use `BRANCH_NAME` without the `env` keyword (it hasn't been required since Pipeline Groovy Plugin 2.18).

Lastly, if you're using Amazon ECR as a private registry, you need to authenticate first with the AWS CLI to the remote repository before issuing the push instructions. For AWS CLI 2 users, use the shell instruction in the following listing to invoke the `aws ecr` command.

Listing 9.15   Publishing the Docker image to ECR

```
def imageName = 'mlabouardy/movies-loader'
def registry = 'ACCOUNT_ID.dkr.ecr.eu-west-3.amazonaws.com'
def region = 'REGION'

node('workers'){
    ...
    stage('Push'){
        sh "aws ecr get-login-password --region ${region} |
docker login --username AWS
--password-stdin ${registry}/${imageName}"

        docker.image(imageName).push(commitID())
        if (env.BRANCH_NAME == 'develop') {
            docker.image(imageName).push('develop')
        }
    }
}
```

Make sure to substitute the `ACCOUNT_ID` and `REGION` variables with your own AWS account ID and AWS region, respectively. If you're using a 1.x version of the AWS CLI, use this code block instead:

```
stage('Push'){
        sh "\$(aws ecr get-login
--no-include-email --region ${region}) || true"
        docker.withRegistry("https://${registry}") {
            docker.image(imageName).push(commitID())
            if (env.BRANCH_NAME == 'develop') {
                docker.image(imageName).push('develop')
            }
        }
}
```

Before triggering the CI pipeline, you will need to give access to Jenkins workers to perform the push operation on the ECR registry. Therefore, you need to assign an IAM instance profile to Jenkins worker instances with the AmazonEC2Container-RegistryFullAccess policy. Figure 9.28 illustrates the IAM instance profile assigned to Jenkins workers.

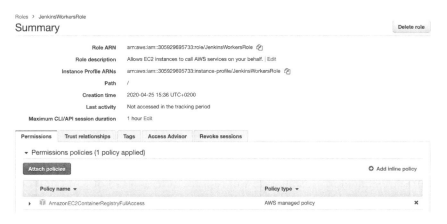

Figure 9.28   Jenkins workers' IAM instance profile

Once you've made the required changes, a new build should be triggered. A new image tag should be pushed to the ECR repository, at the end of the CI pipeline, as shown in figure 9.29.

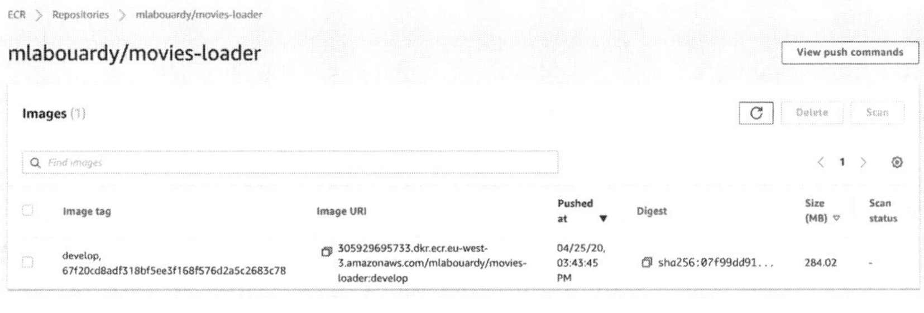

Figure 9.29   Movie loader ECR repository images

Repeat the same procedure for the rest of the microservices, to push their Docker image to the end of the CI pipeline, as shown in figure 9.30.

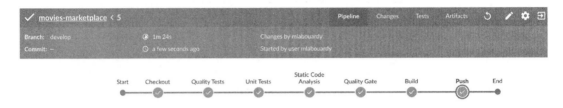

Figure 9.30   Movie marketplace CI pipeline

In a typical workflow, the Docker images should be analyzed, inspected, and scanned against security rules for compliance and auditing. That's why, in the upcoming section, we will integrate a container inspection and analytics platform within the CI pipeline to continuously inspect built Docker images for security vulnerabilities.

9.4   *Scanning Docker images for vulnerabilities*

Anchore Engine (https://github.com/anchore/anchore-engine) is an open source project that provides a centralized service for inspection, analysis, and certification of container images. You can run Anchore Engine as a standalone service or as a Docker container.

> **NOTE**   A standalone installation will require at least 4 GB of RAM and enough disk space available to support the container images you intend to analyze.

You can bake your own AMI with Packer from scratch to install Anchore Engine and set up the PostgreSQL database. Then, use Terraform to deploy the stack, or you can simply deploy the configured stack out of the box with Docker Compose. Refer to chapters 4 and 5 for instructions on how to use Terraform and Packer.

Launch a private instance in the *management* VPC with Docker Community Edition (CE) pre-installed, and then install the Docker Compose tool from the Docker official guide page. Issue the following command to deploy Anchore Engine:

```
curl https://docs.anchore.com/current/docs/
engine/quickstart/docker-compose.yaml > docker-compose.yaml
docker-compose up -d
```

After a few moments, your Anchore Engine services should be up and running, ready to use. You can verify that the containers are running with the `docker-compose ps` command. Figure 9.31 shows the output. Make sure to allow inbound traffic on port 8228 (Anchore API) from the Jenkins master security group ID only, as shown in figure 9.32.

```
        Name                    Command                      State              Ports
-------------------------------------------------------------------------------------------------
ec2-user_analyzer_1       /docker-entrypoint.sh anch ...   Up (health: starting)   8228/tcp
ec2-user_api_1            /docker-entrypoint.sh anch ...   Up (health: starting)   0.0.0.0:8228->8228/tcp
ec2-user_catalog_1        /docker-entrypoint.sh anch ...   Up (health: starting)   8228/tcp
ec2-user_db_1             docker-entrypoint.sh postgres    Up                      5432/tcp
ec2-user_policy-engine_1  /docker-entrypoint.sh anch ...   Up (health: starting)   8228/tcp
ec2-user_queue_1          /docker-entrypoint.sh anch ...   Up (health: starting)   8228/tcp
```

Figure 9.31   Docker Compose stack services

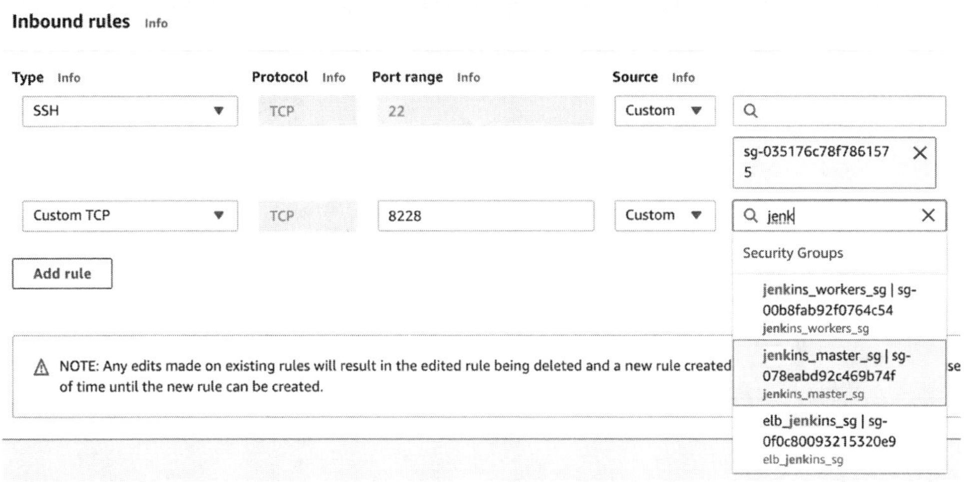

Figure 9.32   Anchore instance's security group

> **NOTE** You can take this further and deploy a load balancer in front of the EC2 instance and create an A record in Route 53 pointing to the load balancer FQDN.

When it comes to Jenkins, an available plugin already makes the integration much easier. From the main Jenkins menu, select Manage Jenkins and jump to the Manage Plugins section. Click the Available tab and install the Anchore Container Image Scanner plugin, as shown in figure 9.33.

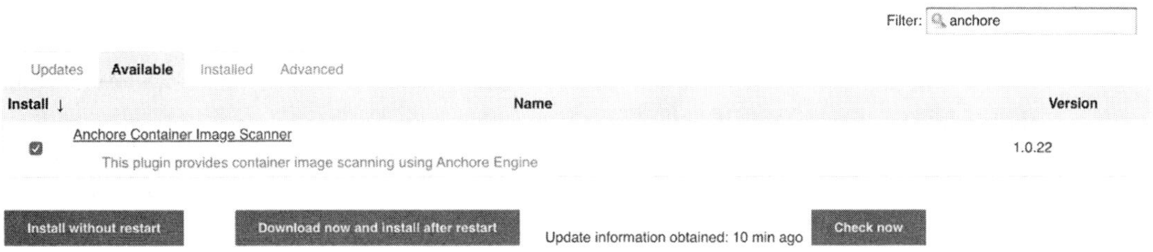

Figure 9.33   Anchore Container Image Scanner plugin

Next, from the Manage Jenkins menu, choose Configure System and scroll down to the Anchore Configuration. Then, set the Anchore URL with the /v1 route included and credentials (the default is admin/foobar), as shown in figure 9.34.

Anchore Container Image Scanner

Engine URL	http://10.0.0.229:8228/v1
Engine Username	admin
Engine Password	......
Verify SSL	☐
Enable DEBUG logging	☐

Figure 9.34   Anchore plugin configuration

Finally, integrate Anchore into the Jenkins pipeline by creating a file named *images* in the project workspace. This file should contain the name of the Docker image to be scanned and optionally include the Dockerfile. Then, call the Anchore plugin with the file created as a parameter, as shown in the following listing.

Listing 9.16   Analyzing Docker images with Anchore

```
stage('Analyze'){
        def scannedImage =
"${registry}/${imageName}:${commitID()}
${workspace}/Dockerfile"
        writeFile file: 'images', text: scannedImage
        anchore name: 'images'
}
```

Push the changes with the following commands to the remote repository on the develop branch:

```
git add Jenkinsfile
git commit -m "image scanning stage"
git push origin develop
```

The CI pipeline will be triggered upon the push event. After the image has been built and pushed to the registry, the Anchore Scanner should be called. It will throw an error due to Anchore not being able to pull the Docker image from the private registry for analysis and inspection.

Fortunately, Anchore integrates and supports analyzing images from any registry compatible with Docker v2. To allow access to the remote images from Anchore, install the anchor-cli binary from the Anchore EC2 instance:

```
yum install -y epel-release python-pip
pip install anchorecli
```

Next, we define credentials for the private Docker registry. Run this command; the REGISTRY parameter should include the registry's fully qualified hostname and port number (if exposed):

```
anchore-cli registry add REGISTRY USERNAME PASSWORD
```

NOTE The same command can be used to configure a Docker registry hosted on Nexus or other solutions.

Since we're using Amazon ECR repositories and running Anchore from an EC2 instance, we will assign an IAM instance profile instead with the AmazonEC2Container-RegistryReadOnly policy. In this case, we will pass awsauto for both USERNAME and PASSWORD and instruct the Anchore Engine to inherit the role from the underlying EC2 instance:

```
anchore-cli --u admin --p foobar registry add ACCOUNT_ID.dkr.ecr.REGION
    .amazonaws.com awsauto awsauto --registry-type=awsecr
```

To verify that credentials have been properly configured, run the following command to list the defined registries:

```
anchore-cli --u admin --p foobar registry list
```

```
[ec2-user@ip-10-0-0-229 ~]$ anchore-cli --u admin --p foobar registry add 305929695733.dkr.ecr.eu-west-3.amazonaws.com awsauto awsauto --registry-type=awsecr
Registry: 305929695733.dkr.ecr.eu-west-3.amazonaws.com
Name: 305929695733.dkr.ecr.eu-west-3.amazonaws.com
User: awsauto
Type: awsecr
Verify TLS: True
Created: 2020-05-15T16:48:03Z
Updated: 2020-05-15T16:48:03Z

[ec2-user@ip-10-0-0-229 ~]$ anchore-cli --u admin --p foobar registry list
Registry                                        Name                                            Type      User
305929695733.dkr.ecr.eu-west-3.amazonaws.com    305929695733.dkr.ecr.eu-west-3.amazonaws.com    awsecr    awsauto
[ec2-user@ip-10-0-0-229 ~]$
```

Rerun the pipeline with the Replay button. This time, Anchore will examine the contents of the image filesystem for vulnerabilities. If high-severity vulnerabilities are found, this will fail the image build, as shown in figure 9.35.

```
[Pipeline] anchore
2020-05-15T17:08:17.605 INFO    AnchoreWorker    Jenkins version: 2.204.1
2020-05-15T17:08:17.605 INFO    AnchoreWorker    Anchore Container Image Scanner Plugin version: 1.0.22
2020-05-15T17:08:17.605 INFO    AnchoreWorker    [global] debug: false
2020-05-15T17:08:17.605 INFO    AnchoreWorker    [build] engineurl: http://10.0.0.229:8228/v1
2020-05-15T17:08:17.605 INFO    AnchoreWorker    [build] engineuser: admin
2020-05-15T17:08:17.605 INFO    AnchoreWorker    [build] enginepass: ****
2020-05-15T17:08:17.605 INFO    AnchoreWorker    [build] engineverify: false
2020-05-15T17:08:17.605 INFO    AnchoreWorker    [build] name: images
2020-05-15T17:08:17.605 INFO    AnchoreWorker    [build] engineRetries: 300
2020-05-15T17:08:17.605 INFO    AnchoreWorker    [build] policyBundleId:
2020-05-15T17:08:17.605 INFO    AnchoreWorker    [build] bailOnFail: true
2020-05-15T17:08:17.605 INFO    AnchoreWorker    [build] bailOnPluginFail: true
2020-05-15T17:08:17.614 INFO    AnchoreWorker    Submitting 305929695733.dkr.ecr.eu-west-3.amazonaws.com/mlabouardy/movies-
loader:02c7fc2863f49d176a1738c722b2b601eb9d122f for analysis
2020-05-15T17:08:17.923 INFO    AnchoreWorker    Analysis request accepted, received image digest
sha256:c0ef9fd3ce1fa82adee2796cf53d2e467ff9e0a0739515357e34a8c05254fc3d
2020-05-15T17:08:17.924 INFO    AnchoreWorker    Waiting for analysis of 305929695733.dkr.ecr.eu-west-3.amazonaws.com/mlabouardy/movies-
loader:02c7fc2863f49d176a1738c722b2b601eb9d122f, polling status periodically
```

Figure 9.35   Image scanning with Anchore

Once the scanning is finished, Anchore will return with a nonzero exit code if the image has any known high-severity issues. The result of the Anchore policy evaluation will be saved in JSON files. Also, the pipeline will show the status of the build (STOP, WARN, or FAIL), as shown in figure 9.36.

Figure 9.36 Anchore report results

The HTML report is automatically published, as well, on the newly created page. Clicking the Anchore Report link will display a graphical policy report showing the summary information and a detailed list of policy checks and results; see figure 9.37.

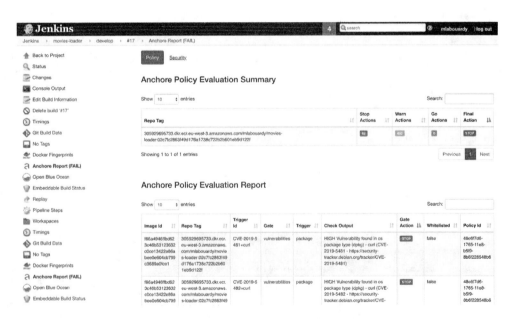

Figure 9.37   Anchore Common Vulnerabilities and Exposures (CVE) report

NOTE You can customize Anchore Engine to use your own security policies to allow/block external packages, OS scanning, and so forth.

And that's how to define a continuous integration pipeline on Jenkins from scratch for Dockerized microservices.

NOTE An alternative solution is Aqua Trivy (https://github.com/aquasecurity/ trivy), which is a freely available community edition. Paid solutions also can be integrated easily with Jenkins such as Sysdig (https://sysdig.com/) and Aqua.

9.5   *Writing a Jenkins declarative pipeline*

Along with the previous chapters, we have used the scripted pipeline approach to define the CI pipeline for our project because of the flexibility it gives while using Groovy syntax. This section covers how to get the same pipeline output with a declarative pipeline approach. This is a simplified and friendlier syntax with specific statements for defining them, without a need to learn or master Groovy language.

Let's take as an example the scripted pipeline used for the movies-loader service. The following listing provides the service Jenkinsfile (cropped for brevity).

Listing 9.17   Jenkinsfile scripted pipeline

```
node('workers'){
    stage('Checkout'){
        checkout scm
    }
    stage('Unit Tests'){
        def imageTest= docker.build("${imageName}-test",
"-f Dockerfile.test .")
        imageTest.inside{
            sh "python main_test.py"
        }
    }
    stage('Build'){
        docker.build(imageName)
    }
    stage('Push'){
        docker.withRegistry(registry, 'registry') {
            docker.image(imageName).push(commitID())

            if (env.BRANCH_NAME == 'develop') {
                docker.image(imageName).push('develop')
            }
        }
    }
}
```

This scripted pipeline can be easily converted to a declarative version, by following these steps:

1 Replace the `node('workers')` instruction with a `pipeline` keyword. All valid declarative pipelines must be enclosed within a `pipeline` block.

2 Define an `agent` section at the top level inside the `pipeline` block, to define the execution environment where the pipeline will be executed. In our example, the execution will be on Jenkins workers.

3 Wrap `stage` blocks with a `stages` section. The `stages` section contains a stage for each discrete part of the CI pipeline, such as `Checkout`, `Test`, `Build`, and `Push`.

4 Wrap each given `stage` command and instruction with a `steps` block.

Create a Jenkinsfile.declarative file with the required changes. The end result should look like the following listing.

Listing 9.18   Jenkinsfile declarative pipeline

```
pipeline{                              Defines where the pipeline should be executed.
    agent{                             In the example, the pipeline stages will be
        label 'workers'    ◁───        performed on the agents with the workers label.
    }
    stages{
        stage('Checkout'){             Clones the GitHub
            steps{                     repository configured in
                checkout scm    ◁───   the Jenkins's job settings
            }
        }
        stage('Unit Tests'){
            steps{                                                    ◁───
                script {
                    def imageTest= docker.build("${imageName}-test",
"-f Dockerfile.test .")
                    imageTest.inside{          Builds a Docker image based on
                        sh "python test_main.py"   Dockerfile.test and provisions
                    }                          a container from the image
                }                              to run the Python unit tests
            }                                                         ◁───
        }
        stage('Build'){                    ◁───
            steps{
                script {
                    docker.build(imageName)    Builds the application Docker
                }                              image from the Dockerfile
            }
        }                                  ◁───
        stage('Push'){                                               ◁───
            steps{
                script {
                    docker.withRegistry(registry, 'registry') {
                        docker.image(imageName).push(commitID())

                        if (env.BRANCH_NAME == 'develop') {
                            docker.image(imageName).push('develop')
                        }
                    }                          Authenticates with the Docker
                }                              remote repository and pushes the
            }                                  application image to the repository
        }                                                            ◁───
    }
}
```

NOTE The declarative pipeline might also contain a `post` section to perform post-build steps such as notification or cleaning up the environment. This section is covered in chapter 10.

Update the Jenkins job configuration to use the new declarative pipeline file instead by updating the Script Path field, as shown in figure 9.38.

Build Configuration

Mode	by Jenkinsfile ⬍
Script Path	Jenkinsfile.declarative

Figure 9.38 Jenkinsfile path configuration

Push the declarative pipeline to the remote repository with these commands:

```
git add Jenkinsfile.declarative
git commit -m "pipeline with declarative approach"
git push origin develop
```

The GitHub webhook will notify Jenkins upon the push event, and the new declarative pipeline should be executed, as you can see in figure 9.39.

	Declarative: Checkout SCM	Checkout	Unit Tests	Build	Push
Average stage times: (Average full run time: ~16s)	1s	1s	1s	4s	44ms
#6 May 02 15:14 1 commit	1s	1s	3s	7s	55ms

Figure 9.39 Jenkinsfile declarative pipeline execution

You can now restart any completed declarative pipeline from any top-level stage that ran in that pipeline. You can go to the side panel for a run in the classic UI and click Restart from Stage, as shown in figure 9.40.

Jenkins › movies-loader › develop › #6 › Restart from Stage

- ⬆ Back to Project
- 🔍 Status
- 📝 Changes
- 🖼 Console Output
- 📄 Edit Build Information
- 🚫 Delete build '#6'
- ⏱ Timings
- 🔧 Git Build Data
- 🏷 No Tags
- 🐳 Docker Fingerprints
- 🌊 Open Blue Ocean
- 🟢 Embeddable Build Status
- 🔄 Restart from Stage

Restart #6 from Stage

Stage Name
- ✓ Checkout
- Unit Tests
- Build
- Push

Run

Figure 9.40 Restart from Stage feature

You will be prompted to choose from a list of top-level stages that were executed in the original run, in the order they were executed. This allows you to rerun a pipeline from a stage that failed because of transient or environmental considerations.

NOTE   Restarting stages can also be done in the Blue Ocean UI, after your pipeline has completed, whether it succeeds or fails.

Docker can also be used as an execution environment for running CI/CD pipelines in the agent section, as shown in the following listing.

Listing 9.19   Declarative pipeline with a Docker agent

```
pipeline{
    agent{
        docker {
            image 'python:3.7.3'
        }
    }
    stages{
        stage('Checkout'){
            steps{
                checkout scm
            }
        }
        stage('Unit Tests'){
            steps{
                script {
                    sh 'python test_main.py'
                }
            }
        }
    }
}
```

If we try to execute this pipeline, the build will quickly fail because the pipeline assumes that any configured machine/instance is capable of running Docker-based pipelines. In this example, the build ran in the master machine. However, because Docker is not installed in this machine, the pipeline failed:

```
+ docker inspect -f . python:3.7.3
/var/lib/jenkins/workspace/movies-loader_develop@tmp/durable-efd13a52/script.sh: line 1: docker: command not f
[Pipeline] isUnix
[Pipeline] sh
+ docker pull python:3.7.3
/var/lib/jenkins/workspace/movies-loader_develop@tmp/durable-7f4fd486/script.sh: line 1: docker: command not f
```

To run the pipeline on Jenkins workers only, update the Pipeline Model Definition settings from the Jenkins job configuration and set the workers label on the Docker Label field, as shown in figure 9.41.

When the pipeline executes, Jenkins will automatically start the specified container and execute the steps defined within it. This pipeline executes the same stages and the same steps.

Pipeline Model Definition

Docker Label	workers
Docker registry URL	
Registry credentials	- none - ⬩ ⬅ Add ▼

Figure 9.41
Pipeline model
definition

9.6 Managing pull requests with Jenkins

For now, we push directly to the develop branch; however, we should create feature branches and then create pull requests to run tests and provide feedback to GitHub and block submission approval if tests fail. Let's see how to set up a review process with Jenkins for pull requests.

Create a new feature branch from the develop branch with the following command:

```
git checkout -b feature/featureA
```

Make some changes; in this example, I have updated the README.md file. Then, commit the changes and push the new feature branch to the remote repository:

```
git add README.md
git commit -m "update readme"
git push feature/featureA
```

Head over to the GitHub repository, and create a new pull request to merge the feature branch to the develop branch, as shown in figure 9.42.

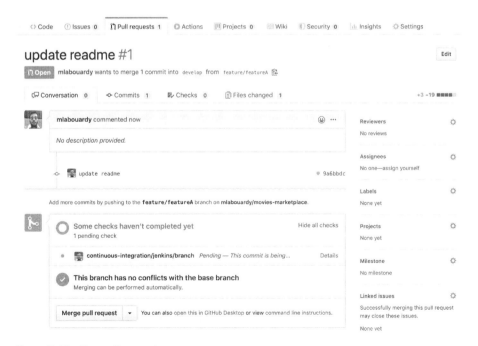

Figure 9.42   New pull request

On Jenkins, a new build will be triggered on the feature branch, as you can see in figure 9.43.

Figure 9.43   Build execution on the feature branch

Once the CI is finished, Jenkins will update the status on GitHub (figure 9.44). The build indicator in GitHub will turn either red or green, based on the build status.

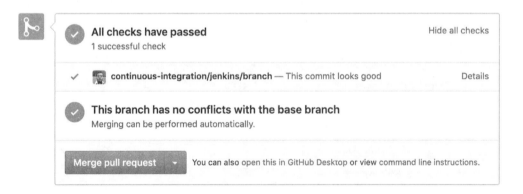

Figure 9.44   Jenkins post-build status on GitHub PR

NOTE   You can also configure SonarQube to analyze pull requests so you can ensure that the code is clean and approved for merging.

This process allows you to run a build and subsequent automated tests at every check-in so only the best code gets merged. Catching bugs early and automatically reduces the number of problems introduced into production, so your team can build better, more efficient software. We can now merge the feature branch and delete it; see figure 9.45.

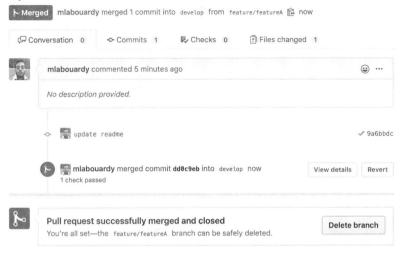

Figure 9.45   Merge and delete the feature branch.

And that will trigger another build on the develop branch, which will trigger the CI stages and push the image with the `develop` tag to the remote Docker registry.

Once the build is completed, we can check the status of previous commits by clicking the Commits section from the GitHub repository. A green, yellow, or red check mark should be displayed, depending on the state of the build; see figure 9.46.

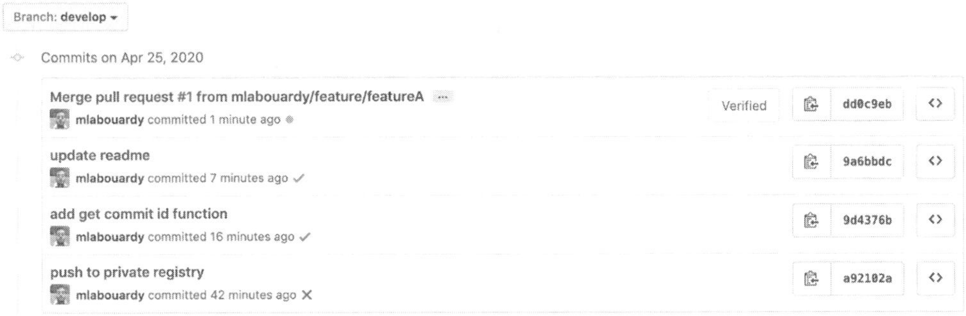

Figure 9.46   Jenkins build status history

Finally, to disable developers from pushing directly to the develop branch and also merging without a Jenkins build being passed, we will create a new rule to protect the develop branch. On the GitHub repository settings, jump to the Branches section and add a new protection rule that requires the Jenkins status check to be successful before merging. Figure 9.47 shows the rule configuration.

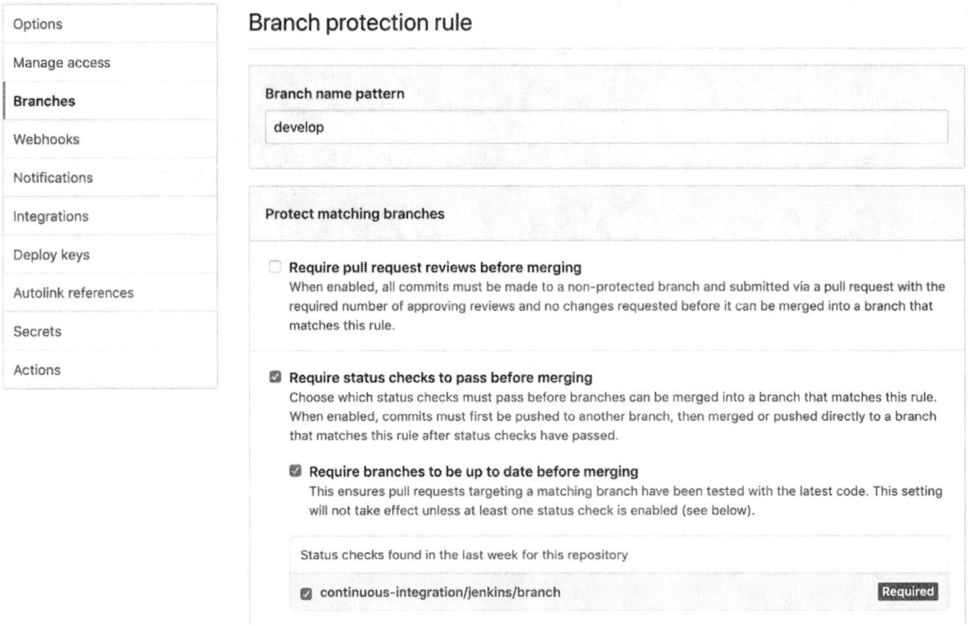

Options	Branch protection rule
Manage access	
Branches	
Webhooks	**Branch name pattern**
Notifications	develop
Integrations	
Deploy keys	**Protect matching branches**
Autolink references	
Secrets	☐ **Require pull request reviews before merging**
Actions	When enabled, all commits must be made to a non-protected branch and submitted via a pull request with the required number of approving reviews and no changes requested before it can be merged into a branch that matches this rule.

☑ **Require status checks to pass before merging**
Choose which status checks must pass before branches can be merged into a branch that matches this rule. When enabled, commits must first be pushed to another branch, then merged or pushed directly to a branch that matches this rule after status checks have passed.

☑ **Require branches to be up to date before merging**
This ensures pull requests targeting a matching branch have been tested with the latest code. This setting will not take effect unless at least one status check is enabled (see below).

Status checks found in the last week for this repository

☑ continuous-integration/jenkins/branch   `Required`

Figure 9.47   GitHub branch protection

Apply the same rule for the preprod and master branches. Then, repeat the same procedure for the rest of the GitHub repositories of the project.

With the Docker images safely stored in the private registry and the build status posted to GitHub, we've completed the implementation of the CI pipeline of Dockerized microservices with Jenkins multibranch pipelines. The next two chapters cover how to implement continuous deployment and delivery practices with Jenkins for two of the most used container orchestration platforms for cloud-native applications: Docker Swarm and Kubernetes.

Summary

- You can optimize Docker images for production with Docker caching layers, multistage build features, and lightweight base images such as an Alpine base image.
- The commit ID and Jenkins build ID can be used to tag Docker images for versioning and rollback to a working version in case of application deployment failure.
- Binary repository tools like Nexus and Artifactory can manage and store build artifacts for later use.
- Anchore Engine is an open source tool that lets you scan Docker images for security vulnerabilities during CI workflow.
- In a CI environment, the frequency of a build is too high, and each build generates a package. Since all the built packages are in one place, developers are at liberty to choose what to promote and what not to promote in higher environments.

Cloud-native applications on Docker Swarm

This chapter covers

- Deploying a self-healing Swarm cluster on AWS and using an S3 bucket for node discovery
- Running SSH-based commands within Jenkins pipelines and configuring SSH agents
- Automating deployment of Dockerized applications to Swarm
- Integrating Slack to manage releases and build notifications of CI/CD pipelines
- Continuous delivery to production and user manual approvals within Jenkins

The previous chapter covered how to set up a continuous integration pipeline for a containerized microservice application with Jenkins. This chapter covers how to automate the deployment and manage multiple application environments. By the end of this chapter, you will be familiar with continuous deployment and delivery (figure 10.1) for containerized microservices running in a Docker Swarm cluster.

CI/CD workflow

Figure 10.1   A complete CI/CD pipeline workflow

One of the basic solutions to run multiple containers across a set of machines is Swarm (https://docs.docker.com/engine/swarm/), which comes bundled with Docker Engine. By the end of this chapter, you should be able to build a CI/CD pipeline from scratch for services running inside a Docker Swarm cluster, as shown in figure 10.2.

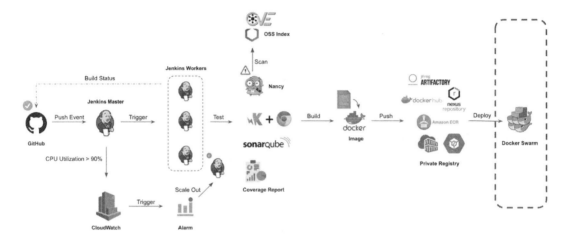

Figure 10.2   Target CI/CD pipeline

10.1   Running a distributed Docker Swarm cluster

Docker Swarm was originally released as a standalone product that ran master and agent containers on a cluster of servers to orchestrate the deployment of containers. This changed with the release of Docker 1.12 in 2016. Docker Swarm became officially part of Docker Engine and was built right into every Docker installation.

> **NOTE**   This is just a brief overview of the capabilities of Docker Swarm in Docker. For further reading, feel free to explore the Docker Swarm official documentation (https://docs.docker.com/engine/swarm/).

To illustrate the deployment of containers into a Swarm cluster from a CI/CD pipeline defined in Jenkins, we need to deploy a Swarm cluster.

The Swarm cluster will be deployed inside a VPC with two Auto Scaling groups: one for Swarm managers and another for Swarm workers. Both ASGs will be deployed within private subnets that spin up across multiple availability zones for resiliency.

Once the ASGs are created, setting up the Swarm requires manual initialization of the managers, and adding new nodes to the cluster requires additional information (a cluster join token) provided by the first manager when the Swarm is created.

This step can be automated with configuration management tools like Ansible or Chef. However, it requires manual interaction. To address this, and to provide automatic Swarm initialization, we will run a one-shot Docker container on instance launch; the container uses an S3 bucket as a cluster discovery registry to find active managers and join tokens.

Figure 10.3 summarizes the architecture we will deploy. We will focus on AWS, but the same architecture can be applied in other cloud providers or locally.

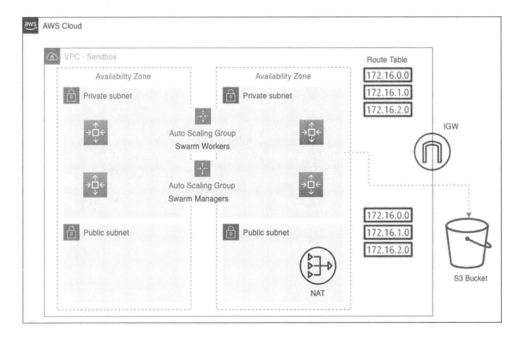

Figure 10.3   Swarm architecture in AWS

NOTE   A distributed, consistent key-value store such as etcd (https://etcd.io/), HashiCorp's Consul (www.consul.io), or Apache ZooKeeper (https://zoo keeper.apache.org/) can be used as service discovery to make the nodes auto-join the Swarm cluster.

To deploy Swarm instances, we need to provide an AMI with Docker Engine preinstalled. By now, you should be familiar with Packer. We will create a template.json file with the content in the following listing. (The full template can be downloaded from chapter10/swarm/packer/docker-ce/template.json.)

Listing 10.1   Docker AMI's Packer template

```
{
    "variables" : {},
    "builders" : [
        {
            "type" : "amazon-ebs",
            "profile" : "{{user `aws_profile`}}",
            "region" : "{{user `region`}}",
            "instance_type" : "{{user `instance_type`}}",
            "source_ami" : "{{user `source_ami`}}",
            "ssh_username" : "ec2-user",
            "ami_name" : "18.09.9-ce",
            "ami_description" : "Docker engine AMI",
        }
    ],
    "provisioners" : [
        {
            "type" : "shell",
            "script" : "./setup.sh",
            "execute_command" : "sudo -E -S sh '{{ .Path }}'"
        }
    ]
}
```

The base image is Amazon Linux 2, which will be provisioned with a shell script that installs the most recent Docker Community Edition package. Then it adds the `ec2-user` username to the `docker` group, to be able to execute Docker commands without using the `sudo` command; see the following listing.

Listing 10.2   Docker Community Edition installation

```
#!/bin/bash
yum update -y
yum install docker -y
usermod -aG docker ec2-user
systemctl enable docker
```

Issue a `packer build` command to bake the Docker AMI. Once the provisioning process is completed, the new baked AMI should be available on the Images section on the AWS Management Console (figure 10.4).

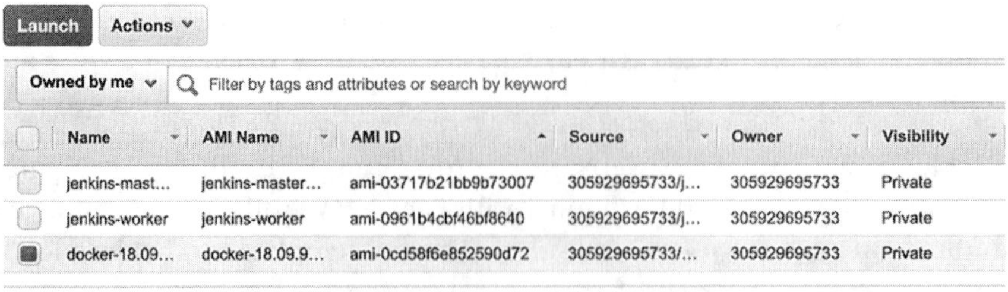

	Name	AMI Name	AMI ID	Source	Owner	Visibility
☐	jenkins-mast...	jenkins-master...	ami-03717b21bb9b73007	305929695733/j...	305929695733	Private
☐	jenkins-worker	jenkins-worker	ami-0961b4cbf46bf8640	305929695733/j...	305929695733	Private
☑	docker-18.09...	docker-18.09.9...	ami-0cd58f6e852590d72	305929695733/...	305929695733	Private

Figure 10.4   Docker Community Edition AMI

Next, deploy the infrastructure with Terraform, and create a dedicated VPC called `sandbox` with a 10.1.0.0/16 CIDR block to isolate the sandbox application and workload. Define the block in listing 10.3 in the vpc.tf file.

> **NOTE** Deploying the cluster on a different VPC is not mandatory, but following the best practices by isolating your workload environments for auditing and security compliance is strongly recommended.

Listing 10.3   Sandbox VPC resource

```
resource "aws_vpc" "sandbox" {
  cidr_block          = var.cidr_block
  enable_dns_hostnames = true

  tags = {
    Name   = var.vpc_name
    Author = var.author
  }
}
```

The Swarm manager needs a way of passing the worker token to the workers after it has initialized. The best way to do that is to have the Swarm manager's user data trigger generating the token and putting it into an S3 bucket. Define a private S3 bucket resource in s3.tf with the code in the following listing.

Listing 10.4   Swarm discovery S3 bucket resource

```
resource "aws_s3_bucket" "swarm_discovery_bucket" {
  bucket = var.swarm_discovery_bucket
  acl    = "private"

  tags = {
    Author = var.author
    Environment = var.environment
  }
}
```

> **NOTE** The AWS Systems Manager Parameter Store (http://mng.bz/r6GX) can also be used as a shared encrypted store to store and retrieve the join token for Swarm workers.

An IAM instance profile is necessary for EC2 instances to be able to interact with the S3 bucket to store or fetch the Swarm token for an autojoin operation. Define an IAM role policy within the iam.tf file, as shown in the next listing.

Listing 10.5   Swarm nodes IAM policy

```
resource "aws_iam_role_policy" "discovery_bucket_access_policy" {
  name = "discovery-bucket-access-policy-${var.environment}"
  role = aws_iam_role.swarm_role.id
```

```
  policy = <<EOF
{
  "Version": "2012-10-17",
  "Statement": [
    {
      "Action": [
        "s3:*"
      ],
      "Effect": "Allow",
      "Resource": "*"
    }
  ]
}
EOF
}
```

Then, we create a launch configuration for Swarm managers that uses the Docker AMI baked with Packer and run a startup script configured on user data. Use the following listing to define the code in swarm_managers.tf.

> **Listing 10.6   Swarm managers launch configuration**

```
resource "aws_launch_configuration" "managers_launch_conf" {
  name                 = "managers_config_${var.environment}"
  image_id             = data.aws_ami.docker.id
  instance_type        = var.manager_instance_type
  key_name             = var.key_name
  security_groups      = [aws_security_group.swarm_sg.id]
  user_data            = data.template_file.swarm_manager_user_data.rendered
  iam_instance_profile = aws_iam_instance_profile.swarm_profile.id

  root_block_device {
    volume_type = "gp2"
    volume_size = 20
  }

  lifecycle {
    create_before_destroy = true
  }
}
```

The startup script uses the name of the cluster discovery S3 bucket and the role of the running instance (manager or worker), as shown in the next listing. Based on the instance role, the docker swarm join command will use the right token (workers token or managers token).

> **Listing 10.7   Swarm managers user data**

```
data "template_file" "swarm_manager_user_data" {
  template = "${file("scripts/join-swarm.tpl")}"
  vars = {
    swarm_discovery_bucket = "${var.swarm_discovery_bucket}"
    swarm_name             = var.environment
```

```
    swarm_role              = "manager"
  }
}
```

The shell script joint-swarm.tpl, shown in the following listing, uses EC2 metadata to fetch the instance private IP address. The script then executes a container that uses the S3 bucket to store the state of the Swarm once it's created or creates a new Swarm if no state already exists in the bucket.

Listing 10.8 Swarm nodes startup script

```
#!/bin/bash
NODE_IP=$(curl -fsS http://169.254.169.254/latest/meta-data/local-ipv4)
docker run -d --restart on-failure:5 \
    -e SWARM_DISCOVERY_BUCKET=${swarm_discovery_bucket} \
    -e ROLE=${swarm_role} \
    -e NODE_IP=$NODE_IP \
    -e SWARM_NAME=${swarm_name} \
    -v /var/run/docker.sock:/var/run/docker.sock \
    mlabouardy/swarm-discovery
```

NOTE The mlabouardy/swarm-discovery full Python script and Dockerfile is given in the GitHub repository: pipeline-as-code-with-jenkins/tree/master/chapter10/discovery.

From there, we will create an ASG of managers. By default, we will create one manager for the cluster. But I recommend using an odd number when running Swarm in production, as a majority vote is needed among managers to agree on proposed management tasks. An odd—rather than even—number is strongly recommended to have a tie-breaking consensus. However, for a sandbox cluster, we will keep it simple and go with one Swarm manager. In swarm_mangers.tf, define the ASG resource as shown in the following listing.

Listing 10.9 Swarm managers Auto Scaling group

```
resource "aws_autoscaling_group" "swarm_managers" {
  name                 = "managers_asg_${var.environment}"
  launch_configuration = aws_launch_configuration.managers_launch_conf.name
  vpc_zone_identifier  = [for subnet in aws_subnet.private_subnets:
    subnet.id]
  depends_on = [aws_s3_bucket.swarm_discovery_bucket]
  min_size        = 1
  max_size        = 3
  lifecycle {
    create_before_destroy = true
  }
}
```

NOTE You can define autoscaling policies with CloudWatch alarms to trigger scale-out or scale-in events based on CPU utilization or custom metrics of the Swarm nodes.

Similarly, we will create an ASG for workers, and we will go with two Swarm workers. Note the use of the `depends_on` keyword to create an implicit dependency on the `swarm_managers` resource. Terraform uses this information to determine the correct order for creating resources.

In this example, Terraform will create Swarm managers first. That way, we guarantee the Swarm initialization and the availability of a join token in the S3 bucket. Add the resource in the following listing in the swarm_workers.tf file.

Listing 10.10   Swarm workers ASG

```
resource "aws_autoscaling_group" "swarm_workers" {
  name                   = "workers_asg_${var.environment}"
  launch_configuration   = aws_launch_configuration.workers_launch_conf.name
  vpc_zone_identifier    = [for subnet in aws_subnet.private_subnets:
      subnet.id]
  min_size               = 2
  max_size               = 5
  depends_on = [aws_autoscaling_group.swarm_managers]
  lifecycle {
    create_before_destroy = true
  }
}
```

Finally, allow the firewall rules in table 10.1 on the security group assigned to the Swarm cluster instances.

Table 10.1   Swarm cluster security group rules

Protocol	Port	Source	Description
TCP	2377	Swarm	Cluster management and raft sync communications
TCP	7946	Swarm	Control-plane gossip discovery communication among all nodes
UDP	7946	Swarm	Container network discovery from other Swarm nodes
UDP	4789	Swarm	Data-plane VXLAN overlay network traffic
TCP	22	Jenkins and Bastion SGs	SSH traffic from Jenkins master and bastion security groups

The following listing provides the security group definition.

Listing 10.11   Swarm nodes security group

```
resource "aws_security_group" "swarm_sg" {
  name        = "swarm_sg_${var.environment}"
  description = "Allow inbound traffic for
swarm management and ssh from jenkins & bastion hosts"
  vpc_id      = aws_vpc.sandbox.id
```

```
  ingress {
    from_port       = 22
    to_port         = 22
    protocol        = "tcp"
    security_groups = [var.bastion_sg_id, var.jenkins_sg_id]
  }
  ingress {
    from_port   = "2377"
    to_port     = "2377"
    protocol    = "tcp"
    cidr_blocks = [var.cidr_block]
  }
  …
  egress {
    from_port   = "0"
    to_port     = "0"
    protocol    = "-1"
    cidr_blocks = ["0.0.0.0/0"]
  }
}
```

NOTE I recommend using an S3 backend with encryption and versioning enabled to remotely store the Terraform state files.

Define the required Terraform variables in variables.tfvars as listed in table 10.2.

Table 10.2   Swarm Terraform variables

Variable	Type	Value	Description
region	String	None	The name of the region, such as `eu-central-1`, in which to deploy the Swarm cluster
shared_credentials _file	String	~/.aws/ credentials	The path to the shared credentials file. If this is not set and a profile is specified, `~/.aws/credentials` will be used.
aws_profile	String	profile	The AWS profile name as set in the shared credentials file
author	String	None	Name of the owner of the Swarm cluster. It's optional, but recommended, to tag your AWS resources to track the monthly costs by owner or environment.
key_name	String	None	SSH key pair
availability_zones	List	None	Availability zone where you'll spin up the VPC subnet
bastion_sg_id	String	None	The bastion host security group ID
jenkins_sg_id	String	None	The Jenkins master security group ID
vpc_name	String	sandbox	The name of the VPC

Table 10.2   Swarm Terraform variables *(continued)*

Variable	Type	Value	Description
`environment`	String	`sandbox`	The runtime environment name
`cidr_block`	String	`10.1.0.0/16`	The VPC CIDR block
`cluster_name`	String	`sandbox`	The Swarm cluster's name
`public_subnets_count`	Number	2	The number of public subnets to create
`private_subnets_count`	Number	2	The number of private subnets to create
`swarm_discovery_bucket`	String	`swarm-discovery-cluster`	The S3 bucket where the Swarm tokens will be stored
`manager_instance_type`	String	`t2.small`	The EC2 instance type for Swarm managers
`worker_instance_type`	String	`t2.large`	The EC2 instance type for Swarm workers

Then, use the `terraform apply` command to start the deployment process. Once deployed, the ASGs will be created, the Swarm discovery container will be launched on each instance, and the first manager to be run will execute the `swarm init` command and store the token on the S3 bucket (figure 10.5), which will be used by other instances to join the cluster.

> **NOTE**   You can have as many or as few worker groups as you wish, running in as many different configurations as you choose (CPU or memory-optimized workers alongside general-purpose Swarm workers).

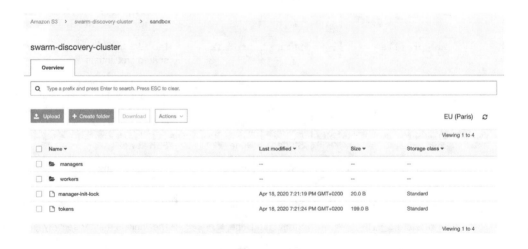

Figure 10.5   Swarm state stored in an S3 bucket

If you decide to create a dedicated VPC for the Swarm cluster, you need to set up VPC peering between management and sandbox VPCs, as shown in figure 10.6. For a step-by-step guide on how to set up peering with Terraform, refer to the official Terraform documentation at http://mng.bz/VBw5.

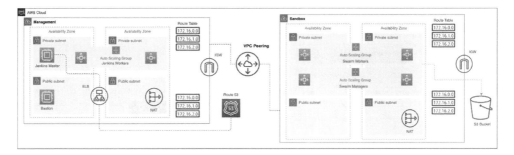

Figure 10.6   VPC peering between management and sandbox VPCs

> **NOTE**   If you intend to use the VPC peering connection, make sure the VPCs don't have matching or overlapping IPv4 CIDR blocks. In our example, the management and sandbox CIDR blocks are 10.0.0.0/16 and 10.1.0.0/16, respectively.

From the VPC dashboard, navigate to Peering Connections and create a new one. Configure the peering as shown in figure 10.7.

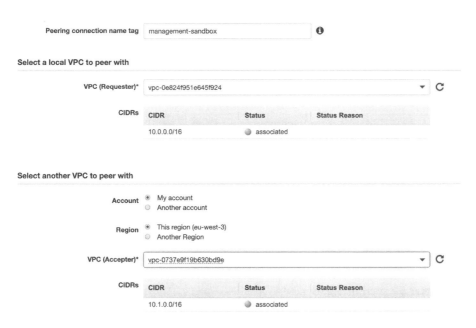

Figure 10.7   Configuring the peering of management and sandbox VPCs

After creating the peering connection, you'll see Pending Acceptance in the status bar. If you are using a different account or different region, go to the corresponding VPC console, where you can see Pending Acceptance in the status bar of the peering connection. From the Actions drop-down, choose Accept Request, as shown in figure 10.8. Then, in the Accept VPC Peering Connection Request prompt box, click Yes, Accept.

Figure 10.8   Accepting VPC peering request

To send and receive traffic across this VPC peering connection, you must add a route to the peered VPC in one or more of your VPC route tables. In the route tables associated with the subnets of the VPC, create a route with the CIDR block of the peer VPC as a destination, and the ID of the VPC peering connection as a target.

Repeat the same setups for all other VPC route tables. Once everything is set up, your routing table will look like figure 10.9.

Route Tables > Edit routes

Edit routes

Destination	Target	Status	Propagated	
10.1.0.0/16	local	active	No	
0.0.0.0/0	nat-0f4ecaa35c041e21c	active	No	✕
10.0.0.0/16	pcx-01e772e9f9e4fc5a5		No	✕

Add route

* Required   Cancel   Save routes

Figure 10.9   Sandbox VPC's route table update

To view the Swarm state, set up an SSH tunnel by using the bastion host deployed in chapter 5's section 5.2.4:

```
ssh -N 3000:SWARM_MANAGER_IP:22 ec2-user@BASTION_IP
ssh ec2-user@localhost -p 3000
```

Replace SWARM_MANAGER_IP with the Swarm manager private IP address. Once connected, if you type the docker info command, the Swarm: active attribute should confirm that Swarm has been properly configured:

```
[[ec2-user@ip-10-1-2-168 ~]$ docker info
 Containers: 1
  Running: 0
  Paused: 0
  Stopped: 1
 Images: 1
 Server Version: 18.09.9-ce
 Storage Driver: overlay2
  Backing Filesystem: extfs
  Supports d_type: true
  Native Overlay Diff: true
 Logging Driver: json-file
 Cgroup Driver: cgroupfs
 Plugins:
  Volume: local
  Network: bridge host macvlan null overlay
  Log: awslogs fluentd gcplogs gelf journald json-file local logentries splunk syslog
 Swarm: active
  NodeID: zv2gyvahz61mthzr3z29e16v1
  Is Manager: true
```

Run docker node ls from the manager machine to view your Swarm's connected nodes. As you can see in figure 10.10, we now have one manager and two workers.

```
docker node ls
```

```
[[ec2-user@ip-10-1-2-168 ~]$ docker node ls
ID                              HOSTNAME          STATUS    AVAILABILITY    MANAGER STATUS    ENGINE VERSION
uoxlczrw3f17bsuegqdcst4o1       ip-10-1-0-91      Ready     Active                            18.09.9-ce
wyo0uo4sjigu0fa030aim809m       ip-10-1-2-155     Ready     Active                            18.09.9-ce
zv2gyvahz61mthzr3z29e16v1 *     ip-10-1-2-168     Ready     Active          Leader            18.09.9-ce
[ec2-user@ip-10-1-2-168 ~]$ 
```

Figure 10.10   Swarm cluster nodes list

With our Swarm up and running, let's deploy the Dockerized-based application with Jenkins.

10.2   *Defining a continuous deployment process*

Create a new GitHub repository for deployment. Because deployment options are often changed, we will store the deployment part on a different Git repo. Then, create three main branches: develop, preprod, and master, as in figure 10.11.

Docker Swarm mode now integrates directly with Docker Compose v3 and officially supports the deployment of *stacks* (groups of services) via docker-compose.yml files. The same docker-compose.yml file you would use to test your application locally can now be used to deploy your application to Swarm.

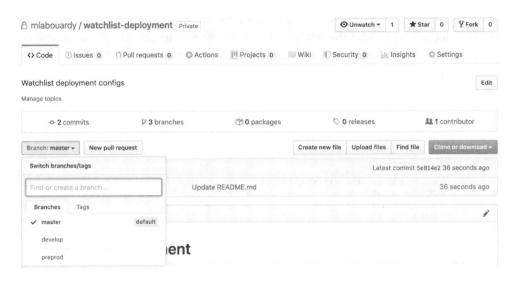

Figure 10.11   GitHub deployment repository

To do a Docker Swarm deployment from Jenkins, we need a docker-compose file that contains the references to Docker images along with the configuration settings such as port, network name, labels, and constraints. To run this file, we need to execute the `docker stack deployment` command over SSH on a manager machine.

On the develop branch, create a docker-compose.yml file by using your favorite text editor or IDE, with the content in the following listing.

Listing 10.12   Application Docker Compose

```
version: "3.3"
services:
  movies-loader:
    image: ID.dkr.ecr.REGION.amazonaws.com/USER/movies-loader:develop
    environment:
      - AWS_REGION=REGION
      - SQS_URL=https://sqs.REGION.amazonaws.com/ID/movies_to_parse_sandbox

  movies-parser:
    image: ID.dkr.ecr.REGION.amazonaws.com/USER/movies-loader:develop
    environment:
      - AWS_REGION=REGION
      - SQS_URL=https://sqs.REGION.amazonaws.com/ID/movies_to_parse_sandbox
      - MONGO_URI=mongodb://root:root@mongodb/watchlist
      - MONGO_DATABASE=watchlist
    depends_on:
      - mongodb

  movies-store:
    image: ID.dkr.ecr.REGION.amazonaws.com/USER/movies-store:develop
```

```
    environment:
      - MONGO_URI=mongodb://root:root@mongodb/watchlist
    ports:
      - 3000:3000
    depends_on:
      - mongodb

  movies-marketplace:
    image: ID.dkr.ecr.REGION.amazonaws.com/USER/movies-marketplace:develop
    ports:
      - 80:80

  mongodb:
    image: bitnami/mongodb:latest
    environment:
      - MONGODB_USERNAME=root
      - MONGODB_PASSWORD=root
      - MONGODB_DATABASE=watchlist
```

NOTE Substitute the `ID`, `REGION`, and `USER` with your own AWS Account ID, AWS region, and ECR URI.

Each service uses the image we built in chapter 9 and references the `develop` tag. This tag is dedicated to sandbox deployment and contains the codebase of the develop branch. Also, we have defined a MongoDB service that will be used by both the movies-store and movies-parser services.

The MongoDB service credentials are in plaintext. However, you shouldn't commit sensitive information under any circumstances and opt for managed solutions like HashiCorp Vault or AWS SSM Parameter Store to encrypt your credentials and access tokens. You can also use an integrated feature of Docker called Secrets to create database credentials:

```
openssl rand -base64 12 | docker secret create mongodb_password -
```

And update docker-compose.yml to use the secret instead of the plaintext password:

```
mongodb:
    image: bitnami/mongodb:latest
    environment:
      - MONGODB_USERNAME=root
      - MONGO_ROOT_PASSWORD_FILE: /run/secrets/mongodb_password
      - MONGODB_DATABASE=watchlist
```

NOTE If the MongoDB service crashes for unknown reasons or has been removed, its data will be lost. To avoid this loss of data, you should mount a persistent volume. Depending on the cloud provider used, Docker volumes support use of external persistent storage such as Amazon EBS.

To decouple the crawling and parsing of HTML pages, we are using a distributed queue between the movies-loader and movies-parser services. In addition to its high availability, this will allow us to deploy additional movies-parser workers based on the number of HTML pages to parse. Create an SQS for the sandbox environment called `movies_to_parse_sandbox` with Terraform (chapter10/swarm/terraform/sqs.tf), as shown in figure 10.12. This queue will be used by movies-loader to push movies into, and then it will be consumed by movies-parser workers.

Figure 10.12   Sandbox queue settings

With Docker Compose out of the way, we can proceed and create a Jenkinsfile, shown in listing 10.13, with these steps:

1 Clone the GitHub repository (chapter10/deployment/sandbox/Jenkinsfile) and check out the develop branch.

2 Send the docker-compose.yml file over SSH to the manager node and execute the command `docker stack deploy`.

NOTE   We use the master label to constrain the pipeline to be executed on the Jenkins master only. Workers' machines might also be used for this job.

Listing 10.13   Deployment Jenkinsfile

```
def swarmManager = 'manager.sandbox.domain.com'
def region = 'AWS REGION'                              Replace with your own
node('master'){                                        AWS default region.
    stage('Checkout'){
        checkout scm
    }
    stage('Copy'){
        sh "scp -o StrictHostKeyChecking=no
docker-compose.yml ec2-user@${swarmManager}:/home/ec2-user"
    }
    stage('Deploy stack'){
        sh "ssh -oStrictHostKeyChecking=no ec2-user@${swarmManager}
    '\$(\$(aws ecr get-login --no-include-email
    --region ${region}))' || true"
```

```
        sh "ssh -oStrictHostKeyChecking=no
ec2-user@${swarmManager} docker stack deploy
--compose-file docker-compose.yml
--with-registry-auth watchlist"
    }
}
```

This Jenkinsfile uses Amazon ECR as a private registry. If you're using a private registry that requires username and password authentication (such as Nexus, DockerHub, Azure, or Cloud Container Registry), you can use the Credentials Binding plugin https://plugins.jenkins.io/credentials-binding/), which is installed by default, to allow registry credentials to be bounded to USERNAME and PASSWORD variables. Then, pass those variables to the docker login command for authentication:

```
stage('Deploy'){
    withCredentials([[
$class: 'UsernamePasswordMultiBinding',
credentialsId: 'registry',
usernameVariable: 'USERNAME',
passwordVariable: 'PASSWORD']]) {
        sh "ssh -oStrictHostKeyChecking=no
ec2-user@${swarmManager}
docker login --password $PASSWORD --username $USERNAME
${registry}"
        sh "ssh -oStrictHostKeyChecking=no
ec2-user@${swarmManager}
docker stack deploy --compose-file docker-compose.yml
--with-registry-auth watchlist"
    }
}
```

Push the Jenkinsfile and docker-compose.yml files to the develop branch with the following commands:

```
git add .
git commit -m "deploy watchlist stack to sandbox"
git push origin develop
```

Head over to Jenkins, and create a new multibranch pipeline job called watchlist-deployment.

> **NOTE** For a step-by-step guide on how to create and configure multibranch pipeline jobs on Jenkins, check out chapter 7.

Set the GitHub repository HTTPS clone URL and allow Jenkins to discover all branches looking for a Jenkinsfile on the root repository, as shown in figure 10.13.

Figure 10.13   Branch sources configuration

For now, the job pipeline should discover the develop branch and execute the stages
defined in the Jenkinsfile, as shown in figure 10.14.

Figure 10.14   Deployment job on Jenkins

The pipeline should fail and turn red at the Copy stage, as shown in figure 10.15. The Jenkins master cannot SSH to the Swarm manager because the Jenkins master has the wrong private SSH key.

Stage Logs (Copy)
Shell Script -- scp -o StrictHostKeyChecking=no docker-compose.yml ec2-user@manager.sandbox.slowcoder.com:/home/ec2-user
(self time 270ms)
+ scp -o StrictHostKeyChecking=no docker-compose.yml ec2-user@manager.sandbox.slowcoder.com:/home/ec2-user
Warning: Permanently added 'manager.sandbox.slowcoder.com,10.1.2.147' (ECDSA) to the list of known hosts.
Load key "/var/lib/jenkins/.ssh/id_rsa": Permission denied
Permission denied (publickey).
lost connection

Figure 10.15 SCP command logs

For Jenkins to continuously deploy to the Swarm, it needs access to the Swarm manager. Create a new credential of type SSH Username with Private Key on Jenkins to access the Swarm sandbox. On a private-key field, paste the content of the key pair used while creating Swarm EC2 instances. Then, call it `swarm-sandbox`, as shown in figure 10.16.

Kind
SSH Username with private key
Scope
Global (Jenkins, nodes, items, all child items, etc)
ID
swarm-sandbox
Description
SSH keypair to SSH to Swarm sandbox
Username
ec2-user
Private Key
Enter directly
Key
Enter New Secret Below
-----BEGIN RSA PRIVATE KEY-----
MIIEpQIBAAKCAQEAvk51M+Z7VRE28OC82VNOlkIJYkSDY3eQjREe2iQgK3KER+a7TAyM+/uYrsYG
Passphrase

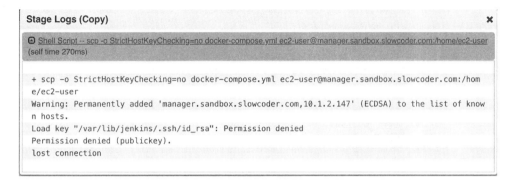

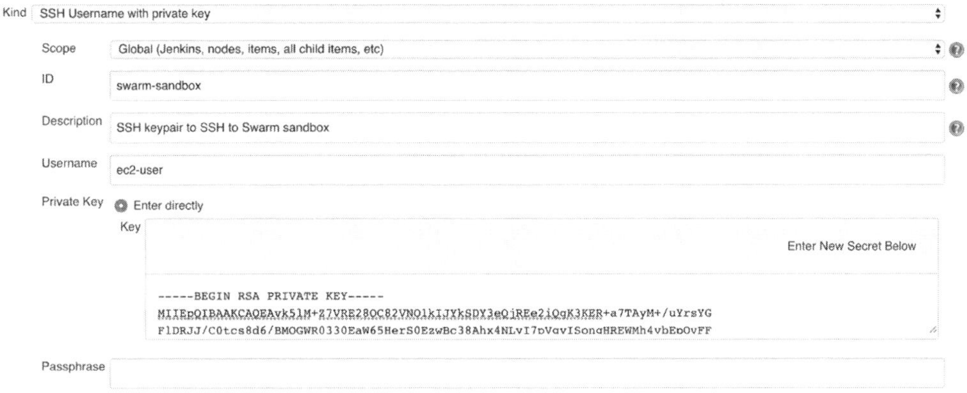

Figure 10.16 Jenkins credential with Swarm SSH key pair

NOTE Jenkins would need access to only the Swarm manager. The other nodes are managed by the Swarm manager, so Jenkins does not need direct access to them.

Update the Jenkinsfile to use the SSH agent plugin (Credentials Binding plugin) to inject the credentials. The `sshagent` block should wrap all SSH- and SCP-based commands, as shown in the following listing.

Listing 10.14 SSH agent configuration

```
sshagent (credentials: ['swarm-sandbox']){
    stage('Copy'){
        sh "scp -o StrictHostKeyChecking=no
docker-compose.yml ec2-user@${swarmManager}:/home/ec2-user"
    }

    stage('Deploy stack'){
        sh "ssh -oStrictHostKeyChecking=no
ec2-user@${swarmManager}
'\$(\$(aws ecr get-login --no-include-email --region ${region}))'
|| true"
        sh "ssh -oStrictHostKeyChecking=no
ec2-user@${swarmManager}
docker stack deploy --compose-file docker-compose.yml
--with-registry-auth watchlist"
    }
}
```

Push the changes to the develop branch. A new build should be triggered on the develop branch's nested job of the watchlist-deployment item.

NOTE For continuous deployment, create a GitHub webhook on the GitHub repository to notify Jenkins on push events.

This time, the pipeline should be successful and turns green (figure 10.17).

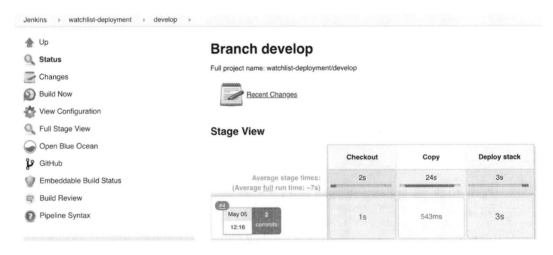

Figure 10.17 Continuous deployment pipeline

On the build logs side, Jenkins will run `docker stack deploy` over SSH on the Swarm manager, and the services in figure 10.18 will be deployed based on the `develop` tag image.

```
+ ssh -oStrictHostKeyChecking=no ec2-user@manager.sandbox.slowcoder.com docker stack deploy --compose-file docker-compose.yml --with-
registry-auth watchlist
Creating network watchlist_default
Creating service watchlist_mongodb
Creating service watchlist_movies-loader
Creating service watchlist_movies-parser
Creating service watchlist_movies-store
Creating service watchlist_movies-marketplace
[Pipeline] }
[Pipeline] // stage
[Pipeline] }
$ ssh-agent -k
unset SSH_AUTH_SOCK;
unset SSH_AGENT_PID;
echo Agent pid 4018 killed;
[ssh-agent] Stopped.
[Pipeline] // sshagent
[Pipeline] }
[Pipeline] // node
[Pipeline] End of Pipeline
```

Figure 10.18 Output from `docker stack deploy`

> **NOTE** If you plan to use Amazon ECR as a remote repository, you need to assign an ECR IAM policy to the IAM instance profile assigned to Swarm instances.

On Swarm, type the following command, and we should be able to view the status of the stack and the services running within it:

```
docker service ls
```

The four microservices should be deployed alongside a MongoDB service, as shown in figure 10.19.

```
[ec2-user@ip-10-1-2-147 ~]$ docker service ls
ID              NAME                          MODE         REPLICAS   IMAGE
ro2ee4qwup7k    watchlist_mongodb             replicated   1/1        bitnami/mongodb:latest
rkmslcb50mr9    watchlist_movies-loader       replicated   0/1        305929695733.dkr.ecr.eu-west-3.amazonaws.com/mlabouardy/movies-loader:develop
rkymrina4zi6    watchlist_movies-marketplace  replicated   1/1        305929695733.dkr.ecr.eu-west-3.amazonaws.com/mlabouardy/movies-marketplace:develop
afsaadidilfs    watchlist_movies-parser       replicated   0/1        305929695733.dkr.ecr.eu-west-3.amazonaws.com/mlabouardy/movies-loader:develop
ftlt8tunlir2    watchlist_movies-store        replicated   1/1        305929695733.dkr.ecr.eu-west-3.amazonaws.com/mlabouardy/movies-store:develop
[ec2-user@ip-10-1-2-147 ~]$
```

Figure 10.19 Stack successfully deployed on Swarm sandbox

Next, we will deploy an open source tool called Visualizer to visualize Docker services across a set of machines. Execute these commands on the Swarm manager machine:

```
docker service create --name=visualizer
--publish=8080:8080/tcp
--constraint=node.role==manager \
    --mount=type=bind,src=/var/run/docker.sock,dst=/var/run/docker.sock \
    dockersamples/visualizer
```

Once the service is deployed, we will create a public load balancer to forward incoming HTTP and HTTPS (optional) traffic to port 8080, which is the port the Visualizer UI is exposed to. Declare the ELB resource in the following listing or download the resources file from chapter8/services/loadbalancers.tf.

Listing 10.15   Visualizer load balancer

```
resource "aws_elb" "visualizer_elb" {
  subnets                    = var.public_subnets
  cross_zone_load_balancing = true
  security_groups            = [aws_security_group.elb_visualizer_sg.id]
  listener {
    instance_port     = 8080
    instance_protocol = "http"
    lb_port           = 443
    lb_protocol       = "https"
    ssl_certificate_id = var.ssl_arn
  }
  listener {
    instance_port     = 8080
    instance_protocol = "http"
    lb_port           = 80
    lb_protocol       = "http"
  }

  health_check {
    healthy_threshold   = 2
    unhealthy_threshold = 2
    timeout             = 3
    target              = "TCP:8080" resource "aws_autoscaling_attachment"
      "cluster_attach_visualizer_elb" {
    autoscaling_group_name = var.swarm_managers_asg_id
    elb                     = aws_elb.visualizer_elb.id
}

    interval            = 5
  }
}
```

Then, we attach the load balancer to the ASG of the Swarm managers. The load balancer can also be assigned to the Swarm workers. In fact, all of the nodes within the Swarm cluster are aware of the location of every container within the cluster via the gossip network. If an incoming request hits a node that is not currently running the service for which that request was intended, the request will be routed to a node that is running a container for that service.

This is so nodes don't have to be purpose-built for specific services. Any node can run any service, and every node can be load balanced equally, reducing complexity and the number of resources needed for an application. This feature is called *mesh routing*:

```
resource "aws_autoscaling_attachment" "cluster_attach_visualizer_elb" {
  autoscaling_group_name = var.swarm_managers_asg_id
  elb                     = aws_elb.visualizer_elb.id
}
```

The following listing (chapter8/services/dns.tf) is not mandatory, but can be used to create a friendly DNS record pointing to the Visualizer load balancer FQDN.

Listing 10.16 Visualizer DNS configuration

```
resource "aws_route53_record" "visualizer" {
  zone_id = var.hosted_zone_id
  name    = "visualizer.${var.environment}.${var.domain_name}"
  type    = "A"
  alias {
    name                   = aws_elb.visualizer_elb.dns_name
    zone_id                = aws_elb.visualizer_elb.zone_id
    evaluate_target_health = true
  }
}
```

NOTE Update the security group of the Swarm cluster to allow incoming inbound traffic on port 8080 from the load balancer security group. Add an ingress rule for port 8080 and use `terraform apply` for changes to take effect.

Once changes are issued, point the browser to the load balancer URL displayed in the `Outputs` section in your terminal session. This handy tool, shown in figure 10.20, helps you see which containers are running, and on which nodes.

NOTE This tool works only with Docker Swarm mode in Docker Engine 1.12.0 and later. It does not work with the separate Docker Swarm project.

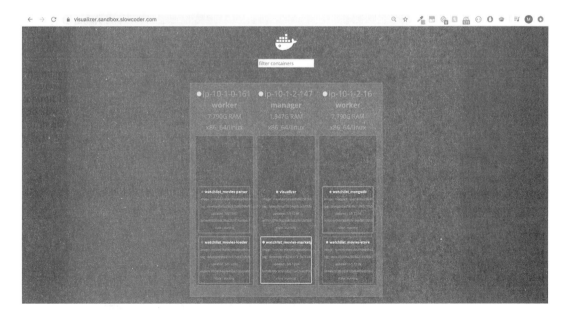

Figure 10.20   Visualizer dashboard

NOTE   Containers are deployed on the manager, too. If you want to restrict deployment to workers, use Docker constraints with labels.

We have successfully deployed our application stack to Swarm. However, for now, the deployment is triggered manually. Ultimately, we want the deployment job to be executed at the end of each CI pipeline's successful execution.

To do so, update the Jenkinsfile (chapter10/pipelines/movies-loader/Jenkinsfile) to trigger the external job with the `build job` keyword. For example, on the movies-loader Jenkinsfile, add the following `Deploy` stage code block to the end of the pipeline:

```
stage('Deploy'){
        if(env.BRANCH_NAME == 'develop'){
            build job: "watchlist-deployment/${env.BRANCH_NAME}"
        }
}
```

Commit and push the changes to a feature branch. Then create a pull request (PR) to merge to develop. A new build should be triggered on the feature branch, and once it's done, Jenkins will post the build status on the PR, as shown in figure 10.21.

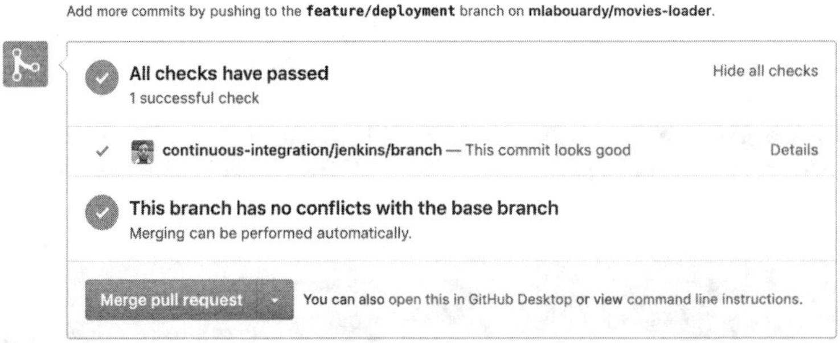

Figure 10.21
Pull request
build status

Once the pull request is validated, we merge to the develop branch, and a new build will be triggered on that branch, as shown in figure 10.22.

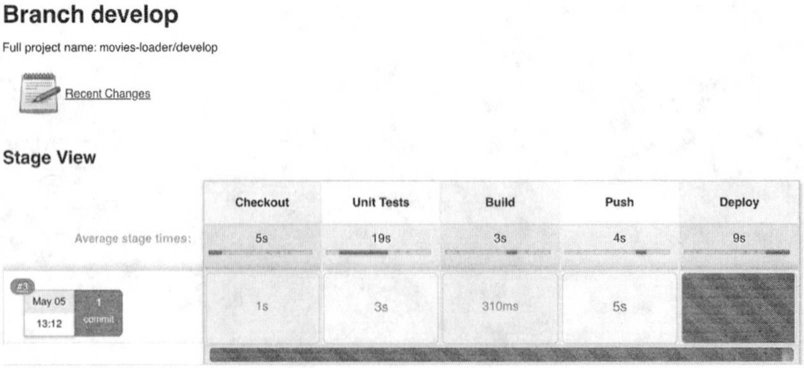

Figure 10.22   Jenkins CI/CD pipeline for the movies-loader project

At the end of the CI pipeline, the deploy stage will be executed, and watchlist-deployment will be triggered on the develop branch, as shown in figure 10.23.

Figure 10.23 External job triggering

That will trigger the deployment job, which will deploy the stack and force the pull of new Docker images with the `develop` tag. Repeat the same process for other GitHub repositories. In the end, each repository will trigger a deployment to sandbox if the CI is successfully executed, as shown in figure 10.24.

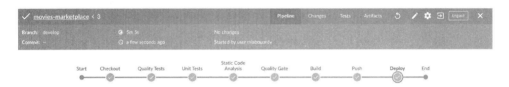

Figure 10.24 Marketplace CI/CD pipeline execution

> **NOTE** In chapters 11 and 12, we will cover how to run automated health checks and post-integration tests on the deployed application from Jenkins within the CI/CD pipeline.

By now, our application is deployed to the Swarm sandbox environment. To access the application, we need to create two public load balancers: one for the API (movies-store) and another for the frontend (movies-marketplace). Use Terraform template files available in the GitHub repository (under the /chapter8/services folder) to create the AWS resources, and then issue `terraform apply` to provision the resources. At the end of the deployment process, the marketplace and store API access URLs will be displayed in the `Outputs` section, as shown in figure 10.25.

```
aws_route53_record.movies_store: Creating...
aws_route53_record.movies_marketplace: Creating...
aws_route53_record.movies_marketplace: Still creating... [10s elapsed]
aws_route53_record.movies_store: Still creating... [10s elapsed]
aws_route53_record.movies_store: Still creating... [20s elapsed]
aws_route53_record.movies_marketplace: Still creating... [20s elapsed]
aws_route53_record.movies_store: Still creating... [30s elapsed]
aws_route53_record.movies_marketplace: Still creating... [30s elapsed]
aws_route53_record.movies_store: Still creating... [40s elapsed]
aws_route53_record.movies_marketplace: Still creating... [40s elapsed]
aws_route53_record.movies_store: Creation complete after 47s [id=Z2TR95QTU3UIUT_api.sandbox.slowcoder.com_A]
aws_route53_record.movies_marketplace: Creation complete after 48s [id=Z2TR95QTU3UIUT_marketplace.sandbox.slowcoder.com_A]

Apply complete! Resources: 2 added, 0 changed, 0 destroyed.

Outputs:

marketplace = https://marketplace.sandbox.slowcoder.com
store = https://api.sandbox.slowcoder.com
visualizer = https://visualizer.sandbox.slowcoder.com
```

Figure 10.25 Terraform apply output

NOTE   Make sure to allow inbound traffic on ports 80 (frontend), 8080 (visualizer), and 3000 (API) from the security group attached to the Swarm EC2 instances.

For the marketplace to be able to interact with the RESTful API to show a list of crawled movies, we need to inject the API URL at the build time of the marketplace Docker image. The source code of the marketplace contains multiple files based on the target environment (figure 10.26).

```
∨ src
  > app
  > assets
  ∨ environments
    TS environment.production.ts
    TS environment.sandbox.ts
    TS environment.staging.ts
    TS environment.ts
```

Figure 10.26   Angular environment files

Each file contains the right API URL. For the sandbox environment, the environment .sandbox.ts file will be used, as shown in the following listing.

Listing 10.17   Marketplace sandbox environment variables

```
export const environment = {
  production: false,
  apiURL: 'https://api.sandbox.slowcoder.com',
};
```

The marketplace Docker image will be built using the `ng build -c sandbox` flag, which will replace the environment.ts file with environment.sandbox.ts values; see figure 10.27.

Branch develop

Full project name: movies-marketplace/develop

 Recent Changes

Stage View

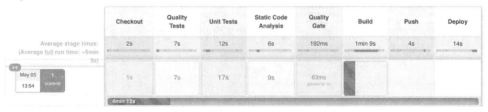

	Checkout	Quality Tests	Unit Tests	Static Code Analysis	Quality Gate	Build	Push	Deploy
Average stage times: (Average full run time: ~5min 5s)	2s	7s	12s	6s	192ms	1min 9s	4s	14s
May 05 13:54 1 commit	1s	7s	17s	9s	63ms (passes for 5s)			
4min 12s								

Figure 10.27   Docker image build execution

Once the new image is deployed to Swarm, point your browser to the marketplace URL. It should display the top 100 IMDb best movies in history, as shown in figure 10.28.

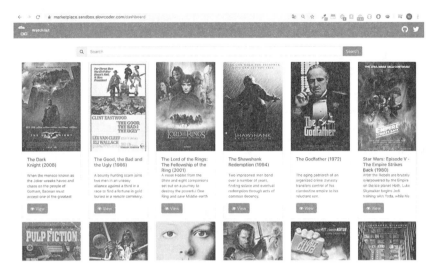

Figure 10.28   Watchlist marketplace dashboard

That's how to reach continuous deployment. However, we want to alert the development and product teams of the deployment and CI/CD status of the project.

10.3   *Integrating Jenkins with Slack notifications*

At certain stages of the pipeline, you may decide you want to send out a Slack notification to your team to inform them of the build status. To send Slack messages through Jenkins, we need to provide a way for our job to authorize itself with Slack.

Luckily for us, Slack has a prebuilt Jenkins integration that makes things pretty easy. Install the plugin from http://mng.bz/xXOB. Replace `WORKSPACE` with your Slack workspace name, as shown in figure 10.29.

Figure 10.29   Jenkins CI Slack integration

Click the Add to Slack button. Then select the channel on which you want Jenkins to send notifications, as shown in figure 10.30.

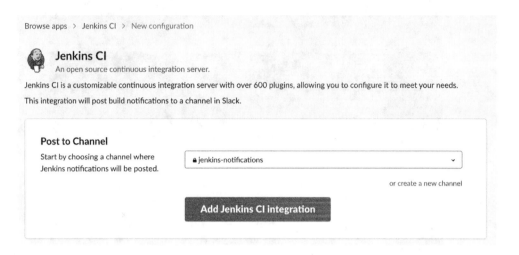

Figure 10.30   Slack channel configuration

After that, we need to set the configuration on the Jenkins Slack Notification plugin (https://plugins.jenkins.io/slack/), which is already installed on the baked Jenkins master machine image. Enter the team workspace name, integration token created on your slack, and channel name, as shown in figure 10.31, and click the Apply and Save buttons.

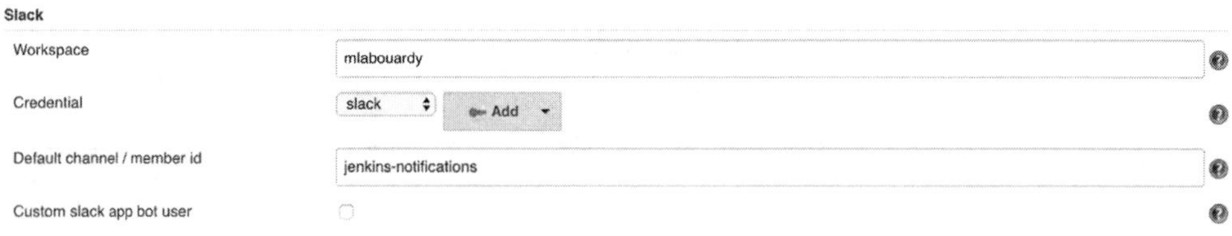

Figure 10.31   Jenkins Slack Notification plugin

Now that we have Slack properly configured in Jenkins, we can configure our CI/CD pipeline to send a notification to broadcast the status of the build with the following method:

```
slackSend (color: colorCode, message: summary)
```

Let's add this instruction at the end of the CI/CD pipeline for the movies-loader service as an example; see the following listing.

Listing 10.18   Jenkins Slack plugin DSL

```
node('workers'){
    stage('Checkout'){}

    stage('Unit Tests'){}

    stage('Build'){}

    stage('Push'){}

    stage('Deploy'){}

    slackSend (color: '#2e7d32',
message: "${env.JOB_NAME} has been successfully deployed")
}
```

NOTE   For simplicity, I skipped steps that run unit tests, build the image, and push the image to the registry. You're advised to put them inside the workflow we are about to explore.

Push the changes to a feature branch, and then merge to develop. At the end of the pipeline, a new Slack notification will be sent, as shown in figure 10.32.

 Mohamed Labouardy 3:30 PM
added an integration to this channel: Jenkins

 Jenkins APP 3:32 PM
Slack/Jenkins plugin: you're all set on https://jenkins.slowcoder.com/

 **Jenkins** APP 3:41 PM
movies-loader/develop has been successfully deployed

Figure 10.32   Jenkins Slack notification

While this works, we also want to be notified when the pipeline fails. That's where `try-catch` blocks come into play to handle errors thrown by pipeline stages; see the following listing.

Listing 10.19   Slack notifications within Jenkins

```
node('workers'){
    try {
        stage('Checkout'){
            checkout scm
            notifySlack('STARTED')
        }

        stage('Unit Tests'){}
        stage('Build'){}
```

```
        stage('Push'){}
        stage('Deploy'){}
    } catch(e){
        currentBuild.result = 'FAILED'
        throw e
    } finally {
        notifySlack(currentBuild.result)
    }
}
```

This time, a `notifySlack()` method is used, which sends a notification with a different color based on the pipeline build status, as shown in the following listing.

Listing 10.20   Custom Slack notification message color

```
def notifySlack(String buildStatus){
    buildStatus =  buildStatus ?: 'SUCCESSFUL'
    def colorCode = '#FF0000'

    if (buildStatus == 'STARTED') {
        colorCode = '#546e7a'
    } else if (buildStatus == 'SUCCESSFUL') {          Colors the border along the
        colorCode = '#2e7d32'                          left side of the message
    } else {
        colorCode = '#c62828c'
    }
    slackSend (color: colorCode,
message: "${env.JOB_NAME} build status: ${buildStatus}")   ◁──┐
}
```

Sends a Slack message with the job name by
using the env.JOB_NAME, and build status
by using the buildStatus variable

Based on your build result, the code sends Slack notifications as shown in figure 10.33.

Jenkins APP 3:48 PM

movies-loader/feature%2Fdeployment build status: STARTED

movies-loader/feature%2Fdeployment build status: SUCCESSFUL

movies-loader/develop build status: STARTED

movies-loader/develop build status: SUCCESSFUL

Figure 10.33   Build status notification

Let's simulate a build failure by throwing an error, by adding the following instruction to the `Build` stage:

```
error "Build failed"
```

Push the changes to GitHub. The pipeline will fail at the `Build` stage (figure 10.34).

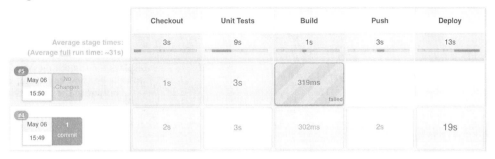

Figure 10.34   Throwing an error within the Jenkins pipeline

On the Slack channel, this time we will receive a notification with the build status set to Failure, as you can see in figure 10.35.

> movies-loader/develop build status: STARTED

> movies-loader/develop build status: FAILURE

Figure 10.35   Build failure Slack notification

In the following listing, we take this further. We'll add more information to the notification, such as the author of the push event, Git commit ID, and message.

Listing 10.21   Custom Slack notification message attributes

```
def notifySlack(String buildStatus){
    buildStatus =  buildStatus ?: 'SUCCESSFUL'
    def colorCode = '#FF0000'
    def subject = "Name: '${env.JOB_NAME}'\n
Status: ${buildStatus}\nBuild ID: ${env.BUILD_NUMBER}"
    def summary = "${subject}\nMessage: ${commitMessage()}
\nAuthor: ${commitAuthor()}\nURL: ${env.BUILD_URL}"

    if (buildStatus == 'STARTED') {
        colorCode = '#546e7a'
    } else if (buildStatus == 'SUCCESSFUL') {
        colorCode = '#2e7d32'
    } else {
        colorCode = '#c62828c'
    }
    slackSend (color: colorCode, message: summary)
}
```

Displays the job's name, its status, and build number

Holds the subject's value and Git info (author, commit message) and build URL

The `notifySlack()` method will call `commitAuthor()` and `commitMessage()` to get the appropriate information. The `commitAuthor()` method will return the name of the commit author by executing the `git show` command, as shown in the following listing.

Listing 10.22   Git helper function to fetch the author

```
def commitAuthor(){
    sh 'git show -s --pretty=%an > .git/commitAuthor'
    def commitAuthor = readFile('.git/commitAuthor').trim()
    sh 'rm .git/commitAuthor'
    commitAuthor
}
```

> Displays the commit message's author with the git show command, saves the output to the commitAuthor file

> Reads the commitAuthor file and trims extra spaces

And the `commitMessage()` method will use the `git log` command alongside the `HEAD` flag to fetch the commit message description; see the following listing.

Listing 10.23   Git helper function to fetch the commit message

```
def commitMessage() {
    sh 'git log --format=%B -n 1 HEAD > .git/commitMessage'
    def commitMessage = readFile('.git/commitMessage').trim()
    sh 'rm .git/commitMessage'
    commitMessage
}
```

> Displays the last commit message description and saves the output in a commitMessage file

> Reads the commitMessage content and trims extra spaces

If we push the changes, at the end of the CI/CD pipeline, the Slack notifications should contain the name of Jenkins job, build ID and its status, author name, and commit description, as shown in figure 10.36.

Jenkins APP 3:57 PM
Name: 'movies-loader/develop'
Status: STARTED
Build ID: 6
Message: Merge pull request #5 from mlabouardy/feature/deployment

commit message & author
Author: LABOUARDY Mohamed
URL: https://jenkins.slowcoder.com/job/movies-loader/job/develop/6/

Name: 'movies-loader/develop'
Status: SUCCESSFUL
Build ID: 6
Message: Merge pull request #5 from mlabouardy/feature/deployment

commit message & author
Author: LABOUARDY Mohamed
URL: https://jenkins.slowcoder.com/job/movies-loader/job/develop/6/

Figure 10.36   Slack notification with Git commit details

Apply the same changes for the movies-store, movies-marketplace, and movies-parser Jenkinsfiles.

> **NOTE** Chapter 11 covers how to use the Jenkins Slack Notification plugin to send a notification with a changelog as an attachment.

10.4 Handling code promotion with Jenkins

Maintaining multiple Swarm cluster environments makes sense to avoid breaking things while promoting code to production. Also, having a production-like environment can help you keep a mirror of your application running in production and reproducing issues in the staging environment without impacting your clients. But this comes at a price.

> **NOTE** You can reduce the costs of the sandbox and staging environments by shutting down instances outside of regular business hours.

With that being said, create a new Swarm cluster for the staging environment in a dedicated staging VPC with a 10.2.0.0/16 CIDR block, or deploy it within the same management VPC where Jenkins is deployed, as shown in figure 10.37.

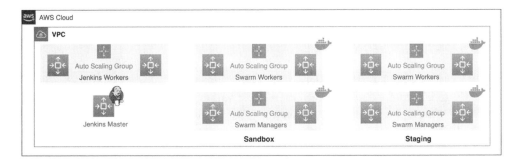

Figure 10.37 Deployment of sandbox and staging Swarm clusters and Jenkins within the same VPC

Create a preprod branch on the watchlist-deployment GitHub repository by running this command:

```
git checkout -b preprod
```

Create a docker-compose.yml file that uses the `preprod` tag, and update the SQS URL to use the staging queue, as shown in the following listing.

Listing 10.24 Docker Compose for staging deployment

```
version: "3.3"
services:
  movies-loader:
    image: ID.dkr.ecr.REGION.amazonaws.com/USER/movies-loader:preprod
```

```
    environment:
      - AWS_REGION=eu-west-3
      - SQS_URL=https://sqs.REGION.amazonaws.com/ID/movies_to_parse_staging
  movies-parser:
      image: ID.dkr.ecr.REGION.amazonaws.com/USER/movies-parser:preprod
```

Create a Jenkins credential of type SSH Username with Private Key with the SSH key pair used to deploy the Swarm staging cluster. Give it a name of `swarm-staging`, as shown in figure 10.38.

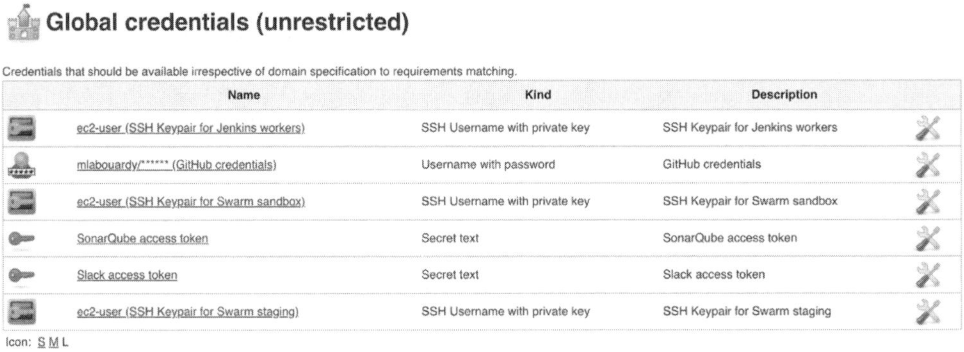

🔐 Global credentials (unrestricted)

Credentials that should be available irrespective of domain specification to requirements matching.

	Name	Kind	Description	
🖥️	ec2-user (SSH Keypair for Jenkins workers)	SSH Username with private key	SSH Keypair for Jenkins workers	🛠️
👤	mlabouardy/****** (GitHub credentials)	Username with password	GitHub credentials	🛠️
🖥️	ec2-user (SSH Keypair for Swarm sandbox)	SSH Username with private key	SSH Keypair for Swarm sandbox	🛠️
🔑	SonarQube access token	Secret text	SonarQube access token	🛠️
🔑	Slack access token	Secret text	Slack access token	🛠️
🖥️	ec2-user (SSH Keypair for Swarm staging)	SSH Username with private key	SSH Keypair for Swarm staging	🛠️

Icon: S M L

Figure 10.38 Swarm staging cluster SSH credentials

Create a Jenkinsfile similar to the one in the develop branch, as shown in the following listing. Update the `swarmManager` variable to reference the manager staging the IP or DNS record instead. Also update the SSH agent credentials to use the Swarm staging credential.

Listing 10.25   Jenkinsfile for staging deployment

```
def swarmManager = 'manager.staging.domain.com'          ⟵── Swarm manager DNS alias
def region = 'AWS REGION'                        ⟵         record or private IP address

node('master'){
    stage('Checkout'){                AWS region where the ECR
        checkout scm                  repositories are created
    }

    sshagent (credentials: ['swarm-staging']){
        stage('Copy'){
            sh "scp -o StrictHostKeyChecking=no
docker-compose.yml ec2-user@${swarmManager}:/home/ec2-user"          ⟵──
        }
                                      Copies docker-compose.yml
                                      to the Swarm manager
        stage('Deploy stack'){                 instance over SSH
            sh "ssh -oStrictHostKeyChecking=no
ec2-user@${swarmManager}
```

```
'\$(\$(aws ecr get-login --no-include-email --region ${region}))'
|| true"
            sh "ssh -oStrictHostKeyChecking=no
ec2-user@${swarmManager}
docker stack deploy --compose-file
docker-compose.yml --with-registry-auth watchlist"
        }
    }
}
```

→ **Authenticates with ECR and redeploys the application stack over SSH**

Push the changes to the preprod branch. A new preprod nested job should be triggered on the watchlist-deployment item on Jenkins upon the push event, as shown in figure 10.39.

Figure 10.39 Stack deployment on staging

At the end of the pipeline, the application stack will be deployed to Swarm staging. Similarly, to access the application, use Terraform to deploy a public load balancer for the marketplace and the store API.

Finally, to trigger autodeployment on preprod, we need to update the Jenkinsfile for each project to trigger the watchlist-deployment on preprod—for example, for movies-loader Jenkinsfile. We build and push a Docker image with the `preprod` tag, as shown in the next listing.

Listing 10.26 Tagging a Docker image based on the Git branch

```
stage('Push'){
    sh "\$(aws ecr get-login --no-include-email --region ${region}) || true"
    docker.withRegistry("https://${registry}") {
        docker.image(imageName).push(commitID())
        if (env.BRANCH_NAME == 'develop') {
            docker.image(imageName).push('develop')
        }
        if (env.BRANCH_NAME == 'preprod') {
            docker.image(imageName).push('preprod')
        }
    }
}
```

Tags the image with the current Git commit ID and stores it in ECR

Authenticates with ECR by using AWS CLI

Based on the current Git branch name, the Docker image is tagged with a unique tag.

In the following listing, we update the `Deploy` stage's `if` clause condition to trigger the deployment of the external job if the branch name is preprod.

Listing 10.27   Triggering external deployment job

```
stage('Deploy'){
    if(env.BRANCH_NAME == 'develop' || env.BRANCH_NAME == 'preprod'){
        build job: "watchlist-deployment/${env.BRANCH_NAME}"
    }
}
```

Push the changes to the develop branch. Then create a pull request to merge develop to the preprod branch after Jenkins posts the build status regarding develop changes (figure 10.40).

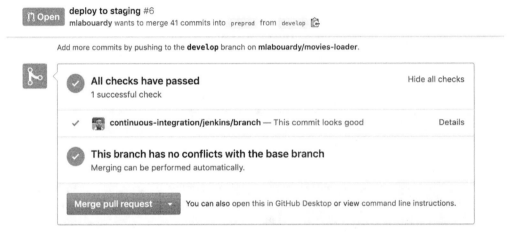

Figure 10.40   Pull request build status

When the merge occurs, a new build should be triggered on the preprod branch, as you can see in the Blue Ocean view in figure 10.41.

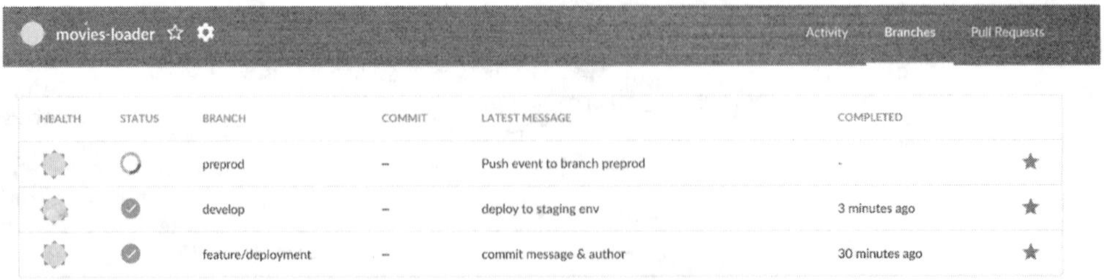

Figure 10.41   Build trigger on preprod branch

Once the `Push` stage is executed, a new image with a `preprod` tag should be pushed to the Docker registry (figure 10.42).

Figure 10.42 Docker image with `preprod` tag stored in ECR

Then, the deployment job on the preprod branch will be executed to deploy the changes on the Docker Swarm staging environment (figure 10.43).

Figure 10.43 Staging deployment triggered automatically

Make the same changes for other microservices, except for movies-marketplace. For movies-marketplace, we need to update the build stage, as shown in the following listing, to inject the appropriate environment and point the frontend to the right API URL.

Listing 10.28 Injecting API URL during build

```
stage('Build'){
    switch(env.BRANCH_NAME){
        case 'develop':
            docker.build(imageName, '--build-arg ENVIRONMENT=sandbox .')
            break
        case 'preprod':
            docker.build(imageName, '--build-arg ENVIRONMENT=staging .')
            break
        default:
```

> If the branch name is develop, we set the environment to sandbox, so the sandbox settings are loaded.

```
              docker.build(imageName)
          }
    }
}
```

> If the branch name doesn't match develop or preprod, the sandbox settings will be loaded by default.

Push the changes to GitHub. This time, the Docker build process will be executed with the ENVIRONMENT argument set to staging (when the current branch is preprod), as shown in figure 10.44. This will replace the environment.ts file with environment .staging.ts values.

Figure 10.44   Docker build with the environment as an argument

10.5   *Implementing the Jenkins delivery pipeline*

Finally, to deploy our application stack to production, you need to spin up a new Swarm cluster for the production environment. Once again, I opted to isolate the production workload in a dedicated production VPC with the 10.3.0.0/16 CIDR block and to set up a VPC peering between the management VPC (where Jenkins is located) and production VPC (where Swarm production is deployed). Figure 10.45 summarizes the deployed architecture.

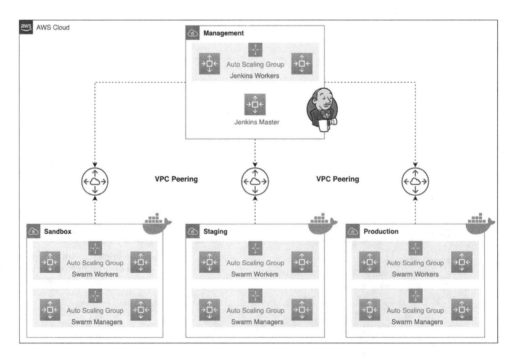

Figure 10.45   VPC peering with multiple Swarm cluster VPCs. The management VPC where the Jenkins cluster is deployed has access to the sandbox, staging, and production VPCs.

NOTE VPC peering doesn't support transitive peering. The production, staging, and sandbox environments are fully isolated, and packets cannot be routed directly from sandbox to production, for example, through the management VPC.

On the master branch of the watchlist-deployment repository, create a docker-compose .yml file. This time, we use the `latest` tag for services running in production, as shown in the next listing.

Listing 10.29 Docker Compose for production deployment

```
version: "3.3"
services:
  movies-loader:
    image: ID.dkr.ecr.REGION.amazonaws.com/USER/movies-loader:latest
    environment:
      - AWS_REGION=eu-west-3
      - SQS_URL=https://sqs.REGION.amazonaws.com/ID/
    movies_to_parse_production
  movies-parser:
    image: ID.dkr.ecr.REGION.amazonaws.com/USER/movies-parser:latest
```

Create a Jenkins credential with the SSH key used to deploy the Swarm cluster for the production environment and call it `swarm-production`, as shown in figure 10.46.

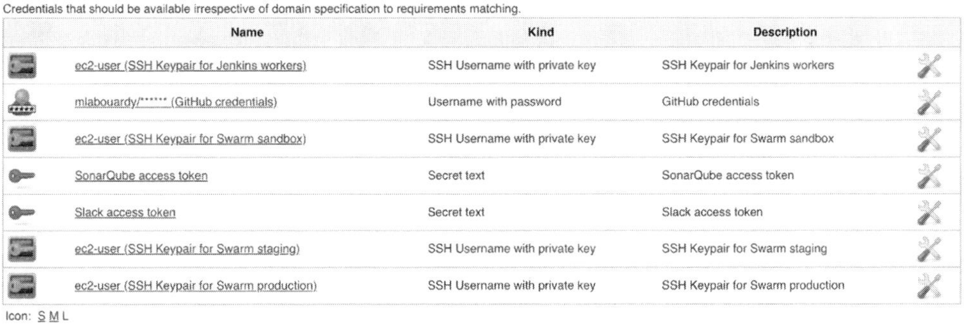

Credentials that should be available irrespective of domain specification to requirements matching.

	Name	Kind	Description	
	ec2-user (SSH Keypair for Jenkins workers)	SSH Username with private key	SSH Keypair for Jenkins workers	
	miabouardy/****** (GitHub credentials)	Username with password	GitHub credentials	
	ec2-user (SSH Keypair for Swarm sandbox)	SSH Username with private key	SSH Keypair for Swarm sandbox	
	SonarQube access token	Secret text	SonarQube access token	
	Slack access token	Secret text	Slack access token	
	ec2-user (SSH Keypair for Swarm staging)	SSH Username with private key	SSH Keypair for Swarm staging	
	ec2-user (SSH Keypair for Swarm production)	SSH Username with private key	SSH Keypair for Swarm production	

Icon: S M L

Figure 10.46 Swarm production cluster SSH credentials

Then, create a Jenkinsfile, shown in the following listing, to remotely upload the docker-compose.yml file to the manager machine. Execute the `docker stack deploy` command to deploy the application.

Listing 10.30 Jenkinsfile for production deployment

```
def swarmManager = 'manager.production.domain.com'
def region = 'AWS REGION'
node('master'){
    stage('Checkout'){...}
```

Clones the GitHub repository—refer to listing 10.25 for instructions.

```
    sshagent (credentials: ['swarm-production']){
        stage('Copy'){...}                              ◄─────    Copies docker-compose.yml to the
                                                                  Swarm manager over SSH—refer
        stage('Deploy stack'){...}     ◄───┐                      to listing 10.25 for instructions
    }
}                                          Redeploys the Docker Compose stack over
                                           SSH—refer to listing 10.25 for instructions
```

Push the changes to the master branch. The GitHub repository should look like figure 10.47.

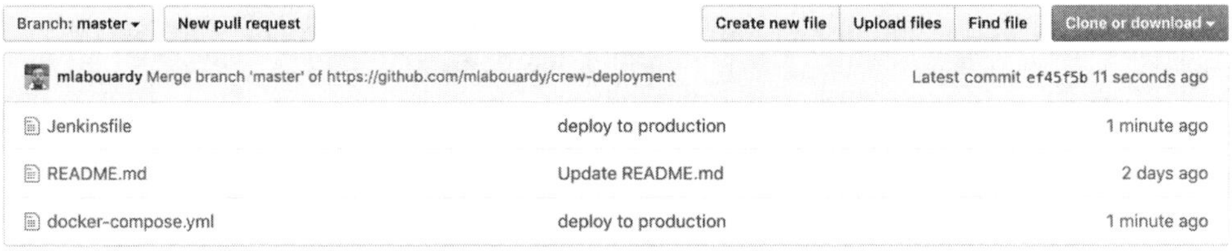

Branch: master ▾	New pull request			Create new file	Upload files	Find file	Clone or download ▾
📷 **mlabouardy** Merge branch 'master' of https://github.com/mlabouardy/crew-deployment					Latest commit ef45f5b 11 seconds ago		
📄 Jenkinsfile		deploy to production					1 minute ago
📄 README.md		Update README.md					2 days ago
📄 docker-compose.yml		deploy to production					1 minute ago

Figure 10.47   Deployment files stored in the GitHub repository

The Jenkins pipeline will be triggered on the master branch. Once the pipeline is finished, the application stack will be deployed to the production environment, as you can see in figure 10.48.

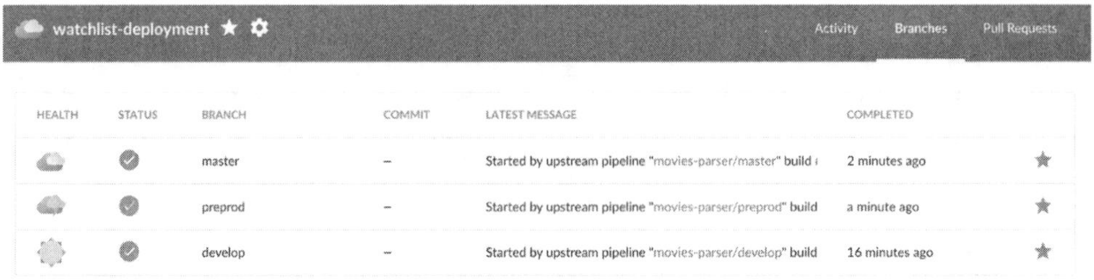

☁ watchlist-deployment ★ ⚙						Activity Branches Pull Requests
HEALTH	STATUS	BRANCH	COMMIT	LATEST MESSAGE	COMPLETED	
☁	✓	master	–	Started by upstream pipeline "movies-parser/master" build :	2 minutes ago	★
☁	✓	preprod	–	Started by upstream pipeline "movies-parser/preprod" build	a minute ago	★
❄	✓	develop	–	Started by upstream pipeline "movies-parser/develop" build	16 minutes ago	★

Figure 10.48   Deployment triggered in the master branch

To trigger the deployment of production at the end of the CI pipeline, update the GitHub repository to trigger the deployment job if the current branch is master. For instance, update the movies-loader's Jenkinsfile to build the image for production and push the result to the Docker registry with the `latest` tag, as shown in the following listing.

Listing 10.31   Tagging the production image

```
stage('Push'){
    sh "\$(aws ecr get-login --no-include-email --region ${region}) || true"
    docker.withRegistry("https://${registry}") {
```

```
        docker.image(imageName).push(commitID())
        if (env.BRANCH_NAME == 'develop') {
            docker.image(imageName).push('develop')
        }
        if (env.BRANCH_NAME == 'preprod') {
            docker.image(imageName).push('preprod')
        }
        if (env.BRANCH_NAME == 'master') {
            docker.image(imageName).push('latest')
        }
    }
}
```

For the deployment part, we can simply update the `if` clause to support deployment on the master branch too:

```
stage('Deploy'){
            if(env.BRANCH_NAME == 'develop'
|| env.BRANCH_NAME == 'preprod'
|| env.BRANCH_NAME == 'master'){
                build job: "watchlist-deployment/${env.BRANCH_NAME}"
            }
}
```

However, we want to require manual validation before deploying to production to simulate the product/business validation (or QA team running tests before approving for production) before deploying releases to production.

To do so, you can use the Input Step plugin to pause the pipeline execution and allow the user to interact and control the deployment process to production, as shown in the following listing.

Listing 10.32 Requiring user approval before production deployment

```
stage('Deploy'){
    if(env.BRANCH_NAME == 'develop' || env.BRANCH_NAME == 'preprod'){
        build job: "watchlist-deployment/${env.BRANCH_NAME}"
    }
    if(env.BRANCH_NAME == 'master'){
        timeout(time: 2, unit: "HOURS") {
            input message: "Approve Deploy?", ok: "Yes"
        }
        build job: "watchlist-deployment/master"
    }
}
```

Here, we set the time-out to be 2 hours to give developers enough time to validate the release. When the 2-hour time-out is reached, the pipeline will be aborted.

> **NOTE** To avoid having a Jenkins worker doing nothing for 2 hours, you can move the `Deploy` stage outside a node block. You can also send a Slack reminder when waiting for user input.

Push the changes to a feature branch, and raise a pull request to merge changes to the develop branch after the feature branch is successfully built and approved by Jenkins (figure 10.49).

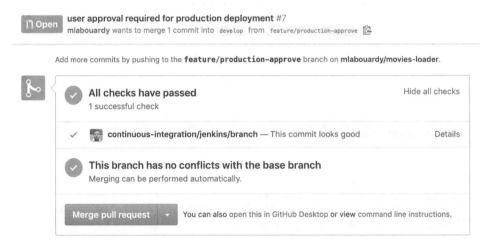

Figure 10.49   Merging the feature branch into develop

Merge the changes to the develop branch and delete the feature branch. A new build should be triggered on the develop branch, which will deploy the image to the Swarm sandbox cluster; see figure 10.50.

Figure 10.50   Deployment to sandbox triggered

Next, raise a pull request to merge develop into the preprod branch (figure 10.51).

Once the PR is merged, a new build will be triggered on the preprod branch, at the end of the CI/CD pipeline. The changes will be deployed into the Swarm staging cluster, as shown in figure 10.52.

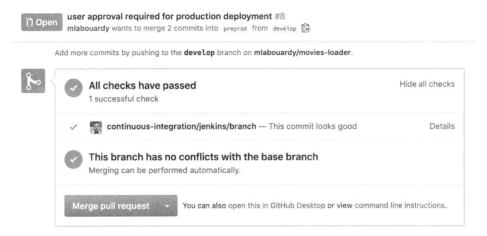

Figure 10.51 Merging the develop branch into preprod

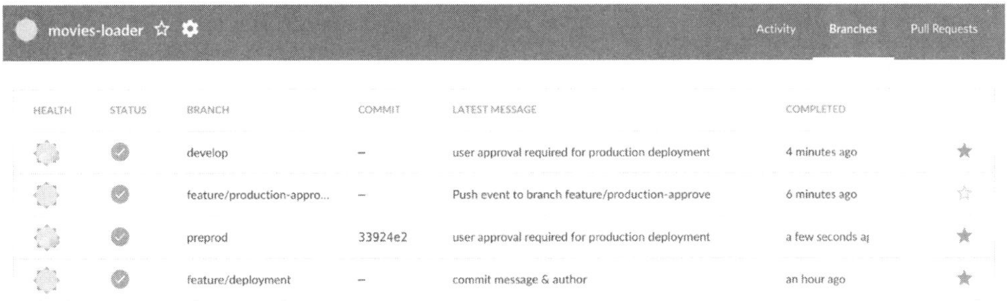

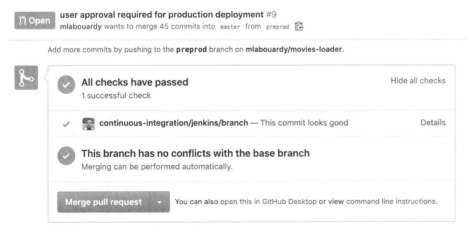

Figure 10.52 Deployment to staging cluster triggered

Finally, create a pull request to merge preprod into the master branch (figure 10.53).

Figure 10.53 Merging the preprod branch into master

When the merge occurs, Jenkins will trigger a build on the master branch of the movies-loader service, as illustrated in figure 10.54. However, this time, once it reaches the deploy stage, an input dialog will pop up for deployment confirmation.

Figure 10.54   CI/CD pipeline execution on the master branch

As you can see in figure 10.55, the interactive input will ask whether we approve the deployment.

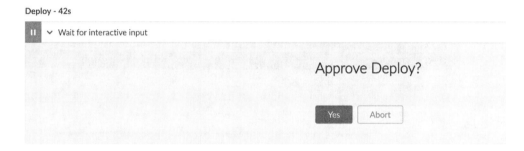

Figure 10.55   Deployment user input dialog

If we click Yes, the pipeline will be resumed, and the deployment job will be triggered on the master, as shown in figure 10.56.

Figure 10.56   Production deployment approval

At the end of the deployment process, the new stack will be deployed to Swarm production, and a Slack notification will be sent to the configured Slack channel (figure 10.57).

Jenkins APP 5:29 PM
Name: 'movies-loader/master'
Status: STARTED
Build ID: 2
Message: Merge pull request #9 from mlabouardy/preprod
user approval required for production deployment
Author: LABOUARDY Mohamed
URL: https://jenkins.slowcoder.com/job/movies-loader/job/master/2/
Name: 'movies-loader/master'
Status: SUCCESSFUL
Build ID: 2
Message: Merge pull request #9 from mlabouardy/preprod
user approval required for production deployment
Author: LABOUARDY Mohamed
URL: https://jenkins.slowcoder.com/job/movies-loader/job/master/2/

Figure 10.57 Production deployment success notification

With the production deployment covered, you have seen how to deploy containerized microservice applications to multiple environments and how to handle code promotion within a CI/CD pipeline. However, because we're managing only three environments (sandbox, staging, and production), we will limit the discovering behavior of the deployment job to the three main branches by defining a regular expression, as shown in figure 10.58.

GitHub
Credentials
mlabouardy/****** (GitHub credentials)
Add
User mlabouardy
Repository HTTPS URL
Repository HTTPS URL
https://github.com/mlabouardy/watchlist-deployment.git
Validate
Repository Scan - Deprecated Visualization
Behaviours
Discover branches
Strategy
Exclude branches that are also filed as PRs
Filter by name (with regular expression)
Regular expression
(master|preprod|develop)
Add

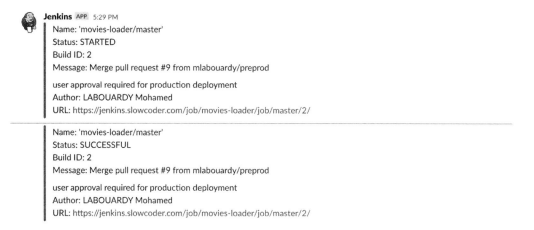

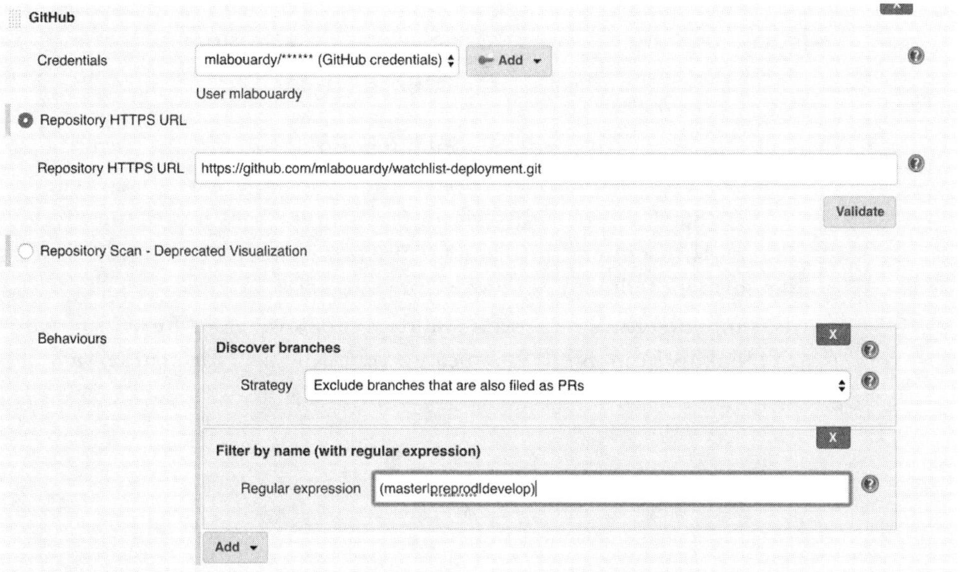

Figure 10.58 Jenkins discovery behavior based on a regular expression

As a result, Jenkins will discover and be triggered only if one of the three main branches has changed; see figure 10.59.

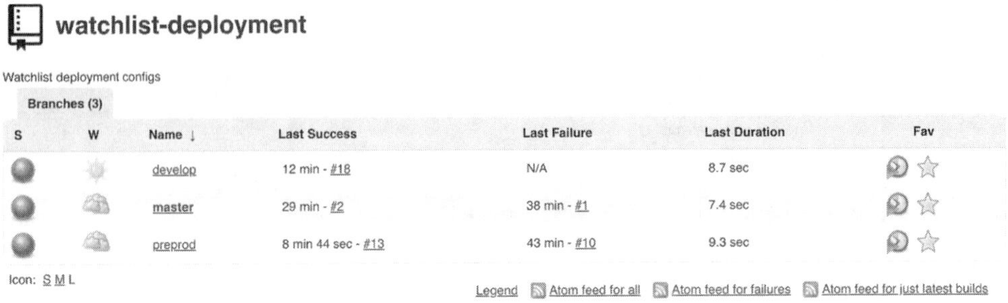

watchlist-deployment

Watchlist deployment configs

Branches (3)

S	W	Name ↓	Last Success	Last Failure	Last Duration	Fav
●	☀	develop	12 min - #18	N/A	8.7 sec	◎ ☆
●	☁	master	29 min - #2	38 min - #1	7.4 sec	◎ ☆
●	☁	preprod	8 min 44 sec - #13	43 min - #10	9.3 sec	◎ ☆

Icon: S M L

Legend 🔊 Atom feed for all 🔊 Atom feed for failures 🔊 Atom feed for just latest builds

Figure 10.59   Deployment multibranch job

So now if we make any change to our application, CI/CD pipelines will be triggered and `docker stack deploy` will be executed, which will update any services that were changed from the previous version.

> **NOTE**   If the deployment target is one single host, a swarm is not needed. The same docker-compose.yml and procedure explained in this chapter should be sufficient to continuously deploy your application on a single-host deployment environment.

Summary

- An S3 bucket or distributed consistent key-value store such as etcd, Consul, or ZooKeeper can be used as service discovery to make the nodes autojoin a Swarm cluster.
- Continuous deployment of containers on a Swarm cluster can be reached by executing `docker stack deploy` over SSH on a Swarm manager.
- Adding Slack notifications within CI/CD pipelines makes the product delivery faster. The sooner the team members are aware of a build, integration, or deployment failure, the quicker they can act.
- To simulate business/product validation before deploying a production release, the Jenkins Input Step plugin can prompt the user for manual validation before deployment.

11

Dockerized microservices on K8s

This chapter covers

- Setting up a Kubernetes cluster on AWS with Terraform
- Automating application deployment on Kubernetes with Jenkins pipelines
- Packaging and versioning Kubernetes Helm charts
- Converting Compose files to Kubernetes manifests with Kompose
- Running post-deployment tests and health checks within CI/CD pipelines
- Discovering Jenkins X and setting up serverless CI/CD pipelines

The preceding chapter covered how to set up a CI/CD pipeline from scratch for containerized applications running in Docker Swarm (figure 11.1). This chapter covers how to deploy the same application in Kubernetes (K8s) and automate the deployment. In addition, you'll learn how to use Jenkins X to simplify the workflow of cloud-native applications running in Kubernetes.

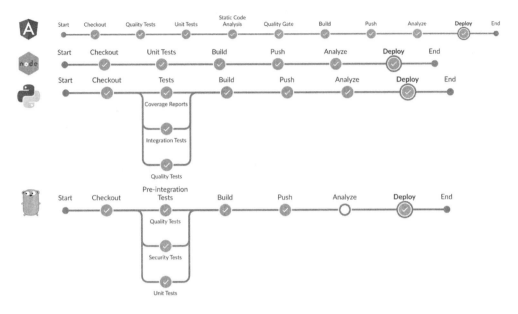

Figure 11.1   Current CI/CD pipeline workflow

Docker Swarm might be a good solution for beginners and smaller workloads. However, for large deployment and at a certain scale, you might want to consider shifting to Kubernetes.

For those of you who are AWS power users, Amazon Elastic Kubernetes Service (EKS) is a natural fit. Other cloud providers offer managed Kubernetes solutions, including Azure Kubernetes Service (AKS) and Google Kubernetes Engine (GKE).

11.1   *Setting up a Kubernetes cluster*

As I've said, AWS offers the Amazon Elastic Kubernetes Service (https://aws.amazon .com/eks). The EKS cluster will be deployed in a custom VPC within multiple private subnets. EKS runs the Kubernetes control plane for you across multiple AWS availability zones to eliminate a single point of failure, as shown in figure 11.2.

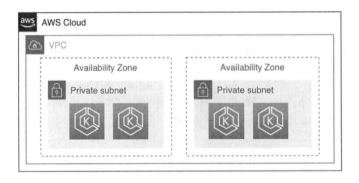

Figure 11.2   The AWS EKS architecture consists of node groups deployed in private subnets.

A few tools (including AWS CloudFormation, eksctl, and kOps) allow you to get up and running quickly on EKS. In this chapter, we picked Terraform because we were already using it to manage our Jenkins cluster on AWS.

To get started, provision a new VPC to host the sandbox environment and divide it into two private subnets. Amazon EKS requires subnets in at least two availability zones. The VPC is created to isolate the Kubernetes workload. For EKS to discover the VPC subnets and manage network resources, we tag them with `kubernetes.io/cluster/<cluster-name>`. The `<cluster-name>` value matches the EKS cluster's name, which is `sandbox`. Create a file called vpc.tf with the content in the following listing.

Listing 11.1   Kubernetes custom VPC

```
resource "aws_vpc" "sandbox" {
  cidr_block          = var.cidr_block
  enable_dns_hostnames = true
  tags = {
    Name   = var.vpc_name
    Author = var.author
    "kubernetes.io/cluster/${var.cluster_name}" = "shared"
  }
}
```

Then, define the subnets and set up the appropriate route tables. Refer to chapter11/eks/vpc.tf for the full source code, or head back to chapter 10 for a step-by-step guide on how to deploy a custom VPC on AWS.

Next, we create a new eks_masters.tf file and define the `sandbox` EKS cluster, which is a managed K8s control plane, as shown in the following listing.

Listing 11.2   EKS sandbox cluster

```
resource "aws_eks_cluster" "sandbox" {
  name      = var.cluster_name
  role_arn  = aws_iam_role.cluster_role.arn
  vpc_config {
    security_group_ids = [aws_security_group.cluster_sg.id]
    subnet_ids         = [for subnet in aws_subnet.private_subnets :
      subnet.id]
  }
  depends_on = [
    aws_iam_role_policy_attachment.cluster_policy,
    aws_iam_role_policy_attachment.service_policy,
  ]
}
```

The managed control plane uses an IAM role with the AmazonEKSClusterPolicy and AmazonEKSServicePolicy policies. These attachments grant the cluster the permissions it needs to take care of itself.

Now it's time to spin up some worker nodes. A node is a simple EC2 instance that runs the Kubernetes objects (pods, deployments, services, and so forth). The master's automatic scheduling takes into account the available resources on each node. Define an EKS node group resource within eks_workers.tf as shown in the following listing.

Listing 11.3 Kubernetes node group resource

```
resource "aws_eks_node_group" "workers_node_group" {
  cluster_name     = aws_eks_cluster.sandbox.name
  node_group_name  = "${var.cluster_name}-workers-node-group"
  node_role_arn    = aws_iam_role.worker_role.arn
  subnet_ids       = [for subnet in aws_subnet.private_subnets : subnet.id]
  scaling_config {
    desired_size = 2
    max_size     = 5
    min_size     = 2
  }
  depends_on = [
    aws_iam_role_policy_attachment.worker_node_policy,
    aws_iam_role_policy_attachment.cni_policy,
    aws_iam_role_policy_attachment.ecr_policy,
  ]
}
```

We also create an IAM role that the worker nodes are going to assume. We grant the AmazonEKSWorkerNodePolicy, AmazonEKS_CNI_Policy, and AmazonEC2Container-RegistryReadOnly policies. Refer to chapter11/eks/eks_workers.tf for the full source code.

> **NOTE** This section assumes that you are familiar with the usual Terraform plan/apply workflow; if you're new to Terraform, refer first to chapter 5.

Lastly, define the variables listed in table 11.1 in the variables.tf file.

Table 11.1 EKS Terraform variables

Variable	Type	Value	Description
region	String	None	The name of the region, such as `eu-central-1`, in which to deploy the EKS cluster
shared_credentials_file	String	`~/.aws/credentials`	The path to the shared credentials file. If this is not set and a profile is specified, `~/.aws/credentials` will be used.
aws_profile	String	profile	The AWS profile name as set in the shared credentials file
author	String	None	Name of the owner of the EKS cluster. It's optional, but recommended, to tag your AWS resources to track the monthly costs by owner or environment.
availability_zones	List	None	Availability zone for spinning up the VPC subnets

Table 11.1   EKS Terraform variables *(continued)*

Variable	Type	Value	Description
`vpc_name`	String	`sandbox`	The name of the VPC
`cidr_block`	String	`10.1.0.0/16`	The VPC CIDR block
cluster_name	String	`sandbox`	The EKS cluster's name
public_subnets_count	Number	2	The number of public subnets to create
`private_subnets_count`	Number	2	The number of private subnets to create

Then, issue the `terraform init` command to initialize a working directory and download the AWS provider plugin. In your initialized directory, run `terraform plan` to review the planned actions. Your terminal output should indicate that the plan is running and the resources that will be created. This should include the EKS cluster, VPC, and IAM roles.

If you're comfortable with the execution plan, confirm the run with `terraform apply`. This provisioning process should take a few minutes. Upon successful deployment, a new EKS cluster for the sandbox environment will be deployed and available in the AWS EKS console, as shown in figure 11.3.

Figure 11.3   EKS sandbox cluster

Now that you've provisioned your EKS cluster, you need to configure kubectl. This is a command-line utility for communicating with the cluster API server. At the time of writing this book, I'm using version v1.18.3.

> **NOTE**   The kubectl tool is available in many operating system package managers; refer to the official documentation (https://kubernetes.io/docs/tasks/tools/) for installation instructions.

To grant kubectl access to the K8s API, we need to generate a kubeconfig file (located under .kube/config in your home directory). You can create or update a kubeconfig file with the AWS CLI `update-kubeconfig` command. Issue this command to get the access credentials for your cluster:

```
aws eks update-kubeconfig --name sandbox --region AWS_REGION
```

To verify that your cluster is configured correctly and running, execute the following command:

```
kubectl get nodes
```

The output will list all of the nodes in a cluster and the status of each node:

```
[jenkins:eks mlabouardy$ kubectl get nodes
NAME                                    STATUS   ROLES    AGE   VERSION
ip-10-1-0-25.eu-west-3.compute.internal   Ready    <none>   73s   v1.15.10-eks-bac369
ip-10-1-2-225.eu-west-3.compute.internal  Ready    <none>   69s   v1.15.10-eks-bac369
```

> **NOTE** To optimize K8s costs, you can use EC2 Spot instances, as they cost about 30–70% less than their on-demand counterparts. However, this requires some special considerations, as they could be terminated with only a 2-minute warning.

At this point, you should be able to use Kubernetes. In the next section, we will automate the deployment of the Watchlist application described in chapter 7 into the K8s cluster with Jenkins following the PaC approach.

11.2 *Automating continuous deployment flow with Jenkins*

To complete a Kubernetes deployment from Jenkins, all we need are K8s deployment files, which will contain references to the Docker images, along with the configuration settings (for example, port, network name, labels, and constraints). To run this file, we will need to execute the `kubectl apply` command.

On the develop branch of the watchlist-deployment GitHub repository, create a deployments folder. Inside it, create a movies-loader-deploy.yaml file by using your favorite text editor or IDE, with the content in the following listing. The deployment instructs Kubernetes on how to create and update the movies-loader service.

Listing 11.4 Movie loader deployment resource

```
apiVersion: apps/v1
kind: Deployment
metadata:
  name: movies-loader
  namespace: watchlist
spec:
  selector:
    matchLabels:
      app: movies-loader
  template:
    metadata:
      labels:
        app: movies-loader
```

```
spec:
  containers:
  - name: movies-loader
    image: ID.dkr.ecr.REGION.amazonaws.com/USER/movies-loader:develop
    env:
    - name: AWS_REGION
      value: REGION
    - name: SQS_URL
      value: https://sqs.REGION.amazonaws.com/ID/movies_to_parse_sandbox
```

NOTE As a reminder, the movies-loader and movies-store services are using Amazon SQS to load and consume movie items, respectively. To grant those services permission to interact with SQS, you need to assign the AmazonSQS-FullAccess policy to the EKS node group.

The movies-loader service can be deployed to Kubernetes through a deployment resource. The deployment definition uses the `develop` tag of the movies-loader Docker image and defines a set of environment variables, such as the SQS URL and AWS region. The MongoDB resource can also be deployed with the mongodb-deploy.yaml file in the following listing.

Listing 11.5 MongoDB deployment resource

```
apiVersion: apps/v1
kind: Deployment
metadata:
  name: mongodb
  namespace: watchlist
spec:
  selector:
    matchLabels:
      app: mongodb
  template:
    metadata:
      labels:
        app: mongodb
    spec:
      containers:
      - name: mongodb
        image: bitnami/mongodb:latest
        env:
        - name: MONGODB_USERNAME
          valueFrom:
            secretKeyRef:
              name: mongodb-access
              key: username
        - name: MONGODB_PASSWORD
          valueFrom:
            secretKeyRef:
              name: mongodb-access
              key: password
        - name: MONGODB_DATABASE
          valueFrom:
            secretKeyRef:
              name: mongodb-access
              key: database
```

The most interesting thing about this deployment definition is the environment variables part. Instead of hardcoding the MongoDB credentials, we are using K8s secrets. We're creating secret store authentication credentials so only Kubernetes can access them.

Before we create a Kubernetes secret, we need to maintain a space in the Kubernetes cluster where we can get a view on the list of pods, services, and deployments we use to build and run the application. We will create a dedicated namespace to associate all of our Kubernetes objects with the following command:

```
kubectl create namespace watchlist
```

Then, invoke the following Kubernetes command on your local machine to create MongoDB credentials secrets:

```
kubectl create secret generic mongodb-access --from-
    literal=database='watchlist'
--from-literal=username='root'
--from-literal=password='PASSWORD' -n watchlist
```

```
[jenkins:chapter11 mlabouardy$ kubectl get secrets
NAME                  TYPE                                    DATA   AGE
default-token-wbzr7   kubernetes.io/service-account-token     3      59m
mongodb-access        Opaque                                  4      5s
```

Create deployment files for the rest of the services: movies-store, movies-parser, and movies-marketplace. The deployments folder structure should look like this:

```
mongodb-deploy.yaml
movies-store-deploy.yaml
movies-loader-deploy.yaml
movies-parser-deploy.yaml
movies-marketplace-deploy.yaml
```

All the source code can be downloaded from the GitHub repository, under the chapter11/deployment/kubectl/deployments folder.

To deploy the application with Jenkins, create a Jenkinsfile.eks file at the top-level directory of the watchlist-deployment project, as shown in the following listing. The Jenkinsfile will configure kubectl with the `aws eks update-kubeconfig` command. Then it issues a `kubectl apply` command to deploy the deployment resources. The `kubectl apply` command takes as an argument the deployments folder.

Listing 11.6   Jenkinsfile deployment stages

```
def region = 'AWS REGION'                                                    ◁──┐
def accounts = [master:'production', preprod:'staging', develop:'sandbox']

node('master'){                                          AWS region where the
    stage('Checkout'){                                   EKS cluster is deployed
        checkout scm
    }
```

```
stage('Authentication'){
    sh "aws eks update-kubeconfig --name ${accounts[env.BRANCH_NAME]} --
region ${region}"                        ◁──
}                                               Configures kubectl so that you can
                                                connect to an Amazon EKS cluster

stage('Deploy'){
    sh 'kubectl apply -f deployments/'   ◁──  Deploys the new
}                                              changes to EKS
}
```

Before pushing the Jenkinsfile and deployment files to the Git remote repository, we need to install the kubectl command line on the Jenkins master. Also, we need to provide access to EKS with IAM roles. To grant Jenkins master permissions to interact with the K8s cluster, we must edit the `aws-auth` ConfigMap within Kubernetes. On your local machine, run the following command:

```
kubectl edit -n kube-system configmap/aws-auth
```

A text editor will open; add the Jenkins instance's IAM role to the `mapRoles` section. Then, save the file and exit the text editor. Check whether the ConfigMap is properly configured with the following command:

```
kubectl describe -n kube-system configmap/aws-auth
```

```
Name:          aws-auth
Namespace:     kube-system
Labels:        <none>
Annotations:   <none>

Data
====
mapRoles:
----
- groups:
  - system:bootstrappers
  - system:nodes
  rolearn: arn:aws:iam::305929695733:role/terraform-eks-demo-node
  username: system:node:{{EC2PrivateDNSName}}
- groups:
  - system:masters
  rolearn: arn:aws:iam::305929695733:role/JenkinsMasterRole
  username: system:node:{{EC2PrivateDNSName}}

Events:   <none>
```

Once the ConfigMap is configured, install aws-iam-authenticator, which is a tool to manage AWS IAM credentials for Kubernetes access. Refer to the AWS documentation at http://mng.bz/AOWW for the installation guide. Then, generate a kubeconfig with the AWS CLI `update-kubeconfig` command. The command should create a `/home/ec2-user/.kube/config` file with no warning. Now we can issue the `kubectl get nodes` command:

```
[[ec2-user@ip-10-0-0-216 ~]$ kubectl get nodes
NAME                                     STATUS   ROLES    AGE    VERSION
ip-10-1-0-43.eu-west-3.compute.internal  Ready    <none>   4h8m   v1.16.8-eks-e16311
ip-10-1-2-182.eu-west-3.compute.internal Ready    <none>   4h8m   v1.16.8-eks-e16311
```

Now, we're ready to push the Jenkinsfile and Kubernetes deployment files to the Git repository under the develop branch:

```
git add .
git commit -m "k8s deployment files"
git push origin develop
```

The GitHub repository content should look similar to figure 11.4 after pushing K8s deployment files.

Branch: develop ▾	New pull request		Create new file	Upload files	Find file	Clone or download ▾
This branch is 16 commits ahead, 4 commits behind master.				⏷ Pull request	⏷ Compare	
mlabouardy k8s deployment files				Latest commit aef7e57 14 seconds ago		
📁 deployments		k8s deployment files		14 seconds ago		
📄 Jenkinsfile		fix region		15 days ago		
📄 Jenkinsfile.eks		deploy to eks		18 minutes ago		
📄 Jenkinsfile.swarm		deploy to eks		17 minutes ago		
📄 README.md		update readme		14 days ago		
📄 docker-compose.yml		deploy to eks		17 minutes ago		

Figure 11.4   Kubernetes deployment files in the Git repository

Once the changes are committed, the GitHub webhook we created in section 7.6 will trigger a build on the watchlist-deployment multibranch job on the develop branch's nested job; see figure 11.5.

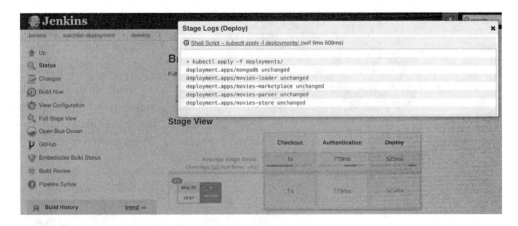

Figure 11.5   The kubectl apply command's output

At the `Deploy` stage, the `kubectl apply` command will be executed to deploy the application deployment resources. On your local machine, run this command to list deployments running in the sandbox K8s cluster:

```
kubectl get deployments --namespace=watchlist
```

The four components (loader, parser, store, and marketplace) of our application will be deployed alongside a MongoDB server:

```
NAME                              READY   STATUS    RESTARTS   AGE
mongodb-7b647bdd54-rdczs          1/1     Running   0          33s
movies-loader-7895fcc9cc-vgpj4    1/1     Running   1          7s
movies-marketplace-7749dc4fd8-wtgf8  1/1  Running   0          16m
movies-parser-7d4fd8f7-9lxkk      1/1     Running   1          3m9s
movies-store-584658766b-b5b2c     1/1     Running   0          16m
```

These deployment resources are referencing Docker images stored in Amazon ECR. At the time of deploying the EKS cluster, we have granted permissions to the K8s cluster to interact with ECR. However, if your Docker images are hosted on a remote repository that requires username/password authentication, you need to create a Docker Registry secret with the following command:

```
kubectl create secret docker-registry registry
--docker-username=USERNAME
--docker-password=PASSWORD
--namespace watchlist
```

Then, you need to reference this secret in your deployment file under the `spec` section as follows:

```
spec:
  containers:
  - name: movies-loader
    image: REGISTRY_URL/USER/movies-loader:develop
  imagePullSecrets:
  - name: registry
```

Our application is deployed. To access it, we need to create a K8s service for both the marketplace and store, as shown in the following listing. Create a services directory in the root repository, and then create a service for movies-store called movies-store.svc.yaml. The service creates a cloud network load balancer (for instance, AWS Elastic Load Balancer). This provides an externally accessible IP address for accessing the Movies Store API.

Listing 11.7 Movie store service resource

```
apiVersion: v1
kind: Service
metadata:
  name: movies-store
```

```
  namespace: watchlist
spec:
  ports:
  - port: 80
    targetPort: 3000
  selector:
    app: movies-store
  type: LoadBalancer
```

Additionally, we create another service to expose the Movies Marketplace (UI). Add the content in the following listing to movies-marketplace.svc.yaml.

Listing 11.8 Movies Marketplace service resource

```
apiVersion: v1
kind: Service
metadata:
  name: movies-marketplace
  namespace: watchlist
spec:
  ports:
  - port: 80
    targetPort: 80
  selector:
    app: movies-marketplace
  type: LoadBalancer
```

The movies-store and movies-parser services store the movie metadata in a MongoDB service. Therefore, we need to expose the MongoDB deployment through a Kubernetes service to allow MongoDB to receive incoming operations. The service is exposed to an internal IP in the cluster. The `ClusterIP` keyword makes the service reachable from only within the cluster. The MongoDB pod targeted by the service is determined by `LabelSelector`. Add the following YAML block to mongodb-svc.yaml.

Listing 11.9 Movies Marketplace service resource

```
apiVersion: v1
kind: Service
metadata:
  name: mongodb
  namespace: watchlist
spec:
  ports:
    - port: 27017
  selector:
    app: mongodb
    tier: mongodb
  clusterIP: None
```

Finally, we update the Jenkinsfile in listing 11.6 to deploy the Kubernetes services by providing the services folder as a parameter to the `kubectl apply` command:

```
stage('Deploy'){
        sh 'kubectl apply -f deployments/'
        sh 'kubectl apply -f services/'
}
```

Push the changes to the develop branch. A new build will be triggered, and the services will be deployed, as shown in figure 11.6.

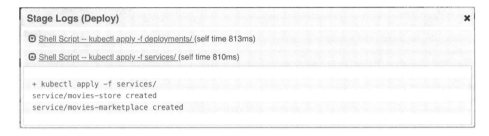

Figure 11.6   The kubectl apply output

Type the following command on your local machine:

```
kubectl get svc -n watchlist
```

It should show the load balancers for the three K8s services:

```
NAME                 TYPE          CLUSTER-IP       EXTERNAL-IP
mongodb              ClusterIP     None             <none>
movies-marketplace   LoadBalancer  172.20.140.150   a5149491400274ac2a7b15f0140133ed-1717030020.eu-west-3.elb.amazonaws.com
movies-store         LoadBalancer  172.20.68.115    a9b485440ea404dc68a60e0973954b70-1525632852.eu-west-3.elb.amazonaws.com
```

On AWS Management Console, two public-facing load balancers should be created in the EC2 dashboard (http://mng.bz/Zx7Z), as shown in figure 11.7.

Figure 11.7   Movies Store and Marketplace ELBs

> **NOTE**   Make sure to set the load balancer FQDN in the environment.sandbox.tf file of the movies-marketplace project. The API URL will be injected while building the marketplace Docker image. Refer to section 9.1.2 for more details.

To secure access to the Store API, we can enable an HTTPS listener on the public load balancer by updating the movies-store service with the changes detailed in the following listing.

Listing 11.10   HTTPS listener configuration

```
apiVersion: v1
kind: Service
metadata:
  name: movies-store
  namespace: watchlist
  annotations:
    service.beta.kubernetes.io/aws-load-balancer-backend-protocol: http
    service.beta.kubernetes.io/aws-load-balancer-ssl-cert:
     arn:aws:acm:{region}:{user id}:certificate/{id}
    service.beta.kubernetes.io/aws-load-balancer-ssl-ports: "https"
spec:
  ports:
  - name: http
    port: 80
    targetPort: 3000
  - name: https
    port: 443
    targetPort: 3000
  selector:
    app: movies-store
  type: LoadBalancer
```

> **Used on the service to specify the protocol spoken by the backend (pod) behind a listener**

> **Exposes port 443 (HTTPS) and forwards requests internally to port 3000 of the movies-store pod**

Push the changes to the remote repository. Jenkins will deploy the changes and update the load balancer listener configuration to accept incoming traffic on port 443 (HTTPS), as shown in figure 11.8.

Load Balancer Protocol	Load Balancer Port	Instance Protocol	Instance Port	Cipher	SSL Certificate
HTTP	80	HTTP	31123	N/A	N/A
HTTPS	443	HTTP	30757	Change	fecce01b-9c10-41ae-8a1a-345d9f89efad (ACM) Change

Figure 11.8   Load balancer HTTP/HTTPS listeners

It's optional, but you can create an A record in Amazon Route 53 pointing to the load balancer FQDN and update environment.sandbox.ts to use the friendly domain name instead of the load balancer FQDN; see the following listing.

Listing 11.11   Marketplace Angular environment variables

```
export const environment = {
  production: false,
  apiURL: 'https://api.sandbox.domain.com',
};
```

If you point your browser to the marketplace URL, it should call the Movies Store API and list the movies crawled from IMDb pages, as shown in figure 11.9. It might take several minutes for DNS to propagate and for the marketplace to show up.

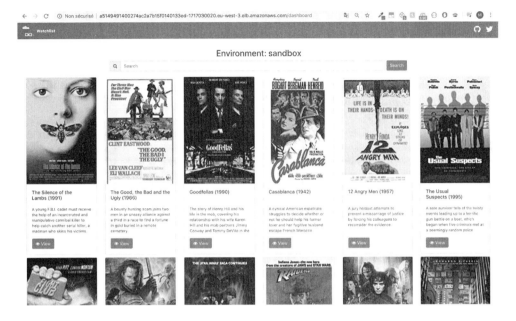

Figure 11.9 Watchlist Marketplace application

Now, every time you change the source code of any of the four microservices, the pipeline will be triggered, and the changes will be deployed to the sandbox Kubernetes cluster, as shown in figure 11.10.

Stage View

	Checkout	Quality Tests	Unit Tests	Static Code Analysis	Quality Gate	Build	Push	Analyze	Deploy
Average stage times: (Average full run time: ~3min 31s)	3s	10s	23s	3s	287ms	2min 12s	4s	22ms	17s
May 20 15:55 No Changes	2s	8s	17s	11s	287ms added to DB	2min 12s	4s	22ms	17s pushed to DB

Figure 11.10 Movies Marketplace CI/CD workflow

Finally, to visualize our application, we can deploy the Kubernetes dashboard by issuing the following commands in a terminal session:

```
kubectl apply -f https://github.com/kubernetes-sigs/
metrics-server/releases/latest/download/components.yaml
```

```
kubectl apply -f https://raw.githubusercontent.com/kubernetes/
dashboard/v2.0.5/aio/deploy/recommended.yaml
```

These commands will deploy the metrics-server and K8s dashboard v2.0.5 under the kube-system namespace. The metrics-server, which collects resource metrics from Kubelet, has to be running in the cluster for the metrics and graphs to be available in the Kubernetes dashboard.

To grant access to cluster resources from the K8s dashboard, we need to create an eks-admin service account and cluster role binding to securely connect to the dashboard with admin-level permissions. Create an eks-admin.yaml file with the content in the following listing (`apiVersion` of the `ClusterRoleBinding` resource may differ between Kubernetes versions).

Listing 11.12   Kubernetes dashboard service account

```
apiVersion: v1
kind: ServiceAccount
metadata:
  name: eks-admin
  namespace: kube-system
---
apiVersion: rbac.authorization.k8s.io/v1beta1
kind: ClusterRoleBinding
metadata:
  name: eks-admin
roleRef:
  apiGroup: rbac.authorization.k8s.io
  kind: ClusterRole
  name: cluster-admin
subjects:
- kind: ServiceAccount
  name: eks-admin
  namespace: kube-system
```

Then, create a service account with the following command:

```
kubectl apply -f eks-admin.yaml
```

Now, create a proxy server that will allow you to navigate to the dashboard from the browser on your local machine. This will continue running until you stop the process by pressing Ctrl-C. Issue the `kubectl proxy` command, and the dashboard should be accessible from http://localhost:8001/api/v1/namespaces/kubernetes-dashboard/services/https:kubernetes-dashboard:/proxy/#/login.

Opening this URL will take us to the account authentication page for the Kubernetes dashboard. To get access to the dashboard, we need to authenticate our account. Retrieve an authentication token for the eks-admin service account with the following command:

```
kubectl -n kube-system describe secret
$(kubectl -n kube-system get secret
```

```
| grep eks-admin
| awk '{print $1}')
```

Now copy the token and paste it into the Enter Token field on the login screen. Click the Sign In button, and that's it. You are now logged in as an admin.

The Kubernetes dashboard, shown in figure 11.11, provides user-friendly features to manage and troubleshoot the deployed application. Awesome! You have successfully built a CI/CD pipeline for a cloud-native application in K8s.

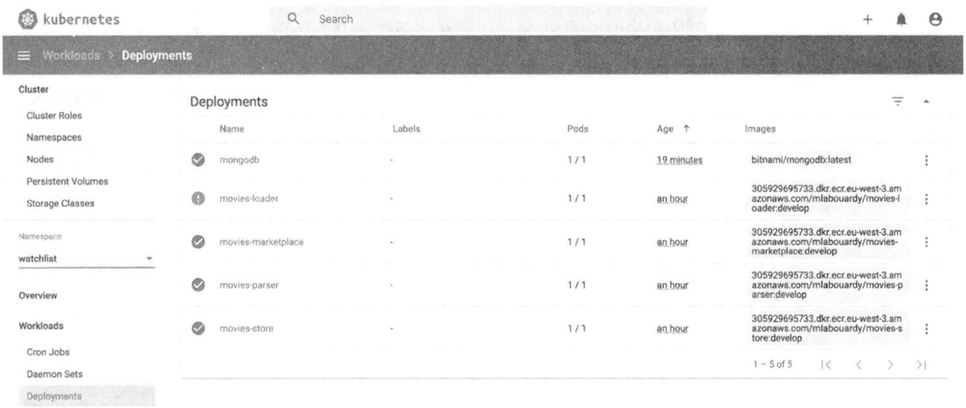

Figure 11.11   Kubernetes dashboard

11.2.1 *Migrating Docker Compose to K8s manifests with Kompose*

Another way of creating deployment files is by converting the docker-compose.yml file defined in chapter 10's listing 10.12 with an open source tool called Kompose. Refer to the project's official GitHub repository (https://github.com/kubernetes/kompose) for an installation guide.

Once Kompose is installed, run the following command against the docker-compose.yml file provided in chapter 10 (chapter10/deployment/sandbox/docker-compose.yml):

```
kompose convert -f docker-compose.yml
```

This should create the Kubernetes deployments and services based on the settings and network topology specified in docker-compose.yml:

```
INFO Kubernetes file "movies-marketplace-service.yaml" created
INFO Kubernetes file "movies-store-service.yaml" created
INFO Kubernetes file "mongodb-deployment.yaml" created
INFO Kubernetes file "movies-loader-deployment.yaml" created
INFO Kubernetes file "movies-marketplace-deployment.yaml" created
INFO Kubernetes file "movies-parser-deployment.yaml" created
INFO Kubernetes file "movies-store-deployment.yaml" created
```

You can push those files to the remote Git repository, and Jenkins will issue the `kubectl apply -f` command to deploy the services and deployments.

However, writing and maintaining Kubernetes YAML manifests for all the required Kubernetes objects can be a time-consuming and tedious task. For the simplest of deployments, you would need at least three YAML manifests with duplicated and hard-coded values. That's where a tool like Helm (https://helm.sh/) comes into play to simplify this process and create a single package that can be advertised to your cluster.

11.3   *Walking through continuous delivery steps*

Helm is a useful package manager for Kubernetes. It has two parts: the client (CLI) and the server (which is called Tiller and was removed in Helm 3). The client lives on your local machine, and the server lives on the Kubernetes cluster to execute what is needed.

To fully grasp Helm, you need to become familiar with these three concepts:

- *Chart*—A package of preconfigured Kubernetes resources
- *Release*—A specific instance of a chart that has been deployed to the cluster by using Helm
- *Repository*—A group of published charts that can be made available to others through a remote registry

Check out the getting started page for instructions on downloading and installing Helm: https://helm.sh/docs/intro/install/.

> **NOTE**   Helm is assumed to be compatible with n-3 versions of Kubernetes. Refer to the Helm Version Support Policy documentation to determine which version of Helm is compatible with your K8s cluster.

At the time of writing this book, Helm v3.6.1 is being used. After installing Helm, create a new chart for the application called `watchlist` in the top-level directory of the watchlist-deployment project:

```
helm create watchlist
```

This should create a directory called watchlist with the following files and folders:

- *Values.yaml*—Defines all values we want to inject into Kubernetes templates
- *Chart.yaml*—Can be used to describe the version of the chart we're packaging
- *.helmignore*—Similar to .gitignore and .dockerignore, contains a list of files and folders to exclude while packaging the Helm chart
- *templates/*—Contains the actual manifest such as Deployments, Services, Config-Maps, and Secrets

Next, define template files inside the templates folder for each microservice. The template file describes how to deploy each service on Kubernetes:

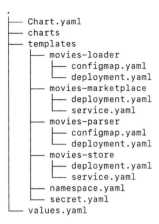

```
.
├── Chart.yaml
├── charts
├── templates
│   ├── movies-loader
│   │   ├── configmap.yaml
│   │   └── deployment.yaml
│   ├── movies-marketplace
│   │   ├── deployment.yaml
│   │   └── service.yaml
│   ├── movies-parser
│   │   ├── configmap.yaml
│   │   └── deployment.yaml
│   ├── movies-store
│   │   ├── deployment.yaml
│   │   └── service.yaml
│   ├── namespace.yaml
│   └── secret.yaml
└── values.yaml
```

For instance, the movies-loader template folder uses the same deployment files we defined in listing 11.4, except it references variables defined in values.yaml.

The deployment.yaml file is responsible for deploying a deployment object based on the movies-loader Docker image. This definition pulls the built Docker image from the Docker Registry and creates a new deployment with it in Kubernetes; see the following listing.

Listing 11.13 Movie loader deployment

```yaml
apiVersion: apps/v1
kind: Deployment
metadata:
  name: movies-loader
  namespace: {{ .Values.namespace }}
  labels:
    app: movies-loader
    tier: backend
spec:
  selector:
    matchLabels:
      app: movies-loader
  template:
    metadata:
      name: movies-loader
      labels:
        app: movies-loader
        tier: backend
      annotations:
        jenkins/build: {{ .Values.metadata.jenkins.buildTag | quote }}
        git/commitId: {{ .Values.metadata.git.commitId | quote }}
    spec:
      containers:
        - name: movies-loader
          image: "{{ .Values.services.registry.uri }}/
mlabouardy/movies-loader:{{ .Values.deployment.tag }}"
          imagePullPolicy: Always
```

```
    envFrom:
      - configMapRef:
          name: {{ .Values.namespace }}-movies-loader
      - secretRef:
          name: {{ .Values.namespace }}-secrets
    {{- if .Values.services.registry.secret }}
    imagePullSecrets:
    - name: {{ .Values.services.registry.secret }}
    {{- end }}
```

Helm charts use {{}} for templating, which means that whatever is inside will be interpreted to provide an output value. We can also use a piping mechanism to combine two or more commands for scripting and filtering.

The movies-loader container reference environment variables like AWS_REGION and SQS_URL are defined in configmap.yaml, as shown in the following listing.

Listing 11.14   Movie loader ConfigMap

```
apiVersion: v1
kind: ConfigMap
metadata:
  name: {{ .Values.namespace }}-movies-loader
  namespace: {{ .Values.namespace }}
  labels:
    app: {{ .Values.namespace }}-movies-loader
data:
  AWS_REGION: {{ .Values.services.aws.region }}
  SQS_URL: https://sqs.{{ .Values.services.aws.region }}
.amazonaws.com/{{ .Values.services.aws.account }}/
movies_to_parse_{{ .Values.environment }}
```

The deployment file also references sensitive information such as MongoDB credentials. These credentials are stored securely in Kubernetes secrets, which are provided in the following listing.

Listing 11.15   Application secrets

```
apiVersion: v1
kind: Secret
metadata:
  name: {{ .Values.namespace }}-secrets
  namespace: {{ .Values.namespace }}
data:
  MONGO_URI: {{ .Values.services.mongodb.uri | b64enc }}
  MONGO_DATABASE : {{ .Values.mongodb.mongodbDatabase | b64enc }}
  MONGODB_USERNAME : {{ .Values.mongodb.mongodbUsername | b64enc }}
  MONGODB_PASSWORD : {{ .Values.mongodb.mongodbPassword | b64enc }}
```

Helm charts make it easy to set overridable defaults in the values.yaml file, allowing us to define a base setting. We can move as many variables as we want out of the template and into the values.yaml file. This way, we can easily update and inject new values at installation time:

```
namespace: 'watchlist'
services:
  registry:
    uri: ''
    secret: ''
deployment:
  tag: ''
  workers:
    replicas: 2
```

This allows us to create a portable package that can be customized during runtime by overriding the values.

Also, note the use of custom annotations or metadata in the deployment file. We will inject the Jenkins build ID and Git commit ID during the build of the Helm chart. This can be useful for debugging and troubleshooting running Kubernetes deployments:

```
annotations:
        jenkins/build: {{ .Values.metadata.jenkins.buildTag | quote }}
        git/commitId: {{ .Values.metadata.git.commitId | quote }}
```

MongoDB offers a stable and official Helm chart that can be used for straightforward installation and configuration on Kubernetes. We define the MongoDB chart as a dependency in Chart.yaml under the `dependencies` section:

```
dependencies:
  - name: mongodb
    version: 7.8.10
    repository: https://charts.bitnami.com/bitnami
    alias: mongodb
```

Now that our chart is defined, on your terminal session, issue the following command to install the watchlist application via the Helm chart we just created:

```
helm install watchlist ./watchlist -f values.override.yaml
```

The command takes the values.override.yaml file, which contains the values to override at runtime, such as the environment name and MongoDB username and password:

```
environment: 'sandbox'
mongodb:
  mongodbUsername: 'watchlist'
  mongodbPassword: 'watchlist'
deployment:
  tag: 'develop'
  workers:
    replicas: 2
```

Check installation progress by checking the status of deployments and pods. Type `kubectl get pods -n watchlist` to show the running pods:

```
NAME                                 READY   STATUS      RESTARTS   AGE
movies-loader-748c544c6b-17c15       0/1     Completed   0          4s
movies-marketplace-57659fbcc-b5jh5   1/1     Running     0          32m
movies-parser-84df877c4-7mn6h        1/1     Running     0          32m
movies-parser-84df877c4-mr5md        1/1     Running     0          32m
movies-store-76d74646bc-v7rsx        1/1     Running     0          32m
```

NOTE To check the generated manifests of a release without installing the chart, use the `--dry-run` flag to return rendered templates.

We can now update the Jenkinsfile (chapter11/Jenkinsfile.eks) to use the Helm command line instead of kubectl. Since our application chart is already installed, we will use the `helm upgrade` command to upgrade the chart. This command takes as a parameter values to override, and sets the annotation values from the Jenkins environment variable `BUILD_TAG` and the `commitID()` method, as shown next.

Listing 11.16 Helm upgrade within the Jenkins pipeline

```
stage('Deploy'){
        sh """
            helm upgrade --install watchlist
./watchlist -f values.override.yaml \
            --set metadata.jenkins.buildTag=${env.BUILD_TAG} \
            --set metadata.git.commitId=${commitID()}
        """
}
```

Helm tries to perform the least invasive upgrade. It will update only things that have changed since the last release.

Push the changes to the develop branch. The GitHub repository should look similar to figure 11.12.

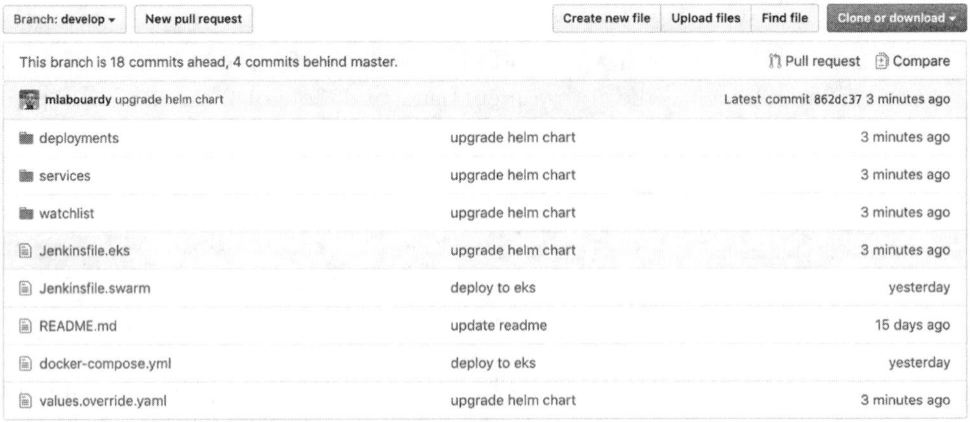

Branch: develop ▾	New pull request		Create new file	Upload files	Find file	Clone or download ▾
This branch is 18 commits ahead, 4 commits behind master.					Pull request	Compare
mlabouardy upgrade helm chart				Latest commit 862dc37	3 minutes ago	
deployments	upgrade helm chart				3 minutes ago	
services	upgrade helm chart				3 minutes ago	
watchlist	upgrade helm chart				3 minutes ago	
Jenkinsfile.eks	upgrade helm chart				3 minutes ago	
Jenkinsfile.swarm	deploy to eks				yesterday	
README.md	update readme				15 days ago	
docker-compose.yml	deploy to eks				yesterday	
values.override.yaml	upgrade helm chart				3 minutes ago	

Figure 11.12 Watchlist Helm chart

On Jenkins, a new build will be triggered. At the end of the `Deploy` stage, the `helm upgrade` command will be executed; the output is shown in figure 11.13.

⬤ Console Output

```
+ helm upgrade --install watchlist ./watchlist -f values.override.yaml --set metadata.jenkins.buildTag=jenkins-watchlist-deployment-develop-8 --
set metadata.git.commitId=58a23e4fbd3a22ba9c9a7f58f5e780747b63f75e
Release "watchlist" has been upgraded. Happy Helming!
NAME: watchlist
LAST DEPLOYED: Thu May 21 14:51:29 2020
NAMESPACE: default
STATUS: deployed
REVISION: 2
TEST SUITE: None
```

Figure 11.13   Helm upgrade output

Now every change on the develop branch will build a new Helm chart and create a new release on the sandbox cluster. If the Docker image has been changed, Kubernetes rolling updates provide the functionality to deploy changes with 0% downtime.

> **NOTE**   If something does not go as planned during a release, rolling back to a previous release is easy by using the `helm rollback` command.

For code promotion to the staging environment, we just need to update the values .override.yaml file to set the environment value to `staging` and use the `preprod` image tag, as shown in the following listing.

Listing 11.17   Staging variables

```
environment: 'staging'
mongodb:
  mongodbUsername: 'watchlist'
  mongodbPassword: 'watchlist'
deployment:
  tag: 'preprod'
  workers:
    replicas: 2
```

If you push the changes to the preprod branch, the application will be deployed to the Kubernetes staging cluster, as shown in figure 11.14.

Stage View

	Checkout	Quality Tests	Unit Tests	Static Code Analysis	Quality Gate	Build	Push	Analyze	Deploy
Average stage times: (Average full run time: ~3min 27s)	3s	6s	16s	10s	336ms	2min 10s	4s	19s	19ms
May 22 14:04 No Changes	3s	6s	16s	10s	336ms	2min 10s	4s	19s	19ms

SonarQube Quality Gate

movies-marketplace OK
server-side processing Success

 Latest Anchore Report (PASS)

Figure 11.14   CI/CD workflow on preprod branch

We can verify that the preprod version has been deployed by typing the following command:

```
kubectl describe deployment movies-marketplace -n watchlist
```

The movies-marketplace deployment has annotations with git/commitId equal to the GitHub commit ID responsible for triggering the Jenkins job, and the jenkins/build annotation's value is the name of the Jenkins job that triggered the deployment (figure 11.15).

```
Name:                   movies-marketplace
Namespace:              watchlist
CreationTimestamp:      Fri, 22 May 2020 14:32:51 +0200
Labels:                 app=movies-marketplace
                        app.kubernetes.io/managed-by=Helm
                        tier=frontend
Annotations:            deployment.kubernetes.io/revision: 3
                        meta.helm.sh/release-name: watchlist
                        meta.helm.sh/release-namespace: default
Selector:               app=movies-marketplace
Replicas:               1 desired | 1 updated | 1 total | 1 available | 0 unavailable
StrategyType:           RollingUpdate
MinReadySeconds:        0
RollingUpdateStrategy:  25% max unavailable, 25% max surge
Pod Template:
  Labels:       app=movies-marketplace
                tier=frontend
  Annotations:  git/commitId: b82100da404cf03670124001cecbbd72d8f365b3
                jenkins/build: jenkins-watchlist-deployment-preprod-4
  Containers:
   movies-marketplace:
    Image:      305929695733.dkr.ecr.eu-west-3.amazonaws.com/mlabouardy/movies-marketplace:preprod
    Port:       <none>
    Host Port:  <none>
```

Figure 11.15   Movies Marketplace deployment description

For production deployment, update values.override.yaml with proper values, as shown in the following listing. In this example, we set the image tag to `latest`, the environment to `production`, and we configure five replicas of the movies-parser service.

Listing 11.18   Production variables

```
environment: production
mongodb:
  mongodbUsername: 'watchlist'
  mongodbPassword: 'watchlist'
deployment:
  tag: 'latest'
  workers:
    replicas: 5
```

Push the new files to the master branch. At the end of the pipeline, the stack will be deployed to the K8s production cluster.

Now if a push event occurs on the master branch on any of the four microservices, the CI/CD pipeline will be triggered, and user approval will be requested, as shown in figure 11.16.

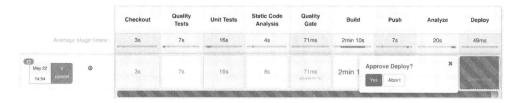

Figure 11.16 User approval for production deployment

If the deployment is approved, the watchlist-deployment job will be triggered, and the master nested job will be executed. As a result, a new Helm release of the watchlist application will be created in production, as shown in figure 11.17.

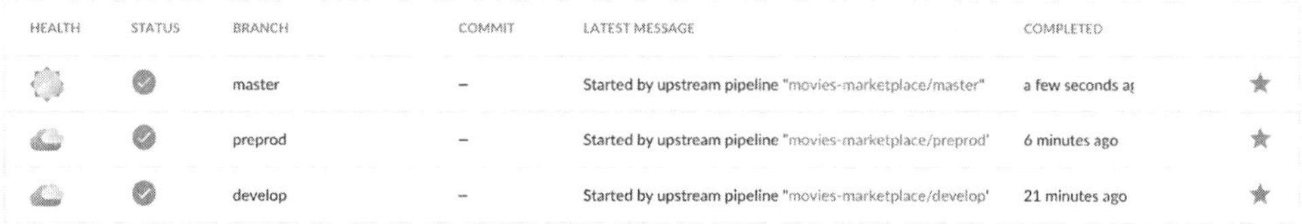

HEALTH	STATUS	BRANCH	COMMIT	LATEST MESSAGE	COMPLETED	
	✓	master	—	Started by upstream pipeline "movies-marketplace/master"	a few seconds a	★
	✓	preprod	—	Started by upstream pipeline "movies-marketplace/preprod"	6 minutes ago	★
	✓	develop	—	Started by upstream pipeline "movies-marketplace/develop"	21 minutes ago	★

Figure 11.17 Application deployment in production

Upon the completion of the deployment process, a Slack notification will be sent to a preconfigured Slack channel, as shown in figure 11.18.

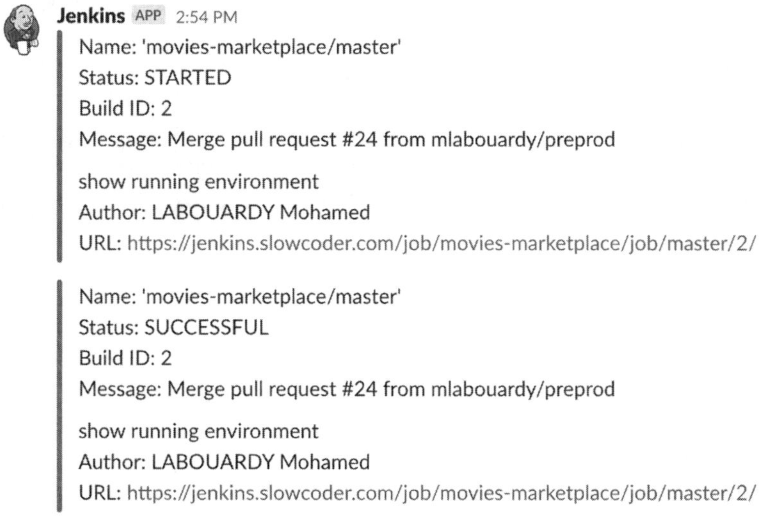

Jenkins APP 2:54 PM
Name: 'movies-marketplace/master'
Status: STARTED
Build ID: 2
Message: Merge pull request #24 from mlabouardy/preprod

show running environment
Author: LABOUARDY Mohamed
URL: https://jenkins.slowcoder.com/job/movies-marketplace/job/master/2/

Name: 'movies-marketplace/master'
Status: SUCCESSFUL
Build ID: 2
Message: Merge pull request #24 from mlabouardy/preprod

show running environment
Author: LABOUARDY Mohamed
URL: https://jenkins.slowcoder.com/job/movies-marketplace/job/master/2/

Figure 11.18 Production deployment Slack notification

Run the `kubectl get pods` command. This should display five pods based on the movies-parser Docker image:

```
NAME                                  READY   STATUS      RESTARTS   AGE
movies-loader-5fc5b6847b-7zrsg        0/1     Completed   1          12s
movies-marketplace-6b7898d567-xvhrh   1/1     Running     0          4m6s
movies-parser-7fd8c9498d-nv427        1/1     Running     5          4m6s
movies-parser-7fd8c9498d-slp7t        1/1     Running     5          4m6s
movies-parser-7fd8c9498d-tpw44        1/1     Running     5          4m6s
movies-parser-7fd8c9498d-x87qv        1/1     Running     5          4m6s
movies-parser-7fd8c9498d-xdlvs        1/1     Running     5          4m6s
movies-store-58d9ffc7d9-9ml5c         1/1     Running     0          4m6s
```

To view the marketplace dashboard, locate the external IP of the load balancer in the EXTERNAL-IP column of the `kubectl get services -n watchlist` output:

```
NAME                 TYPE           CLUSTER-IP      EXTERNAL-IP
movies-marketplace   LoadBalancer   172.20.93.31    a3b35d67b360f4a5e9dd8ebc81bdf8ec-167487368.eu-west-3.elb.amazonaws.com
movies-store         LoadBalancer   172.20.230.116  aa8091de87549426cac6f128b0e73512-633343171.eu-west-3.elb.amazonaws.com
```

Navigate to that address in your browser, and the Movies Marketplace UI should be displayed, as you can see in figure 11.19.

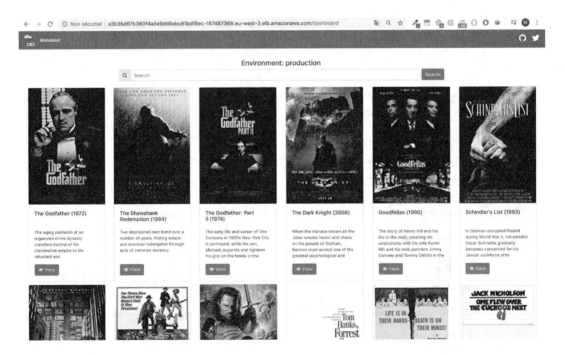

Figure 11.19   Marketplace production environment

Under a production environment, you would replace the load balancer FQDN with an alias in Route 53. Refer to the official AWS documentation for instructions: http://mng.bz/Rq8P.

11.4 Packaging Kubernetes applications with Helm

So far, you have seen how to create one single chart for the microservices-based application and how to create a new release with Jenkins upon new Git commits. Another way of packaging the application is to create separate charts for each microservice, and then reference those charts as dependencies in the main chart (similar to a MongoDB chart). Figure 11.20 illustrates how Helm charts are packaged within a CI/CD pipeline.

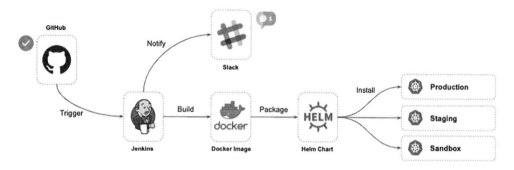

Figure 11.20   CI/CD of containerized application with Helm

On a push event, a Jenkins build will be triggered to build the Docker image and package the new release in a Helm chart. From there, the new chart is deployed to the corresponding Kubernetes environment. Along the way, a Slack notification is sent to notify the developers about the pipeline status.

On the movies-marketplace project, create a new Helm chart in the top-level directory by typing the following command:

```
helm create chart
```

It should create a new folder called chart with the following structure:

```
.
├── Chart.yaml
├── charts
├── templates
│   ├── deployment.yaml
│   └── service.yaml
└── values.yaml
```

As mentioned earlier, a Helm chart consists of metadata used to help describe the application, define constraints on the minimum required Kubernetes and/or Helm version, and manage the version of the chart. All of this metadata lives in the Chart.yaml file (chapter11/microservices/movies-marketplace), shown in the following listing.

Listing 11.19   Movie loader chart

```
apiVersion: v2
name: movies-marketplace
description: UI to browse top 100 IMDb movies
type: application
version: 1.0.0
appVersion: 1.0.0
```

To be able to reference this chart from the main watchlist chart, we need to store it somewhere. Many open source solutions are available for storing Helm charts. GitHub can be used as a remote registry for Helm charts. Create a new GitHub repository called watchlist-charts and create an empty index.yaml file. This file will contain the metadata about available charts in the repository.

> **NOTE** Nexus Repository OSS supports Helm charts as well. You can publish charts to a Helm-hosted repository on Nexus.

Then, push this file to the master branch by issuing these commands:

```
git clone https://github.com/mlabouardy/watchlist-charts.git
cd watchlist-charts
touch index.yaml
git add index.yaml
git commit -m "add index.yaml"
git push origin master
```

The GitHub repository will look like figure 11.21.

Figure 11.21   Helm charts GitHub repository

The Helm repository is an HTTP server that has a file index.yaml and all your chart files. To turn the GitHub repository into an HTTP server, we will enable GitHub pages.

Click the Settings tab. Scroll down to the GitHub Pages section and select the master branch as a source, as shown in figure 11.22.

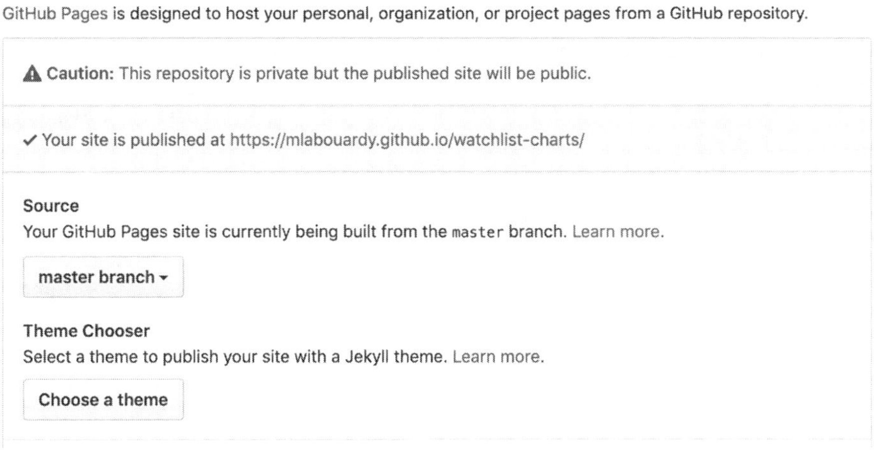

GitHub Pages is designed to host your personal, organization, or project pages from a GitHub repository.

⚠ **Caution:** This repository is private but the published site will be public.

✓ Your site is published at https://mlabouardy.github.io/watchlist-charts/

Source
Your GitHub Pages site is currently being built from the master branch. Learn more.

    master branch ▾

Theme Chooser
Select a theme to publish your site with a Jekyll theme. Learn more.

    Choose a theme

Figure 11.22   Enabling GitHub pages

With the private Helm repository ready to be used, let's package and publish our first Helm chart. On the movies-marketplace project, update the `Build` stage to use a parallel build to build the Docker image and the Helm chart. The `Build` stage should look like the following listing. (The complete Jenkinsfile is available at chapter11/pipeline/movies-marketplace/Jenkinsfile.)

Listing 11.20   Building the Docker image and Helm chart

```
stage('Build') {
 parallel(
  'Docker Image': {
    switch (env.BRANCH_NAME) {
    case 'develop':
       docker.build(imageName, '--build-arg ENVIRONMENT=sandbox .')    ⊲┐
      break
    case 'preprod':
       docker.build(imageName, '--build-arg ENVIRONMENT=staging .')    ⊲┘
      break
    ...
   }
  },
  'Helm Chart': {
    sh 'helm package chart'    ⊲┐ Packages the application
  }                               in a Helm chart
 )
}
```

Builds the appropriate Docker
image by injecting the target
environment settings

The `helm package` command, as its name indicates, packages the chart directory into a chart archive (movies-marketplace-1.0.0.tgz). Finally, update the `Push` stage to use a parallel step as well, as shown in the following listing.

Listing 11.21   Storing the Docker image in a private registry

```
stage('Push') {                                     Authenticates with ECR in order to
 parallel(                                           push the Docker images afterward
   'Docker Image': {
     sh "\$(aws ecr get-login --no-include-email --region ${region}) || true"  ◁─
     docker.withRegistry("https://${registry}") {
        docker.image(imageName).push(commitID())
        if (env.BRANCH_NAME == 'develop') {          Tags and stores
           docker.image(imageName).push('develop')   the image in ECR
        }
        ...
     }
   },
   'Helm Chart': {        ◁─┐  Publishes the Helm chart to
     ...                     GitHub—see listing 11.22 for
   }                         complete instructions.
 )
}
```

The `Helm Chart` stage will clone the watchlist-charts GitHub repository with the `git clone` command, and add the metadata of the new packaged Helm chart to index.yaml with the `helm repo index` command. Then it pushes index.yaml and the archive chart to the Git repository; see the following listing.

Listing 11.22   Publishing the Helm chart to GitHub

```
                                                    Generates an index file, given a
                                                 directory containing packaged charts
'Helm Chart': {
    sh 'helm repo index --url https://mlabouardy.github.io/watchlist-charts/ .'  ◁─
    sshagent(['github-ssh']) {                                   ◁─   Provides SSH
       sh 'git clone git@github.com:mlabouardy/watchlist-charts.git'   credentials to
       sh 'mv movies-marketplace-1.0.0.tgz watchlist-charts/'          builds via an
       dir('watchlist-charts'){                                    ◁─  ssh-agent
           sh 'git add index.yaml movies-marketplace-1.0.0.tgz
&& git commit -m "movies-marketplace"
&& git push origin master'              ◁─    Changes current
       }                                             directory to
    }                    Commits and pushes the     watchlist-charts
}                        archive and index file to GitHub   folder
```

If you push the new Jenkinsfile to the Git remote repository, a new pipeline will be triggered, as shown in figure 11.23. At the `Build` stage, the movies-marketplace Docker image and Helm chart will be packaged. Next, the `Push` stage will be executed to push the Docker image to the Docker private registry and the Helm chart to the GitHub repository.

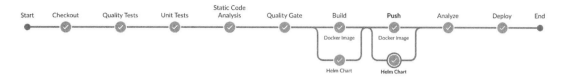

Figure 11.23   CI/CD workflow with Helm and Docker

Upon the completion of the CI/CD pipeline, a new archived chart will be available in the GitHub repository, as shown in figure 11.24.

Figure 11.24   Packaging the Movies Marketplace chart

The index.yaml file will reference the newly built Helm chart under the `entries` section, as you can see in figure 11.25.

Figure 11.25   Helm repository metadata

You can override the chart version set in Chart.yaml by providing the new version with the `--version` flag at the time of packaging a Helm chart:

```sh
'helm package chart --app-version ${appVersion} --version ${chartVersion}'
```

Repeat the same steps for other repositories to create a Helm chart per service. Once done, the Helm charts repository should contain four archived files (figure 11.26).

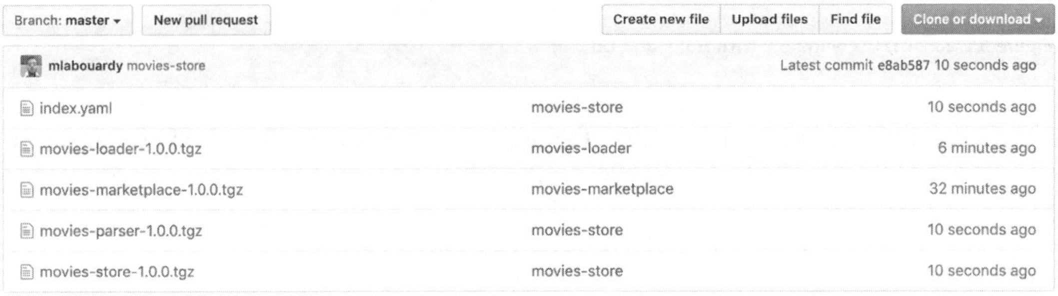

Branch: master ▾	New pull request		Create new file	Upload files	Find file	Clone or download ▾
mlabouardy movies-store					Latest commit e8ab587 10 seconds ago	
index.yaml		movies-store			10 seconds ago	
movies-loader-1.0.0.tgz		movies-loader			6 minutes ago	
movies-marketplace-1.0.0.tgz		movies-marketplace			32 minutes ago	
movies-parser-1.0.0.tgz		movies-store			10 seconds ago	
movies-store-1.0.0.tgz		movies-store			10 seconds ago	

Figure 11.26   Application charts stored in the GitHub repository

Next, we configure the GitHub repository as a Helm repository:

```
helm repo add watchlist https://mlabouardy.github.io/watchlist-charts
```

Finally, we can reference these charts in the watchlist Chart.yaml file under the `dependencies` section, as shown in the following listing.

Listing 11.23   Watchlist application charts

```
apiVersion: v2
name: watchlist
description: Top 100 iMDB best movies in history
type: application
version: 1.0.0
appVersion: 1.0.0
maintainers:
    - name: Mohamed Labouardy
      email: mohamed@labouardy.com
dependencies:
  - name: mongodb
    version: 7.8.10
    repository: https://charts.bitnami.com/bitnami
    alias: mongodb
  - name: movies-loader
    version: 1.0.0
    repository: https://mlabouardy.github.io/watchlist-charts
  - name: movies-parser
    version: 1.0.0
    repository: https://mlabouardy.github.io/watchlist-charts
  - name: movies-store
    version: 1.0.0
```

```
   repository: https://mlabouardy.github.io/watchlist-charts
 - name: movies-marketplace
   version: 1.0.0
   repository: https://mlabouardy.github.io/watchlist-charts
```

Now that all pieces are running together and we checked the core functionality, let's validate that the solution is up for a typical GitFlow development process.

11.5 *Running post-deployment smoke tests*

The microservices are deployed. However, that doesn't mean these services are properly configured and correctly performing all the jobs that they're supposed to be doing.

You want to have a health check that indicates the current health operation of your services. You can set up a simple one by implementing an HTTP request to a service URL and check whether the response code is 200.

For instance, let's implement a health check for the movies-store service. Update the Jenkinsfile of the movies-store project (chapter11/pipeline/movies-store/Jenkinsfile) to add the function shown in the following listing.

Listing 11.24 Groovy function to return API URL

```
def getUrl(){
    switch(env.BRANCH_NAME){
        case 'preprod':
            return 'https://api.staging.domain.com'
        case 'master':
            return 'https://api.production.domain.com'
        default:
            return 'https://api.sandbox.domain.com'
    }
}
```

The function returns the service URL based on the current Git branch name. Finally, we add a `Healthcheck` stage at the end of the pipeline to issue a cURL command on the service URL:

```
stage('Healthcheck'){
    sh "curl -m 10 ${getUrl()}"
}
```

The `-m` flag is used to set a time-out of 10 seconds, to give Kubernetes enough time to pull the latest built image and deploy the changes into the cluster before checking the service health status.

Once you push the changes to the Git remote repository, a new build will be triggered. Upon the completion of the CI/CD pipeline, a cURL command will be executed with a GET request on the service URL, as shown in figure 11.27.

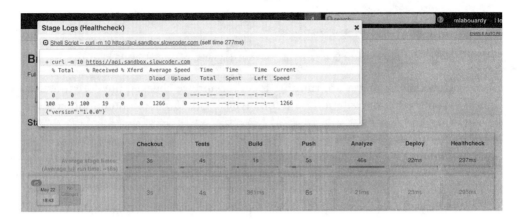

Figure 11.27   cURL command output

If the service responds before the expiration time-out, the cURL command will return a successful exit code. Otherwise, an error will be thrown to make the pipeline fail.

However, if the service is responding, that doesn't mean it's working correctly or a new version of the service has been successfully deployed.

To be able to issue advanced HTTP requests against the service URL, we will install the Jenkins HTTP Request plugin (www.jenkins.io/doc/pipeline/steps/http_request/) from the Jenkins Plugins page, as shown in figure 11.28.

Updates	**Available**	Installed	Advanced		
Install ↓		Name			Version
	Generic Webhook Trigger				
☐	Can receive any HTTP request, extract any values from JSON or XML and trigger a job with those values available as variables. Works with GitHub, GitLab, Bitbucket, Jira and many more.				1.67
	HTTP Request				
☑	This plugin sends a http request to an url with some parameters				1.8.26
	CORS support				
☐	This plugin allows Jenkins to serve Cross-site HTTP requests				1.1

Figure 11.28   Jenkins HTTP Request plugin

We can now update the movies-store's Jenkinsfile. The plugin offers an `httpRequest` DSL object that can be used to call a remote URL. In the following listing, `httpRequest` returns a response object that exposes the response body through a `content` attribute. Then, we use the `JsonSlurper` class to parse the response to a JSON object. The updated `Healthcheck` stage is shown in the following listing.

Listing 11.25   Movie store Healthcheck stage

```
stage('Healthcheck'){
    def response = httpRequest getUrl()
```

```
    def json = new JsonSlurper().parseText(response.content)
    def version = json.get('version')

    if version != '1.0.0' {
        error "Expected API version 1.0.0 but got ${version}"
    }
}
```

The service returns the version number deployed in Kubernetes. This value is fixed in the service source code, but you can inject the Jenkins build ID as a version number while building the Docker image of the service and check whether the returned version is equal to the Jenkins build ID at the `Healthcheck` stage.

Figure 11.29 shows the end result of the CI/CD pipeline of each microservice running in Kubernetes.

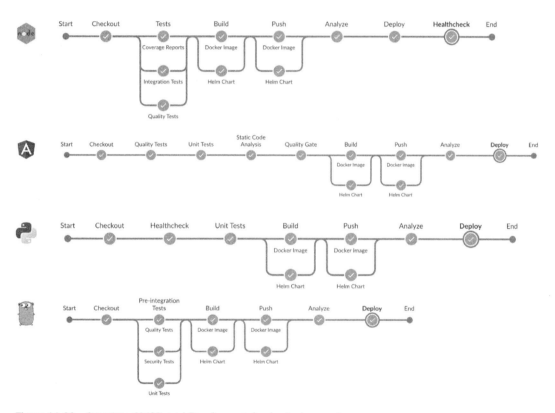

Figure 11.29   Complete CI/CD workflow for containerized microservices

When you opt for Jenkins to build cloud-native applications running in Kubernetes, you're required to create extensive configurations, as well as spending considerable time learning and using all of the necessary plugins to make it happen. Fortunately, Jenkins X comes into play to offer simplicity and ready-to-go templates.

11.6 *Discovering Jenkins X*

Jenkins X (https://jenkins-x.io/) is a CI/CD solution for modern cloud applications on Kubernetes. It's used to simplify the configurations and lets you harness the power of Jenkins 2.0. It also lets you use open source tools like Helm, Artifact Hub, Chart-Museum, Nexus, and Docker Registry to easily build cloud-native applications.

Jenkins X adds what's missing from Jenkins: comprehensive support for continuous delivery and managing the promotion of projects to preview, staging, and production environments running in Kubernetes. It uses GitOps to manage the configuration and version of the Kubernetes resources that are deployed to each environment. So each environment has its own Git repository that contains all the Helm charts, their versions, and the configuration for the applications to be run in the environment.

When following this methodology, Git is the single source of truth for both the infrastructure as code and the application code. All changes to the desired state are Git commits. So it's easy to see who made changes when, and more importantly, it's then easy to revert changes that cause bad things to happen.

With that being said, let's get our hands dirty and cover how Jenkins X works. To get started, install the Jenkins X CLI, and pick the most suitable instructions for your operating system: http://mng.bz/20ZX. Run `jx version --short` to make sure you're on the latest stable version. I'm using version 2.1.71 at the time of writing this book.

Jenkins X runs on a Kubernetes cluster. If you're running on one of the major cloud providers (Amazon EKS, GKE, or AKS), Jenkins X provides multiple approaches for creating this cluster:

```
jx create cluster eks --cluster-name=watchlist
Jx create cluster aks --cluster-name=watchlist
Jx create cluster gke --cluster-name=watchlist
Jx create cluster iks --cluster-name=watchlist
```

> **NOTE** You can run Jenkins X on the existing EKS cluster by referring to the official guide at https://jenkins-x.io/v3/admin/setup/operator/.

Install Jenkins X on a K8s cluster by issuing the following command from your terminal session:

```
jx boot
```

You will be asked a series of questions that will configure the installation, as shown in figure 11.30.

When the installation is done, you will be presented with useful links and the password for your Jenkins X–related services. Don't forget to save it somewhere for future use.

Jenkins X also deploys a set of supporting services, including the Jenkins dashboard, Docker Registry, ChartMuseum, and Artifact Hub to manage Helm charts, and Nexus, which serves as a Maven and npm repository.

```
Creating staging Environment in namespace jx
Created environment staging
Namespace jx-staging created
Created Jenkins Project: http://jenkins.jx.35.198.184.208.nip.io/job/mlabouardy/job/environment-watchlist-staging/

Note that your first pipeline may take a few minutes to start while the necessary images get downloaded!

Triggered Jenkins job:  http://jenkins.jx.35.198.184.208.nip.io/job/mlabouardy/job/environment-watchlist-staging/
Creating GitHub webhook for mlabouardy/environment-watchlist-staging for url http://jenkins.jx.35.198.184.208.nip.io/github-webhook/
Using Git provider github.com at https://github.com
? Using Git user name: mlabouardy
? Using organisation: mlabouardy
Creating repository mlabouardy/environment-watchlist-production
Creating Git repository mlabouardy/environment-watchlist-production
Pushed Git repository to https://github.com/mlabouardy/environment-watchlist-production

Creating production Environment in namespace jx
Created environment production
Namespace jx-production created
Created Jenkins Project: http://jenkins.jx.35.198.184.208.nip.io/job/mlabouardy/job/environment-watchlist-production/

Note that your first pipeline may take a few minutes to start while the necessary images get downloaded!

Triggered Jenkins job:  http://jenkins.jx.35.198.184.208.nip.io/job/mlabouardy/job/environment-watchlist-production/
Creating GitHub webhook for mlabouardy/environment-watchlist-production for url http://jenkins.jx.35.198.184.208.nip.io/github-webhook/

Jenkins X installation completed successfully


      *********************************************************

            NOTE: Your admin password is: u?zTUzZFGMH79UN0C~4u

      *********************************************************
```

Figure 11.30   Jenkins X installation output

The following is the output of the `kubectl get svc` command:

```
NAME               HOSTS                                        ADDRESS        PORTS   AGE
chartmuseum        chartmuseum.jx.34.89.183.25.nip.io           34.89.183.25   80      2m52s
docker-registry    docker-registry.jx.34.89.183.25.nip.io       34.89.183.25   80      2m53s
jenkins            jenkins.jx.34.89.183.25.nip.io               34.89.183.25   80      2m53s
nexus              nexus.jx.34.89.183.25.nip.io                 34.89.183.25   80      2m53s
```

Point your browser to the Jenkins URL printed during the installation process and sign in with the admin username and password displayed previously in figure 11.30. The dashboard in figure 11.31 should be served.

Figure 11.31   Jenkins web dashboard

It is possible to run Jenkins in serverless mode while installing Jenkins X. Then, instead of running the Jenkins web dashboard, which continuously consumes CPU and memory resources, you can run Jenkins only when you need it.

The Jenkins X installation also creates two Git repositories by default: one for your staging environment and one for production, as shown in figure 11.32:

- *Staging*—Any merge performed on the project master branch will automatically be deployed as a new version to staging (auto promote).
- *Production*—You will have to manually promote your staging application version into production by using a `jx promote` command.

environment-watchlist-production `Private`   ☆ Star

● Makefile ⚖️ Apache License 2.0   Updated 2 minutes ago

Figure 11.32
Application
deployment
environments

environment-watchlist-staging `Private`   ☆ Star

● Makefile ⚖️ Apache License 2.0   Updated 2 minutes ago

Jenkins X uses these repositories to manage deployments to each environment, and promotions are done via Git pull requests. Each repository contains a Helm chart that specifies the applications to be deployed to the corresponding environment. Each repository also has a Jenkinsfile to handle promotions.

Now that you have a working cluster with Jenkins X installed, we are going to create an application that can be built and deployed with Jenkins X. For clarity, I have created a RESTful API in Go that serves an HTTP endpoint with a list of the top 100 IMDb movies. We will import this project inside Jenkins with this command:

```
jx import
```

If you wish to import a project that is already in a remote Git repository, you can use the `--url` argument:

```
jx import --url https://github.com/mlabouardy/jx-movies-store
```

The following is the output of the import command:

```
WARNING: No username defined for the current Git server!
[? Do you wish to use mlabouardy as the Git user name: Yes
The directory /Users/mlabouardy/github/jx-movies-store is not yet using git
[? Would you like to initialise git now? Yes
[? Commit message: Initial import

Git repository created
performing pack detection in folder /Users/mlabouardy/github/jx-movies-store
--> Draft detected JSON (63.955137%)
--> Could not find a pack for JSON. Trying to find the next likely language match...
--> Draft detected Go (36.044863%)
selected pack: /Users/mlabouardy/.jx/draft/packs/github.com/jenkins-x-buildpacks/jenkins-x-kubernetes/packs/go
? Who should be the owner of the repository? mlabouardy
replacing placeholders in directory /Users/mlabouardy/github/jx-movies-store
app name: jx-movies-store, git server: github.com, org: mlabouardy, Docker registry org: crew-sandbox
skipping directory "/Users/mlabouardy/github/jx-movies-store/.git"
Draft pack go added
[? Would you like to define a different preview namespace? No
Using Git provider github.com at https://github.com
? Using organisation: mlabouardy
[? Enter the new repository name: jx-movies-store
Creating repository mlabouardy/jx-movies-store
Pushed Git repository to https://github.com/mlabouardy/jx-movies-store
Created Jenkins Project: http://jenkins.jx.35.198.184.208.nip.io/job/mlabouardy/job/jx-movies-store/
```

Jenkins X will go over the code and choose the right default build pack for the project based on the programming language. Our project was developed in Go, so it will be a Go build pack. Jenkins X will generate a Jenkinsfile, Dockerfile, and Helm chart based on the project runtime environment. The import command will create a remote repository on GitHub, register a webhook, and push the code to the remote repository, shown in figure 11.33.

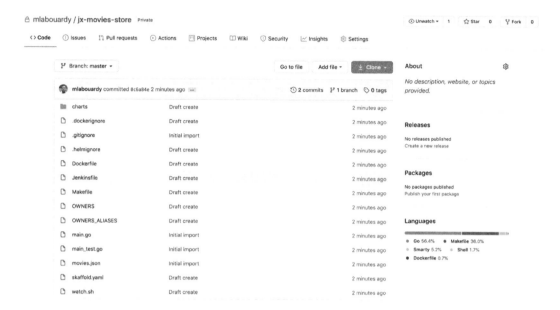

Figure 11.33 Application GitHub repository

Jenkins X will also automatically create a Jenkins multibranch pipeline job for the project, and the pipeline will be triggered. You can check the progress of the pipeline with this command:

```
jx get activity -f jx-movies-store -w
```

```
[jenkins:jx-movies-store mlabouardy$ jx get activity -f jx-movies-store -w
STEP                                      STARTED AGO DURATION STATUS
mlabouardy/jx-movies-store/master #1          39s            Running
mlabouardy/jx-movies-store/master #1        2m13s            Running
   Checkout Source                             1s            Pending
mlabouardy/jx-movies-store/master #1        2m25s            Running
   Checkout Source                            13s       11s  Succeeded
   CI Build and push snapshot                  2s            NotExecuted
   Build Release                               1s            Pending
```

You can also track the progress of the pipeline from the Jenkins dashboard by clicking the project job; figure 11.34 shows the result.

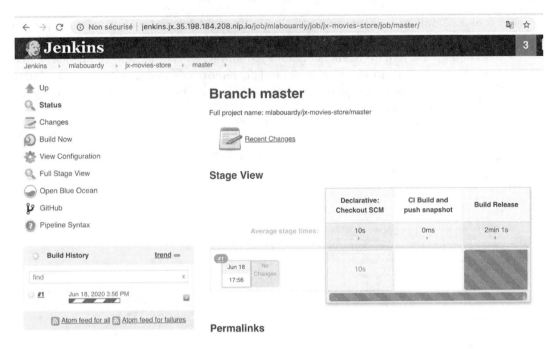

Figure 11.34   Application build pipeline

The pipeline stages are executed on a Kubernetes pod running in the Kubernetes cluster we provisioned earlier, as you can see in figure 11.35.

S	Name ↓	Architecture	Clock Difference	Free Disk Space	Free Swap Space	Free Temp Space	Response Time
🖥	go-msm84	Linux (amd64)	In sync	86.40 GB	⊖ 0 B	86.40 GB	95ms
🖥	master	Linux (amd64)	In sync	28.96 GB	⊖ 0 B	89.93 GB	0ms ⚙
	Data obtained	3 min 59 sec	3 min 59 sec	3 min 59 sec	3 min 59 sec	3 min 59 sec	3 min 59 sec

Refresh status

Figure 11.35   Jenkins workers based on Kubernetes pods

The executed pipeline will clone the repository, build the Docker image, and push it to a Docker registry, as shown in the following listing.

Listing 11.26   Build stage when an event occurs on master branch

```
stage('Build Release') {
      when {
        branch 'master'
      }
      steps {
```

```
        container('go') {
          dir('/home/jenkins/agent/go/src/
github.com/mlabouardy/jx-movies-store') {
            checkout scm
            sh "git checkout master"
            sh "git config --global credential.helper store"
            sh "jx step git credentials"
            sh "echo \$(jx-release-version) > VERSION"
            sh "jx step tag --version \$(cat VERSION)"
            sh "make build"
            sh "export VERSION=`cat VERSION`
&& skaffold build -f skaffold.yaml"
            sh "jx step post build --image $DOCKER_REGISTRY/$ORG/
      $APP_NAME:\$(cat VERSION)"
          }
        }
      }
}
```

A Helm chart will be packaged and pushed to the ChartMuseum repository, and a new release will be published on the project GitHub repository, as shown in figure 11.36. Jenkins X uses semantic versioning for tagging.

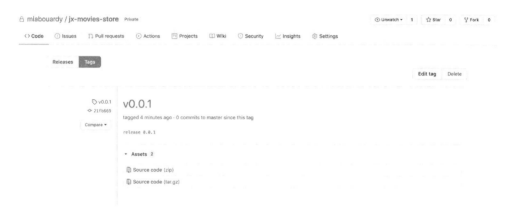

Figure 11.36 Publishing the application release

The release will be pro-moted automatically to the staging environment, as shown in figure 11.37.

During the promotion stage, a new PR will be cre-ated by Jenkins X to

Figure 11.37 Jenkins pipeline on the master branch

deploy the new release to staging. This PR will add our application and its version in the env/requirements.yaml file inside the Git repository, as shown in figure 11.38.

Figure 11.38   **Promoting the application to staging**

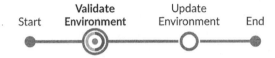

Figure 11.39   **Deploying an application to staging**

Now you can see that the multi-branch jx-movies-store pipeline is triggered for the pull request. It will check out the PR, perform a `helm build`, and execute tests on the environment along with code review and approval. When it's successful, it will merge the PR with the master, see figure 11.39.

Once the application is deployed, we can type `jx get applications` to get the access URL for the application, as shown in figure 11.40.

```
← → C   ⓘ Non sécurisé | jx-movies-store.jx-staging.35.198.184.208.nip.io

{
    "message": "up"
}
```

Figure 11.40   **Application overall health status**

Now we will update our application and see what will happen! Let's create a new feature branch:

```
git checkout -b feature/readme
git add README.md
git commit -m "update readme"
git push origin feature/readme
```

Jenkins X creates a GitHub webhook during the import of our application. This means we can just commit a change, and our application will be updated automatically, as shown in figure 11.41.

Figure 11.41   Building GitHub pull request

Jenkins X automatically spins up preview environments for our pull request, so we can get fast feedback before changes are merged to the master:

```
+ jx preview --app jx-movies-store --dir ../..
Creating a preview
Found commit author match for: mlabouardy with email address: mohamed@labouardy.com
Created environment mlabouardy-jx-movies-store-pr-1
Namespace jx-mlabouardy-jx-movies-store-pr-1 created
expose:
  Annotations:
    helm.sh/hook: post-install,post-upgrade
    helm.sh/hook-delete-policy: hook-succeeded
  config:
    domain: 35.198.184.208.nip.io
    exposer: Ingress
    http: "true"
preview:
  image:
    repository: 10.15.244.126:5000/crew-sandbox/jx-movies-store
    tag: 0.0.0-SNAPSHOT-PR-1-1
Cloning the Jenkins X versions repo https://github.com/jenkins-x/jenkins-x-versions.git with ref refs/heads/master to
/root/.jx/jenkins-x-versions
Updating PipelineActivities mlabouardy-jx-movies-store-pr-1-1 which has status Running
Preview application is now available at: http://jx-movies-store.jx-mlabouardy-jx-movies-store-pr-1.35.198.184.208.nip.io
```

Jenkins X creates a preview environment in the PR for the application changes and displays a link to evaluate the new feature, as shown in figure 11.42.

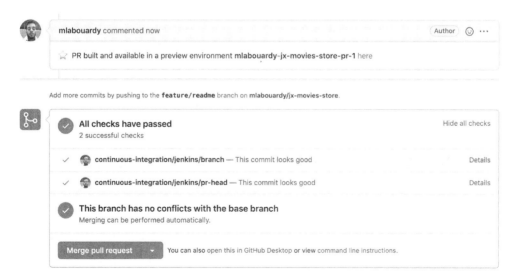

Figure 11.42   Pull request preview environment

The preview environment is created whenever a change is made to the repository, allowing any relevant user to validate or evaluate features, bug fixes, or security hot-fixes. If we click the preview environment URL, we should have access to the service REST API, as shown in figure 11.43.

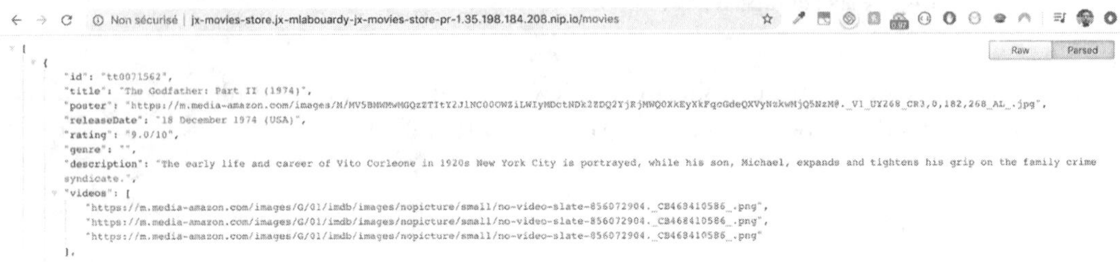

Figure 11.43   Movies Store API

Once the new changes are validated, we can confirm the code and functionality changes with an `/approve` comment, as shown in figure 11.44. This simple comment will merge the code changes back to the master branch and initiate a build on the master branch.

mlabouardy commented 6 minutes ago   (Author) ☺ ⋯

   ☆ PR built and available in a preview environment **mlabouardy-jx-movies-store-pr-1** here

mlabouardy commented 14 seconds ago   (Author) ☺ ⋯

   /approve

   mlabouardy merged commit **9b3630c** into `master` now   [View details] [Revert]
   2 checks passed

Figure 11.44   ChatOps commands within Git PR

Jenkins X offers multiple commands that can be used while managing pull requests. Each command triggers a specific action. Table 11.2 summarizes the most used commands.

Upon the completion of the build on the master branch, a new release will be published, as shown in figure 11.45.

Table 11.2   ChatOps commands

Command	Description
/approve	This PR can be merged. This command must be from someone in the repo OWNERS file.
/retest	Rerun any failed test pipeline contexts for this PR.
/assign USER	Assign the PR to the given user.
/lgtm	This PR looks good to me. This command can be from anyone with access to the repo.

Figure 11.45   New application release

When you're satisfied with your application, you can use the `jx` CLI to promote the application to a different environment using a GitOps approach. For example, we can promote our application to production with the following command:

```
jx promote --app jx-movies-store --version 0.0.3 --env production
```

A new PR will be created, but this time on our production repository, and the environment-watchlist-production job is triggered, as shown in figure 11.46.

Figure 11.46   Promoting the application to production

Once the pull request is validated, the production pipeline runs Helm, which deploys the environment, pulling Helm charts from ChartMuseum, and Docker images from the Docker Registry. Kubernetes creates the project's resources, typically a pod, service, and ingress.

Jenkins X uses Git branch patterns to determine which branch names are automatically set up for CI/CD. By default, the master branch, and any branch starting with *PR-* or *feature* will be scanned. You can set up your own branch discovery mechanism with the following command:

```
jx import --branches "develop|preprod|master|PR-.*"
```

> **NOTE** If you are done with your Amazon EKS cluster, you should delete it and its resources so that you do not incur additional charges. Issue a `terraform destroy` command to delete the AWS resources.

Summary

- Kubernetes manages containerized applications on clusters of nodes by helping operators deploy, scale, update, and maintain their services, and providing mechanisms for service discovery.
- The `kubectl apply` command can be used from Jenkins pipelines to perform deployments on K8s clusters.
- A Helm chart encapsulates Kubernetes object definitions and provides a mechanism for configuration at deployment time.
- GitHub pages have built-in support for installing Helm charts from an HTTP server.
- Jenkins X creates a Kubernetes pod for each agent started, defined by the Docker image to run, and stops it after each build.
- Jenkins X preview environments are used to get early feedback on changes to applications before the changes are merged into the master branch.
- Jenkins X does not aim to replace Jenkins but builds on it with best-of-breed open source tools. It's a great way to achieve CI/CD with batteries included, without having to assemble things together.

12

Lambda-based
serverless functions

This chapter covers

- Implementing a CI/CD pipeline for a serverless-based application from scratch

- Setting up continuous deployment and delivery with AWS Lambda

- Separating multiple Lambda deployment environments

- Implementing API Gateway multistage deployments with Lambda alias and stage variables

- Delivering email notifications with attachments upon completion of CI/CD pipelines

In the previous chapters, you learned how to write a CI/CD pipeline for a containerized application running in both Docker Swarm and Kubernetes. In this chapter, you will learn how to deploy the same application written in a different architecture.

Serverless is the fastest-growing architectural movement right now. It allows developers to develop scalable applications faster by delegating the full responsibility of managing the underlying infrastructure to the cloud provider. That said, going serverless carries several key challenges, one of which is CI/CD.

12.1 *Deploying a Lambda-based application*

Multiple serverless providers are out there, but to keep it simple, we'll use AWS—and specifically, AWS Lambda (https://aws.amazon.com/lambda/), which is the best known and most mature solution in the serverless space today. AWS Lambda, launched at AWS re:Invent 2014, was the first implementation of serverless computing. Users can upload their code to Lambda, which then performs operational and scaling activities on behalf of the users.

The service follows an event-driven architecture. This means the code deployed in Lambda can be triggered in response to events like HTTP requests coming from services like Amazon API Gateway (https://aws.amazon.com/api-gateway/).

Before going into further detail about how to create a CI/CD pipeline for a serverless application, we will look at the corresponding architecture. Figure 12.1 shows how serverless services like Amazon API Gateway, Amazon DynamoDB, Amazon S3, and AWS Lambda fit into the application architecture.

AWS Lambda empowers microservice development. That being said, each endpoint triggers a different Lambda function. These functions are independent of one another and can be written in different languages. Hence, this leads to scaling at the function level, easier unit testing, and loose coupling. All requests from clients first go through API Gateway. It then routes the incoming request to the right Lambda

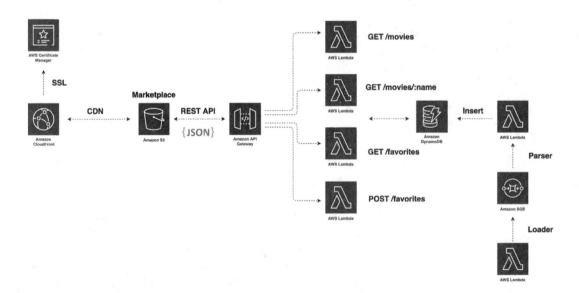

Figure 12.1   Watchlist application based on serverless architecture. Each Lambda function is responsible for a single API endpoint. The endpoints are managed through API Gateway and consumed by the Marketplace service hosted on an S3 bucket.

function accordingly. The functions are stateless, so that's where DynamoDB comes into the scene, to manage data persistence across Lambda functions. The Amazon S3 bucket is used to serve the marketplace static web application. Finally, an Amazon CloudFront distribution (optional) is used to deliver static assets such as Cascading Style Sheets (CSS) or JavaScript files from edge cache locations around the globe.

To deploy a Lambda function, we need to create an AWS Lambda resource and an IAM execution role with a list of AWS resources that the Lambda function has access to during runtime. For instance, the Lambda function `MoviesStoreListMovies` issues a `Scan` operation on a DynamoDB table to fetch a list of movies. Therefore, the Lambda execution role should grant access to the DynamoDB table.

To avoid duplication of code and provide a lightweight abstraction for creating Lambda functions, we will use Terraform modules. A *module* is a container for multiple resources that are used together.

NOTE You can use Terraform Registry (https://registry.terraform.io/) to download well-tested modules built by the community or publish your own modules remotely.

The module responsible for creating an AWS Lambda resource is located under the modules folder (chapter12/terraform/modules). Create a new lambda.tf file with a module block for each Lambda function, as shown in the following listing. The module resource references the custom module through the `source` argument and overrides default variables such as the Lambda runtime environment and environment variables.

Listing 12.1 Creating Lambda functions with the Terraform module

```
module "MoviesLoader" {
  source = "./modules/function"
  name = "MoviesLoader"
  handler = "index.handler"
  runtime = "python3.7"
  environment = {
    SQS_URL = aws_sqs_queue.queue.id
  }
}

module "MoviesParser" {
  source = "./modules/function"
  name = "MoviesParser"
  handler = "main"
  runtime = "go1.x"
  environment = {
    TABLE_NAME = aws_dynamodb_table.movies.id
  }
}

module "MoviesStoreListMovies" {
  source = "./modules/function"
  name = "MoviesStoreListMovies"
```

```
    handler = "src/movies/findAll/index.handler"
    runtime = "nodejs14.x"
    environment = {
      TABLE_NAME = aws_dynamodb_table.movies.id
    }
}

module "MoviesStoreSearchMovies" {
    source = "./modules/function"
    name = "MoviesStoreSearchMovies"
    handler = "src/movies/findOne/index.handler"
    runtime = "nodejs14.x"
    environment = {
      TABLE_NAME = aws_dynamodb_table.movies.id
    }
}

module "MoviesStoreViewFavorites" {
    source = "./modules/function"
    name = "MoviesStoreViewFavorites"
    handler = "src/favorites/findAll/index.handler"
    runtime = "nodejs14.x"
    environment = {
      TABLE_NAME = aws_dynamodb_table.favorites.id
    }
}

module "MoviesStoreAddToFavorites" {
    source = "./modules/function"
    name = "MoviesStoreAddToFavorites"
    handler = "src/favorites/insert/index.handler"
    runtime = "nodejs14.x"
    environment = {
      TABLE_NAME = aws_dynamodb_table.favorites.id
    }
}
```

This code will provision a `MoviesLoader` Lambda function based on the Python 3.7 runtime environment, a `MoviesParser` function based on the Go runtime, and a `MoviesStoreListMovies` function based on the Node.js environment.

Next, we will deploy a RESTful API with Amazon API Gateway and define HTTP endpoints to trigger the Lambda functions upon incoming HTTP/HTTPS requests. The Terraform code in listing 12.2 exposes a GET method on the /movies resource. When a GET method is invoked on the /movies endpoint, the `MoviesStoreList-Movies` Lambda function will be triggered to return a list of IMDb movies stored on the DynamoDB table. Add the code shown in the following listing to apigateway.tf.

> **Listing 12.2   GET /movies endpoint definition**

```
resource "aws_api_gateway_resource" "path_movies" {
    rest_api_id = aws_api_gateway_rest_api.api.id
    parent_id   = aws_api_gateway_rest_api.api.root_resource_id
```

```
    path_part    = "movies"
}
module "GetMovies" {
  source = "./modules/method"
  api_id = aws_api_gateway_rest_api.api.id
  resource_id = aws_api_gateway_resource.path_movies.id
  method = "GET"
  lambda_arn = module.MoviesStoreListMovies.arn
  invoke_arn = module.MoviesStoreListMovies.invoke_arn
  api_execution_arn = aws_api_gateway_rest_api.api.execution_arn
}
```

> **NOTE** In addition to providing a unified entry point for Lambda functions, API Gateway comes with powerful features such as caching, cross-origin resource sharing (CORS) configuration, security, and authentication.

Define the rest of the API endpoints, or download the complete apigateway.tf file from chapter12/terraform/apigateway.tf.

The Movies Marketplace content—including HTML, CSS, JavaScript, images, and other files—will be hosted in an Amazon S3 bucket. The end users will then access the application by using the public website URL exposed by Amazon S3. Hence, we don't need to run any web server such as NGINX or Apache to make the web application available. The Terraform code in the following listing (s3.tf) creates an S3 bucket and enables website hosting.

Listing 12.3   S3 website hosting configuration

```
resource "aws_s3_bucket" "marketplace" {
  bucket = "marketplace.${var.domain_name}"
  acl    = "public-read"
  website {
    index_document = "index.html"
    error_document = "index.html"
  }
}
```

The bucket access-control list (ACL) must be set to `public-read`. The `website` block is where we define the index document for the application. Also, we grant access to the static content by attaching a bucket policy. The bucket policy grants `s3:GetObject` to all principals for any object in the bucket.

> **NOTE** Unless you want to access the marketplace via the S3 bucket URL, you can use CloudFront on top of S3 to serve the application content by using a custom domain name over SSL.

Install the local modules with the `terraform init` command and run `terraform apply` to provision the AWS resources. Creating the whole infrastructure should take a few seconds. After the creation steps are complete, the API and marketplace URLs will be displayed in the `Outputs` section, as you can see in figure 12.2.

```
Apply complete! Resources: 57 added, 0 changed, 0 destroyed.

Outputs:

api = https://kvgfot7n4l.execute-api.eu-west-3.amazonaws.com/test
marketplace = marketplace.slowcoder.com.s3-website.eu-west-3.amazonaws.com
```

Figure 12.2 API Gateway and S3 website URLs

The `api` variable holds the RESTful API URL powered by API Gateway, and the `marketplace` variable is the S3 website URL for the marketplace application. If you head to AWS Lambda console (http://mng.bz/10Qg), the Lambda functions in figure 12.3 should be deployed.

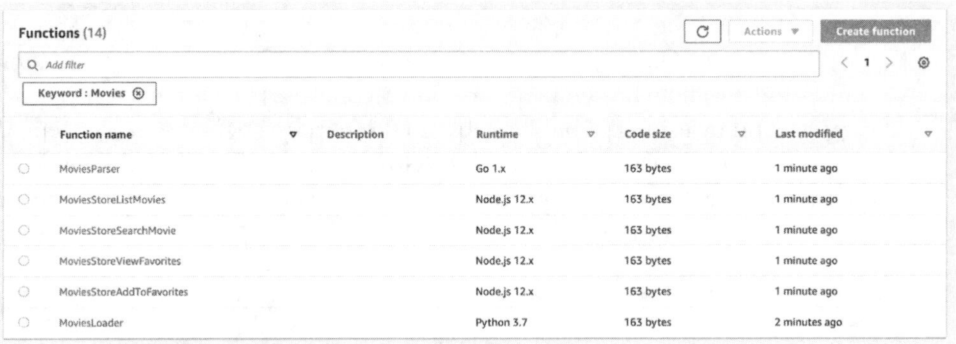
Functions (14)
Actions
Create function
Add filter
Keyword : Movies
Function name
Description
Runtime
Code size
Last modified
MoviesParser
Go 1.x
163 bytes
1 minute ago
MoviesStoreListMovies
Node.js 12.x
163 bytes
1 minute ago
MoviesStoreSearchMovie
Node.js 12.x
163 bytes
1 minute ago
MoviesStoreViewFavorites
Node.js 12.x
163 bytes
1 minute ago
MoviesStoreAddToFavorites
Node.js 12.x
163 bytes
1 minute ago
MoviesLoader
Python 3.7
163 bytes
2 minutes ago

Figure 12.3 Watchlist application's Lambda functions

Point your favorite browser to the API Gateway URL, and navigate to the /movies endpoint. The HTTP request should trigger the `MoviesStoreListMovies` Lambda function responsible for listing movies. The error message in figure 12.4 will be displayed.

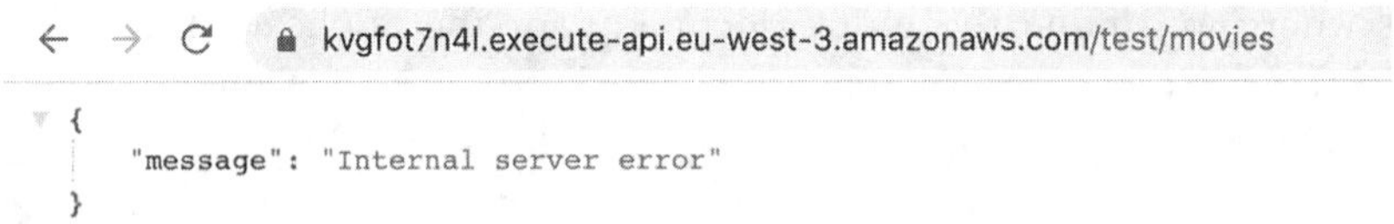
kvgfot7n4l.execute-api.eu-west-3.amazonaws.com/test/movies
{
"message": "Internal server error"
}

Figure 12.4 `MoviesStoreListMovies` HTTP response

Right now, no code is deployed to Lambda functions, so there would be nothing to see. To list movies, we need to deploy the function's code to the Lambda resource. In the upcoming section, we will create a CI/CD pipeline in Jenkins to automate the deployment of Lambda functions. Figure 12.5 illustrates the target CI/CD workflow.

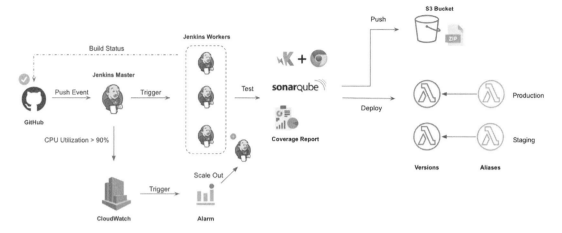

Figure 12.5 CI/CD workflow for a serverless application

A pipeline will be triggered whenever you make a change to your application's source code. The Jenkins master will schedule the build on one of the available Jenkins workers. The worker will execute the stages described in the Jenkinsfile located in the root directory of the application Git repository. The stages `Checkout` and `Tests` are given in chapter 8. The `Build` stage will compile the source code, install needed dependencies, and generate a deployment package (zip archive). Next, the `Push` stage will store the zip file in a remote S3 bucket and finally, the `Deploy` stage will be executed to update the Lambda function's code with the newest changes.

12.2 Creating deployment packages

Before integrating the serverless application in Jenkins, we need to store the Lambda functions' source code in a centralized remote repository for versioning. When it comes to serverless applications, two strategies are most used to organize functions into repositories:

- *Mono-repo*—Everything is put into the same repository; cohesive functions that work together to serve a business feature are grouped together under the same repository.
- *One repository per service*—Each Lambda function gets its own Git repository, with its own CI/CD pipeline.

This section doesn't go into the details around which is better, but instead shows how to build a CI/CD pipeline with the two approaches.

12.2.1 Mono-repo strategy

The MoviesLoader service, which consists of a single Lambda function written in Python, is responsible for loading a list of movies into a message queue. Create a GitHub repository, shown in figure 12.6, for the movies-loader Lambda function, and

Branch: develop ▾	New pull request			Create new file Upload files Find file Clone or download ▾

mlabouardy creating deployment packages		Latest commit d012270 10 seconds ago
☐ .gitignore	creating deployment packages	10 seconds ago
☐ Dockerfile.test	creating deployment packages	10 seconds ago
☐ Jenkinsfile	creating deployment packages	10 seconds ago
☐ index.py	creating deployment packages	10 seconds ago
☐ movies.json	creating deployment packages	10 seconds ago
☐ requirements.txt	creating deployment packages	10 seconds ago
☐ test_index.py	creating deployment packages	10 seconds ago

Figure 12.6   MoviesLoader Lambda function GitHub repository

then push the source code available in the book's repository (chapter12/functions) to the develop branch.

The Jenkinsfile (chapter12/functions/movies-loader/Jenkinsfile) is stored in the root repository. It's similar to the one provided in chapter 8's listing 8.3. Upon a push event, it will check out the function source code and run unit tests inside a Docker container. Having proper unit tests in place safeguards against subsequent Lambda code updates. This definition file, shown in the following listing, must be committed to the Lambda function's code repository.

Listing 12.4   Running function unit tests inside a Docker container

```
def imageName = 'mlabouardy/movies-loader'
node('workers'){
    try {
        stage('Checkout'){
            checkout scm
            notifySlack('STARTED')          ◁── Sends a Slack notification when
        }                                        the build starts, by using the
                                                 custom notifySlack method
        stage('Unit Tests'){
            def imageTest= docker.build("${imageName}-test", "-f
    Dockerfile.test .")
            imageTest.inside{
                sh "python test_index.py"
            }
        }
    } catch(e){
        currentBuild.result = 'FAILED'      ◁── When an error occurs, it's cached here,
        throw e                                  and the currentBuild.result variable is
    } finally {                                  set to FAILED so the right Slack
        notifySlack(currentBuild.result)    ◁──  notification will be sent afterward.
    }
}
```

When the pipeline is completed (success or failure), a Slack notification is sent to raise awareness about the pipeline status.

In listing 12.5, we create a deployment package, which is a zip file that includes both the Python code and any dependencies that the code needs to run. The `Build` stage generates a zip file and uses the Git commit ID as a name. Finally, we push the zip file to an S3 bucket for versioning and delete the file to save space.

Listing 12.5 Generating a deployment package

```
def functionName = 'MoviesLoader'
def imageName = 'mlabouardy/movies-loader'
def bucket = 'deployment-packages-watchlist'
def region = 'AWS REGION'

node('workers'){
    try {
        stage('Checkout'){...}

        stage('Unit Tests'){...}

        stage('Build'){
            sh "zip -r ${commitId}.zip index.py movies.json"
        }

        stage('Push'){
            sh "aws s3 cp ${commitId}.zip s3://${bucket}/${functionName}/"
        }
    } catch(e){
        currentBuild.result = 'FAILED'
        throw e
    } finally {
        notifySlack(currentBuild.result)
        sh "rm -rf ${commitId}.zip "
    }
}
```

The name of the S3 bucket where the deployment packages (zip files) are stored

Clones the Git repository. The instruction was omitted for brevity; see chapter 12/functions/movies-loader/ Jenkinsfile for the command.

Runs unit tests within a Docker container. See chapter 12/ functions/movies-loader/Jenkinsfile for instructions.

Stores the archive to an S3 bucket

Creates an archive (zip file) with the function entrypoint (index.py) and the movies JSON array. The commitId function is used to create a unique ID for the archive based on the current Git commit ID.

Deletes the archive at the end of the pipeline to save hard disk space

> **NOTE** We use the Git commit ID as a name for the deployment package to give a meaningful and significant name for each release and be able to roll back to a specific commit if things go wrong.

On Jenkins, create a new multibranch pipeline job for the `MoviesLoader` lambda function (refer to chapter 7 for a step-by-step guide). Jenkins will discover the develop branch, and a new build will start; see figure 12.7.

	Checkout	Unit Tests	Build	Push
Average stage times: (Average full run time: ~11s)	2s	3s	888ms	1s
#5 May 28 19:36 — No Changes	2s	3s	888ms	1s

Figure 12.7 MoviesLoader Lambda function pipeline

You can drill down to see the steps on the UI that match our steps in the Jenkinsfile. While Jenkins is executing each stage, you can see the activity. You can see the tests running as part of the Unit Tests stage (figure 12.8). If tests are successful, a zip file will be generated and stored in an S3 bucket.

```
[Pipeline] sh
+ zip -r 5e8eb15d2de87a28572a4489e868b1b642e877b8.zip index.py movies.json
  adding: index.py (deflated 47%)
  adding: movies.json (deflated 79%)
[Pipeline] }
[Pipeline] // stage
[Pipeline] stage
[Pipeline] { (Push)
[Pipeline] sh
+ git rev-parse HEAD
[Pipeline] readFile
[Pipeline] sh
+ rm .git/commitID
[Pipeline] sh
+ aws s3 cp 5e8eb15d2de87a28572a4489e868b1b642e877b8.zip s3://deployment-packages-watchlist/MoviesLoader/
Completed 2.7 KiB/2.7 KiB (6.1 KiB/s) with 1 file(s) remaining
upload: ./5e8eb15d2de87a28572a4489e868b1b642e877b8.zip to s3://deployment-packages-
watchlist/MoviesLoader/5e8eb15d2de87a28572a4489e868b1b642e877b8.zip
```

Figure 12.8   Pipeline execution logs

Open the S3 console and click the bucket used by the pipeline for package storage. A new deployment package should be available with a key name identical to the Git commit ID, as shown in figure 12.9.

Figure 12.9   S3 bucket for deployment packages storage

Similarly for the movies-parser function, push the function source code to a dedicated GitHub repository, shown in figure 12.10.

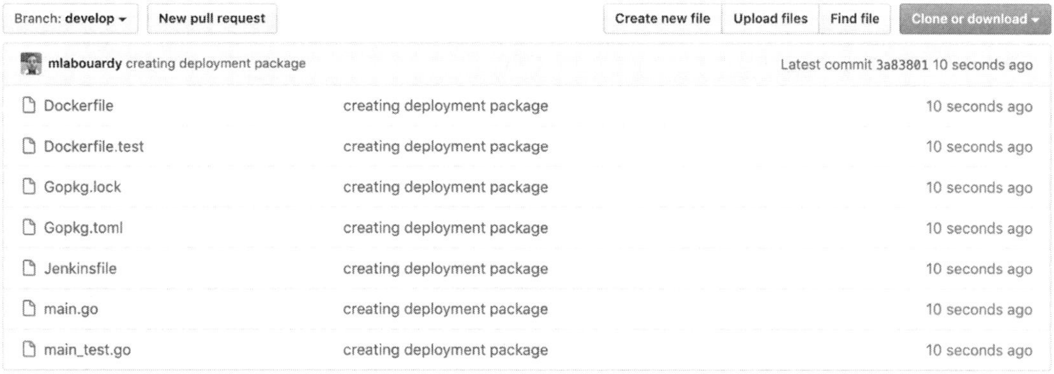

Figure 12.10   MoviesParser Lambda function GitHub repository

Create a Jenkinsfile (chapter12/functions/movies-parser/Jenkinsfile) with similar stages to chapter 8's listing 8.8 in the top-level directory of the Git repository; see the following listing.

Listing 12.6   Running function pre-integration tests in parallel

```
def imageName = 'mlabouardy/movies-parser'

node('workers'){
    try{
        stage('Checkout'){
            checkout scm
        }

        def imageTest= docker.build("${imageName}-test",
"-f Dockerfile.test .")
        stage('Pre-integration Tests'){
            parallel(
                'Quality Tests': {
                    imageTest.inside{
                        sh 'golint'
                    }
                },
                'Unit Tests': {
                    imageTest.inside{
                        sh 'go test'
                    }
                },
                'Security Tests': {
                    imageTest.inside('-u root:root'){
                        sh 'nancy /go/src/github/mlabouardy/
movies-parser/Gopkg.lock'
                    }
                }
            )
```

```
        }
    } catch(e){
        currentBuild.result = 'FAILED'
        throw e
    } finally {
        notifySlack(currentBuild.result)
    }
}
```

The function is written in Go, so we need to build a binary with the Docker multistage build feature, as explained in listing 9.2. Then, we copy the built binary from the Docker container and generate a zip package. Finally, we push the deployment package to the S3 bucket, as shown in the following listing.

Listing 12.7 Building a Go-based Lambda deployment package

```
def functionName = 'MoviesParser'
def imageName = 'mlabouardy/movies-parser'
def region = 'eu-west-3'

node('workers'){
    try{
        stage('Checkout'){...}              Refer to listing 12.6
        stage('Pre-integration Tests'){...} for the instructions.

        stage('Build'){
          sh """
          docker build -t ${imageName} .
          docker run --rm ${imageName}
          docker cp ${imageName}:/go/src/github.com/mlabouardy/
movies-parser/main main
          zip -r ${commitID()}.zip main
          """
        }

        stage('Push'){
          sh "aws s3 cp ${commitID()}.zip s3://${bucket}/${functionName}/"
        }
    } catch(e){
        currentBuild.result = 'FAILED'
        throw e
    } finally {
        notifySlack(currentBuild.result)
        sh "rm ${commitID()}.zip"
    }
}
```

Push the changes to the movies-parser Git repository, and create a new multibranch pipeline job for movies-parser. The pipeline stages should be executed. Upon completion, the pipeline should look like figure 12.11 in the Blue Ocean view.

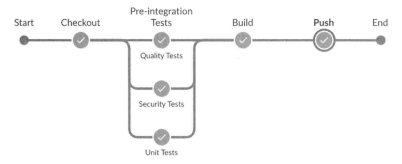

Figure 12.11 MoviesParser Lambda function workflow

Figure 12.12 shows the console output of the Push stage. The function deployment package will be stored under the MoviesParser subfolder.

 **Console Output**

```
+ aws s3 cp 1b073885e88d279e5948dce042ebc364862252ac.zip s3://deployment-packages-watchlist/MoviesParser/
Completed 256.0 KiB/6.9 MiB (540.0 KiB/s) with 1 file(s) remaining
Completed 512.0 KiB/6.9 MiB (1.0 MiB/s) with 1 file(s) remaining
Completed 768.0 KiB/6.9 MiB (1.5 MiB/s) with 1 file(s) remaining
Completed 1.0 MiB/6.9 MiB (2.0 MiB/s) with 1 file(s) remaining
Completed 1.2 MiB/6.9 MiB (2.5 MiB/s) with 1 file(s) remaining
Completed 1.5 MiB/6.9 MiB (3.0 MiB/s) with 1 file(s) remaining
Completed 1.8 MiB/6.9 MiB (3.5 MiB/s) with 1 file(s) remaining
Completed 2.0 MiB/6.9 MiB (3.8 MiB/s) with 1 file(s) remaining
```

Figure 12.12   Publishing deployment package to S3

The obvious counterpart to the multi-repo pattern is the mono-repo approach. In this pattern, a single repository holds a collection of Lambda functions grouped by business capabilities.

12.2.2 *Multi-repo strategy*

The Movies Store API is split into multiple Lambda functions (MoviesStoreList-Movies, MoviesStoreSearchMovie, MoviesStoreViewFavorites, Movies-StoreAddToFavorites). The easiest way to share code among these functions is by having them all together in a single repository. Create a new GitHub repository (chapter12/functions/movies-store), shown in figure 12.13.

The src/ folder at the root is made up of a collection of services. Each service deals with a relatively small and self-contained function. For instance, the movies/findAll folder is responsible for serving a list of movies from the DynamoDB table. The package.json file is located at the root of the repo. However, it is fairly common to have a separate package.json inside each service directory.

Branch: develop ▾ New pull request		Create new file Upload files Find file Clone or download ▾
🖼 **mlabouardy** create deployment package		Latest commit 516b628 15 seconds ago
📁 src	create deployment package	15 seconds ago
📁 test	create deployment package	15 seconds ago
📄 .dockerignore	create deployment package	15 seconds ago
📄 .eslintrc.json	create deployment package	15 seconds ago
📄 .gitignore	create deployment package	15 seconds ago
📄 Dockerfile	create deployment package	15 seconds ago
📄 Dockerfile.test	create deployment package	15 seconds ago
📄 Jenkinsfile	create deployment package	15 seconds ago
📄 package-lock.json	create deployment package	15 seconds ago
📄 package.json	create deployment package	15 seconds ago

Figure 12.13   Multiple Lambda functions stored in single repository

On the movies-store repository, create a Jenkinsfile (chapter12/functions/movies-store/Jenkinsfile) by using your favorite text editor or IDE with the content in the following listing. Refer to listing 8.14 for more details about the implemented stages.

Listing 12.8   Running quality tests and generating code coverage reports

```
def imageName = 'mlabouardy/movies-store'
node('workers'){
    try {
        stage('Checkout'){
            checkout scm
            notifySlack('STARTED')
        }

        def imageTest= docker.build("${imageName}-test",
"-f Dockerfile.test .")

        stage('Tests'){
            parallel(
                'Quality Tests': {
                    sh "docker run --rm ${imageName}-test npm run lint"
                },
                'Unit Tests': {
                    sh "docker run --rm ${imageName}-test npm run test"
                },
                'Coverage Reports': {
                    sh "docker run --rm
-v $PWD/coverage:/app/coverage ${imageName}-test
npm run coverage"
                    publishHTML (target: [
                        allowMissing: false,
                        alwaysLinkToLastBuild: false,
                        keepAll: true,
                        reportDir: "$PWD/coverage",
                        reportFiles: "index.html",
```

```
                    reportName: "Coverage Report"
                ])
            }
        )
    }
} catch(e){
    currentBuild.result = 'FAILED'
    throw e
} finally {
    notifySlack(currentBuild.result)
}
}
```

Next, we run a Docker container from a Node.js base image to install external dependencies by running the npm install command. Then, we copy the node_modules folder from the running container to the current workspace and create a zip file, as shown in the next listing. The deployment package size will impact the functions' cold start. To keep the deployment package size smaller, we install only the runtime dependencies by passing --prod=only to the npm install command.

Listing 12.9 Building a Node.js-based Lambda deployment package

```
stage('Build'){
    sh """
      docker build -t ${imageName} .
      containerName=\$(docker run -d ${imageName})
      docker cp \$containerName:/app/node_modules node_modules
      docker rm -f \$containerName
      zip -r ${commitID()}.zip node_modules src
    """
}
```

> **NOTE** One drawback of dynamic provisioning is a phenomenon called *cold start*. Essentially, functions that haven't been used for a while take longer to start up and to handle the first request.

Then, in the following listing, we push the generated zip file to an S3 bucket, use a loop to go through each function name, and save the zip in an S3 bucket under the function folder. You can use the Serverless framework (www.serverless.com) to create a zip file per function and exclude unused dependencies and files.

Listing 12.10 Publishing Node.js deployment packages to S3

```
def functions = ['MoviesStoreListMovies',
'MoviesStoreSearchMovie',
'MoviesStoreSearchMovie',
'MoviesStoreAddToFavorites']
def bucket = 'deployment-packages-watchlist'

node('workers'){
    try {
        stage('Checkout'){...}
        stage('Tests'){...}
```

```
        stage('Build'){...}

        stage('Push'){
            functions.each { function ->
                sh "aws s3 cp ${commitID()}.zip s3://${bucket}/${function}/"
            }
        }
    } catch(e){
        currentBuild.result = 'FAILED'
        throw e
    } finally {
        notifySlack(currentBuild.result)
        sh "rm --rf ${commitID()}.zip"
    }
}
```

Head back to the Jenkins dashboard, create a new multibranch pipeline job for the movies-store project, and commit the changes to the develop branch. In a few seconds, a new build should be triggered on the movies-store job for the develop branch. On the resultant page, you will see the Stage view for the develop branch pipeline, shown in figure 12.14.

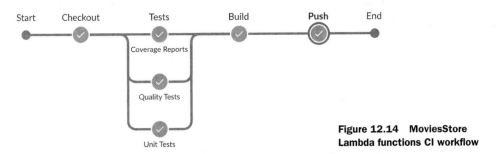

Figure 12.14 MoviesStore Lambda functions CI workflow

For common situations, the build and push stages can take a good amount of the CI/CD execution time. Therefore, we can use the `parallel` key, as shown in the following listing, to run the push stage in parallel, to keep the pipeline turnaround time short.

Listing 12.11   Parallel directive with a map structure

```
stage('Push'){                                          Sets the archive's name
    def fileName = commitID()        <──┘               to the Git commit ID
    def parallelStagesMap = functions.collectEntries {
      ["${it}" : {
         stage("Lambda: ${it}") {
           sh "aws s3 cp ${fileName}.zip s3://${bucket}/${it}/"
         }
      }]
    }
    parallel parallelStagesMap    <──┐
}
                  Runs the stages in parallel
```

Parallel directive is expecting a map structure, so we're building one. We iterate over the functions list and create the corresponding command to store the archive file to the appropriate S3 folder.

The `parallel` directive takes a map of the string and closure. The string is the display name of the parallel execution (name of the function), and the closure is the actual `aws s3 cp` instruction to copy the deployment package to the corresponding function folder in S3. As a result, storing the deployment packages for each function will be run in parallel, as shown in figure 12.15.

Figure 12.15   MoviesStore CI workflow

Once the pipeline execution is completed, in the S3 bucket, a deployment package should be stored for each Lambda function, as shown in figure 12.16.

Viewing 1 to 5

	Name ▼	Last modified ▼	Size ▼	Storage class ▼
☐	📁 MoviesLoader	--	--	--
☐	📁 MoviesParser	--	--	--
☐	📁 MoviesStoreAddToFavorites	--	--	--
☐	📁 MoviesStoreListMovies	--	--	--
☐	📁 MoviesStoreSearchMovie	--	--	--

Figure 12.16   Lambda functions deployment packages

By now, the deployment packages are stored in an S3 bucket, so we can go ahead and update the Lambda function source code with the built zip files.

12.3   *Updating Lambda function code*

For `MoviesLoader` and `MoviesParser` Lambda functions, add the following `Deploy` stage to their Jenkinsfiles (chapter12/functions/movies-loader/Jenkinsfile and chapter12/functions/movies-parser/Jenkinsfile). The stage uses the AWS Lambda CLI to issue an `update-function-code` command to update the function code with the zip file stored previously in the S3 bucket; see the following listing.

Listing 12.12   Updating the Lambda function's code with AWS CLI

```
stage('Deploy'){
    sh "aws lambda update-function-code --function-name ${functionName}
            --s3-bucket ${bucket} --s3-key ${functionName}/${commitID()}.zip
            --region ${region}"
}
```

The command takes as an argument the name of the S3 bucket where the zip file is stored as well as the Amazon S3 key of the deployment package.

Once you push the changes to the Git remote repository, Jenkins will update the Lambda function's code with the `update-function-code` command. The output in figure 12.17 confirms that.

Console Output

```
+ aws lambda update-function-code --function-name MoviesLoader --s3-bucket deployment-packages-watchlist --s3-key
MoviesLoader/5e8eb15d2de87a28572a4489e868b1b642e877b8.zip --region eu-west-3
{
    "FunctionName": "MoviesLoader",
    "LastModified": "2020-05-29T15:43:27.094+0000",
    "RevisionId": "46414431-f7c6-4199-9ade-80a385ccbe3d",
    "MemorySize": 128,
    "Environment": {
        "Variables": {
            "SQS_URL": "https://sqs.eu-west-3.amazonaws.com/305929695733/movies_to_parse"
        }
    },
    "Version": "$LATEST",
    "Role": "arn:aws:iam::305929695733:role/MoviesLoaderRole",
    "Timeout": 10,
    "Runtime": "python3.7",
    "TracingConfig": {
        "Mode": "PassThrough"
    },
    "CodeSha256": "udtoEDeFVkn73aQr9S9kmoBgqbyQzLB7pA+RCeyMmK0=",
    "Description": "",
    "CodeSize": 2725,
    "FunctionArn": "arn:aws:lambda:eu-west-3:305929695733:function:MoviesLoader",
    "Handler": "index.handler"
}
```

**Figure 12.17
UpdateFunction-
Code operation logs**

The CI/CD pipelines for the `MoviesLoader` and `MoviesParser` functions should contain the stages shown in figure 12.18.

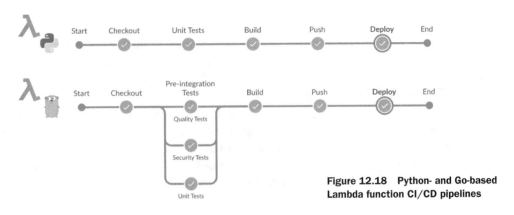

**Figure 12.18   Python- and Go-based
Lambda function CI/CD pipelines**

> **NOTE** The Serverless framework (https://serverless.com/) or AWS Serverless Application Model (SAM) can also be used to write and deploy Lambda functions within Jenkins pipelines.

Similarly, add the same stage to the `MoviesStore` Lambda functions—except this time, we will wrap the `update-function-code` command with a `for` loop to update each function versioning within the same GitHub repository; see the following listing.

Listing 12.13 Updating multiple Lambda functions

```
stage('Deploy'){
  functions.each { function ->
    sh "aws lambda update-function-code
--function-name ${function}
--s3-bucket ${bucket}
--s3-key ${function}/${commitID()}.zip
--region ${region}"
  }
}
```

When the new stage is committed, the pipeline will be triggered upon a push event, and the CI/CD stages in figure 12.19 will be executed.

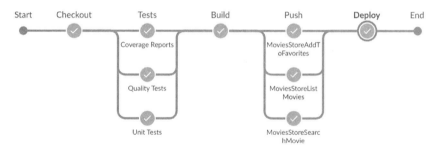

Figure 12.19 MoviesStore CI/CD pipeline

Before we automate the deployment of the marketplace, we need to load some data into the DynamoDB table. Trigger the `MoviesLoader` function from AWS Management Console, or by issuing the following command from your terminal session:

```
aws lambda invoke --function-name MoviesLoader --payload '{}' response.json
```

> **NOTE** Make sure to assign the `AWSLambda_FullAccess` policy to the IAM user configured with your AWS CLI.

The preceding command will invoke the `MoviesLoader` function and save the function's output in the response.json file. The function will load movies to SQS and trigger the `MoviesParser` Lambda function, which will crawl the movie's IMDb page and store its information in the Movies DynamoDB table, shown in figure 12.20.

Figure 12.20   Movies DynamoDB table

Each message in SQS will invoke the `MoviesParser` function; once the queue is empty, the DynamoDB table should contain the top 100 IMDb movies.

12.4   *Hosting a static website on S3*

The Movie Marketplace is a single-page application (SPA), written in TypeScript, using the Angular framework. The application serves static content (HTML, JavaScript, and CSS files), which can be a good fit for S3 website-hosting features.

Let's automate the deployment of the marketplace to an S3 bucket, as shown in the next listing. First, create a GitHub project to version the marketplace source code. Then, write a Jenkinsfile to run quality, unit tests, and static code analysis with SonarQube. Refer to chapter 8 for more details.

Listing 12.14   Integrating an Angular application with the Jenkinsfile

```
def imageName = 'mlabouardy/movies-marketplace'
def region = 'AWS REGION'

node('workers'){
    try{
        stage('Checkout'){
            checkout scm
            notifySlack('STARTED')
        }

        def imageTest= docker.build("${imageName}-test",
"-f Dockerfile.test .")
        stage('Quality Tests'){
            sh "docker run --rm ${imageName}-test npm run lint"
        }
        stage('Unit Tests'){
            sh "docker run --rm
-v $PWD/coverage:/app/coverage
${imageName}-test npm run test"
```

Builds a Docker image based on Dockerfile.test to run automated tests

Runs the code linting process

Runs unit tests and generates a coverage report

```
            publishHTML (target: [
                allowMissing: false,
                alwaysLinkToLastBuild: false,
                keepAll: true,
                reportDir: "$PWD/coverage/marketplace",
                reportFiles: "index.html",
                reportName: "Coverage Report"
            ])
        }
        stage('Static Code Analysis'){
            withSonarQubeEnv('sonarqube') {
                sh 'sonar-scanner'
            }
        }
        stage("Quality Gate"){
            timeout(time: 5, unit: 'MINUTES') {
                def qg = waitForQualityGate()
                if (qg.status != 'OK') {
                    error "Pipeline aborted due to
quality gate failure: ${qg.status}"
                }
            }
        }
    } catch(e){
        currentBuild.result = 'FAILED'
        throw e
    } finally {
        notifySlack(currentBuild.result)
    }
}
```

- **Consumes the coverage report with the Jenkins Publish HTML plugin** — (points to publishHTML block)
- **Runs code-quality inspection with SonarQube** — (points to Static Code Analysis block)
- **Interrupts SonarQube inspection if it takes more than 5 minutes** — (points to Quality Gate block)

Add a `Build` stage to create a Docker container to install the npm dependencies and copy the dependencies folder as well as the generated static web application files to the current workspace, as shown in the following listing. Note the use of the `--build-arg` argument to inject the API Gateway URL at the build time.

Listing 12.15 Building the Angular application

```
stage('Build'){
        sh """
            docker build -t ${imageName} --build-arg ENVIRONMENT=sandbox .
            containerName=\$(docker run -d ${imageName})
            docker cp \$containerName:/app/dist dist
            docker rm -f \$containerName
        """
 }
```

Then, in the following listing, use the AWS CLI to push the generated static web application to the S3 bucket where website hosting is enabled.

Listing 12.16 Storing the Angular static application to S3

```
stage('Push'){
    sh "aws s3 cp --recursive dist/ s3://${bucket}/"    <-- Recursively copies local files to S3
}
```

Push the changes to the develop branch. A new pipeline should be triggered, and the stages in figure 12.21 will be executed successfully.

Start
Checkout
Quality Tests
Unit Tests
Static Code Analysis
Quality Gate
Build
Push
End

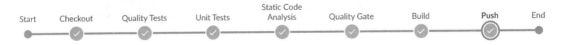

Figure 12.21 Marketplace CI/CD workflow

You can verify that the files have been successfully stored from the Amazon S3 bucket dashboard, or by running the `aws s3 ls` command in your terminal session. Figure 12.22 shows the content of the marketplace S3 bucket.

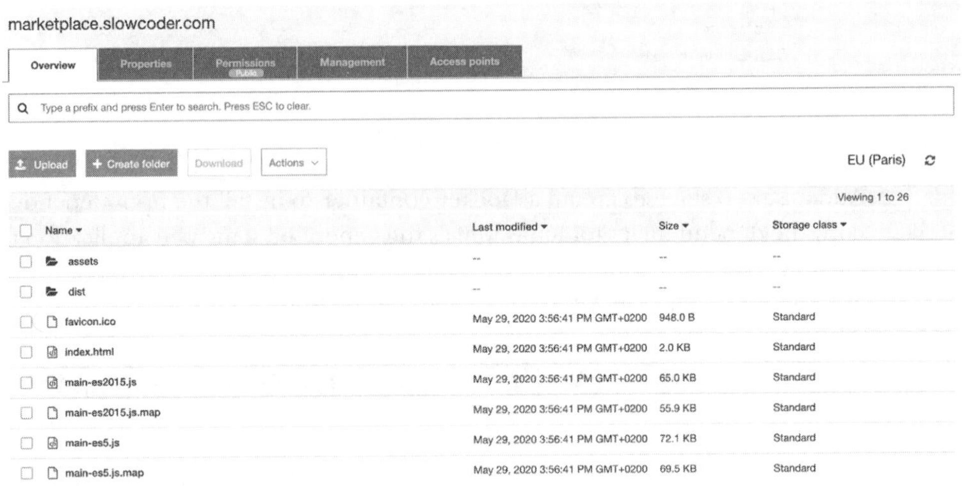

marketplace.slowcoder.com
Overview
Properties
Permissions
Public
Management
Access points
Type a prefix and press Enter to search. Press ESC to clear.
Upload
Create folder
Download
Actions
EU (Paris)
Viewing 1 to 26
Name
Last modified
Size
Storage class
assets
dist
favicon.ico
May 29, 2020 3:56:41 PM GMT+0200
948.0 B
Standard
index.html
May 29, 2020 3:56:41 PM GMT+0200
2.0 KB
Standard
main-es2015.js
May 29, 2020 3:56:41 PM GMT+0200
65.0 KB
Standard
main-es2015.js.map
May 29, 2020 3:56:41 PM GMT+0200
55.9 KB
Standard
main-es5.js
May 29, 2020 3:56:41 PM GMT+0200
72.1 KB
Standard
main-es5.js.map
May 29, 2020 3:56:41 PM GMT+0200
69.5 KB
Standard

Figure 12.22 Marketplace S3 bucket content

If you head to the S3 website URL (http://BUCKET.s3-website-REGION.amazonaws.com/), it should display the marketplace UI, shown in figure 12.23.

That's great! However, when you're building your serverless application, you must separate your deployment environments to test new changes without impacting your production. Therefore, having multiple environments makes sense while building serverless applications.

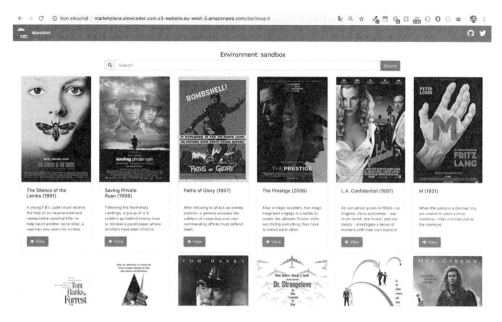

Figure 12.23   Marketplace dashboard running in the sandbox environment

12.5   *Maintaining multiple Lambda environments*

AWS Lambda allows you to publish a version, which represents the state of the function's code and configuration in time. By default, each Lambda function has the $LATEST version pointing to the latest changes deployed to the function.

To publish a new version from the $LATEST version, update the Jenkinsfile (chapter12/functions/movies-loader/Jenkinsfile) to add a new stage to publish a new Lambda function's version, as shown in the following listing.

Listing 12.17   Publishing a new Lambda version

```
stage('Deploy'){
    sh "aws lambda update-function-code --function-name ${functionName}
        --s3-bucket ${bucket} --s3-key ${functionName}/${commitID()}.zip
        --region ${region}"

    sh "aws lambda publish-version --function-name ${functionName}
        --description ${commitID()} --region ${region}"
}
```

When you publish a new version of your Lambda function, you should give it a meaningful version name that allows you to track different changes made to your function through its development cycle. In listing 12.17, we're using the Git commit ID as a version scheme. However, you can use an advanced version mechanism like semantic versioning (https://semver.org/).

When the pipeline is executed, at the `Deploy` stage the preceding commands will be executed. Figure 12.24 shows their execution logs.

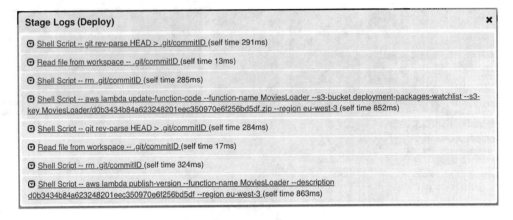

Stage Logs (Deploy)   ✖

⊙ Shell Script -- git rev-parse HEAD > .git/commitID (self time 291ms)

⊙ Read file from workspace -- .git/commitID (self time 13ms)

⊙ Shell Script -- rm .git/commitID (self time 285ms)

⊙ Shell Script -- aws lambda update-function-code --function-name MoviesLoader --s3-bucket deployment-packages-watchlist --s3-key MoviesLoader/d0b3434b84a623248201eec350970e6f256bd5df.zip --region eu-west-3 (self time 852ms)

⊙ Shell Script -- git rev-parse HEAD > .git/commitID (self time 284ms)

⊙ Read file from workspace -- .git/commitID (self time 17ms)

⊙ Shell Script -- rm .git/commitID (self time 324ms)

⊙ Shell Script -- aws lambda publish-version --function-name MoviesLoader --description d0b3434b84a623248201eec350970e6f256bd5df --region eu-west-3 (self time 863ms)

Figure 12.24   Update and Publish commands executed within the deploy stage

NOTE   Versions are immutable: once they're created, you cannot update their code or settings (memory, execution time, VPC config, and so forth).

On the MoviesLoader Lambda dashboard, a new version will be published based on the develop branch source code, as shown in figure 12.25.

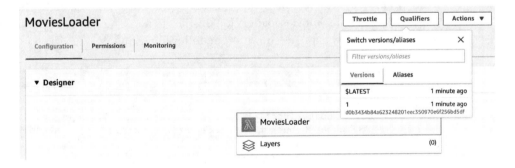

Figure 12.25   MoviesLoader Lambda new published version

The publication of Lambda versions for the MoviesStore API will be done in parallel to reduce the execution time of the pipeline; see figure 12.26.

As a result, you can work with different variations of your Lambda function in your development workflow.

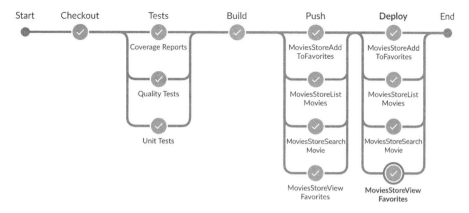

Figure 12.26   Running the publish command in parallel

For now, API Gateway triggers the `MoviesStore` Lambda functions based on the `$LATEST` version, so every time a new version is published, we need to update API Gateway to point to the newest version (figure 12.27)—a tedious and not handy task.

Figure 12.27   GET /favorites integration request

Fortunately, there's the concept of a *Lambda alias*. The alias, a pointer to a specific version, allows you to promote a function from one environment to another (such as staging to production). Aliases are mutable, unlike immutable versions. Now, instead of directly assigning a Lambda function version in an API Gateway integration request, you can assign Lambda alias, where the alias is a variable. The variable will be resolved from a value during runtime.

That being said, create an alias for the sandbox, staging, and production environments that points to the latest version published by using the AWS command line:

```
aws lambda create-alias --function-name MoviesStoreViewFavorites --name
    sandbox    --version 1
```

Once created, the new aliases should be added to the list of Aliases under the Qualifiers drop-down list (figure 12.28).

Figure 12.28   Using multiple aliases to reference different environments

We can update the Jenkinsfile to update the alias directly. Update the `Deploy` stage with the code in the next listing. It updates the Lambda function code, publishes a new version, and then points the alias corresponding to the current Git branch (master branch = production alias, preprod branch = staging alias, develop branch = sandbox alias) to the newly deployed version.

Listing 12.18   Updating the Lambda alias to point to the newest version

```
sh "aws lambda update-function-code --function-name ${it}
        --s3-bucket ${bucket} --s3-key ${it}/${fileName}.zip
        --region ${region}"

def version = sh(
    script: "aws lambda publish-version --function-name ${it}
                --description ${fileName}
--region ${region} | jq -r '.Version'",
    returnStdout: true
).trim()

if (env.BRANCH_NAME in ['master','preprod','develop']){
    sh "aws lambda update-alias  --function-name ${it}
            --name ${environments[env.BRANCH_NAME]}
--function-version ${version}
            --region ${region}"
}
```

The `publish-version` operation returns JSON output with the deployed version number as an attribute. The `jq` command is used to parse the `Version` attribute and store its value in a `version` variable. Then, based on the current Git branch, the corresponding alias will point to the published version number.

Push the changes to the develop branch. The function code will be updated, a new version will be created, and the sandbox alias will point to the newest published version, as you can see in figure 12.29.

Stage Logs (Lambda: MoviesStoreAddToFavorites)   ✖

⊙ Shell Script -- aws lambda update-function-code --function-name MoviesStoreAddToFavorites --s3-bucket deployment-packages-watchlist --s3-key MoviesStoreAddToFavorites/13743ba401a327940c767100ceb45de969829c0d.zip --region eu-west-3 (self time 1s)

⊙ Shell Script -- aws lambda publish-version --function-name MoviesStoreAddToFavorites --description 13743ba401a327940c767100ceb45de969829c0d --region eu-west-3 | jq -r '.Version' (self time 916ms)

⊙ Shell Script -- aws lambda update-alias --function-name MoviesStoreAddToFavorites --name sandbox --function-version 1 --region eu-west-3 (self time 1s)

Figure 12.29   Updating the Lambda alias to the deployed version

On the `MoviesStoreListMovies` Lambda, for instance, the sandbox alias should point to the version with the develop branch source code, as shown in figure 12.30.

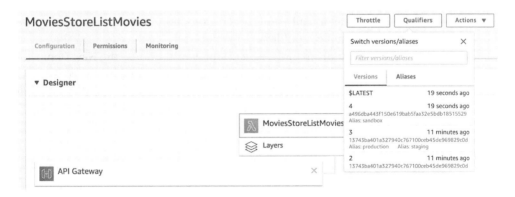

Figure 12.30   Sandbox alias pointing to the new Lambda version

Now that you have seen how to create aliases and switch their values within a Jenkins pipeline, let's configure the API Gateway to use these aliases with stage variables.

Stage variables are environment variables that can be used to change the behavior at runtime of the API Gateway methods for each deployment stage.

On the API Gateway Console, navigate to the Movies API, click the GET method for the instance, and update the target Lambda function to use a stage variable instead of a hardcoded Lambda function version, as shown in figure 12.31.

Figure 12.31   Using a stage variable while configuring the API integration request

In the Lambda Function field, the ${stageVariables.environment} tells API Gateway to read the value for this field from a stage variable at runtime.

When you save the configuration, a new prompt will ask you to grant the permissions to API Gateway to call your Lambda function aliases. At this point, we need to deploy our API to make it publicly available.

From the Actions drop-down, select Deploy API. Choose the New Deployment Stage option, enter sandbox as a stage name, and deploy it. Or use the Terraform code in listing 12.19. The sandbox stage will set the environment stage variable to sandbox. As a result, if a user invokes an HTTP request on any endpoint of the sandbox deployment, the corresponding Lambda function with the sandbox alias will be triggered.

Listing 12.19   API Deployment with an alias stage variable

```
resource "aws_api_gateway_deployment" "sandbox" {
  depends_on = [
    module.GetMovies,
    module.GetOneMovie,
    module.GetFavorites,
    module.PostFavorites
  ]

  variables = {
    "environment" = "sandbox"
  }
}
```

```
    rest_api_id = aws_api_gateway_rest_api.api.id
    stage_name  = "sandbox"
}
```

Create additional deployment stages for staging and production environments. On completion of the `terraform apply` command, the three deployment stage URLs will be displayed, as shown in figure 12.32.

```
Apply complete! Resources: 3 added, 0 changed, 0 destroyed.

Outputs:

api = https://rth65vizrb.execute-api.eu-west-3.amazonaws.com/test
marketplace = marketplace.slowcoder.com.s3-website.eu-west-3.amazonaws.com
production = https://rth65vizrb.execute-api.eu-west-3.amazonaws.com/production
sandbox = https://rth65vizrb.execute-api.eu-west-3.amazonaws.com/sandbox
staging = https://rth65vizrb.execute-api.eu-west-3.amazonaws.com/staging
```

Figure 12.32 API Gateway deployment URLs

If you open the API at https://id.execute-api.region.amazonaws.com/sandbox/movies, you will get the response from Lambda `MoviesStoreListMovies` with the alias `sandbox`.

To deploy the serverless application to the staging environment, create a pull request to merge the develop branch to the preprod branch. Jenkins will post the build status of the develop job on the PR (figure 12.33). Then, merge develop to preprod.

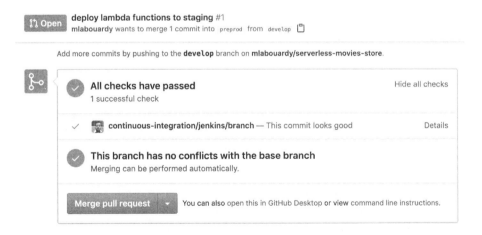

Figure 12.33 Jenkins post build status on GitHub PR

Once the PR is merged, a new build will be triggered on the preprod branch. At the end of the CI/CD pipeline, the staging alias will point to the newly deployed version, as you can see in figure 12.34.

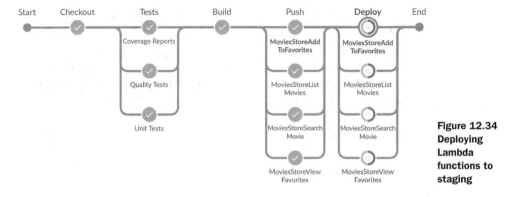

Figure 12.34 Deploying Lambda functions to staging

Now, to deploy the marketplace on multiple environments, we will inject the environment name based on the current branch name; see the following listing.

Listing 12.20 Injecting the environment name during the build

```
stage('Build'){
  sh """
    docker build -t ${imageName}
--build-arg ENVIRONMENT=${environments[env.BRANCH_NAME]} .
    containerName=\$(docker run -d ${imageName})
    docker cp \$containerName:/app/dist dist
    docker rm -f \$containerName
  """
}
```

Then, in listing 12.21, we update the `aws s3 cp` instruction to push the static files to a folder named as the environment name under the S3 bucket. You can also create an S3 bucket per environment, but for simplicity, we use a single S3 to store different environments of the marketplace.

Listing 12.21 Pushing static files to an S3 bucket

```
if (env.BRANCH_NAME in ['master','preprod','develop']){
  stage('Push'){
    sh "aws s3 cp --recursive dist/ s3://${bucket}/
      ${environments[env.BRANCH_NAME]}/"
  }
}
```

Push these changes to a feature branch. Then raise a pull request to merge to the develop branch. When the merge occurs, the new pipeline in figure 12.35 will be executed.

Figure 12.35   Marketplace new CI/CD pipeline

Merge the changes to preprod to deploy the application to staging. Then, merge from preprod to master branch for production deployment. As a result, the S3 bucket should contain three folders. Each folder holds a different runtime environment of the marketplace, as you can see in figure 12.36.

Figure 12.36 S3 bucket with multiple environments

If you point to the S3 bucket website URL and add the /staging endpoint, it should serve the staging environment of the marketplace, as shown in figure 12.37.

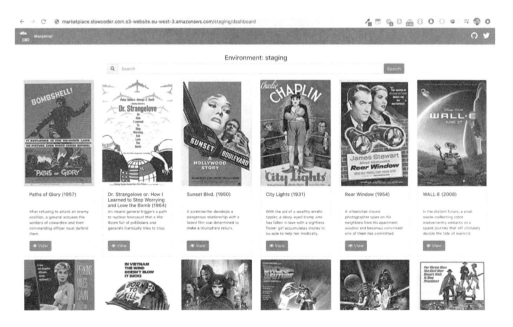

Figure 12.37 Marketplace staging environment

Now, to deploy the Lambda functions to production, merge the preprod branch to the master branch by raising a pull request, as shown in figure 12.38.

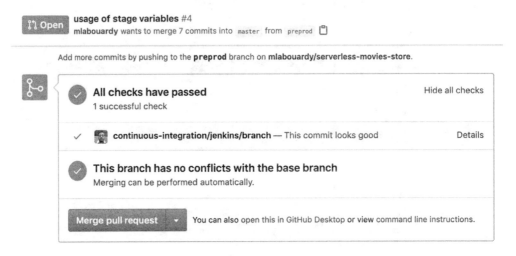

Figure 12.38   Merging the movies-store Lambda functions' preprod branch to master

When the merge occurs, the pipeline will be triggered on the master branch; see figure 12.39.

HEALTH	STATUS	BRANCH	COMMIT	LATEST MESSAGE	COMPLETED	
✿	✓	develop	—	usage of stage variables	3 minutes ago	★
✿	✓	preprod	—	usage of stage variables	a minute ago	★
✿	✓	feature/stage-variables	—	Push event to branch feature/stage-variables	4 minutes ago	★
✿	◯	master	2f9f888	Push event to branch master	-	★

Figure 12.39   Deploying Lambda functions to production

The movies-store functions will be updated, a new version will be created, and the production alias will point to the newly deployed version.

You can take this further and ask for developer authorization before actual deployment to production by using the Jenkins Input Step plugin; see the following listing. When the `Deploy` stage is reached, an input dialog will pop up for deployment confirmation.

Listing 12.22 Asking for user approval before production deployment

```
if (env.BRANCH_NAME == 'preprod' || env.BRANCH_NAME == 'develop'){
    sh "aws lambda update-alias  --function-name ${it}
            --name ${environments[env.BRANCH_NAME]}
--function-version ${version}
            --region ${region}"
}

if(env.BRANCH_NAME == 'master'){
    timeout(time: 2, unit: "HOURS") {
        input message: "Deploy to production?", ok: "Yes"
    }
    sh "aws lambda update-alias  --function-name ${it}
            --name ${environments[env.BRANCH_NAME]}
--function-version ${version}
            --region ${region}"
}
```

The interactive input will ask whether we approve the deployment. If we click Yes, the pipeline will be resumed, and the production alias will point to the newly deployed version, as shown in figure 12.40.

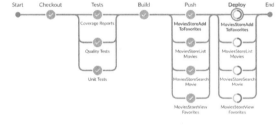

Figure 12.40 Production deployment confirmation within the Jenkins pipeline

So now if we make any change to our serverless application, CI/CD pipelines will be triggered, and the newly published Lambda function code will be promoted to production. A Slack notification will also be sent with the deployment job status, as shown in figure 12.41.

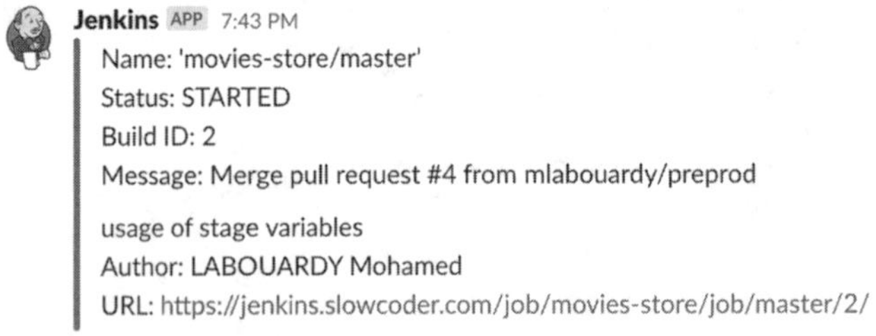

 Jenkins `APP` 7:43 PM
Name: 'movies-store/master'
Status: STARTED
Build ID: 2
Message: Merge pull request #4 from mlabouardy/preprod

usage of stage variables
Author: LABOUARDY Mohamed
URL: https://jenkins.slowcoder.com/job/movies-store/job/master/2/

**Figure 12.41
Production
deployment Slack
notification**

Sending notifications on pipeline triggering and progress helps to communicate the work among team members. So far, we have used it to send start, completed, and failure notifications. but Slack can also be used to take actions or execute commands from the chat window to confirm the production deployment, for instance, or trigger the build of a Jenkins job.

Another way of raising awareness of job build status and reporting testing results is through email notifications.

12.6 *Configuring email notification in Jenkins*

Email notification within Jenkins can be done with the help of an Email Extension plugin (https://plugins.jenkins.io/email-ext/). This plugin comes with a list of essentials plugins installed on Jenkins.

To enable email notification, you need to configure an SMTP server. Go to Manage Jenkins, then Configure System. Scroll down to the Extended E-mail Notification section. Enter your SMTP credentials, if you're using Gmail, and then type `smtp.gmail.com` for the SMTP server and enter your Gmail username and password. Select the use of SSL and enter the port number as 465.

To be able to send an email, you need to configure a list of recipient addresses. Next, click the Apply and Save buttons, as shown in figure 12.42.

Extended E-mail Notification

SMTP server	smtp.mail.eu-west-1.awsapps.com
Default user E-mail suffix	
☑ Use SMTP Authentication	
User Name	mohamed@labouardy.com
Password	....
Advanced Email Properties	
Use SSL	☑
SMTP port	465

Figure 12.42   Extended email notification configuration

You can test configurations by entering the recipient email address and clicking Test Configuration. If all is good, you will see the message `Email sent successfully`.

Now that the plugin is configured, type the following listing in your Jenkinsfile to define a function responsible for sending an email with customizable attributes based on the job build status.

Listing 12.23   Sending email to report job build status

```
def sendEmail(String buildStatus){
    buildStatus =  buildStatus ?: 'SUCCESSFUL'
    emailext body: "More info at: ${env.BUILD_URL}",
            subject: "Name: '${env.JOB_NAME}' Status: ${buildStatus}",
            to: '$DEFAULT_RECIPIENTS'
}
```

Finally, you can invoke the function upon the completion of the CI/CD pipeline by calling the `sendEmail()` method on the `finally` block. In the following listing, an email notification is sent only if a build is running on the master branch to avoid spamming developers.

Listing 12.24   Sending email when a production deployment is happening

```
node('workers'){
    try {
        stage('Checkout'){...}
        stage('Tests'){...}
        stage('Build'){...}
        stage('Push'){...}
        stage('Deploy'){...}
    } catch(e){
        currentBuild.result = 'FAILED'
        throw e
    } finally {
        notifySlack(currentBuild.result)

        if (env.BRANCH_NAME == 'master'){
            sendEmail(currentBuild.result)
        }
    }
}
```

Push the new Jenkinsfile to GitHub. When a build is occurring on the master branch, an email will be sent. Once the pipeline is finished, you should be able to see an email like the one in figure 12.43.

Figure 12.43   Email notification reporting job build status

The email's subject contains the name of the Jenkins job as well as its build status. The email's body has a link to the job output.

The declarative approach of writing Jenkinsfiles provides a `post` section, which can be used to place post-execution scripts. You can invoke the `sendEmail()` method by placing it in the `post` build section, as shown in the following listing.

Listing 12.25   Post steps in Jenkins declarative pipeline

```
pipeline {
    agent{
        label 'workers'
    }
    stages {
        stage('Checkout'){...}
        stage('Unit Tests'){...}
        stage('Build'){...}
        stage('Push'){...}
    }
    post {
        always {
            if (env.BRANCH_NAME == 'master'){
                sendEmail(currentBuild.currentResult)
            }
        }
    }
}
```

You can also attach the job build logs by enabling the `attachLog` attribute with the following listing.

Listing 12.26   Attaching log files in a notification mail

```
def sendEmail(String buildStatus){
    buildStatus =  buildStatus ?: 'SUCCESSFUL'
    emailext body: "More info at: ${env.BUILD_URL}",
            subject: "Name: '${env.JOB_NAME}' Status: ${buildStatus}",
            to: '$DEFAULT_RECIPIENTS',
            attachLog: true
}
```

As a result, email sent by Jenkins will now contain the job status as well the full console output as an attachment, as shown in figure 12.44.

Figure 12.44 Sending job logs as an email notification attachment

Summary

- Terraform modules allow you to better organize your infrastructure configuration code and make the resources reusable.
- When building a serverless application as a collection of Lambda functions, you need to decide whether you're going to push each function individually to its own Git repository, or bundle them all together as a single repo.
- AWS Lambda supports aliases, which are named pointers to a particular version. This makes it easy to use a single Lambda function for sandbox, staging, and production environments.
- The API Gateway stage variable feature enables you to dynamically access different Lambda function environments.
- The Email Extension plugin allows you to configure every aspect of email notifications. You can customize when an email is sent, who should receive it, and what the email says.

Part 4

Managing, scaling, and monitoring Jenkins

This final part is about combining and coalescing everything you've learned and moving even further. You'll learn how to monitor and troubleshoot a running Jenkins cluster. We'll start by exposing Jenkins metrics with Prometheus and build an interactive dashboard with Grafana. Next, I will demonstrate how to stream Jenkins logs to a centralized logging platform based on the ElasticSearch, Logstash, and Kibana (ELK) stack. Finally, I will share tips and best practices to secure and maintain Jenkins.

Collecting continuous delivery metrics

This chapter covers

- Monitoring Jenkins and its jobs effectively
- Forwarding Jenkins build logs to a centralized logging platform
- Parsing Jenkins logs into something structured and queryable
- Exposing Jenkins internal metrics with Prometheus
- Building interactive dashboards with Grafana
- Creating metric-based alerts for Jenkins

In the previous chapters, you learned to design, build, and deploy a Jenkins cluster from scratch by using automation tools; you also learned to set up a fully working CI/CD pipeline for several cloud-native applications. In this chapter, we will dive into advanced Jenkins topics: monitoring a running Jenkins server and detecting anomalies and resource starvation. Along the way, we will cover how to build a centralized logging platform for Jenkins logs.

13.1   *Monitoring Jenkins cluster health*

The cluster we built in chapter 5 consists of a Jenkins master and workers, with each node running inside an EC2 instance. Figure 13.1 shows a typical Jenkins node configuration.

S	Name ↓	Architecture	Clock Difference	Free Disk Space	Free Swap Space	Free Temp Space	Response Time	
	ip-10-0-0-29.eu-west-3.compute.internal	Linux (amd64)	In sync	27.82 GB	⊖ 0 B	27.82 GB	23ms	⚙
	ip-10-0-2-216.eu-west-3.compute.internal	Linux (amd64)	In sync	27.82 GB	⊖ 0 B	27.82 GB	34ms	⚙
	master	Linux (amd64)	In sync	27.46 GB	⊖ 0 B	27.46 GB	0ms	⚙
	Data obtained		30 ms	31 ms	32 ms	30 ms	24 ms	26 ms

Figure 13.1   **Jenkins distributed build architecture**

So far, the Jenkins cluster is working as expected. However, you should never take your IT infrastructure for granted. Your Jenkins master or workers one day will break and will need to be replaced. So, how do you know if your Jenkins cluster is working effectively if you aren't monitoring it?

Monitoring Jenkins should become a crucial part of your IT management. Monitoring helps you look for abnormalities and spot issues on instances running the cluster, saves you money as it minimizes the network downtime, and enhances efficiency.

In AWS, you can monitor Jenkins instances by using Amazon CloudWatch (https:// aws.amazon.com/cloudwatch). The platform consumes data coming from all AWS services and allows the user to visualize, query, and take action on the data. By default, Amazon EC2 sends metrics data to CloudWatch.

> **NOTE** You can use Azure Monitor (http://mng.bz/wQYQ) or Google Cloud's operations (https://cloud.google.com/monitoring/quickstart-lamp) if you want to monitor the overall health and performance of Jenkins instances running in Azure or GCP environments.

Navigate to the Amazon CloudWatch console and jump to the All Metrics tab. Then, under EC2, look for instances running the cluster by typing their instance ID on the search bar, as shown in figure 13.2.

All metrics	Graphed metrics	Graph options	Source

Paris ∨	All > EC2 > Per-Instance Metrics	i-028df42588cd8919a ⊗	Q Search for any metric, dimension or resource id	Graph search

	Instance Name (14) ▲	InstanceId	Metric Name
☐	jenkins_master	i-028df42588cd8919a	NetworkPacketsIn
☐	jenkins_master	i-028df42588cd8919a	NetworkPacketsOut
☐	jenkins_master	i-028df42588cd8919a	CPUUtilization
☐	jenkins_master	i-028df42588cd8919a	NetworkIn
☐	jenkins_master	i-028df42588cd8919a	NetworkOut
☐	jenkins_master	i-028df42588cd8919a	DiskReadBytes

Figure 13.2   **Key metrics for EC2 monitoring**

You will see a pretty long list of reported metrics for your Jenkins EC2 instances. You can scroll and select one or more metrics to display (for example, EC2 instance CPU utilization) and create a graph widget to display them, as shown in figure 13.3.

| ✓ | ■ | i-04a75885117ca95b7 (jenkins_worker) | EC2 • CPUUtilization • InstanceId: i-04a75885117ca95b7 | Average | 5 Minutes | ‹ › ∿ △ ▱ ✕ |
| ✓ | ■ | i-0c97ff1fba9af2db4 (jenkins_worker) | EC2 • CPUUtilization • InstanceId: i-0c97ff1fba9af2db4 | Sum | 5 Minutes | ‹ › ∿ △ ▱ ✕ |

Figure 13.3   **The percentage of allocated EC2 compute units currently in use on the Jenkins instances**

By default, EC2 reports metrics to CloudWatch in 5-minute intervals. However, if your Jenkins cluster is being extensively used (for example, hosting multiple jobs and scheduling many CI/CD pipelines), you can enable the enhanced monitoring feature (http://mng.bz/GOZR) on each instance to get metrics in 1-minute intervals (though an additional cost applies).

CloudWatch also offers dashboards, which provide a quick view of how your instances are performing as well as tremendous flexibility in terms of data visualization—for example, zooming in or rescaling.

You can customize the dashboard and add additional graphs showing, for example, the number of bytes received and sent out on all network interfaces, or disk usage (bytes written and read from all instance store volumes), as demonstrated in figure 13.4.

Now you know how to monitor Jenkins instances using CloudWatch. However, it can be error-prone and tedious to set up CloudWatch monitoring for all your Jenkins instances (and remembering to do it for Jenkins workers created for scaling events). Additionally, some metrics are unavailable through CloudWatch (such as memory usage). Hence, we will use an advanced monitoring stack.

Figure 13.4   **Building the CloudWatch dashboard to monitor Jenkins instances**

NOTE   The Amazon CloudWatch agent can be installed on EC2 instances to report additional and useful metrics. This feature is seldom used, but it is good to know it exists. Refer to the official guide at http://mng.bz/q5J2 for instructions.

Many tools, from open source to a commercial level, can help you monitor your infrastructure and notify you of any failure. (Section 13.3 covers how to set up alerts that will notify you in near real-time.) The good thing is that a powerful open source monitoring solution is available, thanks to the open source community that maintains it. Figure 13.5 summarizes the open source solution we're going to implement.

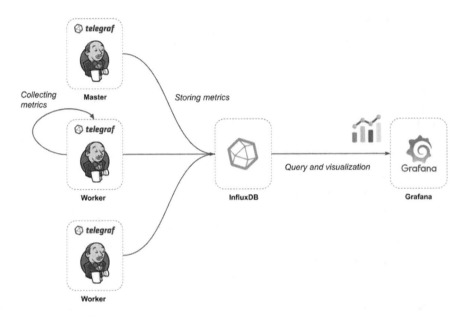

Figure 13.5   Telegraf will collect metrics, store them in InfluxDB, and from there we can visualize them in Grafana.

This monitoring solution can be split into three parts:

- *Telegraf*—A metric collector agent, installed on each Jenkins instance. It collects the internal metrics and ships them to a time-series database.
- *InfluxDB*—An open source time-series database (TSDB), optimized for fast, high-availability storage. It consumes the telemetry coming from Telegraf agents.
- *Grafana*—An open source visualization platform, used to build dynamic and interactive dashboards based on data stored in InfluxDB.

Now that the architecture is clear, we need to deploy an InfluxDB server on an EC2 instance. Check out the InfluxDB official documentation at http://mng.bz/7lJy for a step-by-step guide on how to install and configure InfluxDB.

Once the instance is up and running, SSH to the InfluxDB instance and type the `influx` command on the terminal. The `influx` CLI, which is included in all InfluxDB packages, is a lightweight and simple way to interact with the database. We need to create two databases:

- *instances*—To store metrics about resource usage, such as CPU utilization, memory, network traffic, disk usage, and so forth.
- *containers*—To store metrics about containers running in the Jenkins workers. The containers are basically build jobs scheduled for Jenkins workers.

Create the databases by using the `CREATE DATABASE` Influx Query Language (InfluxQL) statement:

```
CREATE DATABASE containers;
CREATE DATABASE instances;
```

The databases can also be created by making raw HTTP requests to an InfluxDB API over port 8086 (see http://mng.bz/m1z2).

Now that we have databases, InfluxDB is ready to accept queries and writes. To collect Jenkins instance metrics, we need to install a Telegraf agent on each server. One way to do this is to install Telegraf on the existing instances, but this solution won't scale, as we need to install and configure a Telegraf agent each time a new Jenkins worker is deployed. Therefore, the best way is to ship Telegraf within the Jenkins AMI. Once again, we will use Packer to bake the Jenkins master and worker AMIs with a pre-installed and configured Telegraf agent.

Add the code in the next listing to the setup.sh (chapter13/telegraf/setup.sh) script provided in chapter 4, listings 4.4 and 4.5. This code will install the latest stable version of Telegraf (at the time of writing this book, version 1.19.0 is available).

Listing 13.1 Installing the Telegraf agent with the Yum utility

```
wget https://dl.influxdata.com/telegraf/releases/telegraf-1.19.0-1.x86_64.rpm
yum localinstall telegraf-1.19.0-1.x86_64.rpm
systemctl enable telegraf
systemctl restart telegraf
```

Next, we tell Telegraf what metrics to collect, by creating a configuration file at /etc/telegraf/telegraf.conf. The config file consists of *inputs* (where the metrics come from) and *outputs* (where the metrics go). The following listing specifies three inputs (CPU memory usage, and Docker), and specifies InfluxDB as the output. The Docker input reads metrics about the Docker daemon and then outputs this data to InfluxDB.

Listing 13.2 Telegraf configuration file with various inputs

```
[global_tags]
hostname="Jenkins"        ⟵┘ Overrides default hostname;
                             if empty, use os.Hostname()

[[inputs.cpu]]            ⟵┐ Gathers metrics on
  percpu = false             the system CPUs
```

```
    totalcpu = true
    fieldpass = [ "usage*" ]
    name_suffix = "_vm"

[[inputs.disk]]
    fielddrop = [ "inodes*" ]
    Mount_points = ["/"]
    name_suffix = "_vm"

[[inputs.mem]]
    name_suffix = "_vm"

[[inputs.swap]]
    name_suffix = "_vm"

[[inputs.system]]
    name_suffix = "_vm"

[[inputs.docker]]
    endpoint = "unix:///var/run/docker.sock"
    container_names = []
    name_suffix = "_docker"

[[outputs.influxdb]]
    database = "instances"
    urls = ["http://INFLUXDB_IP:8086"]
    namepass = ["*_vm"]

[[outputs.influxdb]]
    database = "containers"
    urls = ["http://INFLUXDB_IP:8086"]
    namepass = ["*_docker"]
```

Gathers metrics about disk usage. By default, stats are gathered for all mount points, and setting Mount_points will restrict the stats to the root volume.

Collects system memory metrics

Collects system swap metrics

Gathers general stats on system load, uptime, and number of users logged in. It is similar to the Unix uptime command.

Uses the Docker Engine API to gather metrics on running Docker containers

Writes system metrics to the InfluxDB instance database

Writes Docker metrics to the InfluxDB container database

Make sure to replace the INFLUXDB_IP variable with the IP address of the instance where the InfluxDB server is running.

Bake a new Jenkins AMI and redeploy a Jenkins cluster with the newly built image by following steps described in section 5.3. Once the new Jenkins cluster is up and running, Telegraf will start collecting metrics and streaming them to InfluxDB for storage and indexing.

To explore the metrics, we will use Grafana. You can install Grafana from a Yum repository or by running a Docker image. (Check out the Grafana official documentation at http://mng.bz/5ZY1 for more details.) Once Grafana is installed, head your browser to HOST_IP:3000. On the login page, enter admin for the username and password.

Before we create a dashboard to monitor the overall health of the Jenkins instances, we need to link the InfluxDB databases to Grafana. To do so, we need to create a data source for each InfluxDB database.

In the side panel, click the cog icon and then click Configuration > Data Sources. Click the Add Data Source button, shown in figure 13.6. Then fill the settings page with the following values:

- *Name*—The data source name. (This is how you'll refer to the data source in queries.)

Figure 13.6   Configuring InfluxDB-based data sources in Grafana

- *URL*—The HTTP, IP address, and port of your InfluxDB API. (By default, the InfluxDB API port is 8086.)
- *Database*—Name of the InfluxDB database (*instances* or *containers* database).

With your InfluxDB connection configured, use Grafana and InfluxQL to query and visualize time-series data stored in InfluxDB. From the left panel, click Dashboards. From the top menu, click Home to get a list of dashboards. Click the Create New button at the bottom to create a new dashboard. To add a graph, just click the graph button in the panel filter. In the Query section, type the following InfluxQL statement:

```
SELECT mean("used_percent") FROM "mem_vm"
WHERE $timeFilter
GROUP BY time($__interval), "host" fill(null)
```

This query selects the memory usage from the mem_vm measurement and groups the results by Jenkins node. The query results in the graph in figure 13.7.

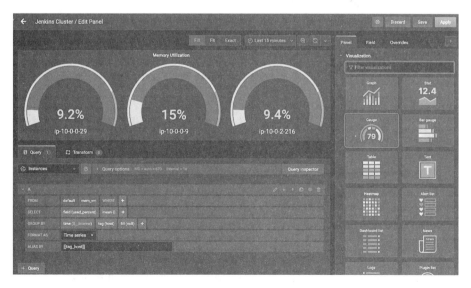

Figure 13.7   Building a memory utilization gauge chart

To monitor the Jenkins jobs build time, you can use the following statement:

```
SELECT mean("uptime_ns") FROM "docker_container_status_docker"
WHERE ("hostname" = 'Jenkins') AND $timeFilter
GROUP BY time($__interval), "container_name" fill(null)
```

This selects the uptime value (the amount of time the container is online and operational) from the `docker_container_status_docker` measurement and groups the results by the container name (figure 13.8).

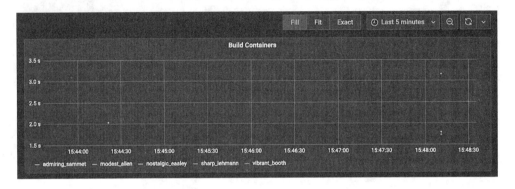

Figure 13.8   Monitoring containers built within CI/CD pipelines

Back to Grafana, you can create multiple graphs to monitor various metrics of the Jenkins cluster:

- CPU usage of Jenkins nodes (master and worker instances)
- Network traffic (in and out bytes)
- Memory utilization of each Jenkins node
- Number of running build jobs
- Overall health and number of workers

Figure 13.9 shows host-level details for the Jenkins cluster. The complete dashboard can be imported from the JSON file (chapter13/grafana/dashboard/influxdb.json). Refer to http://mng.bz/6mGD for instructions.

As mentioned earlier, monitoring the state of your instances is imperative to keeping your Jenkins cluster healthy, and by using the preceding metrics (and the many others) provided by Telegraf, you can achieve this with relative ease.

So far, you have seen how to monitor the Jenkins instances (server side). Let's explore monitoring the Jenkins server itself (application side). As you may have already guessed, a monitoring plugin for Jenkins can provide a lot of data about what's going on within Jenkins and about the tasks being performed by Jenkins. For example, the Metrics plugin (https://plugins.jenkins.io/metrics/) provides health

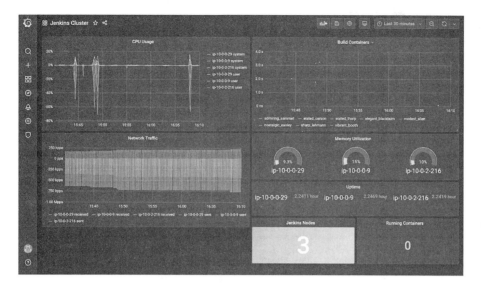

Figure 13.9 Jenkins host metrics

checks by exposing an API on the Jenkins server at the $JENKINS_URL/metrics endpoint. The API provides information on the following:

- HTTP sessions and current HTTP requests
- Detailed statistics of the build times and the build steps by period
- Threads, process list of OS, and heap dumps

For instance, the API call in figure 13.10 returns statistics about the number of executors available to Jenkins.

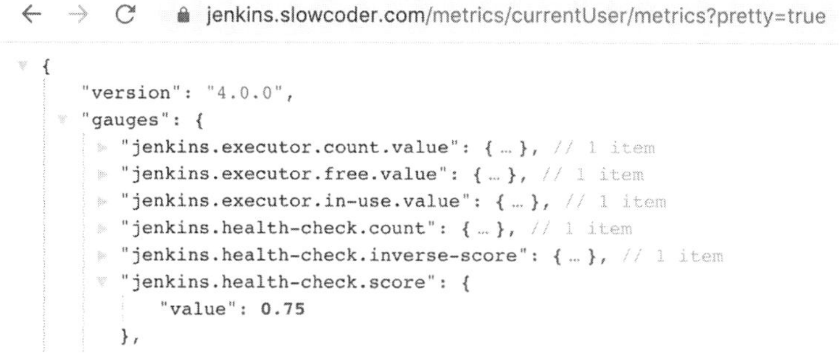

```
←  →  C     🔒 jenkins.slowcoder.com/metrics/currentUser/metrics?pretty=true

{
    "version": "4.0.0",
    "gauges": {
        "jenkins.executor.count.value": { … }, // 1 item
        "jenkins.executor.free.value": { … }, // 1 item
        "jenkins.executor.in-use.value": { … }, // 1 item
        "jenkins.health-check.count": { … }, // 1 item
        "jenkins.health-check.inverse-score": { … }, // 1 item
        "jenkins.health-check.score": {
            "value": 0.75
        },
```

Figure 13.10   Metrics API with health-check endpoints

To create a dashboard based on those metrics, we can write a custom script to save those values regularly to InfluxDB, or use a Prometheus metric plugin (https://plugins .jenkins.io/prometheus/) to expose an endpoint (the default is /prometheus) with metrics that a Prometheus server can scrape.

Prometheus (https://prometheus.io/) is an open source monitoring system with a dimensional data model, flexible query language, efficient time-series database, and modern alerting approach.

> **NOTE** The Packer template file and Terraform HCL files for baking and deploying a Prometheus server are available in the chapter13/prometheus folder.

First, install the Prometheus Metrics plugin (https://plugins.jenkins.io/prometheus/) from the Manage Plugins section. Once it's installed, you can see the plugin's output through JENKINS _URL/prometheus (figure 13.11).

```
←  →  C      🔒 jenkins.slowcoder.com/prometheus/
# HELP default_jenkins_builds_last_build_start_time_milliseconds Last build start timestamp in milliseconds
# TYPE default_jenkins_builds_last_build_start_time_milliseconds gauge
default_jenkins_builds_last_build_start_time_milliseconds{jenkins_job="movies-loader/develop",repo="NA",} 1.591019270526E12
default_jenkins_builds_last_build_start_time_milliseconds{jenkins_job="movies-store/develop",repo="NA",} 1.59102046462E12
default_jenkins_builds_last_build_start_time_milliseconds{jenkins_job="movies-store/preprod",repo="NA",} 1.59102046274E12
default_jenkins_builds_last_build_start_time_milliseconds{jenkins_job="movies-parser/develop",repo="NA",} 1.591021820595E12
default_jenkins_builds_last_build_start_time_milliseconds{jenkins_job="movies-store/master",repo="NA",} 1.59102046629E12
# HELP default_jenkins_builds_stage_duration_milliseconds_summary Summary of Jenkins build times by Job and Stage
# TYPE default_jenkins_builds_stage_duration_milliseconds_summary summary
default_jenkins_builds_stage_duration_milliseconds_summary_count{jenkins_job="movies-store/develop",repo="NA",stage="Tests",} 4.0
```

Figure 13.11   Prometheus endpoint serves a list of metrics

Then, you need to configure a Prometheus server to scrape metrics from Jenkins. Edit the configuration file at /etc/prometheus/prometheus.yml (listing 13.3). In the `scrape_configs` section, add a job for the Jenkins server. The format for writing this config file can be found at http://mng.bz/o8Vr.

Listing 13.3   Configuring Prometheus to scrape metrics from Jenkins

```
global:
  scrape_interval: 10s

scrape_configs:
  - job_name: 'prometheus_master'
    scrape_interval: 5s
    static_configs:
      - targets: ['localhost:9090']
  - job_name: 'jenkins'
    metrics_path: '/prometheus/'
    scheme: https
    static_configs:
      - targets: ['JENKINS_URL']
```

On the Prometheus dashboard (the default port is 9090), you can explore the metrics collected from Jenkins. You will be greeted will the screen in figure 13.12.

Collected metrics are not very useful unless they are visualized. Connect Prometheus with Grafana by creating a new data source. To create a Prometheus data source in Grafana, follow these steps:

1 Click the cogwheel icon in the side panel to open the Configuration menu.
2 Click Data Sources.

Figure 13.12   Exploring Jenkins metrics from the Prometheus dashboard

   3 Click Add Data Source.

   4 Select Prometheus as the type.

   5 Set the appropriate Prometheus server URL to http://prometheus:9090.

   6 Click Save & Test to save the new data source.

Then, create a dashboard based on the available metrics. The dashboard features application-level metrics (which track the total number of jobs in a queue, how many are pending, and how many are stuck or otherwise delayed), followed by internal operation metrics (JVM), and finally system-level metrics (disk I/O, network, memory, and so forth). Figure 13.13 shows a part of the dashboard.

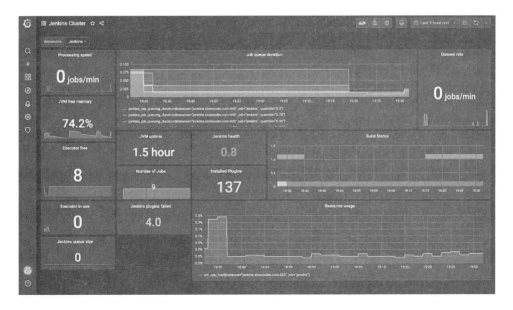

Figure 13.13   Comprehensive Jenkins monitoring summary of jobs and builds

The complete dashboard can be imported from the following JSON file: chapter13/ grafana/dashboard/prometheus.json.

Another popular solution for monitoring Jenkins is the Monitoring plugin (previously called JavaMelody). This plugin produces comprehensive HTML reports about the state of Jenkins, including CPU and system load, average response time, and memory usage; see https://plugins.jenkins.io/monitoring/ for more details. Moreover, the reports are served from the Jenkins dashboard, as shown in figure 13.14.

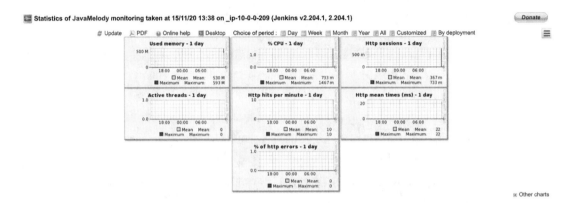

Figure 13.14   Statistics of JavaMelody monitoring

Great! You should now be able to monitor a Jenkins cluster running in production. To provide even further visibility into your Jenkins environment, you can collect and analyze Jenkins logs of real-time system and security events and correlate them with performance and server metrics to identify and resolve issues.

13.2   *Centralized logging for Jenkins logs with ELK*

By default, Jenkins logs are located at /var/log/jenkins/jenkins.log. To view those logs, SSH to the Jenkins master instance with the bastion host, and then issue the following command:

```
tail -f -n 100 /var/log/jenkins/jenkins.log
```

Figure 13.15 shows the command output.

```
[root@ip-10-0-0-130 ec2-user]# tail -f /var/log/jenkins/jenkins.log
        at hudson.remoting.SingleLaneExecutorService$1.run(SingleLaneExecutorService.java:131)
        at jenkins.util.ContextResettingExecutorService$1.run(ContextResettingExecutorService.java:28)
        at jenkins.security.ImpersonatingExecutorService$1.run(ImpersonatingExecutorService.java:59)
        at java.util.concurrent.Executors$RunnableAdapter.call(Executors.java:511)
        at java.util.concurrent.FutureTask.run(FutureTask.java:266)
        at java.util.concurrent.ThreadPoolExecutor.runWorker(ThreadPoolExecutor.java:1149)
        at java.util.concurrent.ThreadPoolExecutor$Worker.run(ThreadPoolExecutor.java:624)
        at java.lang.Thread.run(Thread.java:748)
2020-06-02 11:00:36.938+0000 [id=167]    INFO    c.s.o.i.Platform$JdkWithJettyBootPlatform#getSelectedProtocol:
2020-06-02 11:02:33.304+0000 [id=418]    INFO    c.s.o.i.Platform$JdkWithJettyBootPlatform#getSelectedProtocol:
```

Figure 13.15   Viewing Jenkins logs at /var/log/jenkins/jenkins.log

You can also view those logs from the web dashboard (figure 13.16). Head to the Jenkins dashboard and select System Log from the Manage Jenkins page.

 **Jenkins Log**

Figure 13.16   Viewing Jenkins logs from the Jenkins dashboard

By default, Jenkins records every `INFO` log to stdout, but you can configure Jenkins to record logs of a specific Jenkins plugin by creating a custom log recorder. From the System Log page, click the Add New Log Recorder button and choose a name that makes sense to you. The example in figure 13.17 creates a log recorder for the Slack plugin (the Java package is located at jenkins.plugins.slack).

Figure 13.17   Capturing the Slack plugin's login with a custom log recorder

Now, if any Slack notification is sent from a Jenkins pipeline, a log should be captured as shown in figure 13.18.

 **Slack plugin logs**

Figure 13.18   Display of Slack plugin's logs

You can also view the build logs for a particular job by navigating to the job item from the dashboard and clicking Console Output, or by viewing the content of the logfile at $JENKINS_HOME/jobs/$JOB_NAME/builds/$BUILD_NUMBER/log.

Depending on a log rotation configuration, the logs could be saved for *X* number of builds (or days, and so forth), meaning the old job logs might be lost. That's why you need to persist the logs in a centralized logging platform for auditing and potential troubleshooting.

> **NOTE**   You can enable the Discard Old Build plugin (https://plugins.jenkins .io/discard-old-build/) in each project or job configuration page to configure the interval to keep old builds (for example, once a month, once in 10 builds, and so forth).

Additionally, analyzing Jenkins logs can provide a lot of information that helps with troubleshooting the root cause of pipeline job failure. Build logs contain a full set of records such as build name, number, execution time, and other things. However, to analyze those logs, you need to ship them to an external logging platform. That's where a platform like the ELK stack (Elasticsearch, Logstash, and Kibana) comes into play.

13.2.1 *Streaming logs with Filebeat*

Filebeat (www.elastic.co/beats/filebeat), a lightweight agent that will be installed on the Jenkins master instance, will ship the logs to Logstash (www.elastic.co/logstash) for processing and aggregation. From there, the logs will be stored in Elasticsearch (www.elastic.co/elasticsearch) and visualized in Kibana (www.elastic.co/kibana) through interactive dashboards. Figure 13.19 summarizes the entire workflow.

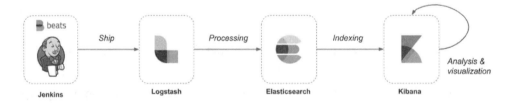

Figure 13.19   Shipping Jenkins logs to the ELK platform with Filebeat

To deploy this architecture, we need to create a machine image for each component. You can use Packer to bake the AMIs (figure 13.20). The Packer templates are available in the GitHub repository at chapter13/COMPONENT_NAME/packer/template .json.

Once the AMIs are created, you can use Terraform to deploy the ELK stack. The template resources are available in the GitHub repository at chapter13/ COMPONENT_NAME/terraform/*.tf.

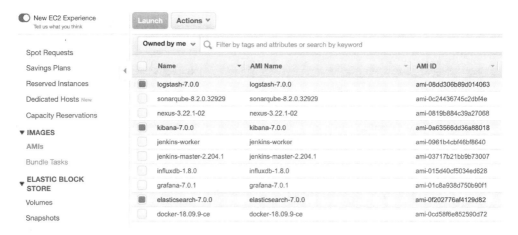

Figure 13.20   Logstash, Kibana, and Elasticsearch AMIs built with Packer

By the end of the provisioning process, three EC2 instances should be created, as shown in figure 13.21.

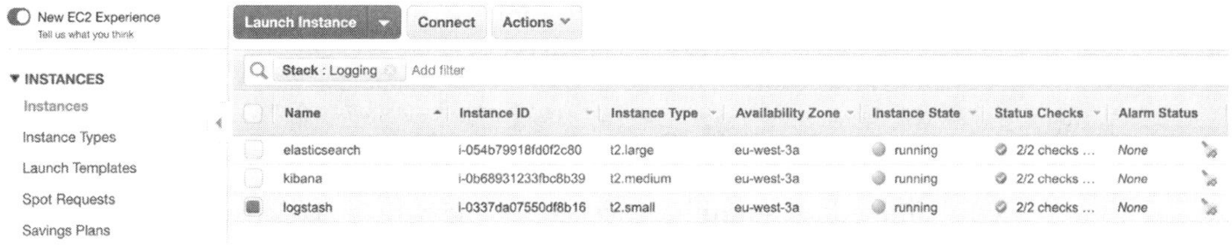

Figure 13.21   Deployed ELK stack on AWS

With the logging platform ready to consume incoming Jenkins logs, we need to install Filebeat on the Jenkins master instance. SSH to the Jenkins server, and run the commands in the following listing to install the latest stable version of Filebeat (at the time of writing this book, version 7.13.2 is available).

Listing 13.4   Installing the Filebeat agent on the Jenkins server

```
curl -L -O https://artifacts.elastic.co/downloads/beats/
filebeat/filebeat-7.13.2-x86_64.rpm
sudo rpm -vi filebeat-7.13.2-x86_64.rpm
```

Next, we need to set the path of the log files that we want to forward to ELK. Here we want to forward logs to /var/log/jenkins/jenkins.log. Go to the configuration directory of Filebeat under the location /etc/filebeat, and update filebeat.yml with the following listing.

> **Listing 13.5   Filebeat input configuration**

```
filebeat.inputs:
- type: log
    enabled: true
    paths:
      - /var/log/jenkins/jenkins.log      ◁
    fields:
      type: jenkins
    multiline.pattern: '[0-9]{4}-[0-9]{2}-[0-9]{2}'
    multiline.negate: true
    multiline.match: after
output.logstash:
    hosts: ["LOGSTASH_HOST"]

processors:
  - add_host_metadata: ~
  - add_cloud_metadata: ~
  - add_docker_metadata: ~
  - add_kubernetes_metadata: ~
```

Harvests lines from the
/var/log/jenkins/jenkins.log file

Adds a field called type to the output, so we
can easily identify logs coming from Jenkins

Configures Filebeat to
handle a multiline message

Sends logs directly to Logstash

Annotates each log event
with relevant metadata
from the host machine

Multiline messages are common in Jenkins logs, especially for log messages containing Java stack traces. Here's an example of a Java stack trace:

```
2020-10-22 20:06:58.217+0000[id=124635] FATAL: Ping failed.
                      java.util.concurrent.TimeoutException:
                      at
      hudson.remoting.PingThread.ping(PingThread.java:134)
              at hudson.remoting.PingThread.run(PingThread.java:90)
```

To correctly handle these multiline messages, we use the `multiline` settings to specify which lines are part of a single log message.

Replace the `LOGSTASH_HOST` variable, with the IP address of the Logstash server. Then restart the Filebeat agent with the following command:

```
systemctl restart filebeat
```

Head to the Kibana dashboard (at `KIBANA_IP:5601`), jump to the Management tab, and to Index Patterns. We have to create a new index pattern. Creating an index pattern means mapping Kibana with an Elasticsearch index. Since Logstash stores incoming Jenkins logs to a series of indices in the format *jenkins-YYYY.MM.DD*, we will create an index pattern `jenkins-*` to explore all the logs, as shown in figure 13.22.

Click the Next Step option. From the Time Filter Field Name drop-down, select @timestamp. Then click the Create Index Pattern button.

Now, to view logs, go to the Discover page. You can see your index data coming in (figure 13.23).

Figure 13.22   Connecting an Elasticsearch index to Kibana

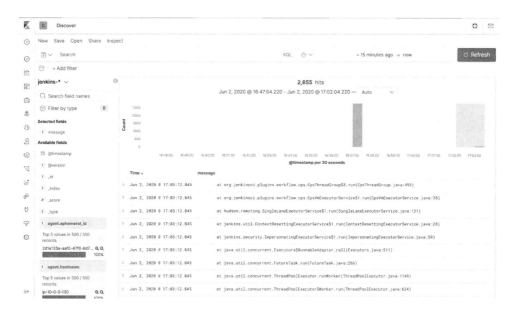

Figure 13.23   Visualizing Jenkins logs from Kibana

Now you have a working pipeline that reads Jenkins logs. However, you'll notice that the format of the log messages is not ideal. You want to parse the log messages to create specific, named fields from the logs. Let's take, as an example, the following Jenkins log:

```
2020-06-02 15:21:56.990+0000 INFO   o.j.p.workflow.job.WorkflowRun#finish:
    movies-loader/develop #7 completed: SUCCESS
```

The timestamp at the beginning of the line is easy to define as the level of the log (INFO, WARNING, DEBUG, etc.). To parse the line, we can write a Grok expression.

Grok works by parsing text patterns, using regular expressions, and assigning them to an identifier. The syntax is `%{PATTERN:IDENTIFIER}`. We can write a sequence of Grok patterns and assign various pieces of the preceding log message to various identifiers, as you can see in the following listing.

Listing 13.6   Grok expression to parse Jenkins log message

```
%{TIMESTAMP_ISO8601:createdAt}
    %{LOGLEVEL:level}%{SPACE}%{JAVACLASS:class}%{DATA:state}:%{SPACE}%{JOBNA
    ME:project} #%{NUMBER:buildNumber} %{DATA:execution}: %{WORD:status}
```

Grok comes with its own dictionary of patterns that you can use out of the box. But you can always define your own custom pattern, as shown in the following listing.

Listing 13.7   Grok custom patterns definition

```
JAVACLASS (?:[a-zA-Z0-9-]+\.)+[A-Za-z0-9$]+
JOBNAME [a-zA-Z0-9\-\/]+
```

You can use the Kibana Grok Debugger console to debug the expression. This feature, which is automatically enabled in Kibana, is located on the DevTools tab.

Enter the log message in the Sample Data field, and the Grok expression in the Grok Pattern field. Then click Simulate. You will see the simulated event that results from applying the Grok pattern (figure 13.24).

Note that the Grok pattern references the `JAVACLASS` and `JOBNAME` custom patterns. They are defined in the Custom Patterns section. Each pattern definition is specified on its own line.

> **NOTE**   If an error occurs, you can continue iterating over the custom pattern until the output matches the event that you expect.

Figure 13.24   Simulating Grok parsing with Grok Debugger tool

The Grok expression is working, but we want the parsing mechanism to be done before storing logs to Elasticsearch. That's why we will update the Logstash config (chapter13/logstash/packer/jenkins.conf) to parse incoming logs from Filebeat. The `filter` section will attempt to match messages coming from Jenkins with the Grok expression defined earlier, as shown in the following listing.

Listing 13.8   Parsing Jenkins logs at the Logstash level

```
filter {
  if [type] == "jenkins" {
    grok {
      patterns_dir => ["/etc/logstash/patterns"]
      match => {
        "message" =>
      "%{TIMESTAMP_ISO8601:createdAt}%{SPACE}\[id=%{INT:buildId}\]
%{SPACE}%{LOGLEVEL:level}%{SPACE}%{JAVACLASS:class}
%{DATA:state}:%{SPACE}%{JOBNAME:project}
#%{NUMBER:buildNumber} %{DATA:execution}: %{WORD:status}"
      }
    }
  }
}
```

This code takes the Jenkins logs collected by Filebeat, parses them into fields, and sends the fields to Elasticsearch. The `pattern_dir` setting tells Logstash where your custom patterns directory is. You can customize the parsing mechanism by adding more processing, such as dropping unused fields or renaming fields. See the Mutate Filter plugin at http://mng.bz/J6Av for more information.

Restart Logstash to reload the configuration. Your Jenkins logs will be gathered and structured into fields (figure 13.25). Right now, not much is in there because you are gathering only Jenkins logs. Here, you can search and browse through your logs.

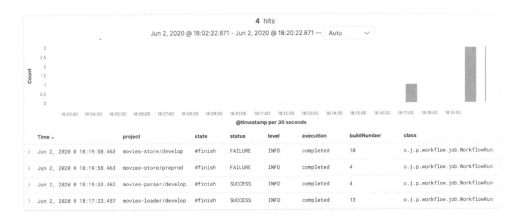

Figure 13.25   Structuring Jenkins logs into separated queryable fields

Each log message coming from Jenkins will match and result in the fields listed in table 13.1.

Table 13.1   Jenkins index fields in Elasticsearch

Field	Description
`time`	The data and time of the message in UTC format
`level`	The log message level (INFO, WARNING, DEBUG, FATAL, ERROR)
`project`	The Jenkins job's build name
`buildNumber`	The build number of the job, which identifies how many times Jenkins runs this build process
`status`	The status of the build (FAILURE or SUCCESS)
`execution`	The current state of the build (running, pending, terminated, or completed)

You can create a stacked bar chart showing the number of failed versus successful builds based on the `status` field over a period of time; see figure 13.26.

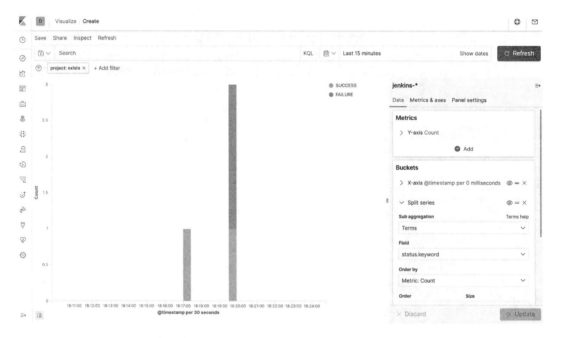

Figure 13.26   Building interactive widgets based on Jenkins structured fields

You can save the bar chart as a widget and import it to a dashboard. With a dashboard, you can combine multiple visualizations onto a single page, and then filter them by providing a search query or by selecting filters by clicking elements in the visualization.

Dashboards are useful when you want to get an overview of your Jenkins logs and make correlations among various visualizations and logs; see figure 13.27.

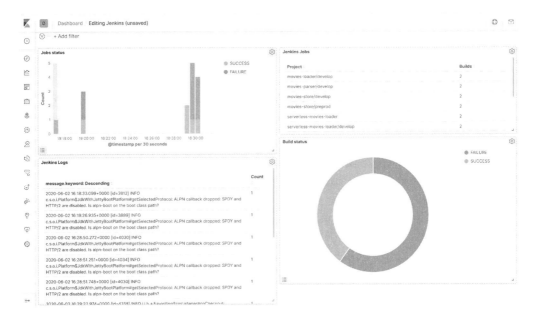

Figure 13.27 Analyzing Jenkins logs from a Kibana dashboard

The complete dashboard can be imported from the following JSON file: chapter13/kibana/dashboard/jenkins.json.

That's it! You've successfully created a pipeline that uses Filebeat to take Jenkins logs as input, forwards those logs to Logstash for parsing, and writes the parsed data to an Elasticsearch server.

13.2.2 *Streaming logs with the Logstash plugin*

You can skip the Filebeat and Logstash configurations by shipping Jenkins logs directly to an Elasticsearch instance via the Logstash plugin (https://plugins.jenkins .io/logstash/) on Jenkins. This solution is ideal if you're not already using external Logstash agents to stream your infrastructure or application logs to Elasticsearch, and if you don't need to enrich the parsing mechanism of logs with custom Grok expressions. Plus, the Logstash plugin can stream the log data from a Jenkins instance to any indexer solution (including Redis, RabbitMQ, and Elasticsearch). In the current scenario, we will use Elasticsearch.

After successfully installing the Logstash plugin in the global configuration of the Jenkins dashboard, we need to configure the plugin with the target indexer. Configure the URI, where the Elasticsearch server is running, as shown in figure 13.28.

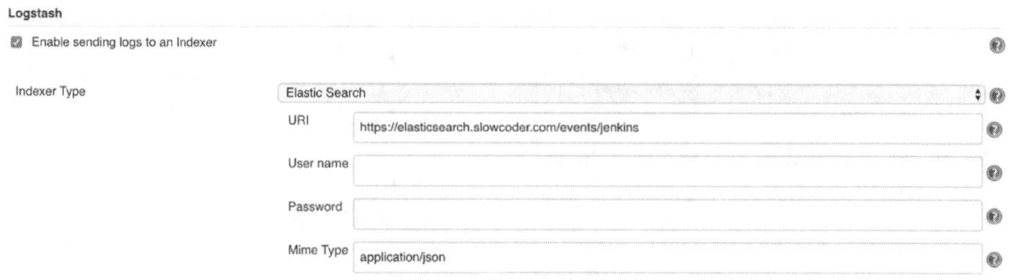

Logstash

☑ Enable sending logs to an Indexer   ⑦

Indexer Type | Elastic Search   ⬍ | ⑦

              URI | https://elasticsearch.slowcoder.com/events/jenkins | ⑦

        User name | | ⑦

        Password | | ⑦

        Mime Type | application/json | ⑦

Figure 13.28   Configuring the Logstash plugin to stream logs to the Elasticsearch server

After configuring the Elasticsearch endpoint in the Logstash configuration, you can add the following block to your pipelines. That way, all the logs produced within the `logstash` step will be streamed into Elasticsearch:

```
logstash {
    echo "Job:${env.JOB_NAME}"
}
```

You can view the streamed logs by accessing the Kibana dashboard, shown in figure 13.29.

Figure 13.29   Example of a log message sent to Elasticsearch

Now we are able to stream the log data from the Jenkins instance to Elasticsearch and finally to Kibana.

13.3   *Creating alerts based on metrics*

We can take the logging and monitoring solutions further and set up alerts. One of the most common use cases is DevOps teams getting notifications of events, such as when the failure build rate is significantly higher than usual. Needless to say, this issue can have a significant impact on the release of new features, hence having an impact on business and user experience.

You can use Kibana to define a meaningful alert on a specified condition; see figure 13.30. For instance, you can define an alert to periodically check the failure build rate. For the notification channel, you can use Slack, OpsGenie, or a simple email notification.

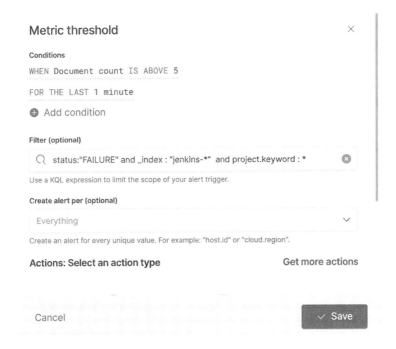

Figure 13.30   Configuring an alert on Kibana

You can also create alerts based on metrics collected by Prometheus or Telegraf, by using the Grafana alerting feature.

> **NOTE**   While it's easy to set up and use Grafana alerting, it's more limited in terms of the alert rules you can apply to your metrics queries. If you're looking for an advanced solution, go with Prometheus Alertmanager (https:// prometheus.io/docs/alerting/latest/alertmanager/).

Before creating monitoring alerts, we need to add the notification channel through which we will be notified. Here, we will be adding Slack as the notification channel.

To set up Slack, you need to configure an incoming Slack webhook URL. Create a Slack application by going to https://api.slack.com/apps/new. After creating the application, you'll be redirected to the Settings page of the new app (figure 13.31). From there, enable the Incoming Webhook feature by switching the radio button to On.

Figure 13.31   Enabling the incoming webhook on a Slack application

Now that incoming webhooks are enabled, the Settings page should refresh, and some extra options will appear. One of those options will be a really helpful button marked Add New Webhook to Workspace, and you should click it.

Go ahead and pick a Slack channel that Grafana will post to, and then click Authorize Your App. You'll be sent back to your app settings, where you should now see a new entry under the webhook URLs for the Your Workspace section, with a webhook URL. Copy it.

After creating the webhook URL, you need to create a notification channel in Grafana. In the Grafana sidebar, hover your cursor over the Alerting icon and then click Notification Channels, as shown in figure 13.32. Create a Slack notification channel as follows:

1 Input the name of the channel.
2 Change Type to Slack and input a webhook URL that you have created.

Figure 13.32
Configuring a new
Slack notification
channel

You can test the setup by clicking the Send Test button at the bottom. After setting up all the fields, just click the Save button.

Now let's create the alert. Select the panel where you want to create an alert. For instance, we can create an alert on the memory usage metric. Click the Alert tab and then click Create Alert. This will open a form for configuring the alert, where you can set the following options:

- *Evaluate Every*—The time interval on which you want the alert rule to be evaluated. For this example, we can set the option to Evaluate Every 1m for 1m. It means that Grafana will evaluate the rule every minute. If the metrics violate the rule, Grafana will wait for 1 minute. If, after 1 minute, the metrics are not recovered, Grafana will trigger an alert.
- *Conditions*—We can use the `avg()` function as we want to validate our rule against the average memory utilization.

This alert will be triggered when the average memory utilization is above 90%, as shown in figure 13.33.

Figure 13.33   Defining an alert rule for memory usage

Additionally, we need to add the notification channel where the alert needs to be sent, as well as the alert message. If the alert is triggered, you will see the message in figure 13.34 on your Slack channel.

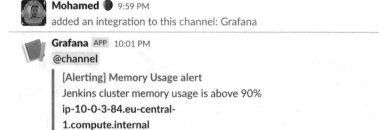

Figure 13.34   Slack notification upon memory threshold exceeded

Creating an alert to a messaging application like Slack is very beneficial. This ensures that you and your teammates get notifications immediately if something wrong happens. You can mention your team Slack group or use @here or @channel to make sure your team gets the message.

Summary

- You can build a monitoring stack with Telegraf, InfluxDB, and Grafana to collect, store, and visualize Jenkins instance metrics.
- You can collect and parse Jenkins logs into structured fields by writing Grok expressions.
- The Prometheus plugin can be used to expose internal and client-side metrics in Jenkins.
- The Logstash plugin is an easy way to integrate Jenkins logs with the ELK stack.
- Filebeat can be installed as an agent on your Jenkins master instance to ship logs to Logstash for parsing. From there, logs will be stored in Elasticsearch and analyzed from Kibana within an interactive dashboard.

Jenkins administration
and best practices

This chapter covers

- Sharing common code and steps across CI/CD pipelines
- Granting job permissions for a user
- Using GitHub for authentication information to secure a Jenkins instance
- Backing up and restoring Jenkins plugins and jobs
- Using Jenkins as a scheduler for cron jobs
- Migrating build jobs to a new Jenkins instance

Chapter 13 covered how to monitor a Jenkins cluster, and how to configure alerts and correlate Jenkins logs and metrics to identify issues and avoid downtime. In this chapter, you will learn how to enforce security on Jenkins by setting up granular access with role-based access control (RBAC) for logged-in users and how to add an extra security layer by using the GitHub authentication mechanism.

We also will discuss a few tips and tricks that you might find useful when maintaining a Jenkins instance. We will look at things like how to back up, restore, and archive build jobs or migrate them from one server to another.

14.1   *Exploring Jenkins security and RBAC authorization*

The current configuration of Jenkins allows not-logged users to have read access, and logged users to access almost everything. To override this default behavior, head to the Configure Global Security section from Manage Jenkins (figure 14.1).

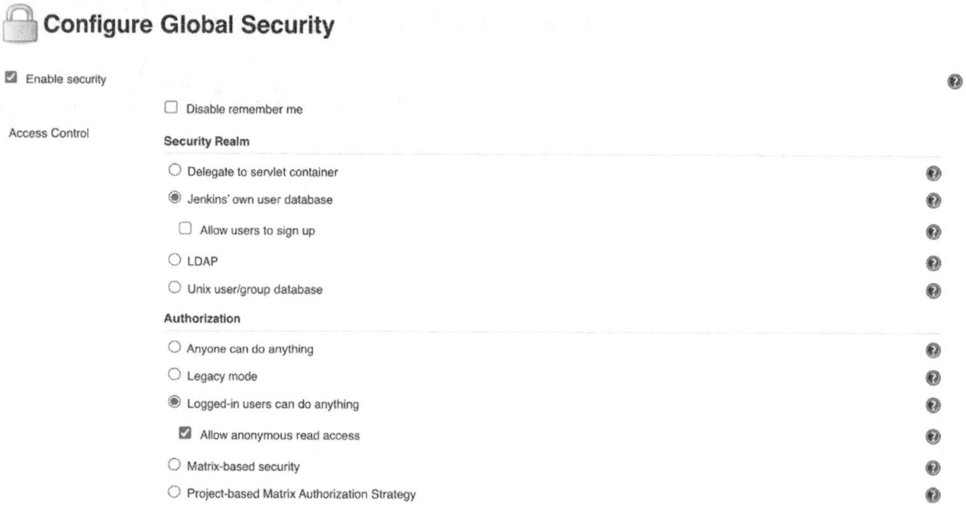

Figure 14.1   Enabling security in Jenkins

Disable Allow Anonymous Read Access and enable Allow Users to Sign Up, and you will be redirected to the sign-in page. This option allows users to create accounts by themselves via the Create an Account link, shown in figure 14.2.

Figure 14.2   Jenkins sign-in page

Click the Create an Account link. You will be prompted to add a new user. In figure 14.3, we are setting up a developer account.

Create an account!

If you already have a Jenkins account, please sign in.

Username

developer

Full name

John Doe

Email

developer@labouardy.com

Password   ☐ Show

●●●●●●●●●●●●●●●●

Strength: Strong

A strong password is a long password that's unique for every site. Try using a phrase with 5-6 words for the best security.

Create account

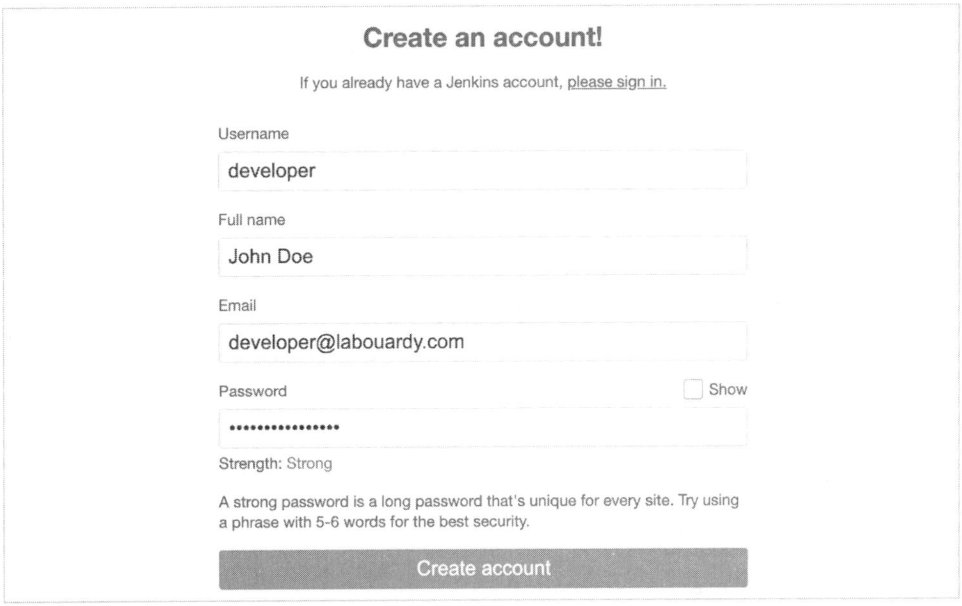

Figure 14.3   Setting up a developer account

Once the new account is created, sign in. You'll notice that it has full control of Jenkins. Letting signed-in users do anything is certainly flexible, and maybe all you need for a small team. For larger or multiple teams, or when Jenkins is being used outside the development environment, a more secure approach is generally required.

> **NOTE** By default, Jenkins does not use CAPTCHA verification if the user creates an account. If you'd like to enable CAPTCHA verification, install a support plugin such as the Jenkins JCaptcha plugin (https://plugins.jenkins.io/jcaptcha-plugin/).

14.1.1 *Matrix authorization strategy*

To set up granular access for logged-in users, we can use the Jenkins Matrix Authorization Strategy plugin (https://plugins.jenkins.io/matrix-auth/). This plugin allows you to control job permission on each project with specific users who can do something on that job.

Once the Matrix Authorization Strategy plugin is installed, head to Configure Global Security. In the Authorization section, enable Project-Based Matrix Authorization Strategy. Jenkins will display a table containing authorized users, and check boxes corresponding to the various permissions that you can assign to these users (figure 14.4).

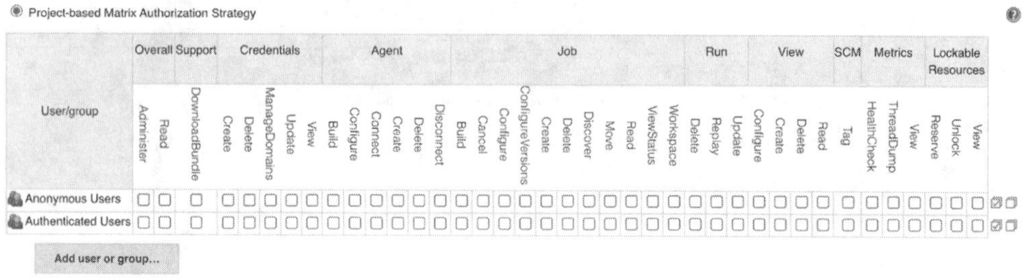

Figure 14.4   Matrix-based security configuration

The permissions are organized into several groups, such as these:

- *Overall*—Covers basic system-wide permissions.
- *Credentials*—Covers managing Jenkins credentials.
- *Agent*—Covers permissions about build nodes or workers (adding or removing Jenkins nodes).
- *Job*—Covers job-related permissions (creating a new build job, updating or deleting an existing build job).
- *Run*—Covers rights related to particular builds in the build history.
- *View*—Covers managing views. Views in Jenkins allow us to organize jobs and content into tabbed categories.
- *SCM*—Covers permissions related to a version-control system (such as Git or SVN).

The matrix controls what users can do (read jobs, execute builds, install plugins, and so forth). We have a couple of built-in authorizations to consider:

- *Anonymous*—Anyone who has not logged in
- *Authenticated*—Anyone who has logged in

You can configure permissions for a specific user by clicking Add User or Group. Add two users: one administrator (say, `mlabouardy/admin`) and a regular user (say, `developer`).

All the check boxes next to users are for setting global permissions. Select all check boxes to give admin full permissions. For Developer (aka John Doe), we are selecting read permissions under Job. With this, Developer would now have read permission to view all jobs that we created in the previous chapters; see figure 14.5.

Click Save, and the login page opens if you log in using developer credentials. In this mode, the developer account has only read permissions, as shown in figure 14.6 (for example, the developer can't trigger a build or configure job settings).

The table shown in the image contains the following permission matrix:

User/group	Overall Support			Credentials						Agent								Job													Run				View					SCM	Metrics			Lockable Resources		
	Administer	Read	DownloadBundle	Create	Delete	ManageDomains	Update	View	Build	Configure	Connect	Create	Delete	Disconnect	Build	Cancel	Configure	ConfigureVersions	Create	Delete	Discover	Move	Read	ViewStatus	Workspace	Delete	Replay	Update	Create	Configure	Delete	Read	Tag	HealthCheck	ThreadDump	View	Reserve	Unlock	View

Rows:

- Anonymous Users: View (Lockable Resources) ✓
- Authenticated Users: View (Lockable Resources) ✓
- John Doe: Read ✓, Read (Job) ✓
- mlabouardy: Administer ✓ (all checked)

Figure 14.5   Fine-tuning user permissions

Figure 14.6   Jenkins read-only access

So far, you have seen how to create and manage Jenkins users as well as how to give granular access to these users. However, in a large organization, assigning granular permissions to multiple users can be tedious. Luckily, you can create different roles with the appropriate permissions and assign them to different users in Jenkins.

14.1.2   Role-based authorization strategy

To manage different roles, install the Role-Based Authorization Strategy plugin (https://plugins.jenkins.io/role-strategy/) from the Plugin Manager page. Then activate the Role-Based Strategy option from the Manage Global Security page, as shown in figure 14.7.

Figure 14.7   Enabling the Role-Based Authorization Strategy plugin

Then you can define global roles on the Manage Jenkins page by selecting the Manage and Assign Roles option (figure 14.8). Note that Manage and Assign Roles will be visible only if you have installed the plugin correctly.

Manage Roles

Global roles

Role	Overall		Support	Credentials					Agent												Job					
	Administer	Read	DownloadBundle	Create	Delete	ManageDomains	Update	View	Build	Configure	Connect	Create	Delete	Disconnect	Provision	Build	Cancel	Configure	ConfigureVersions		Create	Delete	Discover	Move	Read	ViewStatus
admin	☑	☑	☑	☑	☑	☑	☑	☑	☑	☑	☑	☑	☑	☑	☑	☑	☑	☑	☑		☑	☑	☑	☑	☑	☑
developer	☐	☐	☐	☐	☐	☐	☐	☐	☐	☐	☐	☐	☐	☐	☐	☑	☐	☐	☐		☐	☐	☐	☐	☑	☑
qa	☐	☐	☐	☐	☐	☐	☐	☐	☐	☐	☐	☐	☐	☐	☐	☐	☐	☐	☐		☐	☐	☐	☐	☑	☑

Figure 14.8 Defining custom roles

Click the Manage Roles option to add new roles. Create three custom roles with the appropriate permissions:

- *Admin*—Will be assigned to Jenkins administrators for full access to Jenkins
- *Developer*—Will be assigned to developers for permissions to build jobs and view their logs and status
- *QA*—Will be assigned to software quality assurance engineer for permissions to view jobs status/health

Assign Roles

Global roles

User/group	admin	developer	qa
John Doe	☐	☑	☐
Anonymous	☐	☐	☐
Marcus Bergson	☐	☐	☑
Mohamed Labouardy	☑	☐	☐

Figure 14.9 Managing and assigning roles

Then, assign these roles to specific users from the Assign Roles screen (figure 14.9). In these settings, we assign the admin's role to the administrator account, the developer's role to a member of the development team, and QA's role to a software QA.

If you're using Jenkins within an organization, creating and managing users' access might be a tedious task. You can use GitHub as an authentication mechanism.

NOTE You can configure many OAuth2 authentication services with Jenkins, including GitLab, Google, and OpenID.

14.2 *Configuring GitHub OAuth for Jenkins*

Jenkins supports several authentication plugins, in addition to built-in username and password authentication. If you're using GitHub as your version-control system within your organization, you can also use the GitHub OAuth service for user authentication and privileges management.

On Jenkins, install the GitHub Authentication plugin (https://plugins.jenkins.io/github-oauth/) from Manage Plugins. Once it's installed, head to your GitHub account and create a new application (https://github.com/settings/applications/new) called `Jenkins` with the settings in figure 14.10.

Register a new OAuth application

Application name *

> Jenkins

Something users will recognize and trust.

Homepage URL *

> http://jenkins.slowcoder.com

The full URL to your application homepage.

Application description

> Application description is optional

This is displayed to all users of your application.

Authorization callback URL *

> http://jenkins.slowcoder.com/securityRealm/finishLogin

Your application's callback URL. Read our OAuth documentation for more information.

[Register application] Cancel

Figure 14.10 Configuring the GitHub OAuth application

The authorization callback URL must be JENKINS_URL/securityRealm/finishLogin. Click the Register Application button. A Client ID and secret will be generated, as shown in figure 14.11. Keep the page open to the application registration, so this information can be copied into your Jenkins configuration.

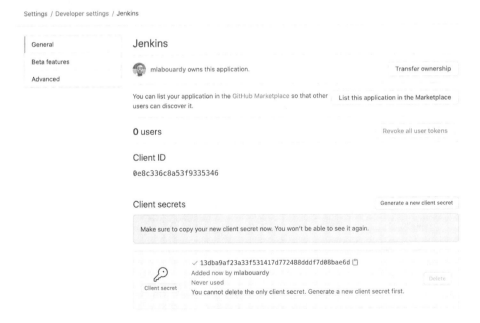

Settings / Developer settings / Jenkins

| General |
| Beta features |
| Advanced |

Jenkins

mlabouardy owns this application.   Transfer ownership

You can list your application in the GitHub Marketplace so that other users can discover it.   List this application in the Marketplace

0 users   Revoke all user tokens

Client ID

0e8c336c8a53f9335346

Client secrets   Generate a new client secret

Make sure to copy your new client secret now. You won't be able to see it again.

Client secret   ✓ 13dba9af23a33f531417d772488dddf7d08bae6d
Added now by mlabouardy
Never used
You cannot delete the only client secret. Generate a new client secret first.   Delete

Figure 14.11 Application client ID and client secret

Head back to Jenkins, and in the Global Security configuration, set the Security Realm option to GitHub Authentication Plugin. Then set the Client ID, Client Secret, and OAuth scopes as shown in figure 14.12.

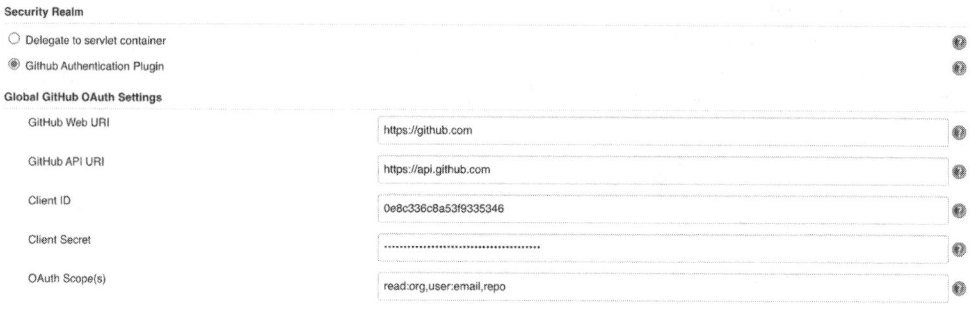

Security Realm

○ Delegate to servlet container

● Github Authentication Plugin

Global GitHub OAuth Settings

GitHub Web URI	https://github.com
GitHub API URI	https://api.github.com
Client ID	0e8c336c8a53f9335346
Client Secret	••••••••••••••••••••••••••••••••••
OAuth Scope(s)	read:org,user:email,repo

Figure 14.12   Configuring the Jenkins client settings for OAuth

Click the Save and Apply buttons to reload the configuration. You can now sign in with your GitHub account, as shown in figure 14.13.

Figure 14.13   Authorizing Jenkins to access your GitHub account

Similar to classic username and password authentication, you can use a project-based matrix authorization strategy to determine Jenkins permissions for each GitHub account.

Another option is to use the GitHub Committer Authorization strategy. If you check this option, you can use GitHub repository permissions to determine permissions for each Jenkins project. If the GitHub repository of the project is public, all authenticated users will have read-only access, while project collaborators can build, edit, configure, cancel, or delete the Jenkins job. However, if the GitHub repository of the project is private, only collaborators can manage the Jenkins job.

To determine Jenkins access based on GitHub access, head to the Configure Global Security section from Manage Jenkins (figure 14.14).

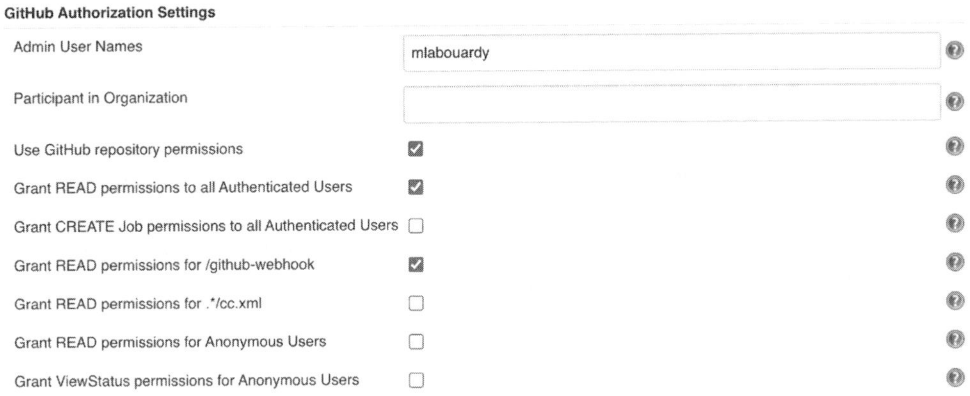

GitHub Authorization Settings

Admin User Names	mlabouardy
Participant in Organization	
Use GitHub repository permissions	☑
Grant READ permissions to all Authenticated Users	☑
Grant CREATE Job permissions to all Authenticated Users	☐
Grant READ permissions for /github-webhook	☑
Grant READ permissions for .*/cc.xml	☐
Grant READ permissions for Anonymous Users	☐
Grant ViewStatus permissions for Anonymous Users	☐

Figure 14.14   Configuring GitHub Authorization settings

NOTE   We have authorized the use of the /github-webhook callback URL to receive post-commit hooks from GitHub.

14.3   *Keeping track of Jenkins users' actions*

In addition to configuring user accounts and access rights, keeping track of individual user actions can also be useful: in other words, who did what to your Jenkins configuration. This sort of audit trail facility is even required in many organizations for security compliance.

The Audit Trail plugin (https://plugins.jenkins.io/audit-trail/) keeps track of the main user actions in a set of rolling log files. To set this up, go to the Plugin Manager page and select the Audit Trail plugin in the list of available plugins. Then, as usual, click Install and Restart Jenkins after the plugin has been downloaded.

To enable audit logging, configure the plugin from the main Jenkins configuration page. Select Logfile as a Logger; that way, the plugin will produce a system-style log file. Then, set the log location (the directory in which the log files are to be written), as shown in figure 14.15. Of course, you need to ensure that the user running your Jenkins instance is allowed to write to this directory.

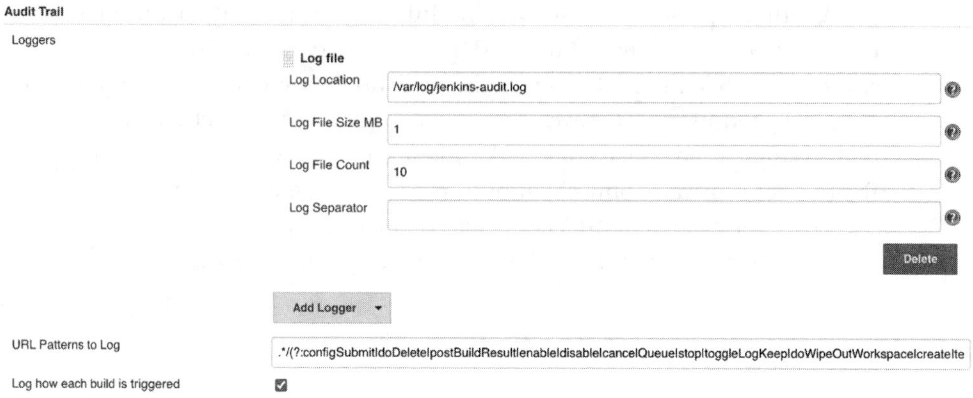

Audit Trail

Loggers

> **Log file**

Log Location	/var/log/jenkins-audit.log
Log File Size MB	1
Log File Count	10
Log Separator	

Delete

Add Logger ▾

URL Patterns to Log   .*/(?:configSubmit|doDelete|postBuildResult|enable|disable|cancelQueue|stop|toggleLogKeep|doWipeOutWorkspace|create|te

Log how each build is triggered   ☑

Figure 14.15   Configuring the Audit Trail plugin

By default, the details recorded in the audit logs are fairly sparse—they effectively record key actions performed, such as creating, modifying, or deleting job configurations or views, and the user who performed the actions. The log also shows how individual build jobs started. Figure 14.16 shows an extract of the default log.

```
[[root@ip-10-0-0-61 jenkins]# tail -f jenkins-audit.log.0
Nov 15, 2020 5:14:19,421 PM/configSubmit by mlabouardy
Nov 15, 2020 5:14:28,449 PMjob/movies-marketplace/job/develop/ #3 Started by user mlabouardy, Parameters:[]
Nov 15, 2020 5:14:49,331 PMjob/movies-store/job/develop/ #3 Started by user John Doe, Parameters:[]
Nov 15, 2020 5:14:50,821 PMmovies-store » develop #3 Started by user John Doe, Parameters:[] on node #unknown# started
Nov 15, 2020 5:15:01,971 PMmovies-marketplace » develop #3 Started by user mlabouardy, Parameters:[] on node #unknown#
```

Figure 14.16   Viewing audit logs for the authorized user activity

You can also configure the number of log files to be maintained and the maximum size of each file. In the previous configuration, we have the Log File Count set to 10; in this case, Jenkins will write to log files with names like jenkins-audit.log.0, jenkins-audit.log.1 . . . jenkins-audit.log.9. Now, you can access the configuration history for the whole server, including system configuration updates, as well as the changes made to the configuration of each project.

> **NOTE**   You can take the preceding configuration further and stream those log files to a centralized ELK platform and set up alerts on unauthorized user activities. For a step-by-step guide, head back to chapter 13.

14.4   *Extending Jenkins with shared libraries*

Throughout this book, you have learned how to write a CI/CD pipeline for multiple applications, and while implementing those pipeline steps, we have invoked multiple custom functions. Those functions, shown in the following listing, were duplicated in multiple Jenkinsfiles.

Listing 14.1 Helper functions for Git and Slack

```
def commitAuthor(){
    sh 'git show -s --pretty=%an > .git/commitAuthor'
    def commitAuthor = readFile('.git/commitAuthor').trim()
    sh 'rm .git/commitAuthor'
    commitAuthor
}

def commitID() {}
def commitMessage() {}
def notifySlack(String buildStatus){}
```

Therefore, we had some common code across different pipelines. To avoid copying and pasting the same code into different pipelines, and to reduce redundancies, we can centralize the common code in a shared library within Jenkins. That way, we can reference the same code in all of the pipelines.

A *shared library* is a collection of independent Groovy scripts stored in a Git repository. This means you can version, tag, and do all the stuff you're used to with Git. Before writing our first shared library in Jenkins, we need to create a GitHub repository where Groovy scripts will be stored.

Inside the repository, create a vars folder and write a Groovy script per function. For example, create a file named commitAuthor.groovy and define a function called `call`. The body of the function is what will be executed when the `commitAuthor` instruction is invoked, as shown in the following listing.

Listing 14.2 Defining a global variable in the shared library

```
                             Searches your path
                             looking for Groovy to
                             execute the script
#!/usr/bin/env groovy   ⟵                              Allows the global variable
                                                       to be invoked in a
def call() {                                      ⟵    manner similar to a step
  sh 'git show -s --pretty=%an > .git/commitAuthor'
  def commitAuthor = readFile('.git/commitAuthor').trim()    Prints the Git
  sh 'rm .git/commitAuthor'                                  commit author
  commitAuthor
}
```

Notice that the Groovy script must implement the `call` method. Write your custom code within the braces {}. You can also add parameters to your method. Do the same for other functions and push the changes to the remote repository. Eventually, your repository should look like figure 14.17.

Figure 14.17   Shared library custom global variables

Now that you've created your library with custom steps, you need to tell Jenkins about it. To add a shared library, head to a job configuration. Under Pipeline Libraries, add a library with the following settings:

- *Name*—A short identifier that will be used in pipeline scripts
- *Default version*—Could be anything understood by Git—for example, branches, tags, or commit ID hashes

Next, load the library from the GitHub repository at the master branch, as shown in figure 14.18.

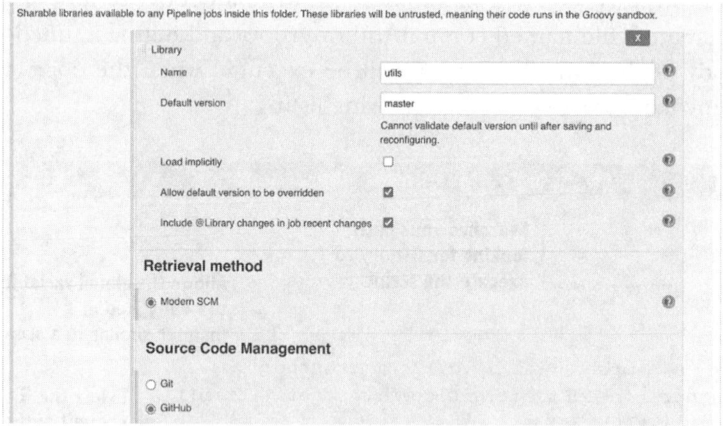

**Figure 14.18
Loading a shared
library from GitHub**

NOTE   You can also define a shared library globally, from Manage Jenkins > Configure System > Global Pipeline Libraries. That way, all pipelines can use functionality implemented in this library.

To load the shared library in a pipeline, you need to import it with the @Library annotation at the top of your pipeline definition. Then call the target function by its name, as shown in the following listing.

Listing 14.3 Importing the shared library in the scripted pipeline

```
@Library('utils')_          ◁────┐  The underscore is required if the line
                                  │  immediately after the @Library
node('workers'){                  │  annotation is not an import statement.
  stage('Checkout'){
     checkout scm
     notifySlack 'STARTED'
  }
}
```

The underscore is not a typo or mistake; you need this if the line immediately after the @Library annotation is not an import statement. You can override the default version defined for the library with the @Library('id@version') annotation.

If you're using a declarative pipeline, you need to wrap the library name inside a libraries section, as shown in the following listing.

Listing 14.4 Importing shared library in the declarative pipeline

```
libraries {
     lib('utils')
}
pipeline {
     // Your pipeline would go here....
}
```

When using a library, you may also specify a version with the following format:

```
libraries {
     lib('utils@VERSION')
}
```

Run the previous pipeline, and the output should look something like figure 14.19.

```
Examining mlabouardy/pipeline-library
Attempting to resolve master as a branch
Resolved master as branch master at revision e8dadc3faa6d861591acee8dd2bcbdbe3c9bd587
using credential github
 > git rev-parse --is-inside-work-tree # timeout=10
Fetching changes from the remote Git repository
 > git config remote.origin.url https://github.com/mlabouardy/pipeline-library.git # timeout=10
Fetching without tags
Fetching upstream changes from https://github.com/mlabouardy/pipeline-library.git
 > git --version # timeout=10
using GIT_ASKPASS to set credentials github
 > git fetch --no-tags --progress -- https://github.com/mlabouardy/pipeline-library.git +refs/heads/master:refs/remotes/origin/master
# timeout=10
Checking out Revision e8dadc3faa6d861591acee8dd2bcbdbe3c9bd587 (master)
 > git config core.sparsecheckout # timeout=10
 > git checkout -f e8dadc3faa6d861591acee8dd2bcbdbe3c9bd587 # timeout=10
Commit message: "shared library"
 > git rev-list --no-walk e8dadc3faa6d861591acee8dd2bcbdbe3c9bd587 # timeout=10
Replacing contents of vars/notifySlack.groovy
Replacing contents of vars/commitID.groovy
Replacing contents of vars/commitMessage.groovy
Replacing contents of vars/commitAuthor.groovy
[Pipeline] Start of Pipeline
```

Figure 14.19 Loading the shared library from Git within a pipeline

Another way to write a library is to define the functions within a Groovy class. Create the `Git.groovy` class in src/com/labouardy/utils, as shown in the following listing.

Listing 14.5   Writing a shared library

```groovy
#!/usr/bin/env groovy
package com.labouardy.utils

class Git {
    Git(){}

    def commitAuthor() {
        sh 'git show -s --pretty=%an > .git/commitAuthor'
        def commitAuthor = readFile('.git/commitAuthor').trim()
        sh 'rm .git/commitAuthor'
        commitAuthor
    }

    def commitID() {
        sh 'git rev-parse HEAD > .git/commitID'
        def commitID = readFile('.git/commitID').trim()
        sh 'rm .git/commitID'
        commitID
    }

    def commitMessage() {
        sh 'git log --format=%B -n 1 HEAD > .git/commitMessage'
        def commitMessage = readFile('.git/commitMessage').trim()
        sh 'rm .git/commitMessage'
        commitMessage
    }
}
```

You can load classes defined in the library by selecting their fully qualified name:

```groovy
@Library('utils') import com.labouardy.utils.Git
this.commitAuthor()
```

Or you can create an object constructor function and then call the method from the object:

```groovy
def gitUtils = new Git(this)
gitUtils.commitAuthor
```

> **NOTE**   It is possible to use third-party Java libraries, typically found in Maven Central (https://search.maven.org/), from trusted library code by using the `@Grab` annotation. Refer to the Grape documentation for details (http://mng.bz/nrxg).

14.5   *Backing up and restoring Jenkins*

Backing up your data is a universally recommended practice, and your Jenkins server should be no exception. Fortunately, backing up Jenkins is relatively easy. In this section, we will look at a few ways to do this.

In Jenkins, all the settings, build logs, and archives of the artifacts are stored under the $JENKINS_HOME directory. You can back up the directory manually, or by using a plugin like ThinBackup (https://plugins.jenkins.io/thinBackup/). The plugin provides a simple user interface that you can use to back up and restore your Jenkins configurations and data.

Once you install the plugin, you need to configure the backup directory, as shown in figure 14.20. Specify the backup directory to be /var/lib/backups. Be sure Jenkins has write rights!

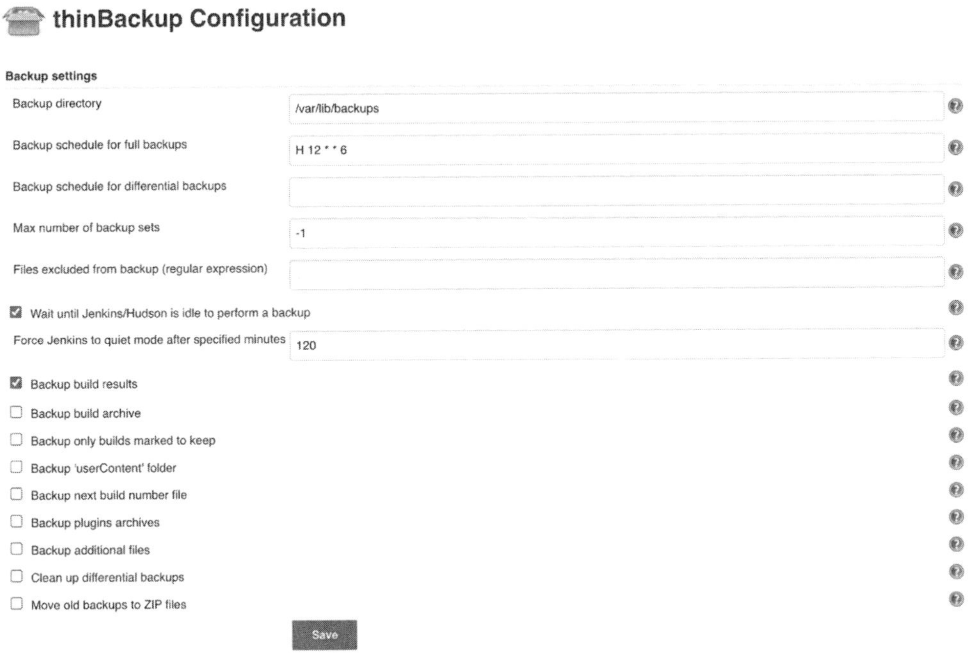

thinBackup Configuration

Backup settings

Backup directory	/var/lib/backups
Backup schedule for full backups	H 12 * * 6
Backup schedule for differential backups	
Max number of backup sets	-1
Files excluded from backup (regular expression)	

☑ Wait until Jenkins/Hudson is idle to perform a backup

Force Jenkins to quiet mode after specified minutes   120

☑ Backup build results
☐ Backup build archive
☐ Backup only builds marked to keep
☐ Backup 'userContent' folder
☐ Backup next build number file
☐ Backup plugins archives
☐ Backup additional files
☐ Clean up differential backups
☐ Move old backups to ZIP files

Save

Figure 14.20   Configuring the ThinBackup plugin

Now, you can test whether the backup is working by clicking the Backup Now option. It will create a backup of Jenkins data in the backup directory you specified in the settings:

```
[[root@ip-10-0-0-116 backups]# pwd
/var/lib/backups
[[root@ip-10-0-0-116 backups]# ls
FULL-2020-11-14_19-11   FULL-2020-11-14_19-12
[root@ip-10-0-0-116 backups]#
```

To restore a previous configuration, just go to the Restore page and choose the date of the configuration you wish to reinstate, as shown in figure 14.21. Once the configuration has been restored to the previous state, you need to reload the Jenkins configuration from disk or restart Jenkins.

📞 Restore Configuration

Restore options

restore backup from [2020-11-14 19:12 ▾]   ❷

☐ Restore next build number file (if found in backup)   ❷

☐ Restore plugins   ❷

[Restore]

Figure 14.21   Restoring a previous configuration

As a result of the backup, you can restore Jenkins from an earlier point in time in case of data corruption or a human-caused event.

> **NOTE** The ThinBackup plugin stores the backup locally for production usage. It's highly recommended to store your backups on a remote server or mount an external data storage.

If you're not a fan of plugins, you can set up a cron job (see the next section for more details) on Jenkins to schedule regular backups. It will back up everything located at /var/lib/jenkins to a remote repository such as S3 bucket, as shown in the following listing.

Listing 14.6   Backing up the $JENKINS_HOME folder to an S3 bucket

```
cd $JENKINS_HOME
BACKUP_TIME=$(date +'%m.%d.%Y')
zip -r backup-${BACKUP_TIME} .
aws s3 cp  backup-${BACKUP_TIME} s3://BUCKET/
```

Sometimes you need to move or copy Jenkins build jobs from one Jenkins instance to another, without copying the entire Jenkins configuration. For example, you might be migrating your build jobs to a Jenkins server on a brand-new instance.

You can copy or move build jobs between instances of projects simply by copying or moving the build job directories to the new Jenkins instance. I have built an open source CLI called Butler (https://github.com/mlabouardy/butler) to import/export Jenkins jobs and plugins easily.

To get started, find the appropriate package for your system and download it. Here's the command for Linux:

```
wget https://s3.us-east-1.amazonaws.com/butlercli/1.0.0/linux/butler
chmod +x butler
cp butler /usr/local/bin/
```

Verify that the installation worked by opening a new terminal session and checking whether Butler is available. To export Jenkins plugins, you need to provide the Jenkins URL:

```
butler jobs export --server JENKINS_URL --username USERNAME --password
    PASSWORD
```

A new jobs/ directory will be created with every job in Jenkins. Each job will have its own configuration file, config.xml.

To import the plugins, issue the `butler plugins export` command. Butler will dump a list of plugins installed to stdout, and a new file, plugins.txt, will be generated, with a list of installed Jenkins plugins with name and version pairs, as shown in figure 14.22.

```
[mlabouardy@Mohameds-MBP-001 github % butler jobs export --server jenkins.slowcoder.com  --username mlabouardy --password mlabouardy
Exporting job: movies-loader
Exporting job: movies-marketplace
Exporting job: movies-parser
Exporting job: movies-store
[mlabouardy@Mohameds-MBP-001 github % butler plugins export --server jenkins.slowcoder.com  --username mlabouardy --password mlabouardy
+-----------------------------------+-----------+-------------------------------+
|              NAME                 |  VERSION  |          DESCRIPTION          |
+-----------------------------------+-----------+-------------------------------+
| blueocean-personalization         | 1.21.0    | Personalization for Blue Ocean |
| subversion                        | 2.13.0    | Jenkins Subversion Plug-in     |
| trilead-api                       | 1.0.5     | Trilead API Plugin             |
| mapdb-api                         | 1.0.9.0   | MapDB API Plugin               |
| structs                           |      1.20 | Structs Plugin                 |
| blueocean-dashboard               | 1.21.0    | Dashboard for Blue Ocean       |
| managed-scripts                   |       1.4 | Managed Scripts                |
| token-macro                       |      2.10 | Token Macro Plugin             |
| favorite                          | 2.3.2     | Favorite                       |
| amazon-ecr                        |       1.6 | Amazon ECR plugin              |
| workflow-api                      |      2.38 | Pipeline: API                  |
| blueocean-bitbucket-pipeline      | 1.21.0    | Bitbucket Pipeline for Blue    |
|                                   |           | Ocean                          |
| workflow-job                      |      2.36 | Pipeline: Job                  |
```

Figure 14.22   Listing of installed Jenkins plugins

You can import exported jobs and plugins with the `butler plugins/jobs import` commands. Butler will use the exported files to issue API calls to the target Jenkins instance to import plugins and jobs.

So, all in all, migrating build jobs between Jenkins instances isn't all that hard—you just need to know a couple of tricks for the corner cases, and if you know where to look, Jenkins provides some nice tools to make the process smoother.

If you want $JENKINS_HOME content to be persisted on disk even if the Jenkins master instance has been restarted or shut down, you can mount a remote filesystem on the $JENKINS_HOME folder.

If you're running Jenkins on AWS, you can use an AWS service called Amazon Elastic File System, or EFS (https://aws.amazon.com/efs/). Create a filesystem on EFS by clicking the Create File System button (figure 14.23).

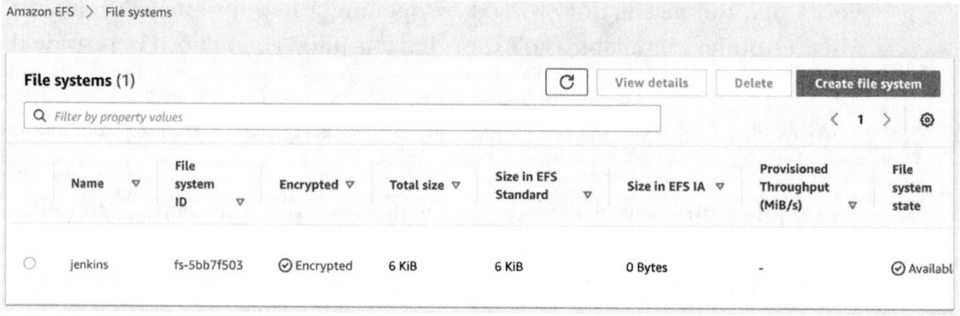

Figure 14.23   Creating an Amazon EFS filesystem

Once the filesystem is created and its state is Available, mount the EFS filesystem in the /var/lib/jenkins directory, so all the configuration will be saved in EFS:

```
sudo mount -t nfs4
-o nfsvers=4.1,rsize=1048576,wsize=1048576,
hard,timeo=600,retrans=2,noresvport
EFS_ID.efs.REGION.amazonaws.com:/ /var/lib/jenkins/
```

If you want to test it, terminate your EC2 instance and a new one will be launched automatically with the same configuration (make sure to add the mount commands to the Packer template while baking the Jenkins master AMI).

14.6 *Setting up cron jobs with Jenkins*

Jenkins provides a cron-like feature to periodically build a project. This feature is primarily used to run scheduled builds, like nightly/weekly builds or running tests. For example, you might want to run performance tests or integration tests for Android or iOS releases at night, when users do not access the backend under test.

To configure a scheduled nightly build that runs at a certain day and time, head over to Jenkins dashboard. Create a new job and select Freestyle Project. Configure the job accordingly by adding the job details shown in figure 14.24.

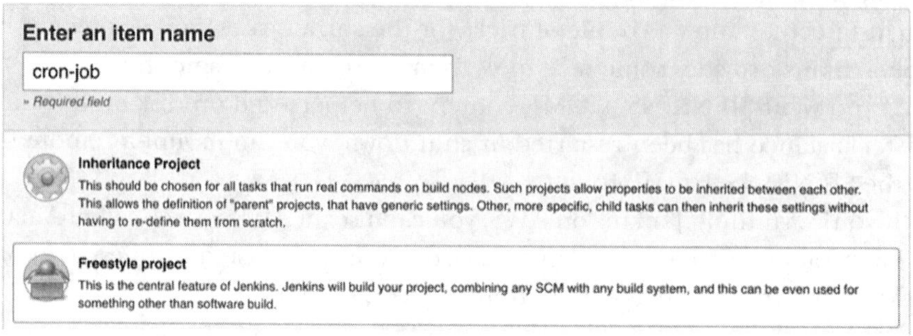

Figure 14.24   Creating a Freestyle project

Schedule your build from the Build Triggers tab by writing the cron syntax shown in figure 14.25, and then select the Build Periodically option. Fill in a cron-like value for the time you wish to trigger the pipeline execution.

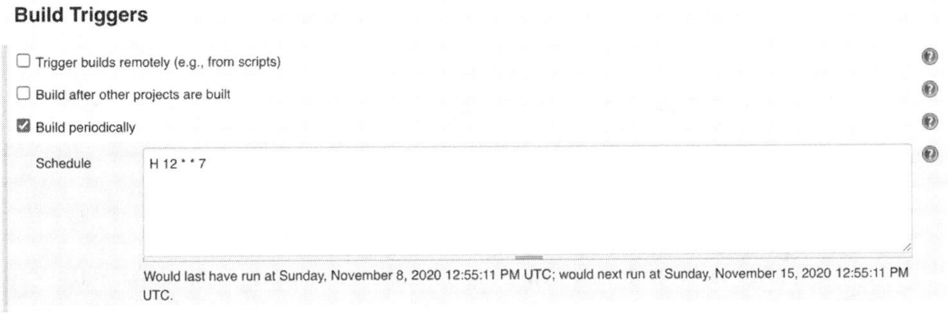

Build Triggers

☐ Trigger builds remotely (e.g., from scripts)

☐ Build after other projects are built

☑ Build periodically

Schedule `H 12 * * 7`

Would last have run at Sunday, November 8, 2020 12:55:11 PM UTC; would next run at Sunday, November 15, 2020 12:55:11 PM UTC.

Figure 14.25   Defining a cron job expression

Jenkins uses a cron expression, with fields as follows:

- MINUTES—Minutes in one hour (0–59)
- HOURS—Hours in one day (0–23)
- DAYMONTH—A day in a month (1–31)
- MONTH—Month in a year (1–12)
- DAYWEEK—Day of the week (0–7), where 0 and 7 are Sunday

For example (figure 14.26), to trigger a build at midnight on Sunday, the cron value `H 12 * * 7` will do the job.

NOTE   You should be aware that the time zone is relative to the location where your Jenkins virtual machine is running. This example uses Coordinated Universal Time (UTC).

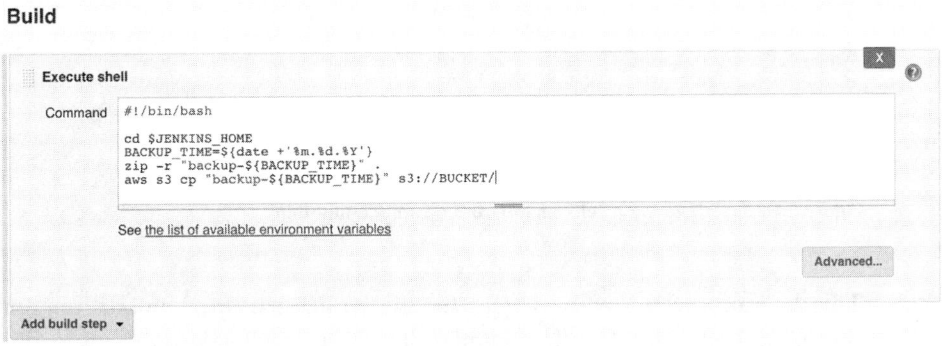

Build

Execute shell

Command
```
#!/bin/bash

cd $JENKINS_HOME
BACKUP_TIME=${date +'%m.%d.%Y'}
zip -r "backup-${BACKUP_TIME}" .
aws s3 cp "backup-${BACKUP_TIME}" s3://BUCKET/
```

See the list of available environment variables

Advanced...

Add build step ▾

Figure 14.26   Shell script to back up the $JENKINS_HOME folder

Build your job to test that everything is working as you've expected. Your build results should look like figure 14.27.

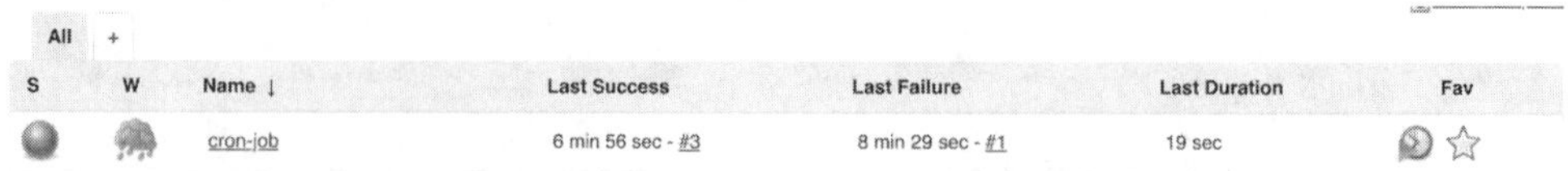

All
+
S
W
Name ↓
Last Success
Last Failure
Last Duration
Fav
cron-job
6 min 56 sec - #3
8 min 29 sec - #1
19 sec

Figure 14.27 Triggering a cron job manually

Next time, your job will automatically execute at 12:00 A.M. since you have scheduled it to run at this time using cron syntax.

Jenkins jobs could be run programmatically, using API calls or the Jenkins CLI. That opens up the opportunity to implement complex schedule builds by integrating an external service like AWS Lambda to invoke a Jenkins build job based on different events; see figure 14.28.

API Gateway
Incoming event
CloudWatch Event Rule
Trigger
AWS Lambda
Query
REST API
Jenkins
Build Job
Worker
Worker

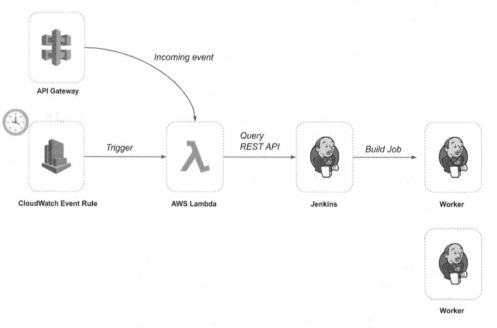

Figure 14.28 Triggering a Jenkins job from a Lambda function

This diagram covers how to trigger a Jenkins build job from a Lambda function through the Jenkins RESTful API. The Lambda function is invoked on the upcoming CloudWatch event rule (cloud-managed cron job) or HTTPS requests from API Gateway.

14.7 Running Jenkins locally as a Docker container

If you need to debug Jenkins or test a new plugin, you can deploy Jenkins locally on your machine and run it as a Docker container. That way, you can easily create and destroy a Jenkins server.

You can use the official Jenkins Docker image from the DockerHub repository (https://hub.docker.com/_/jenkins). The image contains the current LTS release of Jenkins (v2.60.3 at the time of this writing).

To get started, on your terminal, create a bridge network in Docker with the following command:

```
docker network create jenkins
```

We will need the Docker daemon to be able to provision Jenkins workers dynamically. That's why we will deploy a Docker container based on the Docker image:

```
docker run -d --name docker --privileged
--network jenkins --network-alias docker
--env DOCKER_TLS_CERTDIR=/certs
--volume jenkins-docker-certs:/certs/client
--volume jenkins-data:/var/jenkins_home
--publish 2376:2376 docker:dind
```

To avoid exposing the Docker daemon (/var/run.docker.sock) running in the host machine, we will run a Docker container providing a self-service and ephemeral Docker Engine, which Jenkins will use instead of the worker machine's Docker engine. This pattern is referred to as *Docker in Docker*, or *nested containerization*.

We will override the Jenkins official image to install the Docker CLI and needed plugins for Jenkins. Create a Dockerfile with the content in the following listing.

Listing 14.7 Dockerfile to build custom Jenkins image

```
FROM jenkins/jenkins:lts
MAINTAINER mlabouardy <mohamed@labouardy.com>

USER root
RUN apt-get update && apt-get install -y apt-transport-https \
    ca-certificates curl gnupg2 \
    software-properties-common
RUN curl -fsSL https://download.docker.com/linux/debian/gpg | apt-key add -
RUN apt-key fingerprint 0EBFCD88
RUN add-apt-repository \
    "deb [arch=amd64] https://download.docker.com/linux/debian \
    $(lsb_release -cs) stable"                                          Installs Docker
RUN apt-get update && apt-get install -y docker-ce-cli                  community edition (CE) client
USER jenkins                                      Switches to Jenkins user to avoid running the container by default in privileged mode
RUN jenkins-plugin-cli
--plugins blueocean:1.24.3 workflow-aggregator:2.6
github:1.32.0 docker-plugin:1.2.1     Installs the Jenkins plugins
```

This Dockerfile does the following:

- Installs the Docker Community Edition CLI
- Installs Jenkins plugins, including the following:
  - *Blue Ocean*—Sophisticated visualizations of CD pipelines for fast and intuitive comprehension of software pipeline status
  - *Workflow*—A suite of plugins that lets you write pipelines as code (Jenkins-files)
  - *GitHub*—GitHub API integration and support of Git operations
- *Docker*—Lets you provision Jenkins workers on Docker containers

Build a new Docker image from this Dockerfile and assign the image a meaningful name:

```
docker build -t jenkins-custom:lts .
```

Then, deploy a container based on the built image with the following `docker run` command:

```
docker run -d --name jenkins --network jenkins
--env DOCKER_HOST=tcp://docker:2376
--env DOCKER_CERT_PATH=/certs/client
--env DOCKER_TLS_VERIFY=1
--publish 8080:8080 --publish 50000:50000
--volume jenkins-data:/var/jenkins_home
--volume jenkins-docker-certs:/certs/client:ro
jenkins-custom:lts
```

This command will map a Docker volume to the /var/jenkins_home folder. In case you need to restart or recover your Jenkins instance, all of the state is stored inside the Docker volume.

You can also build and deploy all the services by writing a docker-compose.yml file, as shown in the following listing.

Listing 14.8 Grok custom patterns definition

```
version: "3.8"

services:
 docker:
   image: docker:dind
   ports:
     - "2376:2376"
   networks:
     jenkins:
         aliases:
           - docker
   environment:
     - DOCKER_TLS_CERTDIR=/certs
   volumes:
     - jenkins-docker-certs:/certs/client
```

```
      - jenkins-data:/var/jenkins_home
    privileged: true

  jenkins:
    build: .
    ports:
      - "8080:8080"
      - "50000:50000"
    networks:
      - jenkins
    environment:
      - DOCKER_HOST=tcp://docker:2376
      - DOCKER_CERT_PATH=/certs/client
      - DOCKER_TLS_VERIFY=1
    volumes:
      - jenkins-data:/var/jenkins_home
      - jenkins-docker-certs:/certs/client:ro

volumes:
 jenkins-docker-certs: {}
 jenkins-data: {}

networks:
 jenkins:
```

Run `docker-compose up`, and Docker Compose starts and runs Jenkins.

Visit localhost:8080; you should see the login page. As a part of the Jenkins setup, we need to view the password inside the container instance; use the container ID (or the name) and run the `docker exec` command:

```
docker container exec ID sh -c "cat /var/jenkins_home/secrets/
    initialAdminPassword"
```

After running the command, you should see the code. Copy and paste it on the dashboard to unlock Jenkins; see figure 14.29.

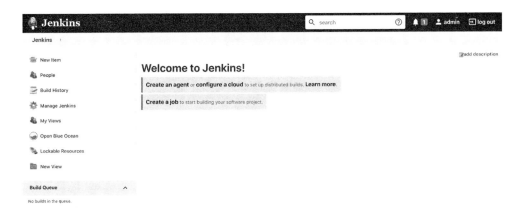

Figure 14.29   Jenkins server running inside a Docker container

To set up workers, choose Manage Jenkins and System Configuration. Then click the Configure tab in the Cloud section. The Docker option will be available. Set the Docker URI to `tcp://docker:2376`, as shown in figure 14.30. Click the Test button to check the connection.

☁Configure Clouds

Docker	
Name	docker
Docker Host URI	tcp://docker:2376
Server credentials	docker (docker) ⌄ ⊷Add ▾

Figure 14.30   Configuring Docker remote API on Jenkins

The Docker API should return an error: `server gave HTTP response to HTTPS client`. You need to configure the client TLS certificates to connect with the Docker daemon. The certificates can be found at the /certs/client folder within the Jenkins container.

Create a new Jenkins credential of type Certificate with the following settings:

- *Client Key*—/certs/client/key.pem content
- *Client Certificate*—/certs/client/cert.pem content
- *Server CA Certificate*—/certs/client/ca.pem content

The credential settings should look similar to those in figure 14.31.

Figure 14.31   Jenkins server deployed locally inside a Docker container

Then, we need to define an agent template, as shown in figure 14.32; this template is the blueprint used to spin up Jenkins workers. You need a Docker image that can be used to run the Jenkins agent runtime. You can use the jenkins/ssh-agent (https:// hub.docker.com/r/jenkins/ssh-agent) as a base for Jenkins workers. The image has SSHD installed (this listens for an incoming connection when you attempt to connect via SSH).

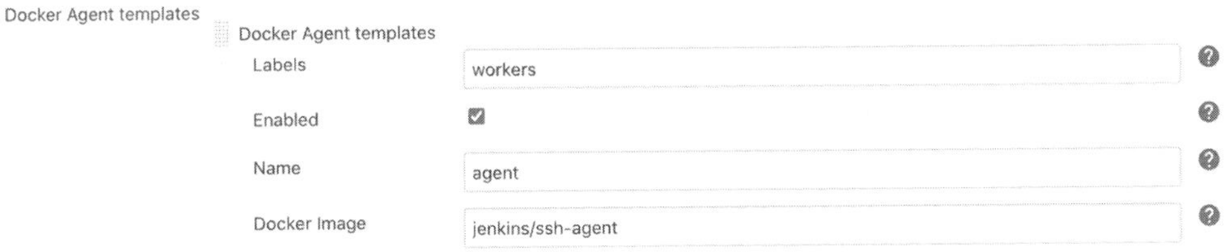

Figure 14.32 Configuring a new Docker agent template

You can also build a custom Docker agent image with all dependencies and packages needed to build your projects. To test it out, create a new Jenkins pipeline with the content shown in figure 14.33.

```
Pipeline

Definition     Pipeline script                                        ˅

      Script    1 ▾ node('workers'){
                2 ▾      stage('Stage 1'){
                3            echo "test"
                4      }
                5 }
```

Figure 14.33 New inline pipeline

Trigger the pipeline by clicking the Build Now link from the left navigation menu; the job will launch a container and execute the pipeline (figure 14.34).

Figure 14.34 Spinning up the Jenkins agent based on a Docker container

The agents are provisioned dynamically and stopped after each build.

Summary

- You can share common code and steps across multiple pipelines by writing a Jenkins shared library.
- You can define fine-grained control over user/group permissions per project with the Matrix Authorization Strategy plugin.
- You can also create a custom role with a list of permissions and assign the role to users instead of assigning appropriate permissions to each user with the Role Strategy plugin.
- Use GitHub's own authentication scheme for implementing authentication in your Jenkins instance.
- The Docker plugin will run dynamic Jenkins agents inside Docker containers.

Wrapping up

We're at the end of our journey in this book. You learned about Jenkins and the pipeline-as-code approach. You discovered several CI/CD implementations for cloud-native applications, such as containerized applications in Kubernetes and serverless applications. You designed and deployed a Jenkins cluster on the cloud for scale and mastered monitoring and troubleshooting Jenkins.

Technology changes quickly, so it's great to have a few resources to go to for recent news and information. The weekly newsletter DevOps Bulletin (https://devopsbulletin .com) features a great collection of posts regarding PaC and the latest wonders in the DevOps space. I also recommend keeping an eye on DevOps World (www.devopsworld .com), where you can be inspired by experts and your peers and gain the tools you need to shape the future of software delivery at your organization and at large.

I hope you've enjoyed the book and learned something from it. PaC is still new, but awareness is growing rapidly. Over the next few years, you'll see many organizations, small and large, embrace PaC to release faster and reduce the feedback loop.

index

Symbols

_repositories_push scope 288
–build-arg argument 421
–dry-run flag 376
–no-sandbox flag 257
–prod 415
–region command-line option 69
–url argument 392
–version flag 385
-auth option 219
-cover flag 241
-i flag 220
-set_exit_status 239
.helmignore 372
*testing.T 240
/* tslint:disable */ instruction 256
/approve comment 398
%{PATTERN:IDENTIFIER} syntax 458
${stageVariables.environment} 428
$JENKINS_HOME directory 64, 124
$JENKINS_HOME/init.groovy.d directory 85
$LATEST version 423, 425

A

Acceptance tests stage 24
ACCOUNT_ID variable 287, 294
ACLs (access-control lists) 57, 405
ACM (AWS Certificate Manager) 63, 124
AD (Azure Active Directory) 163
admin 263, 446
agent directive 51

Agent permission 470
agent section 33, 302, 304
AKS (Azure Kubernetes Service) 356
alerts 462–466
allowMissing parameter 252
always directive 34
always post condition block 34
Amazon ECR (Elastic Container Registry)
    286–287
Amazon Elastic File System (EFS) 124
Amazon Elastic Kubernetes Service (EKS) 356
Amazon Resource Name (ARN) 125
Amazon S3 420–422
Amazon Simple Queue Service (SQS) 200
amazon-ebs builder 78
AMIs (Amazon Machine Images) 55
    master, baking 85–96
        configuring Jenkins upon startup 85–88
        Jenkins plugins 88–96
    worker, baking 96–99
Anchore Engine 296
Anonymous 470
api variable 406
API_TOKEN variable 218
apiVersion 370
applications, microservices-based 199–203
ARG instruction 278
ARN (Amazon Resource Name) 125
AS NAME 276
ASG (Auto Scaling group) 57, 131–133
assertEqual() function 234
Authenticated authorization 470
Auto Scaling groups 128

automated tests 231–270
  code analysis 246–248
  code coverage reports 240–242
  code linter integration 238–240
  HTML coverage reports 250–254
  mocked database tests 248–250
  parallel tests 244–246
  security in CI pipeline 242–244
  SonarQube Scanner 260–270
  UI testing with Headless Chrome 254–260
  unit tests inside Docker containers 233–238
autoscaling 9
autoscaling workers 128–139
  Auto Scaling group 131–133
  CPU utilization load 136–139
  launch configuration 128–131
  scaling policies 133–135
avg() function 465
AWS (Amazon Web Services) 141
  architecting Jenkins for scale in 55–69
    configuring CLI (command-line interface) 65–66
    creating and managing IAM (Identity and Access Management) user 66–69
    preparing environment 64–65
  provisioning VPC (virtual private cloud) 103–117
    overview 104–108
    VPC bastion host 114–117
    VPC route tables 111–114
    VPC subnets 108–111
AWS Certificate Manager (ACM) 63, 124
AWS CLI update-kubeconfig command 360, 363
aws configure command 69
aws ec2 describe-availability-zones command 109
aws ecr command 294
aws eks update-kubeconfig command 362
aws provider 104
aws s3 cp instruction 417, 430
aws s3 ls command 422
AWS_ACCESS_KEY_ID variable 104
aws_ami data source 114
aws_autoscaling_group resource 131
AWS_DEFAULT_REGION environment variable 69
aws_instance resource 117
aws_key_pair resource 115
aws_launch_configuration resource 128
AWS_PROFILE environment variable 104
aws_profile variable 107
AWS_REGION 374
AWS_SECRET_ACCESS_KEY variable 104

aws-auth ConfigMap 363
awsauto 299
AWSLambda_FullAccess 419
Azure 162–183
  applying autoscaling to Jenkins workers 178–183
  building Jenkins VM images in 162–166
  deploying Jenkins master virtual machine 171–177
  deploying private virtual network 166–170
Azure Active Directory (AD) 163
Azure Bastion offering Remote Desktop Protocol (RDP) managed service 169
Azure Container Registry 288–290
Azure Instance Metadata Service (IMDS) 179
azure-arm builder 163
AzureBastionSubnet 167, 170
azurerm 167
azurerm_public_ip resource 170

B

backing up 480–484
baking machine images 70–99
  immutable infrastructure 71–72
  master AMI 85–96
    configuring Jenkins upon startup 85–88
    Jenkins plugins 88–96
  with Packer 72–85
    baking machine image 75–85
    installation and configuration 74–75
    process 73–74
  worker AMI 96–99
BasicSSHUserPrivateKey constructor 87
bastion host 61, 114–117
BDD (behavior-driven development) 24
before keyword 247
Blue Ocean plugin 26–29, 488
BRANCH_NAME 294
build arguments, Docker 277–279
build job keyword 332
Build stage 24, 31, 274, 276, 302, 338–339, 383–384, 407, 409, 421
BUILD_TAG environment variable 376
build() method 274, 278
builders 74, 145
butler plugins export command 483
butler plugins/jobs import commands 483

C

CA (certificate authority) 124
CD (continuous delivery)
  defined 14

metrics 441–466
  centralized logging for Jenkins logs with
    ELK 452–462
  creating alerts based on 462–466
  monitoring Jenkins cluster health 442–452
  on K8s (Kubernetes) 372–381
CD (continuous deployment)
  automating flow with Jenkins 360–372
  defined 13–14
  on Docker Swarm 321–335
CE (Docker Community Edition) 296
centralized logging 452–462
  streaming logs with Filebeat 454–461
  streaming logs with Logstash plugin 461–462
certificate authority (CA) 124
chaos engineering 10
Chart.yaml 372
Checkout stage 24, 31, 209, 222, 302
chkconfig command 79
CI (continuous integration) pipeline 197
  Docker images within 271–308
    building 273–279
    deploying Docker private registry 279–291
    managing pull requests with Jenkins
      305–308
    scanning for vulnerabilities 296–301
    tagging 291–296
    writing Jenkins declarative pipeline 301–304
  security in 242–244
CI/CD (continuous integration/continuous
    deployment) 3–20
  cloud native approaches 4–12
    cloud native 8–10
    microservices 5–8
    monolithic 4–5
    serverless 10–12
  embracing practices 15–16
  tools for 16–20
    choosing 17–18
    Jenkins 18–20
CIDR (Classless Inter-Domain Routing) 60
cidrsubnet(prefix, newbits, netnum) method 109
CLI (command-line interface) 53, 64–66, 372
Client Certificate 490
Client Key 490
client_certificate_password 169
client_certificate_path 169
cloud native 3–20
  approaches for going 4–12
    cloud native 8–10
    microservices 5–8
    monolithic 4–5
    serverless 10–12

CI/CD (continuous integration/continuous
  deployment)
  CD (continuous delivery), defined 14
  CD (continuous deployment), defined
    13–14
  CI (continuous integration), defined 12–13
  embracing practices 15–16
  tools for 16–20
Docker Swarm, applications on 309–354
  defining continuous deployment
    process 321–335
  handling code promotion with Jenkins
    341–346
  implementing Jenkins delivery
    pipeline 346–354
  integrating Jenkins with Slack
    notifications 335–341
  running distributed Docker Swarm
    cluster 310–321
cloud providers 140–193
  DigitalOcean 183–192
    building Jenkins worker Droplets 190–192
    creating Jenkins DigitalOcean
      Snapshots 183–185
    deploying Jenkins master Droplet 186–189
  Google Cloud Platform (GCP) 141–161
    building Jenkins VM images 141–147
    configuring with Terraform 147–153
    deploying Jenkins on Google Compute
      Engine 153–157
    launching automanaged workers on
      157–161
  Microsoft Azure 162–183
    applying autoscaling to Jenkins
      workers 178–183
    building Jenkins VM images in 162–166
    deploying Jenkins master virtual
      machine 171–177
    deploying private virtual network 166–170
cloud-native architecture 4
ClusterIP keyword 366
ClusterRoleBinding resource 370
clusters
  monitoring health of 442–452
  running distributed Docker Swarm 310–321
  setting up Kubernetes 356–360
code
  analysis 246–248
  linter integration 238–240
  promotion 341–346
cold start 415
command-line interface (CLI) 53, 64–66
command-line pipeline linter 41–43

commitAuthor instruction 477
commitAuthor() method 340
commitID() function 293
commitID() method 376
commitMessage() method 340
communication 6
complexity 8
Conditions option 465
consistency 22
containers, Docker
    running Jenkins locally as 487–491
    unit tests inside 233–238
continuous everything 7
continuous integration. *See* CI (continuous integration) pipeline
CORS (cross-origin resource sharing) 405
cost optimization 11
cost-effectiveness 5
count variable 191
coverage reports
    code 240–242
    HTML 250–254
CPU utilization load 136–139
CREATE DATABASE InfluxQL (Influx Query Language) statement 445
create_before_destroy life cycle setting 132
Credentials 470
credentials file 66
credentials() helper method 34
cron jobs 484–486
cross-origin resource sharing (CORS) 405
CSRF (cross-site request forgery) 41
CSS (Cascading Style Sheets) 403
currentBuild.result variable 34

D

database tests, mocked 248–250
DEBUG 457
declarative pipeline 31–35, 301–304
declarative-lint option 43
Default version 478
delivery pipeline 346–354
dependencies section 375, 386
depends_on keyword 316
deploy machine learning (ML) models 141
Deploy stage 24, 332, 344, 349, 365, 377, 407, 417, 424, 426, 432
deployment 6
deployment packages 407–417
    mono-repo strategy 407–413
    multi-repo strategy 413–417
describe keyword 247

Develop 294
develop branch 38–39
develop tag 307, 323, 329, 333, 361
Developer permission 472
development speed 10
development velocity 4, 7, 10
DevOps 4
DigitalOcean 183–192
    building Jenkins worker Droplets 190–192
    creating Jenkins DigitalOcean Snapshots 183–185
    deploying Jenkins master Droplet 186–189
digitalocean builder 183, 185
digitalocean Packer builder 183
digitalocean_droplet type 186
Docker 488
docker build command 235–236
Docker Community Edition (CE) 296
Docker containers
    running Jenkins locally as 487–491
    unit tests inside 233–238
docker cp command 237
Docker DSL 273–277
docker exec command 489
docker group 312
Docker images 271–308
    building 273–279
        Docker build arguments 277–279
        using Docker DSL 273–277
    deploying Docker private registry 279–291
        Amazon Elastic Container Registry (ECR) 286–287
        Azure Container Registry 288–290
        Google Container Registry (GCR) 290–291
        Nexus Repository OSS 279–286
    managing pull requests with Jenkins 305–308
    scanning for vulnerabilities 296–301
    tagging Docker images right way 291–296
    writing Jenkins declarative pipeline 301–304
Docker in Docker 487
docker info command 321
docker login command 34, 285, 325
docker node ls 321
Docker plugin 488
docker push command 290
docker push operation 288
docker run command 235, 488
docker stack deploy command 322, 324, 329, 347, 354
Docker Swarm 309–354
    defining continuous deployment process 321–335
    handling code promotion with Jenkins 341–346

implementing Jenkins delivery pipeline 346–354

integrating Jenkins with Slack notifications 335–341

running distributed Docker Swarm cluster 310–321

docker swarm join command 314

docker_container_status_docker measurement 448

docker-compose ps command 296

docker-compose up 489

docker.build() method 236, 238, 240

Dockerfile.test 234

Droplet deployments 186–189

DSL (domain-specific language) 23

E

EC2 (Amazon Elastic Compute Cloud) 55

ec2-user username 312

ECR (Elastic Container Registry) 286–287

efficiency 22

EFS (Amazon Elastic File System) 124

EKS (Amazon Elastic Kubernetes Service) 356

ELB (Elastic Load Balancing) 121

ELK stack (Elasticsearch, Logstash, and Kibana) 452–462

streaming logs with Filebeat 454–461

streaming logs with Logstash plugin 461–462

email notifications 434–437

entries section 385

ENTRYPOINT instruction 239

ENV instruction 278

env keyword 294

env.BRANCH_NAME variable 294

env.BUILD_ID keyword 291

env.JOB_NAME variable 35

ENVIRONMENT argument 346

environment credentials 66

environment section 34

environment tag 168

Environment Variables 65

ETL (extract-transform-load) pipelines 141

Evaluate Every option 465

extract-transform-load (ETL) pipelines 141

F

failFast true instruction 245

failure post condition block 34

false 252

fast infrastructure deployment 73

fault tolerance 7

feature/X branch 38

Filebeat 454–461

finally block 435

Folder 205

for loop 419

FQDN (fully qualified domain name) 125

Freestyle project 204

FROM instruction 276

function code 417–420

G

GCE (Google Compute Engine) console 145

gcloud command 290

gcloud compute images list command 144

GCP (Google Cloud Platform) 4, 141–161

building Jenkins VM images 141–147

configuring with Terraform 147–153

deploying Jenkins on Google Compute Engine 153–157

launching automanaged workers on 157–161

GCP virtual machines (VMs) 141

GCR (Google Container Registry) 290–291

Get-AzSubscription 163

Git 205–215

git clone command 384

git log command 340

git show command 340

Git.groovy class 480

GitFlow branch model 38–39

GitHub 488

integrating 205–215

triggering builds with webhooks 222–230

GitHub OAuth 472–475

GitHub plugin 488

GitHubWehookForwarder Lambda function 228

GKE (Google Kubernetes Engine) 141, 356

go build command 275

go test command 239–241

golint command 238–239

Google Cloud Platform. *See* GCP

Google Compute Engine 153–157

Google Compute Engine (GCE) console 145

Google Kubernetes Engine (GKE) 141, 356

GOOGLE_APPLICATION_CREDENTIALS environment variable 144

googlecompute builder 143, 145

@Grab annotation 480

Grafana platform 444

granularity 6

H

HCL (HashiCorp Configuration Language)
    declarative language 104
HEAD flag 340
Headless Chrome 254–260
Healthcheck stage 387–389
Helm 381–387
helm build 396
Helm Chart stage 384
helm package command 384
helm repo index command 384
helm rollback command 377
helm upgrade command 376–377
horizontal autoscaling 11
hotfix/X branch 38
HTML 240
HTML coverage reports 250–254
httpRequest DSL object 388
HTTPS 124–127
Hudson plugin 91

I

IaaS (infrastructure-as-a service) provider 100,
    140
IaC (infrastructure as code) 22, 101–103
IAM (AWS Identity and Access
    Management) 66–69
IAM roles 66
ID 323
IDE (integrated development environment)
    integrations 43–45
identified by a client ID (aka application ID) 162
if clause 344, 349
IGW (internet gateway) 60
images file 298
IMDS (Azure Instance Metadata Service) 179
immutable infrastructure 71–72
influx CLI 445
influx command 445
InfluxDB 444
INFLUXDB_IP variable 446
INFO log 453, 457
infrastructure as code (IaC) 22, 101–103
infrastructure-as-a service (IaaS) provider 100,
    140
Inheritance project 204
inputs 445
–insecure-registry flag 285
inside() instruction 238–239
instance.save() statement 86
instances 445

integrated development environment (IDE)
    integrations 43–45
Integration tests 13
internet gateway (IGW) 60

J

Java Network Launch Protocol (JNLP) 53–54
Java Web Start (JWS) 53
JAVACLASS custom pattern 458
JDK (Java Development Kit) 79
Jenkins 18–46, 49–69, 140–193
    administration 467–492
        backing up and restoring 480–484
        configuring GitHub OAuth 472–475
        running locally as Docker container 487–491
        security and RBAC authorization 468–472
        setting up cron jobs 484–486
        shared libraries 476–480
        users actions, keeping track of 475–476
    architecting for scale in AWS 55–69
        configuring CLI 65–66
        creating and managing IAM user 66–69
        preparing environment 64–65
    as code with Terraform 100–139
        autoscaling worker pool 128–139
        infrastructure as code (IaC) 101–103
        provisioning AWS VPC 103–117
        running with native SSL/HTTPS 124–127
        setting up self-healing master 117–124
    automated tests with 231–270
        code analysis 246–248
        code coverage reports 240–242
        code linter integration 238–240
        HTML coverage reports 250–254
        mocked database tests 248–250
        parallel tests 244–246
        security in CI pipeline 242–244
        SonarQube Scanner 260–270
        UI testing with Headless Chrome 254–260
        unit tests inside Docker containers 233–238
    baking machine images 70–99
        immutable infrastructure 71–72
        master AMI 85–96
        with Packer 72–85
        worker AMI 96–99
    code promotion, handling 341–346
    configuring SSH authentication with 219–222
    DigitalOcean 183–192
        building Jenkins worker Droplets 190–192
        creating Jenkins DigitalOcean
            Snapshots 183–185
        deploying Jenkins master Droplet 186–189

email notifications in 434–437
GitFlow branch model 38–39
Google Cloud Platform (GCP) 141–161
    building Jenkins VM images 141–147
    configuring with Terraform 147–153
    deploying on Google Compute Engine
        153–157
    launching automanaged workers on
        157–161
Jenkinsfile 22–35
    Blue Ocean plugin 26–29
    declarative pipeline 31–35
    scripted pipeline 29–31
managing pull requests with 305–308
managing workers 52–55
    command line 53
    JNLP 53–54
    SSH 52–53
    Windows service 54–55
master-worker architecture 50–52
Microsoft Azure 162–183
    applying autoscaling to Jenkins
        workers 178–183
    building Jenkins VM images in 162–166
    deploying Jenkins master virtual
        machine 171–177
    deploying private virtual network 166–170
monitoring cluster health 442–452
multibranch pipelines 36–37
Slack notifications, integrating with 335–341
test-driven development with 39–45
    command-line pipeline linter 41–43
    IDE integrations 43–45
    Jenkins Replay button 40–41
triggering builds with GitHub webhooks
    222–230
writing declarative pipeline 301–304
XML configuration 215–219
Jenkins agent 29
Jenkins Long-Term Support (LTS) 56
Jenkins master 50
Jenkins plugin 91
jenkins user 97
Jenkins worker 50
Jenkins X 390–400
JENKINS_HOME directory 481, 483
JENKINS_HOSTNAME and JENKINS_SSH-
    D_PORT variables 43
JENKINS_JAVA_OPTIONS 86
jenkins_master.tf file 154
JENKINS_URL environment variable 227
jenkins_worker 132
jenkins_workers.tf file 131, 178, 181, 190

jenkins-* index pattern 453
jenkins-master 140, 173
Jenkinsfile 209
JNLP (Java Network Launch Protocol) 52, 54
Job 470
JOBNAME custom pattern 458
JsonSlurper class 388
jump box 61, 114
JVM (Java Virtual Machine) 85
JWS (Java Web Start) 53
jx CLI 399
jx promote command 392
jx version –short 390

K

K8s (Kubernetes) 355–400
    automating continuous deployment flow with
        Jenkins 360–372
    continuous delivery steps 372–381
    Jenkins X 390–400
    packaging with Helm 381–387
    running post-deployment smoke tests 387–389
    setting up Kubernetes cluster 356–360
Kompose 371–372
kubectl apply -f command 372
kubectl apply command 360, 362, 365–366
kubectl get nodes command 363
kubectl get pods -n watchlist 375
kubectl get pods command 380
kubectl get services -n watchlist output 380
kubectl get svc command 391
kubernetes.io/cluster/ 357

L

labels 29
LabelSelector 366
Lambda aliases 425
Lambda-based serverless functions 401–437
    configuring email notification in Jenkins
        434–437
    creating deployment packages 407–417
        mono-repo strategy 407–413
        multi-repo strategy 413–417
    deploying Lambda-based application 402–407
    hosting static website on S3 420–422
    maintaining multiple Lambda
        environments 423–434
    updating Lambda function code 417–420
latest 294, 378
latest tag 294, 347–348
launch configuration 58

Less operational overhead 11
@Library annotation 478–479
@Library('id@version') annotation 479
logging, centralized 452–462
    streaming logs with Filebeat 454–461
    streaming logs with Logstash plugin 461–462
logstash step 462
LOGSTASH_HOST variable 456
LTS (Jenkins Long-Term Support) 56

M

machine images, baking 70–99
    immutable infrastructure 71–72
    master AMI 85–96
        configuring Jenkins upon startup 85–88
        Jenkins plugins 88–96
    with Packer 72–85
        baking machine image 75–85
        installation and configuration 74–75
        process 73–74
    worker AMI 96–99
maintainability 5
management resource group 171, 176
management visual network 167
management VPC 108, 296
managers token 314
mapRoles section 363
marketplace variable 406
master AMI
    baking 85–96
        configuring Jenkins upon startup 85–88
        Jenkins plugins 88–96
    deploying Jenkins Droplet 186–189
    self-healing master 117–124
master branch 38–39
master-worker architecture 50–52
Matrix authorization strategy 469–471
mem_vm measurement 447
mesh routing feature 330
metrics, CD (continuous delivery) 441–466
    centralized logging for Jenkins logs with
        ELK 452–462
    creating alerts based on 462–466
    monitoring Jenkins cluster health 442–452
microservices
    on K8s (Kubernetes) 355–400
        automating continuous deployment flow
            with Jenkins 360–372
        continuous delivery steps 372–381
        discovering Jenkins X 390–400
        packaging applications with Helm 381–387
        running post-deployment smoke tests
            387–389

        setting up Kubernetes cluster 356–360
    overview 5–8
    pipeline as code for 197–230
        configuring SSH authentication with
            Jenkins 219–222
        Git and GitHub integration 205–215
        Jenkins jobs' XML configuration 215–219
        microservices-based applications 199–203
        multibranch pipeline jobs 203–205
        triggering Jenkins builds with GitHub
            webhooks 222–230
microservices architecture pattern 5
mocha 248
mocked database tests 248–250
modules 403
mono repository 201
mono-repo strategy 407–413
monolithic architecture 4–5
movies_to_parse_sandbox 324
MoviesLoader Lambda function 404, 409,
    417–419
MoviesParser Lambda function 404, 417–420
MoviesStore Lambda functions 419, 425
MoviesStoreAddToFavorites Lambda
    function 413
MoviesStoreListMovies Lambda function
    403–404, 406, 413, 427, 429
MoviesStoreViewFavorites Lambda function 413
multi-repo strategy 413–417
multibranch pipelines 36–37, 203, 205
multiline settings 456
multiple repositories 201
multiprovider support 73

N

Name 478
name query parameter 217
NAT (Network Address Translation) 61
native SSL (Secure Sockets Layer) 124–127
nested containerization 487
Network Address Translation (NAT) 61
Nexus Repository OSS 279–286
NFS (Network File System) server 64
ng build -c sandbox flag 334
ng build command 277
no operational overhead 9
node block wrapper 51
node:latest floating tag 276
node:lts floating tag 276
node('workers') instruction 301
node{} 269
notifySlack() method 338, 340

npm (Node Package Manager) 249
npm install command 277, 415
npm run lint alias command 254
npm run test command 249–250, 258
npm start command 277
nx-*-registry-add permission 271
nx-*-registry-read permission 285

O

one repository per service strategy 407
operational overhead 8
Organization 205
os_profile section 172
output section 126
output variable 152
outputs 445
Outputs section 283, 331, 333, 405
Overall 470

P

PaaS (platform-as-a-service) provider 140
PaC (pipeline as code) 22
  for microservices 197–230
    configuring SSH authentication with
      Jenkins 219–222
    Git and GitHub integration 205–215
    Jenkins jobs' XML configuration 215–219
    microservices-based applications 199–203
    multibranch pipeline jobs 203–205
    triggering Jenkins builds with GitHub
      webhooks 222–230
  with Jenkins 21–46
    GitFlow branch model 38–39
    Jenkinsfile 22–35
    multibranch pipelines 36–37
    test-driven development with Jenkins 39–45
Packer 72–85, 142
  baking machine image 75–85
  installation and configuration 74–75
  process 73–74
packer build command 80–81, 94, 98, 144, 146,
    164, 185, 281, 312
packer build template.json command 184
packer validate command 94, 185
packer validate template.json command 146
parallel directive 417
parallel DSL step 244
parallel key 416
parallel keyword 244
parallel section 244
parallel tests 244–246

ParseMovie() method 240
PASSWORD 299
PATH variable 65, 75, 103, 242
pattern_dir setting 459
pip install command 274
Pipeline 204
pipeline as code. *See* PaC (pipeline as code)
pipeline block 301–302
pipeline keyword 301
plan step 150
plan/apply 175
platform-as-a-service (PaaS) provider 140
plugins
  Blue Ocean 26–29
  Jenkins 88–96
  Logstash 461–462
policies, scaling 133–135
PoLP (principle of least privilege) 66
polyglot 11
post build section 436
post section 34, 303, 436
powershell step 235
PR (pull request) 332
PR- or feature 400
Preprod 294
preprod branch 38–39
preprod image tag 377
preprod tag 294, 343, 345, 377
principle of least privilege (PoLP) 66
private registry, Docker 279–291
  Amazon Elastic Container Registry
    (ECR) 286–287
  Azure Container Registry 288–290
  Google Container Registry (GCR) 290–291
  Nexus Repository OSS 279–286
production 378, 392
programming language and architecture 17
provider section 167
provisioner file 91
provisioners section 74
provisioners stage 78
public_repo scope 207
public-read 405
publish-version operation 427
publishHTML command 252
pull requests (PR) 305–308, 332
Push stage 24, 291, 293–294, 302, 345, 384, 407,
    413
python main.py command 274
python test_main.py command 234

Q

QA 472
QA permission 472
quality tests 13, 24
Quality Tests stage 238, 247

R

RBAC (role-based access control) 288, 467, 472
  Matrix authorization strategy 469–471
  role-based authorization strategy 471–472
RDP (Remote Desktop Protocol) 169
REGION log 323
REGION variable 287, 294
REGISTRY parameter 299
REGISTRY_CREDENTIALS_USR and REGIS-
  TRY_CREDENTIALS_PSW environment
  variables 34
release 372
Replay button 40–41
repo scope 207
repo:status 207
repositories 372
resiliency 10
resource block 181
restoring 480–484
risk management 22
role-based access control. See RBAC (role-based
  access control)
route tables, VPC 111–114
Run 470

S

s-1vcpu-2gb 186
S3 420–422
s3:GetObject 405
SAM (Serverless Application Model) 419
sandbox 428
sandbox EKS cluster 357
sandbox VPC 313
scalability 5, 7, 73
scaling 55–69
  configuring CLI 65–66
  creating and managing IAM (Identity and
    Access Management) user 66–69
  policies 133–135
  preparing environment 64–65
scaling and resiliency 5
scaling policy 58
Scan operation 403
SCM 470

scrape_configs section 450
scripted pipeline 29–31
Secure Shell (SSH) 52–53, 219–222
security 468–472
  in CI pipeline 242–244
    Matrix authorization strategy 469–471
    role-based authorization strategy 471–472
security compliance 9
security group 56
security tests 13, 24
Security Tests stage 243
security_groups.tf 175
self-healing master 117–124
sendEmail() method 435–436
Server CA Certificate 490
server gave HTTP response to HTTPS client
  error 490
Serverless 401
Serverless Application Model (SAM) 419
serverless functions
  defined 10–12
  Lambda 401–437
    configuring email notification in
      Jenkins 434–437
    creating deployment packages 407–417
    deploying application 402–407
    hosting static website on S3 420–422
    maintaining multiple environments 423–434
    updating function code 417–420
serverless movement 401
service jenkins status command 121
service nexus restart command 280
service principal (SP) 162
service_account variable 144
service-oriented architecture (SOA) 6
setUpClass() method 234
Shared Credentials file 66
shared libraries 477, 480
sharing, component 6
Slack notifications 335–341
slave or build agent 50
slave term 50
smoke tests 387–389
Snapshots, DigitalOcean 183–185
SOA (service-oriented architecture) 6
sonar-scanner command 266
SonarQube Scanner 260–270
source argument 403
SP (service principal) 162
SPA (Movie Marketplace is a single-page
  application) 420
spec section 365
speed 22

SQS (Amazon Simple Queue Service) 200
SQS_URL 374
SSH (Secure Shell) 52–219, 222
ssh_keys section 172
ssh-keygen command 92, 115
sshagent block 328
SSL (Secure Sockets Layer) 62, 124–127
stacks 321
stage blocks 302
stage command 302
stage variables environment variables 427
stages 23
stages section 302
staging 346, 377, 392
static code analysis 13
static website 420–422
status field 460
steps block 302
steps section 35
strategy.setAllowAnonymousRead(true)
    instruction 86
streaming logs
    with Filebeat 454–461
    with Logstash plugin 461–462
subnets, VPC 60, 108–111
success post condition block 34
SUCCESS status 236
sudo command 312
swarm init command 318
SWARM_MANAGER_IP 321
swarm_managers resource 316
swarm-production 347
swarm-sandbox 327
swarm-staging 342
swarmManager variable 342
synchronization 8

T

t.Error() method 240
t2.large instances 119, 136
t2.micro instance 83
tagging Docker images 291–296
tags 83
target block 252
target platform 17
TDD (test-driven development) 24
team experience and skills 17
Telegraf 444
Template validated successfully 94
templates 372
Terraform
    configuring GCP network with 147–153

Jenkins as code with 100–139
    autoscaling workers 128–139
    infrastructure as code (IaC) 101–103
    provisioning AWS VPC (virtual private
        cloud) 103–117
    running with native SSL/HTTPS 124–127
    setting up self-healing master 117–124
terraform apply command 110, 112–113, 116,
    126, 131–132, 135, 149–150, 152, 155–156,
    160, 169, 171, 173, 176, 182, 189, 228, 262,
    283, 318, 331, 333, 359, 405, 429
terraform destroy command 400
terraform init command 359, 405
terraform output command 116, 157
terraform plan command 106–107, 110, 119
Terraform vX.Y.Z 103
Test keyword 240
test prefix 234
Test stage 35, 302
test-driven development with Jenkins 39–45
    command-line pipeline linter 41–43
    integrated development environment (IDE)
        integrations 43–45
    Jenkins Replay button 40–41
testing package 239–240
TF_VAR environment variable 107
TF_VAR_aws_profile variable 107
tools 16–20
    choosing 17–18
    Jenkins 18–20
top command 136
true 248

U

UI testing 13, 254–260
Unit testing 233
unit tests 13, 24, 233–238
Unit Tests stage 234, 240, 410
unstable post condition block 34
update-function-code command 417–419
USER 323
user variables 74
user-data 129
USERNAME variable 299, 325
username:token argument 219
users 475–476
UTC (Coordinated Universal Time) 485

V

Validate Jenkinsfile command 44
Values.yaml file 372
variable block 105

VCS (version-control system) 31, 272
version variable 427
View 470
VMs (virtual machines)
   Azure
      building Jenkins images 162–166
      deploying Jenkins master 171–177
   GCP 141–147
VPC (virtual private cloud) 60, 103–117
   bastion host 114–117
   overview 104–108
   route tables 111–114
   subnets 108–111
VPN (virtual private network) 114, 166–170
VSCode (Visual Studio Code) 43
vulnerabilities 296–301

W

waitForQualityGate step 269
WARNING 457
Watchlist 219
watchlist application 372
webhooks 222–230
website block 405
Windows service 54–55

withForQualityGate step 268
withRegistry block 291
withSonarQubeEnv block 266
workers 52–55
   applying autoscaling to 178–183
   autoscaling 128–139
      Auto Scaling group 131–133
      launch configuration 128–131
      scaling policies 133–135
      workers CPU utilization load 136–139
   baking AMI 96–99
   building Droplets 190–192
   command line 53
   JNLP 53–54
   launching on GCP 157–161
   SSH (Secure Shell) 52–53
   Windows service 54–55
workers label 51, 131, 209, 304
workers token 314
Workflow plugins 488
WORKSPACE 335

X

XML (Extensible Markup Language) 22,
   215–219

A new online reading experience

liveBook, our online reading platform, adds a new dimension to your Manning books, with features that make reading, learning, and sharing easier than ever. A liveBook version of your book is included FREE with every Manning book.

This next generation book platform is more than an online reader. It's packed with unique features to upgrade and enhance your learning experience.

- Add your own notes and bookmarks
- One-click code copy
- Learn from other readers in the discussion forum
- Audio recordings and interactive exercises
- Read all your purchased Manning content in any browser, anytime, anywhere

As an added bonus, you can search every Manning book and video in liveBook—even ones you don't yet own. Open any liveBook, and you'll be able to browse the content and read anything you like.*

Find out more at www.manning.com/livebook-program.

*Open reading is limited to 10 minutes per book daily